Individualized Education for Preschool Exceptional Children

John T. Neisworth, Ph.D.
The Pennsylvania State University

Sara J. Willoughby-Herb, Ph.D.
Clarion State College

Stephen J. Bagnato, Jr., D.Ed.
University of Maryland

Carol A. Cartwright, Ph.D.
The Pennsylvania State University

Karen W. Laub, Ph.D.
Arizona State University

AN ASPEN PUBLICATION®

Aspen Systems Corporation
Germantown, Maryland
London, England
1980

Library of Congress Cataloging in Publication Data

Main entry under title:

Individualized education for preschool exceptional children.

Bibliography: p. 153.
Includes index.

1. Handicapped children—Education (Preschool)—
Addresses, essays, lectures.   2. Individualized
instruction—Addresses, essays, lectures.   3. Problem
children—Education (Preschool)—Addresses, essays,
lectures.   I. Neisworth, John T.
LC4661.I53   371.9'043   80-12722
ISBN: 0-89443-285-0

Library of Congress Catalog Card Number: 80-12722
ISBN: 0-89443-285-0

Printed in the United States of America

1 2 3 4 5

Table of Contents

Preface

We must take care of our children in the best way possible. Whatever the promise or problems, caregivers and educators must use the best of what is available to assist children in their development. We all can agree that children deserve proper nutrition. To deny an advantageous diet to children would be unthinkable. Yet children often are denied adequate nurturance in other ways. Proper stimulation, adequate opportunities for responding, a systematic educational program, active parent involvement, and other concerns contribute to children's development as surely as do food and drink. Today's preschools and day-care centers have the responsibility of providing the best possible developmental assistance to young children.

In this book, we have presented an effective and systematic approach to early education for children. Whether the children are handicapped or nonhandicapped, and regardless of social or ethnic group, the procedures and curriculum described will provide an effective program for today's young children.

Acknowledgments

It is not possible to thank all those who contributed to this book. The development of the COMP-Curriculum took about three years and involved a number of students, faculty, and preschool teachers. Joyce Wilder assisted in the initial phases of the format and structure for the curriculum. John Worobey was a great help with the infant items. Carol Wegley Brown reviewed portions of the curriculum for revision. Many who used the curriculum offered their suggestions, and to them we are grateful. Susan McFadden provided expert consulting in the development of the Motor section of the curriculum.

Special thanks go to Susan Devenney, whose enthusiasm and studied use of our materials provided a continual source of encouragement for and correction of the curriculum.

As always, we are deeply appreciative for the assistance of Jo-Ann Dreibelbis. She prepared, typed, proofread, and in many ways prodded us through the manuscript. Her work was, indeed, of inestimable value. Thanks, also, to Howard Gallop and Erica Wolf for assisting with the final proofreading of the manuscript. Finally, we feel delighted and obliged to thank the hundreds of children and their parents who participated in the development of this book.

The HICOMP Preschool Project, which developed the COMP-Curriculum (Appendix A), is supported in part through funds provided by the Bureau for the Education of the Handicapped of the Department of Health, Education, and Welfare, Grant #G00-74-02712.

Chapter 1

Today's Early Educator

OBJECTIVES

1. State several concerns you and others might have regarding early education philosophy and practice.
2. List three reasons why families desire early education programs for their children.
3. Briefly describe the eight major roles of today's early educator.
4. Explain what is meant by developmental instruction.

1

"*TWENTY-FIVE OF THEM! Twenty-five. Can you believe it? This is just the first week. I'm already out of my mind. Martha, this is just my first year as a preschool teacher — what am I going to do? I have an aide but I don't even know what to tell her to do. Can you sit down and give me some suggestions?*"

"*Well, Jane, I've been teaching nine years now and I know what you're feeling. It's a real panic, there you are in the middle of 25 kids who are doing their own thing while you're trying to carry on something that looks like early education. Actually, I've got just about the same problems and they keep happening every year. But I've learned some things that seem to help. Some of the problems just kind of go away on their own, but others keep hounding you all year and there's nothing I've learned to do about them. But, Jane, why don't we get together tomorrow afternoon and go over some of your problems and I'll just tell you how I try to handle them. Okay?*"

Next afternoon:

"*Okay, Martha, I've scribbled down a few of the things that are troubling me in the classroom. I've just got to get rid of some of these problems or I won't be able to carry on this great educational program I had planned. You recall that we learned in college about objectives and strategies and wonderful developmental activities for children. But, with all this confusion, I can hardly begin to do any real teaching.*"

"*I know what you mean, Jane, let's hear the list.*"

"*Okay. Let's start with Robert. He won't even talk. As soon as he gets around other kids, he just clams up. Then there's Janie. She's a bossy little thing and keeps shoving the other kids around. Rebecca cries all morning and Janis runs around all the time. Stevie teases all his friends. Bobby keeps belching. Jackie steals food, Sara whines all day, and Mike jumps from the tables. And I haven't even mentioned the kids who wet their pants."*

"Okay, Jane, hold it. It sounds like you've got the whole array of typical problems encountered by a preschool teacher. You have hand-icapped kids in your room, too, don't you?"

"Yes, six of them. And what am I supposed to do with them? I know it's probably good for them to be mixed in with nonhandicapped children—and it's good for the nonhandicapped kids to learn about individual differences, but it just makes my job harder."

"What sort of handicaps do they have?"

"Let's see—two of them have cerebral palsy. They're in special seats that help to restrain some of their involuntary movements. Otherwise, though, both of them seem alert and very pleasant. Billy and two others—I can't remember their names—apparently are retarded. They're all 5 or 6 years old but seem to be much younger. They aren't even able to do some of the things that my 3-year-olds do. I'm going to try with them. I understand you can sometimes make big changes if you work with handicapped children early enough. Rebecca, the other handicapped child, is what you'd call disturbed. She's afraid to leave her parents, cries constantly, and seems to be afraid of just about everything. Where am I supposed to start?"

"Jane, let's go have a cup of coffee! It's 3:30 and I need time to think over your problems. I'm going to discuss your problems—and mine—with a friend in early education and see if she can recommend some solutions. She probably can also suggest some references."

The foregoing dialogue may seem somewhat contrived but it does include some of the problems encountered by many preschool teachers. Most of the problems mentioned deal with the presence of unwanted behaviors in children. The major objective of education, however, is the building of new behaviors that are devel-opmentally productive and useful to the person throughout life. When and if the new teacher learns how to eliminate or reduce the obstructive behaviors listed, the individual then will be faced with the real job of education: helping children acquire a variety of capabilities across major areas of development.

A preschool or day-care setting is a place for a child to learn, to play, and to develop. The quality of the setting will influence greatly the content, direction, and pace of the child's development. Nursery schools, kindergartens, day-care centers, and other childcare facilities no longer are seen as merely baby-sitting arrangements. They provide crucial experiences or encounters that can help shape a child's life.

Since children's encounters with the environment can be so important, it is vital for teachers to make some decisions regarding their own philosophy and approach to early education.

KEY ISSUES

You should consider several key issues and questions, such as these:

- What are the purposes of early education for the children with whom you work?
- Do you believe that every child can benefit equally from your program?
- Can a preschool program accommodate normal and handicapped youngsters with mutual benefit?
- Is it important, necessary, or even possible to prove that your program helps children develop?
- Is it necessary to apply proved teaching strategies and materials? Isn't it sufficient simply to provide an enriched, interesting play and socialization environment?

Certainly this brief book will not and cannot provide full answers and arguments to these issues. What the authors can do, however, is present their reasoned judgments, some opinions, some arguments, and a few answers. The position and program we advocate has received rather widespread support and is consistent with other related social needs and trends.

MAJOR REASONS FOR EARLY EDUCATION

Not all families have the same reasons for enrolling their children in early education or day-care programs.

For families where both mother and father work, it often is important to find a safe, pleasant, convenient place to leave their child during work hours. These parents have as their primary concern the satisfactory custodial care of their child. A good baby-sitter might do just as well.

Many other working parents are not satisfied with a simple substitute for baby-sitting. They want more than a safe, pleasant, and convenient arrangement for their child. These parents desire circumstances that will provide opportunities for their child to play with others. In other words, socialization experiences become an important consideration in choosing a childcare facility for many parents.

Still other parents, working or not, express even greater concern regarding what their children experience daily. Many parents want to see their children enrolled in some sort of program that intentionally provides not only socialization experiences but also activities that are designed to promote progress in other areas of their development. These parents believe their children can get a better start in life by participating in a program that deliberately attempts to promote intellectual, motor, and emotional development in addition to socialization.

Many families simply do not have the resources to provide full learning opportunities for their children. For these children, early education programs become even more important. No longer is a good program just something that will substitute for a good home experience—a good program becomes something of a developmental necessity.

Finally, some families include handicapped children who are entitled to early education. There is a good deal of evidence that early, planned programming for handicapped children not only is a good socialization experience but also can be of enormous benefit. For these children, quality early education can be pivotal to their developmental progress. Early special education of exceptional children, especially in integrated settings, can provide an optimal arrangement for changing a child's life. It must be done with care and concern.

THE PRIMARY ROLES OF THE EARLY EDUCATOR

For purposes of this book, it is useful to view the teacher as one who performs several major roles or duties as an early educator. These are:

1. early identification, or screening, for developmental problems
2. assessment or analysis of child strengths and weaknesses
3. selection or construction of a curriculum—that is, prescription of objectives for the enrolled children
4. linking of assessment findings on a given child to specific curriculum goals for the child—that is, the prescription of educational objectives
5. keeping records on child progress
6. working with parents
7. management of the classroom
8. developmental instruction

Of course, these roles are not independent of each other; one of them often involves one or several others.

The Education for All Handicapped Children Act (Public Law 94-142) was signed in 1975. The law has changed dramatically the nature of public education, including early education. The law guarantees the right of every child, including those with developmental problems, to a free public education and mandates increased participation of handicapped children in regular school programs. The law applies primarily to children ages 5 to 18 years, but the provisions for integrating handicapped and nonhandicapped children and encouragement to keep the handicapped in the mainstream of life as much as possible are spilling over and influencing programs from cradle to grave.

P.L. 94-142 requires that the handicapped children's education be designed individually through the preparation and use of an Individual Education Program—the IEP. This book devotes Chapter 9 to development of IEPs. The law also includes efforts to find unserved handicapped children and provides certain rights for parents and guarantees of due process throughout the identification, assessment, and placement processes.

Since contemporary enrollment in preschools includes children with a wide range of capabilities and problems, today's early educator must be able to perform several key professional roles. These roles are discussed in greater detail in the remainder of this book. For now, these key duties are simply mentioned, with a brief description of their importance.

Screening and Assessment

Screening refers to a rough kind of sorting into categories. In the case of early identification of developmental difficulties, screening refers to relatively quick and simple ways to decide if the child is generally normal or manifests some significant developmental difficulty. It is desirable for identification of difficulties to occur before a child is enrolled in a preschool program. Child-find efforts under P.L. 94-142 are helping.

Sometimes, however, parents enroll children in a preschool program for reasons other than their recognition of the need for such a program. They may be working parents and simply looking for a place for their child to stay. The vigilant preschool teacher should be able to spot children who may be in need of screening and subsequent assessment. A proper referral, early enough, can make a big difference for the child.

Assessment refers to a closer look at a child's strengths and weaknesses. Assessment can be carried out with standardized tests or with more informal teacher-made instruments. Assessment helps the teacher to make placement decisions about where a child should begin activities as well as instruction in the several developmental areas. A good assessment usually involves gathering information on the child's functioning in the areas of intellectual, motor, language, and social development. Such information is indispensable in planning and evaluating a preschool program for each child.

Construction and Use of a Curriculum

The early educator must be able to specify, in rather clear terms, developmental objectives for each child in the program. This does not mean that most children will not share numerous objectives; indeed, it would be peculiar if they were not reaching for similar developmental gains. But each child is unique and they all deserve special sets of objectives tailored to their specific strengths and weaknesses.

In addition to the common core of developmental objectives, then, specific personalized objectives can be written for each child. Many preschool teachers prepare IEPs for the children in their care even though they are not required to do so. Parents can be very helpful in selecting individual objectives. Fortunately, curricula are available that include objectives for early education of handicapped and nonhandicapped children in the major areas of child development. For example, the COMP-Curriculum (Appendix A) is a set of developmentally sequenced objectives for children from birth to age 5. The curriculum is organized within four basic domains: communication, own-care (personal and interpersonal skills), motor development, and problem solving.

Keeping Records

In order to do most things right, we need feedback on how we are doing. In baking a cake, roasting a turkey, building a bookcase, or painting a picture we usually check progress by measuring or testing or at least judging how much the activity has advanced. The information helps us adjust our own behavior to keep things on the right track. Similarly, the early education of young children demands some degree of recordkeeping. Each child's progress in the preschool program should be recorded in some consistent fashion so that teachers, other professionals, and parents can see, in a summarized way, the direction and rate of progress across several areas of development. Indeed, new legislation and professional standards demand accountability and evidence that a proper program is being carried out. Keeping track of children's progress through periodic or, if possible, continuing assessment can be a powerful and yet routine way to document the quality of the program for young children.

Working with Parents

More and more parents are becoming partners in the preschool education of their children. Of course, many parents work all day and do not have the effort or information to become very involved. They view the preschool simply as a place for their child while they are at work. But even these parents can be encouraged to provide input in the planning of the child's program. Some objectives, especially for children with special needs, must be carried out in the home as well as at the preschool. Thus, for instructional as well as ethical reasons, parents should be drawn into the design and—if possible—the carrying out of the child's program. And, of course, parents should be kept abreast of their child's progress.

The several roles described here will be discussed more fully throughout this book. For now, however, the final two roles are presented in greater detail since classroom *management* and preschool *instruction* are primary roles of the early educator.

MANAGEMENT IN THE PRESCHOOL

For purposes here, management includes dealing with problems similar to those recounted by the teacher at the beginning of this chapter. Management usually refers to objectives relating to discipline and other problems that somehow fall short of more positive educational objectives. Dealing with these problems, however, may be crucial to the child's developmental progress. A sound, well-organized preschool program will minimize or eliminate these problems. This book and references to be suggested should help teachers with the most frequently occurring problems. Of management problems encountered by preschool teachers, the following are perhaps the dominant ones.

Separation Difficulties

Children frequently are reluctant to leave their parents in order to spend time in a strange preschool with people they don't know. An extreme version of this problem is termed separation anxiety. This refers to a condition where children exhibit intense and prolonged crying and depression associated with the absence of familiar persons, especially the parents. The problem can be of clinical proportions and require rather skilled use of certain therapeutic procedures. Most children, however, manifest a milder degree of separation difficulty and soon adjust to their new friends and situation. Teachers can learn what *to* do and what *not* to do in order to make separation problems as minimal as possible.

Toileting Problems

Young children who are toilet trained sometimes will begin to have bladder and even bowel control problems in the preschool. Especially under stress, children may wet themselves. Usually, this is not a true case of developmental regression. More often, the child has learned recently how to use the toilet but is in a stage of transition and may oscillate back and forth between disciplined control and haphazard elimination. Again, teachers can learn right and wrong ways to handle these mistakes so that they will not be increased inadvertently.

Unwarranted Fears

Separation anxiety is a fear shown by some children that teachers usually can understand and manage. But many children have fears that seem quite odd to the teacher. Dogs, beards, red books, bells, piano music, corners, crayons, finger paint, and many other objects and events can produce fear for children. It becomes, then, an important job for the teacher to spot these fears and to attempt to help the child with them. Sometimes, it may be necessary to request help from specialists trained in therapies with young children. Most frequently, however, these fears dissipate rapidly and it is best not to give them too much attention.

Eating

Snack time or lunch time at the preschool can be an enjoyable social event or it can be a nightmare. Polite, hungry, happy children are a delight to supervise. Uncooperative, screaming children who won't eat and who disrupt the meals of others can become a real difficulty for the teacher. The management of these problems becomes essential if the meal time is not to be a time of dread for the teacher.

Cooperation, Compliance, and Independence

Perhaps the most widely accepted goal for the preschool experience is socialization. At a young age, children can learn to share, take turns, and in other ways get along with and enjoy the company of others. Equally important to growing up is the skill of being able to comply with the demands of the social and physical environment. Balancing off cooperation and compliance is independence. Educators and parents want children to become increasingly less dependent on instruction and reward from others, to become self-directed and rewarded. Children may have problems in cooperation, compliance, or independence. It becomes the job of the teacher to make sure that the child's curriculum contains objectives that provide for growth of competence in all three of these important developmental areas.

Attention

Paying attention to relevant stimuli is an absolute essential if intentional learning is to take place. Most children, of course, do benefit from incidental learning. This refers to learning that may take place on a casual or unplanned basis. While incidental learning is a valuable component of early education and should be provided through a generally stimulating environment, planned learning activities in which specific learning outcomes can be expected are essential in the preschool.

Attention then becomes a major consideration in carrying out most learning activities. Children do not come to the preschool ready to pay attention to the things the teacher intends them to. With many children, attention problems will be the primary ones to remediate. Many exceptional children, especially those with general or specific learning problems and those with behavior disorders, exhibit unusual patterns of attention to irrelevant stimuli or problems in sustaining attention to anything.

MODERN DEVELOPMENTAL INSTRUCTION

Evidence is piling up that the early years seem to be the most crucial ones for setting the direction and pace for a child's development. What early educators do during the precious time they have with a child is most important.

The great diversity of children enrolled in the modern preschool has been mentioned. The diversity of family and ethnic backgrounds, economic level, and developmental status of children requires special consideration and tactics for integrating them in instructional activities. Teachers cannot have two children with greatly different capabilities at, for example, cutting and pasting, attempting to do the same task. A cutting and pasting activity may be appropriate for both children but the specific objectives for each child will vary. Having to work, play, and just be together, however, is one strategy to help integrate children. There are other techniques for accomplishing instructional integration that will be presented later.

Because of the range of children encountered in the modern preschool, instructional methods and materials must go beyond the conventional ones. Most activities, such as finger painting, story time, finger plays, crafts, circle time, and many other experiences are worthy activities and make sense for most children. Some children, however, may require additional and more highly structured activities because of problems in their development. Also, while several children may engage in finger painting, how and why they do it may vary, depending on their development and the instructional objective.

New instructional methods are emerging that are based on modern learning theory. These new methods are remarkable in their power to bring about positive changes in children's capabilities. Many of the new techniques are based on behavior principles that have been discovered and refined over the last 20 years or so. It is only in the last ten years, however, that new teaching methods based on behavior principles have been refined sufficiently to make them available for use at the preschool level. The modern preschool teacher can use these new strategies now to bring about sometimes incredible changes in young children. These new techniques will be discussed in subsequent chapters.

Whatever strategies are employed, the early educator must be careful to provide a full spectrum of goals or objectives for children. Each child deserves instruction in all important areas of development. All too often, children (especially the handicapped) are given a lopsided curriculum; they are focused on objectives in one or two areas at the neglect of progress in others. Their development thus continues to be abnormal. All children can be helped to realize some progress in all major developmental areas: intellectual, social, language, and motor abilities. In short, developmental instruction must be *balanced, normalized,* and *mainstreamed.*

Chapter 2

Screening and Assessing the Preschool Child

OBJECTIVES

1. Describe the sequence of goals involved in the developmental assessment of preschool children.
2. Distinguish between screening and comprehensive assessment of preschool children.
3. Discuss general procedures for screening and identifying high-risk preschoolers.
4. Identify and describe specific measures used to screen both normal and handicapped preschoolers.
5. Explain the relationship between comprehensive assessment and goal planning.
6. Discuss general procedures for assessing preschool children comprehensively.
7. Identify and describe specific measures used to assess the skills of both normal and handicapped preschoolers comprehensively.

2

A CRITICAL NEED EXISTS to construct practical bonds between diagnostic assessments and educational programming when serving both normal and handicapped preschoolers.

In the past, the early identification and assessment of developmental differences often was viewed and carried out as an activity separate from instructional planning. Thus, the important link between assessment and intervention rarely materialized. The result of this lack of continuity was that educational programming was based mostly on subjective impressions about child needs and functioning because early childhood educators received relatively little practical guidance from psychologists regarding precise developmental data for initial instructional planning.

Recent trends in early childhood education have seen the rise of mandated services for children with differences in development and learning within a mainstreamed setting. With this trend, educators are accountable for accurately defining educational needs and constructing individualized instructional plans, so that a direct similarity exists between behaviors assessed, observed, and taught (Bagnato & Neisworth, 1979). Jordan, Hayden, Karnes, and Wood (1977) advocate this integrated relationship between assessment and curriculum goals by stating that there should be

> clear logical links between what the curriculum is attempting to do (rationale), how it is organized to accomplish the specific aspects of its effort (content and objectives), and how accomplishment can be determined (evaluation). (p. 153)

In light of the growing practical need to imbed assessment within programming in order to operationalize the provisions of Public Law 94-142, school psychologists, early childhood educators, and parents need to merge their efforts to assess

15

and program comprehensively for the disabled preschooler in a systematic manner. P.L. 94-142 requires educators to (a) describe a child's current levels of functioning across many skill areas, (b) specify short- and long-term educational goals, objectives, strategies, settings, and auxiliary services, and (c) to select appropriate evaluative methods to monitor both child progress and program effectiveness.

To carry out these goals, Chapters 2 and 3 present a step-by-step guide that details and discusses various developmental measures with which early childhood educators should be familiar in order to assess and program effectively for the development of both normal and handicapped children. Moreover, these measures are discussed in terms of several interlinking educational goals and purposes.

PURPOSE AND CONTINUITY IN ASSESSMENT

Tests are selected and administered in educational settings for various purposes, but mainly to enable decisions to be made about children's ranges of skills and deficits as well as the most appropriate instructional programs for them. The kind of decision to be made dictates not only the particular assessment measures to be selected and used but also the kinds of behaviors to be sampled. Assessment should not be viewed as a separate educational activity but rather as an integral and continuing part of the programming process. Specifically, tests are administered to accomplish four major goals and purposes:

1. to screen and identify high-risk children
2. to assess multiple areas of development and learning comprehensively so as to identify strengths and weaknesses and to guide curriculum planning
3. to construct individualized instructional goal plans on the basis of assessment/curriculum linkages
4. to monitor both child progress and program effectiveness

When considered as a sequence, each of these assessment purposes serves as a prerequisite for the succeeding one, culminating in the major goals of individualized programming and the monitoring of each child's developmental progress within a particular program of intervention. Similarly, these goals can help to organize and direct efforts to assess each child's pattern of capabilities in a reliable and systematic manner. In this way the assessment process flows from general to specific and ensures follow-through from screening to individualized programming. Figure 2-1 portrays this goal-based, general-to-specific assessment process. Essentially, the results of initial, global screenings of individual children should be

Figure 2-1 Comprehensive Developmental Assessment and Programming

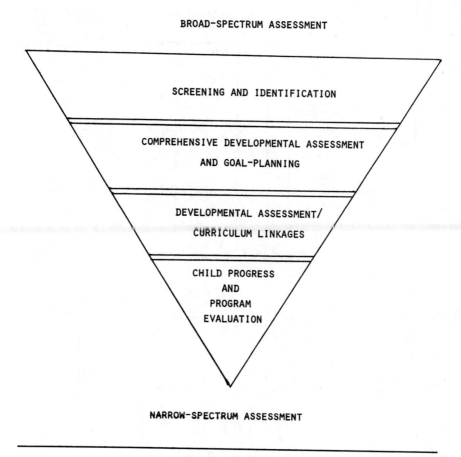

BROAD-SPECTRUM ASSESSMENT

SCREENING AND IDENTIFICATION

COMPREHENSIVE DEVELOPMENTAL ASSESSMENT
AND GOAL-PLANNING

DEVELOPMENTAL ASSESSMENT/
CURRICULUM LINKAGES

CHILD PROGRESS
AND
PROGRAM
EVALUATION

NARROW-SPECTRUM ASSESSMENT

tentative and subject to revision via more comprehensive follow-up assessments that then provide the basis for individualized curriculum goal planning and evaluation.

The series of diagnostic-prescriptive goals in Figure 2-1 encompasses a variety of measures and methods that can be used to assess each child's range of developmental skills in a systematic way so as to facilitate individualized curriculum planning (Exhibit 2-1.) The first step in the sequence is the early identification of developmental problems.

Exhibit 2-1 Developmental Assessment Methods Matrix

Legend:
X Primary focus
O Secondary focus

Instrument	AGES	DOMAINS: Language	Fine/gross motor	Personal-social	Cognitive	Educational Readiness	PURPOSE: Screening	Diagnostic/prescriptio	Evaluation	HANDICAP: Visual	Auditory	Neuro-motor	Language	Socio-emotional	Developmental/learning
Assessment of Child. Lang. Comprehension	3–6 yrs.	X					O	X	O			O		O	X
Alpern-Boll Developmental Profile	Birth–12 yrs.		X		X	X	O	X		O	O	O	O	O	X
Bayley Scales of Infant Development	2–30 mo.		X	O	X			X		O	O	O	O	O	X
Boehm Test of Basic Concepts	K–2nd grade				X	O		X				O	O		X
Callier-Azusa Deaf-Blind Scale	Birth–9 yrs.		X		X	X		X		X	X				X
Carolina Developmental Profile	2–5 yrs.		X		X	X		X							X
Cattell Infant Intelligence Scale	2–30 mo.	O			X	X		X	X						X
Cognitive Skills Assess. Battery	Presch–primary				X	X	X	X	O		X	O	O	O	X
Communication Evaluation Chart	3–60 mo.	O		O			X	X	O	O	O	O	O	O	X
Developmental Activities Screen.	6–60 mo.		O				X	X	O						X
Denver Devel. Screening Test	1–72 mo.		O				X	X							X
Devel. Programming: Infants & Child.	Birth–36 mo.	O	X		X	O		X	X	O	O	O	O	O	X
Down's Syndrome Performance Invent.	Birth–9 yrs.	O			X	O		X		O	O	O	O	O	X
Functional Profile	Birth–6 yrs.	O			X	O		X		O	O	O	O	O	X
Gesell Developmental Schedules	1–72 mo.	O			X	O		X		O	O	O	O	O	X
Haeussermann Educational Evaluation	2–6 yrs.			O	X	O		X		O	O			O	X

Exhibit 2-1 continued

Legend: X Primary focus O Secondary focus

Instrument	Ages	Language	Fine/gross motor	Personal-social	Cognitive	Educational Readiness	Screening	Diagnostic/prescription	evaluation	Visual	Auditory	Neuro-motor	Language	Socio-emotional	Developmental/learning
Learning Accomplishment Profile	Birth–6 yrs.	X	X	X	X	X	X	X	X		O	O	O	O	X
Marshalltown Devel/Behav. Profile	Birth–6 yrs.	O	O		O	O			O		O	O	O	O	X
Maxfield-Buchholz Social Maturity Scale	Birth–6 yrs.	O	O										O		X
McCarthy Scales of Children's Abilities	2½–8½ yrs.	X			X	X			O						X
Memphis Comprehensive Devel. Scale	Birth–5 yrs.					O			O	X	O	X	O	O	X
Milani Motor Devel. Screening Test	Birth–2 yrs.		O				X					X			X
Minnesota Preschool Scale	6–60 mo.		O	O		O				O					X
Preschool Attainment Record	Birth–7 yrs.					X			O	O	O	O	O	O	X
Perceptions of Developmental Skills	Preschool				O				O		O	O	O	O	X
Portage Guide to Early Education	Birth–6 yrs.					X									X
Preschool Profile	Birth–6 yrs.							O							X
Preschool Language Scale	1–8 yrs.	O			O		X	O	O				X		X
Preschool Inventory	2–6½ yrs.								O						X
Pupil Record of Educational Behavior	Presch–Primary			O			X		O						
Receptive Expressive Emerging Language Scale	Birth–36 mo.														X
Umansky Guide: Infants & Preschoolers	Birth–72 mo.									O	O	O	O	O	X

GOAL 1: SCREENING AND IDENTIFICATION

Before discussing how early screening and identification are carried out to detect developmental and learning problems, it is important to define these concepts. The following definitions provide guidelines for understanding this early identification process:

Assessment Activity

Screening: a global process of surveying the behavior of children in an attempt to detect the existence of general developmental problems

Outcome

Identification: the result of the screening process in which apparent developmental deficits are detected and highlighted

Review of Tests and Purposes

The initial goal in comprehensive developmental assessment for individualized curriculum planning is the screening and subsequent identification of suspected deficits in a child's functioning across many behavioral and developmental areas. It is important to collect such screening information from a variety of sources so as to increase the reliability of the results and thus the confidence that can be placed in these data. Screening information directed toward problem identification often is obtained from such diverse sources as problem descriptions from parents, physicians, social workers, and teachers; from behavioral ratings; and even from the administration of brief developmental screening tests or checklists. All such information should be synthesized to gain a complete picture of a child's range of functional skills as perceived by various persons who have observed the individual across situations. Moreover, screening information must cover several major functional areas: language skills, personal-social behaviors, sensorimotor capabilities, and problem-solving skills. This array of information helps to generate a profile of functional skills for each child compared to the skills to be expected of the average child of the same age. Through this global screening procedure, deficit areas requiring more specific follow-up assessment can be highlighted.

Again, such developmental screenings should synthesize information from diverse sources across many behavioral areas. In most cases, early identification efforts are conducted by preschool teachers or by multidisciplinary teams of professionals and paraprofessionals representing various human service agencies. In recent years, professionals interested in early identification of developmental problems have found community-based child-find procedures or "roundups" to be effective in screening large groups of infants and preschoolers to identify those suspected of being at developmental risk (Kurtz, Neisworth, & Laub, 1977; Zehrbach, 1975). Nevertheless, early childhood educators and other cooperating specialists are the most important individuals to organize and conduct these early developmental screenings.

Screening Measures

Individualized curriculum planning to guide instruction is based upon an expanding series of early diagnostic assessments. Screening and assessment measures constructed on the basis of normal child development expectancies have been used to describe a particular current, general developmental status using comparative age norms. This approach is helpful for detecting uneven or delayed patterns of growth and development across a variety of behavioral areas. These global measures may be used to select or identify children who deviate significantly from the average. However, these measures cannot be used to pinpoint specific skill deficits reliably since they survey only a limited number of landmark developmental milestones in these behavioral areas. Thus, screening devices are useful in selecting children in need of help but are inappropriate either for identifying instructional targets or for placing these chidren within a curriculum. Achievement of these instructional goals can be based only upon more detailed and comprehensive developmental assessments.

One of the most frequently employed developmental screening measures is the Denver Developmental Screening Test (DDST) (Frankenburg & Dodds, 1975). Capable of being used with children between the ages of 1 month and 6 years, the DDST surveys the child's development in the areas of gross motor skills, fine motor skills, personal-social skills, and language capabilities. This measure is used most effectively by preschool teachers to detect delays in normal developmental patterns by observing the child's actual performance on a variety of behavioral tasks or activities. Several activities on the scale are placed along points at which normal children generally can accomplish them (Exhibit 2-3). Passes and failures on these activities provide an estimate of how "delayed" a child's development appears to be.

Similarly, the Denver Prescreening Developmental Questionnaire (DPDQ) (Frankenburg & Dodds, 1975) was designed to be used in tandem with the DDST by providing information about *parents' perceptions* of their child's level of developmental functioning.

Many other global screening measures provide quick samples of general functioning; however, few of the currently available scales provide data that can be translated directly into interim educational goals. The Developmental Activities Screening Inventory (DASI) (Dubose & Langley, 1977) is designed as an informal screening device for use with children ages 6 to 60 months. The measure is intended for use by preschool teachers in identifying major developmental skill

Exhibit 2-2 Denver Developmental Screening Results on Andy

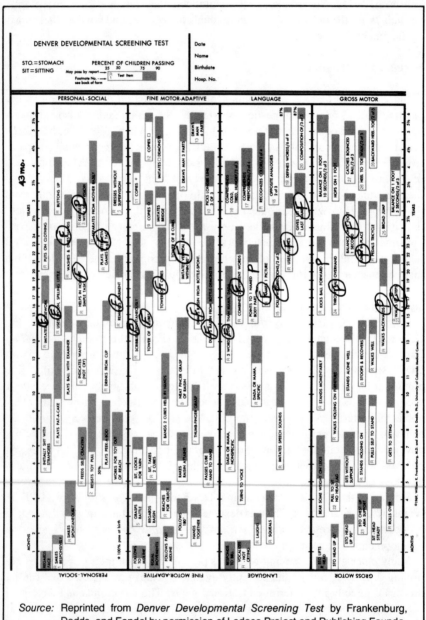

Source: Reprinted from *Denver Developmental Screening Test* by Frankenburg, Dodds, and Fandal by permission of Ladoce Project and Publishing Foundation, © 1974.

Exhibit 2-3 Sample Denver Developmental Screening Test Scoresheet

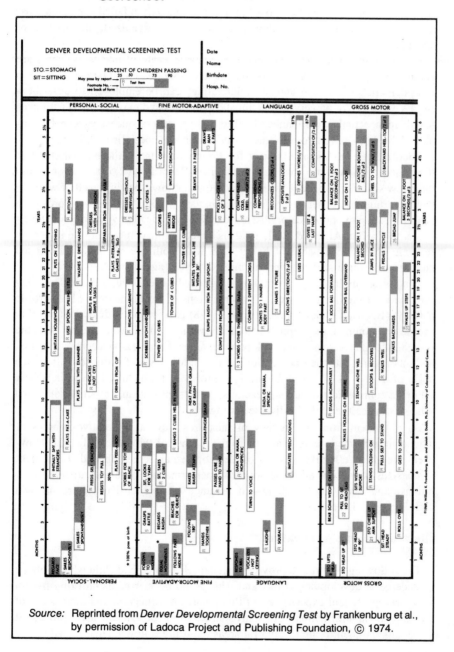

Source: Reprinted from *Denver Developmental Screening Test* by Frankenburg et al., by permission of Ladoca Project and Publishing Foundation, © 1974.

deficits requiring remediation. A nonverbal measure, the DASI can be used with hearing-impaired and language-disordered children. Adaptations for the physically and visually impaired are possible. From an analysis of failed items, diagnostic teaching and initial curriculum planning can be organized, although more detailed assessment is necessary.

For the multihandicapped preschooler, accurate performance assessments are not always possible. Thus, developmental screenings based on parent interviews or systematic observation and behavior ratings can be employed to describe a child's estimated or perceived functional capabilities and to supplement estimates based upon actual performance. In this regard, several measures can be employed by both psychologists and early childhood specialists. The Maxfield-Buchholz Scale of Social Maturity for Preschool Blind Children (Maxfield & Buchholz, 1958) and the Preschool Attainment Record (PAR) (Doll, 1966), both interview scales, can be used with any adult who knows the child well or who has had opportunity to observe the individual in various situations so as to provide a basis for rating the presence or absence of various skills. The Alpern-Boll Developmental Profile (Alpern & Boll, 1972) is a much more comprehensive interview screening measure capable of being used with both normal and handicapped children. All three scales cover the birth to 6-year age range.

In addition, multiple area behavior ratings can be used to supplement screening information from other sources. The Perceptions of Developmental Skills profile (PODS) (Bagnato, Neisworth, & Eaves, 1978) is a screening device intended to profile and compare the impressions of several individuals who interact with the preschool child. Across five developmental areas (Exhibit 2-4) teachers, parents, and other adults rate their perceptions of the child's level of skill acquisition on a scale of 1 to 7 (1 = no problem; 7 = profound problem). Such ratings help facilitate communication among teachers, parents, physicians, psychologists, and others who see the child in diverse settings.

As is evident from this review of measures, several alternative sources of diagnostic information are available to the teacher of the preschool child. However, the most effective system of developmental screening and assessment synthesizes data from all these sources—performance, observation, interview, ratings, and diagnostic teaching—to obtain a comprehensive picture of each child's range of functioning.

Illustration and Application

The following illustration provides an example of a typical child who might be considered at developmental risk and who would be viewed as profiting from a structured preschool experience. At this point, the collection and integration of developmental information from many sources would be valuable in the process of screening and identifying behavioral areas requiring follow-up and remediation.

Exhibit 2-4 Perceptions of Developmental Skills (PODS Profile)

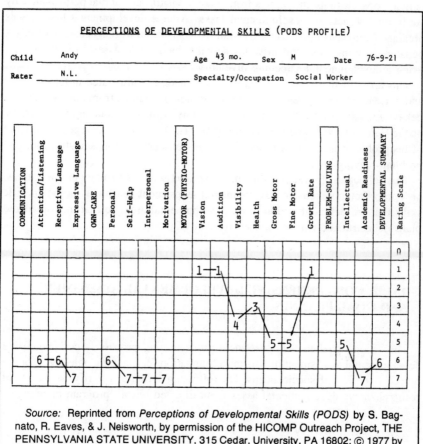

Source: Reprinted from *Perceptions of Developmental Skills (PODS)* by S. Bagnato, R. Eaves, & J. Neisworth, by permission of the HICOMP Outreach Project, THE PENNSYLVANIA STATE UNIVERSITY, 315 Cedar, University, PA 16802; © 1977 by Pennsylvania State University, HICOMP Preschool Project.

Andy, age 3½ (43 months), was referred to the Child Development Center for an assessment of his developmental status. The parents' presenting problems concerned Andy's generalized delay in speech, motor, and socialization skills. Andy appeared to have the physical build of the average child his age, but his social behaviors seemed very maladaptive; i.e., throwing objects, unprovoked screaming and tantrums, self-stimulatory behaviors, head-banging, spinning, distractibility, and resistance to being touched by people.

The initial goal in assessing Andy involved gathering general screening information about the developmental areas (motor, language, personal-social, and problem solving) that seemed to indicate his primary problems. A complete picture of Andy's developmental problems required obtaining descriptions from the parents, observations and ratings from a home visitor, and actual performance by Andy on a variety of developmental tasks. After a developmental history was obtained from the parents, a home visitor (teacher-social worker) observed Andy's behavior at home; subsequently, his actual behavior was assessed in the home, using a developmental screening inventory.

This array of multisource diagnostic information is illustrated in Exhibits 2-2 and 2-4. Note how the developmental information obtained from observation and behavioral ratings (PODS) compares favorably with Andy's actual performance on the Denver Developmental Screening Test (DDST) to provide a general picture of his problems and delays in the language, self-care, motor, socialization, and problem-solving areas.

This collection of screening information draws attention to major problem areas; now, more comprehensive developmental assessment can focus on the specific skills that are deficient within those developmental areas so that individualized plans of instruction can be devised for Andy.

GOAL 2: COMPREHENSIVE DEVELOPMENTAL ASSESSMENT AND GOAL PLANNING

The second goal in the assessment-programming process is comprehensive developmental assessment that forms a foundation for planning objectives for the preschool child with special needs. The following definitions clarify the activity of comprehensive developmental assessment directed toward program planning:

Assessment Activity

Comprehensive Developmental Assessment: a wide-ranging yet specific process of analyzing, describing, and profiling each child's range of developmental skills across multiple behavioral areas in order to determine levels of functioning and provide a basis for individualized educational planning

Outcome

Individualized Instructional Goal Planning: the end result of comprehensive developmental assessment procedures that specifies the child's developmental level functioning and prescribes congruent individual educational targets as a basis for curriculum planning and teaching activities.

Review of Tests and Purposes

Developmental screening measures and the information they yield are vital for identifying children in need of special help and for highlighting problem areas in development but are inappropriate for constructing detailed curriculum plans and teaching strategies. Rather, individualized curriculum planning is based upon a comprehensive assessment and analysis of patterns of acquired, absent, and emerging developmental skills across many areas of functioning.

Many traditional developmental measures as well as recently constructed preschool scales can fulfill this comprehensive assessment purpose quite well for both normal and handicapped preschoolers.

A number of newly developed preschool scales have been constructed primarily for teacher use. They are appropriate not only for comprehensively pinpointing deficient developmental skills but also for planning detailed instructional goals. Some have even been constructed for use with specific curricula.

Both the Learning Accomplishment Profile (LAP) (Sanford, 1974) and the Memphis Comprehensive Developmental Scale (MCDS) (Quick, Little, & Campbell, 1974) fall in this latter category. The LAP is an individually administered developmental profile appropriate for use with children 6 months to 6 years of age. It assesses observable developmental skills within and across fine motor, gross motor, social, self-help, cognitive, and language areas (Exhibit 2-5). The scale yields a profile of each child's variations in acquiring developmental skills and also age ranges that depict the child's current levels of functioning. More specifically, this multiple area assessment of observable skills enables the teacher to determine appropriate learning objectives for each child. The scale also facilitates the continuous monitoring of skill acquisition and, thus, progress within a program.

Similarly, the MCDS is a developmental scale that was constructed for teacher use with the exceptional preschool child in mind. The MCDS covers the age range 3 to 60 months and provides a detailed assessment of skills in fine motor, gross motor, language, personal-social, and perceptual-cognitive areas. A unique and practical characteristic of the MCDS is that it is both a developmental test and a curriculum. After the child has been evaluated developmentally, the teacher notes from the results those skills next in the developmental sequence that the child has not acquired and that are prerequisite behaviors for later learning. The teacher then selects these skills as goals constituting the child's individualized educational plan. Developmental ages also can be derived to describe current levels of functioning.

Finally, the Psychoeducational Evaluation of the Preschool Child (Jedrysek, Klapper, Pope, & Wortis, 1972) is both an assessment device and an instructional format designed for use with both normal and cerebral palsied preschoolers. The scale is teacher-administered and is designed to be employed as a guide in

Exhibit 2-5 Fine Motor Skill Objectives: Manipulation

Developmental Age	Item	Behavior	1st +/−	2nd +/−	Comments
6	FM1	Picks up cube			
6	FM2	Retains cube in one hand			
6	FM3	Thumb and fingers grasp			
9	FM4	Thumb and forefinger			
12	FM5	Picks up 2 objects			
12	FM6	Puts cube in cup			
12	FM7	2 cube tower			
15	FM8	Circle in formboard			
18	FM9	Dumps from bottle			
18	FM10	Turns 2 or 3 pages			
18	FM11	Circle/square in formboard			
18	FM12	4 cube tower			
21	FM13	Folds paper			
24	FM14	Turns twist cap			
24	FM15	7 cube tower			
24	FM16	Turns pages singly			
24	FM17	4 piece formboard			
30	FM18	8 cube tower			
30	FM19	Rolls playdough			
30	FM20	9 cube tower			
36	FM21	Wiggles thumb			
36	FM22	Strings large beads			
36	FM23	Imitates bridge			
36	FM24	10 cube tower			
36	FM25	4-piece formboard, no errors			
36	FM26	Weaves through sewing board			
36	FM27	Puts pegs in pegboard			
36	FM28	Cuts with scissors			
42	FM29	Strings small beads			
42	FM30	Builds 2 steps			
42	FM31	Builds bridge from model			
48	FM32	Laces sewing card			
48	FM33	6-piece puzzle			
48	FM34	Imitates "gate"			
48	FM35	Builds 3 steps			
54	FM36	8-piece puzzle			
54	FM37	Folds triangle			
60	FM38	Builds gate from model			
60	FM39	Imitates 3 folds in paper			
60	FM40	Cuts out diamond			
66	FM41	Builds 4 steps			
66	FM42	Laces			
72	FM43	Ties bow			
		Last Item Administered			
		Less Errors	−	−	
		Manipulation Score			

Source: Reprinted from the *Learning Accomplishment Profile* by LeMay, Griffin, and Sanford, by permission of Kaplan School Supply Corporation, © 1978.

evaluating the educational potential of preschool children. Covering the ages 2½ to 6 years, the scale assesses the child's present functioning and level of achievement in a variety of areas through 41 test items, such as physical and sensory, perceptual, short-term memory and learning, language competence, and cognitive functioning. The scale is not a standardized test but rather serves as an evaluative and curriculum guide for the teacher in planning individualized goals to facilitate each child's learning. Provisions are included to adapt assessment procedures for use with cerebral palsied preschoolers to determine the instructional levels at which they can learn most effectively.

Most recently constructed developmental scales are intended for teacher use. However, these measures actually are modifications of traditional standardized developmental scales such as the Gesell Developmental Schedules (GDS) (Gesell, 1949) and the Bayley Scales of Infant Development (BSID) (Bayley, 1969) that require administration by intensively trained psychologists and clinicians. Nevertheless, many infant stimulation specialists, early childhood special educators, and psychologists with supervised training find the scales to be invaluable tools both for assessing current levels of functioning in infants and preschoolers and for providing a practical base for curriculum planning (Meier, 1976).

The Gesell Developmental Schedules (see Ames, Gillespie, Haines, & Ilg, 1979, for further discussion) is the grandfather of developmental measures from which all other scales have been directly adapted and constructed. Sampling the age range of 4 weeks to 6 years, the GDS provides an excellent and truly comprehensive clinical analysis of the neurological, physical, and psychomotor status of developing children (motor, language, adaptive, and personal-social areas). Separate developmental age ranges instead of a global score are obtained for each of the four major developmental areas to describe variations in current functioning. The scales are particularly useful for identifying and predicting neurological difficulties and developmental retardation as well as establishing short-term, sequential educational goals. The Gesell Schedules' wide age range, broad, specific behavior sampling, and educational relevance make the scales useful for early childhood teachers under supervision of a psychologist.

The most reliable and valid of the comprehensive developmental scales, the Bayley Scales of Infant Development (BSID) cover the age range from 2 to 30 months in the mental and motor areas (Exhibit 2-6). An invaluable infant behavior profile also is included to rate temperament, responsiveness, and other behavioral dimensions. The BSID is an excellent measure of current functioning and provides a reliable base for pinpointing developmental skills and deficits (244 tasks). Developmental ages and rate of growth scores are obtained by comparing each child's score with that of the 1,262 infants to whom the test originally was administered in 1969. In addition, numerous infant stimulation programs use the BSID as a basis for individualized curriculum planning. Standardized procedures

Exhibit 2-6 Sample Tasks from the Bayley Scales of Infant Development

To score: Check P (Pass) or F (Fail). If "Other," mark O (Omit), R (Refused), or RPT (Reported by mother).

Item No.	Age Placement and Range (Months)	Situation	Item Title	Score P	F	Other	Notes
99	11.3 (8-15)		Pushes car along	P			
100	11.8 (9-18)	L	Puts 3 or more cubes in cup	P			
101	12.0 (9-18)	G³	Jabbers expressively	P			
102	12.0 (9-17)	P	Uncovers blue box		F		
103	12.0 (8-18)	Q	Turns pages of book			R	Mother's report but not directly observed
104	12.2 (8-19)		Pats whistle doll, in imitation	P			
105	12.4 (7-18)	D²	Dangles ring by string	P			
106	12.5 (9-18)	N	Imitates words (Record words used)		F		
107	12.9 (10-17)	P	Puts beads in box (6 of 8)	P			
108	13.0 (10-17)	O	Places 1 peg repeatedly	P			Needs prompting
109	13.4 (10-19)	J	Removes pellet from bottle	P			
110	13.6 (10-20)	R	Blue board: places 1 round block (specify)		F		Items 101,121,129,142,155,159,160 ___ No. round placed ___No. square placed ___ Completion time
111	13.8 (10-19)	H¹	Builds tower of 2 cubes (Note number of cubes)		F		Items 111,119,143,161 ___ No. of cubes

Source: Reprinted from *Bayley Scales of Infant Development* by Bayley by permission of Psychological Corporation Division of Harcourt Brace Jovanovich, © 1969.

for adapting the administration of developmental tasks to handicapped infants also are available (Hoffman, 1975).

Finally, most comprehensive developmental scales are only partially useful with multihandicapped infants and preschoolers because they contain activities and require responses that make performance difficult or impossible for the hearing-impaired, blind, and physically-neurologically handicapped child. Seeking to remedy this limitation, specialists have devised scales that exclude tasks that would confound the assessment of these children. One of the most promising of these adaptive scales is the Callier-Azusa Scale for Deaf-Blind Children (Stillman, 1974).

Covering the age range from birth to 9 years, the Callier-Azusa Scale is essentially a profile of sequential developmental skills organized as a checklist to be completed by teachers who are familiar with the child being assessed in motor, perceptual, language, social, and daily living skill areas. The device relies on spontaneous, naturalistic observation of behavior in structured and unstructured settings. The results of observational assessment fulfill three purposes.

1. establishing developmental levels of function
2. measuring child progress and program effectiveness
3. providing behavioral guides to curriculum goal planning and teaching

The scale is especially valuable for assessing the adaptive skills of low-functioning deaf-blind children for whom other developmental scales are inappropriate.

Illustration and Application

A developmental screening attempts to identify children in need of special help and to highlight major problem areas. However, in order to increase the confidence that can be placed in the screening results, comprehensive developmental assessment focuses on those highlighted problem areas and serves to confirm or refute the screening results, to clearly pinpoint and describe deficit skills within those problem areas, and to provide a base for individualized curriculum goal planning.

The previous screening results on Andy revealed generalized developmental delays in several areas: language, self-care, motor, cognitive, and socialization areas.

The next step in the assessment sequence involved an analysis of specific skills and deficits in these areas. After appropriate scales were selected for Andy regarding his age and any observable handicaps that might have limited his performance, a comprehensive developmental assessment was obtained.

In this instance, Andy was given the Gesell Developmental Schedules to establish his levels of developmental functioning in major areas and to pinpoint deficient skills in the normal developmental sequence. Andy's pattern of developmental levels as assessed by his performance on tasks in several GDS areas is shown in Table 2-1.

It can be observed that Andy, age 43 months, demonstrates developmental lags across all areas resulting in skill deficits of nearly two to three years overall, when compared to the capabilities expected of the normal 3½-year-old child. This assessment supports the generalized delay found in the screening procedure and specifies distinct levels of current functioning in several areas.

Establishing Andy's current levels of developmental functioning enables the teacher to enter him at individually appropriate levels within the curriculum. Once he is entered at these levels, individualized curriculum goals are suggested immediately as they occur in the curriculum sequence. However, truly individualized goal planning depends upon an analysis by the teacher of Andy's pattern of acquired (+), absent (−), and emerging skills (±) as revealed in his pattern of test performance and classroom behavior and achievement. This crucial step is discussed thoroughly in the next chapter since it depends on the teacher's matching of assessment goals to similar curriculum goals forming a series of assessment/ curriculum linkages across multiple areas of development.

Table 2-1 Gesell Developmental Schedules Results on Andy

Area	Developmental Level
Language	9-12 months
Personal-social	12 months
Motor	18-21 months
Adaptive	11-15 months

RECOMMENDED ACTIVITIES

1. Obtain copies of both developmental screening and assessment scales to review and to administer to children for practice, *only*. Examples such as the Denver Developmental Screening Test (DDST) and the Memphis Comprehensive Developmental Scale (MCDS) would be manageable starting points.
2. Make arrangements to observe a diagnostic specialist such as a school psychologist conducting a developmental evaluation on a preschool child. Beforehand create a list of developmental behaviors a child of that age should be able to exhibit and tasks that it should be able to complete. During the observation, check off the child's completion of various tasks using this notation: (+) indicates a completed task, (−) indicates a failed task, and (±) indicates a nearly completed task or an emerging skill.
3. Make a list of informal assessment procedures that you as an early childhood educator could use to evaluate a child's capabilities. Indicate the kinds of behaviors and problems you would look for in a child's performance that would be useful to you in program planning.

Linking Developmental Diagnosis and Curriculum Planning

Chapter 3

Linking Developmental Diagnosis and Curriculum Planning

OBJECTIVES

1. Define and discuss the activity of developmental task analysis.
2. Explain and illustrate a procedure for linking assessment and curriculum goals.
3. Complete a simulated assessment/curriculum linkage exercise.
4. Discuss general methods of supplementing developmental assessment information in the classroom.

3

GOAL 3: DEVELOPMENTAL ASSESSMENT/CURRICULUM LINKAGES

GOAL THREE DIRECTS TEACHERS to use developmental assessment results as a practical starting point for curriculum planning. This procedure involves matching assessment and curriculum objectives. The following definitions provide a brief illustration of this linkage activity:

Assessment Activity

Developmental Task Analysis: a process of identifying and analyzing children's ranges of acquired (+), absent (−), and emerging (±) developmental skills as revealed in their performance on assessment tasks in order to select similar tasks and objectives at appropriate curriculum levels

Outcome

Matching Assessment/Curriculum Objectives: the end result of developmental task analysis in which a sequence of individualized curriculum objectives and educational strategies is specified for children within several behavioral areas based upon their current ranges of acquired skills, as revealed through comprehensive developmental assessment

Review of Procedures and Purposes

Comprehensive developmental assessment serves to profile each child's levels of current functioning and to detail the skills within the normal developmental sequence that are fully acquired, emerging, or absent. Because of the comprehensive and specific nature of this assessment, a profile and basis for individualized curriculum goal planning is provided conveniently. Furthermore, early childhood teachers and other specialists readily can use developmental assessment results as a basis for curriculum planning since both scales and curricula contain similar developmental areas and behavioral tasks. This step is essential in the preparation of Individual Education Programs (IEPs).

Using Assessment Results as Guides to Programming

In order to use developmental scales as guides to curriculum goal planning, the early childhood teacher with other specialists must evaluate both the tests and the curricula they employ in terms of their inclusion of similar behaviors, tasks, and objectives. Therefore, it is important that the developmental measures used must match, to a large extent, the objectives of the curriculum used. In effect, "test to the teaching" and match assessment results with congruent curriculum objectives.

Exhibit 3-1 provides a concise, four-phase overview of the steps involved in using developmental assessment results as guides to curriculum planning.

Steps 1 through 3 explain that it is important to select tests that are similar to the curricula used, that developmental screenings help highlight and identify developmental deficits, and that comprehensive assessment procedures help to confirm the screening results and to determine a child's specific levels of functioning in major developmental areas.

Next, Step 4 directs teachers to identify each child's developmental ceilings on the test by doing a developmental task analysis. Specifically, by observing and analyzing the child's quality of performance on a series of tasks along the normal developmental sequence, teachers can identify precisely the tasks the child fully completed (+), failed to complete (−), and only partially completed (±). This range of variable performances will be within the developmental level identified during the comprehensive assessment (for example: 11 to 15 months). Furthermore, there now is present a precise idea of the specific upper limits, or ceilings, that characterize the child's developmental functioning and, therefore, the specific behavioral skills that it has not acquired across many developmental areas. This sequence of ceilings describes a range of skills that need to be taught and acquired before more complex skills can be learned. These skills are viewed as prerequisites to later learning. Therefore, this developmental task analysis identifies crucial skills that need to be focused upon in curriculum planning. Moreover, these developmental ceilings serve as targets for entering children at specific points within the curriculum.

However, once these developmental targets are identified and analyzed in the comprehensive assessment, they must be matched with similar developmental objectives within the particular curriculum used in the preschool before reliable, individualized curriculum planning can occur.

Exhibit 3-1 Steps in Forging an Assessment/Curriculum Linkage

1. Identify Developmental Deficits Requiring More Focused Assessment

2. Match Assessment Devices According to Curriculum Characteristics and Content

3. Determine Developmental Levels in Major Areas of Functioning

C.A. = 43 months........MOTOR	= 18-21 mo.
ADAPTIVE	= 11-15 mo.
LANGUAGE	= 9-12 mo.
PERSONAL-SOCIAL =	12 mo.

4. Identify "Developmental Ceilings" in Each Area of Functioning

Imitates common words	±
Speaks 3-4 words	-
Drinks cup-no spilling	±
Indicates wet pants	-
Jumps both feet	-
Attempts cube tower	-
Finds hidden objects	±
Goes to location	±

5. Match Developmental Ceiling Tasks to Curriculum Target-Objectives in Each Area of Functioning

TEST	CURRICULUM
Imitates common words...	Imitates familiar words
Speaks 3-4 words........	Uses words in speech
Drinks cup-no spilling..	Drinks from cup-unassisted
Indicates wet pants.....	Gestures for wet pants & toilet
Jumps both feet.........	Jumps off floor/both feet
Attempts cube tower.....	Stacks two cubes
Finds hidden objects....	Looks for object out of sight
Goes to location........	Follows direction to go to location

Linking Assessment/Curriculum Target-Objectives

When working with both normal and handicapped preschool populations, it is vitally important that developmental assessment and educational intervention be bonded in ways that are practical for the early childhood teacher. The crucial element in this bond is that a close match must exist between the skills assessed and the skills taught.

In this respect, both developmental scales and most preschool curricula are constructed on the same foundation: the normal sequence of developmental tasks, skills, and behaviors. This relationship between scales and curricula (the developmental task sequence) can be used readily by teachers to plan reliable and individualized educational goal plans based on comprehensive developmental assessments. Exhibit 3-2 demonstrates that the frequently employed developmental scales and curricula focus upon similar behavioral areas—motor, language, cognitive, personal-social, and readiness. This similarity is evident at both general and specific levels in most curricula.

Practical assessment/curriculum linkages can be constructed by capitalizing on this developmental task sequence apparent in both scales and curricula.

Completing this linkage between developmental assessment results and similar curriculum entry target objectives is an important task. Although no clear one-to-one match exists between all tests and all curriculum objectives in any curriculum, the normal developmental sequencing of skills in motor, language, cognitive, and personal-social areas enables many practical linkages to be constructed. Step 5 in Exhibit 3-1 directs the teacher to match a child's developmental ceilings in each behavioral area with similar curriculum objectives that tap those deficient skills. The teacher simply matches the test tasks that were failed $(-)$ or partially completed $(\pm)$ with similar objectives at certain levels in various preschool curricula. The match is made according to the similarity regarding what the child has to do to perform successfully on both tasks, i.e., the physical similarity between test task and curriculum activity, and the kind of response required of the child. For example, repeating a three-digit number sequence and repeating numbers imitating an adult are essentially the same tasks. Exhibit 3-3 illustrates how this assessment/curriculum linkage is accomplished in practice. Note the use of the HICOMP Curriculum, which is given in Appendix A.

The resulting product of this linking procedure is the construction of a sequence of individual curriculum objectives for each child that focuses on many developmental areas and behaviors. These assessment/curriculum linkages are reliable methods of using initial assessment results to construct individualized educational programs, of adapting teaching to the child's deficits and handicaps, and of monitoring both child progress and program effectiveness. Evidence of learning required to complete both test activities and similar curriculum tasks provides

Exhibit 3-2 Developmental Areas Common to Traditional Scales and Preschool Curricula

AREA	DEVELOPMENTAL SCALES				DEVELOPMENTAL PRESCHOOL CURRICULA			
	GESELL	LAP	ALPERN-BOLL	BAYLEY	HICOMP	MEMPHIS	PORTAGE	DEVELOPMENTAL PROGRAMMING
LANGUAGE	Language	Language	Communication	Mental	Communication	Language	Language	Language
PERSONAL/ SOCIAL	Personal/ Social	Social Self-help	Social & Self-help	Infant Behavior Record	Own-care	Personal/ Social	Self-help Socialization	Social/ Emotional/ Self-help
MOTOR	Gross & Fine Motor	Gross & Fine Motor	Physical	Mental/ Motor	Motor	Gross & Fine Motor	Motor	Perceptual & Fine Motor/ Gross Motor
COGNITIVE	Adaptive	Cognitive	Academic	Mental	Problem-solving	Perceptuo-Cognitive	Cognitive	Cognition

Exhibit 3-3 Sample Assessment/Curriculum Linkage Sequence

	GESELL PERFORMANCE CEILING TASKS	-±		HICOMP CURRICULUM SEQUENCE (1977)	÷
L	follows prepositions	-	C	responds with correct prepositions	-
	uses 5-word form—modifiers	±		uses sentences of 4-8 words	±
	uses personal pronouns	-		speech elaborated with personal pronouns	-
	imitates 6-10 syllable form	-		imitates 6 syllable form and elaborated combos.	-
PS	buttons/unbuttons	-	O	buttons and unbuttons	-
	toilet dry at night	±		toileting bowel and bladder	±
	washes hands/face--independently	-		wash and dry/face and hands	-
	emerging associative play	±		sharing play in small groups	±
M	walks on tiptoe	-	M	walks on tiptoe	-
	stands 1 foot-2 secs.	-		balances on 1 foot 2-3 seconds	-
	imitates cross form	-		draws cross-imitates adult	-
	builds bridge form	-		builds bridge imitated	-
A	identifies and describes pictures	-	P	names objects and events	-
	identifies and names colors	-		points to and names secondary-primary colors	-
	counts 1-10 and up	±		counts 1-10 and up	±
	groups as to color, size	-		grouping and sequencing	-

ASSESSMENT ----------- LINK ----------- CURRICULUM

CEILING/TASKS TARGET BEHAVIORS	CEILING BEHAVIORS		CURRICULUM MATCHES	MATCHING CURRICULUM ENTRY OBJECTIVES
	Language ceiling tasks	C3-8.5 C3-4.3 C4-2.6	Matching Communication target objectives	
	Personal-social ceiling tasks	03-5.2/.6 03-2.1 03-2.6 03-3.2	Matching Own-Care target objectives	
	Motor ceiling tasks	M3-1.1 M4-1.2 M3-2.7 M3-2.5	Matching Motor target objectives	
	Adaptive ceiling tasks	P2-4.5 P3-4.2 P4-6.6 P3-6.8	Matching Problem-Solving target objectives	

powerful, dual support of child progress. This final goal of assessment/ programming efforts is discussed in the last section of this chapter.

Supplementing Developmental Assessment Information

To assess developmental capabilities in a comprehensive way, it is important that early childhood teachers and the specialists they work with use many sources of diagnostic information to analyze and program for child problems. The importance of integrating and synthesizing information derived from tests, behavioral ratings, skill checklists, observations, parent interviews, anecdotal records, and the like can not be overstated.

Informal assessment procedures such as these provide one of the most valuable vehicles for planning instructional programs and strategies at a teacher's disposal. When employing informal assessment procedures, the following factors are important elements for defining individual differences in development and learning and, thus, for planning individualized educational strategies:

1. identifying absent, inconsistent, poorly developed, and excessive behavior patterns across multiple areas
2. identifying different settings, events, materials, and activities that appear to control both desirable and undesirable behaviors
3. identifying materials, activities, and rewards that stimulate desirable behavior by children
4. identifying prerequisite goals for children
5. identifying functional handicaps that will affect performance and learning and therefore require adaptive procedures and materials

In addition to informal assessment procedures, other types of standardized and nonstandardized assessment measures can augment the comprehensive developmental assessment results and provide methods for describing the child's range of knowledge in language and conceptual areas, i.e., readiness for adapting to and dealing with preacademic and academic tasks and situations. Such tests as the Boehm Test of Basic Concepts (Boehm, 1971), McCarthy Scales of Children's Abilities (McCarthy, 1972), Preschool Inventory (Caldwell, 1970), and Metropolitan Readiness Tests (Nurss & McGauvran, 1976) can help the teacher accomplish a wide-ranging assessment of learning readiness.

Illustration and Application

Under the comprehensive developmental assessment in Goal 2 administered to Andy, it was determined that serious developmental problems reflecting lags of two to three years were evident in several behavioral areas. This assessment established Andy's current levels of functioning. However, a detailed analysis of his pattern of performance on various developmental tasks was required before individualized curriculum objectives could be specified.

In order to use assessment results to guide curriculum planning, it was necessary to identify and analyze Andy's skills and behaviors along the normal developmental sequence that were absent ($-$), emerging ($\pm$), or fully acquired ($+$) in several behavioral areas, i.e., communication, personal-social, motor, and problem solving. Exhibit 3-4 illustrates Andy's range of developmental ceilings in several of these areas that serve as targets or starting points in curriculum planning.

Finally, in order to link developmental ceilings with appropriate curriculum objectives, Andy's test results on the Gesell Schedules were matched with similar objectives on the HICOMP Curriculum (Appendix A). Andy's completed assessment/curriculum linkage is illustrated in Exhibit 3-5. Now the preschool teacher has a precise idea of the deficit skills that account for Andy's developmental problems as well as specific entry points to start programming in several areas. A simulated exercise at the end of this section can be used to give teachers practice in making assessment/curriculum linkages on a child, using this curriculum as a guide.

As can be seen, this procedure enables teachers to focus on similar objectives in both testing and teaching. Therefore, preschool teachers have a powerful method at their disposal for monitoring child progress and the effectiveness of teaching. The final goal of assessment and programming is discussed in the next section.

GOAL 4: CHILD PROGRESS AND PROGRAM EVALUATION

The final goal in the process of assessment and programming for the preschool child involves evaluation. The concept of evaluation covers the monitoring of both child progress and program effectiveness in the classroom. Several important evaluation terms are defined below. Details and illustrations of evaluation methods appear in the next chapter.

Assessment Activity

Formative/Summative Evaluation: a method of assessing the developmental progress of children as well as the effectiveness of the educational program by using both formal and informal measures continuously to evaluate both everyday progress (formative) and final progress at the end of the program or unit of instruction (summative)

Exhibit 3-4 Andy's Developmental Ceilings

ASSESSMENT–BASED CURRICULUM ENTRY TARGETS

Child Andy   Date 76-9-21

Test Gesell Developmental Schedules   C.A. 43 months

DEVELOPMENTAL CEILINGS	LINK NO.	CURRICULUM-TARGET OBJECTIVES
D.A. = 9–12 mo.	COMMUNICATION	
± Orients to sounds consistently		
± Eye contact with speaker		
− Consistently repeats syllables		
± Gives objects on request		
± Identifies objects on request		
− Looks selectively at pictures		
± Responds to name		
− Imitates common words		
− Speaks 3–4 words		
− Follows 1-level commands		
D.A. = 12 mo.	OWN–CARE	
± Reacts consistently to mirror image		
± Cooperates in dressing		
± Cooperates in toileting		
− Indicates wet pants		
− Toilet/partial regulation		
± Eats with spoon-spilling little		
± Drinks from cup--no spilling		
− Cooperates in washing hands		
D.A. = 18 (18–21) mo.	MOTOR	
± Kicks large ball		
± Stairs/up-down-holds rail		
± Jumps both feet		
− Attempts cube tower		
− Formboard/places circle		
− Imitates horiz./vert. stroke		
D.A. = 11–15 mo.	PROBLEM-SOLVING	
± Finds hidden objects		
± Responds to directions "look at me"		
± Attends to verbalizations		
− Goes to correct location		
± "Show me the . . . ."		

Exhibit 3-5 Sample Developmental Assessment/Curriculum Linkage on Andy

ASSESSMENT-BASED CURRICULUM-ENTRY TARGET LINKS

Child Andy   C.A.   43 months

Test Gesell Developmental Schedules   Curriculum   HICOMP (1977)

TEST PERFORMANCE CEILINGS	LINK INDEX	CURRICULUM-TARGET OBJECTIVES
D.A. = 9–12 mo.	COMMUNICATION	
Orients to sounds consistently	C1-5.2	Head turn to sounds
Eye contact with speaker	C1-5.3	Gaze at speaker
Consistently repeats syllables	C1-1.8	Repeats syllables over/over
Gives objects on request	C1-3.9	Responds to request
Identifies objects when named	C2-3.1	Show me the . . . ."
Looks selectively at pictures	C1-5.6	Looks at pictures in book
Responds to name	C1-3.7	Responds with recognition to name
Imitates common words	C1-4.4	Imitates familiar words
Speaks 3-4 words	C2-2.4	Uses words in speech
Follows 1-level commands	C2-3.3	Follows simple commands
D.A. = 12 mo.	PERSONAL-SOCIAL	
Reacts consistently to mirror image	01-1.7/.8	Smiles at mirror and reaches
Cooperates in dressing	02-5.1/.8	Helps-pants and limb in arm hole
Cooperates in toileting	02-5.8	Helps push down-pull up pants
Indicates wet pants	02-2.5/.14	Indicates wet pants and need
Toilet/partial regulation	02-2.15	Attempts bowel/bladder control
Eats with spoon-spilling little	02-4.15	Spoon-food to mouth/no spilling
Drinks from cup--no spilling	02-4.9	Drinks from cup--unassisted
Cooperates in washing hands	02-2.3	Tries to wash hands
D.A. = 18 (18-21) mo.	MOTOR	
Kicks large ball	M2-1.12	Kicks large ball (stationary)
Stairs/up-down/holds rail	M2-1.11	Stairs up/down-holds rail
Jumps both feet	M2-1.13	Jumps off floor/both feet
Attempts cube tower	M2-2.1	Stacks two cubes
Formboard/places circle	M3-2.9	Places round obj. in round hole
Imitates horiz./vert. stroke	M2-2.8	Imitates vertical stroke
D.A. = 11-15 mo.	PROBLEM-SOLVING	
Finds hidden objects	P1-3.13/.14	Finds hidden object
Responds to directions "look at me"	P2-1.1	"look at me"
Attends to verbalizations	P2-1.6	Attends to verbalizations
Goes to correct location	P2-3.4	Goes where told
"Show me the . . . ."	P2-4.2	"Show me the . . . ."

Outcome

Monitoring Child Progress and Program Effectiveness: the end result of formative and summative evaluation in which the child's curriculum progress is checked continuously and in which the use of special teaching strategies enables the child to function effectively both in and out of the preschool

Review of Procedures in Applications

The final goal of the assessment-programming process brings these efforts full circle—monitoring child progress and evaluating program effectiveness. The series of steps in this process (screening, assessment/curriculum linkage, and progress evaluation) focuses the preschool teacher's attention on each child's range of individual differences and thus on individualized methods of meeting those needs and ensuring each individual's positive growth. Moreover, by continuously monitoring children's progress, preschool teachers gain a clear perspective on the effective impact of these teaching methods as well as the "what," "when," and "how" of selecting and modifying their educational methods. Periodic evaluation is required for IEPs under P.L. 94-142.

Formative and summative evaluation are so important that the next chapter is devoted to the detail and illustration of a number of practical evaluation methods. They demonstrate that teachers can and do use a variety of evaluation methods such as anecdotal records, frequency charts, measures of duration, and others.

CONCLUSION

The growing cooperative involvement of early childhood teachers, special educators, psychologists, speech therapists, and parents in planning programs for both normal and handicapped preschool children underscores the need for devising practical methods of linking developmental assessment curriculum planning and program evaluation.

The more precise the linkage between a child's pattern of capabilities and the plan of instruction, the more effective the total educational experience. Comprehensive methods of developmental assessment, programming, and evaluation help to achieve this practical linkage.

RECOMMENDED ACTIVITY

Forging an Assessment/Curriculum Linkage for the Handicapped
Preschooler: A Simulation Exercise

Assume that you are the head teacher in a preschool program for handicapped children. You are charged with the responsibility of placing preschoolers at individually appropriate levels of your curriculum based upon your analysis of developmental assessment results. Further, you must use these results as a starting point to identify specific appropriate curriculum entry objectives for each child.

On this basis, the exercise (Exhibit 3-6) serves as a method to test your skill in linking or matching appropriate curriculum objectives with information from a developmental assessment in order to develop an IEP for a handicapped preschooler.

Exhibit 3-6 Linking Exercise Sheet

ASSESSMENT–BASED CURRICULUM–ENTRY TARGETS

Child _____   Curriculum _____

Test _____   C.A. _____

PERFORMANCE CEILINGS (TEST)	LINK INDEX	CURRICULUM–TARGET OBJECTIVES
D.A. = 24(21–30) Mo.	COMMUNICATION	
± Follows 2–4 simple directions		
± Uses 20+ vocab. in speech		
– Names pictures & objs. 8–12		
± Uses I, me, you & plurals		
± Identifies objs. & pictures		
– Imitates 5–6 word phrase		
– Gives full name–requested		
± Answers personal/factual		
– Combines 3–4 words in sent.		
± Tells action & experiences		
± Asks for food, toilet, drink		
– Attends & listens to a story		
D.A. = 21(18–24) mo.	SELF–CARE	
± Uses spoon, spilling little		
± Asks to use toilet		
± Tries to contrl bowels/blad		
± Pulls on simple garment		
– Puts on shoes		
– Removes coat		
± Washes/dries hands & face		
– Plays near others, no disturb.		
– Unbuttons		
– Helps put toys away		
± Words/tell wants, food, toilet		
– Careful with toys or hazards		
D.A. = 15–18 mo.	MOTOR	
± Stands momentarily alone		
– Walks a few steps		
– Pulls self to standing		
± Climbs into small chair & sits		
± Rolls, throws, walks into ball		
– Turns book pages singly		
– Builds 3–4 block tower		
– Places in puzzle board		
– Draws horiz & vert lines–imit.		
– Draws circular stroke–imitat.		
– Holds crayon with fingers		
± Puts cubes in–out of cup		
D.A. = 21(18–24) mo.	PROBLEM–SOLVING	
– Matches shapes in puzzle		
– Ident., match, sort colors		
± Understands concept of "one"		
± " prepositions & positions		
± Imit fine motor beh–drawing		
± Names & ident. objects & pict.		
– Imitates a sequence of blocks		
– Repeats 2 digits imit. adult		
– Folds paper imitat. adult		
± Identifies "big" & "small"		
– Follows 2 simple directions		
– Gives use of objects		

Chapter 4

Applying Formative and Summative Evaluation

OBJECTIVES

1. Distinguish between formative and summative evaluation.
2. List, explain, and give an example for each of the 11 formative evaluation methods.
3. Name several major summative evaluation devices available in early education.

4

FORTUNATELY, THERE ARE A number of evaluation methods available to help teachers determine child progress and program success. One or several of these methods may be just what are needed to keep track of child progress—and to display that progress to parents and coprofessionals.

APPLIED FORMATIVE ASSESSMENT

Formative evaluation emphasizes the importance of imbedding assessment within programming. It enables teachers to identify developmental problems in need of special help and to formulate goals, objectives, strategies, and methods of remediating developmental deficits. Formative evaluation procedures reflect the continuous nature of assessment. They also have practical methods for collecting data to determine when a child has learned a given developmental objective and what educational strategies enabled it to learn that skill most effectively. The following types of formative evaluation procedures can be most useful.

Evaluation 1: Developmental Checklists with Simple Criteria to Assess Skill Attainment

Typically, a checklist outlines the behavior of interest to the teacher with a simple "yes, no, and sometimes" format for evaluation. Does the child walk upstairs alternating feet? The behavior can be marked with a check or a plus, minus, or question mark. Checklists in this form are included most effectively as part of each objective in a developmental curriculum (Exhibit 4-1).

Exhibit 4-1 Sample Developmental Checklist

Behavior	Criteria	0 1 2 3 4
Uses spoon for eating		
Drinks from cup		
Uses fork		
Uses Napkin		

Cannot do it	0
Beginning to try	1
Does with help	2
Does much alone	3
Does it alone	4

Evaluation 2: Behavior Rating Scales

Many times a teacher is not as interested in whether or not children can brush their teeth, but in how much of that behavior sequence they can perform. Thus the teacher may devise an evaluation form that gives a range of that behavior and indicates how far along some continuum of can't-can children fall. The teacher may have such categories as "Cannot do it," "Beginning to try," "Does it with help," "Does much alone," and "Does it without assistance." These ratings can be used to evaluate such diverse behaviors as putting on a coat or drawing a picture of a dog (Exhibit 4-2). Depending on the time required to learn the tasks, the teacher may wish to rate the behaviors monthly or weekly or over any other period of time.

Evaluation 3: Frequency of Behavior

Sometimes it is important to know how often children do something. The teacher may want to see how often a child says "Mommy" or names pictures, and need only to record each time the child is heard saying either of these.

Exhibit 4-2 Sample Behavior Rating Scale

Behavior	Criteria	Y	N	S
		✓		
			✓	
			✓	
				✓

Another kind of frequency count is termed rate. Here the number of times something happens is counted. That number then is divided by the amount of time the teacher kept track of it.

For example, the teacher may be interested in knowing how often a child says the word "red," but is unable to follow it around all day. The teacher takes small portions of time, say a minute or two several times a day, and really listens then for what the child is saying. The teacher then could add up all the times the child said "red," total the number of minutes spent listening, and divide the time into the occurrences to determine the rate of the child's saying the word "red." If this is done for a week or two, the teacher should be able to see if the child is saying the word more and more often.

This can be important in looking at behaviors teachers want to increase but it also is useful in keeping a record of those they wish to decrease.

Another important use for recording rate is that occasionally a teacher becomes sensitive to a certain behavior and thinks that it is increasing or decreasing when, in fact, it really is staying at about the same level. Taking rate information may help teachers to be more objective in their perceptions.

Rates or frequencies may merely be listed or can be graphed to show a picture of the behavior (Figure 4-1). In graphing, the days of the week are recorded along the horizontal line and the events counted along the vertical line.

Figure 4-1 Sample Frequency Graph

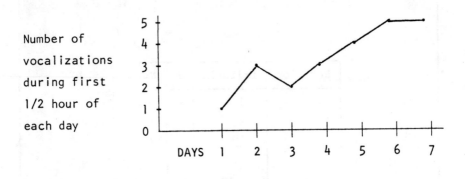

Number of
vocalizations
during first
1/2 hour of
each day

Evaluation 4: Percent Correct

If children are being taught to count, the teacher may be interested in knowing how many numbers out of all those that were counted were counted correctly. Thus, the teacher may write down the number of correct ones and divide that by the total number of answers given. This determines what percentage of answers was correct. Over a period of time, it can be seen whether the child is making more or fewer correct responses.

Percentages can be graphed. In this case the days are indicated along the horizontal line and the percentage correct along the vertical line (Figure 4-2).

Figure 4-2 Sample Percent Correct Graph

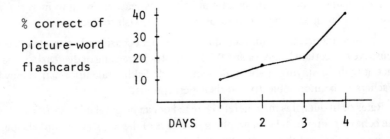

% correct of
picture-word
flashcards

Evaluation 5: Duration of Behavior

A teacher can evaluate behavior or skill attainment continuously by looking at the amount of time a child spends performing the behavior. A stopwatch or clock allows the teacher to monitor how long the child engages in a given behavior (Figure 4-3).

Evaluation 6: Measurement of Latency

Latency can be thought of as the amount of time it takes a child or children to do what they have been instructed to do. A good example of this is the amount of time between the teacher's initial instructions to "clean up" and when children begin to put toys away or cease other activities. Latency also could be measured at outdoor recess. How long does it take for the children to come inside after they have been asked to do so? Latency can be graphed as in Figure 4-4.

Figure 4-3 Sample Duration Graph

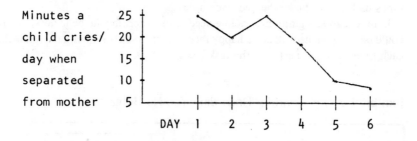

Figure 4-4 Sample Latency Graph

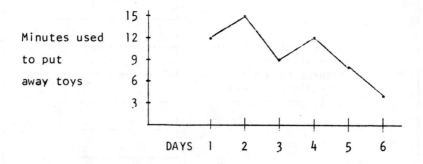

Evaluation 7: Measurement of Intensity

The intensity of a behavior also is of interest. For example, it may be important to decide if the loudness of a child's voice has reached a level that bothers the teacher. The educator could count the number of times this happens and, if it seems greater than what is desirable for the classroom, might implement a strategy to decrease its intensity.

On the other hand, there are children whose voices cannot be heard more than a foot away. It may be advantageous to measure the point at which the teacher cannot hear a child and to employ some procedures to increase the voice volume.

Often, intensity is recorded simply by saving samples of a child's behavior to show changes in intensity. For example, the teacher might save handwriting samples that show changes in the pressure used to write. Tape recordings of voice quality and loudness also illustrate an intensity measure.

Evaluation 8: Sample Yes-No Measurement

At times, the teacher is interested in behaviors that do not happen frequently. A child may be requested to pick up toys only once daily, to use the potty four or five times daily, or to make the bed once a day.

In these cases, a graph may not be needed for recording the behaviors. A chart could be hung on the wall and a happy face sticker, a star, or other marker attached each time the child performs the task (Exhibit 4-3).

Exhibit 4-3 Wall Chart for Recording Yes-No Behavior

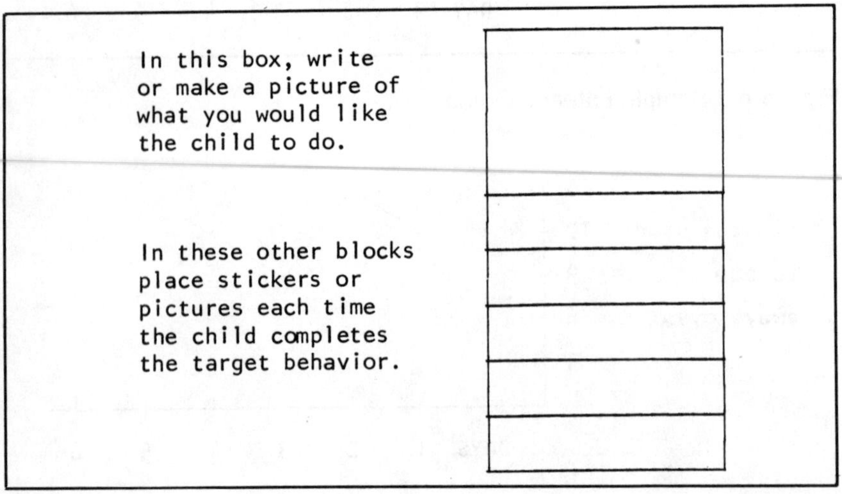

In this box, write or make a picture of what you would like the child to do.

In these other blocks place stickers or pictures each time the child completes the target behavior.

Evaluation 9: Pictorially Supplemented Recording Methods

Some evaluation methods can be modified by replacing some elements on the recording form with pictures. For example, along the ordinate on a simple graph, four backchained spoonfeeding steps (i.e., "Step #1, Step #2, . . .) might be replaced with pictures of faces with spoons in various positions (Figure 4-5). The datakeeper then puts an X across from the picture that shows the lowest position from which the child can successfully complete a bite. With days across the abscissa, for example, progress across time can thus be recorded.

In another example, interval-by-interval recording using a kitchen timer and a series of two-choice pictures was used to record the frequency of tantrums as shown in Figure 4-6.

Figure 4-5 Pictorially Supplemented Chart on Spoonfeeding Steps

Figure 4-6 Pictorially Supplemented Chart on Frequency of Tantrums

Evaluation 10: Critical Incidence Method

This method requires the caregiver to record either unusual behaviors as they are noted or the most or least acceptable behavior observed during a preceding time unit. Thus, the method relies upon memory-influenced judgments or a nonrepresentative sample of running notes.

It is perhaps useful in determining what child behaviors concern parents and/or teachers and when that registered concern is decreased or increased. (The child need not be the person whose behavior is manipulated to meet some objectives.) The method can be valuable in identifying differentially appropriate and rare optimal behaviors.

For example, a mother might record instances when after-nap checks found dry diapers. She might note that these instances occurred when the child did not ingest liquids for at least one hour before the nap. The mother then would withhold liquids until after naps, using its delivery as a reinforcer for dryness.

Evaluation 11: Anecdotal Record

This method simply requires the teacher to define the type of behavior or event to be observed during the day for a given child and a two-part record sheet upon which each occurrence of that behavior and its consequence are listed. Anecdotal recording focuses on the content of the child's behavior rather than its frequency, duration, etc. Exhibit 4-4 was designed for the example of Andy, a child who has language problems and tantrums.

Further samples of formative evaluation procedures with Andy can be seen in Exhibits 4-5 and 4-6. The former presents Andy's pattern of developmental skills in the fine and gross motor areas as determined through the teacher's observation and linkage, using the comprehensive developmental assessment results transferred to the curriculum objectives for Andy. Note Andy's pretest and progress. This simple checklist approach can help the teacher monitor continuing acquisition of crucial, prerequisite developmental skills. This method links assessment with curriculum planning. Furthermore, Exhibit 4-6 illustrates how each of these developmental target objectives can be organized into an Individual Education Program complete with appropriate instructional settings, teaching strategies, adaptive materials, and precise methods to evaluate attainment of objectives in a formative manner (a complete IEP).

Exhibit 4-4 Sample Anecdotal Record

ANECDOTAL RECORD				
			(child's name)	
			(observer)	
			(date)	

CHILD BEHAVIORS			TEACHER BEHAVIORS	
words said	words comprehended	words attempted	reinforcers used	events being paired with reinforcers
up down toy cookie water soda	wheel cup come here	hello hot	raisins crackers	hugs kisses "good-boy"
general tasks enjoyed	specific behaviors at those tasks		vocabulary used	situation in which used
playing piano	playing with 1 finger going up and down keys; humming			
water play	turning water on pouring from cup plugging sink		pour splash hot cold	at the sink
riding toy giraffe	"nibbling" giraffe's ears			with blocks in motor area

OTHER COMMENTS: He began to watch where the teacher kept the reinforcers

Exhibit 4-5 Curriculum-Based Developmental Checklist on Andy

Objective Number	General Objective	Pretest	Date Begun	Date Ended
M-2-1	Fundamental Movement (Gross Motor)			
M-2-1.1	Stoops and recovers	+		
M-2-1.2	Starts and stops walking without falling	+		
M-2-1.3	Climbs into chair, turns around to sit	+		
M-2-1.4	Runs stiffly, sometimes falls	+		
M-2-1.5	Crawls up stairs unassisted	+		
M-2-1.6	Walks up stairs if one hand is held	±	9/15	10/26
M-2-1.7	Walks sideways	-	9/15	
M-2-1.8	Walks downstairs if one hand is held	±	9/17	10/30
M-2-1.9	Squats in play for 2-3 minutes	+		
M-2-1.10	Walks backwards	±	9/17	
M-2-1.11	Walks up and down stairs holding rail, both feet on each step	±	9/22	11/10
M-2-1.12	Kicks large (stationary) ball	±	9/22	11/3
M-2-1.13	Jumps off floor, both feet	±	9/24	12/21
M-2-1.14	Tries to stand on one foot	-	9/24	12/21
M-2-2	Skilled Movement or Visual-Motor or Fine Motor			
M-2-2.1	Stacks two objects	-	9/26	
M-2-2.2	Puts 5-6 cubes (e.g.) in container	±	9/26	1/8
M-2-2.3	Helps turn pages of book	-	9/26	12/4
M-2-2.4	Puts very small object into narrow container	+		
M-2-2.5	Makes random marks on paper with crayon held in fist	±	9/30	11/12

Source: Reprinted from *COMP-Curriculum* by S.J. Forsberg, J.T. Neisworth, and K.W. Laub by permission of the HICOMP Outreach Project, The Pennsylvania State University, 315 Cedar, University Park, PA 16802, © 1977.

Exhibit 4-6 Sample Curriculum Plan by Objectives and Strategies

Objective Number	Specific Objective	Setting	Strategy	Materials	Evaluation
M-2-2.24	Tries to stand on 1 foot	Physical Therapy	Shaping	Furniture to hold onto	Behavioral checklist Frequency measure
M 2-2.1	Stacks two blocks	Individual	Modelling	Puzzle blocks-- multicolored	Behavioral checklist Frequency measure Developmental Scale
M 2-2.5	Makes random marks on paper with cryon in imitation	Group Art Activity	Modelling & prompting	Crayon, paper, fingerpaints	Behavioral checklist Frequency measure Duration measure

APPLIED SUMMATIVE EVALUATION

Whereas formative evaluation focuses on the continuous monitoring of progress, summative evaluation provides the preschool teacher with a method of assessing the overall effectiveness of the programming by evaluating the preschool child at the end of a particular program of intervention.

The most practical and meaningful approach to summative evaluation involves an integration of developmental data derived from multiple sources of assessment, i.e., formal developmental tests, behavior checklists, observations, anecdotal records, curriculum ratings, and parent interviews. However, the most powerful and reliable evidence of progress is that which links assessment measures with curriculum measures to ensure the similarity between behaviors tested and behaviors taught.

Integrating multiple sources of diagnostic information for summative evaluation purposes might involve using the pretest and posttest developmental scores and ratings on each of the measures in Exhibit 4-7 for a particular child. As can be seen, the sources of data from different measures often are in close agreement and provide concurrent evidence both of child progress and of the effectiveness of the IEP.

An additional strategy for evaluating the efficacy of preschool programs is proposed by Bagnato and Neisworth (1980). The Intervention Efficiency Index (IEI), an adaptation of Simeonsson and Wiegerink's method (1975), is a measure of both child progress and program effectiveness that relates changes in child capabilities to time spent in a program of intervention. The index describes individual and group progress in terms of average developmental gains within and across curricular areas for each month's participation in the program. The IEI is based upon two major variables, both expressed in months: (1) an index of developmental gain (pre/post) and (2) length of participation in intervention. A ratio of developmental gain for each month of participation in intervention is generated. Thus, the IEI may be expressed as,

$$\frac{\text{Developmental Gain (Months)}}{\text{Time in Intervention (Months)}} = \text{Intervention Efficiency Rate}$$

For example, when a child shows a developmental gain of 12 months, this finding changes in significance depending upon whether the child has been enrolled in treatment for one year or two. If the child has participated in a program for 12 months and has displayed a 12 months' gain, the IEI is 1.00 (gain/time-in-program); participation for two years (24 months) would lower the index to .50. This index provides evidence of program efficiency and facilitates accountability.

Exhibits 4-8 and 4-9 show the IEI technique applied to the performance and developmental progress of a handicapped preschooler. The child's length of participation in the program was nine months and the range of developmental gain across curriculum areas (language, personal-social, motor, problem solving) was 9-21 months. The overall gain was 13.5 developmental months and the overall IEI, 1.50 (13.5/9) or 1½ months of developmental gain for each month of program participation (Exhibit 4-8). Furthermore, when the results of using four complementary developmental measures are compared for this child, the data provide solid, comparative evidence of apparent progress in the program (Exhibit 4-9).

Finally, then, using these procedures, preschool teachers can maintain both a continuous and overall evaluation of each child's individual progress in intervention as well as the effectiveness of their educational methods.

RECOMMENDED ACTIVITIES

1. Observe a preschool child in some routine situation over a period of about a week. Select for specific attention some behavior about which the teacher or parent is concerned. Record this target behavior, using the most appropriate measure, e.g., frequency, duration, intensity. Display the week's observations in a clear way, such as on a graph or chart.
2. Select a behavior of your own that you are interested in increasing or decreasing. For example, you might wish to alter your smoking or eating behavior, punctuality, orderliness, or any other trait. Keep a record of the target behavior over a 10-day period. Display the results appropriately. (You may discover that simply recording the behavior will change it.)
3. Teach someone else how to use each of the 11 evaluation methods. When they can explain and illustrate them, you will know that you understand them enough to teach someone else about them.

Exhibit 4-7 Sample Multisource Evaluation Procedure

Measure	Source	Pre	Post	Gain
Bayley Scales of Infant Development (BSID)	Performance	9 mo.	21 mo.	12 mo.
Preschool Attainment Record (PAR)	Parent Interview	12 mo.	23 mo.	11 mo.
Project MEMPHIS Curriculum (MCDS)	Curriculum Checklist	11 mo.	21 mo.	10 mo.
Perceptions of Developmental Skills (PODS)	Rating Scale	6 = severe problem	3 = moderate problem	3+ unit gain

Exhibit 4-8 Sample IEI Progress Evaluation

LANGUAGE				PERSONAL-SOCIAL				MOTOR				PROBLEM-SOLVING				Mean Gain Across Developmental Areas	Mean IEI
Pre	Post	Gain	IEI	Pre	Post	Gain	IEI	Pre	Post	Gain	IEI	Pre	Post	Gain	IEI		
12	21	(9)	1.00	12	21	(9)	1.00	21	42	(21)	2.33	15	30	(15)	1.67	13.5	1.50

Exhibit 4-9 Similar IEI Ratings from Different Developmental Measures

Evaluation Measures	IEI	Gesell Developmental Schedules (GDS)	Preschool Attainment Record (PAR)	COMP-Curriculum Sequence	Perceptions of Developmental Skills (PODS)
IEI	1.50	1.50	1.60	1.41	1.64

Using Methods That Make a Difference

OBJECTIVES

1. Name and give an example for the two fundamental principles of behavior.
2. Give a brief description and example for each of the 11 teaching strategies.

5

EDUCATIONAL METHODS ARE NOT new, but good ones are. There are, of course, exceptions to this statement. Some excellent and powerful educational methods have come from the past. Certain of the techniques developed by pioneers such as Montessori, Fernald, Itard, and others have proved to this day to be indispensable in work with children. On the other hand, not all recently developed methods are as useful as could be hoped. For the most part, however, recent research has generated a number of powerful teaching strategies that really do make a difference.

Most of the methods described here are part of an array of techniques generally referred to as behavior modification. The behavioral techniques are based on two general principles. Eleven teaching strategies based on these principles then will be analyzed.

TWO FUNDAMENTAL PRINCIPLES OF BEHAVIOR

The First Principle: Behavior is controlled by its consequences. Learning depends on its outcome.

Some things a child does are followed by positive, rewarding events. Whenever a behavior is followed by positive consequences, that behavior becomes stronger (positive reinforcement). On the other hand, if a behavior is followed by no reinforcement (extinction) or aversive events (punishment), that behavior is weakened. While there is much more that could be said about positive reinforcement and punishment, the crucial point here is that the preschool teacher can attempt to provide strengthening or weakening consequences after a given child behavior. When the teacher is systematic about providing consequences, child behaviors can be changed rapidly.

Teachers probably can name many events that could act as positive reinforcement. Getting a gold star is a familiar example of an old-fashioned technique for encouraging behavior to develop. Many other events reinforce children's learning. In the list below are things or events that typically act to strengthen child behavior:

- food or drink
- prizes
- tokens exchangeable for desirable items or events
- praise
- preferred activities
- positive feedback
- task-imbedded reinforcement (e.g., pieces of puzzle fitting together or task completion)

The Second Principle: Circumstances that exist when a behavior is reinforced become cues or signals for the behavior.

This is known as stimulus control. Many everyday behaviors of everybody are cued or set off by specific stimuli. A good illustration is the signalling of eating by a TV set. If one frequently eats while watching television, the TV set soon becomes a prompt for eating. People may not be hungry at all but because eating has been reinforced while watching TV, they will find themselves wanting to eat when the set is on. If this is the case, it can be said that the TV has been a prompt or cue for eating.

There are, of course, many appropriate prompts for behavior. A green light is a prompt for proceeding; a picture or printed word is a prompt saying the corresponding word; a teacher's finger against the teacher's lips is a signal for being quiet; a bell is a signal for starting or stopping an activity, etc.

Teachers can devise special signals deliberately to prompt specific behavior. Teachers can assure that children more probably will display an appropriate behavior when the right prompt is provided. Children can learn to pay attention, begin work, put away their toys, and talk or not talk to each other when these behaviors come under the control of prompts.

The basic technique for establishing a prompt for a behavior is simple: The behavior must be reinforced when the intended prompt is present and not reinforced when the prompt is absent. A friend who is an excellent preschool teacher uses a kitchen timer as a prompt for seat work. The teacher sets the timer for, say, 15 minutes, instructs the children to work quietly, and rewards those who are diligent. When the timer is absent, children are not rewarded for work at their seats and are permitted to chat. (The timer and instructions become prompts for diligence.)

Teachers may not always want to use the same prompt for a behavior. Often, they will want to shift prompts or fade them. Shifting is done simply by presenting a new signal with one that already is a prompt for a behavior. Gradually, the new prompt gains prominence and can share or replace the control of the original one. Fading is accomplished by gradually reducing the presence of a prompt. These strategies, discussed in this chapter, are powerful techniques for the modern educator.

11 IMPORTANT STRATEGIES

Teachers will want to try many strategies for teaching children new skills and for encouraging the growth of present ones. The COMP-Curriculum (Appendix A) provides hundreds of objectives for children, but does not tell how to teach them. What the curriculum does provide, however, are suggestions of strategies that seem to be successful in teaching particular kinds of objectives. Eleven teaching strategies are suggested throughout the curriculum.

Teachers will not become expert in the strategies overnight. Much practice will be required, but they should keep at it. As in any profession, some persons become more proficient than others, but anyone who tries to use the strategies discussed is bound to become more effective. Teachers probably will notice improvement as soon as they begin. Progressively, they will see even more effective results and will want to expand their expertise. Chapter 8 includes additional resources and suggestions for continuing study of these powerful teaching techniques.

The strategies here have two main uses: management and instruction. Sometimes the big problem with children is discipline or behavior management. Having children be on time, refrain from fighting, eat properly, put away their toys, and many other behaviors often are instances of things children already can do, but don't, or shouldn't. On the other hand, the most important job of educators is teaching new behavior: this is instruction, rather than management. Unfortunately, much time often is spent on management at the expense of instruction. It becomes extremely important, then, to be as effective and efficient as possible in management to assure ample time for real developmental instruction.

The term strategies refers to the teaching methods (shaping, chaining) to be used for getting children to perform the objectives.

The COMP-Curriculum in Appendix A contains numbers in the strategy column. Strategies are suggested for teaching each objective, but they are only suggestions. As teachers become familiar with the strategies and the curriculum, they may develop their own preferred techniques for teaching given objectives. But by making specific suggestions, this book can help as teachers begin their lesson planning. If teachers cross out the number of the suggested strategy and enter the number of their preferred strategy, over time they will be able to evaluate how successful various strategies are in teaching certain objectives.

Each of the suggested strategies is described, along with: (a) general guidelines for using the strategy, and (b) examples of its use in the various curricular areas.

Strategy 1: Shaping

Educators often are faced with teaching new, difficult behaviors to children. A teacher cannot simply ask a 2-year-old to throw a ball across the room and expect that the child will then do it. The child, at first, will experience difficulty in aiming the ball in the correct direction and/or in throwing the ball such a great distance. Nor can the teacher simply wait for the child to accomplish such a difficult task, so that the complete performance can be reinforced. The teacher must reinforce small approximations toward the terminal performance of the task. For example, the child first could be rewarded for simply throwing the ball. After the child becomes proficient at the first approximation of the task, reinforcement is withheld until the performance moves a step closer to the desired behavior. Thus, the child might be told, "Good, but now throw it to *me.*" Then only throws that are toward the teacher would be reinforced.

In shaping, the teacher cannot always predetermine the steps in the shaping process but must watch the child closely and reinforce even slight improvements. Typical shaping sequences are:

- In the communication curriculum is the following terminal objective: Child repeats proper sentence when teacher says, "Mary, say this, 'Give me the pencil.' " The child's typical responses during shaping could proceed from (a) "Pencil," to (b) "Give pencil," to (c) "Give me pencil," and finally to (d) "Give me the pencil."
- In the own-care curriculum is the following terminal objective: Upon entering, the child will leave parent and happily join activities. The child's typical responses during shaping might precede through the sequence (a) child leaves parent, but is in tears; (b) child leaves parent, but looks sad; (c) child leaves parent and watches others play; (d) child leaves parent and walks over to the play group; (e) child leaves parent and joins an activity; (f) child leaves parent and happily joins an activity.
- In the motor curriculum one terminal objective is that the child will walk across the balance beam without falling. The child's typical responses during shaping might begin: (a) child puts one foot on balance beam, (b) child walks along balance beam with one foot on floor, (c) child stands on balance beam upon both feet, (d) child takes two steps and is allowed down. The required number of steps then would be increased gradually until the child walks all the way across the beam.
- In the problem-solving curriculum, a terminal objective is that the child will recall four objects that have been shown. The child's typical responses during shaping would be likely to be (a) child recalls one or two items, (b) child recalls three items, (c) child recalls all four items.

Strategy 2: Chaining Behaviors

Much of what educators wish to teach children involves sequences or chains of behavior, rather than single behaviors. Chaining refers to the putting together of behaviors to form more complex acts. A given sequence of behavior may be built in a forward or backward fashion. Washing one's hands is, for example, a complex act consisting of several steps. After identifying the steps, the child may be taught the initial step and subsequent ones added until the whole sequence is learned. On the other hand, sometimes it is preferable to teach the final step first, and then to work backward to the initial step.

In backward chaining, the teacher initially does every step of a sequence except the last one and then lets the child perform that final step. Because this last bit of behavior is closest to the end and success, it may be learned most easily. When a child can perform that step well, the teacher does everything but the last step and next to last step, leaving those for the child to complete. This procedure continues until the whole sequence can be done by the child. A good example of such chaining might be learning to tie a shoe. The teacher makes the initial tie, loops the loops, and completes all steps in the sequence except for the last pull that tightens the whole bow. The child does this. When the child can do it well, the teacher allows the child to pass the second loop through the space under the first loop and then to tighten the bow. Thus the child completes tying the bow each time.

Forward chaining also involves determining the sequence of steps in a task and having the teacher initially do every step except one. However, in forward chaining the teacher begins by letting the child complete the first step. The teacher then completes the task. When able to do the first step well, the child is required to do the second step, and so on. Because people do have the ability to use language and remember ideas, starting from the beginning and learning the whole sequence in this fashion may be as effective as backward chaining. For example, in shoe tying the child initially might take the two laces and cross them and later pass the top lace around and under the bottom one. Eventually, the child would complete the whole sequence independently.

Strategy 3: Modeling

Many behaviors are taught by having children imitate someone else's behavior. The teacher or another child could model the behavior for the subject child. The teacher should avoid modeling a behavior more difficult than the one the child is to do. Modeling generally is more effective when the demonstrator is reinforced, when the demonstrator is like the observer, and when the observer perceives the model positively.

Modeling also can be encouraged in a less direct manner. For example, the teacher could show a film, read a story, or give a puppet show containing behaviors it is desired that the children imitate.

It often is helpful to talk to the children about what they are watching so that they can more accurately model the behavior when it is their turn to do it. A good demonstration of a behavior can be an effective model for children to imitate. It should be remembered, too, that children may observe and imitate the teacher even when the latter does not intend that they do so. Cigarette smoking, swearing, the use of aggression, and many other unfortunate behaviors are taught to children through unwitting modeling.

INTRODUCTORY COMMENTS REGARDING STRATEGIES 4-7: PROMPTING

The next four strategies involve a technique called prompting. A prompt is a signal or cue that the teacher can use to get a specific behavior. Specially arranged prompts are used to help children perform tasks that they otherwise would not or could not do. However, the eventual goal is for children to perform such tasks without the use of contrived prompts.

In most cases, prompts should be faded (eliminated gradually) as the child learns the new behaviors. Because of this, there are two important considerations to be made in using a prompt: (1) choose a prompt that can be faded easily, (2) choose a prompt that helps the child focus on some significant feature of the task. For example, in teaching children to discriminate between circles and triangles, placing colored dots at the apex of triangles focuses the children's attention on the three points of the triangle.

There are several ways to fade prompts. The intensity of the prompt can be faded. For example, in teaching Peter to recognize his name, one could put a red dot on top of the capital P. This would be the cue. To fade its intensity, the red dot could be made lighter and lighter over trials until it was pink and then lighter and lighter again until it finally blended into the white paper. To fade magnitude of this same prompt, the red dot could be large at first and then get smaller and smaller over trials until it no longer is used. To fade the frequency of this cue, the teacher could begin by presenting the discrimination task occasionally without the cue. As the child came to recognize its name without the cue, the cue would be used less and less often.

Strategy 4: Prompting Attention

Before beginning to teach a task, the educator should consider the children's attention. It may be necessary to direct the children to look or to listen before proceeding with the teaching task. There are two basic approaches a teacher can use to get children's attention on a task. First, the teacher can give a verbal direction (e.g., "Look at me."). Second, the teacher can arouse interest in the direction of the task. It usually is good to pair both of these strategies. Examples of pairing these approaches:

1. *Cueing attention toward a visual task.*

   (verbal direction) "Mary, look at the animal!"
   (arousing interest) The teacher then makes the toy animal tickle Mary's nose.
   Mary now is looking at the animal and the teacher can proceed with the task.

2. *Cueing attention toward an auditory task.*

   (verbal direction) "Mary listen!"
   (arousing interest) The teacher whispers something silly, or talks in a funny voice.
   Mary now is listening and the teacher can proceed with the task.

Strategy 5: Verbal Prompting

Verbal prompts tell the child what to do. In choosing verbal prompts, the teacher must be sure to keep them short and to use simple words. Some examples of verbal prompts from the COMP-Curriculum (Appendix A):

1. In the communication curriculum:
   a. Children can be prompted to make the "th" sound correctly by the teacher's saying, "Put your tongue between your lips."
   b. Children can be prompted to follow verbal directions by teachers' emphasizing critical words of the directions with their voices.
2. In the own-care curriculum:
   a. Children can be prompted to brush teeth correctly by the teacher's saying, "up and down."
   b. Children can be prompted to dress in the proper sequence by the teacher's naming the items of clothing to be put on in the correct order.
3. In the motor curriculum:
   a. Children can be prompted to move scissors correctly by the teacher's repeating, "open, shut."
   b. Children can be prompted to build high block buildings by teaching them to respond to the verbal cue, "steady it," after each new block is added.
4. In the problem-solving curriculum:
   a. Children can be prompted to place objects in the correct sequence by the teacher's repeating the sequence.
   b. Children can be prompted to solve problems involving rules when the teacher repeats the rule frequently.

Strategy 6: Manual Prompting

In manual prompting, the teacher physically helps the child to perform the behavior by leading the child through the activity. In determining which manual prompts to use, the teacher should:

1. Prompt only the necessary parts of the behavior. For example, if a child has difficulty steering a tricycle, help the child steer, but don't also push the tricycle.
2. Try to do manual prompts from behind so that the child is looking at the task and not at the teacher. For example, with the tricycle, steer from behind so that the child watches the "road" and not the teacher. Otherwise, the teacher's presence will have to fade before the child will do the task independently.

Some curricular examples of manual prompting follow:

1. In the communication curriculum:
   a. Children can be prompted to make the "m" sound by the teacher's physically pressing the child's lips together.
   b. Children can be prompted to follow directions ("Put your hand up") by the teacher's moving the child's hand.
2. In the own-care curriculum:
   a. Children can be prompted to stab vegetables with a fork by placing the teacher's hand over the child's.
   b. Children can be prompted to wash all parts of their faces when the teacher guides their hands in the ears, over the eyes, etc.
3. In the motor curriculum:
   a. Children can be prompted to alternate feet by the teacher's tapping first one foot, then the other.
   b. Children can be prompted to draw letters correctly by the use of stencils.
4. In the problem-solving curriculum:
   a. Children can be prompted to find missing objects by the teacher's pointing to them in the proper direction.
   b. Children can be prompted to count objects one at a time by the teacher's manually synchronizing the touching of objects with the saying of the numerals involved.

Strategy 7: Visual Prompting

In discrimination tasks, such as recognizing one name from another, children usually are unable at first to make correct identifications. Two words may be so similar that certain children cannot discriminate between them. A visual prompt adds a dimension to a stimulus in order to make it easier to recognize. For example, if children cannot recognize their names on the bulletin board or lockers, a teacher might paste little pictures very near the first letter so that they can find them more easily. This prompt should be faded eventually, of course.

Visual prompts can be used for both simple and complex tasks. Visual tasks can be prompted by changing the color, texture, location, size, etc., of the stimulus. Some sample visual prompts:

1. In the communication curriculum:
   a. Children's attention to story books can be prompted by using books of exaggerated size.
   b. Children can be prompted to point to an object on request by placement of that object closer to the child.
2. In the own-care curriculum:
   a. Children may be prompted to find their zipper tabs by the addition of a large key chain to the tab.
   b. Children may be prompted to replace their spoons after eating if a spoon outline is drawn on the place mat.
3. In the motor curriculum:
   a. Children may be prompted to alternate feet in walking up steps by color coding their shoes to match footprints on the stairs.
   b. Children may be prompted to hold a pencil in the proper position by placement of marks on the child's hand at points where the pencil should touch.
4. In the problem-solving curriculum:
   a. Children can be prompted to discriminate circles from triangles by the addition of color to the circular shapes.
   b. Children can be prompted to group objects correctly by placing pictures of the objects on the containers into which they are to be sorted.

Strategy 8: Behavior Rehearsal

This technique consists of having children repeatedly practice a given task. In teaching children to count to ten, the teacher might assemble many sets of objects to be counted and then have the children count aloud in various voices (roaring like lions, squeaking like mice). At times the technique resembles the good old-fashioned method of "practice makes perfect."

At other times the teacher is interested not merely in the repeated practice of the task but in the situations under which the task is practiced. Children often must be taught skills that are not typically practiced at school, such as taking a bus ride. It usually is not possible to take the children on a bus ride daily until they learn to step up, pay the driver, take a seat, etc. These behaviors, therefore, are rehearsed in a dramatic play situation until learned. When the children do take a bus ride, they will be likely to use the behaviors they have rehearsed.

At other times, the teacher may want children to rehearse difficult behaviors in comfortable, behavior-conducive settings. In teaching children to play with wooden blocks, the children might rehearse block construction during a small group lesson so that later they will build with them during a free play period.

Two points must be kept in mind while doing behavioral rehearsal: (1) to shape behaviors as the children rehearse, (2) to use task-imbedded reinforcers liberally so that the repetition of tasks does not become tedious.

Strategy 9: Shifting

The procedures here probably are referred to more correctly as shifting of stimulus control. Classical conditioning refers to the pairing of one object or event that leads to a certain behavior with another stimulus that does not lead initially to that behavior. For example, in Level 1 of the communication curriculum is the objective "Laughs when played with." A child could be taught to laugh during play by repeatedly pairing something that already causes laughter (e.g., tickling) with play activity. Eventually the play situation itself will bring on laughter. A teacher might use conditioning to teach an older shy child to play contentedly in groups by pairing the teacher's presence with the group.

In this technique, aspects of the environment become (through pairing) conditioned events for specific behaviors. In the case of the Year 1 objective above, the appropriate behavior is laughing; the stimulus is a play situation. This stimulus would be paired with the tickling stimulus.

Conditioning can be used for a variety of objectives. It frequently is used to teach affective behaviors, such as being brave, friendly, contented.

Strategy 10: Questioning

At times the teacher can arrange for children to engage in certain behaviors merely by questioning them. (Questioning is a special class of prompts.) Children might be encouraged to engage in empathy, for example, by a question such as, "How do you suppose Mary feels now?" Many of the higher level problem-solving skills also are taught through questioning. For example, children are encouraged to notice missing parts of objects by asking, "What's funny about this?"

Questioning allows the teacher to aim the child's behavior toward a given goal, for example, being able to state how another might feel or identifying the missing part.

Often questioning alone will be effective in producing the desired behavior. At other times, children will not respond correctly to the question. What should teachers do then? They could, of course, simply tell the child the correct answer, and at times this is necessary. Then the child can simply imitate the provided answer.

Another correction technique, however, is to provide the child with a prompt for the answer. This technique is more desirable since it still engages the child in more advanced problem-solving behaviors. In fact, the teacher should start with a minimal prompt, adding stronger prompts until the child finally can answer the question. If the child cannot answer the question after several prompts, the teacher should provide the answer.

It is wise to plan ahead when using a questioning strategy, so that prompts will be available. For example:

Objective:

Solves problems involving memory of a fact. In this case, the child is to remember that a toy teddy bear is hidden in the mouth of a large cardboard lion. The bear is hidden as the children watch at the beginning of a 15 minute lesson. Questioning is used at the end of the lesson to encourage the children to recall the fact.

Questioning plan:

1. Primary question: "Do you remember where the bear is? Come whisper the answer to me." (Since the children whisper the answer, they all are forced to recall the fact independently of their peers.)
2. Prompts (minimal to maximal):
    a. "Think back to the beginning of our lesson. I picked up the bear and what did I do with it?"
    b. "Think of how big the bear is." (Teacher demonstrates its size with hands.) "Where could I have put it?"
    c. "Could I have put it in something?"
    d. Teacher points to correct side of room. "Did I put it somewhere over here?"
    e. Teacher narrows the location through hand movements. "I put it near here, do you remember now?"
    f. Teacher again uses hand motions to narrow the vicinity. "I put it inside something over here. Do you remember?"

It is helpful to note which children answer correctly on the first question and which children need minimal or maximal prompts. This information will help in selecting further objectives and materials for specific children.

Strategy 11: Discrimination Training

In using discrimination training, the teacher attempts to establish specific signals for specific behaviors. Sometimes the concern lies in teaching children to discriminate between two or more signals, e.g., to choose the appropriate restroom from the "Men" and "Women" door signs. This might be called a double or multiple discrimination problem since the teacher wants the child to behave appropriately in the presence of two or more sometimes similar signals—a girl should enter the door marked "Women" and look elsewhere when she sees the door marked "Men."

At other times the educator is not concerned directly with teaching children to discriminate between stimuli. In some instances, the teacher wants children to discriminate by choosing appropriate behavior in a certain situation, such as to say "please" at the lunch table, to walk in the classroom, or to sit on chairs during circle time.

In each kind of discrimination task the teacher trains the discrimination in the following way:

1. by providing distinctive prompts for the correct behavior
2. by providing many instances for the children to practice and be reinforced for the correct behavior in the presence of the discriminative signal
3. by reducing opportunities for the children to practice the inappropriate behavior in the presence of the discriminative stimulus
4. by gradually removing any prompts that had to be added to the discrimination—if a picture of a bee had been placed on top of the letter "B" to teach the name of the letter, the picture should be faded gradually.

In addition, when teaching discriminations between or among signals, (e.g., when it is desired that the child say "woman" when seeing a woman, and "man" when seeing a man) the educator should:

1. teach the appropriate answer to one signal and then teach the appropriate answer to the other before finally pairing the two prompts
2. begin with easiest discriminations, i.e., pair the signals that are most different from one another and gradually move to pairing those that are most like one another, e.g., when teaching a child to discriminate triangles from circles a red triangle and a blue circle are paired before a red triangle and a red circle are paired.

Two examples of discrimination training are given next. In the first, a child is taught to discriminate between her printed name and those of the other children in the group. In the second example, children are taught appropriate behaviors for playing in the block area of their classroom.

Example 1: Teaching a Child To Discriminate Own Name

1. State the problem.
   Susan doesn't correctly identify her name tag on her chair and toothbrush.
2. What do you want the student to identify?
   Susan
3. What other stimuli must the child be able to discriminate this from?
   All other names in her group
4. List these words in the order of maximum to minimum difference from the stimulus you are teaching (i.e., Susan).
   1. Joe 2. Henry 3. Marcia 4. Sally
5. List some signals that would even be more different from the word Susan than are these names.
   Colored shapes, animal pictures, lines
6. Order these in terms of maximum to minimum difference from the word Susan.
   a. animal pictures b. colored shapes c. lines
7. Next, think of signals that are not names of children in the group but are very close to the names. List these.
   Individual letters, nonname words, words of similar length, words of similar configuration, other words that start with capitals
8. Order these from maximal to minimal difference from the word Susan.
   a. individual letters
   b. nonname words
   c. words of similar length
   d. words of similar configuration
   e. other words that start with capitals
9. Write a series of paired signals in which the child is to identify Susan by beginning with the order generated above in Step 6, then going to the order in Step 8, and finally to the order in Step 4.

What signals are being paired (easiest to hardest discriminations)?	What do the teaching materials look like?
1. animal pictures, Susan	Susan "Show me your name."
2. colored shapes, Susan	▲ Susan "Show me your name."

What signals are being paired (easiest to hardest discriminations)?	What do the teaching materials look like?
3. lines, Susan	< Susan "Show me your name."
4. individual letters, Susan	Susan B "Show me your name."
5. non-name words, Susan	dog Susan "Show me your name."
6. words of similar length, Susan	jumps Susan "Show me your name."
7. words of similar configuration, Susan (note shape of the words)	Beams Susan "Show me your name."
8. other words that start with capital S, Susan	Short Susan "Show me your name."
9. names of children in group, Susan	Susan Joe "Show me your name."

Example 2: Teaching Children To Discriminate Play Area and Appropriate Behavior for that Area

1. State the problem.
   The children run, "capture" smaller children, and throw blocks in the block area of the classroom.
2. What is your objective for the students?
   To play in block area without engaging in the behaviors listed above.
3. What distinctive signals will you use to prompt the correct behavior?
   In this case the teacher's plan was as follows:
   (a) A large sign was posted that pictured the three inappropriate behaviors with large Xs over them.

   (b) Each free play period in that area was preceded with a pupil-teacher review of the rules about playing there.
   (c) Careful teacher supervision and ample verbal reinforcement for rule-following in the block area were provided until appropriate play behaviors were well established. This reduced opportunities for children to practice inappropriate behaviors in the block area and also provided many opportunities for children to practice and be reinforced for appropriate play behaviors.
4. How will you fade the prompts?
   The teacher decreased the frequency of reinforcement and reduced how often the individual was present during play in that area. Further, on some days the poster was not present and the children were reinforced for remembering the rules anyway.

Before planning discrimination training, teachers must remember that nagging and correcting children is not prompting.

Prompts must come before inappropriate behaviors. If teachers try to prompt after an inappropriate behavior, they might actually be reinforcing that behavior with their attention.

Appropriate use of prompts: Children have just come to the block area to play and the teacher directs them to the chart, asking, "Do you remember the play rules over here?" The teacher reinforces them for remembering and says, "I'll be watching to see who remembers *all* morning." As children play the teacher says intermittently, "You sure are remembering not to throw blocks"; "What nice buildings those are"; "You kids are playing so cooperatively."

Inappropriate use of prompts: The children go to the block area to play. One child hits another. The teacher goes over to the children and says, "Are you forgetting our rules? Let's review them."

RECOMMENDED ACTIVITIES

1. Visit a preschool or day-care facility in order to observe a teacher or aide working with children. See if you can find instances of the use of the teaching strategies described in this chapter. Also, note the degree of actual instruction taking place, as opposed to free time for the children.
2. Select several of the teaching strategies for use with a child. Perhaps a neighbor's or friend's child (or your own) is available so that you can practice some of the strategies. Identify some simple instructional objectives and try to teach with and without a given strategy.
3. Contact someone (a teacher, professor, etc.) who is expert in at least some of the described teaching strategies. Let them demonstrate the skill for you and observe you practicing a skill. A good model will be most helpful.

Chapter 6

Writing Useful Lesson Plans

OBJECTIVES

1. Identify these terms: Premack Principle, behavioral objective, prerequisite skill, distributed practice, antecedent event.
2. Differentiate between: direct and nondirect instructional activities, curricular and instructional (lesson plan) objectives, contrived and task-imbedded antecedents.
3. Describe components of: task analysis, direct and nondirect instructional plans.

6

IN PRESCHOOLS, both direct and indirect teaching situations are planned. Teaching plans must range from providing structured imitation training for a nonverbal child to sequencing art activities for an entire class. The two planning situations are treated separately in this chapter. First, a hypothetical daily schedule (Table 6-1), then how teaching plans might be written to fit such varied activities. This schedule is used for a class of 25 preschoolers, ages 2 to 4½. Several of these children have some sort of developmental delay. The plan, of course, may not exactly correspond to a school's program needs or staffing pattern. However, it has five characteristics that make it a good daily plan for the situation described above:

1. It includes time for both direct and nondirect instruction. The provision for direct instruction is especially important for the individualized program needs of the delayed children, who have specific deficits in language, motor, cognitive, or social development. This may be the time when special objectives from IEPs are included. In this particular program, four direct-instruction periods are set aside so that objectives from each of the four functional domains (language, cognitive, social, motor) can be taught. However, that time also is assigned to nondirected learning activities. At such times, children can choose activities, materials, and playmates freely.

2. The times allotted for direct instruction are short (only 15 minutes each) so that children probably will not tire of those activities. Over a period of a week each child would have one and a half hours of direct instruction in each of the four functional domains. This distribution also allows children to practice newly acquired skills on a daily basis.

3. Reinforcing events have been built into the schedule. Each of the half-hour direct-instructional segments is followed by a more loosely structured activity, e.g., free play, snack. This practice is derived from the Premack Principle of following a low-probability activity (a structured lesson) by a high-probability activity (recess, activity period). In this way, the schedule itself rewards children for engaging in low-probability behaviors.

89

Table 6-1 A Possible Preschool Daily Schedule

Daily Schedule	
8:45 - 9:00	Greetings and Free Play
9:00 - 9:15	Group Circle Time
9:15 - 9:30	Direct Instruction Period #1
9:30 - 9:45	Direct Instruction Period #2
9:45 - 10:10	Toileting and Recess
10:10 - 10:20	Snack
10:20 - 10:35	Direct Instruction Period #3
10:35 - 10:50	Direct Instruction Period #4
10:50 - 11:30	Activity Period
11:30 - 11:40	Dismissal

4. The schedule allows for prompting of low-preference activities. It might be assumed that children will need special reminders and motivators to leave play and go to their direct instructional activities. The first instructional period is preceded by a group circle time, and the third is preceded by a group snack period. These are good times to quiet the group and to get the children's attention in order to announce the "exciting activities" that have been planned for their lessons. For example, this allows a teacher to announce, "At our language centers today we are going to meet some slimy animals (worms). So, when the bell rings, go find your teachers and you can see these creatures." Having the children together in a group (e.g., snack, circle time) before lessons makes it easier to get all children's attention.
5. Finally, the schedule provides varied opportunities for observing child behaviors in unstructured settings. The activity periods at the beginning and end of the session can be used to observe interaction, generalization of skills, independence/dependence behaviors, and others.

Given the daily activity schedule, the discussion now turns to appropriate instructional plans, first for the direct and then for the nondirect instructional activities.

PLANNING FOR DIRECT INSTRUCTIONAL ACTIVITIES

Assuming that all children have been assessed and their curricular placements determined, the teacher can begin to plan "lessons" in order to extend the children's achievement. In these lessons, the aim is to teach the children curricular tasks that they have not yet mastered. The curricular objectives that have been identified through the linkage and observation procedures described earlier become the focal points of lesson planning.

After the child's developmental status has been pinpointed in all curricular subdomains (such as language expression, reception, imitation, play, in the COMP-Curriculum) or on all developmental task hierarchies, objectives are selected for lesson plans in a deliberate manner to assure the child's continuous, sequenced progress through the curriculum. The lesson plans, then, describe the arrangements to be used for teaching curricular objectives to specific children or groups of children.

Good lesson planning is a time-consuming task. Therefore plans should be written for one week at a time, planning for several objectives. In most cases it is preferable to teach preschoolers five to ten objectives during a 15-minute lesson, but practice the objectives over the week. This distributed practice usually results in better learning than in situations where a child is forced to meet the criterion on one objective before going to another. With distributed practice, children are not bored during lessons (since each lesson moves through several objectives), and they maintain learning well (since objectives are practiced daily).

LESSON PLAN COMPONENTS

Recently published guidelines for writing Individual Education Programs recommend formats that include minimum essential content for lesson planning (Exhibit 6-1). However, on this form, emphasis is given to the statement of the objective and to the plan for evaluation. These items, of course, are very important for purposes of accountability. For good teaching, however, the educator must further analyze and categorize the methods component of a teaching plan. That is, teaching strategies must be specified in terms of what will be done to initiate the behavior, how behavior will be rewarded when it does occur, and what will be done if the behavior does not occur. A format more suitable for teaching purposes is presented in Exhibit 6-2. The format consists of eight components.

Exhibit 6-1 Part of an IEP Format

SHORT-TERM OBJECTIVE	INSTRUCTIONAL METHODS MEDIA/MATERIAL TITLE(S) (OPTIONAL)	EVALUATION OF INSTRUCTIONAL OBJECTIVES	
		TESTS, MATERIALS EVALUATION PROCEDURES TO BE USED	CRITERIA OF SUCCESSFUL PERFORMANCE

Source: Reprinted from *An Introduction to Individualized Education Program Plans in Pennsylvania: Guidelines for School Age IEP Development* by National Learning Resource Center of Pennsylvania, Pennsylvania Department of Education, Bureau of Special Education, © 1978.

Exhibit 6-2 Suggested Format for Recording Child's Progress

Curricular Domain _____
Student(s) _____
Date _____

Learner Objectives	Strategy	Antecedent	Consequence	Schedule	Correction	Materials	Evaluation

Learner Objectives

Good objectives have several important characteristics. They should be derived from and sequenced according to the child's curricular placement. Teachers should proceed systematically through the curriculum.

To move from curricular objectives to learner objectives that are appropriate for lesson plans, the teacher must do one of two things: (a) specify the objectives, or (b) task analyze the objective.

Objectives are specified by noting the specific learner behavior desired, specific materials to be used, etc. In Exhibit 6-3, several curricular objectives are identified in a manner appropriate for lesson plans. The lesson plan objectives are much more specific than the curricular objectives. The lesson plan objectives tell the teacher what to do and what to expect of the child.

Some curricular objectives refer to complex tasks, encompassing more than one learner behavior. For example, given the curricular objective, "Grasps number concept 'two,' " it can be predicted that many learner behaviors will be necessary in order to accomplish the objective. The child will have to count to two, count up to two objects, recognize sets of two objects, label sets of two, etc. Since curricular objectives of this type are so complex, they must be broken down into smaller

Exhibit 6-3 Specifying Curricular Objectives

Objective as Stated in a Curriculum*	Objective Specified for Lesson Plan
Identifies three colors	Billy will point to objects (small toys or pictured objects) colored red, blue, or yellow when the teacher says, "Can you find something red?", etc.
Uses plurals	When shown animal pictures depicting one (or more than one) animal, and asked, "What do you see?", Billy will use the plural form correctly in answering.

*These objectives are from the MEMPHIS curriculum (Project MEMPHIS, Memphis, Tennessee, 1974.)

Source: From Quick-Campbell: *Lesson Plans for Enhancing Preschool Developmental Progress.* Copyright ©1976 by Kendall/Hunt Publishing Company, Dubuque, Iowa. Reprinted with permission.

tasks. This activity is called task analysis. Exhibit 6-4 shows how some complex curricular tasks can be task analyzed.

These sample task analyses illustrate the diversity of behaviors required by the curricular objective. The task components may be physical movements, verbalizations, and so on. It should be noted also that the analysis begins with identification of task prerequisites. Prerequisites are behaviors or characteristics that must be present for the child even to begin learning the new objective. For example, following simple verbal directions is a prerequisite to pointing to parts of a doll. If the child cannot follow directions such as "point to," the curricular objective is not appropriate.

Curricular Objective #1:

   This task is broken down in terms of the range of distractors present as the child is asked to identify facial features. This resembles the shaping strategy in that the difficulty of discrimination gradually builds. Such an analysis is especially appropriate for discrimination tasks.

Curricular Objective #2:

   Task component 7 deals with the child's persistence at the task. Many tasks require a disposition toward performance, such as persistence, endurance, concentration, etc. Often, these components must be taught—a child may be able to eat with a spoon, but will not do it reliably.

Curricular Objective #3:

   Task components 5, 6, and 10 refer to coordination of movements. Again, these coordinations often must be taught. A child who can steer and pedal will not necessarily combine the two automatically.

   Task component 12 deals with ending the task. Many tasks require a particular behavior in order to stop—don't forget to consider this. Remember the Homer Price story in which he was taught to use (but not stop) the doughnut machine.

   Task components 9 and 11 refer to an instance in which the child must behave correctly in the presence of certain cues, such as go slow at a corner. It is important to identify these cues (visual, verbal, tactile, etc.) in analyzing tasks.

Finally, the best way to determine the accuracy of the task analysis is to try it out with the child. In this way, the teacher soon will be aware of problems, such as a too-detailed analysis, omitted components, and others.

In summary, lesson plan objectives are derived from curricular objectives by specifying or task analyzing the curricular goals.

Exhibit 6-4 Sample Task Analyses

	1. Points to any five parts of a doll	2. Eats with spoon, spilling little.	3. Pedals appropriately sized tricycle.
Curricular Objective*			
Prereq-uisites	Points at small objects. Follows simple verbal directions.	Grasps and holds spoon-sized objects. Inserts objects in mouth.	Maintains balance on tricycle-sized object. Pushes with feet. Maintains direction in walking.
TASK COMPONENTS	1. Identifies facial components (nose, eyes, mouth, ears, teeth, chin, cheeks) when depicted on stylized drawings of face which has only 1-3 of these components. 2. Identifies those components on stylized drawings containing 4-8 facial components. 3. Identifies same components on more realistic drawings of faces.	1. Grasps spoon handle properly. 2. Brings spoon from table to mouth maintaining proper position of spoon. 3. Scoops soft foods (e.g., applesauce) with spoon. 4. Scoops harder, bite-sized foods (e.g., meat pieces) with spoon. 5. Uses spoon to carry sift foods to mouth, and inserts.	1. Sits on and gets off independently. 2. Places feet on pedals correctly. 3. Places hands on bar correctly. 4. Pushes on pedal with just one foot. 5. Alternates push--first one foot, then the other. 6. Looks ahead while pushing on pedals.

TASK COMPONENTS		
	6. Uses spoon to carry bite-sized food to mouth, and inserts.	7. Continues to push pedals alternately for up to 5 minutes.
4. Identifies same components on doll whose face contains up to 5 of the components.	7. Feeds self several consecutive bites of food without resorting to finger-feeding.	8. Turns steering bar to right/left.
5. Identifies same components on doll whose face has up to 8 of those features.		9. Turns bar in appropriate direction, e.g., turns with sidewalk, or in direction of target.
		10. Continues to pedal while turning.
		11. Adjusts speed to "driving conditions" e.g., slows at corners.
		12. Puts feet down (sole side) to stop.

*These objectives are from the MEMPHIS curriculum (Project MEMPHIS), Memphis, Tennessee, 1974).

Source: From Quick-Campbell: *Lesson Plans for Enhancing Preschool Developmental Progress.* Copyright © 1976 by Kendall/Hunt Publishing Company, Dubuque, Iowa. Reprinted with permission.

Learner objectives should be stated in terms of actual child behavior. For example, an objective should say, "Billy will correctly point to all the red objects, when shown red and green objects." It would not be appropriate to say, "Billy will learn the concept of red." The latter statement is vague. It does not make clear whether the child will point to or label red items nor whether "learning the concept red" means discriminating red from all or a few other colors. The educator must be as specific as possible in stating objectives—telling what, how, and when the child will behave.

Objectives should refer to units of behavior the child can accomplish reasonably in approximately a week. One week is a rough guideline and may not be appropriate for all children. However, if the teacher typically writes objectives that take weeks to accomplish, the objectives probably should be broken down into smaller steps for that learner. That is, there should be a more detailed task analysis. On the other hand, if the teacher writes new teaching plans weekly (as has been suggested here) but some children accomplish the objectives after a day or two, underplanning for those children is evident.

Strategy

Under the strategy section of the lesson plan, the teacher merely identifies the basic teaching strategy to be used. These were discussed in Chapter 5: Prompting (manual, verbal, visual, tactile, etc.), modeling, shaping, chaining, discrimination training. When choosing the teaching strategy, task characteristics as well as learner characteristics should be considered. Exhibit 6-5 summarizes some relationships between task or learner variables and appropriate teaching strategies.

Antecedent

In the column labeled "antecedent" the teacher writes the specific cue(s) that are to precede the behavior. These antecedent cues may be:

1. auditory: "where do you live?"
2. visual: seeing a ⬣stop⬣ sign
3. tactile: feeling the shape of the letter before identifying it

Antecedents may be contrived cues or task-imbedded cues. When teaching young children to tell time by hours and half-hours, it may be necessary to prompt them to read the short hand first so that they will not mistakenly call 6 o'clock 12:30. To prevent such a mistake, a teacher could use this antecedent: "What time is this, Billy? Remember, we read the short hand first." This, of course, is a contrived antecedent. Such a cue is not typically present when Billy sees a clock. On the other hand, only antecedents natural to the task itself are needed. For example, if a child were being taught to recognize when a playdough mixture had

Exhibit 6-5 Relationship of Learner Characteristics and Teaching Strategies

	Prompting	Modeling	Shaping	Chaining	Discrimination Training
TASK Characteristics	Tasks for which shaping alone would be too time-consuming, e.g., handwriting. Tasks where it is important to start, stop, and change behaviors to certain signals	Tasks in which unique performances are not required Behaviors for which the natural environment provides many models --e.g., speaking, social customs	Tasks involving honing of skills --e.g., aiming at targets, learning speech Tasks involving fine motor coordination, e.g., drawing	Tasks involving several steps, e.g., a complicated art activity Sequences of behaviors--which must be performed quickly and in precise sequences, e.g., reciting phone number	Tasks involving attaching labels to concepts, e.g., color names, numbers Tasks in which two or more stimuli are so similar as to result in confusion, e.g., differentiating among similar plants
Learner Characteristics	Learners who do not readily attempt new behaviors Learners who have difficulty focusing on critical stimuli Learners who may have problems in attention	Learners who have acquired generalized imitative skills Learners who enjoy identifying with others--peers, t.v. personalities, etc. Learners who have good attention and observation skills	Learners who lack imitative behaviors Learners who are resistant to acquiring the behavior, e.g., a child who does not want to go to school Learners who are dependent on immediate reinforcement	Learners who are not able to imitate sequences Learners who cannot follow sequenced verbal directions	Learners who currently confuse two stimuli, e.g., red and purple Learners who often overgeneralize, e.g., who call all teachers by the same name

reached the proper consistency, the antecedent events would merely be mixtures of proper or improper consistency (runny) and the question, "Is this playdough ready?" In this case, there is no additional contrived prompt. A contrived antecedent may or may not be needed. This depends on the learner and the difficulty of the task.

A final consideration in selecting antecedents is whether the task is in an acquisition or generalization phase. It will be recalled that acquisition of a task is facilitated by the use of standard, concise cues. In acquisition, then, the teacher would select a clear, simple antecedent that always would precede task performance. In initially teaching the previously mentioned time-telling task, a teacher always would begin the task with "What time is it, Billy? Remember, read the short hand first." However, after Billy has acquired the skill, the contrived antecedent ("Remember, read the short hand first.") should be faded. Then, as the teacher wants Billy's time-telling behaviors to generalize, the antecedent would be varied. At the generalization phase, the teacher might write this in the antecedent column: "Can you tell me the time?", "Please stay here until 10 o'clock," etc.

When choosing antecedents, then, the teacher must consider the nature of the task itself, whether contrived cues are necessary, and whether the task is in an acquisition or generalization stage.

Consequence

The consequence column is for the teacher to identify the positive consequence that will be used for the child's task completion. First, the teacher should label the consequence (e.g., social, food, tangible, token, task-imbedded), then state the particular reinforcer that will be used (social—"What a hard game, but you finished it!" food—apple pieces, wheat cracker pieces).

Schedule

In the schedule column, the educator indicates the relationship between the child's behavior and the delivery of reinforcement. The teacher can assign reinforcers to amounts of behaviors in various ways:

1. Number of tasks performed—Billy will receive a sticker for each puzzle he completes.
2. Amount of a complex task—Billy will be given social reinforcement after taking off each item of clothing while getting ready for his bath.
3. Amount of time passed—Billy will be able to play with his mother after playing independently for half an hour.
4. Correctness of task—Billy will receive a star each time he crosses the balance beam, stepping off no more than once. If he doesn't step off at all, the teacher also will clap for him.

Again, the teacher should determine the type of consequence and the schedule based on both task and child characteristics. Difficult, complex, or uninteresting tasks may require more powerful or frequent reinforcers. Children will function more efficiently with certain types of reinforcers. The teacher should remember, however, to attempt to move children to higher levels of reinforcement. These goals of using the most effective rewards yet gradually changing a child's effective reinforcers can be combined by:

1. Pairing a higher level (social) with a low-level but effective reinforcer. It is quite proper, then, to list two reinforcers for one behavior.
2. Preceding a low-level reinforcer (food) with a high-level one (social), gradually increasing the delay between the two.
3. Using high-level reinforcers at first but only for easier tasks.

Correction

The correction column is for stating what the teacher will do if the child makes an error. First, the teacher must determine whether to allow the child to make errors. Sometimes, when teaching a complex skill or a new skill to a child with learning problems, the teacher does not want errors to occur. In such a case, it should be stated simply that the teacher will prevent errors.

At other times, the teacher may allow errors and might correct them by indicating the behavior is incorrect and (1) modeling the correct behavior and (2) prompting the correct behavior.

Materials

Here, the educator lists materials needed for teaching the lesson. This list should be detailed enough to even include reinforcers so that it is necessary merely to glance at this column when collecting lesson materials.

Evaluation

In this column, the type of formative evaluation to be used for measuring accomplishment of that objective is identified. Some of these (frequency, duration, checklists, and others) have been suggested in Chapter 4. The actual forms for evaluation can be clipped to the lesson plan so that recording can be done quickly at the end of the lesson.

If a predetermined criterion has been set, this also should be noted in the evaluation column. For example, if the child is being taught to draw a house and a checklist will be used to evaluate performance, a teacher may decide to terminate instruction after the child is able to satisfy all items on the checklist for three trials in a row. In most cases, teachers should determine criteria for each objective.

Sometimes, however, it is difficult to predetermine criteria. Often the teacher must begin to teach the task in order to set reasonable criteria. For example, in teaching a child to copy printed letters, the educator may not be able to set a criterion concerning frequency of letters copied per minute before beginning to teach the task.

PLANNING FOR NONDIRECT INSTRUCTION

In a second look at the daily schedule (Table 6-1), the educator will notice that there are several segments in which no direct instruction is to occur: greetings, free play, circle time, toileting, recess, snack, activity period, dismissal. These segments typically are planned in a general way, such as listing steps and materials necessary to complete an art activity. Many teachers, though, do not consider these segments as important components of individualized curricular planning. Although these program segments certainly cannot be planned in the individualized, detailed manner of direct instructional planning, the teacher still should plan for these times. It is important to develop plans for all program segments for two reasons:

1. If teachers only "teach" at certain times during the day and merely supervise at other times, children will learn to "learn" only at those times. In one preschool, children were taught to be neat during their social skills lesson. At that time the teacher always remembered to prompt and reward the children's tidy behaviors since this actually was written on the lesson plan. However, at other times this teacher often forgot to reward or prompt those behaviors. The children learned that there were no consistent rewards or prompts for being neat except at lesson time. The behavior did not generalize because the teacher set up contrasting conditions (prompts, consquences) for the behavior across segments of the school day. The children were taught, quite accidentlly, that there were different expectations of them at different times of the day.

2. Most objectives should transfer to situations outside the lesson times and continue to occur even though the child has met the criterion and no longer is being taught the objective. However, behaviors seldom transfer automatically. Transfer and maintenance must be planned deliberately, prompted, and rewarded by teachers. Although some transfer-facilitating techniques can be implemented during direct instruction (systematically varying cues and/or reinforcers), many behaviors must be rewarded across varied conditions in order to occur reliably. These nondirect instructional segments of preschool programs provide excellent opportunities for the deliberate transfer and maintenance of behaviors.

Content of Nondirect Instructional Plans

Plans for nondirect instruction certainly cannot contain all components of the lesson plans described earlier. It is crucial, however, to indicate the desired behavior and how it is to be evaluated. The teacher might use a variety of daily events to maintain or generalize behaviors that children have learned during lesson segments. Consider that a group of preschool children recently acquired the instructional objectives in Exhibit 6-6 and that the teacher would like these behaviors to be maintained and/or transferred to other settings. Next to each skill, a segment of the daily schedule in which those skills might be maintained or generalized is suggested.

Exhibit 6-6 Specific Skills and Recommended Practice Times and Places

Program Segment	Skills
	Language Skills
activity period, in motor area	1. Reads these sight words: stop, exit, up down.
activity period/ art	2. Listens to and follows a sequence of three instructions.
	Social and Self-care Skills
snack	1. Identifies foods from the four basic food groups.
greetings/ dismissal	2. Buttons and unbuttons small buttons independently.
	Motor Skills
free play at art table	1. Cuts out pictures following a general shape
	Cognitive Skills
circle time, e.g., order characters in a story based on size, voice, etc.	1. Orders objects on basis of degree of specific physical characteristics

It is not difficult to see how curricular objectives are related to children's activities throughout the preschool day. What is difficult, however, is remembering to use the various activity periods for strengthening and transferring children's curricular accomplishments. For example, the teacher can determine easily that an art activity can be used for practicing a newly acquired writing skill (making the letter "S"). However, it also is easy to understand a teacher who, in the midst of ten 4-year-olds "painting" with chocolate pudding, forgets to suggest that Rebecca, Stephanie, and Ryan try writing an "S" shape in their pudding pictures. The task, then, is one of engineering practical techniques that remind teachers to use these activities periods to strengthen and transfer curricular skills.

Formats

It already has been determined that plans for nondirect instruction need only have two components: behavior statement and evaluation method. Since the objectives already have been learned, it is not as important to use standard cues, reinforcers, etc. In some cases, perhaps for children with special learning problems, it may be necessary to specify that a specific method be used. Therefore, the format also should include a column for making special notes. Exhibit 6-7 depicts a very basic format for planning a nondirect instructional activity. Forms such as this one can be printed easily on 4" × 6" index cards. The information recorded in these columns differs from what is recorded on a direct instruction lesson plan:

Child: Only six names are recorded on the form, although all children probably are going to participate in the activity. It simply is not possible to plan strengthening or transfer objectives for all children during each activity period. The teacher must spread emphasis for individual children across the day, according to children's needs.

Objective: Again, objectives chosen are all of one type—writing/drawing. Of course, other behaviors could have been chosen, such as color naming or cutting. By choosing to emphasize one type, however, the teacher increases the chance of being able to cover each one. It probably is not possible to implement a strengthening or transfer plan for all the objectives taught. Therefore, selecting objectives is a two-step procedure. First, the teacher determines which objectives most need additional attention, then assigns them to most reasonable program segments.

Evaluation: Here, the planning form also is the evaluation form. At the end of (or during) the activity, the teacher merely needs to circle yes or no, or put check marks in appropriate columns. It is best to keep the evaluation method simple as has been shown here with yes/no and checklists. A teacher who has chocolate pudding on her/his fingers has limited data recording possibilities.

Exhibit 6-7 Plan for a Nondirect Instructional Segment

_____ (activity)

_____ (teacher)

_____ (date)

Child	Objective	Evaluation		Notes
		form correct	**directionality**	
Rebecca	draw letter - S	y n	y n	
Stephanie	"	y n	y n	
Ryan	"	y n	y n	ask "How many bumps." 1st
		all round | half round	**round | ends meet**	
Greg	draw circle	y n	y n	
		4 equal sides	**3 | 2 | 4L | 3 | 2 | 1**	
Scott	draw square	3 | 2 | 4L	3 | 2 | 1	suggest making square into a t.v., game court, robot
Michelle	"			

Notes: Here the teacher records any information that will help initiate or reinforce the behavior. The person supervising the art activity may not be the same person who taught Rebecca, Stephanie, and the others to draw. The note concerning Ryan suggests that he needs a reminder to make an "S" that has two curves. This will prevent his making a mistake. The note regarding the last two children suggests that their teacher believes they may need some special cajoling to draw rigid squares during a finger painting activity. This suggestion probably will be effective both as a prompt and a reinforcer for drawing squares.

Optimizing Use of Plans

The problem of having to make special arrangements so that teachers actually use plans during nondirect instructional segments was raised earlier. Teachers must consider environmental adaptations that make it both practical and rewarding to use the plans.

First, plans can be considered as prompts for teachers. While the plan in Exhibit 6-7 can fit easily on a 4" × 6" index card, some teachers may find it more practical to record that information elsewhere. For example, the form could be drawn on large pieces of construction paper, then covered with clear contact paper. The specific information could be filled in each week with a wax marker. These charts could be posted in areas of the room where nondirect instructional activities take place—gross motor area, art area, bathroom, cloak room, story area.

Teachers with whom the authors have worked have devised a variety of environmental arrangements to remind themselves to carry out plans. One teacher made colorful center pieces for the snack tables each week. On these she pinned a plan for strengthening snack-related objectives for children assigned to each table. Another teacher kept a notebook in the coat area. It was used for objectives related to self-help skills and for those with which families were expected to help. The teacher and staff made a habit of reading plans from the notebook daily before the children's arrival. This reminded the staff to encourage certain children's independent dressing behaviors and to speak to parents concerning objectives they were to encourage. In another center, having little wall or shelf space, the teachers hung their plans from mobiles suspended over various areas of the room.

Another group of teachers decided to use the children in reminding them to carry out plans. They wrote plans for some activities on large wall charts, as described earlier, but they also illustrated the objectives. Children who recognized their own names (those who didn't learned quickly) enjoyed "reading" the plan, performing the objective, and being permitted to write on the teacher's wall chart. This type of plan seemed to work best in art, motor, and self-help areas. Children eagerly awaited Wednesdays (when charts were changed) to find their names and objectives. Objectives for younger children were treated differently. These children were given plans to "wear." Sometimes plans were written on pendants to be worn around the neck. At other times they were on badges, bracelets, hats, etc. When the teachers put the "plans" on these children each morning (or activity period), they knew what they were to work on (such as, "I can find red objects"). Children were permitted to decorate their "plans" with a star each time they performed the behavior.

These systems not only help teachers but also teach children to be good self-managers. The children learn to work on behaviors without being requested by adults, and they also share in the evaluation (filling out checklists) and delivery of reinforcement (pasting a star on one's pendant). Children begin to see self-management as a natural behavior. For example, a child in one preschool wore a small, attractive hour timer around her neck to remind herself to use the toilet regularly. A new student teacher appeared one day with a similar timer. She was using it for data collection. The child greeted her with, "Do you forget to go to the bathroom, too?"

Effective reward techniques is a second consideration in arranging the environment to encourage teachers' use of plans during nondirect instruction. Teachers need rewards also. It often is difficult enough to conduct a story time for 25 preschoolers, keeping one's place in the story, making certain that all the children are interested and attentive without the added responsibility of remembering to ask one child to recall the sequence of events, another the main characters' names, and so on. Perhaps educators would be more inclined to perform these additional responsibilities if they could make them more rewarding. At one center, teachers initialed all lesson plans they completed. They received a "lottery" ticket for each lesson plan. The tickets were entered into a weekly drawing for a variety of reinforcers: records, books, refreshments, babysitting fee or service, going out to lunch, etc. Others who have described teacher reinforcement systems have recommended rewards such as having a choice in staff scheduling for the week and having one's accomplishments be announced and/or posted. It is not easy to be a good teacher 100 percent of the time. Teachers should consider rewarding themselves for those aspects of their work that seem most difficult to perform.

RECOMMENDED ACTIVITIES

1. Reread the objectives at the beginning of the chapter to assess your learning. Reread to acquire information you missed or forgot.
2. Write a daily schedule appropriate for an infant stimulation program, a day-care center (children 3 to 6 years), or a Head Start program (4-year-olds).
3. Using a preschool curriculum such as the COMP-Curriculum in Appendix A, read through several objectives; note ones you think should be task analyzed and those merely needing specification in order to be used as instructional objectives.

4. Write a task analysis for one of the curricular objectives identified above.
5. Write sample lesson plans for both a direct and a nondirect instructional activity.
6. Write a list of events that would be reinforcing to you as a teacher.
7. Observe in a preschool and write recommendations for implementing nondirect instructional planning.

Chapter 7

Using Relevant Materials

OBJECTIVES

1. State the four major considerations in selecting instructional materials.
2. List the special considerations for mainstream settings, play materials, and instructional kits.
3. Describe the role of prompting in concept teaching.
4. Describe the concerns involved in adapting materials to exceptional children.

7

THIS CHAPTER CONSIDERS the selection of appropriate materials for the classroom. This discussion is confined to toys, teaching materials, and teaching kits. First, a model for evaluating materials (Exhibit 7-1) is described, then special considerations for mainstream settings, for play materials, and for instructional kits. Finally, formats are suggested for systematically assessing and selecting materials.

EVALUATING MATERIALS

Since most preschool programs do not have an abundance of funds, materials must be purchased wisely and for posterity. Teachers continually must resist the powers of good advertising and salesmanship and instead follow a deliberate plan in choosing relevant classroom materials. They must use a deliberate sequence of decision-making processes that will lead to selection of useful and lasting materials.

In the suggested four-step decision-making model (Exhibit 7-1), the process begins with a focus on curricular content, then questions the relevancy of materials based on child characteristics, considers whether materials relate to or utilize learning principles, and finally analyzes cost efficiency. Here are various kinds of questions that should be asked at each step.

Curricular Appropriateness

Just as a good curriculum should represent both breadth and depth of developmental tasks, materials also should represent those areas. Before selecting materials for the classroom, it is wise to list subdomains of the curriculum and to identify related materials systematically (Exhibit 7-2). In initially equipping a

Exhibit 7-1 Steps in Decision-Making Process

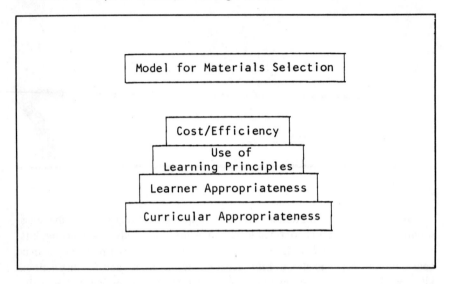

classroom, the educator will be most interested in materials related to several curricular subdomains such as a puzzle box that can be used to teach color and shape differentiation, fine motor skills, and language play. As the materials stock increases, the teacher can become more selective, for example, in choosing a toy that relates to only one curricular area (alphabet tracing cards). Meanwhile, if a matrix relating to curriculum is maintained (Exhibit 7-2), it is easy to determine what kinds of materials are needed to achieve a balance across the curriculum.

In addition to curricular content in choosing materials, the educator also should consider the sequencing characteristics of the curriculum. Is the sequence spiral—that is, are all curricular areas taught in each year of the program as they are in the COMP-Curriculum in Appendix A? Are any domains or subdomains emphasized more in one year than in others? A materials/curriculum matrix could be constructed to reflect this type of information as well. This can be done by coding entries on the matrix, e.g., if appropriate for ages 0 to 12 months, the mark would be entered in red ink, for ages 12 to 36 months, green ink, etc. The teacher then could determine standards for balance across curricular areas, based on sequence of skills through each year of the curriculum. For example, mouth and jaw control has less importance at upper age levels (4- and 5-year olds) than at lower levels (0 to 36 months). In selecting motor materials for infants, if may be desirable to maintain equality among the gross, fine, and mouth and jaw control curricular areas. On the other hand, in selecting motor materials for 4- and 5-year-olds, the teacher would not want equality but rather would choose more materials related to fine and gross motor tasks.

Exhibit 7-2 Relationship of Instructional Material to Curricular Areas

Curricular Areas		Peabody Language Kit	Learning to Dress Board		
Communication:	attention	X			
	imitation	X			
	responding	X			
	self-expression	X			
	play	X	X		
Social Skills:	eating/drinking				
	dressing/undressing		X		
	cleanliness/health				
	social conventions	X			
Motor:	gross				
	fine	X			
	mouth and jaw control				
Problem-Solving:	attention	X			
	imitation	X			
	recall	X			
	concept formation	X	X		
	grouping	X			
	sequencing	X	X		
	application of principles	X			
	creativity	X			

(Materials column header, angled: Peabody Language Kit, Learning to Dress Board)

Source: Reprinted from *COMP-Curriculum* by S.J. Forsberg, J.T. Neisworth, and K.W. Laub, by permission of the HICOMP Outreach Project, The Pennsylvania State University, 315 Cedar, University Park, PA 16802, © 1974.

Learner Appropriateness

The next step in the decision-making process is to evaluate materials based on unique characteristics of the learners. This step is especially important in mainstreamed classes where several children may require special educational consideration.

At this point, it is important to question which unique learner characteristics are relevant for educational planning. Chapter 1 noted that today's early educators are faced with the job of designing programs to fit children and families having diverse needs. They may be asked to provide custodial care, socialization experiences, compensatory education, and/or remedial programming.

Traditionally, educators have attached labels to children in an attempt to identify their educational needs—labels such as culturally disadvantaged, mentally retarded, learning disabled, hyperactive, gifted, emotionally disturbed, and high risk. There is reason (both logical and empirical) to question the usefulness of such labels for educational planning. Furthermore, the use of the labels is debilitating for the persons to whom they are attached. Children so labeled typically develop low self-esteem, are not well-accepted by normal peers, and are treated differentially by their teachers. Practices of labeling children, then, certainly do not lead to educational remediation.

For purposes of individualizing educational programming, it is more important to identify significant behavior characteristics. One approach to this is by developing simplified profiles of child behaviors across curricular areas. Exhibit 7-3 illustrates a simple behavior rating procedure applied to the matrix used earlier. The rating is derived from the child's functioning level within the curriculum. Each child receives a rating of 0, 1, or 2. A zero rating means that the child is functioning within the expected age range, a 1 means that the child's functioning range is one year behind or ahead of the expected age range, and a 2 refers to discrepancies of two or more years.

In choosing materials, teachers should give priority to curricular areas in which individual children or groups of children exhibit atypical functioning.

In addition to selecting materials based on child performance levels, teachers will find many handicapping behaviors will require still further consideration. Some children with sensory deficits or physical limitations will not be able to learn from materials appropriate for nonhandicapped preschoolers. For example, the selection of books for the reading area that included a child with a visual impairment should differ from those of another teacher. The educator of course would attempt to select several books in which a visual approach was not most pertinent to literary enjoyment such as several "scratch-and-sniff" and "pet the bunny" type, as well as several with exciting story lines. In some cases, teachers may even need to adapt materials for children with severe limitations. This will be discussed later.

Exhibit 7-3 Relationship of Learner Behaviors to Curricular Areas

Curricular Areas		Jamie	Jo-Ann	Janis	
Communication:	attention	1	0	1	
	imitation	1	1	2	
	responding	2	1	0	
	self-expression	1	0	0	
	play	2	1	2	
Social Skills:	eating/drinking	0	0	2	
	dressing/undressing	0	0	2	
	cleanliness/health	1	1	1	
	social conventions	0	1	0	
Motor:	gross	0	1	2	
	fine	1	0	0	
	mouth and jaw control	2	0	2	
Problem-Solving:	attention	1	0	0	
	imitation	0	1	1	
	recall	0	2	1	
	concept formation	1	2	1	
	grouping	0	1	0	
	sequencing	0	0	0	
	application of principles	1	1	2	
	creativity	2	0	1	

(Child)

Source: Reprinted from *COMP-Curriculum* by S.J. Forsberg, J.T. Neisworth, and K.W. Laub, by permission of the HICOMP Outreach Project, The Pennsylvania State University, 315 Cedar, University Park, PA. 16802, © 1974.

Use of Learning Principles

After screening materials for curricular and learner appropriateness, the educator must examine them in greater detail in order to see if their design or accompanying procedures are based on modern learning theory. This refers, of course, to the behavior principles discussed in earlier chapters.

Certain of these principles are especially relevant to the construction of educational materials:

1. Reinforcement. Do any reinforcing events occur when the child uses the materials appropriately? For example, one toy company makes a barn with a door that "moos" when opened wide. Young children learning to manipulate the latch and door eagerly anticipate the cow's moo upon opening the door. Materials also can provide reinforcement by way of task feedback. In sorting games, for example, items in like categories may be color coded on the back. After completing the sorting task, a child can turn the items over; if colors match, categorization was done correctly.

2. Prevention of inappropriate behavior. Some toys are designed cleverly so that they can only be used appropriately. For example, some puzzles in which children match words to pictures are designed so that only correct matches will fit together.

Concept Learning

A great deal of learning that takes place in the preschool years concerns concept formation. Children learn to recognize and differentiate among colors, numbers, animals, shapes, people, sounds, etc. Because of this, many commercial materials are designed to teach concepts. Unfortunately, principles for teaching discrimination or generalization often are not employed in these designs.

Teachers should question these characteristics of materials for concept teaching:

1. When using prompts to teach a discrimination, do prompts focus on relevant attributes of the stimulus? For example, in teaching preschoolers the sounds of the alphabet letters, the educator might want to purchase wall charts that would prompt children as to the correct sound. Figure 7-1 shows two sets of wall charts, both using the same prompt. In Set B, however, the prompts are attached to relevant attributes of the letters— that is, they are associated with the shapes of the letters. In Set A, the child's eyes need not even be directed toward the letters to say the appropriate sound. In Set B, the prompts accentuate the letter shapes— they are relevant to the task.

Figure 7-1 Wall Charts to Teach Sounds of Letters

Illustration by Robert Neisworth

2. If irrelevant prompts (such as color) are used to assist in discrimination, can those prompts be faded? The puzzle in Figure 7-2 has been designed to teach concepts of shapes. However, the puzzle board itself provides the learner with two cues other than shape to help solve the puzzle: color and position. Since these cues cannot be faded, the child might learn to complete the puzzle by remembering that red goes on top, yellow in the center, and blue at the bottom. Because the child never would have to discriminate among the shapes in order to perform the task, this puzzle should not be considered as a material for teaching shapes.
3. When matching tasks are used for associating stimuli with concepts, do the operations involved in matching relate to the concept being taught? The materials in Figure 7-3 are to teach children to relate sets of objects with their corresponding numerals. In Set A, the matching behavior required to solve the puzzle could be (a) counting the objects, then selecting the appropriate numeral, or (b) examining the uneven edge of

Figure 7-2 An Ineffective Puzzle Board for Teaching Shape Discrimination

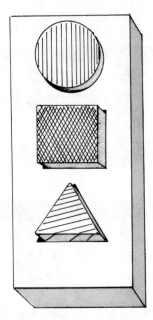

Illustration by Robert Neisworth.

one puzzle piece, and finding the corresponding uneven piece. As in the previous example of the shapes puzzle board, it cannot be assumed that the child has solved the task correctly because it has learned to match sets with numerals. Instead, the child may have learned skills in differentiating among jigsaw shapes. In Set B, however, the matching behavior involves either (a) counting the pegs on the base, then selecting a numeral with a corresponding number of openings (or simply selecting a corresponding numeral), or (b) examining the written word, and selecting the corresponding numeral. In any of these instances, the child is attending to the task of matching number concepts.

Operational Learning

Preschoolers are constantly busy manipulating objects. They are eager to remove clothing, eyes, and hair from stuffed toys. They joyously drop jewelry through holes in radiators, pour goldfish into toilet bowls, and more. Because of this apparent inclination to manipulate everything, teachers often forget that operational (or manipulative) behaviors, too, must be programmed and shaped.

Figure 7-3 Materials for Teaching Number Concepts

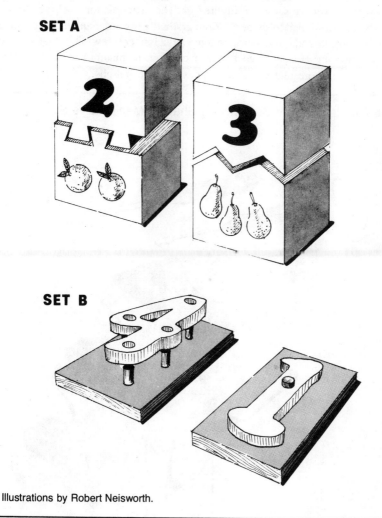

Illustrations by Robert Neisworth.

Materials catalogues for early educators are filled with items for teaching operations such as buttoning, zipping, stacking, pounding, latching. Teachers can choose among these items most wisely by identifying materials that allow for shaping of children's behaviors. They should select materials that permit shaping manipulative tasks sequentially according to patterns of differentiation; for example, moving from gross to fine motor control, moving from simple to complex manipulations.

Examples of materials appropriate for the sequential shaping of buttoning and using a screwdriver are shown in Figure 7-4. The materials for teaching use of a screwdriver are designed to shape children gradually toward manipulating smaller and smaller objects and toward turning longer and longer screws. The materials for teaching buttoning are designed to teach children to manipulate progressively smaller buttons, more buttons, and less easy to grip buttons.

Figure 7-4 Materials for Sequentially Shaping Manipulative Skills

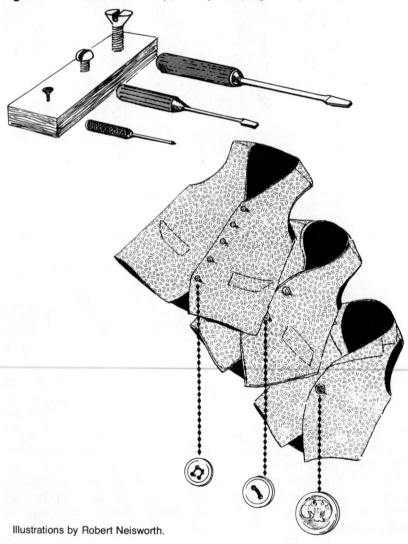

Illustrations by Robert Neisworth.

Materials based on this type of differentiation, of course, are appropriate for teaching beginning operations. They have the additional advantage of being appropriate for a range of learner proficiencies. Beginning "buttoners" can use one buttoning vest, advanced "buttoners" a more difficult vest.

Overlearning

After children have acquired new skills and concepts, educators want to be certain that they will maintain that learning. A good way to ensure children's retention is to arrange for practice of newly learned behaviors. Young children often move naturally from acquisition to practice of skills in their normal development. A toddler who has acquired a few words and speech sounds often can be observed "crowing" this speech over and over in varied intonations throughout the day (as well as wee hours of the morning). Teachers probably have experienced the enthusiasm of a 1-year-old who has just learned to empty a toy box. It seems that the child is willing to empty the box as often as the teacher or parent is willing to fill it.

In selecting materials for the preschool, then, teachers ought to be careful to select some that allow children ample opportunity to practice (overlearn) skills. An important concept in this is the child's motivational characteristics. In general, very young children, up to 2 years, who recently have acquired significant milestone behaviors (walking, talking, picking up small objects, singing, eating finger food) may not need much contrived reinforcement to engage in practice. It appears that these newly acquired activities are rewarding in themselves or that they bring about natural reinforcement. For example, an infant who has learned to grab for objects or to walk can attain many events through these behaviors. On the other hand, a 3-year-old who has learned to count to ten probably will not persist at this counting unless it brings about some reward—adult attention or participation in a game, for example.

The point here is that educators should choose materials that will lead children to practice new behaviors or discriminations that they otherwise might not do. So the teacher might choose a garage and car set in which parking spaces are color coded to match cars or in which certain manipulations are required. In this way, the free play materials provide an opportunity for children to practice color concepts or manipulation skills in a play situation. Teachers especially might consider using this overlearning principle in selecting materials for play areas. This would facilitate the use of free play times for maintenance and transfer of learning (as discussed in Chapter 6 on lesson planning).

Imitational Learning

Educators typically think of imitational learning in terms of live models—a teacher showing a child how to construct a design or how to pronounce a word.

However, once children have acquired generalized imitational skills, they will not always require live models. For example, a teacher may teach visual sequencing by stringing six beads (red round, blue round, yellow round, red square, blue square, yellow square), then asking the child to repeat the sequence on a string, checking its correspondence to the teacher's (string) model. After a few experiences with live modeling, the child probably could use a pictured model. (Many toy companies sell pictured bead sequences along with their wooden bead sets.) Children then can continue modeling sequences independently. Another company sells rubber stamps of the shape and size of its beads. This allows the teacher to stamp sequences appropriate for the children to choose color, shape, length, and size variables that match individual developmental levels.

Cost/Efficiency

The last step in selecting materials involves cost and efficiency. By the time educators make these practical decisions, they already will have narrowed the selection so that they are choosing only among materials that are appropriate to the curriculum and to individual children, and those that make good use of learning principles. At this point, teachers will need to put priorities on item selection, perhaps rating materials from one (absolutely necessary) to three (luxury items). Materials that relate curricular areas to current materials (Exhibit 7-2) and those that relate learner behaviors to curricular areas (Exhibit 7-3) will help determine priority items. In addition, these comparisons will allow teachers to estimate efficiency of items in terms of versatility of given materials.

ADAPTING MATERIALS FOR EXCEPTIONAL LEARNERS

The model for materials selection suggested that the second level of decision making be the screening of materials for learner appropriateness. At times, however, it is impossible to locate materials for certain curricular areas that also are appropriate for certain exceptional child characteristics. While teachers cannot always select materials to match child characteristics, they often can adapt them for appropriateness. It is especially important that teachers in mainstream preschools have skills in identifying child characteristics that might require materials adaptation, and adapting materials for those characteristics.

Identifying Characteristics Requiring Adaptation

Most preschoolers with developmental delays will have one or both of these behavioral characteristics: (1) they will show behavioral deficits, or (2) they will show behavioral excesses. These could be categorized further in terms of the four functional domains. Certain exceptional characteristics are most relevant for materials adaptations:

1. deficits—sensory and perceptual, communication, motor, independence/ self-help, cognitive
2. excesses—emotional, motor

Examples of materials adaptation for each of these exceptional characteristics are considered next.

Sensory and Perceptual Deficits

Many common materials can be adjusted so that they have multisensory aspects. The materials in Figure 7-5 are inappropriate for a visually impaired child. The book is a two-dimensional stimulus: the drawing cards make use of color cues, and the markers on the game board might be upset if tactile feedback was being used to

Figure 7-5 Game Dependent on Visual Cues That Can Provide Multisensory Cues

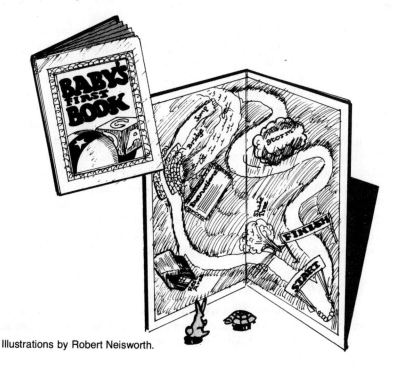

Illustrations by Robert Neisworth.

move from spot to spot. On the other hand, these materials can be adapted easily for visually impaired children. A teacher could purchase two copies of the book (since each page is a simple figure) and cut out and raise the objects on each page so the child could trace object outlines. The colored dots on the drawing cards could be given tactile properties by pasting small circles over the green dots and larger ones over the red dots. Children could learn to draw a line from the small dot to the large one, instead of from green to red dots. The game board and markers also could be adapted. The triangle, square, and circular shapes on the board could be raised by cutting out felt shapes. The markers could have Velcro bottoms so that they would not be upset by someone needing to touch the board.

Communication Deficits

Many games used in preschools involve communication skills. In lotto games, for example, the child chooses a card, names it, and places it on a matching space. A child who cannot speak can participate by signing. The teacher can put finger spelling stick-ons on the lotto boards so that the child's production can be matched with that on the lotto board. In this way, other children also might learn to finger spell.

Motor Deficits

Children with motor delays might exhibit varied motor behaviors: they may show inadequate fine motor control, may not be able to perform certain basic movements, or may have difficulty in coordinating movements. Simple adaptations often allow these children to use typical preschool materials, however. For example, wooden or plastic knobs can be added to puzzle pieces that otherwise would be too difficult to manipulate. The teacher can add larger tabs to zipper pulls or put a stiff plastic around ends of shoe laces. When children have difficulty coordinating movements, materials can be adapted so that they need learn only one movement at a time and then later coordinate the movements. For example, when children can't coordinate pedaling a tricycle and keeping their feet on the pedals, the teacher straps their feet on the pedals. Many preschool materials require similar coordinations for the child with motor deficits. In stringing beads, the string must be held while threading the beads. A bead set could be supplemented with varying lengths of string and varying degrees of stiffness or slickness so that manipulating strings will not interfere with learning to thread beads.

Independence/Self-Help Deficits

In most preschools, children are expected to spend time working and playing independently. Clearly, independence training is an important developmental task. Some handicapping conditions, such as physical disabilities, can limit a child's opportunities to behave independently in a typical preschool. Materials can be modified so that children with limited independence skills can use them. Consider the assortment of containers materials typically are packaged in—cardboard boxes, cylindrical boxes, plastic snap-tops. Materials can be assigned to storage in containers that are low, unbreakable, and easy to open and shut so that all children could use them independently. Other children who have independence deficits are dependent on adult feedback and reinforcement. By adapting materials for corrective feedback (e.g., color coding, sorting materials, accompanying puzzles with pictures of the completed work, etc.), the educator can begin to make these children less dependent on social feedback.

Cognitive Deficits

Many materials (for example, puzzles) that require knowledge of a variety of concepts can be adapted for lower cognitive levels simply by separating the materials into parts requiring knowledge of fewer concepts. The teacher could cut puzzle boards apart, and in fact buy several copies of the same puzzle—gluing some pieces in place and making them into puzzles containing one, two, three, etc., items, shaping the child's performance up to the demands of the original puzzle.

Emotional Excesses

Children who are hyperactive, tantrum-prone, etc., often are steered away from working with many kinds of toys and equipment. For example, teachers may not allow the child to play with small toys that might be thrown, with musical instruments that make loud sounds, etc. By doing this, not only are they preventing those children from educational experiences but they probably are overlooking a great source of reinforcement for those children—sensorimotor events. The objective, then, is to adapt the materials in a manner that maintains children's interests yet prevents them from inappropriate play. One teacher solved this problem somewhat by setting up a play area that was quiet enough (quilts and pads on floors and walls) so that other children were not disturbed by noises. The child was allowed reinforcing play there. In addition, the teacher can fasten down containers in other areas of the room so that children prone to throwing are not rewarded for attempts at upsetting such items.

Motor Excesses

Many handicapped preschoolers have difficulty controlling motor behaviors. The teacher can arrange weights to help them use materials requiring control, such as drawing, walking a pattern, etc. Surfaces (tables) can be covered with rough materials so that these children are not struggling continually with the control of extraneous movements.

MATERIALS FOR PLAY

While it certainly is not difficult to choose high interest play materials for preschoolers, there are several points to consider in buying them. First, it would be wise to choose play materials that provide opportunities for practicing concepts and skills that comprise the curriculum. The teacher also should consider—

- safety, to maximize children's well-being
- novelty, so that school toys have high interest
- cooperative aspects, so that play equipment encourages children to interact
- stereotyping, to avoid subtle teaching of sexist or cultural biases
- mainstreaming, to enhance the social integration of handicapped and nonhandicapped children—for example, the presence of a finger spelling puzzle in a play area might encourage nonhandicapped children to use finger spelling with a handicapped peer

Finally, the educator should consider the purchase of instructional kits. These could be evaluated according to the model presented for materials. This evaluation should be supplemented by a more critical inspection of the stated objectives and program strategies. The teacher can refer to the content from the chapters on curricula and methods to identify critical questions.

RECOMMENDED ACTIVITIES

1. Use the content of this chapter to construct a device for describing/evaluating preschool instructional materials.
2. Use this form together with a curriculum and select instructional materials for a new preschool program. Limit your program to an age group (e.g., 0-2, 3-5) and to a service delivery type (home based, classroom).
3. Look through preschool materials catalogues, identifying play materials that support racial or cultural biases so they can be avoided.
4. From materials catalogues, identify preschool materials that would enhance the social integration of handicapped and nonhandicapped children, such as the finger spelling puzzle.
5. Compile a materials file containing catalogues, brochures, manufacturers' and publishers' addresses, evaluation forms, etc., for your reference when you must select materials.
6. Choose an age group and design a play material for an integrated preschool class that has these characteristics:

   - it uses at least one learning principle
   - it enhances integration of handicapped and nonhandicapped children
   - it can be used independently by that age group

Chapter 8

Keeping Up the Good Work

OBJECTIVES

1. State the seven suggestions that are useful in preparing for conferences or other meetings.
2. Describe the three basic strategies for helping children to generalize their newly acquired skills to circumstances outside the training setting.

8

UP TO THIS POINT, readers have learned techniques for planning, implementing, and evaluating instructional programs. Assuming that these procedures are successful, teachers must consider a final type of program planning, ensuring that children will keep up the good work; that is, they will remember the skills and concepts taught them and they will practice them in a variety of places and with a variety of people. For example, when a 3½-year-old has been taught to put her coat on correctly with buttoning and zipping, the teacher wants her to do it at home as well as at school, with her older sister, grandmother, and others. This child should generalize what she has learned to other people, places, etc. The competent child can perform skills under varied circumstances; therefore, educators must be sure that their teaching responsibilities extend from initial acquisition through the generalization of objectives.

This chapter discusses several techniques to help children generalize their learning. It also analyzes three special situations in which generalization is especially important—generalization between home and school, generalization across various staff persons in the classroom, and generalization when a child is transferred to a new classroom or school. As can be seen, in helping children generalize skills to other situations, the teacher must work with other persons in a cooperative manner. Therefore, the next section considers general techniques for working with others.

WORKING WITH OTHERS TO ENHANCE GENERALIZATION

Teachers who are helping children generalize their skills will need to work out a cooperative relationship with persons with whom the child interacts in other situations—with the child's parents, other teachers, etc. Teachers must communicate information about what to expect of the child, techniques for encouraging and

129

instructing it, and must motivate these persons to follow through with programs so that the child will truly keep up the good work.

For example, there may be a hyperactive child in class. The teacher has controlled this hyperactivity successfully most of the time by using techniques such as reinforcing the child when it is being relatively less active, providing constructive activities for it to engage in, interrupting inappropriate behaviors (such as hand flicking), and providing substitute activities. Now the teacher wants the child to generalize its new, more controlled behavior patterns to other situations. The educator might meet with the child's parents and/or with other teachers with whom the child interacts. Skills in communicating and establishing positive relationships with these other persons are critical to the child and its development. The child either will learn to generalize the new accomplishment or learn that it is not necessary to control hyperactivity except with the teacher. It is of great importance that the educator be able to pass on information and skills to other significant persons in the child's environment. The following list of suggestions is valuable in preparing for conferences as well as in evaluating one's interactions after conferences.

1. Individualize in your interactions with adults just as you do with children. When you have an opportunity to observe in settings such as the home or another classroom, be certain to observe the individual strengths and weaknesses of the parents or teachers. When you are knowledgeable about these characteristics, you can make your interactions and suggestions more relevant. For example, if you are working with parents whom you have observed as being inconsistent with their child, it would be better to demonstrate how to encourage the child to put on its own coat and have the parents practice it a few times, rather than merely to describe what the parents should do.

Another important reason for individualizing interactions with adults is that specific kinds of handicapping conditions often require special adjustments for persons working with that child. For example, a child with a behavioral disorder may do best when the adults around it offer particular kinds and amounts of reassurances. It may not be adequate to tell another teacher to reassure Patty when taking her into new situations (e.g., going on a field trip). It might be more helpful to add that Patty seems most comfortable when she is close to the teacher and with children she knows well, that an occasional smile and hand squeeze seem to comfort her, that she gains confidence if allowed to stand along the sidelines before entering into activities or new rooms.

2. When making suggestions, be practical. It is important to remember that everyone has limitations—whether in skills, time, energy, etc. When making suggestions to others, be sure you are suggesting something that the person can do. It is much better to ask only a little at first and then build on the success. Consider the mother (a single parent) of five children who recently enrolled her son in a preschool program for handicapped children. The son, with severe motor disabilities, was 4 years old and the mother had had no help with him since birth. It was easy to see that this mother was exhausted and needed a respite from "teaching" her son. So even though the child was making progress in toilet training at school, the teacher decided not to try a generalization program at home until the mother seemed more relaxed and expressed an interest in working with her son at home again.

It also is important to be practical in making suggestions to other teachers. For example, make an effort to find out their schedules, class loads, and other responsibilities before making detailed suggestions of activities to do with a mainstreamed child from your class. If you can show this kind of understanding early in your interactions, this teacher is much more likely to continue a cooperative relationship.

3. Make specific arrangements for meetings/conferences. Generalization will not be accomplished simply by remembering to talk with a parent or teacher at the next meeting. Set aside time for the meeting, phone call, etc. This also will make the content seem much more important to the other person. In scheduling, be sure to include arrangements for follow-up. Parents who have agreed to work on a child's hyperactivity, or any other behavior, probably will need support or have questions after a few days. Make plans for a follow-up phone call, note, etc. Also keep in contact even if there are no problems because you are interested in learning whether the generalization has occurred.

4. Establish relations that are interactive as well as supportive. You do not want to limit your relationship with parents and other teaching personnel to a one-way direction in which you merely take the role of adviser. Other persons know the child in situations with which you are less familiar. They probably can make helpful observations and suggestions as well. They also will be more receptive to your suggestions if you listen to and are open to theirs.

5. Be encouraging. Everyone needs support when embarking on a new or difficult task. Even as adults, everyone appreciates and is motivated by an occasional pat on the back. Some persons will need more of this than others, so individualize the frequency and kind of encouragement also. A preschool teacher was working with a low-functioning parent, encouraging the parent to maintain her daughter's grooming skills at home. The child, a 4-year-old, combed her hair regularly at school but still arrived each morning with tangles and sometimes even food in her hair. The teacher met with the mother, reviewed the grooming procedures at school, and gave the mother a brush, comb, and mirror to take home. Still, more often than not, the child arrived with her hair unkempt.

The teacher decided the parent must need more encouragement. One day when the child's hair was somewhat brushed, the teacher sent a note home saying how cute Barbara looked that day. The next day Barbara's hair was brushed and she was wearing a ribbon in it. Again the teacher sent a note home. Evidently this was just the kind of encouragement the parent needed, because the child came to school neatly groomed at least 90 percent of the time from then on. The teacher still sent notes periodically, but they were more subtle. For example she added praise to a drawing Barbara took home (Figure 8-1).

6. **When planning meetings, try to make them rewarding and interesting for others who are involved.** This is especially important in cases where you meet with people on a regular basis. For example, you might work in a program that includes a weekly parent meeting (group or individual). Parents will look forward to these meetings and want to cooperate with school personnel if you can plan ways to keep enthusiasm. Some suggestions are:

Figure 8-1 Sample Note to Parents to Reinforce Their Participation in Skill Generalization

Illustration by Robert Neisworth.

- When recommending a certain kind of interaction with the child, such as talking more in one-to-one situations, provide the parent with concrete materials for the activity. For example, lend the parent a game, books to look at with the child, etc.
- Change your manner of presentation. Don't always talk and discuss. Vary the meeting by using demonstrations, role playing, films, field trips, observations, etc.
- Invite children to your meetings sometimes. This serves two purposes. The child can perform new skills for the parents, and the parents can practice interactions in your presence with guidance and support.
- If you use weekly newsletters to communicate, you might want to include other helpful information, such as recipes, instructions for a craft, a game.

7. Motivate persons to want to work with a particular child. Before beginning any program, be sure to provide information as to why the child needs to generalize its skills to another setting or why it is important that you work together to help the child. Explain clearly the characteristics of the child and why this cooperative program will be so beneficial.

The discussion of techniques for working with other professionals and with parents has highlighted the importance of communicating and sharing pertinent information about the child among all significant persons with whom it interacts. This kind of open communication is necessary if teachers wish the child to practice skills in a variety of situations. In addition to this, however, there are some techniques that teachers can use that will promote the generalization of behaviors to other situations. In general, these techniques all deal with varying the teaching situation in the classroom itself so that there is not a great contrast between the classroom setting and those to which it is desired that the behavior generalize (e.g., home setting). Educators must remember not to practice these generalization techniques until the child has acquired the behavior and it is well-established. Introducing variety before a given objective is well learned will only confuse the child. Generalization techniques are used after an objective is well-established in one situation and the teacher now wants the child to practice it in other situations.

TEACHING TECHNIQUES TO ENHANCE GENERALIZATION

This section presents three major techniques for helping children generalize their learning. These techniques are equally applicable to all of the specific generalization situations discussed—transferring behaviors to the home, interactions with other persons, and new classroom settings such as mainstreamed programs.

Technique 1: Match Conditions in Your Setting to Those in the Generalization Setting

It often is difficult for persons to adjust to new situations that are very discrepant from a familiar, comfortable situation. For young children and for those with learning or behavior problems, the discrepancy often poses great problems that interfere with their ability to generalize. Many children who are shy and withdrawn will learn to interact with one adult in a school setting but will not talk to other adults. Some children learn to take turns and be polite at school but never practice these behaviors at home. Children may attend well in a small group setting but be very distracted in a large group. Perhaps in each of these cases, the two situations are so different that nothing prompts the child to use these new skills. Perhaps the child who is mannerly during meals at school is not that way at home because no one praises taking turns, etc., there or because meal time is more hectic.

What can be done to match the training situation to the generalization situation? First, both situations must be observed carefully, particularly aspects that might be critical for the child. Some of these are:

- The type and amount of reinforcement. A child may be moving to a mainstreamed preschool program in which the teacher uses only verbal praise (no stars, stickers, hugs, etc.) and does this quite infrequently. This discrepancy might cause problems for a child who is dependent on a high ratio of reinforcement from the teacher.
- The materials and equipment that are found in a setting. Children who enjoy reading books at school may not do this in a home because there is no quiet reading area at home.
- The amount of structure provided. Children often find it difficult to move back and forth between situations that are structured and require much compliance and those that are unstructured and require a great deal of independence.

After these and other discrepancies are noted, teachers must determine what can be done to reduce significant discrepancies for the child. Logically, they can do this by changing their own situation or by changing the generalization situation. Let's consider some examples.

Tommy was about to transfer from a preschool handicapped class to a mainstreamed preschool. In the latter, the teacher used only verbal reinforcers and learning centers and expected children to direct their own activities for periods of time up to half an hour. Tommy's teacher observed the mainstreamed class in order to determine how she could better prepare him for the transfer and decided on three approaches:

1. The teacher began to give Tommy tasks he was to complete independently; occasionally he would work on these tasks with two or three other children to simulate a learning center experience.
2. The teacher gradually switched the reinforcement procedures for Tommy to ones that were mainly verbal.
3. The teacher borrowed some materials (books, visual aids, etc.) from the other teacher so that Tommy would be familiar with some of these when he went to the new classroom.

By changing Tommy's existing situation so that it more closely resembled his new, mainstreamed class, the teacher was able to help him make a smooth transition. His new teacher reported that Tommy adjusted nicely, with little regression. He had kept up the good work.

In another example, Mrs. B's preschool was used as a teacher training site for local college students. While most of her children enjoyed and cooperated with her student teachers, one group of four children typically "tested" each new student by their general nonattending, disruptive behavior. For example, during story time with the student teacher, the children talked, did not listen, pushed each other, got up, or lay on their chairs. When Mrs. B. led a circle time, however, these children were attentive and well-behaved.

Mrs. B. decided to work out a plan to make the student teacher's behavior more similar to her own with the hope that the children would respond more similarly. She taught the student to use some of the material and facial and verbal prompts that she used during group instruction.

For instance, Mrs. B. always began group instructions with a rhyme. She held up her hand and said "listen" when it was time to listen. She used special sit-upons for circle time instead of chairs or the floor.

The student teacher was advised to practice all these techniques as well as to reinforce the children for attentiveness. After five or six days, the children were attending well and had stopped their disruptive behaviors. Mrs. B. subsequently passed these techniques on to all other new student teachers and found that the children regularly generalized their appropriate behaviors to the new teachers.

Technique 2: Vary the Practice Conditions After Behaviors Are Learned

Young children and those with learning or behavior problems usually learn tasks better when teaching conditions are very specific. For example, in teaching a 2-year-old to give her whole name (first and last) it is better to use the same question each time: "What's your name?" or "Tell me your name," etc. Initial learning is more efficient with consistent learning conditions; however, learning generalizes better when variety is added to the situation.

As an example of consistent initial learning conditions followed by varied practice conditions, a preschooler with some motor impairment had to learn to walk up stairs unassisted. His teacher first used a specially designed staircase. The steps were smaller in depth and height so the child could master them easily. The child used these stairs time and time again until he could walk up just holding the railing. The child had acquired the skill over very consistent conditions—a special staircase, a consistent adult teacher, and consistent prompting and praising.

At this point the training was varied so that the child would learn to walk up other stairs accompanied by other persons and verbalizations. The training steps were adjusted so that they were slightly higher, other adults worked with the child and were given no specific verbalizations. Periodically, an adult took the child on a building tour, encouraging him to try other stairs. The parents soon reported that the boy was enjoying walking up stairs at home and during outings. The generalization procedures were successful.

Technique 3: Vary the Time During Which the Behavior Is Requested

So often teachers request behaviors only at specific times. For example, please and thank you are encouraged only at meals or snack time, listening and taking turns only at circle time, etc. Teachers must remember to vary these conditions also or children will learn not to generalize. They must guard against this happening by observing and changing their own teaching behaviors. Does the teacher play review games with children or teach them to learn and then forget? Does the teacher request behaviors at unusual times, such as talking about the days of the week during a music activity instead of the usual circle time?

SUMMARY

This chapter has discussed how to enhance generalization and children's learning. Several suggestions were raised concerning teaching procedures that help children generalize. In addition, since generalization involves joint efforts between significant adults (parents and teachers), recommendations were made for working cooperatively with others.

RECOMMENDED ACTIVITIES

1. Choose three behavioral objectives, sampling from various domains of child behavior. For each one describe (a) the specific procedures you would use for initial training and (b) two procedures you would use for generalization training programs.
2. Role-play a meeting with a parent in which the teacher is attempting to persuade the parent to work on a skill with the child.
3. Role-play a meeting between a special class teacher (or a specialist such as a speech therapist) and a regular class teacher. The specialist is to instruct the regular class teacher on procedures for encouraging the child to keep up independent behaviors such as dressing itself.

Chapter 9

Putting It All Together

OBJECTIVES

1. List and describe briefly the major provisions of Public Law 94-142.
2. Write a rationale for parents and professionals cooperating in assessment and program planning activities.
3. Discuss the pros and cons of labels used in special education.
4. List the components of the IEP and describe the process of preparing one.
5. Differentiate between situations in which P.L. 94-142 applies to children in the birth to age 5 range and those in which it does not apply.

9

CENTRAL AMONG the essential roles of the early educator are responsibilities for assessing children's competencies and planning instructional programs that match their current levels of functioning. In the usual routine of assessing, some children with special needs will be identified and additional, more intensive and specialized assessment will be required to identify their needs fully.

On humanitarian grounds, it makes sense to find and serve children with special needs. Recent federal legislation requires that children with special needs be identified and, depending on the age of the child and state laws, that they be served. This chapter clarifies further the links between assessment and instructional programming under Public Law 94-142, The Education for All Handicapped Children Act. Because of the special requirements of P.L. 94-142, the partnership between professionals and parents that must be an element of the process of assessment and instruction also is examined.

MAJOR PROVISIONS OF P.L. 94-142

In 1975, then-President Gerald Ford signed into law the most important piece of legislation ever to be passed for the handicapped. The rights accorded to handicapped children and their parents under the law have important and far-reaching implications for all citizens and especially for those who work in human services fields. Some of the provisions of P.L. 94-142 already were functioning in some way because of previous legislation or litigation but they all were strengthened and brought together under the same umbrella with the passage of this law. This section is not intended to review all relevant litigation and legislation that fed into P.L. 94-142, but to alert educators to the provisions that govern their behavior with children, parents, and colleagues as they go about their daily activities of being early teachers.

141

The federal action in 1975 was official recognition that more than 8 million handicapped children in the United States had special needs that were not being met adequately. Specifically, the law stated that more than half of these 8 million were not receiving appropriate educational services and that as many as 1 million of them were being excluded entirely from the public school system. Responsibilities for correcting these situations were given to state governments and local agencies for action under the law's general guidelines.

In addition, the act said many of the handicapped children in the public schools were not experiencing success because they had special needs that had gone undetected. Procedures such as adequate resources, advanced teacher training, and improved diagnostic and instructional procedures were recommended as ways to remedy these conditions.

In discussing the law, many talk about the fact that educational rights for the handicapped now are guaranteed. This term is not being used lightly. For one thing, the law was passed "in perpetuity," which means that, barring an act of Congress, it is here to stay. Many federal laws have some sort of "sunset" (close-out) provision and it is unusual to pass a law in perpetuity. The law was adopted by huge margins—404 to 7 in the House of Representatives and 87 to 7 in the Senate—an indication of the overwhelming support it generated.

Definitions

Previous chapters encouraged thinking about children in terms of their current functioning, not as some category or group. It is true that labels seldom tell anything about an individual's patterns of strengths and weaknesses. For example, knowing that the 3-year-old in class is diagnosed as mentally retarded offers no help at all in instructional programming.

Nevertheless, many services available to children and families are tied to a label. For example, a child may have to be labeled mentally retarded to qualify for placement in a special program because of the funding for the program or the mandate of the agency operating it. Many persons who do not advocate labels have learned to live with them for this very reason. Often the label is the ticket to the right service for the child. It cannot be emphasized enough that day-to-day work with children cannot be based on generalities about the child's label; it must be based on knowledge of the child's current functioning across developmental domains.

Terms (labels) and their definitions are a part of P.L. 94-142. The law defines what is meant by the term handicapped: children evaluated and diagnosed as being mentally retarded, hard of hearing, deaf, speech impaired, visually handicapped, seriously emotionally disturbed, orthopedically impaired, other health impaired, deaf-blind, multihandicapped, or as having special learning disabilities. All these are eligible for special education and related services.

Another important definition is special education: specially designed instruction to meet the unique needs of the handicapped child, provided at no cost to the parent. Included are classroom instruction, physical education, home instruction, and instruction in institutions and hospitals. Related services is defined as transportation and such developmental, corrective, and other supportive services as are required to assist the handicapped individual to benefit from special education. Related services also includes speech pathology and audiology services, psychological services, physical and occupational therapy, recreation, counseling and medical services needed for diagnostic or evaluation purposes, school health services, social work services in schools, and parent counseling and training. Early identification and assessment of disabilities in children also are considered to be related services.

These special education and related services must be provided at public expense and under public supervision and direction. This provision is referred to as Free Appropriate Public Education (FAPE). FAPE includes guarantees that these services meet standards of the state educational agency; include preschool, elementary, or secondary school education; and are provided in accordance with an Individual Education Program (IEP). Many refer to the act as the "Right to Education" law. It is easy to see how this description would become attached because of the FAPE provisions.

Individual Education Program

The provision for a Free Appropriate Public Education has as a primary purpose the guarantee that the education will be paid for by the state—that it will be at public expense. The objective of the IEP is to assure that the special education and related services will indeed be special for that child. The IEP requires a statement of the child's existing functioning levels. The intent is to match up assessment and special programs and services with another component of the IEP, a statement specifying instructional goals.

The IEP is an ideal mechanism to effect a match between the needs of the child as specified in the annual goals and short-term instructional objectives and the information about its existing functioning levels. The IEP must be written and reviewed to determine child progress annually.

In summary, the IEP must include:

1. information about the child's existing educational levels
2. a statement of annual goals, including short-term instructional objectives
3. a statement of specific services, as needed
4. the special programs required
5. the date when special services are to begin and their estimated duration

6. specification of evaluation procedures, including tests and other information that will be needed to judge the child's progress and determine if the objectives are being met

The IEP is prepared by a team that has a prescribed membership: a committee consisting of a representative of the school district (often the principal of the school), the child's teacher, parents (one or both of them), and the child itself if this is judged to be appropriate. In some cases, a court-appointed parent surrogate is a member of the team when the parents are not present or are unable to participate. If the evaluation and planning for the child is being undertaken for the first time, a member of the multidisciplinary team that conducted the assessment is included on the IEP committee. If a member of the assessment team is not present, someone else who has knowledge of the assessment procedures used with the particular child must be on the team. It is the responsibility of the team to be sure there are appropriate links between assessments and special programming for the child.

Least Restrictive Environment

Whatever special education and related services are planned for the child, the law specifies that the education for handicapped children will take place in the least restrictive environment. Many persons mistakenly refer to this as mainstreaming. In fact, the term mainstreaming is never mentioned in the law. The term used is least restrictive environment. It provides that handicapped children will be placed in special classes or separate schools only when the nature or severity of their handicap is such that education in regular classes, even if the children are provided supplementary aids and services, cannot meet their needs satisfactorily. The intent is, as much as possible, to keep handicapped children in the most normal environments, those that least restrict them and are closest to the mainstream of life.

It is understood that many handicapped children will not be able to participate as fully in the mainstream as their nonhandicapped peers. However, it is expected that many can be moved from rather segregated settings into less restrictive scenes so they can be more in contact with and interact more normally with their peers. The intent definitely is not to dump handicapped children into regular public school classrooms. When it is determined that the handicapped can function appropriately in the regular classroom, that is the placement that is indicated, of course. Under the provision of providing the education in the least restrictive environment, it is assumed regular classrooms will be recommended only when appropriate.

If regular classroom placement is judged to be inappropriate, then the IEP team must consider what other ways are possible and realistic to move the child more into the mainstream of life. Perhaps a person who previously had been institutionalized could be moved into a small, residential group home. Perhaps a child who had been in a segregated school could be moved into a special class in a regular school building where some normal contact would occur in ways other than through regular classroom instruction. Many alternatives are possible. Creative approaches to finding least restrictive environments must be considered by IEP teams. Many attitudes will need to be changed so that handicapped individuals who are moving into the mainstream will feel valued.

Nondiscriminatory Testing

Public Law 93-380 preceded P.L. 94-142 by two years. It specified that evaluation materials and procedures used to classify handicapped children could not be racially or culturally discriminatory. The nondiscriminatory testing concept of P.L. 93-380 is incorporated into the current law. This provision requires that all direct contact with the child is to take place in the language normally used by the child. If there is a difference between the languages used by parents and children, then in situations involving direct contact with the child, including evaluation activities, the mode of communication must be the language normally used by the child, not the one used by the parents. In cases where the person is deaf or blind, the communication mode must be that normally used by the person—for example, sign language or braille.

Certain procedural safeguards are required by P.L. 94-142 and are discussed later. Here, however, it should be noted that the concern for communicating in the language normally used by the child is a concept that spills over to the requirement that communication with the parent about the child must be in the parent's native language.

Confidentiality

The concept of right to privacy is the basic principle underlying laws about the confidentiality of information and recordkeeping. It is true that professionals need information about children and their families in order to provide suitable programs. But the information must be used with care and treated with appropriate safeguards.

The Family Rights and Privacy Act of 1974, popularly known as the Buckley Amendment, was passed in response to concerns about the abuse of students' school records nationwide. Three types of recordkeeping and the confidentiality associated with each were spelled out in the amendment:

1. Type A information includes basic minimum information that schools need to classify students, such as birthdate, attendance records, grades completed in school and other similar basic factors.

2. Type B includes information that must be on hand for the safety of the child, such as special diets, allergies and chronic health problems, and verified information such as test results.
3. Type C information is defined as that which is potentially useful but not yet verified. When verified, this information must be moved to Type B categorization or destroyed.

Assessment information (such as that outlined in previous chapters) being collected for a child in order to determine if it has special needs would be Type C information. This is so because, at the beginning of the assessment process, it would not be known which information eventually would be verified and which would be collected on the basis of false leads and never verified. There is nothing wrong with this situation as long as unverified information is destroyed.

The 1975 law also recognized the rights of handicapped children and their parents to confidentiality of information and recordkeeping. Procedures for notifying parents about identification and evaluation activities are outlined clearly. Parents must be given opportunities to review any educational records related to their children and must be allowed to amend any records found to be inaccurate, misleading, or otherwise violating the rights of privacy held by the child and family. Parents must request a hearing to challenge the accuracy of records they judge to be in error.

Basically, what is needed is full and open communication with parents and informed consent from them to collect and/or disseminate certain information about the children. Careful planning is needed to communicate information that is accurate and useful to parents. Earlier chapters have made clear that assessment and instructional planning for all children is highly complex. It is easy to understand the difficulties involved in communication when the information and decisions involved often are the result of very technical procedures. Full understanding often depends on an adequate background in fields such as psychology, statistics, and education. However, just because the communication is challenging does not mean it should not take place. On the contrary, everyone must work together for the common good of the children while being fully aware of the rights and responsibilities of both parents and professionals.

Due Process

Parents have the right to expect that due process will be followed throughout the screening, assessment, and programming phases of their child's case. These rights are guaranteed by P.L. 94-142, as well as by other legislation and a series of landmark court decisions that led up to the 1975 law. Basically, parents' rights under the law are as follows:

1. Parents have the right to have their child evaluated and must be informed about the results of the evaluation.

2. Parents must be consulted about the child's educational program prior to its implementation (this is provided for by having the parent as a member of the IEP team).

3. Parents have the right to have the child's educational program reviewed periodically as a means of evaluating the child's progress toward the stated goals and objectives.

The key ideas are that parents must be kept informed continually and accurately about what is happening to their child at any step in the process. If they disagree with what is being done or how the case is being handled at any step along the way, the parents have the right to an impartial due process hearing to decide the matter. Parents may request a hearing if they feel their rights have been violated or if they do not agree with the decisions made about their child. In a due process hearing, parents have the right to be represented by legal counsel, to give evidence, to cross-examine, and to receive a written transcript of the hearing and a written decision about the outcome of their case.

It might be helpful to consider briefly how these parental rights and responsibilities are put into action. Routine assessment procedures used in school situations do not require any special parental permission. However, if it is decided that there might be something special or different about the child and further assessment is recommended, permission to go ahead with the assessment must be obtained from the parents. In general, parents must receive written notification, in their native language, describing the tests and other assessment procedures that are proposed for the evaluation, information about who will perform the assessment, and how the results will be used. A permission form, requiring a signature from the parent, should be included with the written notice. The parents must be told, in writing, that they have the right to an independent evaluation, at public expense, if they disagree with the team's findings and that they have a right to a formal hearing, conducted by an impartial officer, if they wish to challenge the recommendations. They also must be told how to go about setting up such a hearing and how to appeal the outcome if they so desire.

Some parents will have requested the special evaluation in the first place, having brought their child's case to the school authorities. In other cases, the request for further assessment may come as a shock or surprise to the parents. It may be helpful to talk informally with parents during early stages so that when the written notification arrives they will be prepared for it. A more effective partnership between parents and professionals will result if everyone is kept well informed, no matter what the requirements are.

If parents refuse to give permission, the school district may request a hearing to substantiate its decision that further assessment is needed. The right to an impartial hearing thus falls to schools as well as to parents. Usually, informal conferences are planned to try to resolve problems before the more formal impartial hearing procedure is begun.

Multidisciplinary Teams

Under P.L. 94-142, states have required school districts to set up multidisciplinary teams to deal with the assessment information gathered about the child. The composition as well as the role of the team is set forth in the law:

- A full and individualized evaluation of each handicapped child's educational needs must take place before the child is placed in a special education program.
- The evaluation must include information about all areas pertinent to the suspected disability and must be made in nondiscriminatory fashion.
- The evaluation must be performed by a multidisciplinary team of professionals designated by the school district. Assessment procedures must be administered in the native language of the child, must be validated for the specific purposes for which they will be used, and must be administered by a trained professional. Further, the use of a single procedure as the sole criterion for determining placement is prohibited; each child's assessment must be comprehensive and individually tailored according to the suspected special needs.

Even if the law did not mandate the use of a multidisciplinary team for assessment and program planning, common sense suggests a team effort is what is needed because of the wide range of differences between possible problems across developmental domains. Another factor is the diversity of assessment procedures needed to obtain more specific information about those problems. It is reasonable to conclude that the talents of several persons are needed. Team evaluation is indicated.

In many cases, the teacher who is working directly with the child is the one who triggers the information-gathering process. It is essential that the evaluation team make use of the information about the child previously obtained by the classroom teacher. It is wasted effort to assign an assessment team member to redo what already has been done by the teacher. In addition, as suggested in earlier chapters, the classroom teacher is in the best position to gather information about the child's normal, everyday interactions and performance in typical learning situations in the classroom setting.

APPLICATIONS FOR PRESCHOOL CHILDREN

The law and regulations that describe implementation procedures seem somewhat contradictory regarding their application to preschool children. In general,

> Each state shall ensure that free appropriate public education is available to all handicapped children aged three through eighteen within the state not later than September 1, 1978 . . . (Federal Register, Vol. 42, No. 163, August 23, 1977, p. 42488)

There are, however, several disclaimers that must be considered. With special reference to children in the age ranges of 3 to 5 years and 18 to 21 years, the following caveat applies:

> If state law or a court order requires the state to provide education to handicapped children in any disability category in any of these age groups, the state must make a free appropriate public education available to all handicapped children of the same age who have that disability. (Federal Register, Vol. 42, No. 163, August 23, 1977, p. 42488)

This provision simply says that FAPE (Free and Appropriate Public Education) cannot be denied to some children and provided for others who have the same disability and are the same age. In addition, the regulations specify:

> If a public agency provides education to nonhandicapped children in any of these age groups, it must make a free appropriate public education available to at least a proportionate number of handicapped children of the same age. (Federal Register, Vol. 42, No. 163, August 23, 1977, p. 42488)

This says that whatever is provided for nonhandicapped children must be provided for handicapped children as well. The picture appears favorable for preschoolers until the following parts are noted.

> A state is not required to make a free appropriate public education available to a handicapped child in one of these age groups if:
> (i) State law expressly prohibits, or does not authorize, the expenditure of public funds to provide education to nonhandicapped children in that age group; or
> (ii) The requirement is inconsistent with a court order which governs the provisions of free public education to handicapped children in that state. (Federal Register, Vol. 42, No. 163, August 23, 1977, p. 42488).

These two disclaimers suggest that not all handicapped preschoolers will receive services under the law. In states in which nonhandicapped preschool children are not provided for, there is no mandate to provide for those who are handicapped.

Interestingly enough, the requirement to identify, locate, and evaluate handicapped children (sometimes referred to as child-find) does apply from birth through age 21:

> Under the statute, the age range for the child-find requirement (0-21) is greater than the mandated age range for providing free appropriate public education (FAPE). One reason for the broader age requirement under "child-find" is to enable states to be aware of and plan for younger children who will require special education and related services. It also ties in with the full educational opportunity goal requirement, which has the same age range as child-find. Moreover, while a state is not required to provide FAPE to handicapped children below the age ranges mandated under 121a.300, the state may, at its discretion, extend services to those children, subject to the requirements on priorities under 121a.320-121a.324. (Federal Register, Vol. 42, No. 163, August 23, 1977, p. 42488).

That final statement is important. It makes clear that states, at their discretion, may extend services to preschool handicapped children. And, if they choose to extend services, the services must be provided in accordance with other provisions of the law. Thus, in situations where preschool services are being provided, the provisions described earlier apply.

SUMMARY

Information about legislation and litigation governing the providing of services to handicapped children, including those in the preschool age range, is not especially interesting to read. Some may even regard it as quite dull and boring. But it is important. A firm understanding of P.L. 94-142 is essential for those who work with children and families. The section on due process and procedural safeguards should have been convincing that what is done for children must be done in accordance with the public laws and court orders that apply.

Regardless of the mandates of P.L. 94-142, it is people who make things happen. Genuine respect for the rights of all concerned, for the special contributions of parents, and for the need for parents and professionals to work together cannot be legislated. In the final analysis, it is peoples' attitudes and values and their concern for fulfilling their responsibilities that will make the system work for the benefit of all children.

RECOMMENDED ACTIVITIES

1. Obtain copies of procedures for implementing P.L. 94-142 in your local school district. Give special attention to determining how the local district provides for child-find, what provisions are made for preschool age children, and what procedures are used by the multidisciplinary assessment team.
2. Interview several teachers who have completed an IEP (for a preschool child, if possible). Ask the teachers, among other questions, how they felt about their preparation for participating in the IEP planning and what suggestions they have for improving the parent-professional communication necessary for successful IEP planning.
3. Obtain a copy of guidelines used in your state for IEP preparation. As you review each guideline, list the competencies a teacher would need. For each one, rate yourself in terms of your ability in performing that competency. Finally, for competencies for which you feel ill prepared, list ways of developing them.

References

Alpern, G.D., & Boll, T.J. *The developmental profile*. Aspen, CO: Psychological Development Publications, 1972.

Ames, L.B., Gillespie, C., Haines, J., & Ilg, F.L. *The Gesell Institute's Child from One to Six: Evaluating the Behavior of the Preschool Child*, New York: Harper & Row, 1979.

Bagnato, S.J., Neisworth, J.T., & Eaves, R.C. *Perceptions of developmental skills profile* (PODS). University Park, PA: HICOMP Preschool Project, The Pennsylvania State University, 1978.

Bagnato, S.J., Neisworth, J.T., & Eaves, R.C. A profile of perceived capabilities for the preschool child. *Child Care Quarterly,* Winter 1978, *7:* 326-335.

Bagnato, S.J., & Neisworth, J.T. Between assessment and intervention: Forging an assessment/curriculum linkage for the handicapped preschooler. *Child Care Quarterly,* Fall 1979, *8:* 179-195.

Bagnato, S.J., & Neisworth, J.T. The intervention efficiency index (IEI): An approach to preschool program accountability. *Exceptional Children,* January 1980, *48*(4): 264-271.

Bayley, N. *Bayley scales of infant development*. New York: Psychological Corporation, 1969.

Boehm, A.E. *Boehm test of basic concepts manual*. New York: Psychological Corporation, 1971.

Caldwell, B. *Preschool inventory revised edition*. Princeton, NJ: Educational Testing Service, 1970.

Chase, J.B. Developmental assessment of handicapped infants and young children: With special attention to the visually impaired. *The New Outlook for the Blind,* October 1975, 341-348.

Cross, J., & Goin, K. (Eds.). *Identifying handicapped children*. New York: Walker & Co., 1977.

Doll, E.A. *Preschool attainment record*. Circle Pines, MN: American Guidance Service, 1966.

Dubose, R., & Langley, B. *Developmental activities screening inventory*. New York: Teaching Resources, Inc., 1977.

Federal Register, Vol. 42, No. 163, August 23, 1977. Washington, D.C.: U.S. Government Printing Office, p. 42488.

Forsberg, S.J., Neisworth, J.T., & Laub, K. *COMP-Curriculum and manual.* University Park, PA: HICOMP Project, The Pennsylvania State University, 1977.

Frankenburg, W.K., & Dodds, J.B. *Denver developmental screening test.* Boulder, CO: University of Colorado Medical Center, 1975.

Frankenburg, W.K., & Dodds, J.B. *Denver prescreening developmental questionnaire.* Boulder, CO: University of Colorado Medical Center, 1974.

Gesell, A. *Gesell developmental schedules.* New York: Psychological Corporation, 1949.

Haeussermann, E. *Developmental potential of preschool children.* New York: Grune & Stratton, Inc., 1958.

Hoffman, H. *The Bayley scales of infant development: Modifications for youngsters with handicapping conditions.* Commack, NY: Suffolk Rehabilitation Center, 1975.

Jedrysek, E., Klapper, E., Pope, L., & Wortis, J. *Psychoeducational evaluation of the preschool child.* New York: Grune & Stratton, Inc., 1972.

Jordan, J., Hayden, A.H., Karnes, M.B., & Wood, M. (Eds.). *Early childhood education for exceptional children.* Reston, VA: Council for Exceptional Children, 1977.

Knoblock, H., & Pasamanick, B. *Developmental diagnosis* (Gesell developmental schedules). New York: Harper & Row, 1974.

Kurtz, P.D., Neisworth, J.T., & Laub, K.W. Issues concerning the early identification of handicapped children. *Journal of School Psychology,* 1977, *15:* 136-139.

Laub, K.W. & Kurtz, P.D *Early identification.* In J.T. Neisworth & R.M. Smith (eds.), *Retardation: Issues, assessment, and intervention.* New York: McGraw-Hill, 1978.

LeMay, D.W., Griffin, P.M., & Sanford, A.R. *Learning accomplishment profile: Diagnostic edition* (revised). Winston-Salem, N.C.: Kaplan School Supply, 1978.

Maxfield, K.E., & Buchholz, S. *The Maxfield-Buchholz scale of social maturity for use with preschool blind children.* New York: American Foundation for the Blind, 1958.

McCarthy, D. *Manual for the McCarthy scales of children's abilities.* New York: Psychological Corporation, 1972.

Meier, J.H. Developmental inventory—profile and base for curriculum planning. In John Meier (Ed.), *Developmental and learning disabilities.* Baltimore: University Park Press, 1976.

National Learning Resource Center of Pennsylvania. *An introduction to individualized education program plans in Pennsylvania: Guidelines for school age IEP development.* King of Prussia, PA: Pennsylvania Department of Education, 1978.

Nurss, J.R., & McGauvran, M.E. *Metropolitan readiness tests.* New York: Harcourt Brace Jovanovich, 1976.

Quick, A.D., Little, T.L., & Campbell, A.A. *Memphis comprehensive developmental schedules.* Belmont, CA: Fearon Publishers, 1974.

Quick, A.D., Little, T.L., & Campbell, A.A. *Project MEMPHIS: Enhancing developmental progress in preschool exceptional children.* Dubuque, Iowa: Kendall/Hunt Publishing Co., 1974.

Sanford, A. *Learning accomplishment profile*. Chapel Hill, NC: University of North Carolina, 1973

Simeonsson, R.J., & Wiergerink, R. Accountability: A dilemma in infant intervention. *Exceptional Children*, 1975, *41*: 474-481.

Stillman, R.D. *The Callier-Azusa scale: Assessment of deaf blind children*. Reston, VA: Council for Exceptional Children, 1974.

Valett, R.D. Developmental task analysis and psychoeducational programming. *Journal of School Psychology*, 1972, *10*: 127-133.

Zehrbach, R. Determining a preschool handicapped population. *Exceptional Children*, 1975, *42*: 76-83.

Appendix A

COMP-Curriculum

by Sara J. Forsberg, John T. Neisworth, Karen W. Laub, and Carol Cartwright

Source: HICOMP Preschool Project, The Pennsylvania State University, University Park, PA., 1977.

Introduction

The HICOMP curriculum is designed to help you work with both handicapped and nonhandicapped children. It provides a comprehensive sequence of objectives to use in planning learning experiences. The curriculum is designed to help you plan overall educational programs for children as well as day-to-day lesson plans.

The objectives that make up the curriculum are arranged in an order that corresponds with the development sequence most children follow. These objectives have been distributed into four general areas, or domains: Communication or Language; Own-Care or Self-Help and Social Skills; Gross and Fine Motor; and Problem-Solving or Cognitive. Because the curriculum covers a broad range of objectives in each of these domains, you can use it to enhance children's development in all areas, not just in areas where they appear to have delays. Also, since the curriculum includes objectives appropriate for children from birth to 5 years, you will find it helpful in working with both nonhandicapped and handicapped children functioning within this age range. In addition, the curriculum can be used with an individual child, a small group, or large group.

To further help you plan lessons and learning experiences, the curriculum provides information which will help you choose appropriate teaching strategies and methods of recording and evaluating children's progress.

Domain and year level are listed at the top of each page of the curriculum. The code number in column 1 indicates the domain, the year, the subdomain which is simply a "broad skill area" within each domain, and the general objective. The general objective is printed in column 2. It serves as a starting point for you to identify the specific goal(s) for your lesson plan. The child's entry level skills should be marked in column 3. In columns 4 and 5, you can record the date when instruction began and ended on a specific objective. Specific teaching strategies (column 6) are recommended for each objective. It is not essential that you use the recommended strategy, but this notation in column 6 indicates which of the strategies described in the COMP Curriculum Guide have been field tested and found appropriate. Similarly, the evaluation techniques listed in column 7 are optional. You may supplement or substitute another means of determining whether a child has achieved a given objective. The remaining columns are self-explanatory.

COMMUNICATION – Year 1 – Page 1

Col. 1	Col. 2	Col. 3	Col. 4	Col. 5	Col. 6	Col. 7			
Objective Number	General Objective	Pretest	Date Begun	Date Ended	Strategy	Evaluation Techniques	Comments:	Activities:	Materials:
C-1-1.1	Vocalizes a pleasant sound				1,3	3			

COMMUNICATION – Year 1 – Page 1

Objective Number	General Objective	Pretest	Date Begun	Date Ended	Strategy	Evaluation Technique	Comments: Activities: Materials:
C-1-1	Language Related Play						
C-1-1.1	Vocalizes a pleasant sound			1,3	3		
C-1-1.2	Vocalizes frequently			1,3	3		
C-1-1.3	Vocalizes varied sounds			1,3	11		
C-1-1.4	Repeats particular sounds (e.g., ah-goo)			1,3	3		
C-1-1.5	Varies loudness, pitch, and speed of sounds playfully			1,3	11		
C-1-1.6	Laughs when played with (e.g., in familiar game)			1,3	11		
C-1-1.7*	Vocalizes amusing sounds (e.g., coughs, animal sounds)			1,3	11		
C-1-1.8	Repeats syllables over and over (e.g., di-di-di, da-da-da-da)			1,3	11		
C-1-1.9	Repeats performance laughed at			1	11		
C-1-1.10	Babbles or hums along with the rhythm of a game or with music			1,3	11		
C-1-1.11	Uses jargon with toys or persons			1,3	11		
C-1-1.12	Cooperates in game (e.g., during "pat a cake")			1	11		
C-1-2	Self Expression						
C-1-2.1*	Attracts attention of the caregiver			1	3		
C-1-2.2*	Babbles back to people and reacts with discomfort to unresponsiveness			1	3		
C-1-2.3	Smiles or brightens at faces and voices			1,3	3		

*Items which are duplicated in other areas of the Curriculum.

COMMUNICATION – Year 1 – Page 2

Objective Number	General Objective	Pretest	Date Begun	Date Ended	Strategy	Evaluation Technique	Comments: Activities: Materials:
C-1-2.4*	Communicates mood						
C-1-2.5	Shows activity preferences by smiles and anticipatory movements				1	11	
C-1-2.6*	Complains about loss of a toy or departure of the caregiver				1	3	
C-1-2.7*	Rejects strangers initially but adapts over time				1	7	
C-1-2.8	Uses "mama", "dada", or equivalent names with evidence of meaningfulness				1,3		
C-1-2.9	Uses exclamations (e.g., "oh-oh")				1,3	3	
C-1-2.10*	Uses a word as an emotional comment				1,3	3	
C-1-3	Language Responding						
C-1-3.1	Startles upon sound				4	7	
C-1-3.2*	Responds to sound				4	7	
C-1-3.3*	Soothed by voice				9	6	
C-1-3.4	Discriminates vocal sound changes (e.g., among different pitches, persons, and phonemes)				11	8	
C-1-3.5*	Anticipates familiar movement (e.g., in being picked up)				9	11	
C-1-3.6*	Responds to inflections (e.g., inhibits response or looks apprehensive upon hearing an angry tone of voice)				11	8	

COMMUNICATION - Year 1 - Page 3

Objective Number	General Objective	Pretest	Date Begun	Date Ended	Strategy	Evaluation Technique	Comments: Activities: Materials:
C-1-3.7*	Responds with recognition when his/her name is stated (e.g., stops activity and listens when he hears his name)			11	3		
C-1-3.8*	Recognizes other familiar words (e.g., looks toward common object or family member named)			11	3		
C-1-3.9	Responds to a simple, familiar signal with appropriate behavior (e.g., gives toy upon request or waves when "bye-bye" is stated)						
C-1-3.10	Responds to a complex, familiar signal with appropriate behavior (e.g., answers the rote question "How big are you?" by putting arms over head)			11,6,7	3		
C-1-3.11*	Indicates "no" or "yes" when asked a question			11,6,7	3		
C-1-4	Imitation Related to Language			5	3		
C-1-4.1*	Repeats model who imitates him/her			3,5	3		
C-1-4.2*	Imitates novel non-speech sounds (e.g., lip smacking, kisses, coughs)			3,5	11		

COMMUNICATION - Year 1 - Page 4

Objective Number	General Objective	Pretest	Date Begun	Date Ended	Strategy	Evaluation Technique	Comments: Activities: Materials:
C-1-4.3*	Imitates motor behaviors that are already part of the child's capabilities (e.g., waves "bye-bye" when someone else waves "bye-bye")				3 6	3	
C-1-4.4*	Imitates familiar words				3 5	3	
C-1-4.5*	Spontaneously uses an appropriate behavior through delayed imitation (e.g., says "ahh" to doll or initiates "peek-a-boo")				3,5	11	
C-1-4.6*	Imitates novel but simple behaviors				3	3	
C-1-4.7*	Imitates novel words				3,5	3	
C-1-5	Language Related Attention						
C-1-5.1*	Shuts down response to repeated sounds				1	6	
C-1-5.2*	Head turns to sound				11	6	
C-1-5.3*	Briefly sustains gaze at speaker				1	5	
C-1-5.4*	Glances from one object or person to another				1	10	
C-1-5.5*	Looks around for visually-removed speaker				1,11	10	
C-1-5.6*	Looks at simple pictures in a book				1	5	
C-1-5.7	Turns the pages of a picture book (with assistance in separating pages if necessary)				6	1/8	

COMMUNICATION – Year 1 – Page 5

Objective Number	General Objective	Pretest	Date Begun	Date Ended	Strategy	Evaluation Technique	Comments: Activities: Materials:

COMMUNICATION – Year 2 – Page 6

Objective Number	General Objective	Pretest	Date Begun	Date Ended	Strategy	Evaluation Technique	Comments: Activities: Materials:
C-2-1	Language-Related Play						
C-2-1.1	Shows or offers toy to adult or peer			1,3	10		
C-2-1.2	Initiates a game (e.g., starts "pat-a-cake")			1,3	10		
C-2-1.3	Provides appropriate vocal responses in accompaniment to a game			1,3	4		
C-2-1.4*	Assumes a familiar role (e.g., pretends to clean house)			1,3	10		
C-2-1.5	Assumes one role in a game which involves two roles (e.g., hide and seek)			1,3	8		
C-2-1.6	Reverses roles in a game			1,3	8		
C-2-2	Self Expression						
C-2-2.1*	Uses gestures to make wants known			1,3	11		
C-2-2.2*	Uses speech to attract attention			1,3	11		
C-2-2.3*	Demonstrates affection by hugging (e.g.)			1,3	10		
C-2-2.4	Names several objects			1,3	3		
C-2-2.5	Makes one word requests			1,3	3		
C-2-2.6*	Expresses gratitude			1,3	10		
C-2-2.7	Narrows use of a word so that it is used more appropriately (e.g., no longer calls all men "dada")			11,3	4		
C-2-2.8	Describes or designates an object (e.g., "hot" or "that")			11,3	3		

COMMUNICATION – Year 2 – Page 7

Objective Number	General Objective	Pretest	Date Begun	Date Ended	Strategy	Evaluation Technique	Comments: Activities: Materials:
C-2-2.9	Names, directs, or describes an action (e.g., "sit", "sitting", "now", or "up")			3	3		
C-2-2.10	Uses real two-word combinations			2,3	3		
C-2-2.11	Uses varied forms of word combinations (e.g., location, possession, nonexistence, negation, questions, action-recipient)			2,3	3		
C-2-2.12	Uses 50 words			3	3		
C-2-3	Language Responding						
C-2-3.1*	Indicates object named in response to "Where is ___? or "show me the ___" (e.g., shows shoe or points to hair)			3,6	3		
C-2-3.2*	Names an object singly presented in response to "What's this?" or a person in response to "Who's that?"			3	3		
C-2-3.3	Follows a simple command relating two objects or an object to a person (e.g., "Give me the cup." or "Put the block in the cup.")			4,6	3		
C-2-3.4*	Points to pictured object (within an array) in response to "Where is ___?" or "Show me the ___?"			11,3	3		

COMMUNICATION – Year 2 – Page 8

Objective Number	General Objective	Pretest	Date Begun	Date Ended	Strategy	Evaluation Technique	Comments: Activities: Materials:
C-2-3.5*	Goes to location specified (e.g., "Go to your bedroom")				3,6	3	
C-2-3.6*	Names a picture (singly presented) in response to "What's this?" or "Who's that?"				3	3	
C-2-3.7*	Indicates self when asked "Who's (child's name)?"				3	3	
C-2-3.8*	Names a picture (within an array) in response to "What's this" or "Who's that?"				3	3	
C-2-3.9*	Selects an object named from among an array				3	3	
C-2-3.10*	Can answer questions in the form "What's ____ doing?"				3	3	
C-2-3.11*	Gives first name when asked, "What is your name?"				3,5	3	
C-2-3.12	Understands the meaning of some personal pronouns (e.g., differentiates "Give it to her." from "Give it to me.")				11,3	11	
C-2-3.13*	Remembers and correctly completes two simple related directions (e.g., "Go to your room and bring back a book to me.")				2,5	3	
C-2-4	Imitation Related to Language						

COMMUNICATION - Year 2 - Page 9

Objective Number	General Objective	Pretest	Date Begun	Date Ended	Strategy	Evaluation Technique	Comments: Activities: Materials:
C-2-4.1*	Imitates a familiar complex behavior (e.g., one involving a limb and an object) when given the signal, "(child's name), do this" and a model (e.g., throwing a ball, hitting one's head)			3,6	4		
C-2-4.2*	Imitates a novel complex behavior			3,6	3		
C-2-4.3*	Imitates a combination of a motor and speech or pre-speech sound when given the signal, "(child's name), do this"			3,5,6	4		
C-2-4.4*	Imitates gross motor behaviors reliably			3,6	3		
C-2-4.5*	Imitates fine motor behaviors reliably			3,6	3		
C-2-4.6*	Imitates speech reliably			3,5	4		
C-2-5	Language Related Attention						
C-2-5.1*	Understands and responds to the direction, "Look at me"			4,6	3		
C-2-5.2*	Varies gaze conversationally when speaking			4	8		
C-2-5.3*	Sits when asked to do so (e.g., teacher points to chair, puts finger up to mouth as if to say, "shh", and says, "(child's name), sit down and be quiet"			11,6	4		

COMMUNICATION – Year 2 – Page 10

Objective Number	General Objective	Pretest	Date Begun	Date Ended	Strategy	Evaluation Technique	Comments: Activities: Materials:
C-2-5.4	Looks at a distant object when his attention is directed to it by parent or teacher (e.g., when teacher holds up a doll and says, "see the doll.")				4	4	
C-2-5.5*	Looks at named objects within an array				4	4	
C-2-5.6*	Looks at pictured object in an array as it is named (one word) by parent or teacher				4	4	
C-2-5.7*	Attends to longer verbalizations when they are accompanied by frequent descriptive actions (attention is defined by the child's looking at the parent or teacher and not engaging in other behavior) (e.g., action songs and finger play rhymes)				4,1	5	
C-2-5.8*	Attends to longer verbalizations not accompanied by descriptive actions (e.g., the reading of a brief story from a picture book)				4,1	5	

COMMUNICATION – Year 2 – Page 11

Objective Number	General Objective	Pretest	Date Begun	Date Ended	Strategy	Evaluation Technique	Comments: Activities: Materials:

COMMUNICATION - Year 3 - Page 12

Objective Number	General Objective	Pretest	Date Begun	Date 2nded	Strategy	Evaluation Technique	Comments: Activities: Materials:
C-3-1	Language Related Play						
C-3-1.1	Performs some short phrases of a rhyme or song (e.g., Mary had a little lamb)			2,3	4		
C-3-1.2	Talks for a doll or puppet			1,3	10		
C-3-1.3	Performs some motions of a song, rhyme or finger play (e.g., Itsy, Bitsy Spider)			2,3	4		
C-3-1.4	Recites several phrases and performs motions to simple songs or rhymes			?,3	4		
C-3-1.4	Recites several phrases and performs motions to several songs or rhymes			2,3	4		
C-3-1.6	Grossly matches pitch of words and sounds (high/low)			11,1	10		
C-3-1.7	Grossly matches volume of words and sounds (high/soft)			11 1	10		
C-3-1.8	Vocalizes "singing" songs or sounds independently			1	10		
C-3-1.9	Responds differentially to music, e.g., "dances," "sings," claps			1	10		
C-3-1.10	Participates in simple group song games, e.g., Ring Around the Rosie			2,3	3		
C-3-1.11	Reverses roles in simple games involving language, e.g., tickles someone while saying "Creep mousie, creep mousie from barn to the housie."			2,3	10		

COMMUNICATION – Year 3 – Page 13

Objective Number	General Objective	Pretest	Date Begun	Date Ended	Strategy	Evaluation Technique	Comments: Activities: Materials:
C-3-1.12	In role-playing familiar persons, uses role appropriate language during dramatic play, e.g., "Mothers" a baby doll, saying "Eat your soup"			1,3	10		
C-3-1.13	Participates in group "sings"			1,2,3	3		
C-3-2	Self Expression						
C-3-2.1	Combines several parts of speech (nouns, objects, verbs, and/or modifiers) to make 3-4 word statements, e.g., "Eat more cake", "Mary eat cake", "Milk all gone".						
C-3-2.2	Speaks clearly enough for most persons to understand			2,5	3		
C-3-2.3	Uses compound sentences			1,5	8		
C-3-2.4	Uses speech to identify concrete objects and events in immediate environment			2,5	3		
C-3-2.5	Appropriately verbalizes common social conventions without an adult's prompting. E.g., "Hello", "Thank you"			3,5	3		
C-3-2.6	Asks 3-4 word questions			1	4		
C-3-3	Language Responding			3,5	3		
C-3-3.1	Responds with an action word when asked, "What's doing?"			1,3	3		

COMMUNICATION – Year 3 – Page 14

Objective Number	General Objective	Pretest	Date Begun	Date Ended	Strategy	Evaluation Technique	Comments: Activities: Materials:
C-3-3.2	Answers specific information questions about self, e.g., "How old are you?"			3,5	3		
C-3-3.3	Reliably follows simple 2-step adult directions, e.g., "Pick it up then give it to Daddy."			3 5	3		
C-3-3.4	Answers with first and last names when asked, "What is your name?"			3,5	3		
C-3-3.5	Recites short rhymes or sings songs on request			2,3,5	3		
C-3-3.6	Responds with modifiers when asked to describe people or events, e.g., "How does the stove feel?" "hot"			3,5	3		
C-3-3.7	Responds with a verb when asked, "What are you doing?" e.g., "I'm washing"			3,5	3		
C-3-4	Imitation Related to Language						
C-3-4.1	Imitates complex single words (e.g., compound words, 2 and 3 syllabled words)			2,3	3		
C-3-4.2	Imitates two-word combinations of nouns, verbs, & modifiers (e.g., "ball go", "get big", "sick baby")			2,3	3		
C-3-4.3	Imitates three word combinations consisting of nouns, verbs, modifiers, & objects e.g., "Mommy plays ball."			2,3	3		

COMMUNICATION – Year 3 – Page 15

Objective Number	General Objective	Pretest	Date Begun	Date Ended	Strategy	Evaluation Technique	Comments: Activities: Materials:
C-3-4.4	Imitates sentences of up to 6 words in length				2,3	3	
C-3-4.5	Articulates these sounds correctly: [phonetic symbols] m b t d w y n h- p- k- -m- -n- -b-				3	8	
C-3-4.6	Imitates 3 to 4 word phrases with expression appropriate for a question				2,3	4	
C-3-5	Language Related Attention						
C-3-5.1	Attends to simple concrete statements or statements involving self				4	5	
C-3-5.2	Looks at pictured objects and events as teacher reads or tells about them.				4	5	
C-3-5.3	Attends to longer verbalizations not accompanied by descriptive actions, e.g., looks at picture book or reader while being read a short picture story book				1,4	5	
C-3-5.4	Attends to short, colorful film or show, e.g., segment of Sesame Street				1,4	5	
C-3-5.5	Attends briefly to adult conversations concerning child and/or concrete events, e.g., listens to a description of the snowman made at recess time.				1,4	5	

COMMUNICATION – Year 3 – Page 16

Objective Number	General Objective	Pretest	Date Begun	Date Ended	Strategy	Evaluation Technique	Comments: Activities: Materials:
C-3-5.6	Listens to short familiar records			1,4	5		

COMMUNICATION – Year 3 – Page 17

Objective Number	General Objective	Pretest	Date Begun	Date Ended	Strategy	Evaluation Technique	Comments: Activities: Materials:

COMMUNICATION - Year 4 - Page 18

Objective Number	General Objective	Pretest	Date Begun	Date Ended	Strategy	Evaluation Technique	Comments: Activities: Materials:
C-4-1	Language Related Play						
C-4-1.1	Performs all hand motions and/or phases of songs or rhymes, e.g., Twinkle, Twinkle, Little Star						
C-4-1.2	Role plays more remote roles e.g., fireman, grocer				2,5,6	4	
C-4-1.3	Provides direction to others during role playing				2,5,6	10	
C-4-1.4	Follows direction of another during role playing				5,1	10	
C-4-1.5	"Guesses" appropriately during verbal guessing games, e.g., when asked "Can you guess what I have in my hand?"				5,6	3	
C-4-1.6	Participates in more complex group games involving roles and reversals, e.g., "Did you ever see a Lassie", "The Farmer in the Dell"				4,10	3	
C-4-1.7	Closely approximates adult pitches that are well within those the child typically uses				2,5,6	8	
C-4-1.8	Closely approximates adult volumes that are well within those the child typically uses				11,3	8	
C-4-1.9	Accompanies rhythm of song by clapping hands				3,4	3	

COMMUNICATION – Year 4 – Page 19

Objective Number	General Objective	Pretest	Date Begun	Date Ended	Strategy	Evaluation Technique	Comments: Activities: Materials:
C-4-1.10	Accompanies rhythm of song by playing a simple instrument			3,4	3		
C-4-1.11	Begins to reproduce a melody line sung by another			3	10		
C-4-1.12	Sings as plays rhythm to a song			3	10		
C-4-1.13	Participates reliably in group "rhythm bands"			3,6	3		
C-4-1.14	Closely approximates another's speech rate in short song or spoken sentences			3	10		
C-4-2	Self Expression						
C-4-2.1	Uses prepositions in combinations with several other parts of speech in talking e.g., "baby get up"			2,3	3		
C-4-2.2	Uses articles (a, an, the) in combination with other parts of speech in talking (e.g., "see the clown")			2,3	3		
C-4-2.3	Often speaks in complete sentences			2,3	3		
C-4-2.4	Begins to use past tense			3	3		
C-4-2.5	Uses sentences of 4-8 words in length			2,3	3		
C-4-2.6	Begins to use language to describe imaginary events			1,5,3	3/10		
C-4-2.7	Uses language for describing and requesting			1,3	3/10		
C-4-2.8	Uses words having abstract meanings, e.g., angry, difficult			1,3	3/10		

Objective Number	General Objective	Pretest	Date Begun	Date Ended	Strategy	Evaluation Technique	Comments: Activities: Materials:
C-4-2.9	Uses both generic and specific names for objects and events, e.g., "It is an animal", "It is a horse"				3	11	
C-4-2.10	Shares (during conversation or show and tell) information about activities or events experienced				5	8	
C-4-2.11	Retells stories of actual events or from books				5	8	
C-4-2.12	Requests favorite activities or objects by asking complete questions or making statements of preference, e.g., "Sesame Street is my favorite show"				5	3/8	
C-4-2.13	Expresses positive emotions, e.g., "I really like this game"				5	3/8	
C-4-3	Language Responding						
C-4-3.1	Names most of major body parts (e.g., arm, leg knee, ankle, elbows, etc.)				3,11	8	
C-4-3.2	Answers factual questions about remote events, objects, or pictures, e.g., while looking at a book and asked, "Where is Swimmy?", child answers "under the rock."				3	3	
C-4-3.3	Understands most adult language directed toward the child; e.g., follows most simple directions				4,5,6	4	

COMMUNICATION – Year 4 – Page 21

Objective Number	General Objective	Pretest	Date Begun	Date Ended	Strategy	Evaluation Technique	Comments: Activities: Materials:
C-4-3.4	Answers simple questions involving prediction of events in story or real-life situations, e.g., "What do you think Billy will do next?"				5	3	
C-4-3.5	Responds with correct prepositions (e.g., on, in on top of) when asked, "Where is _____?"				3,5	3	
C-4-3.6	Responds correctly to simple questions about own family, home, school				3,5	3	
C-4-4	Imitation Related to Language						
C-4-4.1	Imitates more elaborate combinations of parts of speech including conjunctions, articles, and prepositions, e.g., "the birdie flies up".				2,3	3	
C-4-4.2	Imitates three or four word phrases with expression appropriate for an exclamation				2,3	3	
C-4-4.3	Imitates a sequence of 2-3 sentences				2,3	4	
C-4-4.4	Imitates 3-4 syllabled words				2,3	3	
C-4-4.5	Articulates these additional sounds correctly: 1 -g- -p- -k- -p f_ _h_ _w -f_ _ph_				3	8	

COMMUNICATION - Year 4 - Page 22

Objective Number	General Objective	Pretest	Date Begun	Date Ended	Strategy	Evaluation Technique	Comments: Activities: Materials:
C-4-4.6	Imitates a simple, steady rhythm of clapping or beating, e.g., four quarter notes			3,4	8		
C-4-4.7	Imitates a short, simple melody line			2,5	8		
C-4-5	Language Related Attention						
C-4-5.1	Attends to picture story books with longer narratives			4,1	5		
C-4-5.2	Attends to clear pitch changes in music			4,11	8		
C-4-5.3	Attends to clear rhythm changes in music			4,11	8		
C-4-5.4	Attends to clear volume changes in music			4,11	8		
C-4-5.5	Attends to recorded or televised stories, music, etc., for 1/2 hour			4,1	5		
C-4-5.6	Attends to group conversations, e.g., at "sharing time", looks attentively from speaker to speaker			4,1	5		

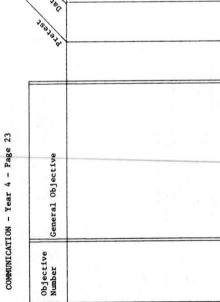

COMMUNICATION – Year 4 – Page 23

Objective Number	General Objective		Pretest	Date Begun	Date Ended	Strategy	Evaluation Technique	Comments: Activities: Materials:

COMMUNICATION – Year 5 – Page 24

Objective Number	General Objective	Pretest	Date Begun	Date Ended	Strategy	Evaluation Technique	Comments: Activities: Materials:
C-5-1	Language Related Play						
C-5-1.1	Participates in simple board games involving turn taking, labeling, etc., e.g., Lotto, Candy Land			3,5,6	5/10		
C-5-1.2	Reverses roles during verbal guessing games involving observation and identification, e.g., "I am thinking of an animal" (where additional verbal cues are progressively given)						
C-5-1.3	Plays group games involving orderly turn taking, e.g., London Bridge, Go in and out the Windows			3,5,6	10		
C-5-1.4	Plays group games involving "if-then" rules, e.g., "Duck, duck, goose," "A tisket a tasket"			3,5,6	5/10		
C-5-1.5	Responds to music in a variety of ways, e.g., sings aloud, claps, dances, plays instrument			3,5,6	5/10		
C-5-1.6	Sings a song accurately reproducing a variance in rhythm, e.g., "wheels on the bus are slowing down"			1,3	2/3		
C-5-1.7	Sings a song accurately reproducing a variance in volume, e.g., "Pop goes the Weasel"			2,3	8		
C-5-1.8	Tells simple jokes			2,3	8 / 10		

COMMUNICATION – Year 5 – Page 25

Objective Number	General Objective	Pretest	Date Begun	Date Ended	Strategy	Evaluation Technique	Comments: Activities: Materials:
C-5-2	Self Expression						
C-5-2.1	Begins to ask "how" and "why" questions in response to information and events				3,5	3	
C-5-2.2	Uses statements of over 7 words in length				2,3	3	
C-5-2.3	Converses with adults and other children				2,3	11	
C-5-2.4	Uses common opposites, e.g., long, short; old, young; light, dark; hot, cold; fast, slow				3,5	3	
C-5-2.5	Uses progressively longer words				1,3	3	
C-5-2.6	Uses personal pronouns correctly				3,5	3	
C-5-2.7	Describes objects and events using varied referents, e.g., color, shape, speed, weight, volume				3,5	3	
C-5-2.8	Purposively expresses ideas through body language, e.g., imitates animals, rhythms, expresses moods				3,6	3	
C-5-2.9	Uses technical words or those specific to particular areas of knowledge, e.g., science, math				11,3	3	
C-5-2.10	Dictates stories for an adult to write				5	5/3	
C-5-2.11	Answers telephone correctly				3,5	8	
C-5-3	Language Responding						
C-5-3.1	Defines simple words				3,5	4	

COMMUNICATION - Year 5 - Page 26

Objective Number	General Objective	Pretest	Date Begun	Date Ended	Strategy	Evaluation Technique	Comments: Activities: Materials:
C-5-3.2	Describes events and objects when requested			3,5	4		
C-5-3.3	Follows a sequence of three instructions			2,3,5	3		
C-5-3.4	Begins to describe how objects are the same or different			11,3,5	8		
C-5-3.5	Answers subjective questions about stories or events, e.g., "How did that make you feel?"			3,5	8		
C-5-3.6	Reads 1-5 sight words, e.g., "stop", child's own name, exit			11,3	4		
C-5-3.7	Reads numbers from 1 to 10			11,3	4		
C-5-3.8	Reads some alphabet letters by name (not by sound)			11,3	4		
C-5-3.9	Reads some alphabet letters by sound			11,3	4		
C-5-3.10	Reads a simple rhythm pattern by clapping or drumming, etc. (e.g., 1 1 2 1) clap-clap – rest-clap			11,3	4		
C-5-3.11	Responds correctly to simple telephone caller requests, e.g., "May I talk to your father?"			8	8		
C-5-3.12	Reliably follows simple instructions told within an hour, e.g., "remember to put your painting on the desk when you have finished"			8,5	10		
C-5-4	Imitation Related to Language						

COMMUNICATION – Year 5 – Page 27

Objective Number	General Objective	Pretest	Date Begun	Date Ended	Strategy	Evaluation Technique	Comments:	Activities:	Materials:
C-5-4.1	Learns songs and rhymes through imitation				2,3	3			
C-5-4.2	Imitates longer words and sentences used by others				2,3	3			
C-5-4.3	Imitates specific technical vocabulary, e.g., "thorax," "insect"				2,3	8			
C-5-4.4	Articulates these sounds correctly: -ng- -t- -ng -ngk -y- -d- -l- -k s- y- -r -ar -mr -pr -dr				3	8			
C-5-4.5	Reproduces pitches sung by a model				4,5	3			
C-5-5	Language Related Attention								
C-5-5.1	Listens politely when adults are talking				4	5			
C-5-5.2	Listens to longer songs and stories not accompanied by pictures				1,4	5			
C-5-5.3	Listens independently to televised and/or recorded songs and stories				1,4	5			
C-5-5.4	Attends to various common signs in environment, e.g., walk-don't walk signs, exit sign, restroom signs				4,11	4			
C-5-5.5	Listens to a set of directions related to a classroom activity, e.g., how to make a wet chalk drawing				4	4			

COMMUNICATION – Year 5 – Page 28

Objective Number	General Objective	Pretest	Date Begun	Date Ended	Strategy	Evaluation Technique	Comments: Activities: Materials:

OWN CARE - Year 1 - Page 1

Objective Number	General Objective	Pretest	Date Begun	Date Ended	Strategy	Evaluation Technique	Comments: Activities: Materials:
0-1-1	Meeting Social Conventions & Developing Values						
0-1-1.1*	Attracts caregiver's attention				1	3	
0-1-1.2	Cuddles or conforms to holding				1,6	2	
0-1-1.3	Orients to near-by sounds and voices				4,6	2	
0-1-1.4*	Briefly sustains gaze at speaker				4,6	5	
0-1-1.5	Smiles or brightens at faces and voices				9	3	
0-1-1.6*	Glances from one object or person to another				4,6	8/5	
0-1-1.7	Smiles at mirror image				9	3/5	
0-1-1.8	Reaches out to mirror image				6	3	
0-1-1.9*	Babbles back to people and reacts with discomfort to unresponsiveness				3,9	3	
0-1-1.10*	Communicates mood				1	10	
0-1-1.11	Responds differentially among persons				9	10	
0-1-1.12*	Complains about loss of toy or departure of caregiver				1,9	3	
0-1-1.13*	Anticipates familiar movement (e.g., in being picked up)				4,9	10	
0-1-1.14	Reaches out to persons				3,6	3	
0-1-1.15*	Rejects strangers initially but adapts overtime				9	7	
0-1-1.16*	Responds to inflections (e.g. inhibits response or looks apprehensive upon hearing an angry tone of voice)				4,9	8	
0-1-1.17	Wary response to sober face				9	8	

OWN CARE – Year 1 – Page 2

Objective Number	General Objective	Pretest	Date Begun	Date Ended	Strategy	Evaluation Technique	Comments:	Activities:	Materials:
0-1-1.18*	Responds with recognition when his name is stated (e.g., stops activity and listens when he hears his name)			4,9	3				
0-1-1.19	Differential responding to adult and peer strangers			9	10				
0-1-1.20*	Uses a word as an emotional comment			1,3,9	3				
0-1-1.21*	Indicates "no" or "yes" when asked a question			1,3	3				
0-1-1.22	Chooses between two objects			1,4,	3				
0-1-1.23	Chooses between two attractive activites			1,4,	3				
0-1-1.24	Shows awareness of household routine			4	11				
0-1-2	Health, Safety, and Personal Cleanliness								
0-1-2.1	Moves limbs vigorously			1,6	7				
0-1-2.2	Relaxes body			1,6	6/8				
0-1-2.3	Enjoys bath			1,9	5/7				
0-1-2.4	Splashes in bath			1,6	8/5				
0-1-2.5	Sleeps through night in own bed			1	5				
0-1-2.6	Adapts to reasonable schedule			1,2	2				
0-1-2.7	Shifts body position freely			1,6	3/8				
0-1-2.8	Plays with wash cloth while being bathed			1,6	8				
0-1-2.9	Makes fairly persistent efforts or repeated attempts to obtain an object								
0-1-2.10	Scrubs body briefly			1,6	7/5				
0-1-2.11	Fusses to be changed after bowl movement			1	6/7/8				

OWN CARE - Year 1 - Page 3

Objective Number	General Objective	Pretest	Date Begun	Date Ended	Strategy	Evaluation Technique	Comments:	Activities:	Materials:
0-1-3	Appropriate and proportional affective reactions to the environment								
0-1-3.1*	Responds to sound			1,4	3				
0-1-3.2*	Is soothed by voice			1,9,4	3/6				
0-1-3.3*	Responds favorably to pleasant smells			1,9	11				
0-1-3.4*	Responds differentially to pleasant and unpleasant tastes			1,11	11				
0-1-3.5*	Orients when stimulation changes			1,4,6	11				
0-1-3.6*	Visually inspects objects			1,7	3/5				
0-1-3.7	Locates an object laid upon his chest at midline			1,4,6	4				
0-1-3.8	Enjoys gentle rocking			1,9	7/5				
0-1-3.9	Reaches for an object bilaterally			1,4,6	3				
0-1-3.10	Waits briefly without crying			1,5,6	5				
0-1-3.11*	Scans environment			1,4,7	8				
0-1-3.12	Reaches for an object unilaterally with either arm			1,4,6	3				
0-1-3.13	Is aware of discrepancies			1,4,11	10				
0-1-3.14	Hits surface to produce sound/movement			1,3,6	3				
0-1-3.15	Shakes objects that rattle			1,3,6	3/5				
0-1-3.16*	Occupies self unattended			1,3,6	5				
0-1-3.17*	Enjoys visual display			4,7,9,1	5				
0-1-3.18*	Explores objects through manipulation			1,3,6	5				
0-1-3.19*	Varies activity in play (i.e., substitutes play for stereotypic activity)			1,3,5,6,7	3				
0-1-3.20	Transfers an object across the midline			1,3,6					

OWN CARE - Year 1 - Page 4

Objective Number	General Objective	Pretest	Date Begun	Date Ended	Strategy	Evaluation Technique	Comments:	Activities:	Materials:
0-1-3.21	Lets an object loose intentionally			1,3,6	3				
0-1-3.22*	Explores a new setting when secure			1,3,5	5				
0-1-3.23	Responds to children with greater interest than to adults			1,3,3	11				
0-1-4	Eating and Drinking								
0-1-4.1*	Sucks well			1,6	2				
0-1-4.2	Swallows semi-solid foods			1,6	3				
0-1-4.3*	Anticipates feeding (e.g., opens mouth on sight of bottle			1,4,	6/3				
0-1-4.4	Regards spoon			1,4,	3				
0-1-4.5*	Accepts food from spoon			1,6	4				
0-1-4.6*	Closes mouth on spoon			1,6	4				
0-1-4.7*	Tries to hold own bottle			1,6	4				
0-1-4.8*	Sucks or chews moistened or soft food			1,6	4				
0-1-4.9*	Takes a bite of cracker (e.g.) held to mouth			1,6	4				
0-1-4.10	Reaches for food or bottle			1,6	4				
0-1-4.11	Tongue protrusion reflex weakened			1,6	7				
0-1-4.12	Assists in spoon feeding by guiding caregiver's hand forward or away			1,6	3				
0-1-4.13	Gag reflex weakened			1	7				
0-1-4.14	Feeds self a cracker (e.g.) after placement in hand			1,2,6	4				
0-1-4.15*	Controls drooling except when teething			1,6	5				
0-1-4.16*	Holds own bottle			1,6	5/3				
0-1-4.17	Picks up and holds spoon			1,2,6	3/5				

OWN CARE - Year 1 - Page 5

Objective Number	General Objective	Pretest	Date Begun	Date Ended	Strategy	Evaluation Technique	Comments: Activities: Materials:
0-1-4.18	Discriminates foods from nonfoods			3,11,6	4		
0-1-4.19	Finger-feeds from feeding surface			3,6,1	3		
0-1-4.20	Discriminates finger foods from spoon foods			3,11,6	4		
0-1-4.21*	Sips from a cup held by caregiver			3,6	3		
0-1-4.22	Helps to hold cup for drinking			6	2		
0-1-5	Dressing and undressing						
0-1-5.1	Relaxes when dressed and undressed			1,9	5/2		
0-1-5.2	Pulls at clothing or feels fabrics			1,6	3		
0-1-5.3	Recognizes a particular item of clothing when it is put on (e.g., the bunting he always wears out-of-doors)			4,11	2/11		
0-1-5.4	Lifts legs when diaper is changed			1,6	3		
0-1-5.5	Offers foot for shoe or sock			1,6	3		

OWN CARE – Year 1 – Page 6

Objective Number	General Objective	Pretest	Date Begun	Date Ended	Strategy	Evaluation Technique	Comments: Activities: Materials:

OWN CARE – Year 2 – Page 7

Objective Number	General Objective	Pretest	Date Begun	Date Ended	Strategy	Evaluation Technique	Comments: Activities: Materials:
0-2-1	Meeting Social Conventions and Developing Values						
0-2-1.1*	Repeats performance laughed at			3/5	1,6		
0-2-1.2*	Uses gestures to make wants known			3/10	1,6		
0-2-1.3*	Demonstrates affection by hugging (e.g.)			3/10	1,4,6		
0-2-1.4*	Varies gaze conversationally			5	4,6		
0-2-1.5*	Assumes a familiar role (e.g., pretends to clean house)				3,5,6,7		
0-2-1.6	Drooling reduced			11	1,6		
0-2-1.7	Points to body part named			5	3,11		
0-2-1.8*	Indicates self when asked "Who's (child's name)?"			4	3,4,6		
0-2-1.9	Recognizes unverbalized approval or disapproval (e.g., reacts to frowning)			3/7	11,1		
0-2-1.10*	Expresses gratitude			3/11	1,3,5		
0-2-1.11*	Goes to room specified (e.g., "Go to your bedroom.")			4	3,6,7		
0-2-1.12	Plays with other children without many disturbances			5	1,5,6		
0-2-1.13	Respects social distance in interaction			2	1,3,6		
0-2-1.14*	Gives first name when asked "What is your name?"			4	11,3,5		
0-2-1.15	Chooses between two unattractive activities			3	3,6		
0-2-1.16	Describes self positively			11	1,3,5		
0-2-1.17	Helps with household chores (e.g., putting toys away)			2	1,3,6		

OWN CARE – Year 2 – Page 8

Objective Number	General Objective	Pretest	Date Begun	Date Ended	Strategy	Evaluation Technique	Comments: Activities: Materials:
0-2-1.18	Shows awareness that some activities must match locations (e.g., eating in the kitchen or ball play out-of-doors)			4,_1	4		
0-2-1.19*	Shares divisible items			3,1 6	8		
0-2-1.20	Helps correct accidents			1,3 6	8		
0-2-1.21	Attempts to state a rule when asked, e.g., "What do we do before snack?"			1,3-5	3		
0-2-1.22	Attempts to follow a simple rule concerning care of materials, e.g., helps to pick up toys before snack			1,3_6	3		
0-2-1.23	Attempts to treat pets and other children with concern, e.g., pets a cat gently but in the wrong direction			1,3_5	3		
0-2-1.24	Attempts to follow a simple rule concerning behavior, e.g., wipes mouth at end of meal but not with complete effectiveness			1,3,5	3		
0-2-1.25	Attempts to follow a simple rule concerning courtesy, e.g., stops talking when told he's interrupting an on-going conversation			1,3,5	3		

OWN CARE – Year 2 – Page 9

Objective Number	General Objective	Pretest	Date Begun	Date Ended	Strategy	Evaluation Technique	Comments: Activities: Materials:
0-2-2	Health, Safety, and Personal Cleanliness						
0-2-2.1	Is dry after nap				1,11	3	
0-2-2.2	Goes to bed without fussing or exceptional ritual				1,11	3	
0-2-2.3	Tries to wash hands				1,3,6	2	
0-2-2.4	Tries to dry hands				1,3,6	2	
0-2-2.5	Indicates when he has wet or soiled pants				1,3,5	6/3	
0-2-2.6	Makes persistent efforts to obtain goal				1,3,5, 6,7	7/5	
0-2-2.7	Tries to wash face				1,3,6	2	
0-2-2.8	Tries to dry face				1,3,6	2	
0-2-2.9	Helps to dry hands or face				1,3,6	2	
0-2-2.10	Shifts freely between activity to inactivity				1,3,6	3	
0-2-2.11	Uses soap in washing				1,3,6	2	
0-2-2.12	Indicates need for the toilet by restlessness and vocalization				1,3,5	6/3	
0-2-2.13	Avoids objects labeled as dangerous (e.g., "hot")				1,11	4	
0-2-2.14	Holds on to one's hand when walking near traffic				1,11	3/5	
0-2-2.15	Attempts to control bowels/bladder				1,5	5	
0-2-2.16	Bowel control complete				1,5	3	
0-2-2.17	Bladder control complete during day				1,5	3	
0-2-3	Appropriate and proportional affective reactions to the environment						

OWN CARE – Year 2 – Page 10

Objective Number	General Objective	Pretest	Date Begun	Date Ended	Strategy	Evaluation Technique	Comments: Activities: Materials:
0-2-3.1	Overcomes simple obstacle (e.g., opens closed door or uses chair for reaching)			1,3,5,6,7	11		
0-2-3.2*	Engages in solitary play if secure			1,5,6,7	5/11		
0-2-3.3*	Explores the out-of-doors			1,4,5,6,7	5/11		
0-2-3.4	Substitutes an appropriate behavior for crying (e.g., waves "bye" to departing mother)			1,3,5	4		
0-2-3.5	Approaches other children			1,3,5,6	3		
0-2-3.6	Attends to the crying of others			1,3,4,5	3		
0-2-3.7*	Enjoys simple discrepancy (e.g., adult peeking from behind a new place)			1,9,4,11	5/11		
0-2-4	Eating and Drinking						
0-2-4.1	Holds cup given by adult and sips, and gives it back			1,2,6	1/5/3		
0-2-4.2*	Chews most solid foods			1,6	3		
0-2-4.3	Holds and lifts cup to sip			1,6	1		
0-2-4.4*	Moves food from side to side in mouth			1,6	3		
0-2-4.5	Puts spoon in dish or returns it to dish, leaving dish in place			2,6	3		
0-2-4.6	Vocalizes to obtain food or drink			1,3,5	3/11		
0-2-4.7	Brings spoon to mouth			6	3		
0-2-4.8*	Sucks liquid through straw			6	2		
0-2-4.9	Drinks from cup unassisted			6	2		
0-2-4.10	Chews meat or other tough foods			6	3/5		

OWN CARE – Year 2 – Page 11

Objective Number	General Objective	Pretest	Date Begun	Date Ended	Strategy	Evaluation Technique	Comments: Activities: Materials:
0-2-4.11	Wipes mouth after eating			5,6	3		
0-2-4.12	Fills spoon			5,6	2		
0-2-4.13	Delivers food to mouth using spoon			5,6	3		
0-2-4.14	Unwraps food (e.g.) candy			1,5,6	2		
0-2-4.15	Brings food to mouth without spilling using spoon			1,6	2		
0-2-5	Dressing and Undressing						
0-2-5.1	Helps put limb into clothing (e.g., arm into sleeve)			1,5,6	2		
0-2-5.2	Tries to take off shoes			1,5,6	2		
0-2-5.3	Takes off simple items of clothing (e.g., hat or socks)			1,5,6	2		
0-2-5.4	Tries to take off unfastened outerwear (e.g., coat)			1,5,6	2		
0-2-5.5	Undresses completely if no fasteners involved			1,5,6	1		
0-2-5.6	Put on simple item of clothing (e.g., hat or mittens)			1,5,6	1		
0-2-5.7	Finds garment holes and puts limb in (e.g., arms and arm holes)			1,11,6	1		
0-2-5.8	Helps push down and pull up pants			1,5,6	2		
0-2-5.9	Takes off unfastened outerwear			5,6	1		
0-2-5.10	Attempts to unzip zipper and to unsnap snap			1,5,6	2		

OWN CARE - Year 2 - Page 12

Objective Number	General Objective	Pretest	Date Begun	Date Ended	Strategy	Evaluation Technique	Comments: Activities: Materials:

OWN CARE - Year 3 - Page 13

Objective Number	General Objective	Pretest	Date Begun	Date Ended	Strategy	Evaluation Technique	Comments:	Activities:	Materials:
0-3-1	Meeting Social Conventions and Developing Values								
0-3-1.1	States simple rule when asked e.g., "What do we do before snack?" "Pick up toys."				5	3			
0-3-1.2	Follows a simple rule concerning care of materials, e.g., picks up toys before snack				3,5,6	3			
0-3-1.3	Follows a simple rule concerning treatment of pets and/or other children, e.g., doesn't squeeze gerbil				3,5,6	3			
0-3-1.4	Follows a simple rule concerning eating behavior, e.g., saying please when asking for food				3,5	3			
0-3-1.5	Follows a simple rule concerning courtesy, e.g., listens while children "share" news				3,5,6	3			
0-3-1.6	Enjoys performing simple tasks independently with minimal prompting by others, e.g., tries to zip own coat				1,5,6	3			
0-3-1.7	Enjoys demonstrating and practicing newly learned skills, e.g., will zip others' zippers				1,3,5	3			
0-3-1.8	Enjoys completing tasks, e.g., assembling a puzzle				9,1,5	3			

OWN CARE - Year 3 - Page 14

Objective Number	General Objective	Pretest	Date Begun	Date Ended	Strategy	Evaluation Technique	Comments: Activities: Materials:
0-3-1.9	Can identify items in the environment as belonging to certain people and as requiring special care			11,3,5	4		
0-3-1.10	Attempts to terminate an inappropriate behavior and to do something more appropriate in its place, e.g., will stop a frustrated cry and go lie down or look at a book						
0-3-1.11	Shares activities and equipment during situations structured for that purpose			3,11,5	4		
0-3-2	Health, Safety, and Personal Cleanliness			3,5	3		
0-3-2.1	Asks to use toilet for urination			3,5	3		
0-3-2.2	Asks to use toilet for bowel movement			3,5	3		
0-3-2.3	Independently uses toilet for urination			3,5	3		
0-3-2.4	Independently uses toilet for bowel movement			3,5	3		
0-3-2.5	Remains dry and unsoiled through the night			1,5	3		
0-3-2.6	Washes and dries face			5,7	2		
0-3-2.7	Washes and dries hands			5,7	2		
0-3-2.8	Attempts to bathe self			3,5,6	2		
0-3-2.9	Attempts to brush teeth			3,5,6	2		
0-3-2.10	Brushes and combs hair			5,7	2		
0-3-2.11	Attempts to use handerchief when coughing or sneezing			3,5,6	2		

OWN CARE – Year 3 – Page 15

Objective Number	General Objective	Pretest	Date Begun	Date Ended	Strategy	Evaluation Technique	Comments:	Activities:	Materials:
0-3-2.12	Can identify some common household items or areas as requiring safety precautions			11,3,5	4				
0-3-2.13	Accurately identifies certain foods as being good for one's health, e.g., vegetables, milk, etc.			3,5,11	4				
0-3-2.14	Daily samples foods comprising a balanced diet, e.g., protein, carbohydrates, fats, vitamins, minerals			3,5,6,7	4				
0-3-3	Appropriate and proportional affective reactions to the environment								
0-3-3.1	Spontaneously joins play involving other children and adults			1,3,5 6,7	3				
0-3-3.2	Engages contentedly in play with small groups of children			1,3,5 6,7	5/11				
0-3-3.3	Engages contentedly in solitary play			1,5,6,7	5/11				
0-3-3.4	Expresses preferences for activities and/or objects within all four curricular areas, e.g., chooses a favorite ball (motor curriculum); requests favorite songs (communication curriculum)			1,3,5 10	3/11				

OWN CARE - Year 3 - Page 16

Objective Number	General Objective	Pretest	Date Begun	Date Ended	Strategy	Evaluation Technique	Comments: Activities: Materials:
0-3-3.5	Laughs at purposive silly behaviors of self and others, e.g., teacher "changes" his/her voice, friend dresses up in a silly costume				1,3,9	3	
0-3-3.6	Attempts to make others laugh by making silly sounds or "performing" antics				1,3,5	3	
0-3-3.7	Attends (by stopping activity or by watching) to others who are hurt or who need assistance				1,3,4	3	
0-3-3.8	Expresses fondness toward certain persons by engaging their attention				1,3,4	3/11	
0-3-3.9	Expresses happiness when presented with a pleasant surprise				1,3,4	10	
0-3-3.10	Accepts, without protest, affection and attention from some persons outside the family				1,3,4,5	3/11	
0-3-3.11	Cooperates by paying attention when being taught new skills				1,3,4,5	5	
0-3-3.12	Cooperates when being given necessary assistance, e.g., takes hand to be helped out of a large leaf pile				3,5,6,7	5	
0-3-3.13	Interacts positively with pets, e.g., pats them, treats them gently				1,3,5 6	5	

OWN CARE - Year 3 - Page 17

Objective Number	General Objective	Pretest	Date Begun	Date Ended	Strategy	Evaluation Technique	Comments:	Activities:	Materials:
0-3-4	Eating and Drinking								
0-3-4.1*	Points tongue straight out of mouth			1,6	8				
0-3-4.2*	Points tongue side to side of mouth			1,6	8				
0-3-4.3	Licks upper and lower lips spontaneously			1,6	8				
0-3-4.4*	Places teeth together in biting position in imitation or on command			1,6	8				
0-3-4.5*	Blows in a controlled stream of air (e.g., blows bubbles)			1,6	8				
0-3-4.6*	Removes food from spoon with upper lip			1,6	3/8				
0-3-4.7*	Chews using rotary motion			1,6	3/8				
0-3-5	Dressing and Undressing								
0-3-5.1	Attempts unzipping a zipper with assistance			1,3,5,6,7	2				
0-3-5.2	Attempts unbuttoning a button			1,3,5,6,7	2				
0-3-5.3	Attempts unbuckling a buckle			1,3,5,6,7	2				
0-3-5.4	Unlaces a shoe			5,6,7	1				
0-3-5.5	Unties a bow			5,6,7	1				
0-3-5.6	Attempts buttoning a button			1,3,5,6,7	2				
0-3-5.7	Puts on and removes elasticized pants with assistance			1,3,5,6,7	2				
0-3-5.8	Puts on and takes off front opening garment with assistance			1,3,5,6,7	2				
0-3-5.9	Attempts taking off and putting on a pullover			1,3,5,6,7	2				

OWN CARE – Year 3 – Page 18

Objective Number	General Objective	Pretest	Date Begun	Date Ended	Strategy	Evaluation Technique	Comments: Activities: Materials:
0-3-5.10	Snaps and unsnaps with assistance				1,3,5, 6,7	2	
0-3-5.11	Attempts taking off and putting on combination clothes (snow suits, overalls, etc.)				1,3,5, 6,7	2	
0-3-5.12	Buttons and unbuttons buttons with assistance				1,3,5, 6,7	2	

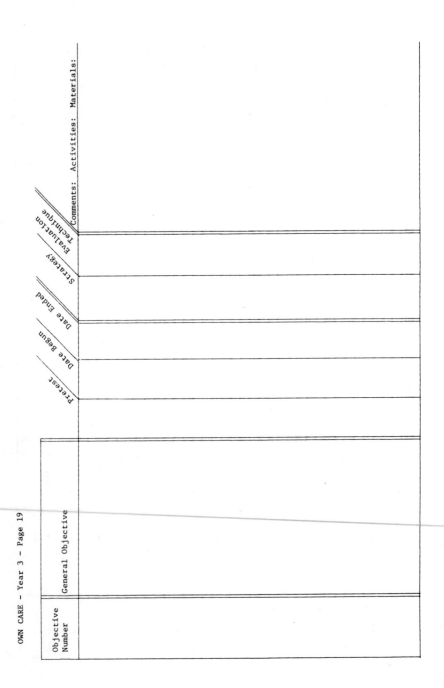

OWN CARE – Year 4 – Page 20

Objective Number	General Objective	Pretest	Date Begun	Date Ended	Strategy	Evaluation Technique	Comments: Activities: Materials:
0-4-1	Meeting Social Conventions and Developing Values						
0-4-1.1	States and follows independently at least 2 rules concerning care of materials, e.g., uses hammer on nails only			3,5,6, 7,11	3		
0-4-1.2	States and follows independently at least 2 rules concerning treatment of pets and/or children (peers)			3,5,6, 7,11	3		
0-4-1.3	States and follows independently at least 2 rules concerning eating behavior			3,5,6, 7,11	3		
0-4-1.4	States and follows independently at least 2 rules concerning courtesy			3,5,6, 7,11	3		
0-4-1.5	Enjoys performing several tasks (from all 4 areas of curriculum) independently			1,3,5	3		
0-4-1.6	Willingly persists at complex or lengthy tasks until completed accurately			1,3,5	5		
0-4-1.7	Expresses eagerness and enjoys learning new and slightly more difficult tasks			1,3,5	3/5		
0-4-1.8	Carefully uses items belonging to others, e.g., is gentle with photographs passed out at circle time			3,5,6,7	2		

OWN CARE – Year 4 – Page 21

Objective Number	General Objective	Pretest	Date Begun	Date Ended	Strategy	Evaluation Technique	Comments: Activities: Materials:
0-4-1.9	Shares activities and objects independently during activities in which sharing was previously taught, e.g., on sliding board take turns				3,5,6, 7,11	3	
0-4-1.10	Identifies self with some positive and realistic self-referent				3,5,10	3	
0-4-1.11	Refers to other children and people in environment as "friends"				3,5,10	3	
0-4-1.12	Approaches diverse people (children and adults) when prompted, e.g., males, females; people in native costumes; people of other ethnic groups				1,3,6,5	3	
0-4-1.13	Participates happily in games and activities both as leader and as follower				3,5,6,8	5/3	
0-4-1.14	Terminates an inappropriate behavior by substituting a more appropriate behavior e.g., when "talking-out" isn't responded to, will raise hand				1,3,5, 6,8	3	
0-4-1.15	Distinguishes between fact and fantasy in own daily life				1,3,5, 10	4	
0-4-1.16	Reports truthfully about very recent activities or events, e.g., "What did you eat for lunch?" (asked 3 minutes later)				1,3,10	4	

OWN CARE - Year 4 - Page 22

Objective Number	General Objective	Pretest	Date Begun	Date Ended	Strategy	Evaluation Technique	Comments: Activities: Materials:
0-4-1.17	Follows through with self-stated plans of an immediate nature, e.g., "I'm going to make this building tall."			1,3,5	4		
0-4-2	Health, Safety, and Personal Cleanliness						
0-4-2.1	Performs toileting procedures successfully			5	2		
0-4-2.2	Washes and dries face independently upon request			5	2		
0-4-2.3	Washes and dries hands independently upon request			5	2		
0-4-2.4	Bathes self			4,5,6	2		
0-4-2.5	Brushes teeth			4,5,6	2		
0-4-2.6	Uses handkerchief when coughing or sneezing			11,5,6	2		
0-4-2.7	Can identify some common objects and/or areas within the community as requiring safety precautions, e.g., construction sites			11,0	4		
0-4-2.8	Reliably avoids potentially hazardous areas, household objects and/or community objects			11,10	5		
0-4-2.9	Willingly eats portions of foods comprising a balanced diet			1,3,5	3		
0-4-2.10	Enjoys some foods from within each of the basic four food groups (protein, vegetables and fruits, grains, dairy products)			1,3,5	3		

OWN CARE – Year 4 – Page 23

Objective Number	General Objective	Pretest	Date Begun	Date Ended	Strategy	Evaluation Technique	Comments: Activities: Materials:
0-4-3	Appropriate and proportional affective reactions to the environment						
0-4-3.1	Cooperates by listening when others are providing short explanations of events				1,3,6,8	5	
0-4-3.2	Often attempts tasks independently before requesting assistance				1,3	3	
0-4-3.3	Plays contentedly in small groups for increasing periods of time				1,5	5	
0-4-3.4	Plays alone contentedly for periods of time in appropriate situation, e.g., when parent is busy with adult guests				1,5	5/11	
0-4-3.5	Has several favorite activities (demonstrated by enthusiasm) within these areas of the curriculum: communication, problem solving, motor skills				1,3,10	3/11	
0-4-3.6	Is reinforced by approval of others				1,9	3	
0-4-3.7	Requires progressively less adult reinforcement for performing many tasks				1	3	
0-4-3.8	Makes statements about own feelings at a fairly concrete level, e.g., "I'm tired," "I'm hungry," "My head hurts."				1,3,10	3/11	

OWN CARE - Year 4 - Page 24

Objective Number	General Objective	Pretest	Date Begun	Date Ended	Strategy	Evaluation Technique	Comments: Activities: Materials:
0-4-3.9	Physically and/or verbally expresses concern for others who are hurt or need assistance, e.g., seeks an adult's help, asks child if she/he is all right				1,3,5,4	10	
0-4-3.10	Shows fondness for others by offering affection, assistance or sharing				1,3 5,6	3/11	
0-4-3.11	Responds without fear in many new situations and with some unfamiliar people, e.g., nurse, policeman				1,3,5	10	
0-4-3.12	Expresses feelings of satisfaction with certain activities, e.g., "I like painting," "I can climb high," "I liked writing that letter."				1,3 5, 10	3/11	
0-4-4	Eating and Drinking						
0-4-4.1*	Licks upper and lower lip in imitation or on command				3,5,6	4	
0-4-4.2*	Places tongue behind upper teeth on command				3,5,5	4	
0-4-4.3*	Imitates speech movements without sound production				3,5,5	4	
0-4-4.4*	Drinks liquids from straw, no spilling				3,5,4	4	
0-4-4.5*	Maintains closed mouth position except for eating, drinking or talking				3,5,6	5	
0-4-5	Dressing and Undressing						

OWN CARE - Year 4 - Page 25

Objective Number	General Objective	Pretest	Date Begun	Date Ended	Strategy	Evaluation Technique	Comments: Activities: Materials:
0-4-5.1	Puts on and removes elasticized pants with assistance			1,3,4,5,6,7	2		
0-4-5.2	Takes off and puts on pullover garments with assistance			1,3,4,5,6,7	2		
0-4-5.3	Puts on and takes off combination clothing (snow suits, overalls) with assistance			1,3,4,5,6,7	2		
0-4-5.4	Snaps independently			4,5,6,7	1		
0-4-5.5	Buckles with assistance			1,3,4,5,6,7	2		
0-4-5.6	Attempts lacing a shoe			1,3,4,5,6,7	2		
0-4-5.7	Independently zips a zipper			4,5,6,7	1		
0-4-5.8	Attempts tying a bow			1,3,4,5,6,7	2		
0-4-5.9	Buttons and unbuttons large buttons independently			4,5,6,7	1		
0-4-5.10	Puts on and removes elasticized pants independently			4,5,6,7	1		
0-4-5.11	Puts on and takes off front opening garment independently			4,5,6,7	1		

OWN CARE – Year 4 – Page 26

Objective Number	General Objective	Pretest	Date Begun	Date Ended	Strategy	Evaluation Technique	Comments: Activities: Materials:

OWN CARE - Year 5 - Page 27

Objective Number	General Objective	Pretest	Date Begun	Date Ended	Strategy	Evaluation Technique	Comments: Activities: Materials:
0-5-1	Meeting Social Convention and Developing Values						
0-5-1.1	States and follows independently more than two rules concerning care of materials				3,5,6,7,11	3	
0-5-1.2	States and follows independently more than two rules concerning treatment of others				3,5,6,7,11	3	
0-5-1.3	States and follows more than two rules concerning eating behavior				3,5,6,7,11	3	
0-5-1.4	States and follows more than two rules concerning courtesy				3,5,6,7,11	3	
0-5-1.5	Enjoys independently performing tasks from all curricular areas				1,3,5	3/5	
0-5-1.6	Persists at progressively more difficult tasks until completed accurately				1,3,5	3/5	
0-5-1.7	Anticipates and enjoys learning new and slightly more difficult tasks				1,3,5,9	3/5	
0-5-1.8	Shares activities and objects during novel play situations, e.g., with unfamiliar children with new toys				3,5,6,7	3	
0-5-1.9	Identifies self positively and accurately in terms of skills, interest, and sociability				3,5,10	3	

OWN CARE - Year 5 - Page 28

Objective Number	General Objective	Pretest	Date Begun	Date Ended	Strategy	Evaluation Technique	Comments: Activities: Materials:
0-5-1.10	Can independently "make friends" with other children or persons when appropriate, e.g., will offer them a toy, ask a question			3,5,6	10		
0-5-1.11	Can distinguish between fact and fantasy in situations remote to own daily life, e.g., "Do elephants fly?"			11,10	4		
0-5-1.12	Reports truthfully about activities and events that happened within twenty-four hours or more			1,3,5, 10	4		
0-5-1.13	Follows through with self-stated plans of beyond an immediate nature, e.g., "I am going to show this to Mommy when I get home."			5,6,10	4		
0-5-1.14	Enjoys participating in games and/or activities in which one cannot always be successful or be the winner			3,5,5	5		
0-5-1.15	Shows self-control by imposing consequences on self that are similar to those used by adults, e.g., goes to "quiet chair" when is upset			1,3,5,3	10		
0-5-1.16	Participates by simple voting in group problem-solving situations			3,5	8		

OWN CARE - Year 5 - Page 29

Objective Number	General Objective	Pretest	Date Begun	Date Ended	Strategy	Evaluation Technique	Comments: Activities: Materials:
0-5-1.17	Abides by consequences of group decisions made as in No. 0-5-1.16			1,3,5,6,7	8		
0-5-1.18	Shows an appropriately balanced concern for "friends" in making decisions, e.g., will choose to look at another book because a friend wants to see the one that the child originally had			3,1,4,5,8	10		
0-5-1.19	Makes accurate statements about the wishes and values of others			1,3,10,8	4		
0-5-2	Health, Safety, and Personal Cleanliness						
0-5-2.1	Performs toileting procedures independently			3,4	2		
0-5-2.2	Washes and dries hands and/or face independently and without adults' prompting, e.g., after toileting, before eating, after painting			3,4	2		
0-5-2.3	Brushes teeth independently			3,4	2		
0-5-2.4	Bathes self independently (may still require final inspection. e.g., behind the ears!)			4,5,6,7	2		
0-5-2.5	Uses handkerchiefs independently			4,5	2		

OWN CARE - Year 5 - Page 30

Objective Number	General Objective	Pretest	Date Begun	Date Ended	Strategy	Evaluation Technique	Comments: Activities: Materials:
0-5-2.6	Carefully uses some potentially hazardous household items, e.g., knives, electric outlets, record players			3,4,5 6,7,1	2		
0-5-2.7	Brushes and combs hair independently			4,5	2		
0-5-2.8	Identifies value of eating foods from the four basic food groups, e.g., protein - for healthy muscles, fruits and vegetables - for healthy skin			3,5,1-, 10	4		
0-5-2.9	Identifies the four basic food groups			3,5,1-	4		
0-5-2.10	Selects a daily menu comprising the four basic food groups			1,3,1-	4		
0-5-3	Appropriate and Proportional Affective Reactions to the Environment						
0-5-3.1	Objectively verbalizes differences among people			1,3,1C	2		
0-5-3.2	Behaves appropriately and comfortably in increasingly more situations, e.g., at doctor's office, at library, at concerts, etc.			1,3,5	10		

OWN CARE - Year 5 - Page 31

Objective Number	General Objective	Pretest	Date Begun	Date Ended	Strategy	Evaluation Technique	Comments: Activities: Materials:
0-5-3.3	Behaves appropriately and comfortably with increasingly more and different people, e.g., people who are "teasers," people who speak differently, etc.			1,3,5	10		
0-5-3.4	In difficult situations (e.g., attempting to complete a difficult puzzle), requests assistance or goes on to another activity rather than become extremely angry or upset			3,5,8	10		
0-5-3.5	Continues to cooperate in learning skills and information within all curricular areas			1,3,5,6,7	2		
0-5-3.6	Expresses pleasure with own performance in activities from all four curricular areas			1,3,10	2/3		
0-5-3.7	Expresses own feelings that are of a more abstract nature, e.g., "I am so happy," "I miss my friend."			1,3,10,8	3		
0-5-3.8	Expresses how others "might" feel, e.g., "I bet Mommy is tired," "John is sad."			1,3,10,8	3		
0-5-3.9	Makes rational statements as to why she/he likes and dislikes people, events or objects			1,3,10	3		

OWN CARE - Year 5 - Page 32

Objective Number	General Objective	Pretest	Date Begun	Date Ended	Strategy	Evaluation Technique	Comments: Activities: Materials:
0-5-3.10	Shows comfort, enthusiasm and spontaneity in most play and learning situations, e.g., asks questions, is not afraid to answer, tries new activities			1,3,5, 6,7	11		
0-5-5	Dressing and Undressing						
0-5-5.1	Takes off and puts on pullover garments independently			4	1		
0-5-5.2	Puts on and takes off combination clothing (snow suits, overalls) independently			4	1		
0-5-5.3	Aligns snap halves and completes closure independently			2,4	1		
0-5-5.4	Buckles independently			2,4	1		
0-5-5.5	Independently laces			2,4	1		
0-5-5.6	Inserts tabs to start zipper			3,5,6,	1		
0-5-5.7	Independently ties a bow			2,4	1		
0-5-5.8	Buttons and unbuttons small buttons independently			2,4	1		
0-5-5.9	Inserts belt in slacks independently			2,4	1		
0-5-5.10	Correctly puts shoes on own feet independently			11,4	1		

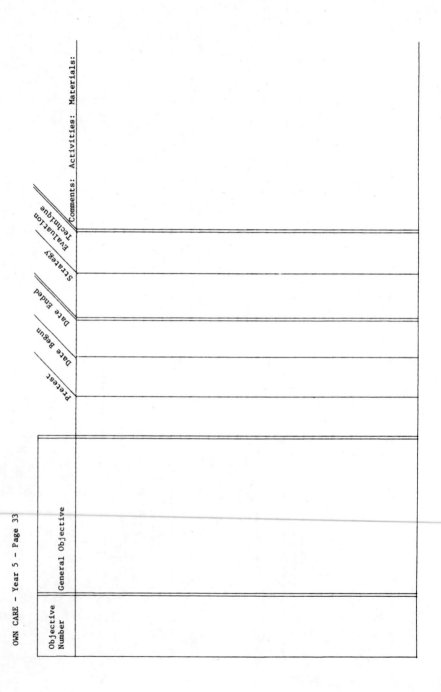

MOTOR – Year 1 – Page 1

Objective Number	General Objective	Pretest	Date Begun	Date Ended	Strategy	Evaluation Technique	Comments: Activities: Materials:
M-1-1	Fundamental Movement (Gross Motor)						
M-1-1.1	Clears nose from bed when lying on abdomen (prone)			5	6/8		
M-1-1.2	Lifts head to 45° when on abdomen (prone)			5	6/8		
M-1-1.3	No head droop if suspended (prone)				8		
M-1-1.4	Head held steady when body supported in sitting			6	5		
M-1-1.5	No head lag when hands held and pulled to sitting			6	8		
M-1-1.6	Pushes whole chest off support, prone			1,5	5/8		
M-1-1.7	Rolls to abdomen from back			1,5	8		
M-1-1.8	Sits supporting self, leaning on hands			1,5	5		
M-1-1.9	Bears weight on legs when body is held			1,6	5		
M-1-1.10	Rolls to back from abdomen			1,6	8		
M-1-1.11	Sits supporting self, leaning on hands			1,6	5		
M-1-1.12	In sitting, shifts weight on extended arms to reach for object			1,6	8		
M-1-1.13	Sits alone for 1 minute			1	5		
M-1-1.14	Pivots body in circle (while prone) using arms			1,6	8		
M-1-1.15	Maintains hands and knees position when placed in that position			1,6	5		
M-1-1.16	Creeps			3,6	1		
M-1-1.17	Assumes hands and knees position			3,6	8		

MOTOR - Year 1 - Page 2

Objective Number	General Objective	Pretest	Date Begun	Date Ended	Strategy	Evaluation Technique	Comments: Activities: Materials:
M-1-1.18	Rocks back and forth in hands and knees position			6	8		
M-1-1.19	Sits independently for indefinite period			1,6	5		
M-1-1.20	Crawls on hands and knees			3,6	5/1		
M-1-1.21	Pulls to standing position			6	1/4		
M-1-1.22	Walks around furniture, holding onto it			1,6	5		
M-1-1.23	Stands from sitting or lying position			1,6	4		
M-1-1.24	Walks with one hand held			6	5		
M-1-1.25	Stands alone, momentarily			1,6	5		
M-1-1.26	Takes 2-3 steps alone			1,6	3		
M-1-1.27	Stands alone for 5 seconds			1,6	5		
M-1-1.28	Stands independently			1,6	5		
M-1-1.29	Walks forward alone			1,6	3/5		
M-1-2	Skilled Movement or Visual-Motor or Fine Motor						
M-1-2.1	Retains briefly an object put in hand			1,6	5		
M-1-2.2*	Glances at object when placed in hand			4,6	8		
M-1-2.3	Holds object put in hand			1,6	3		
M-1-2.4	Brings hands together in midline			1,6	8		
M-1-2.5	Obtains object placed on chest at midline			1,6	8		
M-1-2.6	Reaches for object when lying on back (supine)			1,6	8		
M-1-2.7	Reaches for object unilaterally when lying on back			1,6	8		
M-1-2.8	Reaches for object when supported in sitting			1,6	7/8		

MOTOR - Year 1 - Page 3

Objective Number	General Objective	Pretest	Date Begun	Date Ended	Strategy	Evaluation Technique	Comments: Activities: Materials:
M-1-2.9	Picks up object bilaterally (cube, e.g.)			1,6	8		
M-1-2.10*	Grasps object while looking at it			4,6	3/8		
M-1-2.11	Picks up and retains two cubes (e.g.)			1,6	8/5		
M-1-2.12	Transfers object from hand to hand			1,6	8		
M-1-2.13	Bangs together two objects held in hands			1,6,3	8		
M-1-2.14	Uses whole hand to rake up very small object (e.g., a raisin)			1,6,3	8		
M-1-2.15	Picks up cube (e.g.) with thumb and index finger			1,6,3	8		
M-1-2.16	Reaches for cube (e.g.) inside container			1,6,3	8		
M-1-2.17	Pokes with index finger at very small object			1,6,3	8		
M-1-2.18	Removes one cube (e.g.) from container			1,6,3	8		
M-1-2.19	Puts one cube (e.g.) in container after demonstration			1,6,3	4		
M-1-3	Oral Movement or Mouth and Jaw Control						
M-1-3.1*	Sucks well			6	5/7		
M-1-3.2*	Anticipates feeding (e.g., opens mouth on sight of bottle)			4,6	6		
M-1-3.3*	Accepts food from spoon			6	3		
M-1-3.4*	Tries to hold own bottle			1,6	8		
M-1-3.5*	Closes mouth on spoon			1,6	3		

MOTOR – Year 1 – Page 4

Objective Number	General Objective	Pretest	Date Begun	Date Ended	Strategy	Evaluation Technique	Comments: Activities: Materials:
M-1-3.6*	Sucks or chews moistened or soft food			6	3		
M-1-3.7*	Takes a bite of cracker (e.g.) held to mouth			3,6	3		
M-1-3.8*	Holds own bottle			1,6	5		
M-1-3.9*	Sips from cup held by caregiver			6	3		
M-1-3.10*	Controls drooling except when teething			6	5		

MOTOR – Year 1 – Page 5

Objective Number	General Objective	Pretest	Date Begun	Date Ended	Strategy	Evaluation Technique	Comments: Activities: Materials:

MOTOR – Year 2 – Page 6

Objective Number	General Objective	Pretest	Date Begun	Date Ended	Strategy	Evaluation Technique	Comments: Activities: Materials:
M-2-1	Fundamental Movement (Gross Motor)						
M-2-1.1	Stoops and recovers				1,6	4	
M-2-1.2	Starts and stops walking without falling				1,6	5	
M-2-1.3	Climbs into chair, turns around to sit				1,6	1/4	
M-2-1.4	Runs stiffly, sometimes falls				1,6	8	
M-2-1.5	Crawls up stairs unassisted				1	1/3	
M-2-1.6	Walks up stairs if one hand is held				1,6	1/3	
M-2-1.7	Walks sideways				1/6	1/3	
M-2-1.8	Walks downstairs if one hand is held				1,6	1/3	
M-2-1.9	Squats in play for 2-3 minutes				1,6	5	
M-2-1.10	Walks backwards				1,6,3	1/3	
M-2-1.11	Walks up and down stairs holding rail, both feet on each step						
M-2-1.12	Kicks large (stationary) ball				1,6,3	1/3	
M-2-1.13	Jumps off floor, both feet				1,6,3	3/7	
M-2-1.14	Tries to stand on one foot				1,6,3	3/7	
M-2-2	Skilled Movement or Visual-Motor or Fine Motor						
M-2-2.1	Stacks two objects				2,3,6	3	
M-2-2.2	Puts 5-6 cubes (e.g.) in container				2,3,6	3	
M-2-2.3	Helps turn pages of book				3,6	8	
M-2-2.4	Puts very small object into narrow container				3,6	4	
M-2-2.5	Makes random marks on paper with crayon held in fist				3,6	8	

MOTOR - Year 2 - Page 7

Objective Number	General Objective	Pretest	Date Begun	Date Ended	Strategy	Evaluation Technique	Comments: Activities: Materials:
M-2-2.6	Turns pages of book 2-3 at a time				3,5	8	
M-2-2.7	Builds tower of 3-5 cubes				2,3,6	3	
M-2-2.8	Draws a vertical line, imitating adult				3,5	4	
M-2-2.9	Draws a horizontal line, imitating adult				3,5	4	
M-2-2.10	Puts 10 cubes in cup and hands cup to adult				2,3,6	3	
M-2-2.11	Builds tower of 6-7 cubes				2,3,6	3	
M-2-2.12	Builds tower of 8 cubes				2,3,6	3	
M-2-2.13	Holds crayon in fingers				3,8	8	
M-2-3	Oral Movement or Mouth and Jaw Control						
M-2-3.1	Drooling reduced				1,6	5	
M-2-3.2*	Chews most solid foods				1,6	3	
M-2-3.3*	Moves food from side to side in mouth				1,6	8	
M-2-3.4*	Sucks liquid through a straw				1,6	1/7	
M-2-3.5	Blows in non-specific direction				1,6,3	8	
M-2-3.6	Opens and closes mouth in imitation or on command				1,6,3	4	
M-2-3.7	Presses lips together in imitation or on command (e.g., "m" sound)				1,6,3	4	
M-2-3.8	Purses lips in imitation or on command (e.g., kissing)				1,6,3	4	

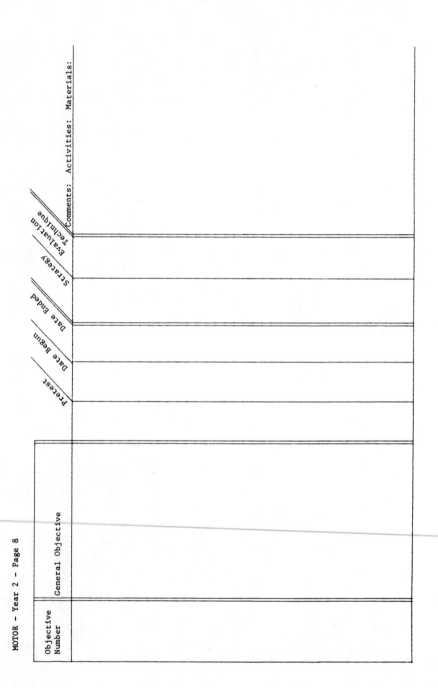

MOTOR - Year 3 - Page 9

Objective Number	General Objective	Pretest	Date Begun	Date Ended	Strategy	Evaluation Technique	Comments:	Activities:	Materials:
M-3-1	Fundamental Movement (Gross Motor)								
M-3-1.1	Walks on tiptoe, demonstrated			1,3,6	1/3				
M-3-1.2	Begins a simple somersault			1,3,6	1/3				
M-3-1.3	Stands on balance beam with both feet			1,3,5	5				
M-3-1.4	Jumps from bottom step			1,3,5,7	8				
M-3-1.5	Walks up stairs, alternating feet			3,5,6,7	1/3				
M-3-1.6	Walks down stairs, alternating feet			3,5,6,7	1/3				
M-3-1.7	Walks on line on floor			3,5,6,7	1/5				
M-3-1.8	Rides a tricycle using pedals			3,5,6	1				
M-3-1.9	Stands on one foot, momentarily			3,5,5	8				
M-3-1.10	Catches large ball by holding it against body			3,5,5	1/4				
M-3-1.11	Jumps with both feet over low objects (1"-2" high)			3,5,5	1/7				
M-3-1.12	Begins to climb a ladder or jungle gym			1,6	1				
M-3-1.13	Slides between two objects sideways			3,5,6	8				
M-3-1.14	Ducks under objects			3,6,5	2				
M-3-1.15	Maintains balance on a variety of surfaces			1,6	2				
M-3-1.16	Walks up and down incline			6	2/8				
M-3-2	Skilled Movement or Visual-Motor or Fine Motor								
M-3-2.1	Draws circle, imitating adult			2,3,5,5	2				
M-3-2.2	Draws vertical line from model			2,5,6	2				
M-3-2.3	Draws horizontal line from model			2,5,6	2				

MOTOR – Year 3 – Page 10

Objective Number	General Objective	Pretest	Date Begun	Date Ended	Strategy	Evaluation Technique	Comments: Activities: Materials:
M-3-2.4	Draws recognizable face			2,3,5,6	2		
M-3-2.5	Builds bridge of 3 cubes, imitating			2,3,5,6	4		
M-3-2.6	Builds tower of 9-10 cubes			2,3,5,6	4		
M-3-2.7	Draws cross, imitating adult			2,3,5,6	2		
M-3-2.8	Paints with large brush			3,5,6	8		
M-3-2.9	Places round object in round hole			3,6	4		
M-3-2.10	Cuts paper with scissors			1,2,3,5,6,7	1		
M-3-2.11	Matches the three primary colors			3,10,11	4		
M-3-2.12	Strings large beads			3,6	4		
M-3-2.13	Builds bridge of five blocks			2,3,5,6	4		
M-3-2.14	Turns (twists) lids or door knobs			3,5,6	7		
M-3-2.15	Folds square paper in half, with crease			3,5,6	2		
M-3-2.16	Turns pages of book singly			3,5,6	4		
M-3-3	Oral Movement or Mouth and Jaw Control						
M-3-3.1*	Points tongue straight out of mouth				8		
M-3-3.2*	Points tongue side to side of mouth			3,6	8		
M-3-3.3	Licks upper and lower lip spontaneously			3,6	8		
M-3-3.4*	Places teeth together in biting position in imitation or on command			3,6	2		
M-3-3.5*	Blows in controlled stream of air (e.g., blows bubbles)			3,6	4		
M-3-3.6*	Removes food from spoon with upper lip			3,6	2/8		
M-3-3.7*	Chews using rotary motion			3,6	2/8		

MOTOR – Year 3 – Page 11

Objective Number	General Objective	Pretest	Date Begun	Date Ended	Strategy	Evaluation Technique	Comments: Activities: Materials:

MOTOR - Year 4 - Page 12

Objective Number	General Objective	Pretest	Date Begun	Date Ended	Strategy	Evaluation Technique	Comments:	Activities:	Materials:
M-4-1	Fundamental Movement (Gross Motor)								
M-4-1.1	Takes two steps on balance beam			3,5,6,7	1/4				
M-4-1.2	Stands on one foot for 2-3 seconds			1,3,6	5				
M-4-1.3	Hops on one foot			1,3,6	3				
M-4-1.4	Turns corners while running			1,3,6	8				
M-4-1.5	Turns wide corner on tricycle			1,3,6	8				
M-4-1.6	Catches bouncing ball, holding it against body								
M-4-1.7	Throws large ball over hand			3,5,6	4				
M-4-1.8	Attempts to skip			3,5,6	2				
M-4-1.9	Performs complete somersault			1,3,5,6	2				
M-4-1.10	Kicks large (stationary) ball with 2 step start			2,3,5,6	2				
M-4-1.11	Walks up and down stairs carrying small object			3,5,6	1				
M-4-1.12	Jumps forward (feet together) a distance of one foot			1,3,5,6	7				
M-4-1.13	Jumps over (feet together) a 3" high rope			1,3,5,6	7				
M-4-1.14	Throws large ball underhand with two hands			1,5,6	2/7				
M-4-1.15	Throws ball to specific target			1,7	2/7				
M-4-2	Skilled Movement or Visual-Motor or Fine Motor								
M-4-2.1	Matches circles, squares, and triangles			3,10,11	4				
M-4-2.2	Puts together simple puzzles			3,10,11	4				
M-4-2.3	Strings small beads			3,5,6	4				
M-4-2.4	Rolls clay into snake shape			3,5,6	2				
M-4-2.5	Cuts on line with scissors			1,3,5,6,7	1				

MOTOR - Year 4 - Page 13

Objective Number	General Objective	Pretest	Date Begun	Date Ended	Strategy	Evaluation Technique	Comments: Activities: Materials:
M-4-2.6	Folds square paper in half (edges meeting), imitating adult			3,5	2		
M-4-2.7	Drives nails and pegs with hammer			3,5,6	1		
M-4-2.8	Draws triangle, imitating adult			3,5,7	2		
M-4-2.9	Draws circle from model			3,5,7	2		
M-4-2.10	Draws square from model			3,5,7	2		
M-4-2.11	Draws cross from model			3,5,7	2		
M-4-2.12	Touches thumb to fingers of same hand, imitating adult			3,6	4		
M-4-2.13	Marches in time to repetitious beat			3,4,6	5		
M-4-2.14	Plays rhythm instruments to familiar song			3,4,6	5		
M-4-2.15	Sings parts of familiar song			1,3,5	3		
M-4-2.16	Points to areas of body touched by adult			3,4,5	4		
M-4-2.17	Draws picture of person with head, body, and eyes			1,3,5,6,7	2		
M-4-3	Oral Movement or Mouth and Jaw Control						
M-4-3.1*	Licks upper and lower lip in imitation or on command			3,6	4		
M-4-3.2*	Places tongue behind upper teeth on command			3,6	4		
M-4-3.3*	Imitates speech movements without sound production			3,6	4		
M-4-3.4*	Drinks liquids from straw, no spilling			1,6	2/5		
M-4-3.5*	Maintains closed mouth position except for eating, drinking or talking			1,6	8		

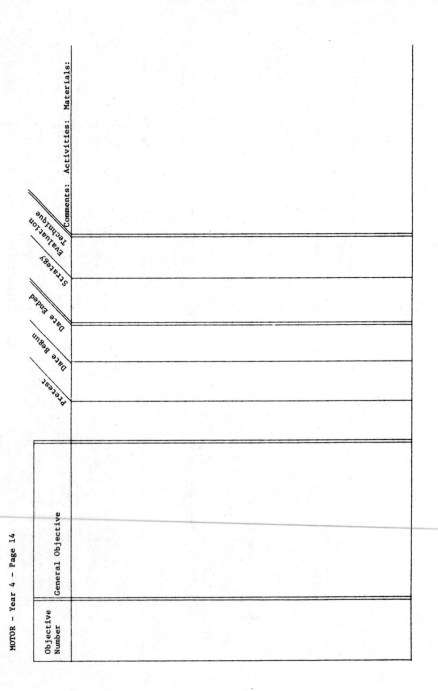

MOTOR – Year 4 – Page 14

Objective Number	General Objective	Pretest	Date Begun	Date Ended	Strategy	Evaluation Technique	Comments: Activities: Materials:

MOTOR – Year 5 – Page 15

Objective Number	General Objective	Pretest	Date Begun	Date Ended	Strategy	Evaluation Technique	Comments: Activities: Materials:
M-5-1	Fundamental Movement (Gross Motor)						
M-5-1.1	Runs through obstacle course, avoiding objects in path			3,5,6,1	2		
M-5-1.2	Runs tiptoe			3,5,6,1	2		
M-5-1.3	Skips on alternating feet			3,5,6,1	1		
M-5-1.4	Takes five steps on balance beam			2,3,5,6	3		
M-5-1.5	Kicks moving large ball			3,5,5	2		
M-5-1.6	Stands on one foot 5 seconds eyes open			1,3,5	5		
M-5-1.7	Catches ball in hands (not against body)			3,6,5	4		
M-5-1.8	Stands on one foot 2-3 seconds, eyes closed			1,3	5		
M-5-1.9	Bounces large ball on floor and catches it with hands			2,3,5,6	1		
M-5-1.10	Maintains momentum on swing			3,5,●	2		
M-5-1.11	Jumps backwards (feet together) a distance of one foot			1,3,5,6	7		
M-5-1.12	Hangs from bar using overhand grip			3,6	2/5		
M-5-1.13	Jumps over 6 inch high rope			3,6	7/3		
M-5-1.14	Turns while jumping			6	8		
M-5-1.15	Throws ball underhand, with one had			1,5,6	2/7		
M-5-1.16	Jumps in different directions			6	8		
M-5-2	Skilled Movement or Visual-Motor or Fine Motor						
M-5-2.1	Winds thread on spool evenly			3,5,6	2		
M-5-2.2	Cuts cloth with scissors			3,5,6	1		
M-5-2.3	Places key in lock and opens lock			6,7	1		

MOTOR – Year 5 – Page 16

Objective Number	General Objective	Pretest	Date Begun	Date Ended	Strategy	Evaluation Technique	Comments:	Activities:	Materials:
M-5-2.4	Matches six colors			3,10,11	4				
M-5-2.5	Draws diamond, imitating adult			3,5,6	2				
M-5-2.6	Prints letters or numbers, imitating adult			2,3,5, 6,7	2				
M-5-2.7	Spreads paste on one side of paper and turns over to stick to another paper			2,3,5, 6,7	2				
M-5-2.8	Cuts out pictures following general shape			3,5,6	2				
M-5-2.9	Connects two dots by drawing a line			3,5,7	2				
M-5-2.10	Rolls clay into a ball			3,6	2				
M-5-2.11	Puts together 8-10 piece puzzles			3,5,10, 11	4				
M-5-2.12	Draws circle, square, triangle, and cross without model			5,6	2				
M-5-2.13	Entertains self looking at books			1	5				
M-5-2.14	Finger paints			3,5,6	2				
M-5-2.15	Sings familiar songs			1,3,5	3				
M-5-2.16	Reproduces actions of familiar songs			1,3,6	4				
M-5-2.17	Plays rhythm instruments in simple pattern			11,3,6	1/5				
M-5-2.18	Draws picture of person with face, body, and extremities			2,3,5 6,10	2				

MOTOR – Year 5 – Page 17

Objective Number	General Objective	Pretest	Date Begun	Date Ended	Strategy	Evaluation Technique	Comments: Activities: Materials:

PROBLEM SOLVING - Year 1 - Page 1

Objective Number	General Objective	Pretest	Date Begun	Date Ended	Strategy	Evaluation Technique	Comments: Activities: Materials:
P-1-1	Attention						
P-1-1.1*	Responds to sound				1,4,5,6,7	3/7	
P-1-1.2*	Briefly sustains gaze at speaker				1,4,5,6,7	5	
P-1-1.3	Focuses on object				1,4,5,6,7	5	
P-1-1.4*	Shuts down response to repeated sounds				1,6	6	
P-1-1.5	Focuses on object and follows its movement briefly				1,4,5,6,7	5	
P-1-1.6	Shifts eyes toward sound				1,4,5,6,7	3/7	
P-1-1.7	Focuses on and follows an object, finding it again when it is momentarily lost				1,4,5,6,7	3	
P-1-1.8	Smoothly follows with eyes a horizontally moving object				1,4,5,6,7	5	
P-1-1.9*	Head turns to sound				1,4,5,6,7	3	
P-1-1.10	Follows horizontally moving object with head and eyes				1,4,5,6,7	5	
P-1-1.11	Visually inspects objects				1,4,5,6,7	5	
P-1-1.12	Follows vertically moving object briefly.				1,4,5,6,7	5	
P-1-1.13	Head turns to sound followed by visual inspection				1,4,5,6,7	3	
P-1-1.14	Follows vertically moving object with head and eyes				1,4,5,6,7	5	
P-1-1.15	Visually follows object through circular movement				1,4,5,6,7	5	
P-1-1.16*	Responds favorably to pleasant smells				1,4,5	7	
P-1-1.17	Responds differentially to pleasant and unpleasant smells				1,4,5,11	3	
P-1-1.18*	Responds differentially to pleasant and unpleasant tastes				11	3	

PROBLEM SOLVING – Year 1 – Page 2

Objective Number	General Objective	Pretest	Date Begun	Date Ended	Strategy	Evaluation Technique	Comments:	Activities:	Materials:
P-1-1.19*	Glances from one object or person to another								
P-1-1.20	Observes hands			1,4	3				
P-1-1.21*	Glances at object when placed in hand			1,4,5	3/5				
P-1-1.22	Scans environment			1,4,5	4				
P-1-1.23*	Looks around for visually removed speaker			1,4,5	5				
P-1-1.24*	Grasps object while looking at it			1,4,5	5/3				
P-1-1.25*	Looks at simple pictures in a book			1,4,5	3/5				
P-1-2	Imitation								
P-1-2.1*	Repeats model who imitates him/her			1,3	4				
P-1-2.2*	Imitates novel non-speech sounds (e.g., lip smacking, kisses, coughs)								
P-1-2.3*	Imitates motor behaviors that are already part of the child's capabilities (e.g., waves "bye-bye" when someone else waves "bye-bye")			1,3	4				
P-1-2.4*	Imitates familiar words			1,3,6	4				
P-1-2.5*	Spontaneously uses an appropriate behavior through delayed imitation (e.g., says "ahh" to doll or initiates "peek-a-boo")			1,3,4, 5,6,7	11				
P-1-2.6*	Imitates novel but simple behaviors			1,3,6	11				
P-1-2.7*	Imitates novel words			1,3,5	11				
P-1-3	Recall								

PROBLEM SOLVING - Year 1 - Page 3

Objective Number	General Objective	Pretest	Date Begun	Date Ended	Strategy	Evaluation Technique	Comments: Activities: Materials:
P-1-3.1*	Orients when stimulation changes				4	2/3	
P-1-3.2*	Anticipates feeding				4,5	6/3	
P-1-3.3	Repeats own action				1,3	3/8	
P-1-3.4	Reacts to sudden disappearance of an object or person				1,4	8	
P-1-3.5	Is aware of discrepancies				1,4	10	
P-1-3.6*	Anticipates familiar movement (e.g., in being picked up)				1,4,5	6/3	
P-1-3.7	Acts and then waits for expected effect to occur				1,3,6	3/5	
P-1-3.8	Finds a partially hidden object				1,3,6	3	
P-1-3.9	Visually anticipates the future position of an object (e.g., in peek-a-boo game in which the puppet keeps reappearing at the same place)				1,3,6	3	
P-1-3.10	Resumes interrupted activity				1,4,5,6,7	7	
P-1-3.11*	Rejects strangers initially but adapts over time				1,3	3	
P-1-3.12*	Responds with recognition when his name is stated (e.g., stops activity and listens when he hears his name)				1,4,5 6,7	4	
P-1-3.13	Finds an object hidden in view of the child in the same place repeatedly				1,3,6	4	
P-1-3.14	Finds an object hidden in view of the child in varied locations				1,3,6,7	4	
P-1-3.15	Recognizes proper orientation of objects (e.g., reverses baby bottle)				1,3,6	4	

PROBLEM SOLVING – Year 1 – Page 4

Objective Number	General Objective	Pretest	Date Begun	Date Ended	Strategy	Evaluation Technique	Comments: Activities: Materials:
P-1-3.16	Keeps goal in mind while using indirect means				1,3,4	10,5	
P-1-4	Concept Formation						
P-1-4.1	Responds differentially to colors (e.g., chooses brightly colored objects over drab objects)				4,3,1	3	
P-1-4.2*	Recognizes familiar words (other than own name), e.g., looks toward common object or family member named				1,4,6	3	
P-1-5	Grouping						
P-1-5.1	Is aware of discrepancy				1,4,5,6,7	10/3	
P-1-6	Sequencing						
P-1-6.1	Matches by size: large and small				1,3	4	
P-1-7	Application of Principles						
P-1-7.1*	Attracts attention of the caregiver				1,3,5,6,7	3/10	
P-1-7.2	Repeats an action involving feedback (e.g., shaking a rattle)				1,3	3/11	
P-1-7.3	Adapts means (e.g., can obtain an object from more than one location, i.e., reach up as well as down)				1,3	11	
P-1-7.4	Uses a single modality to search for an absent object (e.g., sight only)				1,3,=	11	

PROBLEM SOLVING – Year 1 – Page 5

Objective Number	General Objective	Pretest	Date Begun	Date Ended	Strategy	Evaluation Technique	Comments:	Activities:	Materials:
P-1-7.5	Regains a dropped or lost object			1,3,6	4				
P-1-7.6	Child activates object by non-mechanical action			1,3,6	11				
P-1-7.7	Moves several objects in turn			3					
P-1-7.8	Displaces barriers (e.g., climbs over or pushes aside gate)			1,3,6	4				
P-1-7.9	Uses more than one modality at a time in searching for an absent object (e.g., uses cues from sight and hearing)			1,3,5,6,7	11				
P-1-7.10	Waits without distress for an adult to do something for him			1,3,5,6,7	5				
P-1-8	Creativity								
P-1-8.1*	Visually inspects objects			1,4,6	5				
P-1-8.2*	Scans environment			1,4,6	5				
P-1-8.3*	Occupies self unattended			1,4	5				
P-1-8.4*	Enjoys visual display			1,4	7				
P-1-8.5*	Explores object through manipulation			1,4,6	2/5				
P-1-8.6*	Vocalizes amusing sounds (e.g., coughs, animal sounds)			1,5	2/5				
P-1-8.7*	Varies activity in play (i.e., substitutes play for stereotypic activity)			1,4,6, 6,7	2/5				
P-1-8.8*	Explores a new setting when secure			1,4,5, 6,7	2/5				

PROBLEM SOLVING - Year 1 - Page 6

Objective Number	General Objective	Pretest	Date Begun	Date Ended	Strategy	Evaluation Technique	Comments: Activities: Materials:

PROBLEM SOLVING – Year 2 – Page 7

Objective Number	General Objective	Pretest	Date Begun	Date Ended	Strategy	Evaluation Technique	Comments: Activities: Materials:
P-2-1	Attention						
P-2-1.1*	Understands and responds to the direction, "Look at me"			1,4,5,6,7	4		
P-2-1.2*	Sits when asked to do so			1,4,11	4		
P-2-1.3	Looks at a distant object when his attention is directed to it by parent or teacher			1,4,6	3		
P-2-1.4*	Looks at named object within an array			1,4,6,11	4		
P-2-1.5*	Looks at pictured object in an array as it is named (one word) by parent or teacher			1,4,6,11	4		
P-2-1.6*	Attends to longer verbalizations when they are accompanied by frequent descriptive actions			1,4,6	5		
P-2-1.7*	Attends to longer verbalizations not accompanied by descriptive actions			1,4,6	5		
P-2-2	Imitation						
P-2-2.1*	Imitates a familiar complex behavior (e.g., one involving a limb and an object) when given the signal, "(child's name), do this" and a model (e.g., throwing a ball, hitting one's head)			1,3,6	4		
P-2-2.2*	Imitates a novel complex behavior			1,3,6	4/11		

PROBLEM SOLVING - Year 2 - Page 8

Objective Number	General Objective	Pretest	Date Begun	Date Ended	Strategy	Evaluation Technique	Comments: Activities: Materials:
P-2-2.3*	Imitates a combination of a motor and speech or pre-speech sound when given the signal, "(child's name), do this"			1,3,6,5	4		
P-2-2.4*	Imitates gross motor behaviors reliably			1,3,5	4		
P-2-2.5*	Imitates fine motor behaviors reliably			1,3,5	4		
P-2-2.6*	Imitates speech reliably			1,3,5,6	4		
P-2-3	Recall						
P-2-3.1*	Repeats performance laughed at			1,6	5/3		
P-2-3.2	Names absent objects or persons			1,4,1■	3		
P-2-3.3	Finds buried object (i.e., under several layers)			1,4,1■	4		
P-2-3.4*	Goes to location named (e.g., "Go to your bedroom")			1,4,5,6	4		
P-2-3.5	Keeps goal in mind while shifting locations (e.g., going inside to get a cookie)			4			
P-2-3.6*	Assumes a familiar role (e.g., pretends to clean house)				4		
P-2-3.7	Finds object dumped from a container into hiding place			1,3,8	2		
P-2-3.8	Shows awareness of household routines			1,3,10	4		
				1,3,10,3	2		

PROBLEM SOLVING – Year 2 – Page 9

Objective Number	General Objective	Pretest	Date Begun	Date Ended	Strategy	Evaluation Technique	Comments: Activities: Materials:
P-2-3.9	Searches for an object which has "magically disappeared" (e.g., in hands-behind-back hiding game, he knows "it" must be somewhere)				1,3,5,10	5/4	
P-2-3.10*	Remembers and correctly completes two simple related directions (e.g., "Go to your room and bring back a book to me")				1,2,3,5	4	
P-2-4	Concept Formation						
P-2-4.1	Matches on the basis of color (e.g., puts red peg in red cylinder and blue peg in blue cylinder)				11	4	
P-2-4.2*	Indicates object named in response to "Where is ____?" (e.g., shows shoe or points to hair)				4,11	4	
P-2-4.3*	Names an object singly presented in response to "What's this?" or a person in response to "Who's that?"				4,11	4	
P-2-4.4*	Points to pictured object (within an array) in response to "Where is ____?" or "Show me the ____?"				4,11	4	
P-2-4.5*	Names a picture (singly presented) in response to "What's this?" or "Who's that?"				4,11	4	

PROBLEM SOLVING – Year 2 – Page 10

Objective Number	General Objective	Pretest	Date Begun	Date Ended	Strategy	Evaluation Technique	Comments: Activities: Materials:
P-2-4.6*	Names a picture (within an array) in response to "What's this?" or "Who's that?"			11,4	4		
P-2-4.7*	Selects an object named from among an array			4,11	4		
P-2-4.8*	Can answer questions in the form "What's ___ doing?"			3,4,11	4		
P-2-5	Grouping						
P-2-5.1	Recognizes an object misplaced in a homogeneous array (e.g., one car in a set of dolls)			3,4,11	4		
P-2-5.2	Groups objects by kind (e.g., cars and blocks)			3,4,11	4		
P-2-5.3*	Shares divisible items			1,3,5	3		
P-2-6	Sequencing						
P-2-6.1	Following a model, reproduces a sequence of two objects			3,5,6,7	4		
P-2-6.2	Identifies the "big" object			3,11	4		
P-2-6.3	Answers the question relative to one large and one small object, "Which one is big?"			3,1_	4		
P-2-7	Application of Principles						
P-2-7.1*	Uses gestures to make wants known			1,3,5 6	3/11		
P-2-7.2*	Uses speech to attract attention			1,3,5	3/11		
P-2-7.3	Solves a detour problem (e.g., goes around couch to get ball which rolled under it)			3,10	11		

PROBLEM SOLVING - Year 2 - Page 11

Objective Number	General Objective	Pretest	Date Begun	Date Ended	Strategy	Evaluation Technique	Comments: Activities: Materials:
P-2-7.4	Infers causes from observing effects (e.g., looks for person jiggling a mobile)			1,3,10	11		
P-2-7.5	Predicts effects from observing causes (e.g., looks to bottle to see dropped block fall into it)			1,3,10	11		
P-2-8	Creativity						
P-2-8.1	Recognizes when an object is novel			11	10		
P-2-8.2*	Engages in solitary play if secure			1	2/5		
P-2-8.3	Demonstrates a sense of humor			1,3,5	10		
P-2-8.4*	Explores the out-of-doors			1,3,5,6,7	2/5		
P-2-8.5*	Enjoys simple discrepancy (e.g., adult peeking from behind a new place)			9,1	2		
P-2-8.6	Uses own body rhythmically (i.e., as in dance)			1,3,4	2		
P-2-8.7	Uses objects in varied combination to form structures			1,3	2		
P-2-8.8	Uses own body representationally but concretely (i.e., to form a teapot)			1,3	2		
P-2-8.9	Attributes representation to his own drawings			1,3	8		

PROBLEM SOLVING – Year 2 – Page 12

Objective Number	General Objective	Pretest	Date Begun	Date Ended	Strategy	Evaluation Technique	Comments: Activities: Materials:

PROBLEM SOLVING – Year 3 – Page 13

Objective Number	General Objective	Pretest	Date Begun	Date Ended	Strategy	Evaluation Technique	Comments: Activities: Materials:
P-3-1	Attention						
P-3-1.1	Attends to teacher during lesson (e.g., head oriented toward teacher with minimal extraneous body motion)			3,5,6	5		
P-3-1.2	Looks at object(s) for increasing lengths of time (or number of instances) prior to reinforcement when teacher says, "look" and points			1	5		
P-3-1.3	Looks at moving object(s) for increasing lengths of time (or number of instances) prior to reinforcement (e.g. toy train, TV; etc.)			1	5		
P-3-1.4	Attends to sound(s) by looking in that direction for increasing lengths of time (or number of instances) prior to reinforcement			1	5		
P-3-1.5	Engages in play or games for increasing lengths of time (or number of tasks) prior to reinforcement (e.g., building blocks)			1	5		
P-3-1.6	Attends during group "lessons" or activities for 5-10 minutes with some adult prompting, e.g., adult says "look" "listen", etc., periodically			1,4,5,6,7	2/5		

PROBLEM SOLVING - Year 3 - Page 14

Objective Number	General Objective	Pretest	Date Begun	Date Ended	Strategy	Evaluation Technique	Comments: Activities: Materials:
P-3-2	Imitation						
P-3-2.1	Imitates a sequence of two simple motor behaviors involving own body (e.g., pat head, touch nose; or raise hand, clap hands)			1,2,3,6	4		
P-3-2.2	Imitates sequence of two behaviors--one verbal and one motor, e.g., say "hello" and sit down			1,2,3,5	4		
P-3-3	Recall						
P-3-3.1	Indicates object which was removed from a few other objects (e.g., present several objects on tray, then remove one)			3,4	4		
P-3-3.2	Indicates (names or points out) an object when the length of time between presentation and recollection is delayed, e.g., "Do you remember what you ate at snack?"			3,4,1D	4		
P-3-3.3	Recalls (by naming, imitation, etc.) specific labels, movements, locations, etc., from lesson when prompted by "Do you remember ___?"			3,4,1D	4		
P-3-4	Concept Formation						
	Color						
P-3-4.1	Points to correct primary colors when they are named			11	4		

PROBLEM SOLVING – Year 3 – Page 15

Objective Number	General Objective	Pretest	Date Begun	Date Ended	Strategy	Evaluation Technique	Comments:	Activities:	Materials:
P-3-4.2	Points to secondary colors when they are named			11	4				
P-3-4.3	Names primary colored objects when asked; "What color is this?"			5,11	4				
P-3-4.4	Solves match-to-sample problems (e.g., when shown different shapes, the child chooses those that are the same shape as the sample)			4,11	4				
P-3-4.5	Repeats shape names after a model			3,5	4				
	Size (big, little; small, large; long, short; thick, thin)								
P-3-4.6	Points to correct size when it is named			11	4				
	Position (e.g., top-bottom; inside-outside; up-down; above-below-between; front-back-side; on-in-under; near-far; right-left)								
P-3-4.7	Solves match-to-sample position problems (e.g., when shown different positions, child chooses those that are the same as the sample)			4,11	4				
P-3-4.8	Repeats position names after a model			3	4				

PROBLEM SOLVING - Year 3 - Page 16

Objective Number	General Objective	Pretest	Date Begun	Date Ended	Strategy	Evaluation Technique	Comments: Activities: Materials:
P-3-5	Grouping						
P-3-5.1	Groups objects which vary only in color				11,5,6,7	4	
P-3-5.2	Groups objects which vary only in shape				11,5,6,7	4	
P-3-5.3	Groups objects by other single dimensions, e.g., size, sex				11,5,6,7	4	
P-3-6	Sequencing						
P-3-6.1	Following a model, reproduces a sequence of three objects				2,3,5, 6,7	4	
P-3-6.2	Following a model, reproduces a sequence of more than three objects				2,3,5, 6,7	4	
P-3-7	Applications of Principles Solves problems involving deduction of a verbal label						
P-3-7.1	Labels object based on verbal information given (e.g., progressively tell child parts of an animal until child can correctly guess the animal)				4,3,1D	5/3	
P-3-7.2	Labels object based on visual information given (e.g., progressively show child parts of a picture until child can correctly guess the object)				4,3,1D	3/4	

PROBLEM SOLVING – Year 3 – Page 17

Objective Number	General Objective	Pretest	Date Begun	Date Ended	Strategy	Evaluation Technique	Comments: Activities: Materials:
P-3-8	Creativity						
P-3-8.1	Names objects and events even at times when labeling is not the planned objective			1,3,4	11		
P-3-8.2	Prefers novel objects				3		
P-3-8.3	Imitates various behaviors of others, even when imitation is not a planned objective			1,3,5, 6,7,8	11		
P-3-8.4	Uses newly learned behaviors in varied settings, e.g., sings songs at home that have been learned in school			1,3,5, 6,7	11		
P-3-8.5	Uses various objects for several purposes, e.g., uses blocks for buildings, for roads, as cars, as tables, etc.			1,3,5, 6,7	11		
P-3-8.6	Uses own body representatively and abstractly (e.g., to form a letter or to represent anger)			3,5,6,7	11		
P-3-8.7	Attributes representation to program music			1,3,5, 6,7	8		

PROBLEM SOLVING – Year 3 – Page 18

Objective Number	General Objective	Pretest	Date Begun	Date Ended	Strategy	Evaluation Technique	Comments: Activities: Materials:

PROBLEM SETTING – Year 4 – Page 19

Objective Number	General Objective	Pretest	Date Begun	Date Ended	Strategy	Evaluation Technique	Comments: Activities: Materials:
P-4-1	Attention						
P-4-1.1	Persists at most age appropriate tasks (e.g., puzzles, art activity) until completion and with minimal prompts from adults			1	5		
P-4-1.2	Attends for group activities of 10-15 minutes with little prompting from adults (e.g., story times, game circles)			1	5		
P-4-1.3	Switches attention appropriately during lessons or activities, e.g., moves from listening to watching, moves from watching one object to watching another object			1,4	3		
P-4-1.4	Attends to critical incidences in stories, e.g., in the picture story book "The Fat Cat", child notices that the cat gets larger on each page.			1,4	10		
P-4-1.5	Attends to selected aspects of a situation when requested to do so, e.g., looks at the longest stick when teacher requests			1,4	3		
P-4-2	Imitation						
P-4-2.1	Imitates a sequence of two behaviors involving limb and object (e.g., pound with hammer, throw ball, or kick ball, sit down on chair)			2,3	4		

PROBLEM SOLVING - Year 4 - Page 20

Objective Number	General Objective	Pretest	Date Begun	Date Ended	Strategy	Evaluation Technique	Comments: Activities: Materials:
P-4-2.2	Imitates a sequence of two behaviors where one involves a discrimination problem, e.g., touch the red triangle (from an array of red, blue & yellow triangles)			2,3	4		
P-4-2.3	Does repetitive imitation tasks, e.g., plays follow the leader			2,3,4	3/5		
P-4-2.4	Imitates a pictured event, e.g., sticks out tongue as child in picture is doing			3,4	4		
P-4-3	Recall						
P-4-3.1	Indicates which objects from many were shown previously (e.g., show child few objects, child hides eyes while teacher takes objects away, child names objects previously seen)			3,4,5	4		
P-4-3.2	Recites verbal sequences from day to day, e.g., phone number, alphabet, numbers 1-20, spelling of name			2,3,5	4		
P-4-3.3	Recalls by showing or telling a simple daily routine sequence, e.g., at lesson time, "First we find out seats, then we get out boxes, then we take out our felt shapes"			2,3,5 6,7	4		

PROBLEM SOLVING – Year 4 – Page 21

Objective Number	General Objective	Pretest	Date Begun	Date Ended	Strategy	Evaluation Technique	Comments:	Activities:	Materials:
P-4-3.4	Recalls by showing or telling sequences involving an auditory signal, e.g., teacher asks, "What do we do when the timer rings?", child answers, "Pick up"			3,8	4				
P-4-3.5	Recalls various incidental occurrences after a period of time, when questioned, e.g., "Do you remember what Mary was wearing today?" "Do you remember what the policeman had pinned on his shirt?"			1,3,4	4				
P-4-4	Concept Formation								
	Color								
P-4-4.1	Names secondary colored objects when asked, "what color is this?"			11,5	4				
	Shape, (circle, square, triangle, rectangle)				4				
P-4-4.2	Points to correct shape when named. Names shape when asked, "What shape is this?"			11,5	4				
	Size (big, little; small, large; long, short; thick, thin)								
P-4-4.3	Names sizes when asked, "What size is this?"			5,11	4				
	Sensory experiences (tastes, odor, texture, temperature)								

PROBLEM SOLVING – Year 4 – Page 22

Objective Number	General Objective	Pretest	Date Begun	Date Ended	Strategy	Evaluation Technique	Comments: Activities: Materials:
P-4-4.4	Solves match-to-sample problems involving a sensation (e.g., when presented with different textures, the child chooses those that are the same as the sample)			4,5,11	4		
P-4-4.5	Repeats names of sensations after a model			4,5,11	4		
P-4-4.6	Recognizes sensations when named (e.g., "Give me the rough paper")			4,5,11	4		
P-4-4.7	Names sensation when asked (e.g., "How does this taste?")			11	4		
	Properties of sound (pitch, intensity, tempo)						
P-4-4.8	Solves match-to-sample sound problems (e.g., when presented with different sounds child chooses ones that are the same as the sample)			4,11	4		
P-4-4.9	Repeats names of sound properties after a model			3	4		
	Position (top-bottom; inside-outside; up-down; above-below-between; front-back-side; on-in-under; near-far; right-left)						
P-4-4.10	Points to correct position when it is named (e.g., "Show me the top.")			6,11	4		

PROBLEM SOLVING – Year 4 – Page 23

Objective Number	General Objective	Pretest	Date Begun	Date Ended	Strategy	Evaluation Technique	Comments: Activities: Materials:
	Number						
P-4-4.11	Solves match-to-sample number problems (e.g., when shown pictured numerical representations, child chooses those that are the same as the sample)				4,11	4	
P-4-4.12	Repeats numbers after a model				3,5	4	
P-4-4.13	Identifies number symbols 1-10 when named				4,11	4/6	
P-4-4.14	Identifies by naming number symbols 1-10				11	4/6	
	Measurement (long-short; heavy-light; more-less; deep-shallow, etc.)						
P-4-4.15	Solves match-to-sample measurement problems (e.g., when shown a long line, child chooses other long lines)				4,11	4	
P-4-4.16	Repeats measurement names after a model				3,5	4	
P-4-4.17	Recognizes measurement names when they are named (e.g., "Show me the long pencil")				4,11	4	
P-4-4.18	Uses measurement names when asked for specific information (e.g., "Is the book heavy or light?"				11	4	
	Time (day-night; seasons, first, second, third, etc.)						

PROBLEM SOLVING – Year 4 – Page 24

Objective Number	General Objective	Pretest	Date Begun	Date Ended	Strategy	Evaluation Technique	Comments: Activities: Materials:
P-4-4.19	Solves match-to-sample problems involving time names (e.g., when shown different time depictions, child chooses ones that are the same as the sample)			4,11	4		
P-4-4.20	Repeats time name after model			3,5	4		
P-4-4.21	Points to correct time depictions when they are named (e.g., "Show me the winter picture.")			4,11	4/6		

PROBLEM SOLVING – Year 4 – Page 25

Objective Number	General Objective	Pretest	Date Begun	Date Ended	Strategy	Evaluation Technique	Comments:	Activities:	Materials:
P-4-5	Grouping								
P-4-5.1	Groups objects which vary in a single dimension (select dimensions from concepts recently learned, e.g., thick-thin)				4,11	4			
P-4-5.2	Groups objects based on quantitative concepts, e.g., groups sets of one and sets of two (where sets are depicted on cards) groups rods of same length into piles				4,11	4			
P-4-6	Sequencing								
P-4-6.1	Reproduces a sequence of objects from a display of sequenced objects				2,3	4			
P-4-6.2	Reproduces a sequence of objects from a pictured display				2,3,4,5	4			
P-4-6.3	Reproduces a sequence of up to five auditory remarks, e.g., numbers, cords				2,3,4,5	4			
P-4-6.4	Labels sequences of objects or depictions from left to right				2,3,5	4			
P-4-6.5	Says all alphabet letters in sequence				2,3,5	4			
P-4-6.6	Counts by rote in correct sequence up to 10				2,3,5	4			
P-4-6.7	Correctly counts objects and events in time up to 10				2,3,4,5	4			

PROBLEM SOLVING – Year 4 – Page 26

Objective Number	General Objective	Pretest	Date Begun	Date Ended	Strategy	Evaluation Technique	Comments: Activities: Materials:
P-4-7	Applications of Principles						
P-4-7.1	Solves problems involving cause-effect relationships (e.g., when shown a picture of a balloon being popped by a pin, the child selects a picture of a deflated balloon as the result)			1,3,10,8	4		
P-4-7.2	Solves problems involving memory of a fact, e.g., peanut is placed under one of three cups and cups are moved; child is asked to find the peanut.			1,3,4,10	6,4		
P-4-7.3	Solves problems using inductive strategies for sequencing, seriating and grouping, e.g., solves problems by inducing an effective sequencing or sorting strategy, e.g., when presented with 10 cards to sort into two boxes, (one box has one dowel rod protruding from it; the other has two dowel rods protruding from it; the cards have one or two holes in them); solves problems by inducing an effective "rule" for seriating (e.g., correctly stacks a graduate stacking toy)			1,3,4,10	8		

PROBLEM SOLVING – Year 4 – Page 27

Objective Number	General Objective	Pretest	Date Begun	Date Ended	Strategy	Evaluation Technique	Comments: Activities: Materials:
P-4-8	Creativity						
P-4-8.1	Interacts spontaneously with materials and activities going on in room				1,3,4	11	
P-4-8.2	Recognizes and interacts with new equipment and activities in the room				1,3,4	3	
P-4-8.3	Asks questions concerning labels of new objects and events				1,3,4	3	
P-4-8.4	Shows fluency in both verbal and non-verbal tasks, e.g., names many objects in a certain setting even though the child is not there (e.g., "What toys are in your bedroom?")					3	
P-4-8.5	Experiments with color, line, form and space during art and craft activities, e.g., is not restricted by doing only what has been demonstrated by another				1,3	3	

PROBLEM SOLVING – Year 4 – Page 28

Objective Number	General Objective	Pretest	Date Begun	Date Ended	Strategy	Evaluation Technique	Comments: Activities: Materials:

PROBLEM SOLVING – Year 5 – Page 29

Objective Number	General Objective	Pretest	Date Begun	Date Ended	Strategy	Evaluation Technique	Comments: Activities: Materials:
P-5-1	Attention						
P-5-1.1	Persists at tasks in spite of distracting events (e.g., interruptions by sounds or persons)				1	11/5	
P-5-1.2	Attends to progressively more abstract concepts in situations when appropriate, e.g., after seeing the story Hansel and Gretel and asked to tell about the children, child makes some responses concerning how the children might have felt (frightened, hungry, etc.)				1	11	
P-5-1.3	Attends to details of various situations when requested, e.g., when asked to name all the items on the blackboard, when asked to name all the sounds one can hear for 2 minutes				1,4	4	
P-5-1.4	Attends during group activities 20-25 minutes long				1	5	
P-5-2	Imitation						
P-5-2.1	Imitates a sequence of three behaviors involving own body, (e.g., pat head, touch nose, then clap hands; or touch toes, raise arms, then pull ears)				2,3,6	4	

PROBLEM SOLVING – Year 5 – Page 30

Objective Number	General Objective	Pretest	Date Begun	Date Ended	Strategy	Evaluation Technique	Comments: Activities: Materials:
P-5-2.2	Imitates a sequence of three behaviors involving own body (raise hand, close eyes) and involving an object (kick ball, pick up book)			2,3,6, 6,7	4		
P-5-2.3	Imitates a sequence of 3 pictured events				4		
P-5-2.4	Imitates patterns of auditory stimuli, e.g., beats drum first hard, then softly; sings word "Hello" with the first syllable on a high note, the second on a low note			2,3,5, 6,7	4		
P-5-2.5	Imitates procedures of up to four steps, e.g., teacher demonstrates how to make a holiday greeting card and child imitates			2,3,5, 6,7	4		
P-5-3	Recall						
P-5-3.1	Arranges objects to match original sequence viewed (e.g., place three toys in a row, have child look, then ask child to reproduce the original sequence from memory)			2,3,4	4		
P-5-3.2	Recites progressively more verbal information about self, e.g., tells address, name of school, weight			1,3	3		

PROBLEM SOLVING - Year 5 - Page 31

Objective Number	General Objective	Pretest	Date Begun	Date Ended	Strategy	Evaluation Technique	Comments:	Activities:	Materials:
P-5-3.3	Retells stories and events, remembering critical incidents				1,3,4	4/5			
P-5-3.4	Recalls various incidental abstract and complex occurrences after a period of time, e.g., after visiting a dairy, child tells or shows how the cows are milked (complex) or tells how happy everyone was to eat ice cream on such a hot day (abstract)				1,3,4,10	6/3			
P-5-3.5	Recites longer verbal sequences, e.g., nos. 1-50, 1-100				1,2	3			
P-5-4	Concept Formation								
P-5-4.1	Uses color names when asked to describe objects				10,11	4			
P-5-4.2	Recognizes written color names				11	4/6			
P-5-4.3	Uses shape names when asked to describe objects				10,11	4			
P-5-4.4	States relevant characteristics of shapes (e.g., "A square has four sides")				11,3,5	4			
P-5-4.5	Recognizes written shape names				11	4/6			
P-5-4.6	Uses size words when asked to describe objects				10,11,3	4			
P-5-4.7	Recognizes written size words				11	4/6			
P-5-4.8	Uses sensation names when asked to describe objects or events (e.g., "Tell me about your jello.")				3,10,11	4			

PROBLEM SOLVING – Year 5 – Page 32

Objective Number	General Objective	Pretest	Date Begun	Date Ended	Strategy	Evaluation Technique	Comments: Activities: Materials:
P-5-4.9	Recognizes written sensation names			11	4/6		
P-5-4.10	Recognizes sound properties when they are named (e.g., "Tell me when you hear a high sound")			11	4/6		
P-5-4.11	Uses sound labels when asked to describe auditory experiences			3,10,11	4		
P-5-4.12	Uses position names when asked "Where is the object?"			3,10,11	4		
P-5-4.13	Uses position names when asked to describe situations			3,10,11	4		
P-5-4.14	Recognizes written position names			11	4/6		
P-5-4.15	Points to correct number when it is names, 10-20			3,11	4/6		
P-5-4.16	Names number when asked, "What number is this?" 10-20			3,11	4/6		
P-5-4.17	Uses number names when asked "How many (objects) are here?" (objects up to ten)			3,11	4		
P-5-4.18	Uses number names when asked to describe situations			3,10,11	4		
P-5-4.19	Identifies number groups as "smaller" than ___ or "larger" than ___			11	4		
P-5-4.20	Labels number groups as "smaller or larger than ___."			11	4		
P-5-4.21	Identifies group that has "more" than ___.			11	4		

PROBLEM SOLVING - Year 5 - Page 33

Objective Number	General Objective	Pretest	Date Begun	Date Ended	Strategy	Evaluation Technique	Comments:	Activities:	Materials:
P-5-4.22	Labels groups as having "more or less than ___."				11	4			
P-5-4.23	Adds objects to a group when asked to make that group "larger"				3,11	4			
P-5-4.24	Takes away objects from a group when asked to make that group "smaller"				3,11	4			
P-5-4.25	Uses measurement names when asked to describe a situation				3,10,11	4			
P-5-4.26	Recognizes written measurement names				11	4/6			
P-5-4.27	Uses speed names when asked to describe a situation				3,10,11	4			
P-5-4.28	Recognizes written speed names				11	4/6			
P-5-4.29	Uses time names when asked specific questions (e.g., "Where is Mary in the line")				3,10,11	4			
P-5-4.30	Uses time names when asked to describe situations				3,10,11	4			
P-5-4.31	Recognizes written time names				11	4/6			
	Language Arts Concepts								
P-5-4.32	Identifies correct letters when hears specific sound symbols				11	3/4/6			
P-5-4.33	Responds with phonetic sounds when shown specific sound symbols				11	3/4/6			
P-5-4.34	Names lower case letters				11	3/4			
P-5-4.35	Names upper case letters				11	3/4			
P-5-4.36	After reading a word, identifies its meaning by answering a question, pointing to a picture, etc.				3,10,11	4			

PROBLEM SOLVING – Year 5 – Page 34

Objective Number	General Objective	Pretest	Date Begun	Date Ended	Strategy	Evaluation Technique	Comments: Activities: Materials:
P-5-4.37	Reads sentence and indicates its meaning			11,10,3	4		
P-5-5	Grouping						
P-5-5.1	Groups objects which vary in 2 dimensions, e.g., groups objects which vary in color and shape only (red squares, red circles, blue squares, blue circles); Groups objects which vary in shape and size only (large circles, small circles, large triangles, small triangles); Groups objects which vary in size and color only (large red circles, small red circles, large green circles, small green circles)			2,3,11	4		
P-5-5.2	Groups objects or events based on class membership, e.g., groups objects which belong to the class of animals. Groups objects which belong to the class of food. Groups objects which belong to the class of clothing. Groups objects which belong to the class of furniture.			5,3,11	4		

PROBLEM SOLVING – Year 5 – Page 35

Objective Number	General Objective	Pretest	Date Begun	Date Ended	Strategy	Evaluation Technique	Comments: Activities: Materials:
P-5-5.3	Groups objects or events by smaller class membership, e.g., groups objects which belong to the class of animal by species, wild, domestic, etc. Groups objects which belong to the class of food by basic food groups (e.g., fruits, vegetables, meats). Groups objects which belong to the class of furniture of location in the house (e.g., kitchen, bedroom, porch). Groups sounds which belong to classes of animals, e.g., cats, birds.			5,3,11	4		
P-5-5.4	Groups objects or words on the basis of common use or function. Groups objects that are a form of trans-portation (e.g., car, boat, train). Groups objects that are used for protection against weather (e.g., coats, mittens, scarfs). Groups objects that are edible (e.g., orange, bread)			3,5,11	4		

PROBLEM SOLVING – Year 5 – Page 36

Objective Number	General Objective	Pretest	Date Begun	Date Ended	Strategy	Evaluation Technique	Comments: Activities: Materials:
P-5-6	Sequencing						
P-5-6.1	Orders objects on a basis of degree of specific physical characteristics; Puts pictured objects in order of increasing degree of quality (e.g., largeness); Puts pictured objects in order of decreasing degree of quality (e.g., redness)			2,3,5,11	4		
P-5-6.2	"Sounds out" words of three sound units in correct sequence			2,3,7	4		
P-5-6.3	Blends up to three sound units correctly into a word			2,3	3/4		
P-5-6.4	Reads sentences in correct sequence			2,3	4		
P-5-6.5	Correctly counts objects and events in time up to 20			2,3,6,5	4		
P-5-7	Applications of Principles						
P-5-7.1	Solves problems involving deduction of a sequence, e.g., solves problems by completing a given sequence (e.g., boy rolling big snowball, stacking smaller snowball on first one, child selects completed snowman); Solves problems by selecting missing item of a sequence (e.g., girl building tower of blocks, empty space, blocks scattered on floor, child selects picture of tower being kicked)						

PROBLEM SOLVING – Year 5 – Page 37

Objective Number	General Objective	Pretest	Date Begun	Date Ended	Strategy	Evaluation Technique	Comments: Activities: Materials:
P-5-7.2	Solves problems involving the application of facts and principles to specific situations, e.g., Solves problems involving conservation of mass, length, weight and volume by making statements of some, more or less; Solves problems involving sorting and sequencing on the basis of a previously stated rule (e.g., put your beads so they are red, blue, red, blue); Solves problems involving "if--then" statements (e.g., if you see a red light, then you ___ your car); Solves problems involving "if--then" statements in which the child makes a verbal response based on the information given (e.g., if Tom has a red bike, then is this Tom's bike?--point to a green bike)			2,3,10,8	4		
P-5-7.3	Solves problems involving prediction when only partial solutions are given, e.g., Predicts completion of a sequence of concrete objects ("What comes next?"); Predicts completion of a pictured or drawn sequence			2,3,10,8	2/4		

PROBLEM SOLVING – Year 5 – Page 38

Objective Number	General Objective	Pretest	Date Begun	Date Ended	Strategy	Evaluation Technique	Comments: Activities: Materials:
	of objects ("what comes next?"); Indicates (names or points out) an object when only relevant characteristics are given (e.g., "what shape has three sides and three points?")						
P-5-7.4	Solves simple problems involving recall of a rule, e.g., child correctly completes counting tasks when asked to: Count to a specific number; Counts from a specific number; Counts from a specific number to a specific number			2,3,11	4/6		
P-5-7.5	Solves problems involving recall of more than one procedure, e.g., Counts objects and/or events in time and then depicts them by choosing a number; Demonstrates "plussing" by cumulatively adding (counting) two sets of objects and then chooses or writes the correct number			2,3,10,11	1/4		
P-5-7.6	Answers factual questions based on sentences child has read			3,4,10	4/6		

PROBLEM SOLVING – Year 5 – Page 39

Objective Number	General Objective	Pretest	Date Begun	Date Ended	Strategy	Evaluation Technique	Comments: Activities: Materials:
P-5-7.7	Solves problems by verbalizing an effective sequencing or sorting strategy (e.g., when given a sorting box and various geometric shapes, child says "this one (ball) goes in here (points to circle) because it is round.")				1,3,10,8	1/3	
P-5-7.8	Solves problems involving a combination of grouping on the basis of similarities (comparison) and sorting on the basis of differentiation (e.g., when shown four pictures in which one is different, child states which one is different).				1,3,10,8	4	
P-5-7.9	Answers questions concerning extra added features of an object or features that are missing (e.g., "What's funny about this?" While showing picture of table with a missing leg).				3,4,5, 6,7	4	
P-5-7.10	Discusses how two objects are alike or different (e.g., "How are a football and baseball alike?")				3,4,5, 5,7,10	1/3	

PROBLEM SOLVING - Year 5 - Page 40

Objective Number	General Objective	Pretest	Date Begun	Date Ended	Strategy	Evaluation Technique	Comments: Activities: Materials:
P-5-7.11	Makes inferences as to probable 'antecedent' event for a specific consequential event. (e.g., When shown a photo of a burned cake in an oven, child responds to the question, "Why is the cake burned?")			2,3,4,11	3		
P-5-7.12	Makes statements about how to evaluate the correctness of a possible solution when attempting to solve simple problems (e.g., when playing feely-meely and looking for a cotton ball, the child responds to the question, "How do you know it's a cotton ball?" ans. "It feels soft.")			3,4	2/3		
P-5-8	Creativity						
P-5-8.1	Shows flexibility in problem solving; Chooses a factual approach to a problem rather than one that is not factual but has popular support (e.g., even though sufficient adults may say that a piece of metal will float, the child chooses to test it in water)			3,11	3		

PROBLEM SOLVING – Year 5 – Page 41

Objective Number	General Objective	Pretest	Date Begun	Date Ended	Strategy	Evaluation Technique	Comments:	Activities:	Materials:
P-5-8.2	Groups objects in a variety of categories, (e.g., the child responds to "How many things can you tell me about a block?")			3,10,8	3				
P-5-8.3	Changes technique while solving a problem (e.g., first putting a puzzle together using matching colors as cues, then finishing it by using shape of puzzle piece as cue).			2,3,4,10	3				
P-5-8.4	Predicts consequences to "fantasy" situations, (e.g., "What would you do if you lived at the South Pole?")			3,4,8	3				
P-5-8.5	Makes acceptable suggestions when several others have already been made, (e.g., the teacher says, "We are thinking of naming our turtle 'Boxer,' 'Gus,' or 'Spots.' Do you have any suggestions?")			3,10	8				

PROBLEM SOLVING – Year 5 – Page 42

Objective Number	General Objective	Pretest	Date Begun	Date Ended	Strategy	Evaluation Technique	Comments:	Activities:	Materials:

Index

About the Authors

John T. Neisworth, Ph.D., is Professor of Special Education at The Pennsylvania State University. His research and articles have appeared in numerous journals. He is author or coauthor of six widely used textbooks in special and early education. Dr. Neisworth is codirector of the HICOMP Early Intervention Project, a federally funded demonstration and dissemination project in early education for the handicapped; consulting editor for several journals, and a vigorous proponent of noncategorical approaches to the treatment of children with educational problems.

Sara J. Willoughby-Herb, Ph.D., is Associate Professor of Early Education at Clarion State College, Pennsylvania. Her research and publications focus on the developmental integration of handicapped and nonhandicapped youngsters. Dr. Willoughby-Herb is coauthor of and has contributed chapters to several prominent textbooks in special education and early education.

Stephen J. Bagnato, D.Ed., is a developmental school psychologist and Assistant Professor of School Psychology at the University of Maryland. Dr. Bagnato formerly served as Assistant Professor of School Psychology, instructor in special education, and psychological supervisor in the CEDAR Psychoeducational Child Diagnostic Clinic, The Pennsylvania State University. He also has functioned as a school psychologist and consultant for the HICOMP Project and Hershey Medical Center's Neonatal Intensive Care Unit. He has published several articles and applied material for school psychologists and early childhood special educators concerning the developmental assessment and individualized programming of handicapped infants and preschoolers.

Carol A. Cartwright, Ph.D., is Professor of Education in Early Childhood and Special Education at The Pennsylvania State University. Professor Cartwright has taught nonhandicapped and handicapped young children in a variety of special and mainstreamed settings. She has written extensively for regular classroom teachers to prepare them to integrate handicapped children in regular classroom settings. Currently, she is the codirector of the HICOMP Project.

Karen W. Laub, Ph.D., is a member of the Home Economics faculty and coordinator of the Child Development Laboratory of the Center for Family Studies at the Arizona State University. She is the author of articles on infant development and on the early identification of developmental problems. She is consulting editor for the *Family Coordinator* and for the *Journal of the Association for the Care of Children in Hospitals*.

METHODS FOR LEARNING DISORDERS

METHODS FOR LEARNING DISORDERS

PATRICIA I. MYERS

Our Lady of the Lake College
San Antonio, Texas

DONALD D. HAMMILL

Temple University
Philadelphia, Pennsylvania

JOHN WILEY & SONS, INC.

NEW YORK · LONDON · SYDNEY · TORONTO

Library of Congress Catalogue Card Number: 73-93484

SBN 471 62750 X

Printed in the United States of America

PREFACE

Special education in America has long emphasized and attempted to implement a medical model in its approach to the education of exceptional children. Consequently, self-contained classes for medically defined groups of children may be found in the majority of the nation's school districts. These classes provide for children who are mentally retarded, blind, deaf, or crippled; now impetus is being directed toward the establishment of classes for children who are designated as having "brain damage," "neurological impairment," or "minimal brain dysfunction," merely additional medical classifications.

With this group more than any other, the question is whether we are dealing primarily with a medical or an educational problem. If the problem is essentially medical, our approach to these children initially should be preventative and curative, and medical procedures such as drug therapy or even surgery may be applicable. If, however, the problem is primarily educational, the solution may be found in the creation of an instructional program for the child which is based upon his peculiar needs as a learner and which provides him with the skills necessary for environmental adaptation and interaction. Unfortunately, it is not easy to draw the line between the medical and educational aspects of children's learning difficulties. Some children, a distinct minority, may respond well to medical treatment and may require little, if any, special educational attention. The majority, however, do not require medical intervention and, in fact, present either no concrete evidence or at best only presumptive evidence of a medical problem in terms of brain disorders.

The medical orientation ultimately rests upon the assumption that something is wrong with the child. It emphasizes his liabilities and shortcomings, ignores his assets and strengths, and encourages grouping children on the basis of their disabilities. An alternative approach, advocated by the authors, views the so-called brain-damaged child within a behavioral frame of reference and describes him as a learner with a difference. The point is not that he learns poorly but that he learns differently. A behavioral description of his learning style dictates the selection of appropriate instructional techniques and materials as no medical model can.

One should not assume from the tremendous current interest in specific learning disorders that children with these problems have gone unrecognized in American education. Actually children with specific learning disorders have been identified for some time. Historically, the earliest investigators such as Hinshelwood and Orton were concerned with dyslexia or specific reading disabilities. Shortly thereafter, concern for children with reading disabilities was reflected in the remedial techniques set forth by Gillingham and Stillman and Fernald. During the 1950s and early 1960s, McGinnis and Barry developed instructional systems that were concerned with problems of speech and language (congenital aphasia, dysphasia, aphasoid behavior). The 1960s have seen an emphasis upon systems that seek to develop or remediate perceptual-motor processes in children. These systems have come into wide use primarily due to the contributions of Strauss and Lehtinen, Kephart, Cruickshank, Getman, Barsch, Frostig and Horne, and Delacato.

In the past, the identification, assessment, and remediation of one particular learning disability, for example, dyslexia, was undertaken as if it were an independent entity. Relationships among learning problems, regardless of genesis, were not generally recognized. Each problem area was tightly compartmentalized, and specialists tended to go their separate ways. We have seen, therefore, the rise of remedial reading, language pathology, and educational therapy and the development of specialized training programs within noneducational disciplines such as optometry, occupational therapy, and school psychology. Specialists in each of these areas have marked off some special province within the child's learning to which they direct their diagnostic and therapeutic attention. As a result the optometrist has become a specialist in visual-motor problems and generally ignores the often critical influence of audition. On the other hand, the language pathologist may direct himself toward only the child's oral language to the detriment of perceptual-motor processes.

Recent years have witnessed a "growing together" or a recognition of commonality among the disabilities. Reasons for the rapprochement may be (1) the development of theoretical frames of reference to which all the learning disabilities can be related (e.g., the models offered by Osgood, Guilford, and Skinner); (2) the availability and perfection of assessment techniques (e.g., the Illinois Test of Psycholinguistic Abilities, the Marianne Frostig Developmental Test of Visual Perception, and the Purdue Perceptual-Motor Survey) which make possible the demonstration of relationships among disabilities; and (3) the accumulation of research data which point to the etiological and behavioral similarities among the various types of learning disordered children.

Although differences of opinion among professionals still exist on many subjects, there is sufficient agreement relative to functional definitions and useful remedial approaches to permit the development of a new area of interest in special education. The area of specific learning disorders among children, therefore, is experiencing rapid development at the present time. The growth is evidenced by several observable factors.

1. An increase is noted in the number of articles and books published which pertain to children variously labeled as exhibiting learning disability, language disorder, neurological impairment, brain injury, or minimal cerebral dysfunction.

2. An active parent-professional national organization, the Association for Children with Learning Disabilities, has been established.

3. The Division for Children with Learning Disabilities was formed in 1967 within the Council for Exceptional Children, a branch of the National Education Association.

4. An increasing number of state departments of public instruction or state legislatures fund local programs for learning disabled children. Such action has stimulated school districts to initiate services, usually in the form of special classes, resource rooms, or tutoring in regular classes, which take their place in a special education framework along with the services provided for mentally retarded, emotionally and socially disturbed, speech handicapped, physically disabled, and sensory impaired children.

5. College courses and teacher education programs specifically in the learning disabilities area are being established; these reflect the availability of students seeking preparation in this new field. The federal government has been prompt in its support of both program development and financial assistance to students.

Cognizant of these recent developments in the field of learning disabilities, we prepared this book with four major purposes in mind.

To present a theoretical frame of reference within which to view the learning disorders of children. Without a common frame of reference within which individual learning disabilities can be related, the field fragments into disorders of various specialized achievement or skill areas. Trained under such conditions, instructional personnel tend to become proficient in the evaluation and treatment of reading, perceptual-motor problems, and language disorders, to mention a few; but such people often fail to recognize the perceptual, behavioral, and educational relationships among learning disorders. And yet a more broadly based picture of the child's learning is of utmost importance to personnel who are responsible for the evaluation of children with learning disorders. A frame of reference permits the examiner to assess systematically the behavior of children who exhibit learning disorders and allows the teacher to plan a systematic and appropriate program of instruction.

To provide a general textbook in methods of teaching learning disabled children. A great variety of teaching methods and techniques are available in the area of learning disabilities, and classroom teachers as well as those in training need to be oriented in these areas of methodology. Since learning disabled children are likely to be more than just reading disabled, languaged disordered, or poorly integrated motorically, their teachers must be familiar with a wide spectrum of instructional systems developed for use with specific learning disabilities. The success of a teacher who is aware of only one area of disability and/or remediation will be hampered seriously. As a result, one of our purposes in writing the book is to orient students and other personnel to a variety of methodological systems and to provide them with references for the investigation of primary sources.

To prepare an integrated, concise overview of learning disorders for use by professional personnel. In the last few years, several excellent books have been published in the area of learning disability. Some, like the book edited by Frierson and Barbe, are critically selected collections of relevant articles, while other authors, such as Johnson and Myklebust and Barsch, present their unique orientations to the field. This book is neither an anthology nor a presentation of a particular methodological viewpoint. Rather, we advocate a specific theoretical frame of reference which encompasses both evaluation and instructional techniques, the latter being drawn from the work of many authors. Such a work is seen as a potentially valuable reference for teachers, school psychologists, counselors, and therapists who are involved in the assessment and/or remediation of learning disorders.

To suggest a descriptive orientation for assessment and remediation of learning disorders. Because we find the medical model of limited value in the educational sphere, our discussion of learning disabled children and methods suitable for them is presented without special concern toward etiological matters. A behavioral orientation to the field is suggested rather than a medical or psychological one.

The book was conceived and written as an entity. We feel, therefore, that the chapters of the book are complementary and necessary to one another. The teacher needs the first chapter in order to understand the concepts that underlie and provide the basis for remediation; persons concerned with evaluation can use the later chapters to acquaint themselves with available programs and to guide them in making recommendations.

The chapter dealing with a concept of learning disorders is not an exhaustive survey of the literature relative to etiology, research, and characteristics. It is instead a distillation of the authors' viewpoints regarding these topics and is substantiated by experience and acquaintance with the literature. References to the literature are made throughout, and after the reader has acquired the orientation, he should refer to the cited sources and read in detail the primary references. The second chapter presents the comprehensive evaluation of the learning disabled child, and is intended as a guide for assessment. The information provides both the diagnostician and the teacher with knowledge of the kinds of data which should be gathered on each child as well as the rationale for its interpretation. It is not expected that only one professional person will be competent in all areas required for adequate assessment.

In order to eliminate confusion at the onset, the authors do not distinguish between "methods," and "techniques" and as a result frequently use the terms interchangeably. A method is considered a complete system for teaching specific school subjects or skills. A technique, on the other hand, is defined as a procedure or set of procedures aimed at increasing efficiency in some particular skill area whether it be visual-motor perception, motor coordination, auditory discrimination, or other skills. Teachers should be able, using the theoretical framework and the description of the methods, to select an appropriate instructional approach. However, we wish to emphasize that the methods are only summarized and cannot be implemented from the information presented. After selecting a particular approach, the teacher must refer to and study carefully the primary sources.

For the convenience of the reader, a glossary is provided in the appendix. Because many terms used in the book either may be unfamiliar or may have various connotations, we have defined them so that the reader will know how the words are used.

December 1969

Patricia I. Myers
Donald D. Hammill

CONTENTS

xi

METHODS FOR LEARNING DISORDERS

CHAPTER I

A CONCEPT OF SPECIFIC LEARNING DISORDERS

Children with learning disorders constitute a relatively recent addition to special education. Because interest in these children has developed so rapidly in the last decade, both experienced educators and teachers in training may be confused about the limits of the new classification and its connection with other established special education program areas such as those for children with mental retardation, speech and reading difficulty, emotional disturbance, and orthopedic handicaps. This chapter provides a *basic* knowledge of learning disorder and is not intended as a comprehensive presentation. Comprehensive discussions of various topics considered in the chapter are available and are cited throughout the text. Specifically, the chapter aims to familiarize readers with (1) a functional definition of learning disorder, (2) the probable causes of learning disorders, and (3) the characteristics of children with learning disorders.

1

A Definition

In the special education literature, the word *exceptional* is used to describe children who because of their psychological-physical-educational problems require for their instruction special methods and specially trained teachers. Occasionally, and erroneously, exceptional is used as a synonym for *specific learning disabled*. The definitions of the two terms are related, but they are not equivalent. Learning disability is used to describe a specific type of exceptional child; it is not a generic term for all children who have learning problems in school.

Individuals who attempt to find or derive a precise, comprehensive definition of learning disorder are likely to meet with much difficulty partly due to problems related to both taxonomy and semantics. In a paper prepared for the Southern Regional Education Board, McDonald (1967, p. 1) reports the results of a questionnaire to which thirty-five educators and psychologists who work in the general area of learning disorders gave "twenty-two terms which one or more of them use as an exact synonym for the title 'Children with Learning Disorders.'" The collection of terms reflects a wide range of orientations, for example: (1) educational—"remedial education," "educationally handicapped"; (2) medical—"brain injured," "minimal brain dysfunction"; and (3) psycholinguistic—"language disorders," "psycholinguistic disabilities." Some are general terms such as "psychoneurological disorders" and "learning disabilities"; others narrow down to specialized achievement areas such as "problem readers" and "reading disability."

An operational definition is required which is both broad enough to include the diverse educational problems exhibited by children with learning disorders and sufficiently definitive that such a child can be distinguished from other exceptional children. Functional definitions of specific learning disability have appeared with some frequency in the recent special education literature; but the ones reported by Bateman (1964, 1965a, 1965b, 1965c) and Kirk and Bateman (1962) seem well suited to the purpose of a book devoted to methodology because their concepts (1) are educationally oriented, (2) emphasize language behavior, and (3) already are accepted widely by many educators and psychologists.

According to Bateman (1965a, p. 220), children who have specific learning disabilities are those who . . .

1. Manifest an educationally significant discrepancy between their estimated intellectual potential and actual level of performance . . .

2. related to basic disorders in the learning processes . . .

3. which may or may not be accompanied by demonstrable central nervous system dysfunction, and . . .

4. which are not secondary to generalized mental retardation, educational or cultural deprivation, severe emotional disturbance, or sensory loss.

Readers with a background in speech pathology or remedial reading will recognize some similarity between the definition of specific learning disorders and most definitions of dysphasia and dyslexia. Children who demonstrate symptoms characteristic of these latter conditions satisfy every element in Bateman's definition and may be considered learning disabled. The authors maintain that children who evidence perceptual difficulty also are included in the definition.

The definition is in basic agreement with others on such fundamental points as:

1. The principle of disparity.

2. The role of demonstrable central nervous system dysfunction in making educational evaluations.

3. The emphasis upon basic disorder of the learning process.

4. The children excluded by the definition.

THE PRINCIPLE OF DISPARITY

The key word in definitions of learning disability is discrepancy. Even though Rappaport (1966) has referred to "insufficiencies," Gallagher (1966) to "imbalances," and Ashlock and Stephen (1966) to "gaps," most definitions seem to adhere to the principle of disparity. The principle implies that the learning disabled child can be recognized by the presence of a meaningful difference between what he is capable of doing and what he actually is accomplishing, that is, a marked underachievement in school-related activities.

In determining an educationally significant discrepancy, there are apparently no rigid, all-encompassing rules or formulas to follow. With reference to reading, however, children in the first four grades who read at a level one to one and one-half years below that which is expected might be considered candidates for special instruction; for upper-grade pupils, a two or more year lag between actual and expected achievement probably would be a more appropriate criterion. A similar criterion may be employed to determine significant educational deficits relative to arithmetic, spelling, and writing.

Observation of lagging academic performance can be quantified through use of suitable standardized achievement tests. Appropriate tests are readily available; these include the Stanford Achievement Test, the

Metropolitan Achievement Test, the California Achievement Test, and the Sequential Test of Educational Progress, which can be used to ascertain a child's achievement age for specific academic subjects. Yet poor school marks and low achievement scores in themselves are not indicative of specific learning disabilities in children. To satisfy the definition of learning disorder, a child's observed achievement level must be *unexpectedly* low when compared with his mental ability and other factors.

Intelligence must be estimated quantitatively, and such estimations may be accomplished to some extent by evaluation of the pupil's performance on several tests of mental ability, including both verbal and non-verbal measures. Of primary importance would be the results of such tests as the Wechsler (1949, 1955, 1967) scales for school-aged children, adults, and preschool-aged children and the Stanford-Binet Intelligence Scale (Terman & Merrill, 1960), as well as tests of specific cognitive and perceptive abilities. Comprehensive discussions of suitable measures and specific educational diagnostic procedures are presented in Chapter II.

THE ROLE OF DEMONSTRABLE CENTRAL NERVOUS SYSTEM
DYSFUNCTION IN MAKING EDUCATIONAL EVALUATIONS

Frequently, a strong case is made in support of the hypothesis that specific learning disabilities are observable symptoms of underlying neurologic disorganization (Clements, 1966). Most researchers agree that a variety of central nervous system (CNS) impairments appear to be associated with specific learning disability and have noted that groups of learning disabled children present an unusually high incidence of positive neurological signs. But the degree to which these signs are causative of, or merely associative with, learning disability has yet to be fully demonstrated. Nevertheless, many writers have viewed the dyslexias (Gordon, 1965; Johnson & Myklebust, 1965; Bryant, 1964; Orton, 1937), the dysphasias (Eisenson, 1960; Karlin, 1960; West, 1960; Barry, 1961; Taylor, 1958; Myklebust, 1955), and the dysgraphias (Myklebust, 1965) as the result of CNS dysfunction.

However, many pupils who demonstrate one or another of the aforementioned learning disorders have undergone neurological evaluations with results that do not support the supposition of CNS impairment. Whether due to the subtle nature of the hypothesized organic deviations or due to the weakness of present-day medical diagnostic techniques, lack of positive neurological evidence is not an uncommon occurrence among children who manifest learning disorders.

Consequently, Bateman and others have chosen wisely *not to include* demonstrable CNS dysfunction as an essential criterion for the diagnosis and instruction of learning disabled children. Kleffner (1964), Calvert, Ceriotti, and Geile (1966), and McGinnis, Kleffner, and Goldstein (1956) also have eliminated positive neurological findings as criteria necessary for determining dysphasia.

Occasionally, a child who has developed language processes normally will lose some or all of these established abilities as a result of brain injury. Except in such rare cases as these, however, it is quite difficult to determine with any degree of confidence the definite primary etiology for poor reading, arithmetic, or speech performance of any given child. A reading disabled child may demonstrate, for example, letter and word substitutions and omissions; but these deviations are symptomatic of the reading problem and are not the cause of the difficulty.

For the teacher or the clinician who is not engaged in systematic research, the question as to whether these children are brain damaged is of secondary importance because the teacher is concerned with the symptoms manifested by the children. Whether specific learning disorders are symptoms which result from brain injury or developmental delay will not essentially alter the methods of teaching the child. For example, the child who has a reading disorder seemingly related to impaired visual-motor processes and marked by inadequate left-right orientation, reversals, and substitutions may benefit from instructional techniques such as those described by Fernald. The teacher who has demonstrated to his satisfaction that the child can learn to read using the Fernald method is not likely to change his approach if neurological reexamination reveals that the child is or is not brain damaged. A positive diagnosis of brain damage does not dictate any particular teaching method. It is only through an analysis of a child's learning problems and his behavior that the teacher can structure a program for instruction.

Therefore, even though most specific learning disorders probably arise from underlying neurologic disturbances, the educational evaluation of the problem is based upon analysis of the child's present behavior (including both strengths and deficits) and not upon past injuries. Isolation of definite or presumed etiologies for the observed disabilities are of only tangential interest and value to the teacher-clinician and play a minor role in the preparation of an *instructional* program for the child.

THE EMPHASIS UPON BASIC DISORDERS
OF THE LEARNING PROCESSES

In general, the basic learning processes are those necessary for perception (visual decoding, auditory decoding, kinesthetic decoding, among others) and for response formation (vocal encoding and graphic encoding) as well as for the connecting associations; frequently, the terms receptive and expressive are used in place of perception and response formation. The processes, which are discussed later, are essentially brain functions, and inadequate functioning of a process, whether caused by organic or nonorganic factors, can result in learning disability.

Specific learning disorders usually are related to one or more of the three impairments of prelinguistic and/or linguistic function which follow:

1. Loss of an established basic process.
2. Inhibition of the development of such a process.
3. Interference with the function of such a process.

An adult or child who loses his ability to speak after sustaining a cerebral hemorrhage is an example of the first instance; a child who is delayed considerably in speech development, the second; and an individual who speaks but frequently has difficulty with syntax and/or proper word pronunciation exemplifies the third.

Of the three impairments of function, the teacher will be most familiar with the last two. Children so affected are likely to be found among those in the low reading achievement groups and among those referred for speech therapy. While the examples pertain to speech, they may be generalized to disorders of reading, spelling, writing, and other academic activities.

These three impairments affect an individual's perceptual, language, or motor performance by the disruption of his decoding (receptive) pathways, his encoding (expressive) pathways, or the associations between possible combinations of decoding and encoding. The pathways or channels are discussed in Chapter II. The areas of language performance are psychological constructs used to characterize the problems exhibited by children with specific learning disorders. The areas, like all language models, are presented in simplified form.

The possibility exists that a given child could experience an isolated problem in visual decoding with resultant poor reading. The more common educational picture, however, is that affected children experience more than one difficulty in varying degrees of severity.

A child with average or better intelligence who is a nonreader because of inadequate opportunity to learn to read is not necessarily learning disabled. Money (1966) aptly has referred to him as an illiterate. These children suffer from a *lack* of information and not from an inability to process information proficiently. The educational deficits exhibited by culturally disadvantaged children *do* merit special attention from the community; but additional programs of language stimulation and enrichment are necessary rather than placement in classes for children with specific learning disabilities. That deprived children can benefit from a variety of enrichment activities is demonstrated by the work of Stephens, Kirk, and Painter (1967), Carter (1966), Bereiter (1967), Bereiter and Engelmann (1966), and Karnes, *et al.* (1969). Yet one would certainly expect to find a considerable number of learning disabled children among the culturally disadvantaged.

CHILDREN EXCLUDED BY THE DEFINITION

Most definitions of specific learning disability do not provide for children whose *primary* problems are mental subnormality, educational or cultural deprivation, severe emotional disturbance, and/or sensory deficit. Similar exclusions customarily are made regarding diagnosis of specific language disabilities such as dysphasia (Myklebust, 1964; Monsees, 1957) and dyslexia (Kass, 1966; Myklebust & Johnson, 1962).

The decision not to include these other exceptional children among the learning disabled is an arbitrary one; it often is based on sound administrative practices and is not intended as a denial of the presence of learning disorders in children found in these excluded groups. Certainly there are mentally retarded children who can satisfy all the provisions of the definition of specific learning disability, but because their learning difficulties are secondary to the more serious handicap of mental subnormality, they are placed in programs for the mentally retarded rather than the learning disabled. If the retarded child's most outstanding learning disability were corrected, presumably he would still be functioning only at his mental age level in that ability; this is not true of the *pseudo* retarded child who because of a specific learning disability may be misdiagnosed as retarded and mistakenly placed in a classroom for the educable mentally retarded.

However, teachers of the mentally retarded should recognize that children in their classes may have specific learning disorders, as defined, in addition to other problems and should be acquainted with appropriate teaching methods. The same may be said of teachers who have children with educational discrepancies, but who are severely emotionally and socially maladjusted, blind, partially sighted, deaf, or hard-of-hearing.

In short, services for learning disabled children are intended for the particular child who has specific difficulty in one or more basic learning processes but who apparently has normal or near-normal intelligence and who needs special instruction—either in the form of a special class or special tutoring in the regular class provided by his teacher or a special itinerant instructor. These services are not seen as a catchall for problem children in general or for other types of exceptionality, notably the underachiever. A basic understanding of learning disorder and appropriate instructional techniques, however, would be useful to most special education and general teachers.

Probable Causes of Learning Disorders

Specific learning disorders are viewed in this book as symptoms of internal conditions existing within the child, such as suboptimal neurologic functioning or inadequate programing of essentially normal nervous tissue. Examples of neurologic malfunction include such organic deviations as genetic variations, biochemical irregularities, and brain insults (injuries or damages), all of which may cause the brain to function abnormally. Examples of inadequate neural programing include environmentally based deficits in experience which inhibit the development of percepts underlying one or more basic skills. Regardless of etiology, behavioral manifestations or characteristics of learning disabled children are much the same. In children who exhibit problems in auditory or visual perception, it is difficult and often impossible to determine with confidence whether the etiology of the observed disability is essentially organic or environmental in origin. Probably most cases of learning disability are of unknown or very obscure etiology; therefore specific learning disabilities usually are defined, especially for educational purposes, on the basis of symptomatology without undue concern for the establishment of exact cause.

ORGANICALLY BASED ETIOLOGIES

Since brain dysfunction plays a prominent role in any discussion of learning disabilities and since a conspicuous amount of literature is devoted to the subject, teachers need to have a basic comprehension of:

1. The concept of minimal brain dysfunction.
2. The pathologies from which dysfunction may arise.
3. The relationships among types of brain dysfunction.
4. The relationship between brain dysfunction and specific learning disability.

The Concept of Minimal Brain Dysfunction. Many researchers and clinicians in the field maintain that specific learning disabilities are caused primarily by malfunction in the central nervous system. This system is comprised of the brain and spinal cord and serves as a switchboard for the regulation of incoming and outgoing impulses as well as for interconnecting neural associations. Since the system operates as a processor of information, inferior performance in any of its processes can seriously inhibit or retard a child's ability to learn or respond.

Many professionals object strongly to the extensive use of the phrase "minimal brain damage or injury" when referring to children with specific learning disabilities. In a monograph edited by Bax and McKieth (1963), a group of European physicians and other professional personnel points out the inadequacies of this label and suggests instead a more general term—"minimal cerebral dysfunction."

Objections to "minimal brain damage" are centered primarily around the anatomical and etiological implications frequently attached to the phrase. Strictly speaking, a damaged brain is one that has sustained an injury or insult; it has been structurally (anatomically) altered. Yet in children who manifest specific learning disabilities, clear evidence of damage, in the anatomical sense, usually is absent. Frequently nothing in the child's developmental or medical history supports the diagnosis of brain damage. Another objection to the term minimal brain damage is that minimal damage to cortical brain areas can produce comparatively severe behavioral effects, whereas comparatively gross damage to other areas often results in little or no observable disability (Orton, 1937; Cohn, 1964).

All too often, observation of deviant behavior or functioning of children is the basis for the use of the term "minimal brain damage"; this is especially the case when that deviant behavior takes the form of perceptual or language deficits. Since interpretation of a child's performance influences greatly the decisions made relative to which label is to be attached to him, the term "minimal brain dysfunction" according to many authors seems preferable to "minimal brain damage." The more general term, minimal brain dysfunction, implies only that the brain is operating in a suboptimal manner, the results of which are mild or borderline deviations in behavior.

In order to avoid anatomic and semantic pitfalls, teachers and psychologists, when involved in educational evaluations, must make as few inferences pertaining to the structure or condition of the brain as possible. In short, the diagnosis of minimal brain dysfunction does not include any inferences regarding the kind and etiology of the dysfunction or the extent and location of neural tissues involved. The term is applicable only when describing the degree of behavioral disturbance which may be associated with demonstrable or suspected brain malfunction.

Although widely used today, "minimal cerebral dysfunction" has not yet gained the universal acceptance of educators and physicians. The criticism of the term mainly centers upon its lack of precise definition.

To demonstrate that the term has not been sharply defined, Gomez (1967), in a recent article called *Minimal Cerebral Dysfunction* (*Maximal Neurological Confusion*), reported the results of a questionnaire sent to ten pediatricians. The physicians were asked their opinions concerning the usefulness of the phrase. Only one of the physicians found the term useful, though in need of better definition. The other nine "rejected the term because of being too broad and hard to define, because it has become a wastebasket diagnosis for all children who are looked upon as not quite normal" (p. 589). Gomez recommended a more definitive, behavioral approach to terminology and concluded that "minimal cerebral dysfunction" represented a backward step in the attempt to classify disorders of behavior and learning.

Pathologies from which Brain Dysfunctions Arise. Conditions that may result in brain dysfunctions among adults include cerebral hemorrhage, diseases (usually those associated with high fevers), and head injuries. With reference to brain damage in children, Eastman (1959) has stated that unfavorable intrauterine environment is associated with at least two-thirds of the cases and that premature birth, anoxia, physical trauma, Rh factor, and congenital malformations are prime contributors. To these might be added heredity factors and malnutrition.

Of commonly mentioned causes of brain malfunction, the most important, because of their frequency of occurrence, are anoxia and cerebral hemorrhage (Denhoff, 1953). Anoxia is the condition characterized by deprivation of oxygen in the cells of the body. Since oxygen insufficiency is associated directly with many of the causative conditions mentioned, anoxia could be considered a primary cause of brain dysfunction.

Human cells need oxygen in order to perform the metabolic processes necessary for the maintenance of life. Oxygen is transported to the cells of the body by the hemoglobin contained in the red blood cells; anything that interferes with the circulation of the blood (strangulation or hemorrhage, for example) or with its capacity for transporting oxygen (high fevers) can cause oxygen deprivation in body tissues.

Toubin (1960) states that of all the tissues in the body, nerve cells are the most vulnerable to anoxia, and other writers (Best & Taylor, 1939) have noted that the neurons of the cerebral cortex undergo irreparable damage if deprived of their blood supply for five minutes or longer. The cells of the lower centers of the brain, like those of the medulla oblongata, which control vital life processes of the body, are able to undergo longer periods of oxygen deprivation; some of them remain unaffected after as long as sixty minutes of anoxia. A direct relationship exists between the length of time that the central nervous system is deprived of an adequate oxygen supply and the severity of the brain damage incurred.

Relationships among Types of Brain Dysfunction. Brain activities which are pertinent to the study of learning disabilities can be generalized into four areas of cerebral function: motor, mental, sensory, and convulsive. The functions and their associated manifestations of cerebral malfunction are demonstrated in Paine's (1962) outline (Table 1). Suboptimal neural performance which may cause impairment within an area of cerebral function produces either overt (gross) manifestations or borderline (minimal) manifestations. These manifestations or observable behaviors are sometimes referred to as "hard" and "soft" neuro-

Table   1[a]

Area of Cerebral Function	Possible Overt Manifestations	Borderline Manifestations
Motor	Cerebral palsies	Minor choreoathetosis or tremor Isolated hyperreflexia Excessive clumsiness
Mental	Mental deficiency	Mild or minimal retardation Overactivity, impulsiveness, distractibility, short attention span, low frustration tolerance, tantrums Perseveration, concrete patterns of thought, difficulty in abstraction, dyscalculia
Sensory	Cortical blindness or deafness Visual field defects Astereognosis, impaired 2-point discrimination, etc.	Impaired memory for shapes or designs Impaired spatial concept Visual or tactile inattention (extinction)
Convulsive	Epilepsy	Abnormal EEG without seizures

[a] Paine, R. S. Minimal chronic brain syndromes in children. *Develop. Med. Child. Neurol.*, 1962, **4**, 21.

logical signs. When a child exhibits several overt signs, there is solid evidence of brain dysfunction; the presence of borderline signs is less convincing of organicity. For example, if a pupil in a learning disabled classroom were also cerebral palsied and had a tendency toward epileptic seizures, the chances would be highly probable that the child suffered from brain dysfunction. Evidence would be less supportive of such a diagnosis if he were merely awkward in his movements and demonstrated short attention span, perseveration, and temper tantrums.

The function and the manifestations accompanying them are not mutually exclusive, for conditions that result in congenital brain dysfunction usually are diffuse in nature and cause more than one disability in any given pupil. The degree of disabilities in any individual vary from minimal to severe. A severely motor handicapped child may have little or no learning difficulty. Conversely a child who demonstrates gross language deficits might be only slightly awkward or even normal in his motor performance.

Relationship between Brain Dysfunction and Specific Learning Disorders. Perhaps most learning disorders resulting from brain dysfunctions evolve from Paine's system of borderline manifestations. The relationship between brain dysfunctions and learning disorders is demonstrated in Figure 1. Since the incidence of learning disability among children with or without brain dysfunction is not yet clearly established, the circles are not drawn to scale; therefore they should not be interpreted as if they were.

Circle A represents children with medically diagnosed brain dysfunction; circle B represents children with demonstrable, educationally defined, learning disorder. Learning disordered cases arising primarily from or *in association with* brain dysfunction are included in the shaded area common to both circles. A portion of the learning disabled circle

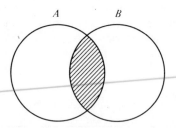

FIGURE 1. Demonstration of relationship between medically diagnosed dysfunction (circle A) and educationally defined learning disability (circle B).

is drawn outside of the brain dysfunction circle; this represents children with problems in learning who have no demonstrable organicity and includes learning disability cases which are actually (1) the result of undiagnosed brain dysfunction or (2) the result of environmental influences. (Nonorganic causes of learning disability are discussed more completely in the following section of this chapter.) Therefore, a child could exhibit any of the following:

1. Symptoms of brain dysfunction but no detectable learning disability.
2. Both brain dysfunction and learning disability.
3. Evidence of learning disability and no observable signs of brain malfunction.

Suggestion is made that pupils chosen to participate in services for the learning disabled generally should be selected from circle *B*. A number of these children, however, will not be placed in classes for the learning disabled because their primary problem is mental retardation, blindness, etc. Of the children who remain, some will exhibit overt evidence of brain malfunction and some will not; however, all should manifest unexpectedly poor school performance, which is related to specific difficulty in a basic learning process.

Ultimately the relationship between the concept of brain dysfunction and that of learning disorder rests upon observations of individual cases. In some instances the relationship is unquestionably causative; in others associative; in still others there may be no relationship at all. The following three examples will illustrate.

1. A child may exhibit dysphasic (language deficiency) behavior which is the direct product of demonstrable cerebral damage (causative). Occasionally a child with well developed language will lose all or some of his ability after a traumatic experience such as a concussion sustained in an automobile accident. If a preconcussion state of language adequacy is demonstrated in such a child, then the possibility of a causative relationship between brain dysfunction and learning disability is supported strongly.

2. Another dysphasic child may exhibit evidence of brain disorder of a type that cannot be related directly to his language difficulty (associative). Children with developmental language disorders frequently are reported to have a history of seizures or other convulsive symptoms. The paroxysmal episodes are accepted as evidence of brain dysfunction which also are suspected to be related in some nebulous and unspecified

way with the learning disability. Since the connection between the brain dysfunction and the language deficit is not established clearly, the relationship probably is described best as associative rather than causative.

3. A third child with dysphasic language patterns may manifest no neurologic signs at all. In a study reported by Landau, Goldstein, and Kleffner (1960), approximately a third of the children they classified as aphasic showed no indication of central nervous system dysfunction.

Note that the terms specific learning disorder and brain dysfunction are not interchangeable. While many, probably most, learning disabled children possess educational inadequacies as a consequence of assorted brain dysfunctions, it does not necessarily follow that all children who have cerebral dysfunctions are learning disabled. Many cerebral palsied and epileptic children, for example, are not educationally or perceptually handicapped even though they suffer from an apparent brain disability. The same is true of children variously described as hyperactive, hyperkinetic, organic and neurologically handicapped. It is equally true that many learning disability cases have no overt evidence at all of brain dysfunction. By definition, therefore, specific learning disorder is reserved for use as a generic term which represents a collection of language or language-related disabilities which in most cases are associated closely with, though not necessarily caused by, brain dysfunction.

ENVIRONMENTALLY BASED ETIOLOGIES

Children may manifest specific learning disability and other behaviors which are believed to be the product of environmental influences rather than of true brain dysfunction. The educational problems exhibited by these children are similar to those associated with children whose learning problems result from brain malfunction. In most instances the diagnostician and teacher are unable to distinguish between etiological groups. In environmentally based learning disorders, the diagnosis of brain pathology usually is untenable because of insufficient medical or psychological evidence. At such time, professionals interested in etiology probe the child's environment seeking factors which might help explain unexpectedly poor school performance. Case histories are evaluated; parents and teachers are interviewed; and the child's personality is assessed by use of assorted projective techniques. The goal of these endeavors is to define factors which may have inhibited the development of or disrupted the function of perceptive, associative, or expressive skills necessary to produce adequate school work. Two environmental factors which seem to affect adversely a child's ability to learn are insufficient early perceptual-motor experience and emotional maladjustment.

Insufficient Perceptual-Motor Experience. Results of studies which used animals as subjects have suggested that mode of rearing has a permanent effect on behavior at maturity, particularily intelligent behavior (Hebb, 1958). An example is afforded by Frantz (1965) who studied the effects of visual experience on perceptual development. Behavior of rhesus monkey infants reared in varying periods of darkness was studied, and the conclusion was that monkeys reared in darkness (two months or more) were inferior to less deprived monkeys both in unlearned visual experience and in later learning. For most monkeys, visual experience, when finally provided, no longer produced expected developmental effects. In addition to impaired visual learning, Frantz postulated other possible detrimental effects of early visual deprivation which included, among others, problems associated with failure to pass a critical period and neural deterioration.

Potentially harmful psychological experiments must necessarily use animals as subjects; thus generalization of results and conclusions to humans are made with understandable caution though some parallels are probable. Writing about children, Frantz has suggested:

Perception precedes action and early perceptual experience is necessary for the development of coordinated and visually directed behavior. The perfection of sensorimotor coordination will in turn increase the efficiency of the perceptual process (1966, p. 144).

Frantz' remarks seem to be in basic agreement with those of Kephart (1960), who comments at length regarding "a modern dilemma" facing today's children. Although present civilization requires the perfection of sensorimotor processes, the practice opportunity necessary for children to develop these processes adequately is decreased. For example, the child of another day who sharpened his sensorimotor skills by taking apart the percolator or other household appliances finds today's appliances too fragile, too difficult, or too dangerous for exploratory activity.

Effect of Emotional Disturbance. Gellhorn and Loofborrow (1963, p. 173) suggest that "emotional reactions, whether overt or not, play an essential role in perception." The validity of their statement is supported in part by (1) the work of Frostig, Lefever, and Whittlesey (1963), who in a study of preschool and primary grade children related disabilities in visual perception to problems in learning and behavior and (2) the findings of Chansky (1958), Bouise (1955), Berkowitz and Rothman (1955), and Tamkin (1960), which report significant correlations between emotional disturbance and reading retardation. Emotional conflicts in children also are attributed as predisposing, precipitating, and maintaining causes of speech disorders (Van Riper, 1954).

Characteristics of Learning Disabled Children

The characteristics observed in children with specific learning disorders may be divided arbitrarily into at least six categories, including disorders of (1) motor activity, (2) emotionality, (3) perception, (4) symbolization, (5) attention, and (6) memory. The categories are not mutually exclusive groupings; in fact, learning disabled children tend to exhibit behavior associated with several, and occasionally all, categories. Though each group of characteristics is discussed as a separate entity, no clear-cut distinctions can be made among the five related categories. For example, a child with hyperactive behavior usually experiences difficulty in attending and manifests some degree of emotional involvement as well. The result of such behaviors is a considerable reduction in a child's educational and social opportunity.

The behaviors are associated with both brain dysfunction and environmental factors and are reported to be characteristics of children from such diverse etiological groups as cerebral palsy, mental retardation, emotional disturbance, convulsive syndrome, minimal cerebral dysfunction, and learning disorder. Such characteristics contribute heavily to the severity of a child's learning problem in school.

DISORDERS OF MOTOR ACTIVITY

Four disorders of motor activity usually are mentioned as associated with specific learning disorders: hyperactivity, hypoactivity, incoordination, and perseveration. The authors' thought is that disorders of motor activity usually contribute to the severity of learning disorders, but seldom cause disorders in academic learning. Probably in many cases, the motor disability and the learning difficulty have a common etiology. Such thinking, however, does not minimize the necessity for perfecting motoric integration in children who exhibit subaverage motor ability.

Hyperactivity. Hyperactivity, that is, excessive mobility, is the most commonly recognized form of motor disability and is mentioned frequently in the reports of psychoeducational evaluations on children with learning disabilities. In general, hyperactive children have been described as frequently restless, engaged in random activity, and erratic in their behavior (Cruickshank & Raus, 1966). The term in general refers to "the child who is always in motion, and whose motion is always in double time. It is not that the particular behavior is necessarily bad, but that there is so much of it" (Rappaport, Hirt, & Decker, 1964, p. 45).

Next to marked underachievement, hyperactivity is perhaps the teacher's most consistent complaint concerning the behavior of learning disabled children. A school-aged child who demonstrates this symptom may be:

1. Constantly engaged in movement.
2. Unable to sit still for even short periods without shuffling his feet, tapping his pencil, or twisting about in his chair.
3. Occasionally given to sustained chatter in class.
4. Almost invariably inattentive.

Hypoactivity. This term is used to describe a child with insufficient motor activity and may be viewed as the reverse of hyperactivity. As pupils so affected are likely to be lethargic, quiet, not given to much action, and the cause of little disturbance in class, the activity problem of these children frequently is not recognized. Therefore, the symptom appears only occasionally in the case histories of learning disabled children.

Incoordination. Physical awkwardness and/or poor motor integration are two signs of incoordination; it is also noted in the behavior of many learning disabled children. The authors have observed that children who experience difficulty in the mastery of school skills often:

1. Do poorly in activities which require a high degree of motor co-ordination such as running, catching, skipping, and jumping.
2. Exhibit walking gaits which may be described as rigid and stiff legged; in extreme cases the arms and legs may move in a homolateral fashion.
3. Perform in a subaverage manner such activities as writing, drawing, and other tasks which require fine motor integration.
4. Appear to experience difficulties in balance as evidenced by frequent falls, stumbling, and clumsy behavior in general.

More detailed discussions concerning clumsy children are found in the contributions of Walton, of Kóng, and of Illingworth in Bax and MacKieth's (1963) monograph. The work of Kephart (1960, 1963) relative to motor development and the distinction between movement patterns and motor skills is of particular value for readers who require further understanding of motoric performance in learning disabled children.

Perseveration. Perseveration has been defined as "the automatic and often involuntary continuation of behavior" (Van Riper, 1964, p. 508) and may be observed in almost any expressive (motor) behavior such as speaking, writing, oral reading, drawing, and pointing (Tansley & Guilford, 1960). Although perseverative behaviors often are seen in individuals with known organic impairment, they are found also among people who have no known brain pathology (Travis, 1957).

In speech, perseveration takes many forms. Generally, however, problems are derived from an inability of the child to shift with ease from one topic, word, or phoneme to another. As a result of his difficulty in changing set, a speech perseverative pupil might repeat a question many times after its clarification or dwell incessantly upon a single topic of conversation. In oral reading, a pupil may have to repeat a phrase several times before he is able to continue.

Perseveration also may occur in writing; for example, a child may repeatedly write the same letter or incorrectly spell a word and then write it again with the same error. Such behavior, as well as the accompanying frustrations, are experienced by college students or teachers who misspell a word while typing a paper or letter and after correction repeat their error.

Gross motor expressive behavior as well as fine motor behavior may be affected by perseveration. A child who exhibits gross motor perseveration may:

1. Continue to pound a nail after it has been fully embedded (Lewis, Strauss, & Lehtinen, 1951).

2. Cover an entire page with one color.

3. Be requested to draw a circle and thereafter continue to draw in a circular motion (Strauss & Lehtinen, 1947).

DISORDERS OF EMOTIONALITY

The chances of emotional lability developing in a child apparently are increased by the presence of brain dysfunction, for Clements (1963, 1966), Beck (1961), and others have reported that emotional instability is one of the most frequently mentioned characteristics in the literature concerning children with brain dysfunction.

Bender (1949) has proposed the following reasons for the high incidence of emotional difficulties among these children:

1. Motor disorders in a child make for prolonged dependency on the mother.

2. Perceptual or intellectual problems which thwart the child's efforts

to make successful contact with the world lead to frustrations, misinterpretations of reality, and bizarre behavior patterns.

3. Disturbed patterning of impulses leads to distortion in actual patterns.

While Bender has offered explanations of why emotional problems arise among these children, specific examples of emotional lability associated with brain malfunction are obtained from the comments of parents and teachers.

1. He seems bright; he is quiet and obedient, but daydreams and can't read.
2. He is high-strung and nervous; his attention is hard to hold.
3. He has frequent temper outbursts, sometimes for no apparent reason.
4. He won't concentrate for more than a few minutes at a time; he jumps from one thing to another, and minds everyone's business but his own.
5. He lacks self control; he cannot work with other children; he picks on them constantly; he is disturbing in the classroom and worse on the playground . . . (Clements & Peters, 1967, p. 186).

Yet the behaviors just outlined are not unique to children with brain dysfunction. Garrison and Force (1965) suggest that deprivation of psychological needs, due to hospitalization or institutional isolation, for example, may damage personality development as much as organic pathology. The developmental nature of emotional and social maladjustment has long been recognized, and no child is immune to an inadequate environment.

DISORDERS OF PERCEPTION

In addition to motor and emotional difficulties, specific learning disabilities in children are characterized by perceptual disturbances as well. Myklebust (1964, p. 359) has defined perceptual disturbance as "inability to identify, discriminate, and interpret sensation." Sensations (actually electrical impulses) occur when environmental stimuli activate sensory receptor cells which are dispersed throughout the body. The impulses are interpreted in the brain as the auditory, visual, olfactory (smell), gustatory (taste), cutaneous (touch), kinesthetic, and vestibular senses depending upon the origin of the sensations. While kinesthetic perception provides awareness about the position of various parts of the body and permits coordinated motor behavior, vestibular perception provides information concerning the location or position of the entire body in space.

Perceptual disorders must be distinguished from sensory defects such as peripheral blindness and deafness. Blind children do not see and, therefore, adequate perception does not take place; but such children cannot be said to suffer from a perceptual disorder.

The terms decoding problem and receptive difficulty are used more or less synonymously to describe any disorder of perception. Thus perceptive disorders in a child may be described behaviorally as poor visual decoding, auditory decoding, kinesthetic decoding, etc. Inadequate reproduction of geometric forms, figure-ground confusions, or letter reversals and rotations are accepted as evidence of a possible visual perception problem. Apparent inability to recognize tunes or to differentiate between sounds may result from auditory misperception. To be unable to identify familiar objects by touch alone (astereognosis) would suggest cutaneous perceptive difficulty. Kinesthetic and vestibular perception malfunction can disrupt internal feedback relative to movement with resultant problems in coordination, directionality, space orientation, and balance. Perceptual problems which pertain to olfaction and gustation probably contribute little to problems in academic learning. Children with perceptive difficulty frequently exhibit symptoms, in varying degree, of more than one type of perceptual problem, though occasionally a child may have a problem in one area and not in the others.

Perceptual adequacy is viewed as the base upon which concept formation, abstraction ability, and/or cognitive symbolic behavior are built. Perceptual disorders in children, if not minimized or corrected, may result in later academic failure or language deficit (Frostig, 1963; Harrington, 1965; Getman, 1965); consequently, early recognition and remediation are recommended. For comprehensive discussions which relate to perceptual aspects of learning disabilities, the reader is referred to the works of Strauss and Lehtinen (1947) and Strauss and Kephart (1955); the programmed text by McGuigan (1964) is suggested for the reader who wishes to acquire a basic understanding of the biological basis of perception.

Disorders of Symbolization

Symbolization is one of the highest forms of mental ability and is involved with both concrete and abstract reasoning. At this level of operation the brain integrates perceptions and memories, as well as other associations, and generates thought processes or chains which may greatly exceed the limits of any given stimulus. For example, a concrete object such as an apple may be abstracted as appleness. Perceptual and symbolic activity therefore differ regarding the amount of meaning (cognition) associated with the symbols.

In addition, the integrity of symbolic processes is an essential criterion which underlies children's acquisition of basic learning skills. Through oversimplification, the symbolic processes can be dichotomized into receptive (decoding) and expressive (encoding) categories. Receptive symbolic activity may be divided further into receptive-auditory and receptive-visual subfunctions, while expressive symbolic activity may be divided into expressive-oral and expressive-motor subfunctions. Other divisions can be derived, but suboptimal performance of these four often is associated with learning disorders.

Receptive-Auditory. Difficulty in this subfunction can take the form of poor understanding of spoken symbols, frequent requests to repeat, echolalia, and confusion of directions or commands. As disorders in this area include conditions referred to as sensory or receptive dysphasia, hearing loss must be eliminated as a cause of the behavior.

Receptive-Visual. Children with problems in this subfunction read with little comprehension and often subvocalize reading to themselves. The difficulty is not secondary to blindness or peripheral visual impairments. Strephosymbolia (Orton, 1937) and congenital word blindness (Morgan, 1896) would be examples of this type of problem.

Expressive-Vocal. The difficulty is essentially one that involves the formulation of thought for speech (expressive or motor dysphasia) and may be evidenced by circumlocutions, inadequate syntax, and dearth of ideas for expression.

Expressive-Motor. The difficulty is concerned with the formulation of thought for writing (dysgraphia) as well as nonvocal communication such as gestures. Spelling errors are frequent among children who have graphic disorders. Letters tend to be omitted, reversed, or poorly formed; occasionally whole words are left out of sentences which are being copied. In addition, difficulty in oral expression may result from poor motor response formation as in dyspraxia.

Notation is made that perceptual activities, as discussed previously, are viewed as receptive processes which are developmentally related to receptive symbolic processes. Therefore, theoretically at least, a first-grade pupil with a visual perception problem who is unable to distinguish one printed letter from another would be expected to experience great difficulty learning to read.

DISORDERS OF ATTENTION

To succeed in school, a child must be able to focus or fix his attention on a given task; he must also be able to break his focus at the appropriate time and move on to a new task. Thus disorders of attention may be categorized as either insufficient attention or excessive attention.

Insufficient Attention. Some children are unable to screen out superfluous, extraneous stimuli; that is, they may be attracted to every available stimulus regardless of its pertinence to the task at hand. The result is a problem of attention variously labeled as distractibility, hyperawareness, hyperirritability, or short attention span.

A pupil with a marked attention problem can be diverted easily from the task of reading, for example, by the almost imperceptible buzzing of the classroom's neon lights, by traffic in the street, or most likely of all by the presence of classmates quietly engaged in their own schoolwork. When the child is required to focus his attention on a particularly complex and perhaps threatening activity, intensive daydreaming and periods of mental blocking (or blanking out) can occur.

Although distractibility often is noted in the behavior of children with brain dysfunctions (Cruickshank et al., 1961; Klapper & Werner, 1950; Fedio, 1965; Strauss & Kephart, 1955), the symptom is not an exclusive characteristic of brain impairment. The results of Cruse's (1961) study indicate that distractibility is a common trait of both brain-injured and familial mentally retarded children; the brain-injured subjects were found to be no more distractible than the familial retardates. The results of Bee's (1964) study, which used mentally normal fourth-grade pupils as subjects, have suggested a possible connection between parent-child interactions and distractibility.

Excessive Attention. Occasionally a teacher will have a child in class who displays abnormal fixations of attention on unimportant details while disregarding the essentials. As an example, Barry (1955) mentions the child who gave all of his attention to a page number instead of looking at the printed material or the picture on a page. She suggests that the apparent lack of attention was actually extreme attentiveness, as far as the child was concerned, but he gave his whole attention to the unimportant detail.

DISORDERS OF MEMORY

In a discussion of memory, one could focus his attention upon the organic aspects, notably the underlying biochemical basis exemplified by the work of Bogoch (1968) and others, which will likely establish a physical basis for memory processes. Teachers, however, will find a behavioral approach to the subject more suitable for their particular needs. Using behavioral criteria, Smith and Smith (1966) have defined memory as a collection of responses of a specialized but integrated kind which can be used appropriately within a context of specified rules. It is noteworthy that memory is a postulated process, it is not directly observable, and it must be hypothesized from interpretation of certain human behaviors.

Interpretation of responses, which are believed to demonstrate memory, have prompted investigators to describe the characteristics and types of memory. Therefore, McDonald (1965) suggests that memory includes, to a considerable extent, the ability to make both meaningful and non-meaningful associations. Piaget (1968) views memory as a developmental phenomenon including recognition, which relies exclusively on perception and sensorimotor schemata, reconstruction, an intermediate stage encompassing elements of the other two stages where the schemata are not adequate to permit direct recall, and evocation, which requires mental imagery or language. Frequently, memory is referred to as long-term memory and short-term or immediate memory. The abstractions necessary for reading with comprehension or for doing complicated arithmetic calculations are mental activities which depend upon long-term memory. Immediate memory is characterized by these mental activities which are most dependent upon rote learning. Obviously, the separation of memory into subtypes is for the most part a theoretical division, and the criteria used for this separation are at best arbitrary and not defined precisely. Most activities are sufficiently complex to include both long- and short-term memory elements, several developmental levels, and both meaningful and nonmeaningful components; it is often difficult to determine which is the most important in any given activity.

Disorders of memory involve difficulty in the assimilation, storage, and/or retrieval of information and may be associated with visual, auditory, or other learning processes. Subsequently one may speak of disorders of visual memory, auditory memory, etc. Inability to reproduce rhythm patterns or sequences of digits, words, or phrases could result from poor auditory memory (as well as from auditory imperception, difficulty in associational and categorizational processes, or perhaps even some form of output deficit). Inability to revisualize letters, words, or forms may be caused by inadequate visual memory. In addition, disorders may be associated with the various developmental levels, the meaningfulness of the material, or the long-term–short-term dichotomy.

Vergason (1968) has pointed out that memory is related highly to such phenomena as (1) the attention of the child, (2) mediation, that is, recognition by the child of the similarities and differences of new material to that which is already learned, (3) the meaningfulness of the new material to the child, (4) overlearning, that is, practice beyond one errorless trial, which is reported to facilitate retention, and (5) interference, the foremost explanation for forgetting. Relative to special education, Johnson and Myklebust (1967) view memory as critical for language development including the ability to read, to calculate, and to write; Van Riper (1954) considers it as basic to oral speech development.

Since memory impairments often occur in association with academic failure, perceptual deficits, symbolic disorder, and other learning disabilities, most authors note the commanding influence of memory on learning. The process, therefore, is accounted for in various behavior models such as McDonald's (1965) Symbolic Model of the Learner, Wepman's (1960) aphasia model, Bateman's (1965) Schematic Model of Selected Contributors to Remediation of Learning Disabilities, and the model offered by the authors in Chapter II.

Summary

The characteristics discussed here were derived from the study of large numbers of children and constitute a clinical picture or stereotype. Although discussed as stereotypes, all characteristics need not be present in one child; neither do the characteristics constitute independent factors in any learning disabled child. Individual characteristics are inseparably meshed in the behavior of children and constitute a formidable problem for teachers and clinicians. Any number of progressions can be posited to demonstrate the influence of one characteristic on another. For example, (1) hyperactivity → lack of attention → poor memory → academic failure → increased hyperactivity or (2) inattention → distractibility → failure to discriminate → poor decoding → lack of generalization → academic failure → emotional overlay → poorer decoding.

References

Ashlock, P., & Stephen, A. *Educational therapy in the elementary school.* Springfield, Ill.: Thomas, 1966.

Barry, H. Classes for aphasics. In M. E. Frampton & E. D. Gall, *Special education for the exceptional.* Vol. II. Boston: Sargent, 1955.

———. *The young aphasic child: Evaluation and training.* Washington, D.C.: Volta Bureau, 1961.

Bateman, B. Learning disabilities—Yesterday, today, and tomorrow. *Exceptional Children,* 1964, 31, 167–176.

————. An educator's view of a diagnostic approach to learning disorders. In J. Hellmuth, *Learning disorders.* Seattle: Special Child Publications, 1965. (a)

————. A summary report of the conference on the child with learning disabilities. Jersey City College, 1965. (b)

————. Learning disabilities—An overview. *Journal of School Psychology,* 1965, **3,** 1–12. (c)

Bax, M., & MacKeith, R. *Minimal cerebral dysfunction.* London: National Spastics Society, Medical Education and Information Unit in association with Heineman Medical Books, 1963.

Beck, H. S. Detecting psychological symptoms of brain injury. *Exceptional Children,* 1961, **28,** 57–62.

Bee, L. The relationship between parent-child interaction and distractibility in fourth grade children. *Dissertation Abstracts,* 1964, **25,** 2024–2025.

Bender, L. Psychological problems of children with organic brain disease. *American Journal of Orthopsychiatry,* 1949, **19,** 404–441.

Bereiter, C. Instructional planning in early compensatory education. *Phi Delta Kappan,* 1967, **48,** 355–356, 358–359.

————, & Engelmann, S. *Teaching disadvantaged children in the preschool.* Englewood Cliffs, N.J.: Prentice-Hall, 1966.

Berkowitz, P., & Rothman, E. Remedial reading for the disturbed child. *Clearing House,* 1955, **30,** 165–168.

Best, C. H., & Taylor, N. B. *The physiological basis of medical practice.* Baltimore, Md.: Williams & Wilkins, 1939.

Bogoch, S. *The biochemistry of memory.* New York: Oxford, 1968.

Boise, L. M. Emotional and personality problems of a group of retarded readers. *Elementary English,* 1955, **32,** 544–548.

Bryant, N. D. Characteristics of dyslexia and their remedial implications. *Exceptional Children,* 1964, **31,** 195–200.

Calvert, D. R., Ceriotti, M. A., & Geile, S. M. A program for aphasic children. Washington, D.C.: Volta Bureau, 1966. (Reprint No. 851.)

Carter, J. The effects of a language stimulation program upon first grade educationally disadvantaged children. *Education and Training of the Mentally Retarded,* 1966, **1,** 169–176.

Chansky, N. M. Threat, anxiety, and reading behavior. *Journal of Educational Research,* 1958, **51,** 333–340.

Clements, S. D. The child with minimal brain dysfunction—A profile. In S. D. Clements, L. E. Lehtinen, & J. E. Lukens, *Children with minimal brain injury.* Chicago: National Society for Crippled Children and Adults, 1963.

————. *Minimal brain dysfunction in children.* Washington, D.C.: Cosponsored by the Easter Seal Research Foundation of the National Society for Crippled Children and Adults and the National Institute of Neurological Diseases and Blindness Public Health Service, 1966.

————, & Peters, J. E. Minimal brain dysfunctions in the school-aged child. *Archives of General Psychiatry,* 1962, **6,** 185–197.

Cohn, R. The neurological study of children with learning disabilities. *Exceptional Children,* 1964, **31,** 179–185.

Cruickshank, W. M., Bentzen, F. A., Ratzeburg, F. H., & Tannhauser, T. *A teaching method for brain-injured and hyperactive children.* Syracuse, N.Y.: Syracuse University Press, 1961.

————, & Raus, G. M. *Cerebral palsy: Its individual and community problems.* Syracuse, N.Y.: Syracuse University Press, 1955.

Cruse, D. B. Effects of distraction upon the performance of brain-injured and familial retarded children. *American Journal of Mental Deficiency,* 1961, **66**, 86–92.

Denhoff, E. A primer of cerebral palsy for the general practitioner. *Medical Times,* 1953, 81, 244–258.

Eastman, N. J. The brain-damaged child: Why does he happen? *The Dallas Medical Journal,* 1959, Special Edition, March 3–7.

Eisenson, J. In R. West (Ed.), *Childhood aphasia.* Proceedings of the Institute on Childhood Aphasia. Stanford University School of Medicine, September, 1960.

Fedio, P. Memory span and sustained attention in children with unilateral temporal lobe and petit mal epilepsy. *Dissertation Abstracts,* 1965, **25**, 4258.

Frantz, R. S. Ontogeny of perception. In A. M. Schrier, H. F. Harlow, & F. Stollnitz, *Behavior of non-human primates: Modern research trends.* Vol. II. New York: Academic, 1965.

————. Pattern discrimination and selective attention as determinants of perceptual development from birth. In A. Kidd & J. Rivoire, *Perceptual development in children.* New York: International Universities, 1966.

Frostig, M. Visual perception in the brain-injured child. *American Journal of Orthopsychiatry,* 1963, **33**, 665–671.

————, Lefever, W., & Whittlesey, J. Disturbance in visual perception. *Journal of Educational Research,* 1963, **57**, 160–162.

Gallagher, J. J. *The tutoring of brain-injured mentally retarded children: An experimental study.* Springfield, Ill.: Thomas, 1960.

————. Children with developmental imbalances: A psychoeducational definition. In W. M. Cruickshank (Ed.), *The teacher of brain-injured children.* Syracuse, N.Y.: Syracuse University Press, 1966.

Garrison, K. C., & Force, D. G. *The psychology of exceptional children.* New York: Ronald, 1965.

Gellhorn, E., & Loofborrow, G. N. *Emotions and emotional disorder.* New York: Hoeber, 1963.

Getman, G. N. The visuomotor complex in the acquisition of learning skills. In J. Hellmuth, *Learning Disorders* Vol I. Seattle, Special Child Publications, 1965, pp 49–76.

Gomez, M. R. Minimal cerebral dysfunction (maximal neurological confusion). *Clinical Pediatrics,* 1967, **6**, 589–591.

Gordon, N. S. Minimal cerebral dysfunction. *Spastic's Quarterly,* 1965, 14, 4–11.

Harrington, D. A. Language and perception. Washington, D.C.: Volta Bureau, 1965. (Reprint No. 848.)

Hebb, D. O. The mammal and his environment. *American Journal of Psychiatry,* 1958, 111, 826–831.

Johnson, D. J., & Myklebust, H. R. Dyslexia in childhood. In J. Hellmuth (Ed.), *Learning disorders.* Seattle, Wash.: Special Child Publications, 1965.

Karlin, I. W. In R. West, *Childhood aphasia*. Proceedings of the Institute on Childhood Aphasia. Stanford University School of Medicine, September, 1960.

Karnes, M. B., Hodgins, A. S., Stoneburner, R. L., Studley, W. M., & Teska, J. A. Effects of a highly structured program of language development on intellectual functioning and psycholinguistic development of culturally disadvantaged three-year-olds, *Journal of Special Education*, 1969, **2**, 405–413.

Kass, C. Psycholinguistic disabilities of children with reading problems. *Exceptional Children*, 1966, **32**, 533–541.

Kephart, N. C. *The slow learner in the classroom*. Columbus, Ohio: Merrill, 1960.

————. *The brain injured child in the classroom*. Chicago: National Society for Crippled Children and Adults, 1963.

Kirk, S. A., & Bateman, B. Diagnosis and remediation of learning disabilities. *Exceptional Children*, 1962, **29**, 73–78.

Klapper, Z. S., & Werner, H. Developmental deviations in brain-injured (cerebral palsied) members of pairs of identical twins. *The Quarterly Journal of Child Behavior*, 1950, **2**, 288–313.

Kleffner, F. R. Teaching aphasic children. *Education*, 1959, **79**, 413–418.

————. In S. R. Rappaport, *Childhood aphasia and brain damage: A definition*. Narberth, Pa.: Livingston, 1964.

Landau, W. M., Goldstein, R., & Kleffner, F. R. Congenital aphasia, a clinicopathological study. *Neurology*, 1960, **10**, 915–921.

Lewis, R. S., Strauss, A. A., & Lehtinen, L. E. *The other child*. New York: Grune & Stratton, 1951.

McDonald, C. W. Problems concerning the classification and education of children with learning disabilities. Report presented to Southern Regional Education Board, Atlanta, Georgia, January, 1967.

McDonald, F. J. *Educational psychology*. Belmont, Cal.: Wadsworth, 1965.

McGinnis, M. A., Kleffner, F. R., & Goldstein, R. Teaching aphasic children. *Volta Review*, 1959, **58**, 239–244.

McGuigan, F. J. *Biological basis of behavior: A program*. Englewood Cliffs, N.J.: Prentice-Hall, 1964.

Monsees, E. K. Aphasia in children: Diagnosis and education. *Volta Review*, 1957. (Reprint No. 693).

Money, J. Dyslexia: A postconference review. In. J. Money (Ed.), *Reading disability*. Baltimore, Md.: Johns Hopkins Press, 1966. pp. 9–33.

Morgan, W. P. A case of congenital word blindness. *British Medical Journal*, 1896, **2**, 1612.

Myklebust, H. R. Training aphasic children. *Volta Review*, 1955, **57**, 149–157.

————. Learning disorders: Psychoneurological disturbances in childhood. *Rehabilitation Literature*, 1964, **25**, 354–360.

————. *Development and disorders of written language*. New York: Grune & Stratton, 1965.

————, & Johnson, D. Dyslexia in children. *Exceptional Children*, 1962, **29**, 14–26.

Orton, S. T. *Reading, writing, and speech problems in children*. New York: Norton, 1937.

Paine, R. S. Minimal chronic brain syndromes in children. *Developmental Medicine and Child Neurology*, 1962, 4, 21.

Piaget, J. *On the development of memory and identity.* Barre, Mass.: Clark University Press, 1968.

Rappaport, S. R. Personality factors teachers need for relationship structure. In W. M. Cruickshank (Ed.), *The teacher of brain-injured children.* Syracuse, N.Y.: Syracuse University Press, 1966.

————, Hirt, J. B., & Decker, R. J. Manifestations of the brain damage syndrome in school. In. S. Rappaport, *Childhood aphasia and brain damage: A definition.* Narberth, Pa.: Livingston, 1964.

Smith, K. U., & Smith, M. F. *Cybernetic principles of learning and educational design.* New York: Holt, Rinehart & Winston, 1966.

Stephens, W. B., Kirk, S. A., & Painter, G. Tutorial program for culturally disadvantaged children, ages eight months to two years. Paper presented at the Society for Research in Child Development, New York City, 1967.

Strauss, A. A., & Lehtinen, L. E. *Psychopathology and education of the brain-injured Child.* Vol. I. New York: Grune & Stratton, 1947.

Strauss, A. A., & Kephart, N. C. *Psychopathology and education of the brain-injured child.* Vol. II. New York: Grune & Stratton, 1955.

Tamkin, A. S. Survey of educational disability in emotionally disturbed children. *Journal of Educational Research*, 1960, 54, 67–69.

Tansley, A., & Guilford, R. *The education of slow learning children.* London: Routledge & Crofts, 1957.

Taylor, M. L. *Understanding aphasia.* New York: The Institute of Physical Medicine and Rehabilitation, 1958.

Terman, L. M., & Merrill, M. A. *Stanford-Binet Intelligence Scale.* Boston: Houghton Mifflin, 1960.

Toubin, A. *The pathology of cerebral palsy.* Springfield, Ill.: Thomas, 1960.

Travis, I. et al. *Handbook of speech pathology.* New York: Appleton-Century-Crofts, 1957.

Van Riper, C. *Speech correction.* Englewood Cliffs, N.J.: Prentice-Hall, 1964.

Vergason, G. A. Facilitation of memory in the retardate. *Exceptional Children*, 1968, 34, 589–596.

Wechsler, D. *Wechsler Adult Intelligence Scale: Manual.* New York: The Psychological Corporation, 1955. (a)

————. *Wechsler Intelligence Scale for Children: Manual.* New York: The Psychological Corporation, 1955. (b)

————. *Wechsler Preschool and Primary Scale of Intelligence: Manual.* New York: The Psychological Corporation, 1967.

West, R. *Childhood aphasia.* Proceedings of the Institute on Childhood Aphasia. Stanford University School of Medicine, September, 1960.

CHAPTER II

THE EDUCATIONALLY ORIENTED EVALUATION

This chapter presents the rationale and procedures relevant to the appraisal of the child's command of the human symbol system which is used for communication. Psychological measures, such as intelligence and personality tests, receive only cursory mention since there are many available texts on the subject of testing persons with specific disabilities (e.g., books by Burgemeister, 1962, and Taylor, 1961). This chapter emphasizes measures of speech, language, and academic achievement as tools to evaluate the child's comprehension of the verbal symbols surrounding him and his ability to formulate and use these symbols. The authors do not expect that any one person will possess the training and competencies necessary for conducting a full psychoeducational evaluation. Rather, we believe that one of the essentials of adequate assessment is the adoption and implementation of the team approach.

29

The Theoretical Model of Evaluation

Any understanding of the impairment of symbol usage must be preceded by the development of a global concept of language function. Without such a concept, evaluation becomes a hodgepodge of unrelated probings about the periphery of the problem. Osgood (1953, 1957; Osgood & Miron, 1963) and Wepman, Jones, Bock, and Van Pelt (1960) have presented schemata encompassing the process of language function which together may prove useful for many diagnosticians and teachers— they provide a frame of reference for diagnosticians in assessment and for teachers in programing instruction. Each of these models is discussed separately before a composite model is presented.

THE OSGOOD MODEL

The Osgood schema is a mediation-integration model of language in which the chief construct is an implicit, stimulus-producing response assumed to mediate between the observable stimulus and the observable response and yielding a two-stage, S-r-s-R process. The covert reaction (r) is a representational process and serves as the meaning of the sign (S) for the individual. The covert reaction is also a mediation process because the self-stimulation (s) may become associated with an overt act (R). The model, shown in Figure 1, encompasses two dimensions of language behavior, language processes and levels of organization.

Language processes. The first dimension of the model includes the language processes—decoding, association, and encoding. In substance, decoding refers to the perception of language, encoding to the use of language for the expression of ideas, and association to the representational mediation process which is elicited by decoding and which, in turn, elicits other processes which result in expressive behavior.

Levels of Organization. Within the second dimension of the model, as shown in Figure 1, the processes may be mediated by any one of three levels of neural organization. The lowest level is the projection level, which relates receptor and muscle events to the brain via "wired-in" neural mechanisms, for example, food powder placed in the mouth will elicit a reliable pattern of food-taking reactions such as salivating and swallowing.

The second and more highly organized level is that of integration,

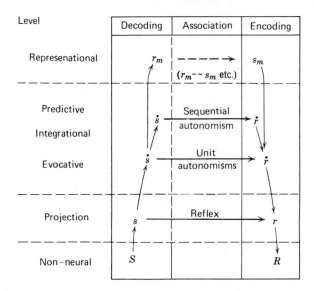

FIGURE 1.   Osgood's model of language behavior.

which is the level that organizes and sequences both incoming and outgoing neural events. The ability to coordinate automatically the muscles
of the lips, tongue, larynx, and diaphragm during speech or to focus
the head and eyes on an object are examples of the contribution this
level makes to language.

The integrations mediated at the second level may be evocative. One
would expect evocative integrations to be formed when external or response events occur with high frequency or temporal contiguity. The
central pattern formed in this manner becomes strong enough to complete itself once it has been initiated. This is a closure function. An
example of an evocative integration or closure would be the seemingly
automatic recognition of a partially completed picture of a familiar object. External events may occur together less frequently or with lesser
temporal contiguity so that the central pattern takes the form of a "set"
and the conditions are merely predictive, rather than evocative. This
suggests that the grammatical and syntactical aspects of language may
be based partly on predictive mechanisms. For example, if the reader
were presented with the sentence "The boy ran up the — — — — — —," he
would be able to predict the missing word, "hill," and would generally
be correct in his prediction. If he were always correct the integration
would be evocative; but in the example given, the correct word might

be "street," "alley," or any other of a set of similar words. The central pattern, therefore, is only predictive.

The third level of organization is the representational or cognitive level. At this point, representational mechanisms are developed for the conception of meaning and all meaningful language activity depends, to some extent, upon cognition. A simple example of activity at the representational level is concept formation.

WEPMAN'S APHASIA MODEL

Clinical experience and research with aphasic patients have led Wepman (1960) and his colleagues to the formulation of an operational schema depicting the levels of function within the central nervous system. In contrast with Osgood's model, the Wepman paradigm takes into account memory, internal and external feedback, and modalities of transmission. As shown in Figure 2, the model describes four dimensions: levels of function, processes, a memory bank, and feedback.

Levels of Function. The three levels of function postulated by Wepman are the reflexive, the perceptual, and the conceptual. The reflexive level is directly analogous to Osgood's projection level and mediates elementary sensorimotor responses, such as the patellar reflex or the reflexive eye blink. The perceptual level mediates language activity which is echoic or imitative and essentially nonmeaningful. Wepman does not discuss the perceptual level of language function as discretely as Osgood, who speaks of sequential and unit autonomisms, but instead he emphasizes the nonmeaningful memory trace left at this level, which allows the individual to repeat words or copy what he sees without understanding the stimulus. The highest degree of symbolic activity— concept formation—is placed at the conceptual level, similar to the representational level in the Osgood model but described as transcending modalities of input and output.

Processes of Language Function. Only two processes are described by Wepman, transmission and integration; the former may be divided into reception and expression or decoding and encoding modes. The transmissive processes are probably modality-bound, that is, for certain activities visual input may be bound to oral expression. In other activities, auditory input may be bound to oral output. According to Wepman, the transmission processes are functional at only the reflexive and perceptual levels. "Transmission across the system . . . is seen as the capacity of the organism to transmit percepts which leave their trace on the memory bank but have no meaning to the individual" (Wepman, 1960,

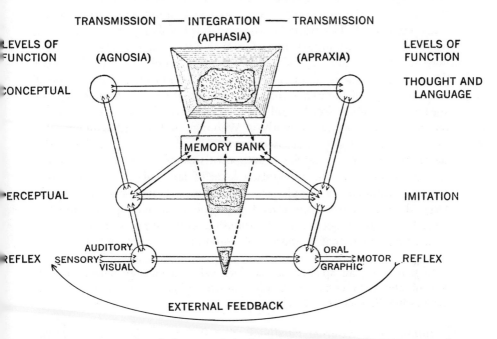

FIGURE 2. An operational diagram of the levels of function in the CNS proposed by Wepman.

p. 327). At the conceptual level, the incoming stimulus affects both the memory bank and the integrative process and triggers comprehension which transcends the modality involved. Wepman, therefore, is able to speak of modality-bound language disorders, which he terms agnosias and apraxias, but describes aphasia "as a disruption of the integrative process after the stimulus is free of its input modality" (p. 328).

The second process of language, integration, is operant at all levels of function, except the reflexive where supposedly no memory trace is left within the central nervous system. Some control, however, of the CNS is shown in Figure 2 since stimulus reception must be translated into motor responses. The integrative process at the perceptual level provides for the decoding and encoding of previously learned patterns by translating the input sign or symbol to an appropriate output pattern. At the conceptual level the integrative process plays its most important role and incoming stimuli combine with past associations to invest the stimuli with meaning.

The Memory Bank. Wepman employs a construct—the memory bank—which receives and stores traces from stimuli transmitted across the system at the perceptual level and which stores associations at the conceptual level. The traces at the two levels differ primarily in being meaningful at the higher level, nonmeaningful at the lower. As one may see from Figure 2, the role of recall is emphasized by Wepman; the memory bank is a prominent part of the model and interconnects with all stages of the perceptual and conceptual levels. Although Osgood speaks of familiar words and past experiences, he does not describe the role of memory as explicitly as Wepman, and it is difficult to determine how he would describe the imitation of a novel stimulus within the framework of his model. Osgood postulates only evocative and predictive mechanisms at the integration level of language, neither of which seems to account for simple echoic responses. Some persons using the Osgood model have been forced into placing matching and imitative activities at the projection level, a solution which appears artificial. Wepman (1960) feels that memory is so important in language that he says:

> In one sense, all aphasia can be decribed as a memory defect since the loss of ability to utilize previously learned verbal constructs so frequently typifies the disorder (p. 329).

Internal and External Feedback. This last dimension of the Wepman schema is, like the memory bank, not demonstrated within the Osgood model. It is difficult to place too great an emphasis upon the role of feedback, both internal and external, in the function of language. Internally, feedback can modify, control, and remove behavior before it is expressed; externally, responses can be controlled and corrected by means of information received from one's own response production or from observation of other people's responses. Wepman does not discuss feedback at length, but he does speak of internal feedback as related to proprioceptive stimulation and hypothesizes that decreased destimulation may lower the accuracy of control or may eliminate some modification of the response before it is expressed.

THE COMPOSITE LANGUAGE MODEL

Many aspects of the Osgood and Wepman models are highly similar and often the difference between the two seems to be one of terminology. In general, we believe that the levels of language function postulated in the separate models are not significantly different and, therefore, for example, the projection level of Osgood is directly comparable to the reflexive level described by Wepman. Also, we see no real difference between the types of language processes discussed; receptive and expressive transmission appear to be the same or nearly the same as decoding and encoding. The central process, be it called integration or association, is again quite similar in the two models.

Ignoring the fact that Wepman is describing a pathological condition, aphasia, and that Osgood speaks of normal language function, the main difference between the schemata is the inclusion by Wepman of a memory bank, feedback, and modalities of input and output. On the surface it appears that the Wepman model could be accepted *in toto* by persons concerned with the assessment and remediation of children's learning disorders. Further inspection of the Wepman paradigm reveals, however, that it would be possible to speak of auditory agnosia in the absence of aphasia, that is, an individual could fail to recognize even the most elementary sounds and still be able to function symbolically. Such may be the case in traumatic aphasia when the disorder occurs after language has developed, but it is impossible to describe in this way a child who has severe auditory receptive problems; if he cannot perceive auditory symbols, he cannot form verbal concepts nor can he express language vocally. On the basis of clinical experience, the authors feel that the Wepman model is unsuitable for describing the child who is still developing language. Nor is the Osgood model appropriate for the practicing clinician or teacher. Too many facets of language, such as memory and feedback, have been ignored or, at best, only implied.

Because we are concerned with children who have *developmental disorders* of language and learning, we cannot use a model which is strictly developmental or disorder-oriented or one which is incomplete in critical areas. Instead, we must search for a schema that describes normal language function in its most important aspects and which simultaneously allows us to observe a variety of specific disorders of function. The authors' present solution to this dilemma is a composite model, shown in Figure 3, that incorporates into Osgood's model the salient features of the Wepman diagram. In the composite model, five dimensions are described: (1) language processes, (2) levels of language function, (3) memory, (4) feedback, and (5) channels of communication.

Language Processes. As stated by Osgood, there are three language processes: decoding, association, and encoding. Decoding is the reception and perception of stimuli which may be meaningful or nonmeaningful but which are necessary to the function of language. Association is the ability to manipulate linguistic symbols in a meaningful or nonmeaningful fashion. Meaningful associative ability is required in activi-

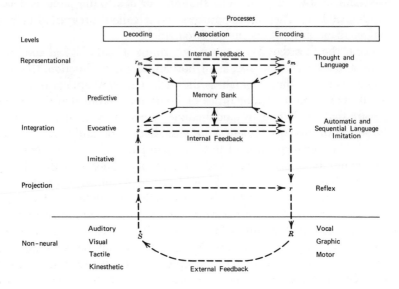

FIGURE 3. The composite model.

ties such as analogies, similarities, and differences. Nonmeaningful associative ability can be demonstrated in the child who is a "word-caller"
in reading; he associates visual and auditory symbols but without meaning. Encoding refers to the expression of linguistic symbols whether
they be meaningful as in verbal discourse or nonmeaningful as in the
repetition of a series of sounds.

Levels of Language Function. The second dimension of the composite
model encompasses three levels which describe the functional complexity
of the organism: the projection, integration, and representational. The
first level, projection, is a reflexive level and differs in no way from
Osgood's description. The second and more complex level of function
in the composite model is integration, which mediates the retention
of linguistic symbol sequences, the execution of automatic habit-chains,
and factors of imitation. The imitation aspect is found in the Wepman
schema and, therefore, the integration level of the composite model
incorporates the basic elements of both Wepman's perceptual and Osgood's integration levels.

A child in the echo babble stage of speech development who has no established meanings for his vocalizations operates at the integration level of language. In general, sequential language behavior ranges from the simple imitation of meaningless sounds or actions to the complex receptive and expressive sequencing of words in sentences.

The most highly organized level of language function is the representational, which mediates activities requiring the meaning or significance of auditory, visual, or other symbols. When a child learns to respond in a given way to a certain object or event, he is operating at the representational level. Thus this level of the composite model is directly comparable to the corresponding level of the Osgood model.

Memory. Imitation is explicitly stated in the Wepman schema and is postulated as a language function by Skinner (1957), who is always parsimonious when hypothesizing constructs. Osgood, however, does not provide directly for the function of imitation or short-term memory for novel stimuli. The authors feel that these factors are of enough importance in learning disorders that they should be incorporated, rather than implicitly assumed, in any model that purports to describe language. Within the composite model, therefore, the memory bank, as described by Wepman, has been included to subserve the function of imitation and memory.

Feedback. The composite model, in common with Wepman's schema, includes both internal and external feedback, although there appears to be a difference in approach. The present authors distinguish internal and external feedback in the following manner. Before an overt response is produced by an individual, an appropriate response pattern must be formulated. Part of this response pattern is fed back into the system for comparison and, if necessary, correction; such feedback is internal. On the other hand, external feedback is accomplished through the auditory, visual, and kinesthetic-tactile modalities, that is, one hears and sees one's response or feels the manner of its production. If the information returning to the system regarding the overt response indicates that an error has been made, the response is corrected. The reader may observe in Figure 3 that internal feedback occurs at both the integration and representational levels to assure that the response pattern formed through the encoding process is appropriate. External feedback as shown is presumed to occur after the overt response is produced and scanned or monitored.

Feedback requires the scanning or monitoring process which entails the constant backflow and inspection of output information. Adequate monitoring demands that the individual listen rather than simply hear, that he look rather than merely see. Children who make and ignore errors in reading when they are familiar with the individual words are said to exhibit poor feedback; they are not monitoring their responses and, therefore, are unaware of errors. One of the aims of remediation is to train the child in *active* scanning so that he listens to himself when he speaks or reads aloud.

Channels of Communication. The last dimension of the composite model deals with channels of communication—the sensory motor paths through which language is transmitted. Wepman's research with aphasic adults indicated that four nonconceptual factors were present in the group: (1) the ability to read aloud; (2) the ability to write words presented auditorially; (3) the ability to repeat auditory stimuli; and (4) the ability to copy printed material. Since the response process seemed to depend upon the stimulus modality, Wepman postulated the concept of transmission as an independent dimension of his model. More recently, Mira (1968) reported that normal and learning disabled children exhibit individual and differing patterns of attention to auditory and visual events. In the authors' experience, many children with learning disabilities appear to be deficient only when presented with stimulus items involving a particular modality. On this basis, the authors hypothesize that children, as well as adult aphasics, have modality preferences and they feel that a model describing language function should include the dimension of modality, although it is unclear whether each discrete encoding process is dependent upon a particular decoding process, as Wepman implies.

The modality combinations, or channels of communication, that may be described are numerous, for example, auditory-vocal, auditory-motor, visual-vocal, visual-motor, tactile-motor. According to Kirk and Mc-Carthy (1961b), the modes of input and output of greatest interest to the teacher and clinician are the auditory-vocal and visual-motor channels. The authors basically agree with this supposition but feel that in view of the multisensory approach to remediation taken by a number of clinicians, other channels deserve consideration.

EXAMPLES DEMONSTRATING THE COMPOSITE MODEL

Although it is theoretical, the composite model can be used to exemplify activities that occur in language. The two examples that follow demonstrate what is presumed to happen when an individual either writes the name of an observable object or imitates a word spoken to him.

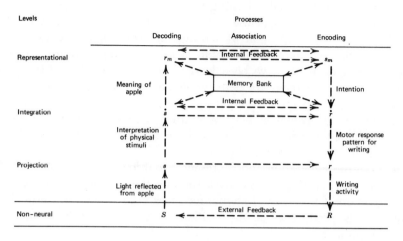

FIGURE 4. The written response of the word "apple" to the sight of an apple.

The first example chosen to demonstrate the model deals with the written response "apple" to the visual stimulus provided by the apple. As may be seen in Figure 4, the apple is a non-neural event, that is, an object that exists external to the individual. The physical stimuli from the apple, in the form of reflected light, are received by the individual and are termed the "sensory signal" at the projection level. The sensory signal is associated with similar past experiences drawn from the memory bank and both are integrated into a whole sensory stimulation which occurs at the integration level. The sensory stimulation assumes the form of a pattern that has been constructed in the past after the person has seen many apples; the sight of the present apple is associated with all of those past experiences of seeing apples. These sensory correlates are activated directly and reliably by the particular sensory signals upon which they are dependent, in this case, the sight of the apple.

At the representational level, the person responds to the sensory integration with the meaning of "apple," and this concept provides the self-stimulation which will elicit previously learned motor integrations. The understanding of "apple" (the significate) is an internal response to the sensory signal and is the point in the model at which meaning is decoded. This internal response, r_m, in turn gives rise to the first stage of encoding, self-stimulation, or s_m.

Self-stimulation elicits on the integration level (through the encoding process) the motor correlates in the memory bank which are associated with the conditioned reflex leading to writing. In many ways the motor correlates are analogous to the sensory correlates on the decoding side of the model. The intention of writing the word "apple" elicits a set of automatic and sequential motor elements geared toward writing. These motor elements have been learned and overlearned and the integrations mediating them are both predictive and evocative. The writing reflex is located on the projection level and, as the reader may observe in Figure 4, the actual activity of writing is carried out at this point. The result of the writing activity is the word on the paper—"apple"—which is, in itself, a non-neural event.

At both the integration and representational levels, part of the encoding product ($\dot{r}$ and s_m) is fed back through the system for modification or correction, if necessary. External feedback occurs when the individual inspects his production of the written word and corrects errors that may be present.

The second example of the model, shown in Figure 5, demonstrates the activities occurring when an individual imitates a word spoken by another person. The imitative response is considered merely echoic and

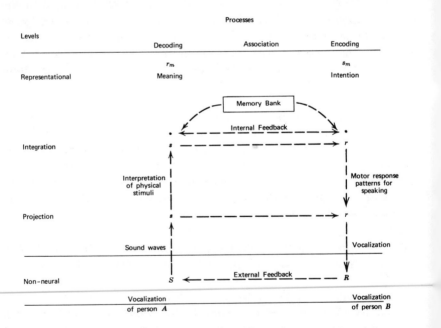

FIGURE 5.   The imitative response.

without meaning. In the example, the non-neural stimulus is a word, syllable, or any vocalization produced by one person. The stimulus in the form of sound waves is heard by a second person at the projection level and is interpreted at the integration level, interpretation which is possible because the sensory signal is familiar although without meaning. The sensory correlates associated with the sensory signal serve to elicit motor correlates, that is, the automatic and sequential imitative patterns for motor activity. The activity itself, in this case vocalization, occurs at the projection level. The result of vocalization is a word or syllable produced by the second person and heard by himself and the other person. Although a spoken word is fleeting and does not occupy space as does the written word, it is still a non-neural event after it has been produced. As in the previous example, feedback occurs at the integration and non-neural levels.

Whenever the various tests administered in the different evaluations are discussed, the readers should refer to Table 1. This particular table has been constructed to demonstrate the level of language organization and channel of communication measured by each test or subtest. This same type of test analysis was given by Miron (Osgood & Miron, 1964) using only the Osgood model of language function as a basis for categorizing tests of adult aphasia. A major difference between the present analysis and that presented by Miron is the elimination in Table 1 of the classification of tests by language process. The decision not to assign a process label to each of the tests was made on pragmatic grounds and reflects the fact that the level of language and the channel are more important therapeutically than is the process. As a result of research with language deficient children Weiner (1969) stated that "the modality concept, as defined in the language model, serves as a major organizing principle in describing the cognitive functioning of these . . . children" (p. 62). In fact, both Wepman (1964) and Myklebust (Johnson & Myklebust, 1967) feel that specific learning disabilities can be better understood if one takes in account the modality functioning of the child.

The first entry in Table 1 refers to tests of articulation and the analysis indicates that such tests measure an ability found at the integration level of language with the channel of communication being auditory or visual input with vocal output. Entries for some tests record the channel utilized as a single modality—"Vocal," as equal input and output—"Visual/Motor," or as primary and secondary modalities—"Auditory(Visual)." For example, Test 3a—Auditory Reception from the ITPA—is judged to utilize only the auditory channel; Test 4e—Auditory

Table 1 Psycholinguistic Analysis of Tests Used in the Educationally Oriented Evaluation

Test and/or Subtest	Level[a]	Channel[b]
1. Articulation tests		
a. Imitation	II	Aud/Voc[d]
b. Picture or sentence tests	I	(Vis)Voc[e]
2. Peripheral speech mechanism examination (motility)		
a. Voluntary movement	I	Motor
b. After stimulation	I	Tac/Mot
3. Illinois Test of Psycholinguistic Abilities, Revised Edition		
a. Auditory Reception	R	Auditory
b. Visual Reception	R	Visual
c. Auditory Association	R	Aud/Voc
d. Visual Association	R	Visual
e. Verbal Expression	R	Vocal
f. Manual Expression	R	Motor
g. Visual Sequential Memory	II	Visual
h. Auditory Sequential Memory	II	Aud/Voc
i. Grammatic Closure	IP	Aud/Voc
j. Auditory Closure	IE	Aud/Voc
k. Visual Closure	I	Visual
l. Sound Blending	IE	Aud/Voc
4. Houston Test of Language Development, Part II		
a. Self-Identity	R	Aud/Voc
b. Vocabulary	R	Vocal
c. Body Parts	R	Auditory Aud/Voc
d. Gesture	R	Aud/Mot
e. Auditory Judgment	R	Aud/Voc
f. Communicative Behavior	R	Vocal
g. Temporal Content	IP	Vocal
h. Syntactical Complexity	IP	Vocal
i. Sentence Length	I	Vocal
j. Propositions	R	Auditory
k. Serial Counting	IE	Vocal
l. Counting Objects	R	(Vis)Voc
m. Repetition: Speech Patterns	II	Aud/Voc
n. Repetition: Melody Patterns	II	Aud/Voc
o. Geometric Designs	II	Vis/Mot
p. Drawing	R	Motor
q. Verbalization while Drawing	R	Vocal
r. Telling about Drawing	R	Vocal

Table 1 (Continued)

Test and/or Subtest	Level[a]	Channel[b]
5. Verbal Language Development Scale: parent report, no testing involved		
6. Speech-sound discrimination tests		
a. Wepman	I	Auditory
b. Templin	I	Auditory
c. Picture tests	I	Aud(Vis)[c]
7. Picture vocabulary tests	R	Aud(Vis)
8. Picture Story Language Test		
a. Productivity Scale	R	Motor
b. Syntax Scale	IP	Motor
c. Abstract-Concrete Scale	R	Motor
9. Tests of oral reading level	I	Vis/Voc[d]
10. Tests of oral reading comprehension	R	Vis/Voc
11. Tests of silent reading	R	Vis(Aud)
12. Tests of listening comprehension	R	Auditory
13. Spelling tests		
a. Oral spelling	IP	(Aud)Voc
b. Written spelling	IP	Vis/Mot
14. Tests of arithmetic computation		
a. Orally presented	R(I)	Aud/Voc
b. Written tests	R(I)	Vis/Mot
15. Bender Gestalt Test	II	Vis/Mot
16. Benton Visual Retention Test	II	Vis/Mot
17. Frostig test		
a. Eye-Hand Coordination	I	(Vis)Mot
b. Figure-Ground	I	Vis(Mot)
c. Form Constancy	I	Visual
d. Position in Space	I	Visual
e. Spatial Relationships	II	Vis/Mot

[a] Level:
    R = representational
    I = integration
  IP = integration predictive
  IE = integration evocative
  II = integration imitative
[b] Channel:
  Aud = auditory
  Mot = motor
  Tac = tactile
  Vis = visual
  Voc = vocal
[c] ( ) = secondary importance of level or channel
[d] / = equal emphasis on each channel

Judgment from the Houston Test—requires both the auditory and vocal modalities; and Test 17a—Eye-Hand Coordination from the Frostig Test—uses the primary modality of motor response but includes vision as a secondary input.

As the various tests used in the educationally oriented evaluation are mentioned in this chapter, the reader should refer to Table 1 and to Figure 3, which demonstrates the composite model of language function. By comparing the entries for each test given in Table 1 with the model in Figure 3, the reader will become increasingly familiar with the theoretical frame of reference advocated by the authors.

The Speech Evaluation

As stated at the beginning of the chapter, the model of language function, developed by Osgood and presented in Figure 1, and the composite model, presented in Figure 3, form the framework of the speech, language, academic, and psychological evaluations. The division of the diagnostic evaluation into categories, such as speech, language, psychological, is artificial, and it must be remembered that the purpose of the evaluation is to gain a broad and varied amount of information about the verbal and nonverbal abilities of the child which will be relevant to the remediation of his learning problems.

We must assume that tests of auditory and visual acuity are administered routinely to rule out the possibility of sensory deficits or to determine to what degree the presence of such deficits may contribute to the learning problem. If one attempts to relate such testing to the theoretical model, it may be seen that the projection level of language and the decoding process are involved in problems of reduced sensory acuity.

The authors relate the various tests described in this section to the language model in an effort to indicate the usefulness of the individual tests in over-all evaluation. The speech evaluation is often the initial contact between the child and the team members and, therefore, it is discussed first. Specialized examinations of vocal output are utilized only when necessary, if there are indications of problems like stuttering, cleft palate, or voice disorders in addition to the learning disability. Detailed descriptions of such testing are not given but may be found in Johnson, Darley, and Spriestersbach (1963). In the routine speech evaluation, information as to the quality of vocal expression in terms of articulation, fluency, and phonation should be obtained as should information concerning the adequacy of the peripheral speech mechanism.

TESTS OF ARTICULATION

Children with specific learning disorders often present problems in articulation and general intelligibility. Articulation tests in general provide the child with a visual stimulus, usually a picture but sometimes a word, and the child is required to respond with the name of the picture or to read the word. The verbal response contains the particular sound or phoneme the examiner wishes to elicit. The reader may observe that the task requires minimal visual decoding (in fact, visual decoding can be eliminated by saying the words for the child to imitate) and requires a motor response. The nature of the task, the production of certain sounds, places it at the integration level. In terms of the language model, learning articulation skills is dependent upon the integrity of the auditory decoding process at the projection and integration levels, upon the organization of adequate motor encoding correlates at the integration level, and upon control of the muscles of articulation at the projection level. In evaluating articulation problems, one must assess auditory and motor skills in addition to the evaluation of the product, namely, articulation.

Several tests of articulatory proficiency are available to the diagnostician; these include the Templin-Darley Tests of Articulation (Templin & Darley, 1960), McDonald's (1964) Deep Test of Articulation, the revised Bryngelson-Glaspey test (1962), and the Arizona test (Barker, 1960). Many of these measures are discussed by Darley (1964) and Johnson, Darley, and Spriestersbach (1963). The tests generally attempt to evaluate the child's ability to produce the standard speech sounds of American English in various positions in words or within varying phonetic contexts. Some of the tests provide norms for articulatory ability, but such norms should be used with caution. The articulation age given by the Templin-Darley test is related to the mean number of errors and thus the child may obtain an age equivalent which does not adequately describe his performance. For example, a child who manifests a problem with the /s/ sound will have a lower articulation age than may be warranted, because the /s/ is a phoneme which is investigated thoroughly on the test in initial, medial, and final positions and in a number of blends while other phonemes are tested only a few times.

As a routine part of the articulation assessment, the examiner subjectively rates the child's speech according to the intelligibility of connected speech and the child's ability to produce correct sounds after stimulation, that is, by imitation. The ability to imitate correct sounds is related to improvement in articulation; the child who produces the correct sound after stimulation has a better prognosis than the child who imitates poorly. Often a child's connected discourse is less or more intelligible than the results of the articulation inventory would lead one to expect.

TESTS OF MOTOR SPEECH

Following the procedures set forth by Johnson, Darley, and Spriestersbach (1963), the diagnostician should examine the child's peripheral speech mechanism, that is, the lips, tongue, palate, and dental arches. Of interest and importance, naturally, are any structural abnormalities that may contribute to faulty articulation. In evaluating children with specific learning disabilities, however, there is perhaps greater interest in the areas of speech mechanism motility, a function located on the integration level of language. Motility may be defined as the movement of any of the movable structures in the oral cavity. The range and the speed of the movement are assessed as well as the coordination of movements involving more than one structure.

Because the total expressive function of the child is under scrutiny, the presence of possible dyspractic qualities should engage the attention of the examiner. Dyspraxia refers to an inability to formulate an appropriate motor response pattern even though there are no paralytic or structural anomalies present. Many of the misarticulations of children with learning disorders are of the distortion type and improvement after stimulation is relatively poor. The hypothesis of verbal dyspraxia should be set forth tentatively when there is evidence from the examination of the peripheral speech mechanism in the form of restricted or reduced motility of the articulators, without evidence of a neuromuscular disorder.

Within the writers' experience many children with learning disabilities do not exhibit articulation problems, but at the same time they do show evidence of poor lip and tongue motility and incoordination. This evidence does not constitute a basis for a diagnosis of dyspraxia at this time; however, it should be noted and, when all the tests have been completed and the total language functioning is reviewed, it may become significant. Johnson and Myklebust (1967) state that many of these children are found to evidence signs of dyspraxia.

The results of the examination of the peripheral speech mechanism fit into the language model as motor encoding processes at the integration and projection levels. The diagnostic questions to be answered are whether the child can formulate an appropriate response pattern and whether he can control and manipulate the appropriate muscles. If the answer to the first is negative, we may assume that the child is dyspractic; however, if the answer to the second question is negative, the child *may* be dyspractic, for he also has some paralytic or neuromuscular disorder. In cases such as this, a neurologist should make the final decision.

The Language Evaluation

Although the speech tests are evaluated within the framework of the theoretical language models which are used as the basis for the complete assessment of specific learning disabilities, there are measures of language ability which are not influenced by articulatory inadequacy. These tests form the core of the language evaluation and are interpreted in terms of the various dimensions of the language paradigm.

COMPREHENSIVE LANGUAGE TESTS

Illinois Test of Psycholinguistic Abilities. The 1968 Revised Edition of the ITPA consists of 10 discrete subtests and 2 supplementary subtests standardized on approximately 1000 children between the ages of 2 and 10 years (Kirk, McCarthy, & Kirk, 1968). Six of the subtests measure aspects of the Representational level of language and include tests of reception, association, and expression. The remaining subtests are located on the Automatic level, a level analogous to the integration level of the composite model (see Table 1). Two of these latter subtests measure what is termed "sequential memory," and the other four are designed to assess closure or the ability to complete or recognize an incomplete stimulus event.

Normative data are provided enabling the examiner to derive both psycholinguistic age equivalents and scaled scores, thereby giving an objective point of reference in judging the performance of a child in any of the 12 abilities tested.

The ITPA is the only comprehensive test of children's language which provides norms derived from systematic standardization, and for this reason it is probably the most useful instrument in the language diagnostician's armamentarium. Because, however, the ITPA does not provide all of the types of linguistic information considered essential in the language evaluation, other test batteries should be included in an assessment.

To date, most of the research studies done with the 1961 ITPA do not lend themselves to drawing conclusions regarding one-to-one relationships between school achievement and performance on the ITPA subtests. Some studies, such as the one by Kass (1966), indicate that poor readers may perform more poorly than expected on subtests at the Automatic-Sequential (integration) level than on Representational level subtests, suggesting a deficiency in reading skills rather than a deficiency in ability to comprehend the material. There is no assurance, however, that training a child in the kinds of abilities assessed by the ITPA will result in increased reading ability. Readers interested in a critical evaluation of the 1961 ITPA should consult Weener, Barritt, and Semmel (1967) and McCarthy's (1967) reply to them.

Houston Test of Language Development. The Houston test, constructed by Crabtree (1963), is divided into two parts—the first for children between the ages of 18 and 36 months; the second for children aged 3 to 6 years. Included at each age level are items which are general in nature and related to the broad linguistic categories of reception, conceptualization, and expression. Also included are items which are more specific in nature, such as melody, rhythm, accent, gesture, articulation, vocabulary, grammatical usage, dynamic content of expression, knowledge of body parts, counting, and geometric designs.

It is difficult, and sometimes impossible, to pinpoint a child's performance in each category of the test in relation to his expected performance at a given age level, but the range of information garnered is significantly broader than that obtained from the ITPA. In order to evaluate the results of the Houston test in terms of the language model described in the opening section of the chapter, the reader should consult Table 1.

Verbal Language Development Scale. This scale, better known as the Mecham (1959), is the result of an extension and restandardization of the communication items from the Vineland Social Maturity Scale (Doll, 1953). The technique used in administering the scale is the same as that used with the Vineland—the informant-interview method—and anyone who knows the child well may serve as the informant.

The scale results are expressed as language ages, and since the age equivalents range from .14 to 15.0 years, the scale may be used with infants or adolescents. Because the school-age child is penalized severely on the scale if he has a reading problem, the suggestion is made that the scale be used with only preschool children if an estimate of oral language development is desired. Otherwise, the estimate one derives is, to some extent, an estimate of the child's academic difficulty. For diagnostic purposes it would seem more desirable to isolate oral language from graphic language when evaluating the child with specific learning disabilities.

SPECIALIZED LANGUAGE TESTS

In contrast to the comprehensive tests of language, the specialized tests assess only one fairly circumscribed area of language function. For example, the first tests described deal with auditory discrimination, the second group with vocabulary comprehension, and the last test with written expression.

Auditory Discrimination Tests. According to Wepman (1958), children with speech and/or learning problems often have inadequate discrimination of speech sounds. To explore this area, three tests of speech sound discrimination have been found useful: the Auditory Discrimination Test (Wepman, 1958), Templin's modification of the Travis-Rasmus test (Templin, 1943), and the Boston University Speech Sound Discrimination Test (Pronovost & Dumbleton, 1953). The Wepman test, which uses paired words alike or differing in only one phonemic quality, is particularly useful as a screening test.

We recommend that the child who performs poorly on the Wepman test be evaluated further in this area through the administration of the other two tests mentioned. The Templin test uses nonsense syllables, a device which eliminates the element of meaning and places the test more firmly on the integration level of organization. The Boston test is used to determine whether a child can discriminate between sounds when contrasting pairs of words or syllables are not used. The test is administered by having the child point to a picture, for example, a cup, on a page of pictures which may include not only the cup but also a cap, a cop, and so on. In this way, the child has to recognize the word without a similar auditory presentation with which to compare it.

Speech sound discrimination tests are usually restricted to auditory input, although the Boston does require minimal visual decoding ability. The response mode may be either vocal, saying "same" or "different," or motor, that is, pointing, nodding, etc.

Interpretation of auditory discrimination tests reveals that they require auditory decoding and motor encoding at the integration level. A certain minimal competency in short-term memory is required by the Wepman and Templin tests but not by the Boston test. The latter, however, introduces another variable, visual decoding, which may contaminate results. The administration of the Boston test and either of the other two should provide adequate information regarding speech sound discrimination.

Peabody Picture Vocabulary Test. The Peabody test (Dunn, 1959) is used in the diagnostic evaluation as a measure of the child's vocabulary comprehension and as a rough estimate of his intellectual functioning. In the presence of a possible learning disorder involving the ability to comprehend the auditorially presented verbal symbols of the test, the results become a part of the language evaluation and are not used as a reflection of the child's intellectual functioning.

Other available tests may serve the same purpose as the Peabody. The Full-Range Picture Vocabulary Test (Ammons & Ammons, 1948) and the Van Alstyne Picture Vocabulary Test (Van Alstyne, 1959) are similar in construction and administration to the Peabody and in at least one study (Dunn & Harley, 1959) were found to have intercorrelation coefficients above .80.

Picture Story Language Test. This test, constructed by Myklebust (1965), endeavors to measure the adequacy of written language and is comprised of three scales.

1. Productivity Scale—a scale which measures the amount of written language expressed under given circumstances and which is related primarily to the length of the written sample (total number of words), although the number of sentences and the mean sentence length are considered.

2. Syntax Scale—a scale which measures the correctness of the written sample in terms of syntax, grammar, and morphology.

3. Abstract-Concrete Scale—a scale which is concerned with the content of the written sample. Five levels of meaningfulness are used in scoring the scale, ranging from the lowest level of meaningless language to the highest level of abstract-imaginative language.

Derived scores for the Picture Story Language Test consist of age equivalents, percentile rankings, and stanines for children between the ages of 7 and 17 years. Because the test has become available only recently, it has not been used extensively by clinicians and its usefulness has yet to be determined. At present, however, it is the only standardized measure of children's written language and, as such, represents a unique contribution to the field of differential diagnosis of specific learning disorders.

INFORMAL TESTING PROCEDURES

Although several diagnostic tests of language development and function are available, the examiner often finds that the published standardized tests do not provide the range of information desired. When very young or severely involved children are being tested, measures such as the ITPA may be beyond the response capacity of the children and much simpler tasks must be substituted. Items from the lower age levels of the Revised Stanford-Binet Intelligence Scale (Terman & Merrill, 1961) may be used as well as items from other well-known instruments, such as the Gesell Developmental Schedules (Gesell, 1949) or the Grace Arthur Point Scale (Arthur, 1930). Bangs (1961) has furnished a language scale composed of items from other batteries, arranged by age levels, which is quite useful in testing young children.

The examiner, however, frequently finds that he desires to investigate areas of language function that are not included in available scales and tests. On these occasions, he will need to improvise his own testing procedures. Usually the need for informal testing arises as a result of the child's performance on standardized test materials; the necessity of investigating thoroughly an area of deficiency becomes obvious.

For example, the Auditory Decoding subtest of the ITPA consists of a series of graded questions requiring a "yes" or "no" response. The subtest purports to measure the child's ability to understand the spoken word without demanding more than minimal expressive ability on the part of the subject. If the child performs poorly on this subtest, the examiner knows only that when compared with other children his age, the subject does not comprehend adequately what is said to him; and yet, auditory language is a highly complex system involving parts of speech, syntax, structure, memory, and even such seemingly simple events as environmental noises. The examiner knows that the child does not understand what he hears on the subtest, but exactly what the child does not comprehend in terms of the complexity of auditory language is unknown. One cannot assume that the child does not comprehend such things as color names, prepositions or other parts of speech, or grammatical endings, just because he does poorly on the Auditory Decoding subtest. At this point, the examiner's clinical curiosity should lead him into informal testing procedures.

The informal procedures employed can be as detailed as the examiner's knowledge of language function, his ingenuity, and time permits. They can be only as lengthy as the child's endurance allows. The informal procedures described in the following section do not include every area of language that can be tested, but the description is detailed enough for the reader to gain insight into the process of informal testing. The suggestions may encourage the examiner to devise his own procedures and to extend them far beyond this outline.

Auditory Functions. These procedures are primarily auditory in nature; although other functions may be tested simultaneously, they are of lesser importance in the child's performance.

1. Auditory decoding
    a. Recognizes environmental noises
    b. Understands parts of speech—nouns, verbs, adjectives, prepositions, etc.

    c. Follows one, two, three, or four instructions
    d. Recognizes names of colors
    e. Understands a story read to him
  2. Auditory association
    a. Matches noisemakers by sound, e.g., two horns or two whistles
    b. Speech-sound discrimination—words, nonsense syllables
  3. Auditory closure
    a. Recognizes incomplete words
    b. Auditory blending of sounds to form words
    c. Simple analogies

Visual Functions. As with the auditory functions, the procedures used to test visual competencies may overlap into other areas of language function, but the tasks are primarily visual in nature.

  1. Visual decoding
    a. Recognizes objects and pictures
    b. Recognizes a picture cut into two, three, or four pieces
    c. Recognizes colors
  2. Visual association
    a. Matches colors, objects, pictures
    b. Matches object with picture
    c. Matches geometric forms—two or three dimensional or three dimensional forms with pictures of forms
  3. Visual closure
    a. Recognizes incomplete pictures
    b. Recognizes incomplete letters, numerals, or words

Tactile-Kinesthetic Functions.

  1. Recognizes by touch alone objects placed in either hand
  2. Matches sandpaper forms by touch
  3. Recognizes simple geometric forms, letters, words, etc., when they are drawn on the back of his hand or on his back

Vocal Functions.

  1. Uses words, phrases, or sentences
  2. Uses adequate grammar—proper inflectional endings, tenses, etc.
  3. Uses adequate sentence structure—words are not omitted, transposed, substituted
  4. Tells a story in logical sequence
  5. Mean sentence length appropriate for age

Motor Functions.

1. Imitates examiner's actions
2. Pantomimes everyday actions—combing hair, brushing teeth, batting a ball
3. Copies geometric designs
4. Draws human figures
5. Writes his name, letters, numerals, words, sentences

Memory Functions.

1. Repeats series of digits in or not in sequence
2. Recalls a set of objects seen
3. Recalls a set of pictures, letters, numerals, words

Sequencing Functions.

1. Recalls a pattern of taps, pitches
2. Recalls in sequence a series of objects, pictures, forms
3. Recalls a series of unrelated words, a sentence, a series of related words

The suggestions given above for testing language functions in an informal manner do not exhaust, by any means, the possibilities of testing. As the reader may have noted, no reference was made to testing sound-letter or letter-sound associations, the reason being that such testing may be more easily done during the academic evaluation which is devoted to the evaluation of the child's command of the graphic symbol system.

The Academic Evaluation

The language evaluation is devoted to the assessment of language processes utilizing the vocal symbol system, although there are a few notable exceptions, such as the Picture Story Language Test, which is concerned with the graphic symbol system, and some of the subtests of the ITPA and the Houston Test, which deal with visual nonverbal symbols. In contrast to the language evaluation, the academic evaluation is concerned solely with the decoding, association, and encoding of graphic symbols. It appears that these two symbol systems, the vocal and graphic, may represent fairly discrete language systems.

Clinical experience with children who have learning disorders has demonstrated that there is a group of children who manifest no *detect-*

able disorders of oral language. In vocal encoding they make no syntactical or structural errors, sentence length is adequate, and there are no indications of word-finding problems or of circumlocution. On the receptive side of the language model, no difficulties arise in the comprehension or oral language. There may be, however, minimal problems of a visual-perceptual nature on test items found at the integration level, particularly in the area of short-term sequential visual memory.

These children with adequate oral language manifest serious problems when confronted with tasks involving the graphic system. In attempting to spell, they may exhibit signs of poor visualization or poor auditorization of graphic symbols. Their sentence structure and syntax in written language may be disordered, and indications of what has been termed dyslexia may be noted.

The discrepancies between the child's performance on the two systems may be an artifact resulting from inadequate testing of oral language, and the discrepancy would disappear if measures of oral language were refined enough to detect minimal disorders. At this point in our knowledge, however, it appears better to treat oral and graphic language as two entities, rather than attempting to generalize test results in one area to the other. For this reason, the distinction between the language evaluation and the academic evaluation is considered appropriate.

DIAGNOSTIC ACADEMIC TESTS

The emphasis of this section is on areas of testing rather than on academic evaluation in terms of specific tests. A good description of various academic tests can be found in Ashlock and Stephen (1966).

In general, all school-age children should be given a battery of diagnostic academic tests; the younger children should be administered a battery of diagnostic readiness tests. Here, as in the other evaluations, the diagnostician is interested in the specific areas of modality input and output that are functioning adequately or inadequately. The overall estimate of academic achievement derived from the testing is important for administrative reasons, but it is the *profile* of academic abilities that is of diagnostic significance.

The academic evaluation is comprised of six general areas:

1. Oral and silent reading ability.
2. Oral and silent reading comprehension.
3. Listening comprehension.
4. Phonic and other word attack skills.
5. Oral and written spelling ability.
6. Oral and written arithmetic ability.

The first five areas of the evaluation may be assessed through the use of any of several good diagnostic reading tests which are administered individually. Among the more adequate are the Diagnostic Reading Scales (Spache, 1963), the Durrell Analysis of Reading Difficulty (Durrell, 1955), and the Gates-McKillop (1963). They have the advantage of providing the examiner with estimates of the child's ability to respond to the graphic symbol system using both visual and auditory input modalities and vocal and motor output modalities, while only a single test battery is administered.

The sixth area of the evaluation is devoted to the assessment of oral and written arithmetic ability. Most of the arithmetic tests available have no separate norms for oral administration; therefore, two equivalent forms of the same test should be used, one given orally, the other given as a written examination. Tests of both arithmetic computation and arithmetic reasoning should be used. Children who are in the upper grades and who have been exposed to arithmetic problems requiring complex computation, difficult without the use of pencil and paper, are administered only the written test of computation. If the child has reading difficulties, he should be permitted to demonstrate his ability in arithmetic reasoning by having the "word" problems read aloud to him.

The previous discussion concerns the child who achieves well enough to respond to academic tests. However, the young school-age child who is in the first or second grade and who manifests specific learning disabilities rarely will be able to handle the type of achievement tests just described. For these children, the academic evaluation consists of a battery of readiness tests. Several readiness tests are useful, but the one that has been found most informative is a relatively old test—the Monroe Reading Aptitude Tests (Monroe, 1935).

The Monroe has five separate scales, each related to reading, and offers percentile ranks derived for each of the five scales—visual, auditory, motor, articulation, and language—as well as for the entire test. In addition to obtaining scores for the various scales, the examiner will find of great benefit the fact that the test provides norms for children five through eight years of age. Number readiness, not measured by the Monroe, is assessed by the Metropolitan Readiness Test (Hildreth & Griffiths, 1950), which is used also for testing reading readiness. Other aspects of reading readiness, not covered in the previously mentioned instruments, are measured by such batteries at the Lee-Clark Reading Readiness Test (Lee & Clark, 1962) and the Gates Reading Readiness Test (Gates, 1939).

The academic test results are viewed in terms of one mode of input against one mode of output. The examiner attempts to answer such questions as: Does the child spell better with a vocal response or with a written one, that is, a motor response? Can he comprehend better what is read to him or what he himself reads, and at what level can he comprehend material read to him? Can he copy a word he has seen better than a word that has been spelled aloud to him? One expects, therefore, that the academic evaluation will provide information as to the best mode of input and of output when the child is confronted with tasks requiring the manipulation of the graphic symbol system.

INFORMAL TESTING PROCEDURES

The informal procedures used by the language diagnostician have been described in a previous section of the chapter; the academic examiner also employs informal testing when he finds that no standardized measures of specific abilities are available. For example, there are no standardized tests of sound-letter or letter-sound associations; the academic diagnostician tests these associations using the following combinations:

1. Auditory-Vocal. The sound is presented by the examiner and the child responds with the name of the letter.
2. Auditory-Motor. The sound of the letter is presented; the child responds by writing the graphic form of the letter.
3. Visual-Vocal. The letter is shown to the child and he responds by giving the name of the letter and the sound associated with it.
4. Visual-Motor. The child looks at the letter, it is withdrawn, and he writes the letter.

In addition to testing combinations of letters and sounds using the different sensory modalities, the examiner also undertakes some short-term teaching to determine, if possible, the manner in which the child best learns to read words. Generally, three techniques should be used in teaching the child several words which he does not know. The first technique used is the traditional "look-and-say" or word method in which the child looks at the word, is told what it is, and says the word; several trials are given. Second, the child is given a word which he must simultaneously view, trace, and say; he then writes the word without the model. This is basically the same technique advocated by Fernald (1943). The third technique employs a phonic approach; the child analyzes the word by sounds and then blends the sounds to form the word. Such short-term teaching should be done at the beginning of the testing period and learning is evaluated by reviewing at the end of the session the words which the child mastered using the different methods. With good fortune the examiner is able to determine which method is most suitable for the child.

Informal testing procedures cannot substitute for standardized procedures, but they may give the diagnostician insight into the specifics of the child's learning problems and may point the way for remediation. Habilitation of specific learning disorders, however, is based upon the results of the total evaluation, not upon results obtained by any one examiner, which may be, and often are, directly contradicted by results obtained by other members of the team.

The Psychological Evaluation

Although the statement may seem repetitive, it must be said that the results of the psychological evaluation of the child with specific learning disabilities should be interpreted in terms of the theoretical model of language function. The interpretation is made with respect to the modes of input and output utilized, the levels of language organization involved, and the psycholinguistic processes concerned. The psychologist bears the primary responsibility for a differential diagnosis which determines whether the problem is that of a learning disorder, mental retardation, or an emotional disturbance. Should the decision be a learning disorder, the psychologist often must defer to the judgment of the other examiners who probably are better able to differentiate the type of learning problem and to recommend remedial procedures.

Burgemeister (1962) and Taylor (1961) have reviewed thoroughly the tests and procedures of testing that are useful in evaluating both adults and children suspected of having specific disabilities. Both of these references are of interest and should be consulted for detailed discussions of psychological appraisal.

The psychological tests of intelligence most frequently administered to children with learning disabilities are the Revised Stanford-Binet Intelligence Scale (Terman & Merrill, 1960), the Wechsler Intelligence Scale for Children (Wechsler, 1949), the Columbia Mental Maturity Scale (Burgemeister Blum, & Lorge, 1959), the Leiter International Performance Scale (Leiter, 1948), Raven Children's Colored Progressive Matrices (Raven, 1947), and the Minnesota Pre-School Scale (Goodenough Maurer, & Van Wagenen, 1932). Other tests of specific abilities and aptitudes include the Bender Visual-Motor Gestalt Test (Bender, 1938), the Marianne Frostig Developmental Test of Visual Perception (Frostig et al., 1964), and the Goodenough-Harris Drawing Tests (Harris,

1963). In addition to these measures of cognitive and perceptual ability, various personality tests are utilized.

Intelligence and personality measures are not discussed in detail in this chapter because such tests have little predictive validity in terms of the selection of appropriate teaching methods. Perceptual and psychomotor tests are classified under the rubric of psychological tests and do have direct relationships to training procedures outlined by many authors discussed in later chapters (Frostig & Horne, 1964; Barry, 1961; Roach & Kephart, 1966; Freidus, 1964; Getman, 1962). Because of these rather direct bonds between testing and training, several of the perceptual and psychomotor measures are discussed at this point. Most of the measures under consideration deal with visual perception; the greater part of auditory perceptual testing is done within the language evaluation.

BENDER VISUAL-MOTOR GESTALT TEST

The Bender, developed in 1938 by Lauretta Bender, purports to estimate the visual motor development of the child; such development is seen as parallel to mental development and as associated with language ability (Bender, 1938). The test consists of nine designs, each on a separate card, which are exposed one at a time before the child. He is requested to copy on a sheet of paper each successive design; no time limits are imposed.

The reproduced designs are judged in terms of distortion, rotation, perseveration, method of reproduction, and other factors. Koppitz (1963) has devised and standardized a scoring technique for the Bender which may be used with children as young as five years of age; it yields derived scores related to developmental age and school grade equivalents. As Taylor (1961) has reported, the examiner often finds it difficult to interpret a specific child's drawings and therefore corroborating evidence from other tests and observations must be gathered.

BENTON VISUAL RETENTION TEST

The Benton (1955) test of visual memory consists of a number of designs shown to the subject for a specific period of time and reproduced by him from memory. Scoring standards are provided for children eight years of age and older and age equivalents may be obtained. The Benton, like the Bender, has been used extensively in attempting to diagnose brain injury in both children and adults; such is not the purpose of the test in a psychoeducational evaluation. Rather these "tests of brain injury" are administered to children with specific learning disabilities in an effort to assess and describe the nature and extent of their difficulties in visual perception.

MARIANNE FROSTIG DEVELOPMENTAL TEST OF VISUAL PERCEPTION

The Frostig (Frostig et al., 1964) is a battery of five reportedly discrete tests of visual perception which may be administered to children with CAs of 4-0 to 8-0 years, either individually or in small groups. The five areas of visual perception measured were selected by the author because of their high degree of relationship to academic skills.

Frostig (Maslow, Frostig, et al., 1964) observed from her work with children who had reading, spelling, and/or writing problems that the following visual perceptual disturbances were observed in the children:

1. Poor *eye-hand coordination* appeared to be related to writing ability.

2. Disturbances in *figure-ground discrimination* were related to poor word recognition.

3. Poor *form constancy* appeared in children who had difficulty recognizing letters or words when the size or type of print was altered or when the color was changed.

4. Children who rotated or reversed letters or words seemed to show a deficiency in their ability to perceive *position in space*.

5. Problems in analyzing *spatial relationships* were related to the transposition of letters in words and also were related to auditory perceptual problems.

The Frostig test was constructed, therefore, to assess the child's ability in each of these five areas of visual perception. No assumption was made relative to these being the only areas of interest in evaluating the total visual perception process, but Frostig believes that these are the areas most relevant to school performance.

PURDUE PERCEPTUAL-MOTOR SURVEY

The Purdue Scale (Roach & Kephart, 1966) has, as its objective, the rating of perceptual-motor development—one area of general development. No claim is made by the authors of the scale that other areas of development, such as verbal and symbolic development, are not of great concern to the diagnostician and to the teacher, but these areas are merely outside the purview of the rating scale. The tasks on the scale are designed for children aged six to nine years, although the scale may be used, with modifications, for both younger and older children

The areas of perceptual-motor development encompassed by the scale are as follows:

1. Balance and postural flexibility.
2. Body image and differentiation.
3. Perceptual-motor match.
4. Ocular control.
5. Form perception.

The scale may be used by teachers, as well as diagnosticians, to determine the level of perceptual-motor development attained by the child so that a training program may be initiated for the child.

Many of the authors discussed here have devised training methods either directly related to specific perceptual assessment techniques, such as Frostig and Horne (1964) and Kephart (1960), or indirectly related to the testing, such as Barry (1961), Getman (1962), and Freidus (1964). There are many other tests of perception, some quite old, others relatively new, for example, the Kohs Block Designs Test (Kohs, 1923), the Goldstein-Scheerer Stick Test (Goldstein & Scheerer, 1941), the Memory-for-Designs Test (Graham & Kendall, 1960). For a detailed review of these and other perceptual tests, the reader is referred to either Burgemeister (1962) or Taylor (1961).

Another consideration in the area of psychological testing is measures of memory. Most of the individually administered intelligence tests include items concerned with the assessment of short-term memory; for example, the WISC measures memory through a digit repetition test and, to some extent, through a digit symbol test. Memory items on the Revised Stanford-Binet include such tasks as repeating digits and sentences; a digit span test is found also on the ITPA.

Two particularly interesting tests of short-term memory are discussed by Taylor (1961) and could be included easily in the psychoeducational evaluation. The first test, devised by Rey in 1941 and adapted by Taylor, consists of two lists of 15 words each which are read to the child, one list at a time. Each list is read five times and after each reading, the child is asked to name all the words he can remember. Rough norms are provided for the successive readings and for the total number of words recalled.

The second test is an adaptation of the previous procedure and requires the child to learn 15 pictures which are named and presented to him at 1-second intervals. When all pictures have been viewed by the child, he is asked to recall as many as he can. Again, the collection of pictures is presented five times and the norms of the auditory test are used. Taylor (1961) states that the visual procedure seems easier for children than the auditory and separate norms are needed.

Short-term memory for auditory and visual symbols is measured by these two techniques, but, in addition, two modes of learning are being tested. From a comparison of the results of the two tests, one may be able to determine which sense modality is more effective for learning in an individual child. Note that in the visual test there is also an auditory element—the examiner's identification of the picture. Although the pictures are supposedly quite familiar to most children, the examiner names the object pictured so that the child will have a name when he responds, recalling all that he can. A child might recall a picture and yet, if he has no name for it, he cannot indicate to the examiner that he remembers. No adaptation of the test is available at present, but the implications of giving an auditory stimulus in a visual test are significant.

The results of the psychological evaluation frequently bear out what has been noted by many workers in the field (Cruickshank, Bice, & Wallin, 1957; Bender, 1959; Strauss & Lehtinen, 1947; Werner & Strauss, 1941):

1. Perceptual disturbances are common in children with specific learning disabilities, and examiners are led to the judgment that many of the children exhibit signs of central nervous system dysfunction. The central processes which interpret the flood of stimuli coming to the brain from the peripheral sensory organs are disrupted in some way, resulting in a disorder on the input side of the theoretical model.

2. Conceptual disorders frequently are noted. The ability to generalize or to classify the communality of elements is mainly, even if not wholly, dependent upon the intactness and integrity of the cerebral cortex. The child with a learning disorder often is found to have great difficulty in the areas of generalization and categorization, and many psychologists feel that such problems are the result of minimal cerebral dysfunction.

There does not exist at present a pattern or a type of response characteristic and specific for the learning disabled child when he is tested on standardized measures of intelligence or perceptual-motor performance. Clements and Peters (1962) suggest that there are three main patterns found on the WISC protocols of children with minimal brain dysfunction:

1. The most frequently encountered pattern is significant intratest scatter.

2. Verbal-scaled scores significantly higher than performance-scaled scores are typical of the second most frequent pattern.

3. The third pattern has a performance scale significantly higher than the verbal scale and is the least frequently seen pattern. This last pattern is said to be typical in children with reading disabilities.

Clements and Peters maintain that these three WISC patterns are indicative of minimal brain dysfunction. For individual children with demonstrable learning disorders, however, such patterns are not always encountered, and the psychologist who would state that these children have impairments of the central nervous system would be hard put to furnish incontrovertible test evidence.

Altus (1956) and Kallos, Grabow, and Guarino (1961) have attempted to discover WISC profiles typical of children with reading problems. Findings indicate that there is not a significant difference between verbal and performance IQs but that there is diagnostic value in the profile. Apparently a low score on the Coding subtest coupled with either a low score on Arithmetic or Information or a high score on Block Design would confirm the diagnosis of reading disability. Such diagnosis by profile may be accomplished for groups of children, but as individuals the children present a multiplicity of problems in varying combinations and diagnosis must be an individual matter.

If the purpose of the psychological evaluation is to provide a differential diagnosis in terms of brain injury versus no brain injury, not much hope can be held out for a positive diagnosis of the syndrome, minimal cerebral dysfunction. If, however, the purpose of the evaluation is to assess the child's cognitive and perceptual status, there is relatively little difficulty. The results of the psychological testing can yield valuable information as to the input and output competencies of the child as well as many data regarding his associational processes when tasks requiring the adequacy of high-order cognitive functions are concerned. Information is gained as to whether the child's ability to handle higher order abstractions is adequate, whether his perceptual-motor and psychomotor processes are intact, and whether he has possible greater potential than is observable from his over-all scores.

Summary

Three general classifications of information have been presented in this chapter:

1. The language model constructed by Osgood (1957) was discussed as a reference point for the diagnosis of language/learning disorders. Because the Osgood model does not incorporate memory, feedback, or

modality functions, the model of language presented by Wepman et al. (1960) also was discussed. The two models were merged into a composite model which was adopted by the authors as the framework for the educationally oriented evaluation of children with specific learning disorders.

2. A review was given of the types of information that should be gleaned from the diagnostic evaluation of the child with a specific learning disorder. This information was presented to the reader in the form of discrete examinations—speech, language, academic, and psychological—and the more important tests and test batteries were examined critically.

3. Third, and most important from the authors' viewpoint, was the presentation of a philosophy of assessment. The use of a diagnostic frame of reference within which to weigh all test data is not necessarily an innovation in diagnosis, but it is a departure from typical discussions of testing and diagnosis. A sincere effort has been made to present a way of looking at the child with a learning disorder that crosses the artificial boundaries separating the psychological evaluation from the speech evaluation or dividing the language and academic evaluations. The method of diagnosis that has been discussed is more than an example of the team approach; it is the team approach with all members functioning within their specific discipline but also operating within a common theoretical frame of reference.

The authors are committed to the belief that programs of remediation grow out of psychoeducational evaluation, and that the diagnostic information gathered from a child can form the structure of the instructional program. In Chapter III, the interpretation of test results and the structuring of remedial programs are discussed.

References

Altus, G. T. A WISC profile for retarded readers. *Journal of Counseling Psychology,* 1956, **20**, 155–156.

Ammons, R. B., & Ammons, H. S. *The Full-Range Picture Vocabulary Test.* Missoula, Mont.: Psychological Test Specialist, 1948.

Arthur, G. *A Point Scale of Performance Test.* New York: Commonwealth Fund, 1930.

Ashlock, P., & Stephen, A. *Educational therapy in the elementary school.* Springfield, Ill.: Thomas, 1966.

Bangs, T. Evaluating children with language delay. *Journal of Speech and Hearing Disorders,* 1961, **25**, 6–18.

Barker, J. O. A numerical measure of articulation. *Journal of Speech and Hearing Disorders*, 1960, **25**, 79–88.

Barry, H. *The young aphasic child: Evaluation and training.* Washington, D.C.: Volta, Bureau, 1961.

Bender, L. *A visual motor gestalt test and its clinical use.* New York: American Orthopsychiatric Association, 1938.

————, *Psychopathology of children with organic brain disorders.* Springfield, Ill.: Thomas, 1959.

Benton, A. L. *Revised Visual Retention Test: Clinical and experimental application.* New York: Psychological Corporation, 1955.

Bryngelson, B., & Glaspey, E. *Speech in the classroom.* (3rd ed.) Chicago: Scott, Foresman, 1962.

Burgemeister, B. B. *Psychological techniques in neurological diagnosis.* New York: Harper & Row, 1962.

————, Blum, L., & Lorge, I. *Columbia Mental Maturity Scale.* (2nd ed.) Yonkers, N.Y.: World Book, 1959.

Clements, S. D., & Peters, J. E. Minimal brain dysfunctions in the school-age child. *Archives of General Psychiatry*, 1962, **6**, 185–197.

Crabtree, M. *Houston Test of Language Development.* Houston, Tex.: Houston Press, 1963.

Cruickshank, W. M., Bice, H. V., & Wallin, N. E. *Perception and cerebral palsy.* Syracuse, N.Y.: Syracuse University Press, 1957.

Darley, F. L. *Diagnosis and appraisal of communication disorders.* Englewood Cliffs, N.J.: Prentice-Hall, 1964.

Doll, E. A. *The measurement of social competence (A manual for the Vineland Social Maturity Scale).* Washington, D.C.: Educational Testing Bureau, 1953.

Dunn, L. M. *Peabody Picture Vocabulary Test.* Minneapolis, Minn: American Guidance Service, 1959.

————, & Harley, R. K. Comparability of Peabody, Ammons, Van Alstyne, and Columbia test scores with cerebral palsied children. *Exceptional Children*, 1959, **26**, 70–75.

Durrell, D. D. *Durrell Analysis of Reading Difficulties.* New York: Harcourt, Brace, & World, 1955.

Fernald, G. *Remedial techniques in basic school subjects:* New York: McGraw-Hill, 1943.

Freidus, E. Methodology for the classroom teacher. In J. Hellmuth (Ed.), *The special child in century 21.* Seattle, Wash.: Special Child, 1964.

Frostig, M., & Horne, D. *The Frostig program for the development of visual perception.* Chicago: Follett, 1964.

Frostig, M., Lefever, D. W., & Whittlesey, J. R. *The Marianne Frostig Developmental Test of Visual Perception.* Palo Alto, Cal. Consulting Psychologists Press, 1964.

Gates, A. I. *Gates Reading Readiness Tests.* New York: Teachers College Press, 1939.

————, & McKillop, A. S. *Gates-McKillop Reading Diagnostic Tests.* New York: Bureau of Publications, Teachers College, Columbia University, 1963.

Gesell, A., et al. Gesell Developmental Schedules. New York: Psychological Corporation, 1949.

Getman, G. N. How to develop your child's intelligence. Luverne, Minn.: Announcer, 1962.

Goldstein, K., & Scheerer, M. Abstract and concrete behavior. Evanston, Ill.: American Psychological Association, 1941.

Goodenough, F. L., Maurer, K. M., & Van Wagenen, M. J. Minnesota Preschool Scale. Minneapolis, Minn.: Educational Test Bureau, 1932.

Graham, F. K., & Kendall, B. S. Memory-for-Designs Test: Revised general manual. Perceptual and Motor Skills, 1960, 11, 147–190.

Harris, D. B. Goodenough-Harris Drawing Tests. New York: Harcourt, Brace & World, 1963.

Hildreth, G. H., & Griffiths, N. L. Metropolitan Readiness Tests. Yonkers, N.Y.: World Book, 1950.

Johnson, D, & Myklebust, H. Learning disabilities. New York: Grune & Stratton, 1967.

Johnson, W., Darley, F. L., & Spriestersbach, D. C. Diagnostic methods in speech pathology. New York: Harper & Row, 1963.

Kallos, G. L., Grabow, J. M., & Guarino, E. A. The Wisc profile of disabled readers. Personnel and Guidance Journal, 1961, 39, 476–478.

Kass, C. Psycholinguistic disabilities of children with reading problems. Exceptional Children, 1966, 32, 533–541.

Kephart, N. C. The slow learner in the classroom. Columbus, Ohio: Merrill, 1960.

Kohs, S. C. Intelligence measurement. New York: Macmillan, 1923.

Kirk, S. A., McCarthy, J. J., & Kirk, W. O. Illinois Test of Psycholinguistic Abilities, examiner's manual. Urbana: University of Illinois Press, 1961. (a)

———. The Illinois Test of Psycholinguistic abilities—an approach to differential diagnosis. American Journal of Mental Deficiency, 1961, 66, 399–412. (b)

Kirk, S. A., McCarthy, J. J., & Kirk, W. O. Illinois Test of Psycholinguistic Abilities, revised edition. Examiner's manual. Urbana: University of Illinois Press, 1968.

Koppitz, E. M. The Bender Gestalt Test for young children. New York: Grune & Stratton, 1963.

Lee, J. M., & Clark, W. W. Lee-Clark Reading Readiness Test, 1962 revision. Monterey: California Test Bureau, 1962.

Leiter, R. S. Leiter International Performance Scale. Chicago: Stoelting, 1948.

Maslow, P., Frostig, M., Lefever, D. W., & Whittlesey, J. R. The Marianne Frostig Developmental Test of Visual Perception, 1963 standardization. Perceptual and Motor Skills, 1964, 19, 463–499.

McCarthy, J. J. A response. Exceptional Children, 1967, 33, 6.

McDonald, E. T. Articulation testing and treatment: A sensory-motor approach. Pittsburgh, Pa.: Stanwix House, 1964.

Mecham, M. J. Verbal Language Development Scale. Minneapolis, Minn.: American Guidance Service, 1959.

Mira, M. P. Individual patterns of looking and listening preferences among learning disabled and normal children. Exceptional Children, 1968, 34:9 649–659.

Monroe, M. Reading Aptitude Tests. Boston: Houghton Mifflin, 1935.

Myklebust, H. *Auditory disorders in children.* New York: Grune & Stratton, 1954.

———. *Development and disorders of written language. Vol. I. Picture Story Language Test.* New York: Grune & Stratton, 1965.

Osgood, C. E. *Method and theory in experimental psychology.* New York: Oxford University Press, 1953.

———. Motivational dynamics of language behavior. In M. R. Jones (Ed.), *Nebraska symposium on motivation.* Lincoln: University of Nebraska Press, 1957.

———, & Miron, M. S. (Eds.) *Approaches to the study of aphasia.* Urbana: University of Illinois Press, 1963.

Pronovost, W., & Dumbleton, C. A picture-type speech sound discrimination test. *Journal of Speech and Hearing Disorders,* 1953, **18,** 258–266.

Raven, J. C. *Progressive Matrices (Coloured) Sets A, Ab, B.* London: Lewis, 1947.

Roach, E. G., & Kephart, N. C. *The Purdue Perceptual-Motor Survey.* Columbus, Ohio: Merrill, 1966.

Skinner, B. F. *Verbal behavior.* New York: Appleton-Century-Crofts, 1957.

Spache, G. D. *Diagnostic Reading Scales.* Monterey: California Test Bureau, 1963.

Strauss, A. A., & Lehtinen, L. *Psychopathology and education of the brain injured child.* Vol. I. New York: Grune & Stratton, 1947.

Taylor, E. M. *Psychological appraisal of children with cerebral defects.* Cambridge, Mass.: Harvard University Press, 1961.

Templin, M. Study of sound discrimination ability of elementary school pupils. *Journal of Speech Disorders,* 1943, **8,** 2.

———, & Darley, F. L. *The Templin-Darley Tests of Articulation.* Iowa City: University of Iowa Bureau of Research and Service, 1960.

Terman, E. L., & Merrill, M. A. *Stanford-Binet Intelligence Scale.* Boston: Houghton Mifflin, 1961.

Van Alstyne, D. *Van Alstyne Picture Vocabulary Test.* (1959 revision.) New York: World Book, 1959.

Wechsler, D. *Wechsler Intelligence Scale for Children.* New York: Psychological Corporation, 1949.

Weener, P., Barritt, L. S., & Semmel, M. I. Forum: A critical evaluation of the Illinois Test of Psycholinguistic Abilities. *Exceptional Children,* 1967, **33,** 6.

Weiner, P. S. The cognitive functioning of language deficient children. *Journal of Speech and Hearing Research,* 1969, **12,** 53–64.

Wepman, J. *Auditory Discrimination Test.* Chicago: Language Research Associates, 1958.

Wepman, J. M. The perceptual basis for learning. In H. A. Robinson (Ed.), *Meeting individual differences in reading.* Suppl. Educ. Monogr. 94. Chicago: University of Chicago Press, 1964. Pp. 25–33.

———, Jones, L. V., Bock, R. D., & Van Pelt, D. Studies in aphasia: Background and theoretical formulations. *Journal of Speech and Hearing Disorders,* 1960, **25,** 323–332.

Werner, H., & Strauss, A. A. Pathology of figure ground relation in the child. *Journal of Abnormal and Social Psychology,* 1941, **36,** 58–67.

CHAPTER III

FROM EVALUATION TO INSTRUCTION

If learning disordered children formed a homogeneous group, all reflecting the same types of problems in learning, both diagnosis and remediation would be immeasurably simpler. Unfortunately, children with specific learning disabilities exhibit all of the variations found in unaffected children as well as a variety of problems in learning, some of which are related to the vocal symbol system, some to the graphic system, and others to the subtle and pervasive elements of learning subsumed under such categories as attention and memory. Some problems manifested by these children are perceptual or psychomotor (integration level) in nature, whereas others are problems of conceptualization (representational level). Some of the children have impaired auditory modalities; others perform poorly in the visual areas, while still another group may have difficulty in translating symbols from one modality to another.

The information from the diagnostic evaluation discussed in Chapter

II must be interpreted as a whole; such interpretation may well be done within the frame of reference provided by the composite model of language function, also described in Chapter II. Parts of tests involving the decoding or perception of language symbols, the association of symbols, and the encoding or expressing of such symbols are grouped together so that each test or subtest may reveal its contribution to the assessment of that dimension of the model within which it is located.

In the same manner, test results are examined in relation to the level of language organization involved, that is, whether it is a test of meaningful language or a test of automatic, sequential, or imitative usage of nonmeaningful symbols. By superimposing the Wepman model upon the Osgood model, one more obligation is assumed in terms of interpretation—that of determining which modes of input and output are utilized by the test. Table 1 in Chaper II describes various tests along the dimensions of the language model.

The general purpose of the educationally oriented evaluation is to determine which language functions and processes have developed to an optimal level and which are defective. For example, a child may be able to understand what is spoken to him but be unable to speak. That is, he interprets auditory symbols but cannot encode or express himself in words. From the results of the tests, one may say that the child has normal auditory decoding ability but exhibits a deficiency in vocal encoding. Sometimes a child can interpret what he hears but cannot comprehend what he sees. In this case, one may say that the child has adequate auditory decoding ability but has a deficit in visual decoding. The examples given are oversimplifications of the learning disorders presented by the great majority of children who are seen diagnostically, but they do represent the type of differential diagnosis that is undertaken.

As may be noted from a comparison of the model of language and the diagnostic tests used, one of the major problems in interpreting results within the framework of a theory is related to the purity of the constructs hypothesized in the model and the "impurity" of the tests as they are constructed. In short, one is unable to measure decoding ability without requiring an overt response, minimal as it may be; similarly, one cannot assess encoding without providing some kind of overt stimulus.

Testing the association process, within the model, presents an even more difficult task than testing decoding or encoding. Association is the implicit mediational process, hypothesized by Osgood (1957) as a central process occurring between the overt stimulus and the overt response. In its pure form, association would have to be tested without reference to the overt events; this would be impossible using our present behavioral techniques.

The only solution to the quandary presented apparently lies in attempting to hold the response requirements to as minimal a level as possible when assessing decoding or to reduce the decoding requirements when testing encoding. The authors have come to the conclusion that by using more than one test of an ability and by varying slightly the process, level, or mode requirements of the tests, a diagnostic decision can be attained—a decision in which one may have a high degree of confidence.

The following diagnostic case study is an example of the evaluation process outlined in Chapter II.

M. S. was referred for examination because of poor speech. According to his mother, he could not make a number of sounds, spoke very rapidly, and ran many of his words together. Even when he spoke slowly, his speech was difficult to understand.

M. S. had entered kindergarten at the age of 5-1 years and had received both individual and group speech therapy for varying periods of time during kindergarten and first grade. At the time M. S. was seen he was 6-7 years old and in the first grade. He was performing poorly in his school work and probably would not be promoted to the second grade. His speech therapist had noted no significant improvement in speech production.

Intelligence tests resulted in an IQ of 87 on the WISC Verbal Scale, 93 on the Performance Scale, and 89 on the Columbia Mental Maturity Scale. There was little discrepancy between M. S.'s WISC verbal and performance IQs, but the range of the subtest scaled scores was nine points—from a low of six on Comprehension to a high of fifteen on Coding. M. S. had been considered by the school authorities for a class of educable mentally retarded children, but the results of the intelligence tests negated this suggestion.

M. S. was given a speech and language evaluation which revealed very poor articulation; one sound was produced correctly on the 50-item screening test of the Templin-Darley, and on a 114-item form of the same test 91 errors were recorded. Normal hearing acuity was found, and on the peripheral speech mechanism examination it was noted that M. S. had poor to fair lip and tongue motility. On the ITPA all areas involving the auditory-vocal channel were depressed as were the encoding areas; visual-motor areas were found to be unimpaired. Auditory discrimination and vocabulary comprehension—both auditory areas—were inadequate. During the informal testing, it was found that M. S.'s auditory-vocal and auditory-motor associations for sounds and letters were poor; and his visual-vocal associations, while below average, were comparatively better than those involving the auditory modality.

The lowest points on M. S.'s language profile were in the auditory-vocal areas involving the representational level of language and in the vocal and motor encoding areas. His short-term memory for auditory and visual sequences was relatively good. The assets of this boy, together with his deficits, provided clues to a training program which could utilize his abilities to develop his poor areas. The following recommendations were made:

1. The superiority in visual decoding and the other visual areas, including memory and sequencing, indicated that M. S. would probably learn to read most easily by the "look-and-say" method of teaching, i.e., an emphasis on the visual approach. Interestingly enough, he had learned word recognition by the whole word method and was reading at about the low first-grade level. He had no ability to sound out words or to recognize unknown words, but he did have a limited sight vocabulary.

2. A program of instruction for training M. S. in his deficient areas was suggested by the profile of test results. The program should be organized to remediate his auditory deficits through utilizing his visual abilities, providing him with visual clues to aid in auditory decoding and in making auditory-vocal associations.

3. Articulation therapy was recommended to ameliorate the speech production problem and to assist in the remediation of what appeared to be a mild dyspraxia, both verbal and nonverbal. M. S.'s difficulties in lip and tongue and in motor encoding as well as his general clumsiness led to the diagnosis of dyspraxia.

The boy in the case study presented was diagnosed as having an auditory receptive language disorder rather than aphasia, although persons familiar with aphasia terminology readily may draw parallels between the terms "auditory receptive problems" and "auditory" or "sensory aphasia." Because of the numerous connotations implicit in aphasia terminology, a behavioral description, such as auditory receptive language disorder, is deemed preferable to auditory aphasia when discussing children.

Diagnostic Teaching

Although the testing done on a specific child may seem exhaustive, there may be many times when the diagnosticians are unsure of the true nature of the child's problem and are not able to provide exact guidelines for the instructional program. At such times, it is the responsibility of the teacher to engage in what is called clinical education by Johnson and Myklebust (1967), educational therapy by Ashlock and Stephen (1966), but which the authors will refer to as diagnostic teaching.

THE AIM OF DIAGNOSTIC TEACHING

Diagnostic teaching is an extension and a continuation of the diagnostic process in which the teacher through careful observation and reporting aids in arriving at a behavioral description of the child's specific difficulties. Because the teacher sees the child on a daily basis, he has the opportunity to discover with some exactitude the parameters of a child's problem in any particular area.

Test results usually yield information regarding the broad outlines of a problem, for example, a visual-motor deficiency manifested in letter and word reversals, poor visual-motor or visual-vocal associations for letters and sounds, and poor visual memory. Recommendations from test results would, in a case such as this one, be related to suggestions for teaching through the auditory modality while strengthening the visual areas. When the teacher begins working with the child, however, he is the one who must make the decision as to where instruction will start. Such fine decisions cannot be made by the diagnosticians in the majority of cases but must be made by the teacher who utilizes the diagnostic reports as a starting point for diagnostic teaching.

In the case of M. S., the teacher would know that the boy has difficulties in the area of auditory understanding and should be encouraged to use his visual modality whenever possible to form adequate auditory associations. But where does instruction begin? If the boy can read a few words by sight, can the teacher assume that he knows the entire alphabet? The truth of the matter is that in the area of academics alone, the teacher can assume little from the reports of the diagnostic evaluation. There are at least two valid reasons for not assuming that the reports are comprehensive enough to provide an exact starting point for teaching.

INTRASUBJECT VARIABILITY

One of the outstanding comments made about children with learning disorders concerns their day-to-day variability. Teachers and parents alike report that what the child has learned to perfection on one day often is not retained the following day. It is not unusual for the diagnostician to be told by the parents that the child can perform a certain task and then find that in the testing situation he is not able to perform. Because of the variability within the child, test results also may vary, and although it can be assumed that the child's true scores lie within a certain range, the teacher will want a more definitive description of his ability. Such a description can be obtained by setting forth specific tasks for the child to perform several days in succession.

The behavioral variations of children with specific learning disabilities are not the only cause of intrasubject variability. One must take into consideration any variations in performance due to other physical or psychological variability, for example, the presence of an undetected low-grade fever may depress the child's performance, heightened emotional states can work to his detriment, and numerous other factors may prevent his performing to the best of his ability. By the same token, all conditions may be optimal, and the child will perform at a level which is above that on which he functions routinely. At any rate, the teacher must realize that the test results do not always reflect the child's actual performance level.

LACK OF TEST INFORMATION

The diagnostic tests, as they have been described, do not purport to assess the parameters of the child's ability in any one academic skill area, but rather they provide a sample of his ability to perform in many areas. The information from the tests is interpreted in terms of the processes the child goes through in responding to the tests. Thus an academic test does not show whether the child is able to recognize all of the letters of the alphabet but, instead, determines whether he recognizes several letters better with a visual or an auditory approach. It is the teacher's responsibility to determine whether the child knows *all* of the letters and then to teach him those he does not know, using the approach suggested by the diagnostician.

SUGGESTED TECHNIQUES IN DIAGNOSTIC TEACHING

Carrow (1968) has developed a sequence of procedures which directs the teacher's attention to the assessment of the child's responses in the auditory-vocal areas. The teacher may devise procedures for investigating the child's responses in other channels, namely, the visual-motor channel, using the following as a guide.

1. *Awareness.* Is the child aware of sound; does he respond in any fashion to sound? He may turn when he hears a sound in an attempt to localize the sound; he may change his facial expression; or he may attempt to imitate the sound. All responses would indicate that he has heard and is aware of the sound being produced.

2. *Recognition.* The teacher must determine whether the child can recognize a *specific* sound; evaluation may consist of presenting a sound stimulus and having the child match or select from a series of sounds

the one he heard. The teacher must decide also whether the child's response to the stimulus is constant, that, is, whether his response varies when his attention is directed toward other kinds of activities. The question of stimulus closure must be investigated: Can the child recognize a sound when it is not completely presented or when it is distorted?

3. *Identification.* Can the child select the source of a sound that has been presented? In order to select a sound source, the child must have adequate figure-ground discrimination, and therefore the teacher must determine whether he can identify the sound when it is surrounded by background noise.

4. *Discrimination.* Is the child able to discriminate between sounds of varying pitch, loudness, direction, or distance? Can he discriminate speech sounds as opposed to environmental sounds or can he differentiate between different speech sounds, for example, /b/ and /p/? Can he make these kinds of distinctions in the presence of competing background noise?

5. *Recall.* Can the child recognize the correct sequence as given in a stimulus? That is, can he recall a sequence of gross sounds or patterns of loudness or rhythm? Can he recall a sequence of speech sounds or a sequence of words? All the child has to do in the recall area is to identify whether the patterns are alike or different and the difficulty of the task may be increased by allowing the child to use both auditory and visual input the first time a series is introduced and then permitting him to use only the auditory input system the second time. The teacher also can determine whether the child can select a series of objects placed in the order of their naming.

6. *Generalization.* Can the child generalize sounds, that is, can he perceive categories into which sounds should be classified? For example, can he recognize that a series of bell sounds can be grouped together and a series of horn sounds can form another, discrete group? Can he select the best classification for a particular sound?

7. *Comprehension.* An evaluation should be made of the child's understanding of various aspects of linguistic structure: (*a*) lexical items such as nouns, verbs, adjectives, and adverbs; (*b*) the function words such as prepositions and articles; (*c*) morphological devices such as the "s" signifying plurality, "ed" denoting past tense; and (*d*) sentence structure

such as active or passive voice. These linguistic constructions can be presented to the child to elicit a motor response (pointing) without requiring vocal expression on the child's part.

8. *Imitation.* Can the child imitate the sound produced by the teacher? Such imitation may involve simultaneous production, that is, having the child begin clapping his hands at the same time the teacher begins. The particular pattern of sound can be maintained or the child can be required to imitate nonsense syllables.

9. *Recall and Reproduction.* Can the child repeat an auditory pattern after it has been presented? In other words, how adequate is his short-term memory for auditory sequences? Can he repeat a clapping pattern, a drumbeat pattern, or a series of object names? How long a series of unrelated abstract words or sentences can he repeat? In each instance, the teacher should determine how the child performs when presented with both auditory and visual stimuli or with auditory stimulation alone. In addition, one would wish to know if the child can repeat the content of a story in sequence. Other areas of investigation would include changes in response behavior when there is a delay between the stimulus presentation and the child's response, and how accurately the child can respond with increasing delay.

10. *Formulation.* What kind of language expression does the child have? Is his sentence length adequate? Does he use compound and/or complex sentences? Does he make grammatical errors? If so, what kind of errors and how consistently do they appear? Are there errors of morphological construction in the child's vocal expression? What is the nature and consistency of the errors? Does he circumlocute, that is, talk "around" a subject without clearly stating his ideas? Does he seem to have word-finding difficulties?

11. *Feedback.* Does the child respond to feedback from an external source, that is, does he discriminate an error if the teacher uses his error in a sentence? When the teacher contrasts the sentence with the error and one without it, can the child select the correct sentence? Can he evaluate his own errors? Can he indicate whether he used the form correctly or incorrectly? Does he monitor his expression only when attention is called to it or does he monitor at all times? Is he aware that he makes errors?

As stated at the beginning of this section, the teacher may adapt the eleven steps of diagnostic teaching to assess the child's performance in areas other than the auditory input system. The teacher who follows such a procedure as the one described will find that the process is on-going—it is not accomplished in one week or even in one month, but only as the child develops. Obviously, the teacher will need to decide at what point to investigate the child's performance and, in some instances, will not investigate unless the child is having particular difficulty with some task. For example, if the child does not seem to be able to follow directions in the form of commands, the teacher will attempt to determine at what level the child in unable to perform—does he comprehend, can he remember one command but not two, etc.

The concept of prescriptive remediation requires the accumulation of information regarding the child's abilities and disabilities, gathered in formal testing and in diagnostic teaching, and requires also the selection of appropriate teaching techniques. The diagnostician should be familiar with various teaching methods so that he may give the teacher guidance in initiating an instructional program; however, the teacher ultimately must be the one who prescribes educational precedures for the child, utilizing both objective and informal test results.

Numerous teaching approaches are available, some developed for the regular classroom, some for children with learning disabilities. The methods used in regular classes are often adapted for special classes, and although we will concentrate upon the specialized methods, an overview of some of the newer classroom instructional programs, particularly in reading, is relevant at this point.

Newer Approaches to Reading

Since the advent of Flesch's (1955) book *Why Johnny Can't Read,* great interest and controversy have been generated among educators as to the appropriate method of reading instruction. The extent of the interest has been demonstrated in the proliferation of reading methods; the controversy may be followed in most educational journals where numerous studies have been published, each indicating that one method is superior to another or that there is no significant difference among methods. The majority of the new approaches devised within the past few years are intended for use in the regular classroom and not in the classroom for children with specific learning disorders. Intention, however, often differs from application and the present writers have found that many of these new approaches to reading instruction are being used in special classes for children with learning disabilities. Teachers using these materials have reported that they are eminently satisfied with the new materials. Although the approaches are not remedial, it appears that some discussion of them in this chapter is warranted, if only because they are being used.

THE LINGUISTIC METHODS OF TEACHING READING

Bernstein (1967) has identified eight linguistic systems of reading instruction. The earliest of these is the method offered by Bloomfield and Barnhart,

> whose central thesis is that an inseparable relationship exists between the words as printed and the sounds for which the letters are conventional signs, and that to learn to convert letters to meaning requires from the start a concentration upon letter and sound to bring about as rapidly as possible an automatic association between them (1961, p. 6).

With this statement all of the authors who have devised linguistic approaches would agree, as would the proponents of the older phonics approach. The linguistic method differs, however, from the phonic methods in the application rather than the teaching of phonetics. In some ways, the linguistic approach may be characterized as a whole-word method in which the emphasis is placed upon the word as a whole. Bloomfield and Barnhart focused upon this point when they said that isolated speech sounds are foreign to our language and they deplored the presentation of single letters as signals for single speech sounds.

The linguistic methods differ from the more traditional approaches in yet another way, namely, the emphasis upon the introduction and teaching of phonetic patterns in a systematic sequence. Words are presented to the student according to the form of the words: regular forms first, irregular forms later. Vocabulary is controlled as in most reading books, but the control is achieved through phonetic regularity rather than word-usage frequency.

The linguistics approach devised by Fries (1962a, 1962b), who is the author if the *Merrill Linguistic Readers,* emphasizes intonation and syntax as well as spelling patterns and meaningful reading. Fries focuses upon oral reading in order to teach the child to use and understand patterns of intonation as clues to comprehension. According to Bernstein (1967), the Fries materials are the most thorough of the approaches she reviewed with respect to application of structural linguistics to reading instruction.

Research dealing with the use of linguistic materials has been sparse and the results have been generally inconclusive (Sheldon & Lashinger, 1966; Wilson & Lindsay, 1963; Wyatt, 1966). Reports in the literature indicate that as with other types of teaching methods, the linguistic approach as used is usually supplemented or modified so that research results are not open to generalization.

PHONETIC CODING BY COLOR

Two methods of teaching reading have been devised in which a color code is used to identify varying phonetic elements within words. The first of these approaches, *Words in Color,* was originated by Gattegno (1962, 1966) and embodies two of the standard elements of the linguistic methods, a strong emphasis on phonics and the avoidance of pronouncing the consonants in isolation. In this system each of the sounds in the English language is represented by a color—over 50 colors in all. In this way, the sound "a" as in "spade" always will be represented in the blue-green color regardless of whether it is spelled "a," "ei," "ea," or any other way.

Children being taught by this method learn first the five short vowel sounds and begin building letter combinations through the utilization of what Gattegno (1962) terms "visual dictation," meaning that the children and teacher point out successions of sounds from written sequences on the chalkboard. Visual dictation is emphasized because in this way the child learns to associate a spatial sequence of letters with a temporal sequence of sounds.

Advantages and disadvantages of the *Words in Color* method have been summarized by Dean (1966), who states that color discrimination may be difficult for a few children and that the children may become proficient in word-calling without comprehension. The latter statement could be made about any of the strongly phonic approaches because the primary school child's experience is limited and he may not understand many of the words which he is able to "read." Bernstein (1967) criticizes the Gattegno method on the grounds that it is too complex and that transition from color to black and white print may complicate the reading process to an unnecessary degree.

The second system of reading instruction which involves coding sounds by color was developed by Bannatyne (1966), who reports that he was inspired to develop his technique, "color phonics," after visiting the Ordblinde Institut in Denmark. The Bannatyne system differs from that developed by Gattegno in that not all letters are color coded by their different sounds; rather, only those letters which have fairly regular duplicate sounds are differentiated by color.

STRUCTURAL READING—A DISCOVERY METHOD
OF TEACHING READING

An almost direct antithesis of the linguistic approach to reading instruction is the discovery method used by Stern (1965), which she calls "structural reading." Basic to this method at every level of instruction are insight and meaning. As with the linguistic methods, the point of departure for Stern is the child's spoken vocabulary, and she emphasizes a type of phonics teaching. Beyond these similarties, the two approaches are quite different in rationale and methodology.

Instruction in structural reading begins with teaching the child to identify sounds he hears in spoken, known words; letters are introduced later. This initial period of instruction is devoted to training in auditory discrimination using objects and pictures. The student progresses from identification to finding several objects whose names begin with the same sound. Still using the spoken word, the child learns to read words; the preparation for sentence reading also begins at the spoken level.

First, children should discover how to read printed words whose structure corresponds exactly to the structure of the spoken word. . . . Since the children gain insight into the structure of these words, they can write them as well as read them. . . . Writing a word includes the knowledge of how it is constructed, that is, how it is spelled. Because reading, writing, and spelling have an integral relationship, they are taught simultaneously (Stern, 1965, p. 54).

As the student progresses through the reading program, the structural characteristics of words and sentences are emphasized. Because of his insight into the structure of reading, the child is able, supposedly, to transfer what he has learned to the comprehension of new tasks.

THE PROGRAMED INSTRUCTION METHOD
OF TEACHING READING

The *Sullivan Programmed Readers* (Buchanan & Sullivan Associates, 1963) combine the technique of the programed instruction with a developmental linguistic approach. Sounds are taught in isolation at the beginning of instruction, but because there is no strict correspondence between sound and graphic symbol in the English language, some elements of the whole-word approach are incorporated. Each child is able to progress at his own rate of learning using the programed workbooks, and as he learns to read a word, he also learns to spell and to write it. Bernstein (1967) questions the motivational value of the programed materials and states that the text is dull and unimaginative; other teachers have found the readers to be of high interest to children in Special Education classes and have noted adequate progress in reading.

Recent literature which pertains to the effectiveness of programed instruction in teaching school subjects indicates that the technique is as effective as other approaches to teaching (Schramm, 1964). With regard to reading instruction, the reports of McNeil (1964), Keislar and McNeil (1961), and Schuell (1966) point to positive gains of experimental groups over control groups where programed materials were in use. Specifically, results of large studies using the Sullivan materials undertaken in Colorado Springs (Liddle, undated) and Denver (Denver Public Schools, 1966) as well as the findings of various pilot studies suggest unexpected gains after one year's study in reading, in favor of experimental groups. A similar study in Philadelphia, however, yielded no difference between groups (Hammill & Mattleman, 1969).

Relative to the Sullivan studies (mostly action research reports), where tests of significance were used, actual reading achievement differences between groups tended to be small although statistically significant. The possibility of Hawthorne effect could not be discounted in any of the studies reviewed. The authors' opinion is that it has yet to be demonstrated conclusively that use of the Sullivan materials will result in a meaningful increase in reading ability over traditional, nonprogramed procedures.

THE INITIAL TEACHING ALPHABET

The i.t.a. is not a method of instruction so much as a teaching tool; it is the Pitman alphabet which consists of 44 characters, each of which represents only one English phoneme (Downing, 1965). For example, the numerous ways of spelling "I" ("eye," "igh," "uy," "ais," "is," etc.) are signified by one symbol—the "i" joined to the "e." Downing (1966) states that he has repeatedly made the comment that the i.t.a. may be used with any type of reading instruction, whether it be phonic, whole-word, programed, or eclectic. In his words, "i.t.a. is not a *method of reading instruction* and, in particular, it is *not* to be associated with the synthetic phonics approach. . . . It might better be termed a teaching aid" (Downing, 1966, 93–94). Downing conceives of the i.t.a. strictly as a writing system and so refers to it throughout his articles.

In his discussion of i.t.a., Downing (1966) emphasizes two points: (1) i.t.a. reduces the number of elements which must be learned before children begin to read, and (2) i.t.a. is designed to provide an easy transition to traditional orthography. At this time there are few children who have completed the transfer stage, but transition appears to present no problems.

Although no specific instructional method is necessitated when i.t.a. is used, the nature of the alphabet lends it most naturally and even inevitably to a phonic approach. Children who rely solely upon the visual characteristics of words printed in i.t.a. may exhibit great difficulty in transferring to the traditional alphabet.

One of the primary advantages in using i.t.a. readers, according to

Mazurkiewicz and Tanyzer (1964), is that the students who use them do not experience the obstacles raised by traditional orthography and are able to read material which is more advanced than that which is usually presented in the primary grades. The problem of reading without comprehension, however, is as real when i.t.a. is used as when any other rote material is emphasized. The authors question whether six- or seven-year-old children have the background of experience and the resultant cognitive ability to comprehend verbal material which is any more sophisticated than that presently found in the majority of the primary reading series.

A significant amount of research is being carried forward to determine the longitudinal effects of reading instruction which incorporates the initial teaching alphabet (Downing, 1966). The results of four years of research, including the research design and methodology, are being prepared by the National Foundation for Educational Research in England and Wales. It appears that one of the problems in interpreting this body of research in terms of teaching methods is that the i.t.a. may have been used with a phonic, word, or sentence approach since it is not supposed to be bound to a specific method of instruction. It is likely, therefore, that different teachers using i.t.a. would employ different teaching procedures, thereby offering little support for one method rather than another.

Insofar as the authors have been able to determine, little research has been done involving Gattegno's *Words in Color,* Bannatyne's color phonics, Stern's structural reading, or any of the other newer approaches to teaching reading. Readers who are interested in the present status of reading research should consult the last two volumes of *Research in Reading* (Traxler & Townsend, 1955; Traxler & Jungblut, 1960), where it may be observed that few, if any, of the questions about the nature of the reading process or the acquisition of the ability to read have been resolved. The authors also suggest Chall's (1967) recent book in which a systematic phonics approach to beginning reading is strongly recommended.

Before undertaking research in this areas, the following statement by Fries should be considered:

> The process of learning to read in one's native language is *the process of transfer* from the auditory signs for language signals, which the child has already learned, to the new visual signs for the same signals. This process of transfer is not the learning of the language code or of a new language code; it is not the learning of a new or different set of language signals. It is not the learning of new "words," or of new grammatical structures, or of new meanings (Fries, 1962, p. 120).

According to Fries, learning to read requires only that the child develop a set of habitual responses to a set of graphic shapes, the content of these responses being

1. The correlation of the spatial sequence of graphic symbols with the temporal sequence of auditory symbols, that is, the child must internalize the fact that reading and writing progresses in a left-to-right direction as spoken symbols progress in a sooner-to-later sequence.
2. The identification of the letters of the alphabet, which means that instant and automatic recognition and discrimination of the graphic symbols have been attained.
3. The learning of graphic symbols other than letters, for example, numerals, punctuation marks, standard abbreviations, and various other symbols, such as the mathematical operation symbols.
4. The learning of language signals which are not expressed in writing, namely, intonation.

In addition to the content of habitual responses which the child must form, Fries postulates three stages in learning the reading process. The first stage covers the period during which the student learns to transfer from the auditory signals to the visual signals. In the second stage these responses to the visual patterns become automatic, and the child no longer attends, on a conscious level, to the specific graphic shapes he is viewing. The third and last stage commences when the child begins reading to acquire new experience and reads as readily as he responds to spoken language for the acquisition of such experience.

An Overview of Specialized Methods

Certain highly specialized approaches to both preacademic training and reading instruction have been developed for children with learning disabilities. Such approaches, for the most part, are completely within the limits of Fries' premises regarding the nature of responses that the child must form in learning to read. By and large these methods differ from those discussed earlier in that they are remedial and emphasize specific modes of learning.

The specialized methods have been designed expressly for children who have some type of learning disorder regardless of the classificatory label attached to them. One will find, therefore, that some of the systems were developed for deaf children, some for aphasic children, and others for children labeled dyslexic, brain damaged, or language disordered.

The futility of labeling methods may be exemplified by recalling Maria Montessori (1912), who developed methods for teaching retarded, deprived children, and who lived to see them used with bright, socially advantaged children. It is not unusual or irrational to use a method devised for teaching language to deaf children when teaching hearing, language delayed children, because the system, with or without modification, may work equally well with both groups.

The important consideration in selecting a teaching method is not for what group it was designed, but for what groups it will work. One may go so far as to use materials prepared for strengthening kinesthetic perception in the blind child when teaching a child with a visual perception problem, thereby utilizing the tactile and kinesthetic senses of the child while, with other materials, reinforcing his visual abilities.

In attempting to categorize the specialized methods for teaching children with specific learning disabilities, several different methods of classification were considered. The teaching methods could be classified as synthetic or analytic, but such a classification was deemed unsuitable for two reasons.

First, there is little agreement as to which methods are analytic and which are synthetic. Diack (1960) states that the analytic methods are the whole word or sentence approaches and that the synthetic methods begin with letters and build them up into words. Lehtinen (Strauss & Lehtinen, 1947), however, refers to her teaching method, which is strongly phonic-oriented, as analytic. To reduce the possibility of confusion accruing from the disagreement on terms, it seemed better to eliminate the analytic-synthetic dichotomy.

The second reason for discarding the categories of analytic and synthetic was quite pragmatic in nature—not all of the methods described could be pigeonholed in these categories. Some of the systems are not methods in the strictest sense of the word but are sets of sequential procedures aimed at developing various skills and, as such, are not "methods" of teaching reading, spelling, writing, or any other academic subject.

In this book, the methods and techniques are presented in the following chapters according to the primary orientation emphasized in the instructional system. Each group of methods is presented in overview at this point along with a brief description of the category; mention is made also of the specialized methods included within the category. The seven categories include the following systems: perceptual-motor, multisensory, language development, phonic, structural test-related and neurological organization.

PERCEPTUAL—MOTOR SYSTEMS

Much of the recent work in developing methods and techniques for teaching learning disabled children has focused upon the perceptual-motor problems presented by many of the children; in actuality, many of the techniques suggested would be considered readiness activities by primary teachers. The systems included in this category are those developed by Barsch (1967), Freidus (1964, 1966), Getman (1962), and Kephart (1960). The techniques emphasize training in visual-perceptual areas; spatial orientation, directionality, eye-hand coordination, etc., are discussed in detail.

Seldom do the authors mentioned above discuss structured programs of instruction in reading or other school subjects. Instead they seem to believe that the child's difficulty in reading has its genesis in a more basic problem—perceptual-motor deficits—and once the child is trained thoroughly in perceptual-motor areas, he can be taught to read by any of the standard teaching methods.

MULTISENSORY SYSTEMS

The best known and best defined of the multisensory methods of teaching is the system designed by Fernald (1943). In the initial stages of the Fernald approach, equal emphasis is placed upon the visual, auditory, kinesthetic, and tactile (VAKT) modalities of the child. Although tracing of letters for tactile-kinesthetic effect is mentioned by Gillingham and Stillman (1965), the tactile and kinesthetic elements are not an integral part of their method. Stuart (1963) recommends the use of multisensory techniques when teaching children with "specific language disabilities" and marshalls an impressive amount of research to buttress her arguments. Although Stuart does not offer a remedial instruction program, she does provide the reader with an excellent approach to teaching a core curriculum of art and music, utilizing many perceptual-motor activities. Also included in the multisensory category are the techniques of Cruickshank (1961) and Lehtinen (Strauss & Lehtinen, 1947).

LANGUAGE DEVELOPMENT SYSTEMS

The methods that best illlustrate the category are those designed by Barry (1961), McGinnis (1963), and Myklebust (1967), which were developed for children with auditory receptive language disorders or, in their term, aphasic children. In the McGinnis system, known also as the "Association Method," children are taught initially to associate sounds with pictures whose names begin with the sound being taught. The graphic symbol is included in the association, but at the beginning the emphasis is upon fostering a meaningful association, that is, an association between a sound and a familiar picture, rather than between two abstract events, such as a sound and a letter.

PHONIC SYSTEMS

The methods that have been included in the auditory category are those relying primarily upon auditory-visual and visual-auditory associations between sounds and letters or letters and sounds. The approach taken in these methods, exemplified by the systems of Spalding (1957) and Gillingham and Stillman (1965), is essentially auditory in nature. It should be mentioned at this point that Spalding's system is the only method devised for regular classroom instruction that is presented in the section on specialized methods. Provisions are made in the phonic systems for strengthening visual associations, but these associations always are related to the graphic symbol, that is, the graphic representation of the *sound*.

STRUCTURAL SYSTEMS

Two authors, Fitzgerald (1963) and Pugh (1946), are discussed in the chapters dealing with teaching methods, although they have not developed methods for teaching specific subjects, such as reading and spelling. Instead, they have devised systems for teaching the structure of the English language as it is expressed vocally and graphically. The techniques were designed originally for deaf children who manifest great difficulty in acquiring the proper structure of the language. The methods, however, have been used successfully with many types of children, although little has been published regarding results.

Time and again, the teacher of learning disordered children is cautioned to provide careful structure for the children under his tutelage, both in the physical surroundings and in the presentation of tasks to be learned. Very seldom are suggestions given as to how structure can be provided in learning; much has been written about structuring the physical environment. The Fitzgerald Key gives the teacher, in at least one area—language expression—a technique for incorporating structure in teaching.

TEST-RELATED SYSTEMS

The systems discussed within this category are related directly to two diagnostic test batteries, the Illinois Test of Psycholinguistic Abilities (ITPA) and the Marianne Frostig Developmental Test of Visual Perception. Without question the procedures classified as "test-related" systems could be discussed in other categories. For example, the remedial techniques developed by Frostig are perceptual-motor, but because the suggestions for remediation are so closely associated with the child's performance on a specific test, as is not true of systems in other categories, the decision was made to discuss the Frostig and Illinois test-related approaches in a separate chapter.

A NEUROLOGICAL ORGANIZATION SYSTEM

Delacato (1959, 1963) has proposed a theory of neurological disorganization as the basis of learning disorders and has developed a system of therapy based upon the theory. The methods suggested by Delacato have produced widespread discussion and controversy, and no attempt is made in this text to resolve the conflict; simply, the theory and treatment program are presented. Many teachers undoubtedly will find that the motor training described by Delacato can produce desirable results in the children they teach, at least in the area of motor development if in no other areas. Many learning disabled children manifest aberrations in motor coordination, both gross and fine, and for this reason, the authors feel that some teachers might wish to incorporate elements of the Delacato regimen in physical education programs.

In addition to Delacato, the authors discussed in the section dealing with perceptual-motor systems often place a strong emphasis upon motor training. For example, both Freidus (1964) and Kephart (1960) present many techniques that focus upon the development of motor skills in children.

From the multitude of methods presented, both the diagnostician and the teacher must have some rational basis for selecting an appropriate method for teaching a particular child. As stated previously, the decision must be made in light of the child's specific learning disabilities as measured and in light of the types of disability best ameliorated by various methods.

In previous chapters, diagnostic procedures were reviewed, and in the present section a brief outline of remedial systems has been provided. At this juncture, before detailed discussion of the systems, a means of systematically relating diagnostic conclusions to appropriate remedial systems should be mentioned.

In an ideal situation diagnosticians and teachers would work together closely within the same theoretical frame of reference. Diagnosticians would have an intimate knowledge of the remedial methods, which was derived from direct observation, and in all likelihood would continue to evaluate the children. Because of this close association, teachers would be familiar with diagnostic information and its implications for instruction. In situations such as the one just described, the transition from diagnosis to remediation is accomplished without hindrance.

In far too many situations, however, the teacher and the diagnostician live in two different worlds. The diagnostician often has no conceptual framework within which to relate his findings; the teacher also lacking a frame of reference cannot use proficiently the diagnostic information which is provided. It appears obvious, therefore, that both need some means of interpreting the child's performance on diagnostic tasks in terms of ways of teaching him.

As shown in Table 1, types of specific learning disabilities may be related to remedial systems. Rather than presenting detailed narrative explanations of the table, its utilization will be demonstrated through the use of case history examples.

1. In the first example, the pupil's test performance leads to the conclusion that his poor reading is associated with impaired visual decoding processes at both the integration (perception) and representational (cognitive) levels. Other information indicates that the child's auditory modality is intact and that he exhibits no deviations in oral language. Referring to Table 1, one may find that the child needs remedial activities related to visual reading problems and visual perceptual disabilities. Methods which may be selected to overcome the visual perceptual problem are those developed by Kephart, Frostig, Lehtinen, among others. An appropriate reading method would be selected from those devised by Gillingham and Stillman, Lehtinen, and, depending upon the severity of the problem, Fernald.

2. Another child with reading problems may reveal inadequacies in the auditory modality, namely, poor speech sound discrimination, auditory memory, and ability to associate sounds with letters. Such a child also may exhibit poor articulation and various deficits in oral language. Appropriate methods geared to remediate the auditory-perceptual and oral language difficulties of the child may be those of Barry and those associated with the ITPA; he could best be taught to read through the use of McGinnis' Association Method.

The discussion of the individual systems in the following chapters provides the reader with reasons for choosing among systems which erroneously appear from Table 1 to be more or less equivalent. For example, after reading the discussion of Fernald and McGinnis, the reader will understand why the McGinnis approach was the method of choice for the child described in case history 2.

Discussion of these systems includes the underlying rationale, a summary of the teaching procedures, and a description of the specific learning disability most efficiently alleviated by the method. It is important

Table 1 Types of Learning Disability and Appropriate Remediation Systems

Motor Problems	Perceptual Problems		Oral Language Problems		Graphic Language Problems			
	Visual	Auditory	Receptive (Speech Comprehension)	Expressive (Speaking)	Receptive (Reading) Associated with: Auditory Deficit	Visual Deficit	Expressive (Writing)	Arithmetic Problems
Delacato (Barsch)[a] (Kephart) (Freidus)	Barsch Lehtinen Kephart Getman Frostig (DPVP) Cruickshank (Freidus) ITPA Barry	(Freidus) ITPA Barry Myklebust	ITPA Barry Myklebust Fitzgerald-Pugh McGinnis	ITPA Barry Myklebust Fitzgerald-Pugh McGinnis	Myklebust Fitzgerald-Pugh McGinnis Fernald	Lehtinen Cruickshank Myklebust Fernald Spalding Gillingham-Stillman	Myklebust	Lehtinen (Freidus) (Myklebust) (Fernald)

[a] ( ) = areas of secondary emphasis.

to remember that *none of the systems discussed can be utilized or imple-mented without study of the primary sources.*

References

Ashlock, P., & Stephen, A. *Educational therapy in the elementary school.* Springfield, Ill., Thomas, 1965.

Bannatyne, A. The color phonics system. In J. Money (Ed.), *The disabled reader: Education of the dyslexic child.* Baltimore, Md.: Johns Hopkins Press, 1966.

Barry, H. *The young aphasic child: Evaluation and training.* Washington, D.C.: Volta Bureau, 1961.

Bernstein, M. C. Reading methods and materials based on linguistic principles for basic and remedial instruction. *Academic Therapy Quarterly,* 1967, **2**, 149–154.

Bloomfield, L., & Barnhart, C. *Let's read.* Detroit: Wayne State University Press, 1961.

Buchanan, C. D., & Sullivan Associates. *Programmed instruction.* New York: McGraw-Hill, 1963.

Carrow, Sister M. A. Some general principles of language therapy. In *A theoretical approach to the diagnosis and treatment of language disorders in children.* San Antonio, Tex.: Harry Jersig Speech and Hearing Center, 1968.

Chall, J. S. *Learning to read: The great debate.* New York: McGraw-Hill, 1967.

Cruickshank, W. M., Bentzen, F., Ratzebury, F. H., & Tannhauser. M. *A teaching method for brain-injured and hyperactive children.* Syracuse, N.Y.: Syracuse University Press, 1961.

Dean, J. Words in color. In J. Downing (Ed.), *The first international reading symposium.* New York: Day, 1966.

Delacato, C. *The treatment and prevention of reading problems.* Springfield, Ill.: Thomas, 1959.

Delacato, C. *The diagnosis and treatment of speech and reading problems.* Springfield, Ill.: Thomas, 1963.

Denver Public Schools. Progress report: Programmed reading in the primary grades. Unpublished report of the Department of Research Services, Denver, Colo., 1966.

Diack, H. *Reading and the psychology of perception.* Nottingham, England: Palmer, 1960.

Downing, J. *The i.t.a. reading experiment.* Chicago: Scott, Foresman, 1965.

————. The initial teaching alphabet. In J. Downing (Ed.), *The first international reading symposium.* New York: Day, 1966.

Fernald, G. M. *Remedial techniques in basic school subjects.* New York: McGraw-Hill, 1943.

Fitzgerald, E. *Straight language for the deaf.* Washington, D.C.: Volta Bureau, 1963.

Flesch, R. *Why Johnny can't read.* New York: Harper & Row, 1955.

Freidus, E. Methodology for the classroom teacher. In J. Hellmuth (Ed.), *The special child in century 21*. Seattle, Wash.: Special Child Publications, 1964.

——. The needs of teachers for specialized information on number concepts. In W. M. Cruickshank (Ed.), *The teacher of brain-injured children*. Syracuse, N.Y.: Syracuse University Press, 1966.

Fries, C. C. *Linguistics and reading*. New York: Holt, Rinehart & Winston, 1962. (a)

——. *Merrill linguistic readers: A basic program*. Columbus, Ohio: Merrill, 1962. (b)

Gattegno, C. *Words in color*. Chicago: Learning Materials, 1962.

——. Words in color. In J. Money (Ed.), *The disabled reader: Education of the dyslexic child*. Baltimore, Md.: Johns Hopkins Press, 1966.

Getman, G. N. *How to develop your child's intelligence*. Luverne, Minn.: Announcer, 1962.

Gillingham, A., & Stillman, B. *Remedial training for children with specific disability in reading, spelling, and penmanship*. (7th ed.) Cambridge, Mass.: Educators Publishing Service, 1965.

Hammill, D., & Mattleman, M. Programmed reading instruction in the primary grades: An evaluation study. *Elementary English*, 1969, 46:3, 310–312.

Johnson, D., & Myklebust, H. R. *Learning disabilities: Educational principles and practices*. New York: Grune & Stratton, 1967.

Keislar, E. R., & McNeil, J. D. Teaching scientific thinking to first grade pupils by auto-instructional devices. *Harvard Educational Review*, 1961, 31, 73–87.

Kephart, N. C. *The slow learner in the classroom*. Columbus, Ohio: Merrill, 1960.

Liddle, W. Colorado Springs tests programmed reading. *Journal of Programmed Reading*, No. 6, undated.

Mazurkiewicz, A. J., & Tanyzer, H. J. *Early to read i.t.a. program*. New York: Initial Teaching Alphabet Publications, 1964.

McGinnis, M. *Aphasic children: Identification and education by the association method*. Washington, D.C.: Volta Bureau, 1963.

McNeil, J. D. Programmed instruction for beginning reading. *Programmed Instruction*, 1964, 3, 7.

Montessori, M. *The Montessori method*. New York: Strokes, 1912.

Osgood, C. E. Motivational dynamics of language behavior. In M. R. Jones (Ed.), *Nebraska symposium on motivation*. Lincoln: University of Nebraska Press, 1967.

Pugh, B. L. *Steps in language development for the deaf*. Washington, D.C.: Volta Bureau, 1955.

Schramm, W. *The research on programmed instruction*. U.S. Department of Health, Education, & Welfare, 1964.

Schuell, H. J. Programmed reading report—so far, so good. *Nation's Schools*, 1966, 78, 39–40.

Sheldon, W. D., & Lashinger, D. R. Effect of first grade instruction using basal readers, modified linguistic materials, and linguistic readers. *Reading Teacher*, 1966, 19, 576–579.

Spalding, R. B., & Spalding, W. T. *The writing road to reading.* New York: Morrow, 1957.

Stern, C. *Children discover reading.* Syracuse, N.Y.: Singer, 1963.

Strauss, A. A., & Lehtinen, L. *Psychopathology and education of the brain-injured child.* Vol. I. New York: Grune & Stratton, 1947.

Stuart, M. F. *Neurophysiological insights into teaching.* Palo Alto, Cal.; Pacific Books, 1963.

Traxler, A. E., & Jungblut, A. *Research in reading during another four years.* New York: Educational Records Bureau, 1960.

Traxler, A. E., & Townsend, A. et al. *Eight more years research in reading.* New York: Educational Records Bureau, 1955.

Wilson, R., & Lindsay, H. G. Applying linguistics to remedial reading. *Reading Teacher,* 1963, **16**, 452–455.

Wyatt, N. M. The reading achievement of first grade boys versus first grade girls. *Reading Teacher,* 1966, **19**, 661–665.

CHAPTER IV

THE PERCEPTUAL-MOTOR SYSTEMS

The methods and techniques included in the category of perceptual-motor systems are strongly developmentalistic in orientation and all place great emphasis upon the early motor learnings and visual-spatial development of the child. In a longitudinal study of three children, Piaget (1952) noted that overt motor learning preceded the covert, inner language method of solving problems and he commented that this method of learning tends to be evident throughout adult life. In fact, beginning with behavior which starts in the embryological stage of development, Sherrington (1948) states that the first neurological system to develop is the motor system. Once it becomes functional, the perceptual system develops. The last neurological system to develop is the association system, which emerges only when the two prior systems have developed and are functioning adequately. According to Kephart, the ability to generalize in the higher mental processes grows out of and has its foundation in the ability to form motor generalizations. The authors believe that Freidus, Getman, and Barsch would agree with this statement, which is, in essence, no different from the observations made by Piaget and Sherrington regarding the importance of motor learning. Our feeling is that the appoaches to specific learning disabilities developed by the authors discussed in this chapter basically are attempts to unify in one framework the physiological and perceptual development of the child but are inadequate to the task of describing disorders of learning which are related to and involve language and thought.

Each of the writers appears to arrive at his particular viewpoint through different routes, for example, Barsch postulates a biological survival basis for his rationale while Kephart adheres to a strictly psychophysiological frame of reference. In the end, however, the basic sensory-perceptual-motor orientation and the suggested remedial activities are very much the same. Barsch and Getman emphasize the visual-motor processes of the learner and Kephart is concerned mostly with the perceptual-motor match (a more cognitive approach), but we find that their suggestions for treating the child with a learning disability are disturbingly similar, and we wonder whether their differing rationales are merely variations on a theme.

Who is the child for whom we would recommend the procedures reviewed in this chapter? In terms of information gathered during the educationally oriented evaluation, what are his strengths and weaknesses? How does he learn or what has he failed to learn? In general, we feel there are several guiding principles to be observed in prescribing any of the perceptual-motor approaches. First, our experience indicates that children younger than eight to nine years of age profit from these systems more than older children and, generally, the younger the child, the more he profits. Second, the child whose major deficits are in the visual-motor channel of communication at either the integration or representational levels makes greater progress under a perceptual-motor program of training than the child with other types of learning disabilities.

To describe the type of child for whom we would suggest one of the perceptual-motor programs, a case history approach seems most efficient and illustrative. The following report describes a preschool child with motor, perceptual, and behavioral problems who made substantial progress while enrolled in a remedial program emphasizing perceptual-motor development.

J. L., a five-year-old girl, was referred for evaluation and treatment on the advice of her pediatrician. Seven months prior to the referral she had experienced a series of convulsions and although the neurological examination and the EEG tracing were negative she had been placed on a drug control program. According to J. L.'s kindergarten teacher, the child's behavior in school had been disruptive, and various signs of a learning disability had been noted.

The results of the speech and hearing evaluations indicated a mild articulation problem, normal function of the speech mechanism, and normal hearing. The language and psychological testing revealed that J. L. was functioning within the low average range of intelligence and that her visual-motor abilities were significantly impaired. She obtained poor scores on drawing tests, the visual, motor, and visual-motor subtests of the ITPA. Her Bender protocol was not scorable nor was her Draw-a-Man. Tests of gross and fine motor coordination also indicated serious problems.

J. L.'s strengths were revealed by such scores as the following: Peabody Picture Vocabulary Test—IQ 103; sentence length and syntax—adequate; vocal, auditory, and auditory-vocal subtests of the ITPA—average to above average.

Because J. L. had been in kindergarten for a year, some limited academic testing was done. The results revealed numerous letter and number reversals and a fixed, although incorrect, order of letters when writing her name.

J. L.'s behavior during the testing sessions was marked by incessant chattering, impulsivity, and mild hyperactivity. The psychiatric report noted some oppositional and provocative behavior on J. L.'s part when with her mother but no signs of a psychotic or neurotic disorder were evident.

Following evaluation, J. L. was enrolled in the training program where she remained for 11 months. During that time techniques suggested by Kephart and Getman were used to improve her motor skills and her visual-motor abilities. Her progress was slow but consistent and when she was dismissed from the program, her teacher felt that she would have little difficulty in the first grade. J. L. was enrolled in a special education class for children with learning disabilities the following year but has since successfully completed the second grade in a regular class.

The case history of J. L. exemplifies the type of child who often makes substantial progress in programs devoted to training perceptual-motor abilities. It is doubtful whether her progress would have been as great in a less intensive program; she attended class five days a week for three hours daily over a period of eleven months. Even at the end of this lengthy time her teacher felt that she should not attend a regular class but instead needed the more protective atmosphere of a special education class for children with learning disabilities. Other children with similar but less severe problems have made more rapid progress than J. L. and after less intensive therapy have been enrolled in regular classes.

Newell C. Kephart

Kephart, director of the Glen Haven Achievement Center, Fort Collins, Colorado, is a psychologist who has long been interested in learning disordered children. He is the author of many articles, co-author with

Strauss of *Psychopathology and Education of the Brain-Injured Child* Volume II, and the author of *The Slow Learner in the Classroom*. Kephart's theory of perceptual-motor learning development, based upon clinical experience as well as upon developmental psychology, is perhaps more systematic than his remedial "method," which is actually a collection of techniques rather than a method. In fact, puzzles, pegboards, fingerpainting, and dot-to-dot pictures, all recommended by Kephart, have been used for some time by kindergarten and special education teachers, although not for the reasons provided by Kephart.

The uniqueness of the Kephart approach lies in his strong emphasis, upon the sensorimotor basis of all learning, which consists of certain generalizations rather than highly specific skills. He notes that reading, writing, and arithmetic involve many perceptual and motor skills; even a so-called basic skill such as drawing a square, however, requires the integrity of even more basic skills, such as gross motor abilities, eye-hand coordination, laterality, directionality, ocular control, dexterity, temporal-spatial translation, and form perception. Rather than basing remediation upon skills such a drawing a square, therefore, Kephart feels that greater success in developing readiness accrues from breaking down simple activities into more basic skills and teaching those skills. Further, he states that no training technique should be considered a goal in itself, but that the technique is merely the vehicle by means of which a child can be taught certain generalized skills and abilities. This attitude toward remediation represents a major shift in emphasis from task-oriented to process-oriented teaching. For example, many authors suggest treating children with reading disabilities by teaching them to read, but Kephart suggests treating them by remediating impairments of the basic skills and generalizations upon which the reading act is dependent.

THE STAGES OF LEARNING DEVELOPMENT

Kephart illustrates his emphasis in his theory, which is organized into three stages of learning development—practical, subjective, and objective—all stages based upon four motor generalizations—posture and the maintenance of balance, contact, locomotor, and receipt and propulsion.

The Practical Stage. The first stage of development is marked by the infant's physical manipulation of objects without any evidence that the infant perceives the objects as being separate and distinct from his own activity. The infant at this motor learning stage in his development is unaware of himself as separate from his environment or of objects in the environment as separate from his handling of them; his major task is to produce a movement of the various, movable parts of the body, a movement combining parts, and to control the movement. This early stage lays the foundation for future learning, and Kephart assumes that all behavior is basically motor, that is, prerequisities for any kind of behavior are muscular and motor responses.

The basic motor generalization upon which the practical stage is based is posture and the maintenance of balance. The only stable environmental condition around which the child may build his postural model of himself is gravity, which he reacts to in two ways:

1. He resists the force of gravity, thus calling upon his righting reflexes to prevent his falling.
2. He learns to maintain a constant balance between antagonistic sets of muscles, thereby keeping himself in the erect position in various settings.

This maintenance of balance requires awareness of the center of gravity and muscular flexibility.

Out of the kinesthetic information of posture and balance arises the balancing generalization, which allows the child to explore space without worrying about gravity. He is able to get from one place to another, changing his movements to meet the changing demands of the situation without direct regard for the movement pattern but with concern only for the purpose of the movement. He need not worry about alterations to be made in specific movements—the movement pattern takes care of the changes.

Kephart notes that specific motor skills, such as walking, may be taught with relative ease but that the teaching of movement patterns presents a much more difficult task. The child taught a specific skill may perform adequately as long as the series of movements he has learned are appropriate, but if the situation changes and alteration in the series of movements must be made, the child has no pattern of movement upon which he can depend. His motor performances are, therefore, often awkward and stilted with infrequent variation.

Motor exploration and the resulting feedback data, facilitated by the balancing generalization, result in motor awareness and lead to the emergence of a second generalization—the concept of body schema. Body schema, according to Kephart (1960), is a "learned concept resulting from observation of the movements of parts of the body and relationships of different parts of the body to each other and to external objects" (p. 51) It is an internal conceptualization of self, fluid and dynamic, and depends upon kinesthetic input relating any new posture to the ones preceding it. Once the child has established his body image, he is able to develop practical directionality or awareness of dimension along body axes.

Directionality consists of verticality, or awareness of the up-and-down axis, and laterality, or awareness of the relative position of one side of the body versus the other. Directionality, in its vertical and lateral aspects, develops with respect always to the body's center of gravity. Awareness of a point in space, that is, practical directionality, is complemented in the child by a growing awareness of a point in time—synchrony. Synchrony, or precise timing, allows control of starting and stopping an activity and is based upon a sense of "nowness" in time. Other aspects of the practical stage of development are:

1. Practical succession—the beginning of directional ordering of objects and temporal ordering of events, which is experienced directly by the child at this stage.

2. Practical continuity—the beginning of figure-ground orientation through exploration of continuous surfaces and related movements.

The Subjective Stage. The second stage of learning development is the subjective or perceptual-motor stage in which perceptual knowledge as well as motor knowledge must be referred always to the self. This stage is based upon the motor generalizations of contact and of locomotion. Contact generalizations, employing patterns of reach, grasp, and release, enable the child to manipulate and to explore object shapes and relationships in terms of movement patterns and body schema. Locomotor generalizations enable the child to explore space and its relationships in the same fashion, employing, however, movement patterns pertinent to moving the body from one place to another. Form perception is based upon contact generalizations; spatial perception is based upon locomotor generalizations, and the two together prepare the way motorically for the perceptual-motor match.

Before discussing Kephart's focal principle, the perceptual-motor match, early motor and early perceptual activity must be clarified. Dunsing and Kephart (1965) define movement as observable response and motor as an internalized neurophysiological event relating to the output system. Thus a covert motor generalization is built upon many movement patterns and frees the child from direct attention to the movement so that he may move unhampered about his environment in a purposeful and exploratory fashion. Motor generalizations are built in two ways:

1. By increasing differentiation of hitherto gross, undifferentiated movement, followed by integration of the movements into total patterns.

2. By integration of reflexes into patterns so that muscles act as part of a total, purposive activity.

While these motor generalizations are developing, perceptual activity, which begins later, follows much the same sequence, that is, from gross generalization to differentiation to integration into meaningful patterns. For example, form perception begins with an innate awareness of globular, undifferentiated masses, which probably differ only in intensity, extension, and color. Such a mass gradually becomes differentiated by the child into its signal qualities, or characteristic details, which are then integrated into a constructive form having a new quality that is characteristic of only this form.

Although one may speak of perception and motor as two different processes, they actually must always be related, according to Kephart (1960), who subscribes to a servomechanistic model of the perceptual process, as illustrated in Figure 1.

In the servo system, part of the output pattern is fed back into the input side of the model in a continuous cycling fashion until input matches output. This process may explain covert activities such as problem-solving in which the greater part of the output pattern is fed back to input instead of to a muscular or overt response. Thus Kephart cannot sanction the "textbook" separation of perceptual and motor activity and feels that such a dichotomy can lead only to error. Learning experiences, then, should be designed in terms of the total perceptual-motor process.

Thus to be meaningful, perceptual information must be matched to basic motor generalizations through the body schema in order for the information to be veridicated. Since motor generalizations develop first, perception must always be matched to motor activity; never is motor

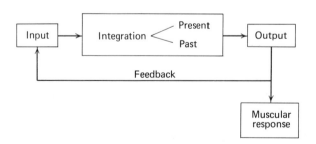

FIGURE 1.   Diagram of feedback mechanisms in perception. (From Kephart, 1960, p. 56.)

activity matched to perception. Kephart speaks of two worlds, perception and motor, which must be combined in order for the child to function objectively and consistently in his environment.

The perceptual-motor match is necessary for veridication of spatial information and for further development of continuity, or figure-ground orientation. Concerning the development of continuity, the child's visual exploration of continuous surfaces must be matched to his motor awareness of them. Objective laterality, or the projection of laterality into space, cannot take place without an intermediary step of perceptual-motor matching, in this case, visual perceptions matched with haptic-motor activity. This step of spatial localization is a difficult one; the child must match his two worlds simultaneously because he has no direct knowledge of space.

The Objective Stage. Subjective continuity, subjective succession, and signal qualities can be used to describe an object, but the awareness of the total configuration is lacking and is not fully developed until the end of the objective or perceptual stage of learning development. In this stage, Kephart feels that perception, particularly vision, assumes primary importance in receiving information. The objective stage is based upon the advanced motor generalizations of receipt and propulsion, patterns which involve dynamic relationships between a moving child and objects that are moving or are about to be moved. In receipt patterns, the child interferes with a moving object; in propulsion patterns, he imparts movement to an object. The child, in his objective spatial structure, perceives relationships among a number of different objects. For knowledge of direction he can utilize information not only about Euclidean coordinates, but about diagonals, slants, and curves. He has developed temporal percepts of rhythm and sequence. Time and space he now sees as different dimensions of the same objective reality and can translate from one to the other. Finally, the child makes the ultimate projection, that is, he projects beyond the range of his visual and temporal fields and is able to learn conceptually as well as perceptually.

Kephart notes that one of the many problems faced by the child in the objective stage of development is that of dealing with activities which require crossing the body midline. The child must learn that an object, when crossing his midline, changes in pattern from outside-in to inside-out but does not change in constancy of movement or of shape.

The highest level of generalization, according to Kephart (1963), is that of the concept which is based upon similarities between objects or situations. The basic point Kephart makes in discussing conceptual development is that the concept can be no better than the perception upon which it is based. "If perceptions lack in generalization, concepts will likely be weak, restricted, or bizarre" (Kephart, 1963, p. 18).

TREATMENT FOR SPECIFIC LEARNING DISABILITIES

Treatment procedures suggested by Kephart are derived through the administration of the Perceptual Motor Rating Scale (Kephart, 1960), which emphasizes the assessment of sensorimotor learning, ocular control, and form perception. Results of the evaluation indicate the developmental stages of learning which are inadequate and which much be treated. Sensorimotor training equipment and activities include walking boards, balance boards, trampolines, games such as " angels-in-the snow," scribbling, fingerpainting, midline-crossing exercises, dot-to-dot drawing, and bilateral and unilateral exercises. Ocular control is developed in a sequential fashion through the use of monocular training, rotary pursuit, and Marsden ball activities, Form perception training is achieved through chalkboard activities, puzzles, matchstick figures, and pegboard designs.

Part III of Kephart's (1960) manual for the classroom teacher is devoted to training activities and is divided into four major sections: (1) chalkboard training; (2) sensory-motor training; (3) training ocular control; and (4) training form perception.

Chalkboard Training. The activities in this section are primarily visual-motor in nature, beginning with random scribbling and progressing through directionality exercises, including those that require the child to cross the midline, to orientation exercises in which the child copies forms, reproduces them from memory, and varies his reproductions with respect to size, speed, direction, etc. Throughout these activities the child is taught to attach the verbal symbol to his productions. In general, however, the child is experimenting with movement patterns and observing closely the pattern left on the chalkboard which results from his activity; both activities comprise the essentials of visual-motor perception. Specific activities recommended are:

1. Scribbling.
2. Fingerpainting.
3. The clock game—a device to teach the child to use various combinations of bilateral movements, namely, movements toward and away from the center, parallel movements, and crossed movements.
4. Drawing circles and other geometric forms.

Sensory-Motor Training. Activities discussed under sensory-motor training generally include exercises requiring the use of the large muscles or groups of muscles. Emphasis first is placed upon the development of balance but progresses through the development of body image and bilaterality and unilaterality. The child is taught balance through a number of activities requiring a walking board: walking forward, backward, sidewise, and turning and bouncing on the board are typical exercises. In addition to the walking board, and usually after proficiency on it has been attained, the child is introduced to the balance board and taught many of the same skills he has learned on the walking board. The trampoline is used in this phase of training as well as the walking and balance boards. Other activities included in the sensory-motor training program include:

1. Angels-in-the-snow—used in teaching bilateral, unilateral, and cross-lateral movements and in teaching the child to change the time and position of his movements.

2. Stunts and games—for example, the duck walk, rabbit hop, crab walk, measuring worm, and elephant walk; all aimed at teaching variations in movements patterns and providing the child with opportunities to elaborate movement patterns which he has learned.

3. Rhythmical activities—both bilateral and unilateral.

Ocular Control Training. The third section dealing with remedial techniques is devoted to activities in the area of control of the eyes. Kephart emphasizes the point that information obtained only through the eyes does not provide adequate data regarding location and orientation in space and, therefore, visual control must be matched to the general motor and kinesthetic patterns that the child has learned. As Kephart states, it is apparent from the foregoing that the child must achieve a measure of competency in motor patterning before ocular control can be expected.

Kephart outlines five stages in ocular-pursuit training which serve as a basis for remediation:

1. Stage one. The child is taught to follow with his eyes an object, such as a pencil, while it is moved first laterally and vertically and then moved diagonally and in rotary fashion. The latter movements are the more difficult and are not employed until the child is able to follow lateral and vertical movements of the target.

2. Stage two. The second stage of training differs from the first in that the target used is a small pen-shaped flashlight, thereby increasing the intensity of the visual stimulus. The same type of target movements are used in training.

3. Stage three. The penlight is the target in the third stage and the same types of movements are used, but the child follows the moving

target with his finger as he simultaneously follows with his eyes. In this stage, kinesthetic information from extraocular muscles is matched to kinesthetic information from the ocular muscles.

4. Stage four. The fourth stage differs from the previous stage only in that the child is asked to put his finger on the light from the penlight and move his finger as the target light moves. In this fashion kinesthetic and tactile stimulation is increased as in stage two visual stimulation was increased. In stage four, however, the intensity of the stimulus is not only increased but is still correlated with other stimuli, that is, the intensified kinesthetic stimulus is associated with the visual stimulus.

5. Stage five. The fifth stage of ocular training requires the use of a ball, first large, such as a beach ball, then smaller, such as a baseball. In this stage, the teacher places both hands, palms flat, on one side of the ball, and the child places his hands on the opposite side. The teacher moves the ball in lateral, vertical, diagonal, and rotary patterns carrying the child's hands along with him and encouraging the child to keep the ball in sight as it is moved. Kephart makes several points in reference to the fifth stage of training: that kinesthetic and tactual information is increased; that both hands are used; and that since the teacher is guiding the ball he may create resistance, thereby increasing tactual stimulation, by pressing against the ball.

Kephart recommends that ocular training begin at the level on which the child is able to perform and that all phases of training in the various stages should be completed. Other ancillary techniques suggested by Kephart include the following:

1. Special practice aimed at increasing the extent or range of the child's eye movements if it becomes apparent that his movement range is restricted.

2. Binocular and monocular training.

3. The Marsden ball—a soft rubber ball is suspended by a string from the ceiling so that when the ball is moved it will swing like a pendulum. Basically, the technique for using the swinging ball consists of having the child touch the ball just as it passes in front of him, which means that he must follow the moving target with his eyes and respond in terms of the position of the ball, an activity requiring accurate time and correlation of visual and motor systems. Other variations and elaborations of the basic technique are provided by Kephart.

Training Form Perception. In training the child with poor constructive form perception, Kephart discusses several specific activities, such as puzzles, stick figures, and pegboards. The tasks, by and large, require the child to match and reproduce various forms and patterns. Several general principles are laid down with respect to the materials and activities.

1. The form or the picture should be more striking than the shape of the individual pieces; puzzles depicting a single human figure are probably best for beginning a training program. Particularly, overlapping figures should not be used on puzzles, nor should pictures poorly differentiated from the background be given to the children. Kephart also suggests that the cutout pieces of the puzzle should conform to the outline of the picture rather than being randomly cut.

2. The teacher should prepare a series of forms made of matchsticks glued to a piece of cardboard or wood. From a supply of separate matchsticks (without striking heads) the child must reproduce the constructive aspects of the forms. The coordination necessary for copying or drawing is not needed, nor are the elements of the forms so emphasized as in drawing.

3. The pegboard tasks suggested by Kephart are modifications of the Strauss Marble Board (Strauss & Lehtinen, 1947; Strauss & Kephart, 1955). The pegs should be fairly large size, for example, golf tees, to provide ease in handling. The pegboard should be about 12 inches square with ⅛-inch diameter holes ½ inch apart. The tasks set for the children involve their copying patterns boards with model figures on them.

4. Two types of activities may be used with both the stick figures and the pegboards. The children either may copy directly from the model or may be asked to construct the forms after having seen the model for only a brief period.

The children for whom the Kephart techniques would be beneficial are legion and may be found among groups classified as "minimally brain injured," "language disordered," "learning disabled," or "perceptually damaged." The classification—the label—is not the important factor in determining whether to use Kephart procedures; rather the developmental level of the child in sensory-perceptual-motor areas is crucial. If a child is found deficient in any of the developmental aspects discussed by Kephart, one may assume that he can profit to a lesser or greater degree from the techniques described by Kephart. The secondary factor in deciding whether to use Kephart techniques should be the diagnostic classification of the child. Teachers of various groups of children—mentally retarded, learning disordered, and developmentally delayed—have reported positive results from the use of the materials and activities recommended by Kephart.

Elizabeth Freidus

Freidus, who has been associated with Lexington School for the Deaf in New York and with Teachers College, Columbia University, has conducted special courses and seminars in the area of learning disabilities at many other institutions. She has lectured to many diverse groups and has made widely known the problems faced by and presented by children with specific learning disorders. Her orientation to the field is primarily developmental and she has drawn upon and modified the ideas of Kephart, Strauss and Lehtinen, Piaget, and Bruner, among others.

THE MODEL OF THE LEARNING PROCESS

The process of learning, according to Freidus (1964), may be best conceptualized as analogous to the storage and retrieval of information within a computer. In other words, Freidus employs a servosystem model as do Kephart (1960), Fairbanks (1954), and Mysak (1966), all of whom see information being received and compared with other information already stored, the rise of a response pattern, the response proper, and the feedback of part of the response to the input side of the model so that the process is self-correcting. Freidus' model is comprised of seven stages:

1. Information is received through the senses.
2. Sensory information is attended to by the individual.
3. The sensory information received is associated with other information, previously received and stored, and invested with meaning.
4. An appropriate response pattern is organized.
5. The response pattern is effected; the overt reponse occurs.
6. The overt response is monitored for quality and correctness.
7. The results of the monitoring function are stored in order to aid in future association—stage 3—and in response organization—stage 4.

In discussing the child with learning disabilities, Freidus (1964) is not concerned with the cause of the problem, for she feels the etiology has little educational significance; however, she is concerned about the stage within the learning process at which the child encounters difficulties. Her analysis of learning disorders and the attendant remediation are dependent upon the utilization of servo theory. For persons in the field of speech pathology, among others, the use of a servosystem model to explain learning is not novel. Fairbanks (1954) and Van Riper and Irwin (1958) have employed such models for some time; Mysak

(1966) recently has used servo mechanisms as the basis for treating a wide variety of speech and language problems. If the model described by Freidus is to be used in analyzing a child's learning disorders, then there are numerous diagnostic questions which must be posed at each stage of learning to determine where in the model the breakdown in learning has occurred.

The Reception of Sensory Information. Questions to be answered at this stage in the learning process are related to the adequacy of the child's sensory acuity. Undoubtedly deficits at this stage, particularly in visual or auditory acuity, have far-reaching consequences in terms of learning. For minor acuity problems, glasses or hearing aids may resolve many of the difficulties; if, however, the acuity problem is severe, the entire orientation toward teaching the child will have to be altered, and even after the best of teaching, he may still have noticeable gaps in learning. Freidus feels that generally the child with a sensory deficit may be more fortunate than the learning disordered child, at least if the acuity problem is dealt with early in the child's life. It is doubtful that Freidus is speaking of the profoundly deaf or totally blind child when she terms him more fortunate than his learning disabled counterpart.

Attention to Sensory Information. At the second stage of the model, diagnostic questions are related to listening and looking rather than to hearing and seeing. The child with normal hearing acuity may find that his hearing is an unreliable source of information and may cease to listen, effectively shutting out most, if not all auditory stimuli. In addition to investigating the child's awareness of sensory information, other questions are posed to determine how constant and efficient his attention is. If he pays attention, he may have difficulty shifting his focus and thereby become perseverative, or his attention may be so fleeting and diffuse that he is described as distractible. He may not be able to analyze a form because he cannot distinguish it as a whole, separate from its background; his attention is not focused upon parts nor in turn are the parts synthesized to form the whole.

Association of Sensory Information and Past Experiences. At this point, sensory information is invested with meaning because it is only through the association of the present sensory event and past experience with similar events that one is able to gain meaning from a sensory experience in the present. Relevant questions to be raised concerning this stage of the learning process are: Does the child, having seen an object, picture, etc., comprehend it? After hearing, does he understand what he has heard? In other words, is he able to use integrated past meaning as a vehicle for interpreting present experience?

Normally, children use past, relevant experience without difficulty, but the child who has problems in storing and retrieving information will manifest significant difficulty in comprehension, abstraction, and generalization.

The Organization of an Appropriate Response. One may find that a child has the sensory acuity to hear, that he has listened, and that he has understood the sensory signal, but he is not able to organize and sequence a response pattern appropriate to the data obtained. Response organization is learned by the child initially during the early motor learning stage of development and continues through the stages of speech and language development. Because Freidus is developmentalistic in outlook and orientation, she feels that earlier stages of development must be adequately and fully completed if the child is to succeed at later levels. In the area of sensory-motor organization, she states that children who have not learned enough about themselves and their relation to the physical environment because of their inadequate experience, awareness, and/or integration of experience, must be provided with opportunities to solve, monitor, and feedback some of the early infantile developmental tasks (Freidus, 1964). Often difficulties in response organization are subsumed under the category of the dyspraxias and, as such, may refer to verbal dyspraxia—difficulty in speech production— or nonverbal dyspraxia—difficulty in executing specific body movements. It should be noted that Freidus does not use the term dyspraxia, but other authors do and the two terms—dyspraxia and inadequate response organization—may be considered synonymous.

Response Production. Once the response pattern has been organized, the child is ready to produce an overt response which is, in essence, a motor act whether it be gross body movement, speech production, or writing. Difficulties in this stage of learning are likely to be manifested in incoordination during walking, jumping, hopping, etc.; asymmetric movements; improper sequencing of motor elements; and/or problems in starting, stopping, maintaining, or shifting a sequence of movement elements.

Monitoring the Response. After the child has produced a response does he monitor that response in terms of its accuracy and its quality? Freidus' (1964) discussion of the monitoring process does not allow for monitoring and the feedback of information except after production. Such thinking of the feedback system as involving a *post hoc* kind of monitoring has been challenged by other disciplines. The neurologists, for example, contend that there are too many neural synapses involved for correction to take place in time for complicated series of movements to continue without significant interruption. The model developed by Freidus (1964) provides for correction after error production and correction of produced errors certainly occurs, but the maintenance of a steady flow of motor responses requires correction before the occurrence of errors. Two solutions to the problem have been offered by Irwin (1966):

1. Internal monitoring of the neural impulse, occurring directly after the response pattern has been organized, takes place.
2. Once a motor act has been learned, it is not monitored, but intsead becomes a habit chain, that is, an automatic process.

Freidus, in her explanation of the monitoring-feedback process, appears to rely upon the second solution. Children, when they are learning, must consciously monitor their responses, but once the act is learned, or probably overlearned, the response becomes automatic and is no longer monitored unless the feedback system is opened and attention is called to the response. Children with feedback problems, therefore, must be taught to attend carefully to the responses they produce, to compare them with an external model provided by the teacher, and to correct their errors, bringing the responses into congruence with the external standard.

Therapeutic Methods

Freidus (1964) contends that there is no one educational methodology that is appropriate for all learning disabled children, but that there are many kinds of learning disorders, each of which dictates its own requirements for training. She states that the individual child's problems must be evaluated in terms of the model of the learning process and treatment must be tailored to fit the child's needs as evidenced by the results of the evaluation.

Problems in the Reception of Sensory Information. Problems arising in the learning process which may be attributed to poor reception of sensory information are problems of sensory acuity, that is, hearing or vision losses. The educational difficulties of children who have hearing losses or who are visually impaired are best met by special programs designed for the hard of hearing, deaf, partially sighted, or blind child and, as such, are not programs for the learning disabled child.

Problems in Attention to Sensory Information. Problems of attending and focusing may be manifested in figure-ground confusion, the habits of not-seeing or not-hearing, distractibility, and difficulty in shifting attention. Exercises in attending are recommended, that is, teaching the child to listen and to look. Sounds can be emphasized through the use of amplification, thereby bringing the sensory signal to the awareness level in a child who has been ignoring sound because he could not comprehend. In the same fashion, visual information can be heightened by heavy, black underlining, by using several colors to delineate the parts of a visual stimulus, or by removing distracting extraneous elements. Such structured auditory or visual experiences will serve to reduce confusion and enable the child to be more receptive when sensory information is presented.

Problems in Association of Present and Past Information. Difficulties in associating present sensory information with meaningful past experience are basically problems in comprehension. Children who comprehend information received through one sensory modality but not that received through another modality can often benefit from training aimed at integrating information from two or more sense modalities. In this way, a child who comprehends auditory material can learn to understand visually if the meaningful visual stimulus is repeatedly paired with the meaningful auditory stimulus.

Children can be trained to use relevant past experience if they are provided with structured opportunities for observing and finding meaning in what they observe. Activities in sorting, matching, categorizing, and sequencing are useful and can be used on any level of treatment from the most concrete to the abstract.

Problems in Organizing the Response. To aid children in the organization of appropriate responses, Freidus (1964) believes that activities which involve motor organization are beneficial. These activities may deal with organizing responses for distance, direction, shifting direction, and orientation; in fact, the tasks may run the gamut of visual-motor activities. Many of the specific suggestions made by Kephart (1960) would be applicable, such as the use of walking rails, balance boards, and other equipment. For many children the difficulty in organizing responses lies in their inability to sequence the component elements of the response pattern and they may be taught to verbalize the sequence in a "first this, then that" fashion. Such a sequence may be memorized by requiring the child to carry out a series of acts over and over without verbalization. Freidus describes an obstacle course through which children may be taken:

The children are asked to creep on their hands and knees through a sequence which they memorize: First, creep under the chair, second, around the table; third, over the bench; and so on, increasing the number of items as they grow proficient. With their eyes covered, they must remember not only sequence of tasks, but the direction and distance of each obstacle in relation to the one before. When they find themselves off course, they must use whatever they happen to touch in order to cue themselves back to where they should be (Freidus, 1964, 314).

Problems in Producing the Response. The majority of the comments and suggestions made by Freidus relative to response production are concerned with the motor coordination of the child. She remarks on the almost universal clumsiness of children with learning disabilities, their poor balance, and their inadequate coordination. A great many of the suggestions for activities to improve response production overlap with activities discussed under previous topics and do not appear to be geared solely toward improving the quality of the motor response. This overlap illustrates quite well the futility of breaking down sensory-motor integration into discrete elements; integration is much more of a unitary process than molecular bits of behavior.

The adequacy of the response is dependent upon how it is organized, whether it has been organized on the basis of previous experience, and involves the sorting, interpreting, and storing of sensory information. According to Freidus (1964), "A motor response becomes stabilized when it successfully meets the requirements of the sensory information which activated it" (p. 315). For example, when a bell rings, before responding, the person must "decide whether it might be the front door, back door, telephone. . . . For this, she uses past experience to help her discriminate between various kinds of bells and their possible location and use. . . . In deciding what to do about answering the bell, she must choose where to go, which impulses to control and which to act upon" (p. 315).

Problems in Monitoring Responses. In view of Freidus' reliance upon monitoring of the error after it has occurred, many of the activities she describes would necessarily require external feedback. The child is given specific instructions related to possible errors and is told to check for errors as they occur. "Coloring within a heavy outline gives him an opportunity to search for uncolored areas, so he can color them" (p. 316). Information regarding the correct response then is assumed to be fedback and stored until the next time it is needed. Self-correcting materials, or at any rate materials that do not allow error, such as form boards, are recommended.

Other monitoring activities, such as having the child work arithmetic problems on paper and then check his work through the use of concrete aids, are suggested. All of these activities allow for independent verification by the child. Similar activities are suggested by Kephart (1963), for example, when a child builds a bridge of blocks he should be required to verify the construction by walking across it. If the bridge is inadequately built, it will fall, and the child has immediate verification of his form construction. All kinds of measuring devices and dictionaries can be used by the child to check his arithmetic, word usage, and spelling activities.

TEACHING ARITHMETIC CONCEPTS

Freidus (1966) has offered a discussion related specifically to the teaching of arithmetic which is separate from her more general discussion of learning disabilities. In teaching number concepts, Freidus states that one needs primarily to recognize that arithmetic is a way of thinking about the quantitative aspects of life, and that it is also a language for expressing and dealing with them. The language of arithmetic is used to describe, measure, manipulate, and record quantitative relationships and problems. Freidus stresses the fact that number concepts should be developed in a sequential fashion. Such sequentiality is particularly important when teaching children who have inefficient or deviant styles of learning. With such children, understanding of number concepts should be based upon concrete experiences, a principle that is valid for all children but more so for children with learning disabilities. The sequence of teaching number concepts as outlined by Freidus is comprised of the following eight stages.

Sets and Matching. The first task in teaching number concepts is to develop the ability to group objects into sets so that they may be counted. The child must first be able to recognize figure and ground so that a single object can be focused upon. When a second object is focused upon and can be matched to the first, the child is ready to learn the concept "same." Any characteristic of the object, such as color, size, form, may be used at this stage to teach the child the idea of sameness.

Relationship Concepts. Matching and sorting activities, used in the first stage, prepare the way for learning to make comparisons and to relate objects. At this point, the child can learn to understand comparisons and relationships, such as bigger-smaller, above-below, sooner-later, more-less. For many children, much of this kind of learning is gained before starting to school. With children who have learning disorders, however, such simple relationships will have to be taught before the children are ready for more complex tasks.

Measuring and Pairing. After the child has learned to group and to compare objects, he is ready to begin comparing sets of objects. Such comparison is done first by estimation: Will this block fit that space? Have we enough cookies for all of us? After estimation, the child's response is verified by measuring, which is characterized by "one for Mary, one for Joe, one for Ruth." In this way the next stage, counting, is prepared.

Counting. The learning of numerals in proper sequence aids the child in matching each object to a number symbol, one to one, for true counting, which is to be distinguished from serial or rote counting. The child may need to move each object as he counts, not just look at it, but he should be impresssed with the necessity of one to one matching—one object, one numeral.

Sequential Values. In our number system, numerals are arranged in a clearly defined sequential order, and from this order the values of the numerals are derived. Each numeral, that is, derives its value from its sequential position in relation to the numeral 1. Thus, since 2 comes after 1, it has the value of 1 more than 1, 3 has the value of 1 more than 2, and so on. The relationship is consistent whether one measures by inches, miles, pounds, or pennies. Having learned to estimate set size, then measuring or counting by pairing a numeral with each object, the child is taught to look for sets of the same measurements or containing the same number of elements, for example, 2 hands, 2 inches, 2 hours. The more sets the child can find which are of like numerical quantity, the more he will understand "twoness," "threeness," etc. in relation to each other. He will also be able more easily to associate a number symbol, oral or written, to a particular quantity.

Relationship of Parts to Whole and Parts to Each Other. At this stage of teaching number concepts, concrete, self-correcting materials should be used so that two given quantities, when combined, always equal the same larger quantity. The child is encouraged to experiment and to discover that given the whole and one part, he can supply the missing part; that given two parts, he can predict what the whole will be; or given a part detached from the whole, he can determine the value of the remainder.

Operations. After working on tasks at the previous stage, the child is ready to develop ease and fluency in expressing and manipulating the facts he has discovered and worked with. The number facts up to 10 are taught and the child deals with them concretely and symbolically.

The Decimal System. The last stage in teaching number concepts, according to Freidus, involves the introduction of the decimal system. The child must learn the system of numeration and notation beyond the number 10 and upon the base 10, in short, the decimal system. Freidus suggests the use of numerous aids in teaching the decimal system, for example, number lines, 10-square counting frames, dimes and pennies, checkers or poker chips for stacking, and any materials which may demonstrate the structure of the system.

Freidus feels that after the child has progressed through these stages, he will have little difficulty with arithmetic. She states that most teachers do not take the time to check back into the child's previously acquired learning to find out exactly what he has learned and on what level he is now functioning. Instead, there is a tendency to continue teaching more and more difficult abstract arithmetic processes.

Freidus has summarized her approach to the education of children with specific learning disabilities in five major points:

1. The teacher must be able to break down a skill into its separate, sequential elements. for example, what is involved in dialing a telephone number.

2. The teacher must have a thorough understanding of how children normally develop the elements of a skill.

3. After analyzing the skill and knowing the sequential stages of development, the teacher must be able to identify the level at which the child's development has been disrupted and what adaptations or compensations the child has made in response to the disruption.

4. The teacher himself must monitor the results of teaching continuously and must modify procedures when necessary.

5. The teacher must look at the child as an individual, not as a member of a group which supposedly exhibits X characteristics and can learn in Y ways. The child, rather than various axioms about the child, must be the guide for teaching.

Freidus' methods are suitable for most of the children classified as learning disordered, although it appears that the activities she suggests would be most beneficial to the child who is manifesting sensory-motor or perceptual-motor integration problems. For the child whose primary difficulties are in the area of learning and using the language code, a more structured approach, such as that devised by McGinnis (1963) or Gillingham and Stillman (1965), would be advisable. Even then, however, the activities recommended by Freidus would often provide valuable supplementary tasks.

Gerald N. Getman

Getman, who emphasizes a developmental approach to visual perception, holds both a Doctor of Optometry and a Doctor of Ocular Science degree. In the 1940s, he served the original Clinic of Child Development at Yale University as Visiting Staff Optometrist and co-authored *Vision, Its Development in Infant and Child* with Gesell. Later he studied the relationships between basic perceptual abilities and reading skills with Betts at Temple University. Currently, Getman is the Director of Child Development at the Pathway School in Norristown, Pennsylvania, a facility dedicated exclusively to brain-injured children who manifest learning and/or behavioral difficulties.

In *How to Develop Your Child's Intelligence* (1962a), Getman has (1) advanced his basic theory, (2) presented six stages of visual-motor development, and (3) suggested a collection of activities to train at each stage. The activities were subsequently revised and presented in more structured form (Getman & Kane, 1964). The theory and stages of development are discussed under "Rationale"; the activities are described under "A Training Program for the Development of Visual Perception."

RATIONALE

Four concepts which seem characteristic of Getman's remedial approach are repeatedly emphasized throughout his work:

1. Educational success depends heavily upon visual adequacy.
2. Direct experience enhances perceptual development.
3. The child learns to perceive and learns to learn as well.
4. Perceptual success follows a logical, systematic sequence of development.

To Getman, a child's growth, behavior, and intellectual achievement conform to a basic sequence of visually related development, regardless of the diagnostic category into which he might be placed. Distinction is made between sight and vision. Sight is considered to be nothing much more than the basic biological response of the eye to light. Vision, by contrast, is the interpretation of what is seen. Sight is a passing ray of light striking the retina. Vision is a lifetime brought to bear upon the optical clue of the moment, which triggers every possible associated and interrelated cognitive response. The importance attached to visual perception by Getman is repeatedly underscored by such statements as:

1. "Vision is intelligence" (Getman, 1962a, p. 20).
2. "It has been estimated that approximately 80% of everything we learn is learned visually" (Getman & Kane, p. III).
3. ". . . recall that children grow up to live in a visual world" (Getman, 1962a, p. 20).
4. "Visual success is reading success" (Getman, 1961, p. 1).

The idea that no knowledge can be as useful as that gained from one's own experience is accentuated in Getman's writings, and consequently the importance of participation and involvement in one's own development is stressed strongly. A frequently emphasized point is that the child learns best when he is most actively involved; that is, learning is intensified when he not only performs a task but also observes himself in the performance. The importance of primary or direct experience is reflected in Getman's (1962a, p. 14) description of intelligence as "the ability to make a judgment, decision, or action best suited to the problem of the moment, based upon the total knowledge gained from one's experiences."

To Getman, an infant has the basic machinery for learning, through which he learns all he knows; the child must even learn how to learn with this machinery. Although it is generally accepted that a child learns to walk and to talk, Getman (1962a, p. 16) points out that he also learns to see, feel, smell, and taste and therefore suggests a training program designed to provide experiences for helping children learn how to learn.

The foundation of Getman's training program is the basic sequence of growth and development associated with the first five years of life. This sequence is organized into six sequential and interrelated developmental areas or stages (Getman, 1962a, p. 23–31), briefly discussed below.

1. *General Movement Patterns.* When the child moves, he learns; without movement, learning does not take place. The body learns to explore—the eyes become the steering mechanism, the bone-frame the supporting structure, the nervous system the start-control-stop circuit, and the muscles the anatomical parts for action.

2. *Special Movement Patterns.* General movement skills are extended to include synchronized use of body parts and manipulation. Eye-hand coordination is achieved early and sets the pattern for subsequent integrations within the body's perceptual system.

3. *Eye Movement Patterns* (to reduce action). Then vision replaces general and/or special movements, and the hands are freed for more economical uses. The less manipulation the hands must exercise, the more available they are to produce shapes, forms, and symbols with greater and greater steering from the visual system. Subsequently the acquisition of information involves less and less manipulation.

4. *Communication or Visual Language Patterns* (to replace action). For the mastery of speech, considerable control of lip, mouth, tongue, and throat muscles must be acquired. According to Getman, nonverbal communication (that is, meaningful gesturing) is related to eye movement patterns and other special movement patterns. Suggestion is made that children with inadequate eye movement development evidence much difficulty with words of distance, direction, and position. Examples of such words include up, down, right, left, near, and far. Language communication gives the child opportunity to verify visual discriminations.

5. *Visualization Patterns.* Sometimes called visual memory, visualization involves (a) the recall of previous learnings, (b) the matching of new learnings against those already known, and (c) the inspection and interpretation of new learnings. Therefore, visualization patterns substitute for action, speech, and time.

6. *Visual Perceptual Organizations.* This level of development makes it possible for an individual to interchange body mechanisms when interpreting the environment. By touching an object, for example, certain reliable inferences can be made regarding its appearance, without sight input. Vision remains most important in interpretation, however, since it characteristically provides more accurate distance reception than audition and yields information on texture, size, shape, direction, and color as well.

Elaboration of Getman's underlying orientation and theory is best presented in recent publications (Getman, 1967, 1966; Getman & Hendrickson, 1966).

A TRAINING PROGRAM FOR THE DEVELOPMENT OF VISUAL PERCEPTION

In outlining a program for the development of visual perception and closely related skills, Getman (1962a, p. 37–106) has organized the activities to correspond to five of the six development stages discussed previously (under Rationale):

1. General Motor Patterns.
2. Special Movement Patterns.
3. Eye Movement Patterns.
4. Visual Language Patterns.
5. Visualization Patterns.

No activities are suggested specifically for the Visual Perceptual Organization stage because Getman is convinced that these patterns emerge when adequate perceptual organization exists at the other four levels.

Examples of activities associated with each stage are listed in Table 1. The table, however, does not provide all the information concerning the individual tasks needed for initiation of the program. For example, consultation with Getman's work is necessary to understand what is meant by "Angels-in-the Snow" or how the trampoline is intended to be used. Although Getman's training procedures are presented only very briefly in Table 1, they illustrate his basic principle that learning takes place best when the child's experience "involves *movement use* of the neuro-muscular system (general movement patterns), practice and repetition for the combination of parts and body mechanisms (special movement patterns), and the resulting interpretation of all information thus received and integrated by all body mechanisms (perception)" (Getman, 1962a, p. 32).

Getman's original training program has been revised and arranged into a more formal, structured format. The improved work was published under the title *The Physiology of Readiness: An Action Program for the Development of Perception for Children* (1964) with Elmer R. Kane as co-author. The philosophy on which the revised systematic training program rests is based upon four premises:

1. Academic performance in today's schools depends heavily upon form and symbol recognition and interpretation.
2. There are perceptual skills which can be developed and trained.

General Movement Patterns	Special Movement Patterns	Eye Movement Patterns	Vision-Language Patterns	Visualization Patterns
1. Basic movements a. Angels-in-the-snow b. Stomach roll c. Rolling sit-ups d. Sit-ups e. Bent-knee sit-ups f. Feet lift g. Roll from back to hands and knees h. Roll from back to hands and feet i. Toe touch 2. Obstacle course 3. Jump board 4. Walking beam 5. Trampoline 6. Rhythmic work with music 7. Running and throwing games	1. Percolator for toy 2. Cupboard or drawer for child 3. Blockcraft and construction blocks (single-color set) 4. Hammer and nails 5. Permission for use of preferred hand 6. Activities requiring bilateral and reciprocal interweaving of the two halves of the body a. Jacks b. Lincoln Logs c. Swings d. Wheelbarrow e. Tricycles and bicycles 7. Tracing blocks or cutouts	1. Fixation practice a. Identifying game b. Making child *look or reach* c. Making child *look and listen* d. Have child look, point, speak 2. Pursuit-golf ball a. to and fro b. side to side c. circular 3. Plane spotter and pilot (pursuit and fixation) 4. Skill of seeing clearly at various distances. Rhythmic fixation. Ability to shift from near to far a. Finger to finger b. Pencil to wall calendar	1. Verb games 2. Encourage talking about interests and activities 3. Adverb games 4. Preposition games 5. Adjective games 6. Naming and classifying 7. Picture description 8. Imitation of sounds 9. Story-telling, main points 10. Opposites 11. Slow, then fast articulation 12. Different types of voices; imagination visualization 13. Let child "rattle on" occasionally 14. Have child retell	1. Simple jigsaw 2. Sorting real objects 3. Visual comparison—size, shape, weight, texture, check with touch or lift 4. Object identification, eyes closed Tactual 5. Matching old labels to new cans 6. Visual comparison outdoors 7. Coloring books 8. Tracing visualizing of a word 9. Visual memory a. Recalling familiar objects b. Telling which is missing c. Recalling items in pictures

General Movement Patterns	Special Movement Patterns	Eye Movement Patterns	Vision-Language Patterns	Visualization Patterns

	8. Catching and throwing
	a. Large, light balloon
	b. Smaller balloons
	c. Heavier beach balls
	d. Softballs and baseballs
	9. Cutting out pictures
	10. Fit objects together
	11. Peg board pictures
	12. Tracing and copying
		5. Chalkboard practice and play
		a. Bimanual circles
		  (1) R-clockwise L-counter-clockwise
		  (2) L-clockwise R-counter-clockwise
		  (3) Both clockwise
		  (4) Both counter-clockwise
		b. Bimanual straight lines
		  (1) All horizontal
		  (2) Both horizontal and vertical
		  (3) Diagonal
		  (4) All possible combinations
		6. Follow the dots
			short stories
			15. Varied tapping for numbers Rhythm
			16. Nursery rhymes, unison
			17. Identification and location of noises
			18. Have child watch for meaning in mouth and facial expression
			19. Initial consonant discrimination
			20. Encourage repetition of radio and T.V. commercials
			21. Provide phone for repetitive listening
			22. Use action/sound records
			23. Voice, identification
			24. Oral directions, increasing number
				d. Reproducing erased forms
				e. Reproduce parts from memory
				f. Label familiar objects: Let child copy
				10. Visual projection
				a. "I am thinking of . . ." Visualize from description
				b. Identify family or friend from description
				c. Identify a place in town from description
				d. Have child describe trip to store, etc.

3. The development of perceptual skills is related to the levels of coordinations of the body systems, that is, the better the coordinations of the body parts and body systems, the better the prospects are for developing perception of forms and symbols.

4. The child whose perceptual skills have been developed and extended is the child who is free to profit from instruction and to learn independently. The greater the development of the perceptual skills, the greater the capacity for making learning more effective (Getman & Kane, 1964, p. III).

Each of these premises has a decidedly visual emphasis, which is consistent with Getman's approach. Though the term *perceptual skills* is utilized, the term *visual perceptual skills* would more adequately reflect Getman and Kane's intent.

Specific activities designed to develop perceptual skills are grouped into six categories. These categories in theory form a developmental sequence corresponding to a considerable degree with the developmental stages described in the section on Rationale. Discussion of the categories and related activities follows.

1. *Practice in General Coordination.* Tasks presented in the first section are designed to develop coordination of the torso, head, and limbs. At this level of training, visually directed gross motor behavior is emphasized and "Angels-in-the-Snow" is a characteristic activity. In the accomplishment of this task, the child is placed in the Starting Position, that is, on his back in a relaxed state with his eyes fixed on a spot on the ceiling. He is instructed to clap his hands overhead while his legs extend to a wide position at the same time. Next the arms return to his sides and his heels are brought back to touch in the center. Arms and legs are relaxed but straight throughout the exercise.

2. *Practice in Balance.* These activities develop balance through visually directed movement, that is, visually interpreted, steered, appraised, and corrected movement. The Walking Board, a 2- × 4-inch board at least 8 feet in length resting upon supports placed under each end, is fundamental to all tasks in this section. The child is taught to walk the board forward and backward with suitable variations.

3. *Practice in Eye-Hand Coordinations.* Tasks included in this section assist children to develop integration of the visual-tactual systems. Getman asserts that these systems are basic to all symbolic interpretations and manipulations. By the use of chalkboard exercises, the child experiences and learns the concepts of the circle and horizontal, vertical, and diagonal lines. Success in these tasks should result in greater speed and accuracy when the child uses workboards and textbooks in school.

4. *Practice in Eye Movements.* Activities presented in this section develop control and accuracy of eye movements. Successful performance results in the acquisition of ocular fixation and pursuit abilities, movements necessary for reading. Included are exercises that require the child to shift his focus from one fixed point to another (ocular fixation) and to follow with the eye his finger moving across a table top (pursuit).

5. *Practice in Form Perception.* Mastery of form perception develops continuity and rhythm of hand movements and permits visual inspection of resulting patterns. The child is given templates (patterns) for the circle, the square, the triangle, the rectangle, and the diamond, and draws each form on the chalkboard. The direction of movements is reinforced by having the child walk out the chalkboard pattern on an open floor space. Transition from the chalkboard to the desk is made, and templates are correspondingly reduced in size. Previous to the publication of *The Physiology of Readiness,* Getman (1962b) developed the School Skill Tracing Board, a useful supplement for children up to the second grade who need practice in form perception. The Tracing Board is slanted and rests upon the child's desk. The template is covered by a transparent sheet on which the child traces various forms. Mistakes are easily wiped off so the child experiences reduced frustration when errors are made. Patterns begin with continuous slanted lines and ovals, proceed to geometric designs, and conclude with mazes, manuscript letters, and cursive exercises.

6. *Practice in Visual Memory.* The final group of activities is designed to develop skill in visual memory through the acquisition of (*a*) greater awareness of size and form relationships, (*b*) increased speed in visual recognition, (*c*) increased span of visual form recognition, and (*d*) more adequate retention of visual images. Practice necessitates the use of a tachistoscope, a projection instrument which flashes a pattern on a screen at regular time intervals. A series of slides is presented to which the child responds in varying ways. For example, he may be required to name the form (oral), trace it in the air (kinesthetic), circle it on a worksheet (matching), trace over it on a worksheet (tactile, or reproduce it (visual memory).

DISCUSSION OF GETMAN'S APPROACH

Concern has been expressed regarding various aspects of Getman's position. Mostly the criticism centers upon (1) the strong emphasis placed by him upon visual perception and (2) the lack of research-established validity.

Hagin (1965) has stated that Getman overemphasizes the role of visual perception in the classroom and has pointed out that classroom learning actually involves a considerable amount of talking and listening (auditory-vocal skills). In fact, the value of auditory training and the contribution of auditory skills to school success are scarcely mentioned in Getman's writings, even though most writers in remedial education would probably agree that auditory processes are most important to adequate language (including reading) development. If this is so, then Getman's unqualified remarks relative to vision and intelligence, some of which were listed previously, would seem to be exaggerated.

Although many clinicians have successfully used the Getman techniques or modifications of these techniques to develop visual adequacy, the validity of either the whole program or of the individual tasks has not been established by carefully designed research. Silver (1965) even questions a basic premise of the approach; saying: "the training of gross motor functional patterns, such as balancing on a rail has not been proven to improve perception and learning" (p. 20). In his discussion of Getman's teaching suggestions, Hagin (1965) concluded: "I am concerned that his training procedures have not been tested through careful sampling and controlled research. I'm concerned about oversimplification and lack of specificity" (p. 25).

The results of one pilot project which used the procedures with matched first-grade pupils has been circulated by the publishers of *The Physiology of Readiness*. The experimental subjects significantly surpassed the control subjects in reading comprehension at the end of a 15-week training experience. As frequently occurs with pilot studies, the design was not completely satisfactory, that is, no mention is made relative to control of Hawthorne effect or to random allocation of subjects into groups. The results, however, do indicate that training in visually related readiness activities may be associated with reading acquisition, though additional research is necessary to conclusively verify the relationship.

In general, most of the questions concerning the validity of Getman's techniques could be, or have been, directed toward the procedures of Delacato, Kephart, and others who train at the perceptual-motor level. Although similarities do exist among these systems, Getman (1967) draws several distinctions between his approach and those advocated by these workers:

1. Neither Kephart or Delacato has a functional, performance-centered concept of child development.

2. Neither sees vision as a dynamic process of cumulative and emerging cognitive performance that involves the entire organism and is merely triggered by light.

3. Neither demands use of the visual system as the ultimate guidance and appraisal system to control and correct the action system.

4. Both see movement as significant unto itself.

5. Both insist that an organism that has lived for years may be returned to actions and experiences characteristic of a much earlier developmental period and function as if it were in tune with that period.

Relative to research support for these techniques, it must be pointed out that Getman views himself as a clinician and as such is not personally interested in undertaking a series of validity studies. To Getman, the accumulated clinical evidence derived from his experience is sufficient validation for the suggested approach. Getman readily agrees, however, that formal investigations into the efficacy of his techniques would be desirable, and he encourages interested persons to research this area.

Ray Barsch

Barsch is a man entranced with the world of space and movement within that space. In his frame of reference even language, that highly auditory and temporal accomplishment, is reduced to a visuospatial phenomenon. He states:

Man is a visual spatial being. At birth he is surrounded by space and "makes his living" in space from one end of life's cycle to the other. . . . Man is a symbolically oriented being. Symbols become his system for logging his journey through space (Barsch, 1965a, p. 3).

In his earlier writing, Barsch was concerned primarily with the child who is brain damaged and he discussed parent counseling (1961), the concept of regression (1960), and a method of evaluation and classification (1962). More recently Barsch has abandoned the concept of minimal brain damage in children and his efforts have been directed toward developing a conceptual schema that describes the child as a learner and provides an approach to education, designated by Barsch as the "physiologic approach," in contradistinction to the more traditional "intellectual" and "psychiatric" approaches (1965b). The implementation of the physiologic approach resulted in an experimental curriculum based on 12 dimensions of learning derived from what Barsch terms "movigenics." He defines movigenics as "the study of the origin and development of movement patterns leading to learning efficiency" (1965b, p. 5).

RATIONALE AND BASIC POSTULATES

Barsch's (1967) theory of movement—movigenics—rests upon ten postulates synthesized from the work of numerous theorists and researchers in many disciplines. Without exception all of the postulates deal with man as a moving being within a spatial world. The basic principle underlying the human species is "movement efficiency," which develops in a sequential fashion throughout its forward thrust toward maturity and which is characterized by a striving for equilibrium or homeostasis. Survival in a spatial world is the prime objective of movement efficiency, which develops in a climate of physical and psychological stress. The ability to process information by means of the "perceptocognitive system" is necessary to the emergence of movement efficiency. This system is composed of the six sense channels—auditory, visual, kinesthetic, tactual, olfactory, and gustatory—as well as a "cognitive sequence," which includes discrimination, categorization, and generalization. Barsch (1967) notes that the adequacy of feedback is essential to the development of movement efficiency, which "is symbolically communicated through the visual-spatial phenomenon called language" (p. 59). Movement and communication are viewed in an antecedent-consequent relationship, that is, communication depends upon the ability to process information from the various portions of the perceptocognitive system, an ability which, in turn, is dependent upon efficient movement patterns.

THE DIMENSIONS OF LEARNING

From the postulates Barsch (1967) derives twelve dimensions pertaining to human learning which serve as the areas constituting the educational curriculum.

Postural-Transport Orientations. The first four dimensions of learning deal with control of the body and movement through space. *Muscular strength,* the first dimension, provides support of the body and the initial impetus for such activities as rolling, crawling, sitting, and standing. Adequate muscular strength implies appropriate muscle tonus, power, and endurance, which, naturally, are expected to vary according to the individual's size and age. Given adequate muscular strength, the second dimension, *dynamic balance,* is necessary for overcoming the pull of gravity; a person may maintain his posture by facilitating and inhibiting muscular contractions. The adjustments made in achieving dynamic balance are bilateral in nature because both sides of the body are brought into play, but bilaterality is considered a separate dimension and is only incidental to dynamic balance. The developing child who has acquired appropriate muscular strength and balance is "ready to move," but before he can interact with his environment in a meaningful way he must arrive at the third dimension, *body awareness*, that distinction between self and not-self. As Barsch explains, the child must answer the question "Who am I?" before he can answer for the next question, "Where am I?" This leads to the fourth dimension, *spatial awareness*. The child integrates muscular strength with information regarding self, places, and positions thereby moving both himself and objects in accordance with his needs and environmental demands.

Perceptocognitive Modes. As the child is learning to transport himself in space, he is learning simultaneously to process information from the four primary modalities, the tactual, kinesthetic, auditory, and visual modes. Barsch (1967) states that the modes are not considered senses but are functional channels of reception and expression, although each mode has a sensory component. The fifth dimension, *tactual dynamics,* is defined as the ability of the child to process information gained from the cutaneous surface of his body. According to Barsch, tactual dynamics implies a process, not the simple sense of touch; but his discussion of the dimension appears to be confined to tactile stimulation and discrimination. All parts of the body are involved and all kinds of tactile stimulation such as heat, texture, and pressure are discussed. Touch is divided into two types: active touch in which the child reaches out for contact and passive touch in which he receives contact. It is somewhat difficult, however, to distinguish the types of touch on physiological or developmental bases.

Kinesthesia, which constitutes the sixth dimension, refers to the ability to feel movement, to remember movement patterns, and to integrate the perceptual and cognitive elements of movement sequences. Barsch (1965b) views kinesthesia as a "function of tactuality and proprioception with the added ingredient of a specific perception of movement to bring the action of the body to a full state of meaning" (p. 24). Tactual dynamics and kinesthesia thus complement one another, and kinesthesia may be necessary to bring the body into contact with another surface but the perception of contact is primary and kinesthesia only facilitates the act.

The seventh dimension of learning is *auditory dynamics,* composed of the perception of sound and the expression of a communication system. The dimension is defined as the ability to process information from the world of sound, that is, to receive and to express. Other than dividing audition into receptive and expressive components and noting the absence of hearing loss in most learning disabled children, Barsch devotes little time to the auditory process. In essence, he says that the "individual must find some way of gaining meaning from the acoustic energy which impinges on his tympanic membrane and passes through the auditory neurologic system" (1965b, p. 23).

Barsch's discussion of auditory dynamics is sparse, but the eighth dimension, *visual dynamics*, is described in great detail (1967). This dimension encompasses far more than vision or sight alone. It includes visual tracking and steering, the visual definition of the limits of surroundings, the discrimination of the details of a task, and the interpretation of the relationship between details of more than one task. Vision describes distance and the relationship of objects in space. "Vision defines distance, color, relationships, textures—and becomes the *true integrating agent* for touch, kinesthesia and audition" (Barsch, 1965b, p. 7; authors' italics). No single statement could better exemplify the emphasis which Barsch places upon the visual processes. Neither Kephart nor Frostig considers vision to be of such primary importance in learning and development, although they do not discuss the auditory processes in detail.

Degrees of Freedom. The last four dimensions of learning set forth by Barsch (1965b) "represent those factors which enlarge, enrich, expand, and explicate the performance efficiency of all others" (p. 8). The ninth dimension is *bilaterality*, the ability to perform efficient, reciprocal movement patterns on both sides of the body midline. In contrast to the findings of Orton (1937), Kephart (1960), and Delacato (1959), Barsch states that most of the children he saw were firmly one-sided and could not perform adequately when using the nonpreferred side of the body. The dimension of bilaterality is included to insure smooth, coordinated movement of the body as a whole. The tenth dimension, *rhythm*, is the ability to coordinate and synchronize movements of the body to achieve harmony and grace. Patterns of movement are labeled arhythmic, dysrhythmic, and rhythmic; the underlying factor is apparently temporal sequencing of movements. Arhythmic movements are random and diffuse while dysrhythmic movement is jerky and spasmodic. Rhythmic movement is graceful and occurs in a well-defined temporal sequence.

Flexibility, the ability to modify or shift patterns of movement in an appropriate fashion, constitutes the eleventh dimension. In order to facilitate the modification or shifting of movement patterns, the child must have at his command a repertoire of responses which enable him to change as the situation dictates. The modifications discussed by Barsch are speed, direction, force, and time, all of which must be available to the child as alternative choices when he is faced with the necessity for changing a movement pattern. The twelfth and final dimension is *motor planning,* which "requires a knowledge of one's own movement repertoire and some spatial estimate of the presented demand"; this is concerned primarily with planning rather than execution of the movement. Such planning necessitates forethought as preparation for movement and, according to Barsch, may be thought of as cognitive rehearsal. The dimensions in the category degrees of freedom are those leading to outstanding performance in motor areas and are exemplified in professional athletes.

The twelve dimensions were employed by Barsch (1965b) in constructing a curriculum for children with learning disabilities which was sponsored by the Wisconsin State Department of Public Instruction and was used experimentally at Longfellow School in Madison.

THE MOVIGENIC CURRICULUM

The curriculum devised by Barsch is based directly upon the twelve dimensions of development and learning discussed above. No provision is made in the curriculum for differential treatment of individual children; instead, the program assumes that each child will receive instruction in each dimension and that no other program will be included. Each dimension is now defined in Barsch's words, and the activities he suggests are given.

Dimension I—Muscular Strength. Muscular strength is "the capacity of the organism to maintain an adequate state of muscle tonus, power and stamina to meet the daily demands appropriate to his body size and chronological age" (Barsch, 1965b, p. 15). The activities suggested for improvement of muscular strength are those that would be included in most physical education programs for young children. A variety of exercises is recommended along with specific instruction in positioning the body for jumping, lifting, pushing, balancing, and so forth.

Dimension II—Dynamic Balance. Barsch (1965b) states that "dynamic balance is the capacity of the organism to activate antigravity muscles in proper relationship to one another against the force of gravitational pull to maintain alignment, sustain his transport pattern and aid in recovery" (p. 16). To aid in recovery of balance the child may use balance boards, imitate animal gaits, and learn to move about a darkened room avoiding obstacles. Walking rails are recommended to teach the maintenance of alignment; also used are twisting, turning, and spinning activities. The child learns to sustain a transport pattern by walking, hopping, tiptoeing, etc., to the beat of a metronome or tom-tom, by performing these same activities on the walking rail, and by maneuvering on a scooter board or on his abdomen, knees, or while sitting.

Dimension III—Spatial Awareness. According to Barsch (1965b), "spatial awareness is the capacity of the organism to identify his own position in space relative to his surround with constant orientation to surface, elevation, periphery, back and front" (p. 18). The activities for training in spatial awareness are arranged in eight categories:

1. Rotation in space. The children turn in the direction they are commanded: left, right, toward various objects in the room while imitating the teacher, later without watching him.

2. Labeling directions in space. The children follow the teacher's directions to point up, down, to the side, etc., in relation to parts of their own bodies.

3. Basic lateral patterning in space. The children are taught to imitate the tonic neck reflex pattern.

4. Visualization of space. Activities consist of describing objects when blindfolded and recalling the identity and position of objects.

5. Reorganization of space. The children are taught to form new designs from materials arranged in patterns by the teacher. Activities progress fom rearranging furniture in the classroom to creating designs using geometric forms, word lists, or parquetry blocks.

6. Reproduction of designs in space. Designs formed in a great variety of materials are copied by the children.

7. Rolling in space. The synchronization of the four count roll is taught, that is, on the count of one, two, three, four, the child lifts his head, turns his shoulder, raises his hips, and rolls over.

8. Variable transport in space. The children walk, run, jump, and perform other transport activities in many different directions in the room.

Dimension IV—Body Awareness. "Body awareness is the capacity of the organism to achieve a conscious appreciation of the relationship of all body segments to movement, to be able to label body parts and to appreciate the functional properties of various body parts" (Barsch, 1965b, p. 19). One series of activities is intended to develop body image and consists of games like "Simon Says," finger games, figure drawings, and identification of body parts. Another series of exercises used in training body awareness is designed to teach the children how various parts of the body function. Exercises are devoted to teaching relaxation and the movement of discrete body parts in isolation as well as an explanation of function taught didactically through questions such as, "What do you see with?" and "What do you walk with?"

Dimension V—Visual Dynamics.

Visual dynamics is the capacity of the organism to fixate accurately on a target at near, mid and far points in space, to scan a surround for meaning in the vertical and horizontal planes, to converge and accommodate, to equalize the use of both visual circuits in a binocular pattern to achieve fusion and to steer the body in proper alignment for movements through space (Barsch, 1965b, p. 20).

The activities for training in visual dynamics suggested by Barsch are grouped in five sections: steering, tracking, attention, shifting, and memory.

1. Visual steering. Although visual steering is included in many of the activities given in following sections, a few are recommended as being specifically related to steering, for example, using visual targets when walking, rolling, or walking the rail and when throwing bean bags.

2. Visual tracking. Any activities which require the child to follow a moving target with his eyes are suitable for training in this area.

3. Sustained attention. While in a darkened room, the children focus their attention on a light beam and keep their eyes on that spot as long as the light remains.

4. Visual shifting. The activities recommended in this area are similar to those described under visual tracking, the primary difference being that the children must shift their eyes from one visual target to another as quickly and as smoothly as possible.

5. Visual memory. Tachistoscopic slides, also used for visual shifting, are recommended to train visual memory. Other activities included are the recall of a number of objects previously seen and the answering of such questions as "What color is a lemon?" and "Can you tell me something that is red?"

Dimension VI—Auditory Dynamics. Barsch (1965b) defines auditory dynamics as "the capacity of the organism to process information on a receiving and a sending basis from the world of sound and to attach appropriate relationships to the world of sound" (p. 22). Activities suggested in this area are aimed at improving receptive and expressive audition through imitation, discrimination, and comprehension tasks. The exercises are not presented in a developmental fashion, instead they seem appropriate to a language enrichment program.

Dimension VII—Kinesthesia. "Kinesthesia is the capacity of the organism to maintain an awareness of position in space and to recall patterns of movement from previous experience for utility in resolving continuing demands" (Barsch, 1965b, p. 23). Exercises for improving kinesthesia are related to gross and fine movement patterning. Activities for gross motor patterning include rolling, homologous, homolateral, and cross-diagonal crawling, Angels-in-the-Snow, and writing in the air with hands, elbows, or feet. To improve fine movement patterning some suggestions are using pegboards, cutting with scissors, and blowing and catching bubbles. Several exercises described under the sections devoted to spatial awareness and body awareness are also appropriate.

Dimension VIII—Tactual Dynamics. Barsch (1965b) says "tactual dynamics encompass the capacity of the organism to gain information from the cutaneous contact of active or passive touching" (p. 25). All activities described in this dimension are related to teaching the child to discriminate and identify tactual stimuli whether he is touching or being touched. He is taught to identify by touch alone geometric shapes, scraps of material (texture), temperature, and whole objects. Many of the activities require that children identify stimuli with their bare feet.

Dimension IX—Bilaterality. Barsch (1965b) describes bilaterality as "the capacity of the organism to reciprocally interweave two sides in a balanced relationship of thrusting and counterthrusting patterns around the three coordinates of vertical, horizontal and depth in proper alignment from initiation to completion of a task" (p. 27). All of the activities which Barsch suggests in this dimension require bilateral movements: the child writes or draws with both hands, he imitates bilateral movements of the teacher, and he performs a variety of exercises with alternating sides of the body and then with both sides simultaneously.

Dimension X—Rhythm. "Rhythm is the capacity of the organism to synchronize patterns of movements according to situational demands, thus achieving harmony, grace and use of movement" (Barsch, 1965b, p. 28). Any rhythmic activity utilizing metronomes, tom-toms, clapping, tapping, etc., and manifested in walking, running, singing, choral speaking, etc., would be appropriate for improving performance in the dimension of rhythm.

Dimension XI—Flexibility. According to Barsch (1965b), "flexibility is the capacity of the organism to modify or shift patterns of movement appropriate to the situational demand" (p. 29). The exercises to improve flexibility are the same as those described in the other dimensions, the only difference being the shifting of patterns as dictated by the teacher. No specific suggestions, therefore, are described.

Dimension XII—Motor Planning. "Motor planning is the capacity of the organism to plan a movement pattern prior to execution in order to meet the demands of a task" (Barsch, 1965b, p. 29). Again, no specific descriptions of activities to improve motor planning are given because the exercises are the same as those recommended in other dimensions of the program. To facilitate motor planning while performing the various exercises, the teacher reminds the children to plan their movements and then check their plans against what happened when they moved.

Barsch (1965b) reported that most of the children enrolled in the experimental program at Longfellow School in Madison, Wisconsin, made substantial progress, although no formal testing was done and the conclusion is by and large subjective. At the end of the training period, the majority of the children were able to perform the tasks in the various dimensions of the program; such was not the case at the beginning of the experiment. At least one other study has been reported which illustrates the efficacy of the Barsch techniques. Painter (1966) reported a study of children enrolled in a movigenic program; they scored significantly higher on several subtests of the ITPA at the end of the experimental period, indicating that improvement of movement efficiency is related, to some extent, to improvement in psycholinguistic areas. Like the approaches of authors discussed previously in this chapter, Barsch's orientation remains essentially nonlanguage with the primary emphasis being upon perceptual-motor learning. The child who exhibits delays in motor and/or visual-perceptual development benefits from these programs, but the child with a severe auditory receptive language disorder can profit most from the language development systems of Barry, McGinnis, and Myklebust.

Conclusion

Most authors discussed in this chapter, as well as Frostig, consider the visual-motor channel the key to the development and mastery of academic skills, conceptualization, and abstract thinking. As a result, auditory training receives less emphasis than visual training in their approaches. The stated or inferred hypothesis that a lack of certain visual-motor skills adversely affects the acquisition of academic skills is not necessarily tenable. Bateman (1964) has observed that "there are children who manifest severe spatial orientation, body image, perceptual, coordination, etc., problems and who are not dyslexic" (p. 11). Relative to children with motor difficulties, Irwin and Hammill (1964, 1965) have consistently failed to find differences in perception, language, or intelligence between mild, moderate, and severe cerebral palsied youngsters. Readers are also referred to the work of Birch and Leford (1964), who report that differences between cerebral palsied and normal children relative to visual form discrimination are of only slight functional significance. Similarly, Dunn (1967) reminds his readers that "efficacy studies in the areas of motor development and perceptual learning with Strauss-type children are nonexistent" (p. 130). Thus these authors should be looked upon as a rich and valuable source of practical suggestions which aid in the development of perceptual-motor skills, but it should not be assumed that a child who lacks some of these abilities will become a slow learner, or necessarily have difficulty with academics.

References

Barsch, R. The concept of regression in the brain-injured child. *Exceptional Children,* 1960, **27**, 84–90.

———. Counseling the parent of the brain-damaged child. *Journal of Rehabilitation,* 1961, **3**, 1–3.

———. Evaluating the organic child: The Functional Organizational Scale. *Journal of Genetic Psychology,* 1962, **100**, 345–354.

———. The concept of language as a visuo-spatial phenomenon. *Academic Therapy Quarterly,* 1965, **1**, 2–11. (a)

———. *A movigenic curriculum.* Madison, Wisc.: State Department of Public Instruction, 1965. (b)

———. *Achieving perceptual-motor efficiency: A space-oriented approach to learning.* Seattle, Wash.: Special Child Publications, 1967.

Bateman, B. Learning disabilities—Yesterday, today, and tomorrow. *Exceptional Children,* 1964, **31**(4), 167–177.

Birch, H. G., & Leford, A. Two strategies for studying perception in "brain-damaged" children. In H. G. Birch, *Brain damage in children.* Baltimore, Md.: Williams & Wilkins, 1964. Pp. 46–60.

Delacato, C. *The treatment and prevention of reading problems.* Springfield, Ill.: Thomas, 1959.

Dunn, L. M. Minimal brain dysfunction: A dilemma for educators. In E. C. Frierson, & W. B. Barbe, *Educating children with learning disabilities.* New York: Appleton-Century-Crofts, 1967.

Dunsing, J. D., & Kephart, N. C. Motor generalizations in space and time. In J. Hellmuth (Ed.), *Learning disorders*. Vol. I. Seattle, Wash.: Special Child Publications, 1965.

Fairbanks, G. Systematic research in experimental phonetics: 1. A theory of the speech mechanism as a servosystem. *Journal of Speech and Hearing Disorders*, 1954, **19**, 133–139.

Freidus, E. Methodology for the classroom teacher. In J. Hellmuth (Ed.), *The special child in century 21*. Seattle, Wash.: Special Child Publications of the Seguin School, 1964. Pp. 303–321.

————. The needs of teachers for specialized information on number concepts. In W. M. Cruickshank (Ed.), *The teacher of brain-injured children: A discussion of the bases for competency*. Syracuse, N.Y.: Syracuse University Press, 1966. Pp. 111–128.

Getman, G. N. Visual success in reading success. *Journal of the California Optometric Association*, 1961, **29**(5), 1–4.

————. *How to develop your child's intelligence*. Luverne, Minnesota: Author, 1962. (a)

————. *The school skill tracing board*. Minneapolis, Minn.: Programs to Accelerate School Success, 1962. (b)

————. Personal communication, 1967.

————, & Kane, E. R. *The physiology of readiness: An action program for the development of perception for children*. Minneapolis, Minnesota: Programs to Accelerate School Success, 1964. Revised and retitled. Getman, G. N., Kane, E. R., Halgren, M. R., & McKee, G. W. *Developing learning readiness*. Manchester, Mo.: Webster Division, McGraw-Hill, 1968.

Gillingham, A. B., & Stillman, B. L. *Remedial training for children with specific disability in reading, spelling, and penmanship*. (7th ed.) Cambridge, Mass.: Educators Publishing Service, 1965.

Hagin, R. I. In symposium: Perceptual training for children with learning difficulties. New Jersey Association for Brain Injured Children, et al., 1965.

Irwin, J. V. *Short course on articulation*. Texas Speech and Hearing Association annual meeting, October, 1966, Austin, Texas.

Irwin, O. C., & Hammill, D. D. Some results with an Abstraction Test with cerebral palsied children. *Cerebral Palsy Review*, 1964, **25**(5), 10–11.

————. Effect of type, extent and degree of cerebral palsy on three measures of language. *Cerebral Palsy Journal*, 1965, **26**(6), 7–9.

Kephart, N. C. *The brain-injured child in the classroom*. Chicago: National Society for Crippled Children and Adults, 1963.

————. Perceptual-motor aspects of learning disabilities. *Exceptional Children*, 1964, **31**, 201–206.

————. Perceptual-motor correlates of learning. In S. A. Kirk, & W. Becker (Eds.), *Conference on children with minimal brain impairments*. Chicago. National Society for Crippled Children and Adults, 1963. Pp. 13–26.

————. *The slow learner in the classroom*. Columbus, Ohio: Merrill, 1960.

McGinnis, M. *Aphasic children: Identification and education by the Association Method*. Washington, D.C.: Volta Bureau, 1963.

Mysak, E. D. *Speech pathology and feedback theory.* Springfield, Ill.: Thomas, 1966.

Orton, S. T. *Reading, writing and speech problems in children.* New York: Norton, 1937.

Painter, G. The effect of a rhythmic and sensory motor activity program on perceptual motor spatial abilities of kindergarten children. *Exceptional Children,* 1966, 33, 113–119.

Piaget, J. *The origins of intelligence in children.* New York: International Universities Press, 1952.

Sherrington, C. S. *The integrative action of the nervous system.* New Haven: Yale University Press, 1948.

Silver, A. A. In symposium: Perceptual training for children with learning difficulties. New Jersey Association for Brain Injured Children, et al., 1965.

Strauss, A. A., & Kephart, N. C. *Psychopathology and education of the brain-injured child.* Vol. II. New York: Grune & Stratton, 1955.

————, & Lehtinen, L. *Psychopathology and education of the brain-injured child.* Vol. I. New York: Grune & Stratton, 1947.

Van Riper, C., & Irwin, J. V. *Voice and articulation.* Englewood Cliffs, N.J.: Prentice-Hall, 1958.

CHAPTER V

THE MULTISENSORY SYSTEMS

Unlike most of the systems reviewed, which are either strongly visual-motor or auditory-vocal in their orientation, those discussed in this chapter emphasize no particular modality or channel. Instead, a decidedly eclectic approach is advocated; in general this approach permits cross-modality stimulation in most training activities. The emphasized tasks use visual-auditory-kinesthetic-tactile inputs, which permit the child to capitalize on any areas of strength while hopefully improving areas of deficit at the same time. This approach often is called the V-A-K-T method of instruction.

What happens in the brain as the various sensory channels send their messages in a coordinated, simultaneous manner? Hebb (1949) says that there are interconnections of the neural cells in the brain, which possibly form connections in patterns. Parts of the patterns can be excited by more than one type of input, because of the interweaving of the pattern elements. Thus, if an auditory input that usually occurs with a visual input happens to enter without the visual input, part of the pattern of the two could be excited by the single input. Consequently, a "set" could consist of forming a word through visual, auditory, and kinesthetic channels, which could eventually be excited by the input of just one channel.

This chapter surveys the multisensory systems of Lehtinen, Cruickshank, and Fernald. The first two are concerned with both preschool and school-aged children and stress the importance of the perceptual buildup as a prerequisite for academic success. Fernald, however, addresses her attention exclusively to the remediation of problems in specific academic subjects, notably reading and to some extent arithmetic and spelling. Therefore, when selecting among these systems, the age of the child and the particular skills in need of development will determine which is the most suitable. Although some clinicians advocate the almost exclusive use of the V-A-K-T method, we recommend its use with children who evidence a mosaic pattern of strengths and weaknesses that cuts across not only sensory modalities but levels of language as well. The case history that follows describes the child for whom use of a multisensory approach is recommended.

The public school coordinator of special education referred S. M. for evaluation because of first-grade failure associated with difficulty in attention and memory. The parents supported the complaints raised by the coordinator and added that S. M. had acquired a considerably negative attitude toward school which was evidenced by: (1) his poor attendance, (2) inadequate peer relationships, (3) his dislike of and/or inability to do homework, and (4) possible psychosomatic episodes probably induced to avoid school. In fact, S. M. missed the first three weeks of school because of "stomach aches." By Christmas, he had finally adapted to school, but the family moved in April and a change of schools was required.

Results of the WISC suggested that S. M. was at least of low average intelligence. His performance on the individual subtests, however, ranged from Scaled Score 2 to 14 and indicated the presence of strengths and deficits on *both* the Verbal and Performance scales. The findings from the ITPA were suggestive of a generalized language problem. Although above CA in Visual Decoding, he scored substantially below CA on all the other subtests (including the visual-motor ones). No modality preference was evident; strengths and weaknesses were apparent in both auditory-vocal and visual-motor channels. Deficiencies at the Representational as well as the Automatic-Sequential levels of language were noted. In speech he was found to have poor discrimination of speech sounds and articulation ability while demonstrating adequate syntax and sentence length.

Due to S. M.'s youth and apparent multiple perceptual difficulties, a perceptual build-up program was recommended, following Lehtinen-Cruickshank percepts. He was referred for placement in a classroom for children with learning disabilities. Should he develop trouble learning to read and should his cross-modality problem persist, the Fernald method would be an appropriate instructional approach.

Laura Lehtinen

In 1947, when Strauss and Lehtinen published *Psychopathology and Education of the Brain-Injured Child,* few educators recognized the existence of the minimally brain-injured child. Only a few years before, in 1941, Gesell had proposed the idea of the minimally brain-damaged child, and little research had been done in this area. Thus Lehtinen was among the pioneers in the education of these children. As the Educational Director of the Cove School for Brain-Injured Children in Racine, Wisconsin, she worked with Strauss, its President, to evolve a means of teaching these children. Lethinen has developed not so much a specific method as a teaching procedure based on Strauss' research and on his theory of cortical damage. The fact that her pioneering efforts have not become outmoded attests to their validity.

In order to make the fullest use of the procedures Lehtinen describes, it is necessary to understand the theories on which they are based. The questions Strauss worked to answer were concerned with how the brain continues to function when portions of it are impaired or even destroyed, and after injury to what extent it functions normally and to what extent pathologically.

CONCEPT OF CORTICAL FUNCTION

In his studies Strauss used three frames of reference, the ontogenetic, the phylogenetic, and the comparative. Since these approaches are familiar ones, it is not necessary to describe them. The most interesting aspect of Strauss' theory is his concept of cortical functioning. Because his concept is not based on commonly accepted theory, one finds Strauss, in the first volume of this work (Strauss & Lehtinen, 1947), cautiously disagreeing with the belief of older clinicians that disordered functions result from injury in localized cortical areas. In the second volume of the series (Strauss & Kephart, 1955), his rejection of this once commonly accepted theory of point-for-point localization at the cortical level is strong and specific. Today rigid localization of function is considered untenable by most authorities.

The clearest description of Strauss' concept of brain functioning appears in the later volume. He visualizes the cortex as a vast network of interconnecting fiber paths by means of which impulses travel in

interconnecting chains or loops. These chains are so intricately intercon-
nected that an impulse can move freely not only from one chain to
another but to any number of chains. The cortex is never at rest. The
chains of neurons are always activated and functioning, so that when a
new stimulus enters the cortex it meets an already functioning activity
and the cortex tries to fit the new stimulus into the ongoing activity; if
it cannot, a rapid repatterning of activity must take place and the new
stimulus sets into activity a new pattern of chains. Thus the activity
of the cortex becomes activity within activity and the new stimulus
travels in a chain with a complex pattern of connecting chains all under
action at the same time. From this complex integration of simultaneous
activity, a single impression fuses and a concept results.

A pattern of activity that develops in the cortex leaves a trace which
influences patterns developed in the future. So the activity of the cortex
is affected not only by the energy entering at a given moment, but
also by energy patterns of the past, which have left their trace, and
further by the pattern of a activity developed in response to a particular
stimulus.

A new stimulus entering the cortex meets simultaneously both the
chains currently in action and the influence of chains developed in the
past. The new pattern that emerges is an interweaving of past and
present activity. This interweaving must be consistent and the total activity must remain pertinent to the stimulating situation. If not, behavior
becomes bizarre and inappropriate. Thus the sometimes strange and
unpredictable behavior of brain-injured children is explained.

Disagreeing with the theory of point-for-point localization, Strauss
believes that a particular stimulus does not have to enter a specific
point in the cortex. A neuron can enter into any one of a number of
chains, its activity being altered according to the chain. Depending on
the orientation of the cerebrum, the same neuron might, five minutes
later, enter an entirely different chain, generating a pattern differing
entirely from the one it would have made on the earlier entrance. It
might enter a long chain with many interconnecting loops or a short
chain with few. Believing that most of the cortex is concerned with
general rather than specific activity, Strauss explains the localized areas
that have been found in the cortex as areas where a large number of
chains all related to certain behavior converge. For example, Broca's
area represents a convergence of chains associated with the motor aspects of speech. He feels that localization of specialized functions in
the cortex is not acceptable but localization of such generalized centers
of convergence is.

In spite of Strauss' rejection of localization of brain function, he says that the effect of brain damage is determined by location of the lesion rather than by its extent. Comparatively minor damage to brain tissue can cause serious disturbance if the damage is close to a convergence center. Here one small unit of damage can cause major interference for it disrupts a great number of complex, interlocking patterns. Conversely, if the damage is in an area removed from a specific convergence point, the same sized unit of damage will create far less disturbance for there are fewer patterns to receive interference. But in either case there will always be general, over-all disturbance because of the interweaving of the chains.

In this phase of his work, Strauss concerns himself only with the forebrain (the new brain and the old brain, or the telencephalon and the diencephalon) in which impairment produces the specific disturbances characteristic of brain-injured children, for the disturbances described by Strauss do not follow the destruction of nerve tissue below the level of the midbrain. Injuries found below the midbrain produce neurological signs but not the disorders found in injuries to the higher centers of the brain.

In general terms Strauss lists these disturbances as distractibility, perceptual disturbances, thinking disorders, and behavior disorders. He delineates the difficult child now categorized as "hyperactive," and his description of the characteristic disorders of this child has become the familiar "Strauss syndrome."

Strauss interprets the strong psychomotor disturbances, which are so prominent a part of the behavior of brain-injured children, through Cannon's theory that emotion is a function of the thalamus and that thalamic processes are a source of affective experiences. The subcortical neurons do not require cortical direction in order to be released into action but can be discharged directly, precipitately, and intensely. This uncontrolled release of powerful impulses results in the intense and disinhibited behavior of the brain-damaged child. Strauss believes that this explosive release of thalamic energies in emotion can be controlled by cortical processes, so that with the increased functioning of the higher mental processes the brain-injured child can learn to control his hyperactivity and drivenness. From this neurophysiological viewpoint, Strauss and Lehtinen received their notions regarding education and their optimism in the belief that methods can be developed to relieve the perceptual and conceptual disturbances of brain-injured children, thereby lessening the behavioral disorders attendant upon the former disabilities.

At the time Strauss and Lehtinen began their work, the "quiet" brain-damaged child had not come to attention and the term "brain-injured child" connoted only the hyperactive, distractible, driven child. It was with these difficult children that they worked, searching for ways to help them tolerate the classroom situation, learn to control themselves, and to advance academically. Although the hypoactive child does not need their behavioral controls, the teaching procedures they developed are equally applicable to him.

EDUCATIONAL PRINCIPLES

Lehtinen bases her methods of educational treatment on Strauss' clinical and psychological findings, on her own observation of the effect of general disturbance on attention, perception, and behavior, and on the effect of general disturbances of particular perceptual fields upon the learning of special academic skills. She finds the brain-injured child with his different mental organization and his characteristic disorders in perception, concept formation, and behavior as abnormally responsive to the stimuli of his environment. His reactibility is beyond his control, and in a situation of constant stimulation, such as that of a regular classroom, he can react only in an undirected, disinhibited manner. Many of the child's educational and emotional problems are the result of his organic restlessness and distractibility. His behavior interferes with group adjustment and learning, which, in turn, leads to repeated failures, producing emotional problems and further poor behavior.

Even with an understanding teacher who is able to make individual adjustments for him, the hyperactive child can be helped little in a regular classroom. He must have an environment tailored to his needs. In seeking the best means of helping this child, Lehtinen extends her efforts in two directions, manipulating and controlling the environment and teaching the child to exercise voluntary control.

To achieve the environment she considers optimal, Lehtinen keeps the class group small—twelve should be the maximum number—and uses a large classroom so that each child can be seated at a distance from the others. The room is devoid of all visually stimulating material, the windows covered, the teacher's dress plain and unornamented. If necessary, she places the child facing the wall or uses screens around him. She divests the child's materials of all but the barest essentials, even cutting away the borders of pictures and using covers over reading material to expose only a small area at a time.

In such a structured environment, many of the children are able for the first time to meet academic requirements adequately. With the decrease in distractibility and hyperactivity, ability to perform in a learning situation increases. The interaction of external control and learning is reciprocal; as control is imposed, learning takes place, and with learning greater control is possible. Direction of the child's behavior must eventually come from within himself; and as his organic disturbance lessens, the protections are gradually removed—the child's desk is placed in the class group, pictures and bulletin boards make their appearance in the classroom.

Having manipulated the situation to achieve behavior control, Lehtinen proceeds with teaching methods based on the child's disabilities. She believes the approach should be an attack on the organic disturbance rather than a psychotherapeutic approach to relieve emotional conflicts or an approach of stimulation intended to increase interest and motivation. She disagrees with the theory that a child should be developed in the areas of his strength so that he can have a better sense of achievement. On the contrary she stresses work in, and development of, the areas of his weakness.

Lehtinen points out that in teaching brain-injured children, the problem presented by the young brain-injured child who is just beginning his academic experience should be differentiated from the problem of teaching the older child who has been in school several years. The theoretical approach is the same for both, but the method differs. The younger child is taught with various readiness materials; the method for the older child is essentially remedial. Here Lehtinen makes an important point: even though many of the techniques employed with the older groups are similar to standard remedial techniques, the orientation to the problem is different. Greater emphasis is placed upon the correction of the disability.

EDUCATIONAL MATERIALS

Lehtinen plans her lessons to include motor activities—sorting, cutting, printing or writing, manipulating counters and gadgets. She uses instructional materials or devices constructed according to the knowledge of the particular disturbances of the child, and she inserts a word of caution in regard to these materials: The materials and devices should not be confused with the method; the materials are simply the vehicle through which the method is implemented and are static devices unless the teacher is familiar with the method.

Lehtinen uses many different kinds of teaching materials. For arithmetic, there are number wheels, counting boards, "takeaway" boxes, various counting devices, number cards, the abacus. For reading she uses word and letter cards, letter puzzles, slotted covers to expose only one word or a sentence at a time. She does not often use pictures because even in a simple picture there can be distracting details. Commercially prepared workbooks, with their pages loaded with distractions, are not suitable for the brain-injured child; but they are valuable source books and can be presented to the child if the pages are cut up, rearranged into simpler form with the unessential, distracting details eliminated. As described by Lehtinen, the materials can be constructed by the teacher and, in many instances, by the children. In fact, she feels it is particularly important for the children to construct their materials, for in measuring, cutting, pasting, etc., they are occupied motorically and at the same time are gaining some insight into how the materials are made and how they will be used. In this fashion, among others, the materials are considered self-tutoring.

These teaching materials are *not* examples of games used to increase motivation or to teach through play. They are materials constructed to present the essential elements of a skill or process so the child can gain insight into it.

Since these instructional materials are constructed to meet the particular needs of a particular child or group of children and vary accordingly, Lehtinen's description of them is not detailed here. It is perhaps more profitable to follow the course she herself stresses—proceed from the underlying principles to whatever method and materials are indicated for a given child.

Arithmetic. Four general principles underlying arithmetic instruction for brain injured children are specified by Lehtinen (Strauss & Lehtinen, 1947):

1. Number concept, based originally upon organized perceptual experiences, depends upon the relationships of objects in space and the resulting development of a number scheme.
2. Development of such a scheme is the outgrowth of ability to organize; it is a semiabstract structure evolved from the understanding of relationships, of parts to parts and parts to the whole.
3. This visuospatial scheme will be abstracted from its perceptual concrete origins when relationships are grasped and meanings understood. This implies the need for perceptual experiences (concrete or semiconcrete) until such organization occurs.
4. For the child with organic disturbances, it may often be necessary to develop special material and technics of instruction based on our knowledge of such disturbances (p. 152).

One must remember that according to Lehtinen the brain-injured child lacks the abilities of the normal child to discover spontaneously the significant relationships of the number system. Thus, although the brain-injured child usually has little difficulty in learning arithmetical processes, he encounters extreme difficulty in understanding the meaning behind the processes. Long before "modern math" made its appearance, she was using methods which stressed meaning and relationships. Lehtinen aims at developing a pattern of visual spatial organization with emphasis upon the relatedness of parts of the pattern. Effort should be directed also toward aiding the child in structuring his pattern of organization as completely and normally as possible.

She cautions that habituation through drill should be the last step of the brain-injured child's learning of arithmetic skills. Many people feel that if material is practiced often enough and in varying contexts, it will be learned and understood; the natural technique for accomplishing such learning is drill. The brain-injured child, however, if exposed to excessive drill may rely upon rote memorization without comprehension, as may any child.

Reading. Approaching the teaching of reading from the standpoint that reading, even when silent, is primarily auditory, Lehtinen (Strauss & Lehtinen, 1947) lays down the following principles:

1. In the auditory perceptual area as well as in the area of visual perception and behavior, the general disturbances of distractibility, disinhibition, erraticism, and perseveration are evident.

2. . . . Individuals whose imagery is predominately visual will have difficulty making auditory images.

3. The disturbances of spatial organization apparent in the visual field is, in many instances, a factor productive of disturbance in the auditory field as well (p. 173).

The beginning of phonetic instruction is entirely oral. It is not until the child can discriminate the sounds and reproduce them in isolation that symbols are used. After the child has developed fairly adequate auditory discrimination, the letter should be presented as the visual symbol for the sound and writing should be correlated with this association. At this point, Lehtinen finds it beneficial to assign a color to each vowel sound and to teach an association between color and sound. She stresses an analytical rather than a global method of making a response to the whole word. The child's attention is drawn to the visual and auditory parts of a word and he builds words from copy. The words are written on paper, letter by letter, using a stamping set, or they are built from letter cards. The child may copy the completed words, emphasizing certain letters or parts of letters through the use of color, or he may write them on the chalkboard.

Writing. Closely allied to reading, the teaching of writing to brain-injured children has two underlying principles which direct its aims.

1. Writing is a valuable and effective means of developing visuomotor perception, a psychological function in which we know the brain-injured child is outstandingly handicapped.
2. It is an important adjunct to learning to read, partly through its stimulating and organizing effect upon the visual perception of words and partly through the additional kinesthetic factors involved (Strauss & Lehtinen 1947, p. 154).

Using cursive writing and appropriately lined paper, Lehtinen begins writing instruction with the teaching of single letters in isolation. She does this because brain-injured children with perceptual disturbances who attempt to structuralize a whole word in order to execute the correct visuomotor patterns find the task exceedingly difficult. The first letter taught is *m* because the abductor movements of the arm (those which proceed outward from the body) develop earlier than the adductor movements (those moving inward across the body). The next easiest letters are the pointed ones, *i, u, w, t,* and *s.* Usually *e* and *l* come next, though this sequence may vary. The most difficult letters are *a, o, d, c,* and *g,* which combine two movements. The order of the remaining letters depends on the child. The seldom used *x* and *q* are taught last.

The child whose perception of letter forms is weak must be given special help since he may confuse the similar forms. The child who perseverates will not be able at first to make letters with movements opposed to the one just mastered. He can be helped by writing with a stylus on modeling clay rolled out in a pan. The child who has a good deal of motor disturbance can be helped by wrapping the pencil in modeling clay, thus enlarging the area which is grasped. It is important that writing be taught together with reading, its reverse activity. In reading a visual symbol is translated into an auditory-verbal one and in writing an auditory-verbal symbol is translated back to the visual symbol.

In teaching academic skills, the brain-injured child's particular disabilities must always be kept in mind. Many of these children have poor work habits stemming from their organic disturbances. Others are over-meticulous and the slightest deviation from the child's standard must be corrected over and over again. The performance of these children is extremely variable. Bright and capable one day, a child may be inert and sluggish the next; a skill or bit of knowledge apparently mastered today may be totally forgotten tomorrow; or the usually good-humored child may become irritable. Bad weather, a very minor, yet exciting occurrence such as a skinned knee, hurt feelings, playground stimulation, all are reflected in school work.

In conclusion, Lehtinen says that the teacher of brain injured children must be a therapist; his aim is habilitation. Specifically, in his role as therapist, the teacher must:

1. Observe behavior precisely and continuously.
2. Be cognizant of each child's personality and organic disturbances.
3. Analyze specific learning disabilities and prescribe appropriate remedial procedures.
4. Analyze behavior disturbances and devise preventative environmental controls.

Thus for the teacher of the brain injured child there is no one specific method, but rather an analytical approach based on understanding of the child and his problems.

In considering Lehtinen's teaching procedures, two points should be made. First, both Strauss and Lehtinen believe that emphasis should be placed on the area of the child's weakness rather than in building up his strengths, but there is other evidence that when the child's strengths are neglected in favor of remediating his weaknesses, the strengths may deteriorate. Second, later studies have shown that brain-injured children are perhaps not so highly stimulated by visual stimuli as Lehtinen maintains. Dunn (1967) warns that we should look at contrasting research in several areas including the Strauss and Lehtinen theory that an excess of incoming stimuli causes hyperactivity. Other authors, he reports, feel that hyperactivity is rather an attempt to increase stimulation. Gardner, Cromwell, and Foshee (1959) report that hyperactivity is decreased with increased visual stimulation. Spradlin, Cromwell, and Foshee (1960) state that the increased auditory stimulation of tapes being played had no effect on the activity level of organic, familial, hyperactive, or hypoactive mentally retarded children. Burnett (1962) found no significant difference in the speed with which a list of words was learned in a regular and in a nonstimulating classroom. If these results are accurate, the barren classroom may be more harmful than good.

Other researchers, Semmel (1960) and Zigler (1962), question whether disinhibited, uncontrolled behavior is more common in brain-injured children than in other children of similar mental ability. Dunn (1967) reports that others have not found significant differences in concept formation between brain-injured and familial mentally retarded children. Frey (1960) tested Lehtinen's techniques in reading and found they appear to be helpful for Strauss Syndrome children.

The teaching procedures are perceptive and flexible, thus escaping the criticism that must be leveled at the rigid methods—that an inflexible teaching procedure cannot meet the extreme variety of problems presented by the very diverse individuals in a brain-damaged class. However, it is important to note that the techniques developed by Lehtinen were devised with a particular type of child in mind—the hyperactive, distractible, brain-injured child described by Strauss. The child with Strauss Syndrome usually displays marked perceptual and conceptual disorders and may differ significantly in many ways from the child who is only dyslexic or the child who, in Myklebust's terms, is an auditory aphasic. Many of the behavioral controls and highly structured perceptual-training procedures would not be applicable to children who do not exhibit signs of the Strauss Syndrome. Keeping in mind the type of child with whom Lehtinen worked, one may conclude that her methods are rational, well-developed, and efficient.

William M. Cruickshank

Cruickshank's (1961) major methodological work, *A Teaching Method for Brain-Injured and Hyperactive Children,* postdated the definitive works of the two other authors discussed in this chapter, Fernald and Lehtinen. Before Cruickshank's study, much research had been done in developing effective grouping and instructional techniques for children with central nervous system disorders and satisfactory results were associated with some of the research. Such has not been the case, however, for children *without* a diagnosis of brain injury, who Cruickshank described as hyperactive underachievers with emotional disturbance. These children "were not responding adequately to existing methods of classroom instructional programs and there remained an urgent need to explore the basic causes of their learning disabilities" (p. 3).

Many methods, techniques, and approaches have been developed in different disciplines in order to meet the needs of emotionally disturbed children with or without brain damage. According to Daley (1962), the first approach is designed to help the child and his parents through individual or group psychotherapy because of the belief that until the emotional problems are resolved, the child cannot organize his energy into learning activities. In the next approach, behavior is treated as a symptom of, or associated with, the frustration of failure resulting from specific learning disabilities. This approach is based on the assumption that if teaching techniques, grouping criteria, and instructional guides can be developed which provide the children with a continuously reinforced experience in the mastery for learning, then the child will benefit from goal-directed teaching and achieve some social and academic success. The Montgomery County—Syracuse University Study and Teacher Demonstration, conducted by Cruickshank, utilized both approaches to meet the needs of a large number of children who were referred to as hyperactive, acting out, and emotionally disturbed.

The purpose of this section is to review the characteristics of the children in question, discuss the principles underlying the project, study in detail the teaching method, and give a critical review of the principles employed in the utilization of the program.

CHARACTERISTICS OF BRAIN-INJURED AND HYPERACTIVE CHILDREN

Cruickshank states that the brain-injured child displays certain characteristics, and the following usually are included: distractibility, motor disinhibition, dissociation, disturbance of figure-ground relationships, perseveration, absence of a well developed self-concept and body image. He contends that the first four of these characteristics are a variation of distractibility and that perseveration and body image are separate entities.

Distractibility is described as "the lack of that cortical control which permits prolonged attention to the task and negative adaptation to the unessential" (p. 4–5). He feels that distractibility is the chief characteristic of these children and under the characteristic of distractibility he places motor disinhibition, which he describes as "the failure of the child to refrain from response to any stimuli which produce a motor activity" (p. 5). Dissociation, or the inability to see things as a whole, also is hypothesized as part of distractibility. The entity has been considered an important factor in the adjustment and learning of the brain-injured child.

Figure-ground disturbance also appears to be related closely to distractibility or hyperactivity. Cruickshank feels that relating all of these entities to distractibility or hyperactivity is important in considering the total problem of the learning situation for the child. He believes that perseveration impedes learning and describes it as the inability to shift with ease from one psychological activity to another. Finally, the ideas of self-concept and body image are considered important in the learning ability of these children. Without an adequate self-concept, the learning experience would be quite difficult. Cruickshank assumes that once the children's problems are recognized, an effective educational program geared to the specific disability of the child will facilitate his educational achievement.

Children who exhibited the preceding characteristics were considered for the original study. Some children who did not exhibit evidence of brain injury were included. These children were also hyperactive and indistinguishable from the children with signs of brain injury. The children were between the chronological ages of 6–11 and 10–11. They had mental ages not less than 4–8 and intelligence quotients not less than 50. All of the children were having difficulties in school. Several of them could not adjust to the discipline and structure of the classroom situation.

THE APPROACH TO EDUCATION

A multidisciplinary diagnostic evaluation was done on each child, developmental and environmental data were collected, and case histories were prepared. The diagnostic team was somewhat reluctant to agree on a diagnosis of brain injury, even though the neurologist and pediatrician did support the fact. The diagnostic and clinical data, however, helped Cruickshank describe the children in terms of behavior and language learning disorders. On the basis of the diagnostic data, 40 candidates were separated into two diagnostic groups: (1) those children with clinically diagnosed neurological and medical evidence of brain injury; and (2) those children whose case histories demonstrated psychological behavior and learning disabilities typical of those of brain-injured children. The children were then placed in four groups matched by chronological age, mental age, instructional level, degree of hyperactivity and perseveration and previous experience in special classes. Two groups of 10 each out of the original 40 were designated as experimental and two were designated control.

Cruickshank believes that the educational program for normal children is completely unsatisfactory for these children. An educational environment designed to meet the needs of the children and to teach directly to the disability is considered the best approach. The plan of education, therefore, involved Cruickshank's modification of Strauss and Lehtinen's concepts of education for brain-injured children and was based upon four essential principles comprising a good teaching environment:

1. The reduction of unessential visual and auditory environmental stimuli.

2. The reduction of environmental space.

3. The establishment of a highly structured daily program.

4. The increase of the stimulus value of the instructional materials themselves.

Further, the program involved the extensive and concentrated use of color in the teaching techniques and materials for all areas, since Strauss and Kephart (Cruickshank, 1961) reported that "color perception and responsiveness to color remain intact in spite of the severest disturbances of perceptual and general integration" (p. 166).

Finally, the program involved many suggestions and detailed teaching techniques borrowed from Montessori to improve visual-motor perception and incorporated Kirk's principles with regard to reading readiness, although all suggestions were modified to meet the needs of the program and of the children.

In discussing the first principle of teaching, Cruickshank describes the normal classroom as one in which many stimuli are present to attract the child, to create an awareness of environment, and to motivate the child to the appropriate activity. He states that this type of setting is not appropriate for the brain-injured child because he is unable to adapt to the negative or unessential stimuli which create for him an undesirable learning situation. He suggests, as does Lehtinen, that the room be completely void of extraneous materials. The colors of the walls, woodwork, and furniture should match the floor; the windows should be opaque; the room should be sound treated; and the number of children should be below normal registration of the elementary classroom. By decreasing all visual and auditory stimuli, the child will be placed in a position where socially positive conditioning is likely to take place.

Relative to the second factor, reduction of space, Cruickshank believes that with such area reduction stimuli also are reduced. He suggests that the place where learning activities take place should be reduced to the smallest practical area; in fact, small cubicles should be constructed for each child. The cubicles should be the same color as other structures in the room, and the child's desk should face the back wall. The cubicle should contain nothing but the child's desk and chair and all teaching materials must be kept out of sight. Under these conditions, the nonstimulating classroom exists. Further controls include restriction of the number of visitors and reduction of all unnecessary auditory and visual stimuli. Later research, including a recent study by Rost (1967), indicates that there is no evidence that it is beneficial for a "brain-injured" or hyperactive child to spend his study time in a separate booth or cubicle.

In his discussion of the third principle, Cruickshank states that these children have never had genuine success in socially approved activities. He notes that their lives have been filled with failure and confused responses which have led others to label them as management and behavior problems. The new educational program, therefore, should be based on success but must be completely teacher oriented with little or no opportunity for pupil choice. The teacher must have at his command all available material regarding achievement levels and abilities of the child.

The structured program includes specific activities to be initiated at specific times. Each single assignment during the day should be checked by the teacher and the child should not be allowed to discontinue his work until the task is correctly completed. Such a practice should introduce into the classroom learning situation a rigid order of sequential procedures in work organization, which increases the child's sense of responsibility for order and cleanliness. The learning tasks must be within the learning capacity, frustration level, and attention span of the child. This structured situation should continue until the child is functioning with success in most of the activities. After this has been accomplished, the teacher may begin to present the child with opportunities for making choices between activities.

The fourth factor of increased stimulus value of teaching materials was chosen because it was hypothesized that "if hyperactive children are distracted to stimuli, then their attention can be drawn to stimuli which are purposefully organized and specifically placed within their visual field" (Cruickshank, 1961, p. 20). Therefore, Cruickshank suggests using material that is intensified in its visual and tactual fields.

As each child enters the program, the teacher tests him to discover his learning needs in visual perception, visual motor and fine motor control, language ability, and number ability. The teacher, in planning a program of instruction, should "begin with work where the child is able to succeed, be sure the child understands what is expected of him, be consistent, use the child's strengths to correct his weaknesses, observe carefully and remember that progress comes slowly" (Cruickshank, 1961, p. 146). It is important that the teacher structure tasks so that the child succeeds with each activity. If he becomes frustrated, the teacher must be close by to help analyze his problem.

In the beginning of instruction, most of the child's work will be on the perceptual level and includes the use of blocks, stencils, pegboards, color cubes, and puzzles. As the child learns to do more kinds of work, the teacher plans a program that includes many areas—perceptual training, writing, arithmetic, and reading. Two kinds of instructional plans are organized: one for individual lessons which are ready for the child when he enters the room, and a second for group plans in which the children are all organized together for strengthening peer relationships and personal worth.

TEACHING METHODS

The specific methods Cruickshank recommends for teaching various subjects are discussed next. As has been stated, all lessons are structured highly, incorporating a multisensory approach. He begins by stating that most of the children are inadequate in visual discrimination; therefore, the teacher must develop elementary tasks so that the child may succeed in perceiving whole objects. He suggests that the teacher use color in teaching the children, because reportedly color perception remains intact. Beginning with sorting forms, both paper and block forms and colors, the teacher moves gradually to puzzles, stencils, and pegboards. Sorting and matching of colors, pictures, letters, and numbers also help the child coordinate his eyes and hands. More effective hand-eye coordination can be accomplished by having the child cut cardboard in straight lines and gradually progress to cutting out geometric forms.

An auditory training program should be provided for those children who have difficulty distinguishing sounds. Instruction begins with listening exercises requiring the child to listen and account for gross sounds, contrasting sounds, and discrimination of sounds. Slowly, the teacher moves to more abstract tasks in which the children are required to listen to poetry or familiar rhymes and fill in missing parts.

Developing the tactual percept is approached by using sandpaper numbers; teaching the distinction between soft and hard, smooth and rough; recognition of wooden forms by feeling; and writing with the finger.

A child's need for motor training can be discovered by the teacher as he observes each child in his particular setting. Cruickshank notes that the program of physical activity does not begin until all of the children have made an adjustment to the structured classroom and have begun to succeed in the learning situation. Useful activities and materials are the jumping board, balance beam, walking blocks, jumping rope, throwing and catching, relay games, etc.

In teaching writing, the developmental kinesthetic approach is recommended as the senses of touch and motion help the child fix the sound and shape of letters. Only cursive writing is taught because it emphasizes left to right progression, the letters are connected in a whole word thus forming a Gestalt, and it helps the child's disorganized movement fall into a coherent pattern. "The first letters to be taught are those requiring motions which develop earliest in the child—those moving away from the body" (p. 197). The pointed letters come next, followed by the a, o, d, c, and g, which require first forward then backward motion.

The teaching of arithmetic is concrete and practical. Number concepts begin with matching patterns and colors, end to end, and independent matching. In introducing numbers, the teacher should begin with number symbols and number names. Moving gradually toward the abstract, the child learns addition, subtraction, telling time, multiplication, and, finally, division.

Reading is taught last because the other subjects are thought of as prerequisites to the ability to read. Cruickshank lists the following factors described by Kirk as prerequisites for reading readiness:

1. A mental age of 6 years or more.
2. Adequate language development.
3. Memory for sentences and ideas.
4. Visual memory and visual discrimination.
5. Auditory memory and auditory discrimination.
6. Correct enunciation and pronounciation.
7. Motor ability.
8. Visual maturity.
9. Motivation.

The approach to teaching reading begins with the basic tools necessary for reading and builds on these to attain a reading level. The teacher begins with visual motor training for hand preference, moves slowly through matching of letters, and then introduces whole words. At the same time, auditory perception training is given with training for imitating sounds and correction of deviant sounds. Having successfully mastered these tasks, the child then learns initial consonants by finding pictures with the sound, writing the sound, and saying it with each presentation. After each initial consonant sound is learned, the child proceeds to learning the final consonants and continues with the same techniques used for learning initial consonants. Vowels are introduced after a few consonants are learned. The short *i* is introduced first because it is the easiest to write. The child then learns to build word families with his consonants and vowels. Sight words are next introduced along with color words, number words, and the words needed to follow simple directions, which are learned first.

EVALUATION OF THE PROJECT STUDY

At the end of the academic year, the children in the study were reevaluated. The results indicated that all of the children made some gain in their ability to differentiate figure from background and that the experimental group demonstrated more pronounced growth in social maturity. The elements essential to the experimental classroom settings were valuable in appraising the gains of the children. The average increase in academic achievement for the four groups was 2.5 years. Psychiatrists' implications indicated that some emotionally disturbed children can achieve academic success without psychotherapy. It was found that the neurological and EEG data were of the least value of any information received. This was because the study was educational in design and such information was not considered significant enough to bear on the educational program. Cruickshank felt that the organized multidisciplinary approach to underachieving emotionally disturbed children resulted in the understanding and successful teaching of the children, which enabled them to achieve both academically and socially.

The results of the study appear to be quite remarkable in that these children improved so quickly. At first glance, it would seem from the study that this method of teaching and diagnosing the brain-injured child is the best approach. Several studies of these same children three years later, however, show quite different results. Bentzen and Peterson (1962) compared the neurological and EEG findings of Cohn with the clinical data of the experiment. The purpose was to determine whether Cohn's neurological and EEG findings would have predicted which children made the most progress, which made the least, and which made a modest gain. There was no correlation. After three years, only six children in the study had been transferred out of the project and into a regular-age grade public school classroom. Of the children who neurologically appeared to have the least chance of profiting from the specialized teaching experience, one was scheduled for residential care, and the others made less than six months' progress. Bentzen (1962) contends that the reason these children did not succeed was "that there was a poverty of language development and lack of integration of the classroom learning experience into a useful, productive mode of life" (p. 140). Bentzen further explores the validity of this study by stating that maybe the teachers were too concerned with the performance of a specific task rather than the comprehension of a given learning experience.

Hewett (1964) suggests that the teacher should provide a hierarchy of educational tasks for children with learning disorders. In this way, the child will be given tasks to perform at different levels of learning. He feels that an effective program depends on the establishment of a point of *meaningful* contact between the child and the teacher. In his hierarchy, he presents an "order task" level which is very similar to the whole Cruickshank program. However, this one level is only a single point on the hierarchy where the teacher can have meaningful contact with the child. The educational program should not be static, but should change from day to day with the teacher increasing control as necessary until the child has progressed to the "achievement task" level.

Hewett, while agreeing with Cruickshank on the "order task" level, quickly goes on to other levels of meaningful functioning, which Cruickshank fails to do.

The authors feel that Cruickshank's procedures, which are modifications of principles and techniques developed by Strauss and Lehtinen, are appropriate for some children, probably the same type of children for whom Lehtinen provided her methods. It appears that the advantages and disadvantages of the two systems are essentially the same. One may speculate that a combined program of procedures taken from Lehtinen, Cruickshank, and Hewett might reveal results quite different from those obtained from the Cruickshank study alone. In such a program, the child would approach academic and social learning through a hierarchy of experiences extending upward through the level of meaningfulness, thereby gaining the ability to structure his needs and cope with his environment by relating to himself, his environment, and other persons in a meaningful fashion.

Grace Fernald

In 1921, the Clinic School was established at the University of California. For several years before that, a reading project had been in progress with total disability cases. The project included an idiot, an imbecile, a moron, a "word-blind" case, several very poor spellers, a case of extreme mental instability, two cases of superior intelligence, an epileptic, a spastic, and a stutterer. Success with these cases brought demand for further experimentation, and a new program was set up in a room of the school.

Included in the new program were children of normal intelligence, most of whom had extreme reading disability. The children were grouped according to type of difficulty and attended classes from nine in the morning until three in the afternoon for eight months of the year. Complete records were kept. The parents were required to give consent for their child to remain in the program until the remedial work was completed and the child was ready to return to the regular classroom. The aim of the Clinic School program was the development of diagnostic, remedial, and preventive techniques that would help the individual adjust to his environment. From this early work, the present program was established in the psychology department of the University of California.

Fernald maintains that in order to make satisfactory adjustment to his environment a child needs successful experiences. School, which a child is forced to attend, makes serious demands for continuous readjustment. Unless the child masters the fundamental subjects of reading, writing, spelling, and arithmetic, he will find no success in school and his future vocational success will be limited. A child may fail to learn because of retarded mental development; he may have superior intelligence and fail because of conditions which interfere with the learning process. Individuals with normal or superior intelligence can overcome or compensate for emotional disabilities, poor physical adjustment, and difficulties in school subjects if proper diagnosis and adequate treatment are employed.

Whenever possible, the application of remedial techniques should be used before a child has met failure. After the child has experienced extreme failure, negative emotional reactions become part of the remedial problem. Constant failure in class activities often creates in the child a chronic state of emotional instability. Every child has an innate desire to learn, but constant failure results in negative reactions of hate or fear related to the learning situation.

Fernald's case histories show that most children with learning problems had *no emotional upset before entering school.* The school is usually a child's first experience with a group and repeated failure to achieve may arouse and condition emotions to such an extent that the mention of reading and writing will send the child into a paroxysm of fear or rage or arouse sullen negative responses. The child may withdraw, assume a fearful or antagonistic attitude toward the group, or compensate for failure by bullying or showing off. Fernald's case histories frequently describe the "solitary child" and the "bombastic child."

The two general methods of handling cases of emotional maladjustment Fernald calls the Analytical Method and the Reconditioning Method. The Analytical Method seeks to discover all the factors that contributed to the individual's emotional problem and then focus the patient's attention upon the factors involved in his particular ideas. Expressing the ideas supposedly relieves the blocking and gives the individual a chance to start constructive voluntary activities which will reduce frustration.

The Reconditioning Method is the opposite of the Analytical Method. Reconditioning first requires an environment in which stimuli that give rise to the emotion which is to be modified are avoided. Second, a substitute stimulus which is connected with a positive emotion is provided. After the pattern has been well established, the event that needs reconditioning is introduced. Reconditioning is completed when the event arouses the desired emotional reaction to the substitute stimulus. Reconditioning directs the individual's attention away from everything connected with the undesirable emotional reaction. The information in the case history is used to avoid arousing the undesirable reaction.

The method of the Clinic School permitted the child to start on the first day with a learning activity that would result in successful learning. No one sympathized or called attention to things the child did not know. The child found out that he was capable of learning any word that he wanted to learn, regardless of its length or complexity. Once the learning process was established, an emotional transformation took place. The child's expression, attitude, and conduct usually improved as the remedial work progressed.

Care was taken to avoid the following conditions because they were emotionally loaded:

1. Extreme pressure upon the child to learn to please the family.
2. Sending the child back into the classroom too soon and forcing him to use a method that would reestablish the negative emotional learning block.
3. Putting the child back into the regular classroom and expecting him to use a method that would cause him to feel embarrassed or conspicuous because his learning procedure was different from that of the other children.

Exposing the child to situations that would set up negative emotional responses during the early stages of learning was suspected of resulting in an emotional reversal more intense than the original one. Such exposure carried the added disadvantage of negative conditioning of the new technique, which would make it more difficult to reinstate the method. For the child's protection, he was not sent back into the regular classroom until sufficient skills had been developed to permit him to compete with pupils of his own age and intelligence level.

Fernald developed a kinesthetic remedial reading method designed to instruct individuals with extreme reading difficulty. Any person with normal or better intelligence was accepted in her program and in most cases they learned to read within a few months to two years. Although the method has elicited some criticism and skepticism, Fernald continued her work and left the controversy to others. Her experience suggested that every child with a reading disability, from extreme nonreaders to those with a partial disability, could succeed by this method. In addition to improved reading ability, she found that the method also raised the level of spelling and composition in the students with whom she worked.

In Fernald's opinion, cases of reading disability may be divided into two groups: (1) those with partial disability; and (2) those with total, or extreme, disability. Fernald first used her tracing method with cases of extreme disability who had attended school regularly and who had no physical or mental subnormalities that could explain their inability to read. Later she worked with partial disability cases and discovered that they also could be successfully taught by the tracing method. The partial disability cases often were more hampered than the extreme cases because of bad habits which tended to interfere with the learning process.

In the course of her work at the Clinic School, Fernald found that the tracing method produced satisfactory results when used with both total and partial reading disability cases. The general method, as opposed to the techniques, consisted of determining the developmental level of the child through the use of an intelligence test, an achievement test, and a diagnostic reading test.

Evaluation was followed by remedial treatment designed to increase the child's reading ability to a point commensurate with his intellectual level and expected educational level. In partial disability cases, three types of difficulty were found:

1. The inability to recognize certain commonly used words.
2. Labored, word-by-word reading.
3. Failure to comprehend content read.

Constant failure with common words tends to attract the attention of the reader to the unknown word and to cause him to block or panic. Repeated negative conditioning toward the printed page sets the negative emotional response. Slow, laborious, word-by-word reading causes a student to lose track of the unit as a whole, and he therefore fails to understand the content of the printed page.

The remedial method allows each child to learn in the manner to which he is best suited. Even children with sensory defects as well as those who learn by visual methods soon adapted to conditions of the remedial program. The stages of the hand-kinesthetic approach are as follows:

1. The discovery of a method by which the child can learn to write correctly.
2. The motivation of such writing.
3. The reading by the child of the printed copy.
4. The extensive reading of other compositions.

STAGE ONE

In stage one, the child is allowed to select a word *he wants to learn,* regardless of its length. The word is written for the child with crayon in plain, blackboard-sized script or print. The child traces the word with his finger and says each part of the word as he traces it. The process is repeated until the word can be written by the child without his looking at the copy. The pupil is allowed as much time as necessary.

The word is written on a scrap of paper first, and then it is incorporated into a story which the child composes. The story is typed, and the child reads his printed story to the teacher. The child places the word or words that have been learned by tracing in his word-file. This file is arranged alphabetically, and the child learns the alphabet incidentally. The practice is excellent training for later learning how to use the dictionary as well as for learning the letters of the alphabet. In cases of extreme disability every word used in the first composition may have to be learned by tracing. Usually the child soon gains sufficient skill and progresses into the second stage.

Pertinent points relative to stage one are:

1. Direct finger contact in tracing. Fernald notes that the child may use one or two fingers in tracing. She found, however, that learning takes place more rapidly when the child uses direct finger contact in tracing rather than when he uses a pencil or stylus.

2. Writing the traced word from memory. Fernald emphasizes the point that the child should never copy the words which he has traced. Looking back and forth between the copy and the word he is writing tends to break the word into fragmentary, meaningless units. In copying, Fernald feels that the flow of the hand in writing is interrupted, and the eyes move back and forth instead of fixing as they should upon the word being written. Fernald contends that the habit of copying words seriously impedes correct writing or spelling, and even interferes with the recognition of words already written.

3. Writing words as units. The word must be learned and written as a whole rather than by sounds or syllables. If a child is unsuccessful in his attempt to write a word after tracing it, the incorrect form is removed from view. The child begins the tracing process anew and again attempts to write the word as a whole. Erasing or correcting single words, letters, or syllables is *not* permitted, since Fernald feels strongly that such procedures break up the word into a jumbled, meaningless entity which does not represent the correct form of the word.

4. Using words in context. By always using his words in context, the child experiences them in meaningful groups, which helps to give exact meaning to all of the words. The child usually has a speaking vocabulary large enough to express those things that are of interest to him. When a child has a limited vocabulary, he should start learning to write and read words which he already uses in speech.

STAGE TWO

Tracing is no longer necessary in stage two of the remedial work. The child has developed sufficient skill to learn words by looking at the word in script, saying the word over to himself as he looks at it, and then writing the word without copying. The child continues to write freely and to read the printed copy of his work. Writing becomes easier for him, and his stories become longer and more interesting. The child is allowed to write on any subject that interests him.

The important connection between stages one and two is that the child continues to vocalize the word he is learning. The individual must establish the connection between the sound of a word and its form so that visual stimulation will immediately stimulate a vocal recall. Vocalization of the word should be natural and not a stilted or distorted sounding out of letters or syllables, which results in the loss of the word as a whole. The sounds of individual letters are never produced separately and are never overemphasized. In a longer word such as *important*, the student says *im* while tracing the first syllable, *por* while tracing the second syllable, and *tant* as he finishes the word. In writing the word, he again pronounces each syllable as he writes it. After a little practice, the two activities, writing and speaking, seem to occur simultaneously without effort.

Fernald suggests no arbitrary limit for the length of the tracing period, because the student usually stops tracing gradually. A decrease in the number of tracings needed to learn a new word is observed first; then a few short words are learned without tracing. Eventually tracing is no longer necessary. The average tracing period is from two to eight months.

Material should not be simplified to a point below the intelligence level of the child, either in terms of vocabulary range or complexity of subject matter. According to Fernald, the student is more highly motivated when reading and writing somewhat difficult material that he can understand rather than when confronted with material that is below his mental level. Once the child discovers that he has acquired a technique by which even long and difficult words can be learned, he takes delight in learning. Actually the longer and more difficult words are easier to recognize on later presentation. When tracing is no longer necessary, the teacher can substitute a small word box file for the larger word box. The words now are written in ordinary-sized script.

STAGE THREE

The child learns directly from the printed word in stage three. He looks at the word and is able to write the word without vocalizing or copying. In this stage books are presented; the student is permitted to read from them and is told the words he does not know. When he is through reading the article, the new words are reviewed and the words then are written from recall. A check is made later to determine whether the words have been retained.

STAGE FOUR

The fourth stage begins when the student can generalize and make out new words from their resemblance to known words. The student's interest in reading increases with his reading skill. Fernald states that the student is *never read to* either at home or at school until he has achieved normal reading skill. However, she does not object to reading to the student after he has developed normal reading skill, because by this time the student prefers to read by himself. Usually he finds that reading for himself is faster, easier, and more pleasant.

In reading scientific or other difficult material, the student is encouraged to glance over a paragraph seeking words he does not know. These new words are learned before he reads so that the paragraph is read as a unit. At first, the new words are retained better if the student pronounces the word as he writes it. He repeats the words, turns the paper over, and rewrites the word. Eventually the child gains enough skill to retain the word and its meaning if the word is identified for him. The teacher records the word for later review so that he may determine whether words learned in this manner are being retained.

The four stages described comprise the instructional method designed by Fernald for use with cases of total or partial reading disability. During each stage of the method a child is continually evaluated in an effort to discover whether he retains the words he has learned. If the retention rate decreases, the teacher returns the pupil to an earlier stage of learning.

In discussing the phonics approach to teaching reading, Fernald comments that the child should never sound out words and that the teacher should never sound out words for the child except in those rare cases where the child, due to previous training, wants to sound out a word. Then the child is allowed to sound out a word if he does it before he reads. Many people believe that phonics must be taught if a student is to develop the ability to recognize new words from their similarity to words that have been experienced in other combinations. As a matter of fact, Fernald says that the student will come to understand word combinations after the development of a varied reading background. The average individual after several years of extensive reading develops a complex apperceptive background and a larger reading vocabulary than either his spoken or written vocabulary.

The amount of reading instruction needed to bring a child with a reading disorder to his optimal reading level depends upon the individual and upon the educational age desired. The younger child is ready to return to regular classes when the reading achievement level of his regular class group is reached. The older child should remain in the remedial group until he can recognize new words, has established an adequate reading vocabulary, and has developed the necessary conceptual background. Many failures occur because the individual does not have the wealth of reading experience necessary for intelligent, rapid reading. Sufficient skill must be achieved before the student can read with speed and comprehension materials suitable to his age and intellect.

Certain bodily adjustments are necessary along with other skills, in order to acquire the particular coordination which characterizes the reading process. Fernald discusses some of the conditions that may affect reading such as farsightedness, nearsightedness, astigmatism, muscle imbalance, aniseikonia, and lack of visual acuity. She states that poor eye coordination is not the reason a child fails to learn to read; some people with monocular vision, nystagmus, and spastic imbalance learn to read with a fair degree of speed and comprehension provided the eye can provide a clear retinal image. Most good readers, however, develop the ability to move across each line of print with a series of sweeps and fixations. Rapid readers make few fixations and only occasional regressions while reading familiar material. A slow reader makes many stops with many regressions.

SUMMARY

Fernald's remedial reading method is mentioned in most texts on the teaching of reading; thus the method is recognized by most authorities on reading. Smith and Carrigan (1959) say that Grace Fernald's "hand-kinesthetic" technique provides all the conditions known to be essential to learning. The child tells a story (insures motivation and maximum meaning). The teacher writes each word to be learned. The child traces and pronounces the word aloud (behaviors which demand maximum attention and also provide multiple sensory input). The child writes the word independently and checks its correctness. Thus reward is immediate (fulfillment of his expectancy).

Johnson (1963) states that Fernald recommends supplementing the visual and auditory stimuli with a kinesthetic stimulus to increase the comparative intensity of the task at hand and to apply the psychological principle of reinforcement. The method insures active attention, presents the material in an orderly sequential manner, and reinforces, re-teaches, and reviews until a word is established thoroughly. The method is applicable to the development of the initial sight vocabulary. When the child has established reading skill, the method may be dropped.

Fernald's approach may be supported by reference to certain neuro-physiological concepts advocated by Rood (1962) and Ayres (1964). The actual tactile sensation and the kinesthetic act of moving send neural impressions to the brain. Rood says that every little muscle spindle and every surface hair that is activated by the least movement will create an afferent or sensory stimulus pattern in the brain. In this way body image and mental alertness are dependent upon the proprioceptive stimuli. The afferent stimulus can be either high threshold (less discriminating) or low threshold (more specific), depending upon the type of fibers activated. The high-threshold fibers are primitive, unmyelinated, and terminate in the reticular formation of the midbrain. The low-threshold fibers are myelinated, fast, and selective and are collaterals into the reticular formation. According to Rood, if a low-threshold stimulus pathway is used first, it is then readied for a speedier transmission of immediate succeeding stimuli along the same pathway. Thus the act of tracing a word several times prepares the mental coordinates for an important message and then follows through on a selective avenue of approach. Thus the auditory and visual pathways are being activated in the same manner as the child sees and says the word as he is tracing it.

Ayres (1964) also builds on an exploration of the two cutaneous systems functioning in man. The protective or spinothalmic system is the more primitive and serves the purpose of arousing and alerting the central nervous system. The protective system, composed of unmyelinated, high-threshold fibers, is activated by light touch or pain. Superimposed upon this system is the discriminating or epicritic system, which differentiates between various tactile sensations. Composed of myelinated, low-threshold, selective fibers, it is activated by pressure. Inhibition of the protective system is achieved by stimulation of the discriminative system. Ayres suggests that tactile discrimination might counteract to some extent the hyperactivity believed to be caused by the action of the protective system. This would account for Fernald's successes with children exhibiting a hyperactive, impulsive behavior pattern. As the child traces over the word, he subdues the protective system by the pressure of tracing. When the protective system is inhibited, the child may attend to the task at hand because he is no longer oversensitive to the tactile influences in his surroundings.

Children with difficulty in visual perception and imagery probably benefit more from Fernald's approach than do children with auditory perceptual problems. Some authors have, in fact, attributed the success of the method to the auditory feedback provided by saying the word as it is traced and viewed. In conclusion, the tracing approach is highly successful with many children but will produce little more than a primtive kind of skill in others. The conditions which limit the acquisition of skills appear to be in the learner, not the method.

References

Ayers, J. Tactile functions, their relation to hyperactive and perceptual-motor behavior. *American Journal of Occupational Therapy*, 1964, **6**, 6–11.

Bentzen, F. B., & Petersen, W. Educational procedures with the brain-damaged child. In W. T. Daley, *Speech and language therapy with the brain-damaged child*. Washington, D.C.: Catholic University of America Press, 1962.

Burnette, E. *Influences of classroom environment on word learning of retarded with high and low activity levels*. Unpublished doctoral dissertation, Peabody College, 1962.

Cohn, R. The neurological study of children with learning disabilities. *Exceptional Children*, 1964, **31**(4), 179–186.

Cruickshank, W. *A teaching method for brain-injured and hyperactive children*. Syracuse, N.Y.: Syracuse University Press, 1961.

Daley, W. T. *Speech and language therapy with the brain-damaged child*. Washington, D.C.: Catholic University of America Press, 1962.

Dunn, L. M., Minimal brain dysfunction: A dilemma for educators. In E. C. Frierson and W. B. Barbe, *Educating children with learning disabilities*. New York: Appleton-Century-Crofts, 1967.

Fernald, G. M. *Remedial techniques in basic school subjects*. New York: McGraw-Hill, 1943.

Frey, R. M. *Reading behavior of brain-injured and non-brain-injured children of average and retarded mental development*. Unpublished doctoral dissertation, University of Illinois, 1960.

Gardner, W. I., Cromwell, R. L., & Foshee, J. G. Studies in activity level. II-visual. *American Journal of Mental Deficiency*, 1959, **63**, 1028–1033.

Hebb, D. O. *The organization of behavior*. New York: Wiley, 1949.

Hewett, F. A hierarchy of educational tasks for children with learning disorders. *Exceptional Children*, 1964, **3**(14), 207–216.

Johnson, W., et al. *Speech handicapped school children*. (3rd ed.). New York: Harper, Row, 1967.

Rood, M. The use of sensory receptors to activate, facilitate, and inhibit motor response, autonomic and somatic, in developmental sequence. In C. Sattley, *Approaches to the treatment of patients with neuromuscular dysfunction*. Dubuque, Iowa: Brown, 1962.

Rost, K. J. Academic achievement of brain injured and hyperactive children in isolation. *Exceptional Children*, 1967, **34**, 125–126.

Semmel, M. I. Comparison of teacher ratings of brain-injured and mongoloid severely retarded (trainable) children attending community day-school classes. *American Journal of Mental Deficiency*, 1960, **64**, 963–971.

Smith, D. E., & Carrigan, P. M. *The nature of reading disability*. New York: Harcourt, Brace, & World, 1959.

Spradlin, J. E., Cromwell, R. L., & Foshee, J. G. Studies in activity level, III-auditory stimulating. *American Journal of Mental Deficiency*, 1960, **64**, 754–757.

Strauss, A. A. & Kephart, N. C. *Psychopathology and education of the brain-injured child*. Vol. II. Progress in theory and clinic. New York: Grune & Stratton, 1955.

———, & Lehtinen, L. E. *Psychopathology and education of the brain-injured child*. New York: Grune & Stratton, 1947.

Zigler, E. Social deprivation in familial and organic retardates. *Psychological Reports*, 1962, **10**, 370.

CHAPTER VI

LANGUAGE DEVELOPMENT SYSTEMS

This chapter is concerned with three widely used systems that emphasize language development: the systems reported by Myklebust, by Barry, and by McGinnis. These authors are concerned primarily with the communication problems of children diagnosed as aphasic, a condition characterized by language deficit emanating from underlying brain pathology. However, since conclusive evidence of brain impairment need not be demonstrated in affected children, the observable presence of inadequate language ability is sufficient to suggest the possible utility of these systems. Much similarity exists among the systems discussed in this chapter, although Barry's techniques seem preferable for use with younger children while McGinnis' approach is better designed for use with older children and adolescents. Myklebust contributes a comprehensive theory of language development as well as a collection of training techniques which are suitable for use with most preschool and school-aged youngsters. The readers should recognize that these systems employ numerous visual and auditory tasks, but the primary purpose of these activities is to facilitate the development of language rather than perceptual-motor integration. For this reason the systems of Myklebust, Barry, and McGinnis are presented under the rubric of language development systems.

These three authors share a rather strong auditory orientation, which is reflected in their training systems. Myklebust's earlier work was concerned with deafness and aphasia; Barry's clinical efforts were directed toward the education of aphasic children; and McGinnis was for many years at the Central Institute for the Deaf, where she worked with children with auditory aphasia. Because of this orientation, the systems devised by these particular authors are probably most suitable for use with children who evidence disorders associated with auditory-vocal deficits. Such a child is described in the case history that follows.

K. C., a four-year-old boy, was referred for evaluation because his speech was unintelligible and occasionally he was thought to have trouble understanding the speech of others. In addition, the father reported that when K. C. related an experience only the main words were used and even these were frequently presented in an improper sequence.

The Revised Stanford-Binet and the Columbia Mental Maturity Scale were administered and the results indicated that K. C. was of at least average intelligence. The examiner noted that the child seemed to have considerable difficulty comprehending some of the directions and was unable to express himself adequately when he did understand. The hypothesis of an auditory receptive language problem was set forth at that time and additional testing was undertaken.

Even though the audiological evaluation revealed a mild bilateral conductive hearing loss, its presence was not so severe as to account for the child's apparent language difficulty. The findings of the speech and language evaluation were indicative of both auditory receptive and expressive language disorder and was characterized by (1) poor articulation and syntax, (2) depression on the ITPA profile on all auditory and/or vocal subtests except the Auditory-Vocal Sequential subtest, and (3) a significantly low score on the Peabody Picture Vocabulary Test. Conversely, comparable strength was noted on all ITPA subtests which involved the visual and/or motor channels with the single exception of performance on Visual-Motor Sequential. During the evaluation, much evidence of hyperactivity and distractibility was noted by all persons involved.

K. C. was placed in a preschool class and because of his age the techniques suggested by Barry were prescribed. This approach was supplemented by standard articulation therapy. Near the end of the year K. C. underwent surgery and suffered unexpected complications. When he returned to school, significant regression had occurred and the Barry program was continued for longer that would be expected otherwise. After two years in the preschool experience, he was promoted to an ungraded primary class where the program was organized according to the McGinnis principles. At dismissal, K. C. was still somewhat hyperactive and distractible, but easily controlled. His articulation problem was corrected and his language showed marked improvement with both verbal expression and comprehension adequate for his age. He was recommended for regular first-grade placement. Although no problems are anticipated, should K. C. have academic difficulty, techniques suggested by Myklebust for problems in specific areas would be recommended on a supportive tutoring basis.

Helmer R. Myklebust

Helmer R. Myklebust is best known for his work in diagnosis and remediation of language problems of children who evidence deafness (1947, 1954, 1960) and/or aphasia (1952, 1954, 1955, 1957a). Drawing upon his knowledge of speech and language pathology he recently has expanded his earlier concepts into a comprehensive theory of learning disorders (Myklebust, 1964, 1968; Myklebust & Boshes, 1960; Boshes & Myklebust, 1964). Since Myklebust's early work in auditory disorders considerably influenced the development of his theory of language and of "psychoneurological learning disorder," frequent reference is made to it in this section. For more than fifteen years, his research and training activities have been directed toward the development of a frame of reference, the formulation of a series of educational principles, and the perfection of effective remedial techniques for use with learning disabled children. Recently, Myklebust was Professor of Language Pathology and Psychology and is Director to the Institute for Language Disorders at Northwestern University.

BASIC PSYCHONEUROLOGICAL AND DEVELOPMENTAL CONCEPTS

Semiautonomous Systems. Myklebust accepts as a starting point the concept of semiautonomous systems within the brain which underlie and control the processes of learning. Such a concept hypothesizes semi-independent systems within the brain which may function almost independently of each other, complement one another, or function in a completely interrelated manner. For example, the auditory system may function independently of the visual or other systems as in the acquisition of spoken language. Learning that occurs through the utilization of basically only one system is referred to by Myklebust as intraneurosensory learning. In addition, he speaks of interneurosensory learning, which implies a dependent relationship between two systems and integrative learning, "which utilizes all these systems functioning simultaneously" (Johnson & Myklebust, 1967, p. 26).

As Myklebust notes, probably no learning is completely and purely intraneurosensory; however, a single system may be of such primary importance in the learning of certain elements that for all purposes it functions relatively independently. As in the example given earlier, mastery of spoken words is interneurosensory learning using primarily the auditory system. Hence, it can be seen that brain dysfunction could impair one system and leave the others relatively intact.

Although there are few examples of strictly intraneurosensory learning, Myklebust says that interneurosensory learning, which occurs when two or more systems function together, is quite common. To account for interneurosensory learning, he introduces the construct of a transducer system within the brain which acts as a mechanism for translating information from one system to the others. Myklebust cites dyslexia and apraxia as examples of disorders that arise from deficits in the transducing mechanism.

Integrative learning occurs when all semiautonomous systems function as a unit. In many respects the integrative function appears to invest the individual's experience with meaning and therefore seems analogous to the process Myklebust calls "inner language" and to the representational mediation hypothesis of Osgood. Integrative learning includes the acquisition of meaning and the ability to conceptualize.

Myklebust postulates as a corollary the concept of overloading, which implies that information received through one sensory modality may interfere with the integration of simultaneous information received through other modalities. Many children with learning disorders can process information from only one sensory avenue at a time and according to Myklebust cannot profit from a multisensory approach to remediation. This concept is obviously important in evaluation of the child in that the data obtained may preclude the use of multisensory techniques.

Psychoneurological Integrities for Learning. Adequate functioning of the peripheral and central nervous systems as well as psychological integrity is considered essential for normal language development (Johnson & Myklebust, 1967). A variety of difficulties may arise when performance in one or more of the necessary integrities is less than optimal. Such problems cannot always be classified as specific learning disabilities in the context used by Myklebust. There is no doubt, however, that suboptimal functioning of any area will result in decreased learning.

When the integrity of the peripheral nervous system is impaired, some sensory limitations probably will ensue. The resultant deafness or blindness can impede language development. For example, before a child can acquire adequate speech in a normal manner, he must hear and understand his own speech as well as that of others; deafness disrupts this essential monitoring process. Myklebust does not consider sensory impairment an example of psychoneurological learning disability.

The central nervous system must be intact or psychoneurological learning disabilities are likely to occur. Such disorders may affect speech, reading, writing, arithmetic, and nonverbal performance. Myklebust suggests four specific categories of problems that arise primarily from CNS dysfunction and adversely influence learning.

1. Perceptual disturbance: Inability to identify, discriminate and interpret sensation. Often seen clinically as poor recognition of every day experience sensorially.

2. Disturbance of imagery: Inability to call to mind common experiences although they have been perceived. Seen as deficiencies in auditorization and visualization.

3. Disorders of symbolic processes: Inability to acquire facility to represent experience symbolically. Seen as aphasia, dyslexia, dysgraphia, and dyscalculia, and as language disorders.

4. Conceptualizing disturbances: Inability to generalize and categorize experience. Seen as a deficiency in grouping ideas that have a logical relationship—concreteness (1964, p. 359).

When considering the integrity of the CNS as related to learning disabilities, both intellectual and motor capacities must be considered. Measured intellectual ability on either verbal or nonverbal tests at some specified level is necessary for efficient learning. The child with limited intellectual capacity reveals overwhelming lack of CNS integrity. Adequate motor capacity is also dependent upon the intactness of the CNS. Poor motor performance ranges from crippling conditions such as cerebral palsy to clumsiness and poor coordination exhibited by many children with learning disability.

A child needs to have not only integrity of the peripheral and central nervous systems but of the psychodynamic processes as well. Myklebust (1957b) believes that three basic psychological processes must be intact: identification, internalization, and assimilation. The first is the recognition of and identification with the human voice. Babbling is the first lingual manifestation of identification. Some relationship between defective babbling and language disorders has been mentioned by Myklebust, who pointed out that hearing-impaired and receptive aphasic children evidence deviant babbling patterns. Internalization is the second pscyhological process that must be intact. This process relates the child's experience to the symbols which represent and communicate that experience. Internalization follows identification, but the periods of development overlap and progress simultaneously. Some children who tend to repeat what they hear (echolalic behavior) may have achieved identification but cannot associate experiences, and the echolalia may result from their attempt to integrate their experience. If a child finds language threatening instead of pleasurable or if he does not identify with the human voice, internalization may be impeded or precluded altogether, and language development may be disturbed. The third required psychological process is assimilation. As identification and internalization develop, experiences become related to one another, that is, assimilation occurs. Through assimilation, abstraction ability becomes possible.

These three processes evolve in a maturational order: identification precedes internalization; internalization precedes assimilation. Necessarily, babbling precedes the understanding of verbal symbols; and a basic verbal competence is essential before echolalia can evidence its negative role. Thus certain psychodynamic factors are seen to exert an influence on language development. Disturbances of these processes can interfere with normal language development and may cause autism or schizophrenia.

Normal Language Development.

DEFINITION OF LANGUAGE. Language is defined by Myklebust (1955) as symbolic behavior; it includes the ability to abstract, to attach meaning to words, and to use these words as symbols for thought and for the expression of ideas, objects, and feelings. Myklebust (1960) hypothesizes five levels of abstraction: sensation, perception, imagery, symbolization, and conceptualization. The individual levels are viewed as overlapping, developmental stages directly related to experience, rather than as mutually exclusive categories. Speech and language, while closely associated, are not considered synonymous. Language is the more inclusive term and is the vehicle for man's symbolic behavior, a faculty which differentiates him from other forms of life (Myklebust, 1954).

DEVELOPMENTAL HIERARCHY OF LANGUAGE. In 1960, Myklebust published a graphic description of his theory for the acquisition of language (Figure 1) in which five developmentally related levels of verbal behavior are presented. The first level is acquisition of meaning or inner language. Next, auditory symbols and experience are associated, resulting in the child's comprehension of spoken words, a process which contributes to the development of auditory receptive language. Auditory expressive language is evidenced in speech. Comprehension of printed words or reading (visual receptive language) is followed by expression of printed words in writing (visual expressive language).

The language processes consist of several receptive-expressive modes, of which the more important are auditory-verbal and visual language.

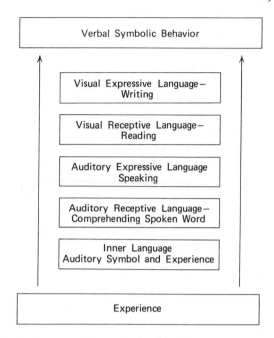

FIGURE 1.   The developmental hierarchy of man's language system. (From Mykle-bust, 1960, p. 232.)

The relationship between the auditory-verbal and the visual language modes is viewed as hierarchical in nature and emerges in a sequential pattern. For example, reading skills are mastered by superimposing visual symbols on the already firmly established auditory language base, and the written form assumes knowledge of the read form (Myklebust, 1960).

INNER LANGUAGE. Inner language is the first aspect of language to develop, emerging at approximately six months of age. The behavior initially is characterized by formation of simple concepts which may be evidenced in the child's play activities, such as his demonstrating knowledge of simple relationships between objects. At a later stage of development, the child can understand more complex relationships and plays with toys in a meaningful fashion, for example, appropriately ar-ranging furniture in a doll house. In its most complex form inner lan-guage permits the transformation of experience into verbal or nonverbal symbols.

RECEPTIVE LANGUAGE. Only after inner language has developed to an unspecified degree can the receptive aspect of language emerge. At about eight months of age, the child begins to indicate that he partially understands what is said to him. He responds properly to his name, several substantives, and simple commands. By the end of approximately four years of age, the child has mastered the acquisition of auditory language and thereafter the receptive processes provide an elaboration of the verbal system. It should be noted that once inner and receptive language have emerged, there is a reciprocal relationship between the two; development of inner language beyond the simple concept formation phase becomes dependent upon comprehension, and receptive language, to be meaningful, must rely on integrative, inner processes.

EXPRESSIVE LANGUAGE. The last aspect of language to appear is expression, which, according to Myklebust, develops after the acquisition of meaningful units of experience and establishment of comprehension. The child's expressive language, which emerges at around one year of age, reflects to a great extent the status and adequacy of his receptive abilities.

PSYCHONEUROLOGICAL LEARNING DISABILITIES

Definition and Etiology. Dissatisfaction with the terms in general use, notably "brain damage" and "learning disorder," prompted Myklebust to select a different label, "psychoneurological learning disability," which he suggests encompasses adequately the behavioral and the physiological parameters involved in the problems exhibited by these children. According to Myklebust and Boshes (1960), children with psychoneurological learning disability often evidence minor awkwardness, certain behavior disturbances, and difficulties in reading, writing, arithmetic, and speaking, all of which are inferred to be the result of brain dysfunction. Irrespective of age of onset or cause, the term refers to all aberrations of behavior in learning that have a neurological base; the disorder is viewed as a behavioral deviation rather than an incapacity to learn. With the exception of Myklebust's strongly stated position that learning disabilities are invariably caused by neurological dysfunction, the definition of "psychoneurological learning disability" resembles those of Bateman and others discussed in detail in Chapter I.

Whereas many writers and researchers in the field do not attempt to establish a relationship between learning disabilities and brain dysfunction, Myklebust makes this association one of the hallmarks of his concept of psychoneurological learning disabilities. Even though objective findings of a disturbance in brain function may be lacking and the disabled learner may appear neurologically intact, evidence of the brain dysfunction can be presumed on the basis of behavioral signs (Johnson & Myklebust, 1967, Myklebust, 1968). But he feels that most dysfunctions can be demonstrated neurologically and when diagnostic techniques become more precise and sophisticated, most learning disabilities will reveal neurological signs. Within this framework, psychoneurological learning disability indicates that the disorder is in the behavior and is attributable to neurological causation. Of interest, here, is the circular reasoning inherent in this aspect of the concept, inasmuch as one of the fundamental criteria for diagnosis and classification frequently must be made on an inferential basis.

Types of Psychoneurological Learning Disabilities. Failure to master skills in any of the semiautonomous learning systems or at any level within the developmental hierarchy will result in a corresponding disability, which in turn reduces the probability of success at higher levels. For example, no child talks until he understands speech, nor does he learn to read normally unless he first has acquired oral language. Further, since written language is the expressive side of read language, the child who cannot read is unable to write. Myklebust (Johnson & Myklebust, 1967) speaks of five general groups of learning disorders: disorders of auditory language, disorders of reading, disorders of written language, disorders of arithmetic, and nonverbal disorders of learning.

DISORDERS OF AUDITORY LANGUAGE. Auditory symbolic language disorder usually is detected when the child is two to four years of age. This disability is more handicapping than a speech problem because normal symbolic language development is prevented. Originally three types were recognized by Myklebust (1955): receptive, expressive, and mixed. Recently, however, Johnson and Myklebust (1967) speak of generalized deficits in auditory learning, disorders of auditory receptive language, and disorders of auditory expressive language.

The child with a generalized problem "hears" but interprets neither speech nor environmental sounds. Since his visual and tactile modalities are relatively intact, he may be confused mistakenly with the deaf. The receptive form affects the ability to comprehend auditory symbols and has serious influence upon language development. Such cases are distinguished from the former type by their apparent mastery of nonverbal-social or environmental sounds. Frequently, the condition is referred to as receptive aphasia, sensory aphasia, auditory verbal agnosia, or word deafness.

In the expressive form, symbolic communication is disrupted, even though the meaning of the symbols is understood. Three common types of expressive disabilities are emphasized. In the first, the problem relates to "reauditorization" and word selection (anomia). An affected child may comprehend words but may be unable to recall them for spontaneous expression. The speech of a young child who experiences difficulty in word recall is characterized by a disproportionate number of circum-

locutions, delayed responses, gestures, nonverbal sounds, and word associations (the substitution of a word from within the same category as
the word being sought, for example, knife for fork). The older child
may resort to written expression as a means of communication and generally prefers silent reading to oral reading. In the second type, the
difficulty centers upon inability to effect the motor habits necessary for
speech rather than upon problems of word retrieval or memory (dyspraxia). The third type is characterized by the presence of defective
syntax. An affected child can communicate adequately when single
words or short phrases are required but does not exhibit the organization
necessary to master complete sentences, as evidenced by unexpected
errors in word order, verb tenses, and other syntactical infractions.

DISORDERS OF READING. When a child enters school and begins learning
to read, dyslexia may be recognized as a problem. Dyslexia is an inability
to read normally as a result of damage to the brain. Such an impairment
may be considered highly disruptive to the language process and debilitating to the total language development of the child. Dyslexia is commonly found in combination with other language inadequacies, notably
impairments in memory, memory for sequence, left-right orientation,
time orientation, body image, spelling and writing, dyscalculia, motor
disturbances, and perceptual disorders. However, dyslexia does not result
from mental retardation, sensory impairment, emotional problems, or inadequate teaching. All facets of childhood dyslexia are not necessarily
present in a given child; generally, however, these symptoms characterize
children having this type of language disability. Other terms used to
describe this condition include word blindness, developmental dyslexia,
and strephosymbolia.

Two common forms of dyslexia are discussed—visual and auditory.
Some, but not all types of visual disturbance result in visual dyslexia.
An affected child has difficulty visually mastering whole words as well
as the letters and syllables of individual words. Characteristics of reading
problems associated with visual dyslexia follow:

1. Confusion of similar words and letters.
2. Slow word recognition.
3. Frequent letter reversals (b for d).
4. Letter inversion tendencies (u for n).
5. Difficulty following and retaining visual sequences.
6. Concomitant visual memory disorders.
7. Inferior drawings.
8. Problems with visual analysis (puzzles).
9. Better at auditory tasks than visual tasks.
10. Tendency to avoid games which require visual integration skills.

In auditory dyslexia, the child is likely to have visual strength, and the whole-word approach to reading will be comparatively easy for him. His difficulties center upon phonetic word attack skills, reauditorizing phonemes and words, and sound blending.

DISORDERS OF WRITTEN LANGUAGE. Written language is considered by Myklebust (1965) to be the culminating verbal achievement of man, necessarily requiring the establishment of all of the preceding levels of abilities. The normal development of written language presumes the integrity of the sensory and motor processes. Oral and written expression are dependent on the adequacy of the receptive functions. Disorders of the written form include dysgraphia, deficits in revisualization, and disorders for formulation and syntax.

In dysgraphia, the child can read and speak but cannot initiate the motor patterns when necessary for expression through writing. He cannot even copy letters, words, or numbers. The difficulty is essentially one of visual-motor integration rather than ideation, although it may accompany an ideation problem. Dysgraphia is viewed by Myklebust as a type of apraxia involving the visual-motor system.

In deficits of revisualization, the problem is basically one of visual memory. The child speaks, reads, and copies, but he cannot revisualize words or letters. As a result he does not write spontaneously or from dictation. In disorders of formulation and syntax, the problem involves ideation; the child can read, spell, copy, and express himself well vocally, but he is unable to put his ideas onto paper. Though difficulties in syntax can exist in isolation, they frequently accompany disorders in ideation and are characterized by word omissions, distorted word order, and improper verb and pronoun usage, word endings, and punctuation.

DISORDERS OF ARITHMETIC. Johnson and Myklebust (1967) state that man developed the spoken and written symbol systems to express thoughts and feelings, but for the expression of certain ideas, namely, quantity, size, and order, the number system was developed and perfected. As with language in general, this system has an inner, receptive, and expressive form. Whereas poor mathematics ability may result from inferior instruction or subaverage mental ability, dyscalculia is associated with a certain type of neurological dysfunction which interferes with quantitative thinking. Two types of arithmetical inadequacy are suggested—those related to other language disorders and those related to disturbances in quantitative thinking.

The child with an auditory receptive language disorder will probably do poorly in arithmetic in school, not because he fails to comprehend the principles involved in calculation but because he has difficulty understanding (1) the teacher's oral discussion of those principles, (2) story problems when they are read aloud, or (3) spoken instructions. The presence of reading disorder places the child at a disadvantage in reading story problems, while dysgraphia may interfere with his ability to write the answers.

Disturbances in quantitative thinking (dyscalculia) involve comprehension of the mathematical principles themselves. The child can read and write but cannot calculate. This condition often is characterized by (1) deficient visual-spatial organization and nonverbal integration, (2) extraordinary auditory abilities, (3) excellence in reading vocabulary and syllabication skills, (4) disturbance in body image, (5) poor visual-motor integration (apraxia), (6) no clear distinction between right and left, (7) low social maturity, and (8) considerably higher scores on standardized tests on verbal tasks than on nonverbal tasks.

NONVERBAL DISORDERS OF LEARNING. Johnson and Myklebust (1967) recognize that not all psychoneurological learning disabilities are verbal. Some youngsters fail to understand many aspects of their environment such as time, space, size, direction, or self-perception. Such a child is categorized as follows:

[He has] a deficiency in social perception, meaning that he has an inability which precludes acquiring the significance of basic nonverbal aspects of daily living, though his verbal level of intelligence falls within or above the average. There are many such children but they are largely unrecognized since test procedures for identifying them, as well as procedures for educational remediation, have been slow in developing (1967, p. 272).

A variety of diverse skills are represented under the heading of Nonverbal Disorders of Learning. Specific types, discussed in detail by Johnson and Myklebust, include problems in gesturing, motor learning, body image, spatial orientation, right-left orientation, social imperception, distractibility, perseveration, and disinhibition.

In addition to being in itself a legitimate form of communication, a gesture often supplements vocal expression. Subsequently, inadequate use of gestures can affect the total communication process of a child. As with other communication skills, inadequacy may result from impairment of either the comprehension or the use of gestures, and occasionally both aspects are involved.

Some children exhibit considerable difficulty in the acquisition of nonverbal motor patterns, such as learning to cut with scissors, jump rope, and comb hair. Such disorder must result from deficits in learning rather than from actual paralysis. Other children may evidence distortions in body image (self-perception or body consciousness). In these cases, the child usually does not know the names of the parts of his body or the relationships among the parts. The child with poor body image is likely to suffer also from difficulties involving spatial orientation. Since he cannot position himself in the spatial world, the child often bumps into things, gets lost, and makes errors in judging distance. Right-left disorientation is another frequently noted nonverbal learning disability which often occurs side by side with poor imagery and spatial orientation. Affected children are not aware of the right-left concept and therefore experience problems in following directions, for example, directions which involve paper and pencil routines. In addition, learning disabled children often have trouble in social situations. Such difficulty is not necessarily the result of autism or severe emotional disturbance, for the child wants to fit in but lacks sufficient social understanding and skill to achieve his goal. His attempts to cope frequently are misjudged and rewarded with punishment.

When present, distractibility, perseveration, and disinhibition complicate the entire remedial undertaking. The distractible child does not or cannot attend sufficiently to environmental events and instead his attention is directed fleetingly to all events without respect for their relevancy. In the case of a perseverative child, attention persists beyond the time required, making it difficult for him to shift his attention, although a shift may be desirable. The child exhibiting disinhibition is unable to hold on to or to control ideation processes. An idea can be held or attended to for but a short time before the mind shifts randomly to another internal event.

Remediation of Psychoneurological Learning Disabilities. Because the brain is comprised of systems that sometimes function semi-independently, supplementary, and in conjunction with other systems, a strong case is made by Myklebust (1964) for the acquisition of an accurate, differential diagnosis for children with psychoneurological learning disorders. In fact, the planning of an educational program for a child with a learning disability begins with the comprehensive diagnostic study, and such a study is viewed as an essential factor in remediation. Therefore appraisal of the brain's capacity to receive, categorize, and integrate information as well as of the intactness of the auditory, visual, motor, and tactile modes is undertaken. In many cases, the total evaluation will include clinical teaching in order to acquire the additional information which makes possible the alteration of training programs and the verification of test data.

The fundamental principles that guide the remediation of psychoneurological learning disorders are presented by Johnson and Myklebust

(1967) in their recent book, *Learning Disabilities: Educational Principles and Practices*. Briefly stated, these considerations are:

1. Teaching must be individualized.
2. Teaching according to readiness in a balanced program is essential.
3. Teaching must be as close to the level of involvement as possible.
4. Consider that input precedes output as a basis for classification or grouping.
5. Teach to the tolerance level, avoiding overloading in particular.
6. Use multisensory stimulation.
7. Raise the deficits without undue stimulation or demand on the disability itself.
8. Teaching to the integrities is necessary but has limitation.
9. Provide training in perception when needed.
10. Control important variables such as attention, rate, proximity, and size as needed.
11. Develop both the verbal and nonverbal areas of experience.
12. Guide the approach by both behavioral criteria and psychoneurological considerations.

Through application of these principles to clinical teaching, a set of specific methods and techniques was developed. These techniques are recommended for use with children who have disorders in auditory language, reading, written language, arithmetic, and nonverbal learning.

REMEDIATION OF AUDITORY LANGUAGE DISORDERS. Appropriate training activities are suggested for generalized, receptive, and expressive auditory language disorders. The goal of training children with generalized auditory language deficits is to teach them to understand the meaning of environmental sounds and of speech; the need for simultaneous matching of sounds and experience is emphasized. Learning is facilitated by the availability of an optimal instructional setting which is free of distracting noise and which is provided with visual materials. After the child is aware of sound, as opposed to no sound, noise-producing toys such as bells, drums, and horns are presented for him to explore. Localization of sound is taught through activities which require the child to respond to noises made to his right or left and which require him to follow the sound of a whistle blown by the teacher while walking around the room. During these activities the child is blindfolded. Sound discrimination is facilitated through the matching of noisemaking toys with the sound each makes. One exercise used to develop auditory memory requires that the child imitate a pattern of hand claps—first one, then two, then three, etc.

Auditory receptive language disorders affect the child's ability to understand speech but do not involve his comprehension of nonverbal-social sounds. Since these children can hear, the primary goal of training is the development of understanding of what is heard. The teacher should remember to begin training early, to provide sufficient input before expecting acceptable output, to structure material into meaningful units, to present the spoken word and the associated experience simultaneously, to use much repetition, to select a vocabulary which is meaningful to the child, and to present the parts of speech beginning with sounds, then nouns, verbs, adjectives, and prepositions.

Children with auditory expressive language disorders usually understand speech adequately but experience difficulty when using spoken words. There are three common forms, involving reauditorization, auditory-motor integration, and syntax. Problems in reauditorization are characterized by inability to recall words or word-finding difficulty, and the aim of training is to facilitate the spontaneous recall of words. To achieve this goal, sentence completion exercises are used in conjunction with picture cues. In addition, such word associations as bread and butter and needles and pins are taught. Children with auditory-motor integration problems are unable to say words (apractic), and the goal of education is to develop voluntary repetition and meaningful oral communication. The child is made aware of the sounds he already can produce before new ones are introduced. The use of mirrors to see oneself talk or watching others talk helps develop a motor plan for speech. Other children experience difficulty in formulating sentences. They hear and understand but speak in single words or brief phrases and manifest problems in syntax and organization. The objective of educational intervention is to "develop a correct, natural, spontaneous flow of language" (p. 136). One suggested approach is to teach the structure of the language using techniques similar to the audiolingual methods of teaching foreign language. In addition, meaningful sentences are spoken and the child internalizes the various sentence patterns. Suggested exercises include scrambled sentences, where the child puts the words into a proper sequence, and incomplete sentences, where the child supplies a suitable word to complete a sentence.

REMEDIATION OF READING DISORDERS. In teaching reading, the printed word generally is associated with a spoken word, which in turn is based upon a concept. For example, the child already has a highly developed impression of cat before he ever uses the spoken word "cat." Later, he associates "cat" with its printed form—cat. Subsequently, the youngster who cannot integrate meaningful experiences or cannot learn through the visual or auditory channels is likely to develop a reading problem. The major objective of training, therefore, is to promote the integration of experience, the spoken word, and the printed word. Since the nature of the dyslexia varies from child to child, precise training procedures are based upon the study of each case. Johnson and Myklebust discuss remedial activities for two common forms of dyslexia—visual and auditory dyslexia.

The visual dyslexic has difficulty in the association of printed words with their meaning, so a phonetic approach is recommended if his auditory modality is intact. Involved in this approach is the teaching of isolated sounds and their eventual blending into words. Initially, several consonants are selected which differ markedly in both sound and appearance (m, t, s). The letters are printed on cards which are flashed before the child. At the same time, the teacher says the letter's *sound*, not the letter's *name*. Then the child is encouraged to say the sound. Next the pupil is requested to think of words beginning with the sound under discussion. After mastering several consonants, the activity is altered, and the child is asked to pick from the group of flash cards the one that goes with a particular sound voiced by the instructor. Sound blends are introduced next, as are long vowels, simple sentences, paragraphs, and stories. Myklebust points out that these activities are related highly to those offered by Gillingham and Stillman (see the discussion of the phonics systems included in this book). While teaching this child to read through his auditory strengths, the teacher is also responsible for improving his visual deficits. A variety of visually oriented matching activities are recommended, including the matching of pictures and printed words, pictures and outline drawings, objects and drawn outlines, among others. Eventually the child learns that words have their own configuration, for example, where ⌐‾⌐ , home ⌐‾⌐ , kitten ⌐‾⌐ .

In teaching children with auditory dyslexia to read, a whole-word approach is emphasized during the early stage of instruction. The first words to be taught are drawn exclusively from the child's speaking vocabulary and differ in both their auditory and visual forms. Whole printed words are matched with objects and experience. For example, in teaching nouns, a card is presented to the child with the word *shoe* on the left and a picture of a shoe on the right; this facilitates the development of the association. For verbs, the child jumps and is presented with the printed word *jump*. The activities progress in complexity, and adjectives, prepositions, short phrases, and sentences are introduced. The teacher also seeks to improve the child's auditory deficits.

REMEDIATION OF WRITTEN LANGUAGE DISORDERS. Johnson and Myklebust have postulated three major forms of written language disorders and have offered remedial suggestions for each. In dysgraphia, a problem of visual-motor integration, affected children must acquire adequate visual and kinesthetic patterns if writing is to be mastered. Initially, the child watches the instructor draw several vertical lines on the blackboard; no attempt is made at this time, however, to have the child reproduce the figure. While the child is blindfolded, his index finger is guided repeatedly over the drawn figure until he can follow the pattern unassisted. The blindfold is removed, and the child is encouraged to coordinate the visual and the motor tasks by reproducing the figure. Additional drawings are presented but the visual, kinesthetic, and combination progression is maintained. Reinforcement techniques are suggested and include the use of stencils (templates), dot-to-dot figures, and tracing with copy paper. Success with these activities indicates that the child is ready to learn manuscript letters and numbers. Each letter to be taught is analyzed thoroughly; thus the child recognizes, for example, that the letter b is comprised of a line and a semicircle. To aid in the beginning stages of letter formulation, practice letters written in dotted lines are provided and the child connects the dots. Arrows are superimposed on these figures to illustrate the direction to be followed in completing the letters. Attention must be directed toward spacing and erasure habits, for they can render the writing difficult to read.

In training children in visual memory (revisualization), special care is devoted to the selection of materials. Words are printed in larger type than usual and may be in color in order to strengthen the visual impression. The use of a pocket flashlight as a pointer as well as many verbal instructions tend to facilitate attention, which is so necessary in remediating memory deficits. Auditory and tactile reinforcements are recommended as aids in improving recall; for example, spelling words can be learned through tracing them several times. Numerous activities are suggested to help develop partial recall; one of them has the child complete partially drawn pictures from memory and another one asks him to make a circle into as many pictures as he can (for example, a sun, a face).

The initial objective in training disorders of formulation and syntax is to make the youngster aware of his errors in writing. This is accomplished to some extent by having him listen to the teacher read aloud sentences he has written. Since the child usually is intact auditorially, he can hear the errors. Later, he reads his own work aloud and monitors the errors. The teacher can construct sentences and stories which contain a variety of mistakes, and the pupil is encouraged to locate as many as possible. To encourage abstraction in writing, the child is given specific and detailed instructions as to what is to be written; outlines and key words are used also. Johnson and Myklebust provide a number of exercises and ideas which are helpful in developing formulation and syntax.

REMEDIATION OF ARITHMETIC DISORDERS. The acquisition of skill in the use of quantitative relationships is the goal of teaching dyscalculic children. Often training must begin at a basic nonverbal level, and the principles of quantity, order, size, space, and distance must be taught. In general, the development of these concepts is facilitated by the use of concrete materials and considerable auditory verbalization.

The reasoning processes required for early quantitative thinking are based to a considerable extent on visual perception, thus puzzles, pegboards, formboards, and jigsaw puzzles are helpful for those dyscalculic children who manifest associated problems in form perception. An adequate grasp of size and length possibly is related to such mathematical concepts as perimeters and areas. One exercise offered to develop this skill requires the child to grade four circles made of felt according to size, beginning with the largest and concluding with the smallest. One-to-one relationships are taught with various matching exercises which stress one-to-one correspondence; for example, a series of paper dolls is placed in a row, and the child is encouraged to draw one hat for each figure. One technique, among others offered, by which a child may be taught to count requires motor responses such as stringing beads or touching pegs as he counts aloud. Having acquired a concept of quantity and the skill to count aloud, the child must learn that numbers refer to visual symbols; the number quantity of three, therefore, can be represented by a spoken word, by "3," or by a written word without altering the basic concept. All suitable activities (number lines, number stepping blocks, etc.) use visual symbols.

The ideas of Piaget (1953) regarding the assessment of conservation of quantity are considered important, and familiar Piagetian tasks are recommended. In one activity reported, the child is requested to fill a cup of water and to pour the contents into a glass; next he is asked to fill the cup again and to pour the water into a flat bowl; when asked to comment about the amounts in each container, the child maintained that the glass contained more water. To develop conservation, concrete materials which can be manipulated are suggested, notably Cuisinaire Rods and toys frequently associated with Montessori schools. Another problem related to dyscalculia is the inability to quickly recognize the number of objects in a group. In one training activity, a plate with small groups of dots is flashed using tachistoscope procedures and the child matches the flashed form with a like form on an answer sheet. In addition, children may need to be taught the language of arithmetic—the meaning of signs, the arrangement of numbers, the sequence of steps for calculation, and problem solving.

REMEDIATION OF NONVERBAL DISORDERS OF LEARNING. The use of realistic pictures and photographs are fundamental to the assessment of and remediation of nonverbal disorders of learning. In the selection of suitable pictures, consideration must be made of their size, color, and background. In general, pictures larger than 4 × 10 inches are avoided, realistically colored pictures are preferred, and the best backgrounds are devoid of confusing shadings and clutter. Exercises are prepared which entail the matching of real objects with their pictures, pictures of objects with their drawn outlines, and other combinations.

In teaching nonverbal motor learnings such as buttoning, typing, and cutting, each act is reduced to its basic movement patterns. For example, when a child is taught to skip, he is instructed how to stand first on one foot then the other foot; he watches himself in a mirror to obtain a visual image of the activity; he listens to the sounds made by others while skipping to obtain the auditory pattern; and, finally, he is encouraged to try the activity himself. Rope jumping, cutting with scissors, and other skills are taught in a similar manner. Some children lack sufficient body image and need special training. One suggested exercise requires the child lie down on a sheet of wrapping paper while the teacher draws his outline. The child then observes the completed drawing and discusses its parts with the teacher. Later, the facial features, fingernails, and other details are added. Work with mirrors and body puzzles also are helpful in the perfection of body image.

Since learning disabled children tend to be highly distractible, the room should be free of excessive visual stimulation and noise. Cupboards are covered; floors are muted with rugs or tile; and rubber tips are placed on the legs of furniture. To control perseveration, which often accompanies distractibility and which may be the by-product of fatigue, the period of instruction should be structured to provide for rest periods and frequent breaks in routine. Toys which stimulate perseveration are removed from the situation as soon as they are recognized as such. Disinhibition in children is managed by the establishment of daily routines, which aids them in mastering desired patterns of behavior. Techniques useful in the management of hyperactivity include teaching an affected child to walk down the hall with his hands in his pockets, which discourages him from touching everything along the way, or to walk down the hall following a pattern marked on the floor, which keeps him from popping in and out of adjacent classrooms. Youngsters who lose control of themselves and exhibit euphoric laughter, excessive gross motor activity, or other disruptive behavior are removed from the cause or scene of the overstimulation and placed in a small, quiet environment, possibly another room or a part of the classroom, until control is restored. Additional remedial suggestions, exercises, and techniques are offered by Johnson and Myklebust for training or developing gestures, right-left orientation, spatial orientation, and social imperception.

Much of Myklebust's recent writings promotes an understanding of his concept of psychoneurological learning disabilities. From this frame of reference he has evolved criteria for diagnosis and classification of learning disabilities in children, as well as appropriate remedial approaches. While he continues to stress the importance of the auditory language system, Myklebust emphasizes the reciprocal relationships of visual, auditory, and graphic channels in verbal and nonverbal learning.

Hortense Barry

For some years, Barry taught children with communication disorders in an experimental classroom. Her book *The Young Aphasic Child: Evaluation and Training* is a compilation of pertinent, practical information, procedures, techniques, and materials found to be of value when used with such children. Much of the information included in the book is derived from Barry's own teaching experience, though she points out that many of her ideas are taken from other sources. An eclectic approach, therefore, is implied by Barry in dealing with aphasic children; she feels that "no one specific method, no one set of tools, no one simple approach is or can be the solution to so complex a problem" (Barry, 1961, p. 1).

ORIENTATION

Barry (1961) describes aphasia as "the inability to use and/or understand spoken language as a result of defect or damage in the central nervous system" (p. 3). Two main types of aphasia are cited: receptive aphasia (sensory or auditory) in which the child lacks understanding of spoken language, and expressive aphasia (motor or verbal) in which speech is understood but the child does not talk normally. The most common diagnosis is that of mixed aphasia, where the child demonstrates characteristics of both receptive and expressive aphasia. In addition to these two types, there are two less frequently seen conditions: central aphasia where the inner language functioning is disturbed, and global aphasia where there apparently is no inner, receptive, or expressive language function.

Barry's approach is based upon principles set forth by Myklebust, the concept of inner, receptive, and expressive language, and the need for presenting language in the same sequence in which normal children are presumed to acquire it. First, training in inner language is given to help the child relate better to his environment. Symbolic toys help familiarize him meaningfully with his environment. Until the child learns to manipulate toys successfully, no attempt is made to teach receptive or expressive language.

Then receptive training, or the "feeding-in process" is begun, and finally, after the child has begun to structure his own auditory world, expressive language training is given. No expressive language is demanded during the training for receptive language, although Barry states that many children spontaneously begin to give back some of the language to which they have been continuously exposed.

EVALUATION

Before aphasia can be diagnosed, other causes for the lack of normal verbal communication must be ruled out. Peripheral hearing loss, mental retardation, and severe emotional disturbance must be eliminated as primary problems before the diagnosis of aphasia is tenable. It is important to note that children admitted to Barry's class for aphasics had average intelligence, which was evidenced through clinical or teacher impressions rather than by formal psychological tests.

In the absence of a team of experts or in the presence of conflicting opinions, Barry suggests that six areas of the child's behavior should be explored by the teacher. The areas to be evaluated include (1) the case history, (2) hearing, (3) language, (4) psychomotor function, (5) emotional and social adjustment, and (6) motor abilities.

The first step in the teacher's evaluation of the child is the taking of a history. This should include pertinent information on pregnancy, delivery, family (siblings, handedness, speech or hearing disorders), motor development (when the child sat up, walked, etc.), illnesses, social development (toilet training, feeding, dressing, sleeping habits, eating habits, behavior), communication, and education. The history is primarily the parent's impression of the child.

The next step is a hearing evaluation with the interest concentrated on auditory perception and memory rather than acuity. The child is tested for awareness of sound, voice, and speech, and then for discrimination of sound, voice, and speech patterns. Auditory perception and auditory memory also are tested.

Step three is a language evaluation in which inner, receptive, and expressive language are tested individually, and always in the stated order. Familiar toy objects such as small figures and furniture are used in these tests rather than pictures, since pictures themselves are symbols.

In step four, the evaluation of psychomotor functioning, which includes figure-ground, visuomotor, body image, and spatial relationship functioning are tested. The fifth area investigated is that of the child's emotional and social adjustment; and the final step is an evaluation of motor abilities including gross motor skills, fine motor skills, and speech motor control.

Barry (1955) compiled a list of characteristic behaviors in speech, language, reading, and writing which are associated with aphasic children. Use of the list could contribute to the informal teacher evaluation. After careful review of the entire evaluation, if the teacher is still unable to reach a definite conclusion upon which to plan suitable therapy or training, he proceeds with "diagnostic teaching," a combination of continued evaluation and therapy.

TRAINING

Three important considerations in the training of aphasic children are (1) the physical setup, (2) corrective therapy for psychomotor dysfunctions and impaired functions, and (3) the development of language and skills related to language.

The Physical Setup. The number of pupils in the special class should be limited; the physical environment should be uncluttered and free from distractions. Pupils are seated apart from one another, and highly distractible children are assigned seats which face a wall with their backs to all activity. Attempt is made to teach children to work without direct supervision on assigned tasks so that the teacher may have the opportunity to give the pupils additional individual help. The materials are selected carefully and should be simple and easy to handle. Any pictures used in these classes need to be free from unnecessary details. All materials should be filed when not in use in order to maintain the uncluttered appearance of the classroom.

Barry (1961, p. 14–21) outlines a sample day complete with time allotments and structured teaching activities that can be used. This highly structured day which begins at nine in the morning and ends at three in the afternoon is planned with routines and time limits, which are carefully observed and which provide the pupil with needed security. Explicit directions are given in simple, direct language. The child is taught step by step where to put his things, when to take turns, and how to walk quietly. All this is accomplished in a kind but firm manner. This approach helps the child, whose perceptions may be unstable, to order his world and to integrate his experiences. Specifically, the day's activities include training in visual perception, reading and number readiness, auditory perception, language, and writing; there is time out for snack, outdoor play, lunch, and rest.

Corrective Therapy for Psychomotor Dysfunctioning and Impaired Perceptions. The child who cannot control or integrate his behavior needs firm and deliberate procedures. For this reason, structure is the key to teaching aphasic children. Barry (1961) divides the training of the impaired functions into four areas and suggests possible activities for each area. Areas to be trained are (1) impaired body image, (2) impaired perceptions, (3) figure-ground disturbance and spatial disorganization, and (4) motor disabilities, in the order listed.

1. TRAINING IMPAIRED BODY IMAGE. If the child's concept of body image (awareness of self as a entity separate from others) is impaired, Barry stresses the need for training in that area before attempting further training.

A number of highly structured procedures are proposed. The child is helped to model a human figure from clay (calling it a boy, a girl, or a daddy). The location of the eyes, nose, mouth, and arms is pointed out. The pupil is taught to make a life-sized outline of another child lying on a large piece of paper on the floor; he then cuts it out and is encouraged to draw parts of the body. Development of adequate body image is facilitated further by having the child look at himself in a mirror. The use of stuffed animals permits the child to feel parts of the body and to discuss the body while dressing the figure. Other suitable procedures can be found in Barry's (1961) book.

2. TRAINING IMPAIRED PERCEPTIONS. Once the child perceives the body and its parts realistically, training can proceed to the remediation of impaired perceptions. After visual perception training, the child should be able to form visual relationships, to make visual contact with objects, to look where he wants to look, and to change his focus both in direction and distance at will. He must be able to organize and synthesize visual fields and to translate into movement what he sees. Specific techniques which are helpful in developing visual perceptions include the child's participation in matching and sorting activities which make use of different colors, forms, and objects; the copying of simple forms; and coloring, cutting, and pasting tasks.

Occasionally a child needs tactile perception training. Activities are designed to develop the child's ability to discriminate and recognize forms, textures, and objects by touch alone. An initial task might require the child, with his eyes closed, to feel one block and to place it with other blocks having different shapes. The child then looks at all the blocks and identifies the one that he had felt. This procedure is varied for use with other tactile stimuli, for example, distinguishing among cans filled with sand, soap flakes, flour.

Training of auditory perception and memory is often necessary. After training in this function, the child should have developed both awareness and discrimination among sound stimuli and symbols. Training proceeds from gross to finer sounds and finally to the sounds of voice and speech. The child must have intensive practice relating motor responses to auditory stimuli. In teaching awareness of sounds, the child is encouraged to raise his hand or jump when he hears a musical instrument, the jingling of coins, or spoken nonsense syllables. In teaching discrimination among sounds, the child is taught to select from a group of instruments the one that was sounded behind him (discrimination between loud and soft sounds is developed at this time). Discrimination among speech sounds may be taught by requiring the child to associate the syllables *moo* and *baa* with the pictures of a cow and a sheep. This task is increased in difficulty as the child succeeds to one-syllable words, to two-syllable words, etc. In teaching auditory memory, cards are prepared with short and long vertical lines to represent high-low or loud-soft patterns (visual clues) produced by the teacher. The child selects the proper card to match the sounds. Imitation of rhythms and nonsense syllables is used to give practice in memory.

3. TRAINING FOR FIGURE-GROUND DISTURBANCE AND SPATIAL DISORGANIZATION. After training in figure-ground discrimination and spatial orientation, the child's fluctuating impressions tend to become stabilized. Having auditory figure-ground disturbance, the child attends to all sounds equally and therefore must be trained to listen and to control the sound background. Auditory figure-ground disturbance may be improved by using the suggestions for training awareness and discrimination against a background of soft music. If visual figure-ground disturbance is present, the child must learn to bring the foreground sharply into focus. Training is designed to help the child attend to the foreground stimulus without being overly aware of the background. The teacher gives practice in finding differences, making a whole from parts, discrimination of figure from ground. This latter is accomplished by use of a cardboard stencil placed over white paper, both tacked onto a board. The child colors within the stencil; as the child becomes more skillful, the stencil is removed and the child colors within an outline. To gain spatial orientation, the child is trained to find a reference point

and to use judgment in spatial matters. Training consists of finding the top, bottom, sides, and back; of learning up, down, over, under, in, bigger, heavier, etc., in concrete situations. The teacher may employ the color cone, the three-hole form board, cut-out forms of different colors to be matched to identical forms pasted on a board, designs of many kinds for the child to copy, puzzles, and sequencing activities involving gradations of color, size, weight, etc.

4. TRAINING IN MOTOR SKILLS. The final section on impaired functions discussed by Barry deals with the training of motor skills. Once again the training begins with gross motor abilities (moving and stopping), proceeds to the fine motor skills (using the fingers), and then progresses to speech motor skills. In training gross motor skills, all practice in moving and stopping is encouraged. Running, skipping, hopping, throwing, kicking, walking up and down stairs, and walking within prescribed limits are suggested activities. In training fine motor skills, activities such as picking up small objects and dropping them into holes or slots, buttoning, stringing beads, folding, and cutting are useful. In training speech motor skills, relaxation exercises such as dropping the head forward and rotating it slowly or babbling and yawning are employed first. Other activities include having the child (1) breathe in and out through the nose, or breathe in through the nose and out through the mouth, or blow a ping-pong ball across a table, (2) imitate or sing nonsense syllables or digits to improve voice production, (3) use articulation exercises such as chewing, with and without voice, raising and lowering the jaw, protruding the tongue and moving it from side to side and up and down, and protruding the lips.

Training Language and Related Skills. Language training usually is started at the same time as, and coordinated with, perception and motor training. In normal language development, inner language begins to function at about eight months of age, receptive language at from eight to thirteen months, and expressive language from thirteen months on. In training language disabilities this same order is followed, but training is begun at the level at which the child is impaired.

In training inner language, the child is helped to relate better to his environment, to "make believe," to use past experience, and to integrate. Until he can do this, receptive and expressive language training are not attempted. Specifically, inner language is developed by manipulation of and play with objects representing items in the child's daily experience until he can make relationships in a meaningful way.

The techniques for training receptive language are described by Barry (1960) as a "feeding-in or pouring-in" process. The use of basic color words is suggested as a beginning point, and two-inch, solid color blocks are used. Red, blue, and yellow are taught first. The color name is given again and again. "This is red, red. See, it's the same as your tie, red. Let's find something else red." The teacher encourages eye-to-eye contact, sits very close to the child in order to focus his visual attention, and uses a hearing tube to focus his auditory attention. The teacher speaks in a low, clear voice, using much repetition, until the child is able to respond by pointing to the correct block. After several colors have been taught, the teacher removes the visual clue by seating herself behind the child, who must now listen attentively to the auditory stimulus. If the child who has difficulty with auditory patterns is at least five years old, the printed form of the word may be given. However, if the child's behavior appears disturbed, caution must be exercised in using the multisensory approach. In this event, the auditory channel should be emphasized. Toy furniture and figures are presented with much conversation regarding their use. These activities are repeated until the child knows the names of a great many things. Action words are then introduced, with prepositional phrases following these. No expressive language is demanded of the child during this training, though. Most likely the child will begin to imitate spontaneously.

In expressive language training, "any vocalizations that are meaningful to the child are accepted by the teacher and are used as a basis of communication" (Barry, 1961, p. 53). Nouns, verbs, and prepositions are presented in the same order as for receptive language. The pronoun "I" is encouraged early and the child is helped to relate his experiences. "What did you do?" "What is this?" "Where is Mommy?" Speech is encouraged and corrections are made casually. As the child progresses, more parts of speech are used. For structure, the Fitzgerald Key is used and accuracy is demanded. Words that have been learned are kept on charts according to "who," "where," "what," "what color," and "how many." These charts are used for reference by the children learning to read and write.

The aphasic child's difficulty in learning to read is part of his general impairment in perception and behavior. Many of the techniques mentioned previously as training for impaired functions are devices used in reading readiness programs. Many of the approaches used in remedial reading programs are adaptable in teaching reading to aphasic children.

In teaching writing, the child first must be proficient in the handling of crayons and pencils. Specially lined paper is used and there is much structuring in all his writing. The child is required to follow dots and to stay within limits. For beginning writing, boxes for each letter may be added to the lined paper. Manuscript is used and cursive writing is not introduced until the child is ready for the adjustment required.

Number concepts are taught in about the same manner as they are taught to a normal child; however, it takes the aphasic child longer to master each step, so more practice is given. Concrete materials are used extensively. Individual bead boards are used so that the child can touch each bead as he counts. The child learns the written symbol and the printed form of the number words and then matches these with the configuration.

The key word in Barry's corrective therapy is "structuring," which means putting things in order, teaching limits and sequence, clarifying, simplifying, concretizing, bringing the foreground sharply into focus, and blocking out nonessentials. Structuring is the performance of a simple activity in deliberate, sequential steps in response to deliberate, sequential commands, and it involves using every technique, device, or trick that will help the child to hear, see, and understand better. Since Barry employs structuring primarily as a device to facilitate the development of language in children who generally experience deficits in that ability, her system is discussed along with the system of McGinnis.

Mildred A. McGinnis

McGinnis taught elementary school for several years and in 1916 joined the staff at Central Institute for the Deaf in St. Louis, Missouri. Two years later she was named Director of the Speech and Correction Division and held that post until she retired in 1963. She was awarded a Fulbright grant to lecture in countries around the world in 1964, one of many lecture tours she made. After McGinnis' death, Silverman (1967) wrote "Courage, staying power and salty Hibernian wit are all part of her rich legacy to CID. But the heart of the legacy is her persistent commitment to the task of bringing the precious skill of communication by speech to whom nature denied it. . . ."

McGinnis (1964) reports that there are nonlanguage children with multiple handicaps who respond adequately to the Association Method, if the primary problem is aphasia. The child who is predominantly aphasic, but who also has a hearing loss, for example, does not learn effectively by educational methods for the deaf. Similarly, the child whose predominant problem is severe emotional disturbance, and whose secondary problem is aphasia, does not respond adequately to the Association Method until the emotional disturbance has been resolved, in part or wholly.

McGinnis (1963) referred to language-delayed children as types of aphasics; namely, expressive or motor aphasics, and receptive or sensory aphasics. The children with expressive or motor aphasia are those with combinations of motor aphasia and normal intelligence, motor aphasia and above normal intelligence, motor aphasia and mild mental retardation, motor aphasia and secondary cerebral palsy and retardation. The second type of child McGinnis refers to is the sensory aphasic who responds well to the Association Method. These children she described as having predominantly sensory aphasia with scribble speech, scribble speech with intelligible words, sensory aphasia and echolalia, and the silent child.

Prall (1964) reports that the role of aphasia in childhood psychosis and autism was little appreciated until McGinnis and others began working in the field of aphasia. In childhood psychosis one of the primary symptoms is lack of speech development; it is important, therefore, to have a clear differential diagnosis and an appropriate method to help the child acquire language in order to help him with his secondary problems.

McGinnis (1963) reports that the method used in teaching aphasic children is called the Association Method because it develops and associates systematically each of the several specific skills that must be coordinated for the development of ability to understand and to use oral communication. The development and organization of the sequence of steps and procedures which constitute the Association Method were completed shortly after World War I and have been applied in the teaching of aphasic children at Central Institute for the Deaf in St. Louis since that time.

There are six essential differences between the Association Method and the approach commonly used with deaf children:

1. There is no formal lipreading of what the child cannot say.
2. There are no voice-building exercises disassociated with words.
3. Nouns are presented sound by sound in the initial stages.
4. The written form accompanies every sound that is taught.
5. The acoustic and lipreading steps are given after, not before, the child can say the nouns and associate them with the objects they symbolize.
6. When sounds and nouns are learned, recall is expected without constant prompting by the teacher.

The educational objective is to prepare aphasic children for entrance into regular schools as near their appropriate age and grade level as possible. Although the Association Method emphasizes the development of speech and language, the over-all program provides for teaching academic subjects as well.

The method initially stresses the mechanics of speech more than the ideas to be expressed or understood through spoken language. McGinnis' observations of the children classified as receptive aphasics lead her to believe that their problem is more an inability to communicate verbally about their daily experiences than a lack of understanding of their experiences. Therefore, the Association Method's approach to teaching emphasizes the development of skill in the use of the tools of communication enabling the child to speak about his experiences and to interpret the speech of others.

McGinnis utilizes the simple-to-complex approach in teaching speech and language to the child. Simple speech acts are taught first and then combined and built into acts requiring more complex expression and understanding. The Association Method is based upon five major principles:

1. Words are taught by a phonetic or elemental approach.
2. Each sound is learned through emphasis on precise articulation production.
3. The correct articulation of each sound is associated with its corresponding letter-symbol written in cursive script.
4. Expression is used as the foundation or starting point in building language.
5. Systematic sensorimotor association is utilized.

The child in therapy is first taught to produce each sound and to associate it with the written letter-symbol for the sound. Sounds are taught using the Northampton-Yale sound designations. Supporters of the Association Method believe it is easier to hold a child's attention on an individual speech sound than on sentences, phrases, or words. The child has a much simpler task upon which to concentrate when learning to produce single sounds and is able to achieve some success, which helps to motivate him to continue trying for speech and language improvement. By teaching the child how to produce a sound accurately and by providing the sound's corresponding visual symbol, a frame of reference is established for the child which he can use in the retention and recall of the language he is being taught. The later associations of speaking and writing (expressive skills) with reading, lipreading, and hearing (receptive skills) are built on the initial association of articulation placement and letter symbols.

Before sound combinations are made, formulating a complete word, the child says each sound in the word separately. At this stage it is important to teach the child to produce sequences of sounds which make up words. At first, the child's speech will appear rather stilted; however, after time and practice, smooth articulation occurs without the loss of accuracy in the production of individual speech sounds. Mc-Ginnis stresses that production of words precedes any attempt to establish recognition of the meanings of words.

She states that the child with receptive aphasia is not expected to understand any word until he has first produced the word for himself (McGinnis, Kleffner, & Goldstein, 1956). As the child progresses from learning of single speech units (sounds) to more complex speech units (words), the principle of systematic association of motor skills and capacities is more fully utilized. This principle can best be illustrated by the advocated method of teaching nouns in the following sequential steps:

1. The child looks at the written noun word and produces each sound contained in the word in the sequence in which it is written.
2. The child matches the *picture* or the *object* represented by this word to the written form of the word.
3. The technique of simultaneous talking and writing is employed as the child writes the word and articulates each sound as he writes the letter(s) for it.
4. After the teacher says the word aloud (first broken into sequence of separate sounds and then blended into a word unit), the child repeats the same procedure and then matches the *object* or *picture* to the written form of the word. This process is repeated three times by the child:
   a. After the teacher says the word.
   b. As he identifies the picture or object named by the word.
   c. As he identifies the written form of the word.
5. The teacher presents pictures representing the nouns already taught, and the child must say the name of the object from memory without the aid of lipreading, auditory stimulus, or written form.

Not all of the vocabulary and language the child learns must be taught in a formal manner. Once he has gained some skill in the use of language, he develops increasing ability to acquire new vocabulary and language in an incidental fashion.

There are primarily two types of programs representing the basic language and speech curriculum the child is expected to complete over a period of time—the vertical and horizontal programs. The vertical program represents the total sequence of items that a child will be expected to learn. The horizontal program represents the daily class program and consists of items from the vertical program.

Vertical Program.

1. Contains the sequence of items to be taught.

2. Is divided into three units of language in which progress is measured not by grades but by language units.

3. Before advancement from one unit to the next, the child must be proficient at using independently all structured language forms within the unit presently under study.

Horizontal Program.

1. Consists of items taken from the vertical program carried out in a daily program in the classroom.

2. Items are presented early in the program and then discontinued after having been mastered by the child.

3. The teacher concentrates on those items in which the child needs the most attention; included should be items necessary to prepare the child for grade work in geography, arithmetic, and other subjects.

In addition to the two basic language programs, correlative programs are employed to reinforce material previously presented. The correlative programs consist of:

1. Attention-getting exercises.

2. Exercises leading to writing.

3. General tongue exercises, which are gradually replaced by specific exercises for the development of individual speech sounds.

4. Number work.

5. Multiplication tables.

6. Calendar work.

7. Specific and special teaching approaches for the motor aphasic child.

McGinnis' training manual (1963) is thorough and presents a concise and detailed description of the method and how it should be implemented. There are many useful and important teaching techniques that could be applied in one way or another to all children having language difficulties.

In the manual, McGinnis states that there are several stages or levels a child must complete if the program is to be considered successful. The initial step is the presentation of Attention Activities. The aim of these activities is to teach habits of attention and exact response, and to train the children to do independent seatwork, which replaces free play periods as the program progresses. The attention-getting exercises are first presented to the group, with each child performing individually while his classmates observe.

The second level of the program is synonymous with the vertical program and is comprised of three language units. The child must learn all the language forms in one unit and be able to use them independently before he can move on to the next unit.

First Unit of Language

In the first language unit the child begins to take the first steps in the acquisition of oral language. Formal teaching is directed toward the child's learning 50 nouns. At the same time other activities help prepare the child for orderly learning and memory.

Interspersed with formal instruction on individual sound production are short play periods. These periods help the child adjust during his first few weeks in school and also help him to distinguish between work and play. Attention-getting exercises are used with the instruction to help the child learn to concentrate. Drawing strings on balloons and imitating tongue movements are some of the exercises that are suggested.

The teacher writes each child's name on a card and then assists the child in learning to respond to his name. Simple commands necessary for class management are placed on a chart, and the child is again taught to respond.

Individual sounds are developed by articulation practice and association with the written symbols on the checkboard. Beginning books are made for each child to keep a record of the sounds learned. Cross-drills and practice in lipreading and acoustic association add further to the child's sound development.

When nouns are introduced the same procedures used for individual sound development are followed. For further clarification, pictures and objects are used along with strip charts on which the nouns that have been taught are recorded. When the proper number of nouns are learned, the child is ready for the second unit of language. The following activities comprise the first language unit:

1. Attention-getting exercises.
2. Single sound development.
3. The combination of sounds into nouns.
4. The association of meaning with nouns.
5. Writing-readiness exercises and writing of nouns.
6. Lipreading and auditory training with individual sounds and then in word combinations as nouns.
7. Association of the meaning of commands that relate to daily class routine from both written and oral stimulation.

Second Unit of Language

In the second unit, the teaching of language is begun. Simple sentences are introduced and a question chart is made. Articles and pronouns are presented. Animal stories are developed by the class through the gradual addition of descriptive sentences. Through use of animal stories, new vocabulary is introduced, memory span is increased, and numbers and adjectives are introduced.

Personal description stories are developed. Prepositions are taught using concrete examples, first with pictures, then with actual objects. Teaching the present progressive of verbs is begun by writing a sentence describing an action. The child then reads and copies the sentence until he has mastered articulation and memory of sentence structure.

The second unit progresses through the following steps:

1. Simple sentences are introduced:
   a. I see——.
   b. This is——.
   c. I want ——.
   With the exception of the pronoun *I*, capital letters are not used at this time. The articles *a* and *an* and the adjective *some* are added to the nouns.
2. Questions are introduced after each sentence is taught. A basic question chart is made using the following questions:
   a. What do you see?
   b. What is this?
   c. What do you want?
3. The pronoun *my* is introduced with the question, "Who is this?" when the child is asked about pictures of parents and siblings.
4. Description stories describing animals and requiring the memory of four sentences are introduced at this point. After description stories progress to eight sentences, the teacher includes descriptions of inanimate objects such as toys, bicycles, cars. Description stories serve as a teaching experience for the development of new vocabulary, adjectives, and number concepts. New nouns and adjectives are recorded on strip charts and the noun chart should record both the singular and plural form.
5. Numbers are introduced as the first description stories about animals are begun. A number chart is made and addition facts are begun. The question, "How many —— has a ——?" is added to the question chart. Characteristics of animals promote the question, "Can a —— fly, swim, climb, etc.?" which is added to the chart.
6. Having the children describe one another provides a medium for teaching the uses and concepts of the pronouns *he, she, his, her,* and *your*. These pronouns are not recorded on a chart.

7. The prepositions *in, on,* and *under* are introduced by the question "Where is ——?" This question is added to the chart.
8. No new language concepts are taught at this stage. Round-up stories are used, and the teacher "rounds up" all the language concepts the children have learned and applies them to the description of pictures. Pictures of rooms, places, and scenes may be used in this exercise.
9. The cross-drill is continued. New vocabulary is taught by writing the new words and then asking the child to pronounce each individual sound and blend the sounds into syllables.
10. The present progressive form of verbs is introduced. Pictures portraying activities of the action verbs are used in teaching this verb form. The question, "What is the —— doing?" is added to the chart.
11. The preceding program is supplemented by the introduction of incidental language. The children learn to say the commands recorded on the chart when they are conducting a lesson, and to make oral requests that have been recorded on the chart.
12. Calendar work is begun.

THIRD UNIT OF LANGUAGE

After the development of language concepts on a concrete level in Units One and Two, Language Unit Three introduces concepts of tense and language forms that are more complex. The items taught in this unit are presented in the following sequence:

1. The past tense of the verb is taught and verb charts are made.
2. Partitives are taught.
3. The past tense of the verb is applied to events other than those occurring in the classroom.
4. Experience stories are developed.
5. Imagination stories are developed.
6. The future tense is introduced.
7. The use of textbooks is begun.
8. Comparisons, categories, and materials are introduced.
9. Language forms as suggested in textbooks are developed.
10. Idioms are explained and direct and indirect conversation is taught.

When the child has completed the third unit of language, he may be ready for regular class placement. His future educational program should be determined, however, by a team comprised of the teacher, the psychoeducational diagnosticians, medical personnel, and the child's parents. Since the child usually will have a residue of language confusion, he undoubtedly will need clinical assistance during the transition period from the special program to the regular classroom.

The approach taken by McGinnis is essentially the same for children who have receptive, expresssive, or mixed language disorders. The key word in the preceding statement probably is language, and the children best able to benefit from the Association Method are those who are delayed in the acquisition and development of vocal language skills, whether the skills be receptive or expressive. Such children would have difficulty with the graphic symbol system but their overriding disabilities are in the auditory-vocal areas, inability to comprehend oral language, poor understanding of the language code, deficits in the ability to associate input signals with appropriate output patterns, and an inability to formulate and express intentions or ideas in vocal language.

Conclusion

In the chapter dealing with language systems the methods and techniques devised and developed by Myklebust, Barry and McGinnis have been explored. The discussion of Barry preceded that of McGinnis as vocal language precedes graphic language and Barry's procedures, by and large, do not include suggestions for the formal teaching of reading, spelling, and arithmetic. McGinnis' methods are more suitable than Barry's for the older, school-aged child; Barry's are geared more toward very young or quite severely involved older children.

References

Barry, H. Classes for aphasics. In M. E. Frampton & E. D. Gall. Vol. II. *The physically handicapped and special health problems.* Boston: Sargent, 1955. P. 362–367.

———. Training the young aphasic child. *Volta Review,* 1960, 7, 362–328.

———. *The young aphasic child, evaluation and training.* Washington, D.C.: Alexander Graham Bell Association for the deaf, 1961.

Boshes, B., & Myklebust, H. R. Neurological behavioral study of children with learning disorders. *Neurology,* 1964, 14, 7–12.

Johnson, D., & Myklebust, H. R. *Learning disabilities: Educational principles and practices.* New York: Grune & Stratton, 1967.

McGinnis, M. A. *Aphasic children.* Washington, D.C.: Volta Bureau, 1963.

———. In S. Rappaport, *Childhood aphasia and brain damage.* Narberth, Pa.: Livingston, 1964.

———, Kleffner, F. R., & Goldstein, R. Teaching aphasic children. *Volta Review,* 1956, 7, 239–244.

Myklebust, H. R. Remedial reading for children with impaired hearing. *Training School Bulletin,* 1947, **43**, 170–176.

———. Aphasia in childhood. *Journal of Exceptional Children,* 1952, **19**, 9–14.

———. *Auditory disorders in children.* New York: Grune & Stratton. 1954.

———. Training aphasic children. *The Volta Review,* 1955, **57**, 149–157.

———. Aphasia in children. In L. Travis (Ed.), *Handbook of speech pathology.* New York: Appleton-Century-Crofts, 1957. Pp. 503–530. (a)

———. Babbling and echolalia in language theory. *Journal of Speech and Hearing Disorders,* 1957, **22**, 356–360. (b)

———. *The psychology of deafness.* New York: Grune & Stratton, 1960.

———. Learning disorders: Psychoneurological disturbances in childhood. *Rehabilitation Literature,* 1964, **25**, 354–359.

———. *Development and disorders of written language.* Vol. 1. New York: Grune & Stratton, 1965.

———. Learning disabilities: Definition and overview. In H. R. Myklebust (Ed.), *Progress in Learning Disabilities.* Vol. I. New York: Grune & Stratton, 1968. Pp. 1–15.

———, & Boshes, B. Psychoneurological learning disorders in children. *Archives of Pediatrics,* 1960, **77**, 247–256.

Piaget, J. How children form mathematical concepts. *Scientific American,* 1953, 185(5), 74–79.

Prall, R. C. In S. Rappaport, *Childhood aphasia and brain damage.* Narberth, Pa.: Livingston, 1964.

Silverman, S. R. Editorial in *News Notes.* Central Institute for the Deaf. Saint Louis, Mo.: Spring, 1967. School newspaper obtained from Central Institute in Saint Louis, Mo.

CHAPTER VII

THE PHONIC SYSTEMS

The teaching methods characterized as phonic systems include the instructional programs developed by Gillingham and Stillman (1965) and Spalding (1957) and are termed auditory due to the emphasis placed upon the teaching of sound-letter associations. The systems' reliance primarily upon the auditory modality does not mean that no other sensory channels are employed, for this is not necessarily true. We have classified these two methods as phonic simply to emphasize the primary reliance upon the auditory input mode which characterizes the methods in contrast to, for example, the method devised by McGinnis (1963), which incorporates at all times *meaningful* visual clues.

The methods of Gillingham and Stillman and of Spalding are most efficacious when used with children who fail to learn to read because of inadequate *visual* modalities; children with poor auditory discrimination and comprehension are penalized unduly when taught through these approaches. The following case history illustrates the type of child who often makes unexpectedly rapid gains when taught with a phonic approach.

S. T., age 8-5 years, was referred by the neurologist because of persistent severe reading and spelling difficulties. He was in the third grade and was receiving remedial reading (of an unspecified nature). Reversals in reading and spelling were reported by his teacher along with poor word memory. S. T.'s developmental and medical histories were unremarkable although his father was reported as being a "slow reader."

Results of the psychological evaluation indicated that S. T. was within the bright-normal range of intelligence. The only problem apparent on the tests was on the WISC Block Design where he tended to reverse the order of stimuli presented and become confused. His Bender protocol was slightly below average but, in the main, adequate. His articulation and hearing were within normal limits, as were his vocabulary comprehension, sentence length and syntax, and speech-sound discrimination. The language evaluation revealed deficits in the Visual-Motor Association and Visual-Motor Sequencing subtests of the ITPA, although visual tests at the representational level were performed adequately. It was found that S. T. was reading and spelling at the first-grade level and that his sound-letter associations were fairly good. He was unable, however, to use a systematic phonics approach to reading or spelling.

Because it appeared that the auditory-vocal channel was S. T.'s best modality for learning and because he did not exhibit severe problems in elementary visual perception, he was enrolled in a Gillingham-type remedial reading program. At the end of two years of therapy S. T. was dismissed from the program. His reading level and comprehension were at the sixth-grade level and no further need for therapy was evident.

Children like S. T. exemplify the cases of reading disability referred to by Myklebust as "visual dyslexia." Their auditory processes are intact and they exhibit few visual discrimination problems when presented with meaningful material. Their ability to recall visual images, however, is poor, particularly when stimuli are nonmeaningful. A review of the work of Orton (1929, 1937, 1939), upon whose hypotheses Gillingham and Spalding base their systems, will provide further insight into the type of learning disability best ameliorated through the phonic systems.

Samuel Torrey Orton

Orton, a neuropathologist, studied the effects of brain injury on language function in adults and applied his findings to the study of developmental language disorders occurring in children. He described a specific reading disability which may be present in a child and which is not commensurate with the child's intelligence, commonly normal or above, or with his visual and auditory acuity, generally adequate. The reading disability, however, is often accompanied by very poor auditory and visual memory, characteristics found common to children with any of the developmental language disorders (Orton, 1937). Symptoms displayed by the group of reading disabled children studied by Orton are:

1. Confusion of lower-case letters.
2. Uncertainty in reading short palindromical words such as saw and was.
3. Tendency to reverse parts of words or whole syllables.
4. Greater facility than usual in reading from the mirror, and frequently a facility in producing mirror writing (1929, p. 140).

The remainder of this section is concerned with a discussion of Orton's theory of the genesis of developmental language disorders, particularly the specific disorder of alexia, which he refers to also as congenital word blindness, strephosymbolia, and specific reading disability. Other points of discussion are findings of recent research in the area of cerebral dominance and a description of the basic principles of remediation.

In 1861, Broca, a French surgeon, performed an autopsy on a patient who had lost the ability to speak. It was found that the man had sustained brain damage to the third frontal convolution of the left hemisphere (Eisenson, Auer, & Irwin, 1963). This finding and all of the subsequent work of other investigators with adult asphasics led Orton to a basic principle:

[I]n the two faculties whence man's superiority derives speech and manual dexterity—a highly novel physiological pattern has been evolved in the brain whereby the functional control of these faculties is restricted sharply to one of the two cerebral hemispheres (Orton, 1937, p. 27).

In other words, it is normal for all of the language processes to be the function of one side of the brain and for this side to be dominant also for manual skills. This theory of contralateral control of language was first stated by Broca and Bouillaud in France. Orton (1937) further explains the relationship of the particular areas of damage to the resulting disability; acquired alexia apparently results from injury to the angular gyrus and its immediate environs. It should be noted that Orton cannot be thought of as a strict localizationist, for he states that reading is a complex activity involving several areas of the brain.

From his work with brain-damaged adults, Orton attempted to explain the occurrence of language disabilities in children who had not suffered brain injury yet displayed symptoms similar to those exhibited by the adults who had sustained language loss. Orton's hypothesis is that children who do not establish hemispheric dominance in particular areas of the brain display specific developmental language disabilities such as reading disability.

The children having specific reading disabilities who were examined by Orton often displayed what he termed "motor intergrading," that is, mixtures of left and right sidedness in handedness, eyedness, and footedness. Though some children showed definite laterality for one side or another, they were for the most part "intergrates" (Orton, 1937). He suggests that if these symptoms of mixed or confused dominance are seen in the motor areas, then a comparable mixing may occur also in the language areas of the brain. How does this mixed dominance occur? Orton (1937) states that, while there is no direct evidence, dominance is due to "transmission of a better brain structure" (p. 155). This quality of being "better" is not due to size and "is probably dependent more on numbers of nerve cells, richness of their interconnections and abundance of blood supply" (p. 156). He further contends that such superiority may be transmitted to one complete hemisphere, to one or more areas of one hemisphere, or to the cortex of one hemisphere and to other areas of the other hemisphere "leading to difficulty in establishing a complete unilateral superiority in function or a use" (p. 156). Possible support for this hereditary transmission, according to Orton, is that there will often be familial history of similar reading problems.

The symptoms of alexic children listed earlier are explained by Orton on the basis of mixed dominance. Reversals and mirror reading occur because when records of the associations of written words and their meaning are stored in the dominant hemisphere, mirrored copies are stored in the nondominant hemisphere. "If then these opposite engrams are not elided through establishment of consistent selection from one hemisphere, we would expect . . . errors or confusion in direction" (Orton, 1929, p. 140).

Orton's theory of the dominant hemisphere being opposite the preferred hand seems to be generally opposed today. A study by Quadfasel and Goodglass reported by Osgood and Miron (1963) states that on the basis of research, "more than 50 per cent of left handers have speech representation in the left hemisphere and that speech representation in the right hemisphere in right handers is extremely rare" (p. 50). Eisenson, Auer, and Irwin (1963) support this statement with the report that evidence which has been collected in the United States and other countries indicates that the left hemisphere is dominant in the control of language function no matter which hand is preferred, and that language and handedness are independent. On the basis of their studies of electrical interference in the brain, Penfield and Roberts (1959) support the same conclusion, as do Russell and Espir (1961).

Localization of language function may also be open to question in the light of recent findings, the most striking of which is reported by Eisenson (1957). Mettler and associates, a group of neurologists, psychiatrists, psychologists, and neurophysiologists, found that in two cases of bilateral removal of Broca's area no aphasia occurred. In fact, one of the patients who had been mute prior to the operation began to speak fluently. Eisenson, Auer, and Irwin (1963) report that although differing opinions are found on this subject, it is generally accepted that language functions cannot be localized.

Another aspect of cerebral functioning is the mission of the nondominant hemisphere. Orton holds that records of mirrored engrams are stored there. Eisenson, Auer, and Irwin (1963) feel that the nondominant hemisphere plays a generalized, although nonetheless important role in cerebral functioning. These authors also quote Weisenburg and Mc-Bride, who observe that "the nondominant hemisphere is apparently concerned with normal language function but to a limited degree" (p. 453). Also discussed is research by Weisenburg in which it was found that damage to the right hemisphere sometimes causes impairment of the quality of language, for example, sentence quality and use of abstract language. Hughlings Jackson, as reported by Eisenson (1957), is of the opinion that the function of the nondominant hemisphere is the affective aspects of language and the lower language functions, for example, serial speech, singing, and memorized repetition. Goldstein is reported to believe that when the child is one or two years old both sides of the brain are equally important in functioning. Later one side becomes dominant and higher mental functions are related to it. The nondominant hemisphere does not lose all of its functions to the dominant one; the differences in function are quantitative rather than qualitative.

Although it appears that Orton's underlying theory for explaining reading disabilities is open to question, consideration should be given to the principles of remediation which arise from it.

Orton experimented in the treatment for language disorders with almost 1000 cases in a 10-year period from 1927 to 1936. Alexic children from kindergarten to college were studied and all types of private, public, and parochial schools were employed. He discovered first that these children had been exposed to the sight-word method in attempting to learn to read. Basing his conclusions on the failure of this method and his theory of mirrored engrams, Orton says that this method must be avoided. In the more detailed book by Gillingham and Stillman, it is recommended that the child be removed from the class during all reading and spelling lessons because the methods by which they should be taught are so opposed to the ones ordinarily used in the classroom.

Second, because it was found that these children are able to remember spoken words, Orton states that their auditory avenues should be capitalized and that a phonetic approach to teaching reading should be employed. The method of choice is explained in detail by Gillingham and Stillman (1965). The sound equivalents for each of the letters are taught; then the most important step is begun—the sounds are blended into words. Blending is important because of the reversal problems which plague these children. In addition the kinesthetic avenue is employed in tracing to help erase reversals and to maintain left to right progression. Sound and movement are linked by simultaneous speaking and writing.

Third, because the reading problem is usually seen in connection with spelling problems, it is necessary also to establish associations between the sound and the letter, so that given the sound the child can produce the letter. Also of importance is auditory analysis of written words because visual recall is so poor. Fine discrimination of sound is stressed.

In defense of his theory, Orton (1939) suggests the following:

1. The theory helps to explain why problems so often are compound, for example, reading, writing, and spelling disabilities all in the same child. These multiple problems occur because they all have the same physiological basis. Such an explanation to the child, his parents, and his teachers will greatly reduce frustrations; the problem is not due to the child's laziness.

2. The theory offers a suggestion as to what direction treatment should take. Reversals in eye movements may be only a secondary symptom of the larger underlying problem of mixed dominance, and so should not be treated.

Although Orton's basis may be subject to criticism, his stress upon individuality is a saving point. As he states: "We have tried to avoid overstandardization lest the procedure become too inflexible and be looked upon as a routine method applicable to all cases of nonreaders" (1937, p. 161).

Anna Gillingham

With her friend Bessie Stillman, Anna Gillingham taught at the Ethical Culture Schools in New York City. She served as mathematics teacher, principal of the Open Air Department, and—in the 1920s—school psychologist, one of the first so designated in this country. She participated in the first use of the Binet intelligence scale for the identification of gifted children.

Growing aware of bright children with reading and related language problems, Gillingham took a leave of absence from the Ethical Culture Schools to become a Research Fellow under Orton at the Neurological Institute, Columbia-Presbyterian Medical Center, New York. She worked closely with Orton and Stillman to devise and refine teaching techniques for children with specific language disabilities.

In 1936 Gillingham and Stillman went to the Punahou Elementary School in Honolulu, Hawaii, to set up and put into operation their program. Other schools became interested and many established similar programs. Both women returned to New York, where they continued to work together until Stillman's death in 1947. Gillingham visited schools to observe and supervise her method and saw her work spread. She revised her training manual several times (it is presently in its seventh edition) and remained actively involved in her work until 1960 when almost total blindness curtailed her activities. She died in 1964.

Gillingham and Stillman base their work upon Orton's theory of incomplete hemispheric dominance as discussed in the preceding section. They state:

> Orton believed that records on that side of the brain not usually in control of language—records usually ignored—are always present and may sometimes assert themselves. Records made on the two hemispheres, according to him, are in reverse pattern, and so the obtrusion of one from the wrong side would account for the "reversals"; collision of two from opposite sides would produce complete confusion (1946, p. 16).

Gillingham reports that such reversals and confusions frequently are seen as characteristics of children who exhibit specific learning disabilities and cites examples:

> In the visual field, for example, the word *go* may be read *og*, *was* may be called *saw*. A well-educated woman glanced at eat and read it tea. In the auditory field one may hear loop called pool. A five-year-old, driving by a pasture in which were black-and-white cattle, remarked, "Those are Steinhols." A little boy wearied with a prolonged ordeal asked querulously, "How last will it long, Daddy?" In the kinesthetic field the same cause probably underlies the much-talked-of-mirror writing (1946, p. 16).

She explains this phenomenon, as would Orton, by saying that the evolution or development of the language function has not achieved completion and is still subject to variations. "The degree to which the language function of an individual is controlled by one hemisphere determines the degree of language or disability in that individual" (p. 16).

The Gillingham method is geared toward those children in the third through sixth grades who:

1. Are of normal or superior intelligence.
2. Have normal sensory acuity (visual and auditory).
3. Have the tendency to reverse letters or words and to mirror write.
4. Have difficulty in pronunciation.
5. Have been unable to acquire reading and spelling skills by "ordinary school methods," that is, "sight word methods, even when these are later reinforced by functional, incidental, intrinsic, or analytical phonics, or by tracing procedures" (p. 17).

In contrast to sight-word procedures in which words are first recognized by the child as ideograms and then broken down by the teacher into letter sounds through functional phonics, Gillingham's Alphabetic Approach proceeds from teaching the sounds of the letters to building these letter sounds into words, like "bricks in a wall." The technique aims to establish close associations between visual, auditory, and kinesthetic records in the brain.

In order to use the technique effectively, Gillingham emphatically stresses two points:

1. The remedial pupil should do no reading or spelling except with the remedial teacher. His schedule should insure that he be out of the classroom when his class is having reading and spelling.
2. The steps of the procedure should be followed rigidly, since they are a "series of logical sequences, the omission of any one of which will jeopardize the complete success of the precedure" (p. 42). To use the technique effectively, she stresses that one must "begin at the beginning" (p. 45).

Gillingham's (1946) approach makes use of six basic combinations of the visual, auditory, and kinesthetic modalities. Although she recommends occasional use of tactile stimuli through finger-tracing, the procedure is not necessary to her word-learning program. Tracing, as she incorporates it, involves kinesthetic rather than tactile stimuli. The six basic patterns for integration of fundamental associations are these:

V-A   Translation of visual symbols into sound, vocalized or not.
A-V   Translation of auditory symbols into visual image.
A-K   Translation of auditory symbols into muscle response, for speech and writing.

K-A Movement of a passive hand by another to produce a letter form, in order to lead to the naming or sounding of the letter.

V-K Translation of visual symbol into muscular action of speech and writing.

K-V The muscular "feel" of the speaking or writing of a letter, in order to lead to association with the appearance of that letter.

Gillingham's methods for effecting the associations mentioned above involve the use of very specific materials and techniques, as well as the dedication of a skillful teacher whose background includes several years of successful classroom experience, thorough familiarity with English phonics (plus—by inference—speech production understanding), and an awareness of the neurological hypotheses of Orton. Her guide (which first appeared in 1934) is thoroughly detailed and divides the instructional program into three sections:

1. General preparation of the child before the actual program is begun. The evolution of written language is explained, as also are the reasons for which the child is having difficulty with reading and spelling.

2. Reading and Spelling with Phonetic Words.

3. Words Phonetic for reading but not for spelling.

READING AND SPELLING WITH PHONIC WORDS

The sequence followed in this section is that of introduction of letters, words, and sentences.

Letters. Each new phonogram is introduced by a key word and is taught by the following processes, which involve the visual, auditory, and kinesthetic linkages.

Association I. This association consists of two parts—association of the visual symbol with the name of the letter, and association of the visual symbol with the sound of the letter: also the association of the feel of the child's speech organs in producing the name of sound of the letter as he hears himself say it. Association I is V-A and A-K. Part b. is the basis of oral reading.

Part a. The card is exposed and the name of the letter spoken by the teacher and repeated by the pupil.

Part b. As soon as the name has been really mastered, the sound is made by the teacher and repeated by the pupil. It is here that most emphasis must be placed if the case is primarily one of speech defect. The card is exposed, the implied question being, "What does this letter (or phonogram) say?" and the pupil gives its sound.

Association II. The teacher makes the sound represented by the letter (or phonogram), the face of the card not being seen by the pupil, and says "Tell me the name of the letter that has this sound." Sound to name is A-A, and is essentially oral spelling.

Association III. The letter is carefully made by the teacher and then its form, orientation, etc., explained. It is then traced by the pupil over the teacher's lines, then copied, written from memory, and finally written again with eyes averted while the teacher watches closely. This association is V-K and K-V. Now, the teacher makes the sound, saying, "Write the letter that has this sound." This association is A-K and is the basis of written spelling. . . . Before the child is asked to write there must be whatever practice is necessary in tracing, copying, and writing from memory to dictation, this last being sometimes carried out with the child's eyes averted. Except in tracing and copying, the teacher dictates the name of the phonogram. In all instances the child says the name of each letter as he writes it. This is called "S.O.S. (Simultaneous Oral Spelling)" (Gillingham & Stillman, 1946, p. 41).

1. Drill Cards. Consonants are printed on white cards and the vowels are printed on salmon-colored cards in order to facilitate recognition of distinction between vowel and consonant sounds. Drills with the preceding associations are continued in almost daily practice.

2. First Group of Letters. These first phonograms are taught as having only one sound:

a	apple	j	jam
b	boy	k	kite
f	fun	m	man
h	hat	p	pan
i	it	t	top

Words. After the ten letters in the first group of phonograms are fairly well known with all associations, blending them together into words is begun. Words such as the following are printed on small yellow cards and placed in the child's box of phonetic words: hat, bat, mat, him, tap, at, mat, hip, if, fat, hit, Jim, bib, pat, pit, bit, fib, kit, jab, it.

1. Reading. First certain Drill Cards that form a word are laid out on the table. The pupil is asked to give in succession the sounds of these letters, repeating the series of sounds again and again with increasing speed and smoothness; if necessary, he is helped to recognize the word he is saying. Then the yellow word cards are exposed one by one by the teacher and read as rapidly as possible by the pupil. Those cards read correctly are laid in one pile, and those read incorrectly

in another. However, no attempt for correction or self-correction is made at this point.

2. Spelling. A few days after blending is begun, the analysis of words into their component sounds is initiated. The procedure followed is referred to as the "Four-Point-Program":

The teacher says a word, then says the word again very slowly, sound by sound. As the child recognizes each sound, its corresponding letter is placed on the table until the word is completed. The teacher says the word again. After the teacher pronounces the word, the child (1) repeats it, (2) names the letters, (3) writes, naming each letter as he forms it, (4) reads the word he has written. At this point, it should become routine to have the child correct his own reading and spelling errors.

After spelling is begun, the following program for daily lessons is suggested:

Association I—All white and salmon cards so far taught.
Practice in Association II for these same phonograms.
Practice in Association III for these same phonograms, sometimes traced, sometimes written to dictation, (sometimes with eyes averted), always S.O.S.
Drill words for reading.
Drill words for spelling and writing: Words are selected from the word box and the Four Point Program is followed, the point being to see how many words can be spelled in this way correctly in succession (Gillingham & Stillman, 1946, p. 54).

As the above daily program is continued, new letters are presented, one or two a day in the following order:

g	go	s	sat
o	olive	sh	ship
r	rat	d	dog
l	lamp	w	wind
n	nut	wh	whittle
th	this	y	yes
u	umbrella	v	van
ch	chin	z	zebra
e	elephant		

Words for each letter are added to the word box for Drill, and a reading graph is charted.

3. Spelling Rule I. After the preceding phonograms have been learned by the pupil, the following spelling rule is introduced: Words of one

syllable ending in f, 1, or s after one vowel usually end in double f, double 1, or double s. Words in which this rule is applied are written on yellow cards and placed in the word box. As soon as these words have become fairly familiar to the pupil, they are shuffled in with the other cards for reading, graphs, and the Four-Point Program.

Stories. After the pupil can read and write any phonetic three-letter word, words are combined into sentences and stories. Some of the stories are stapled into small books and other are printed on tag-board. The stories do not have for their purpose entertainment or literary content, but rather they are steps in the development of skill.

1. Reading Procedures. The pupil reads a sentence silently, and if he has difficulty with a particular word, he may ask for help, which usually consists of helping him sound out the word. When he is ready, the pupil reads the sentence out loud. All nonphonetic words in the story are supplied for the pupil by the teacher.

2. Dictation. The same stories are used as dictation exercises. Nonphonetic words (words underscored in the story) are written on paper and copied by the pupil. No word is repeated in the exercise, since one of the present goals is to increase the child's auditory span.

An example of Group I Stories containing unequivocal consonants, plain vowels, and Rule 1 is the following:

FAT SAM

Fat Sam has *a* bat.
Fat Sam at bat.
Fat Sam sat on *the* mat.
The rat sat on Sam.
Sam ran and *the* rat ran.
This *is Thin Ann.*
Fat Sam met *Thin Ann.*
The rat sat on *the* mat.

Sam hit *Ann.*
Then *Ann* hit Sam.
Sam ran *and Ann* ran.
Ann had a tan *mitten.*
Ann *lost* it.
This is Ann's tan *mitten.*
Sam got *the mitten.*
Sam *sent the mitten to Ann.*

(Gillingham & Stillman, 1946, p. 60).

3. Consonant Blends. Consonant blends are introduced at this point and words containing blends are shuffled into the pack of phonetic word for daily reading, frequent graphing, and for spelling in the Four Point Program. Group II stories containing previously learned phonograms, Rule 1, and consonant blends are then introduced.

4. Spelling Rule 2. After introduction of consonant blends, the following spelling rule is introduced: The sounds of all the vowels are changed by a silent e on the end of the word. The change in pronunciation is indicated by placing a bar over each of the words. Thus the long

vowels are introduced in this particular context. Words ending in silent e are typed in a long list of similar words and the pupil reads the list rapidly. They also are printed on yellow cards and shuffled in with the pack of phonetic words for reading and spelling. Group III stories containing previously learned phonograms, and rules, and words with the final e are introduced.

At this point in the program, the schedule of lesson topics consists of:

    a. Daily Review of Drill Cards.
    b. Graphing of Phonetic Words— probably once a week.
    c. Spelling—Four Point Program—twice a week.
    d. Dictation—twice a week.
    e. Reading whatever Little Stories are now available.

5. Syllable Concept. Drill cards, graphing of words read, spelling by the Four Point Program, and reading of Little Stories continue steadily in daily routine, in addition to exercises three or four times a week to develop the syllable concepts, as follows:

    a. The child is taught to recognize nonsense syllables which are printed on orange cards.
    b. The child is asked to read real words of more than one syllable printed with syllables apart.
    c. Words are typed with syllables for apart and these syllables are then cut out. Words are then built out of their component parts.

6. Accent. The pupil is required to place the accent on each syllable in succession and decide which trial produces a word he recognizes.

Words Phonetic for Reading but not for Spelling. Up to this time, words taught have been purely phonetic, that is, each phonogram has had only one sound and each sound has been represented by only one symbol. Only one possible pronunciation or spelling for the words has been given. Ambiguities in the English language are now introduced. With this introduction of ambiguity, the remedial teacher should give the pupil some understanding of the history of language growth and the fact that words change as they pass from country to country and from century to century.

"From the day when a second sound is introduced for a phonogram or a second spelling for a sound, there will be a radical change in procedure" (Gillingham & Stillman, 1946, p. 79). Association I with the white and salmon cards is constantly reviewed, new cards are added, and some of the familiar phonogram cards acquire new responses. Associations II and III are not applied to any of the new phonograms or responses, and none of the words following each phonogram is to be spelled. The practice words following the new phonograms are typed on blue cards. The Four Point Program for phonetic words should be continued every few days. Spelling of words containing phonograms for which more than one sound is possible is presented gradually as a thought process by means of the introduction of Rules and Generalizations. The pupil begins to keep a notebook divided into sections labeled: Tests; Rules; Generalizations; Learned Words; Dictation.

1. Tests
   a. Ordinary spelling tests: Words are pronounced by the teacher and written by the pupil in columns, S.O.S.
   b. Labeling tests: In a second column the pupil indicates the reason for spelling a word as he has written it by listing the corresponding rule or by indicating if the word is phonetic or a learned word.
2. Rules. Rules are gradually added to those previously taught. Each rule is developed, applied, and in time memorized.
3. Generalizations. Phonograms having the same sound are assembled.
4. Learned Words. Although there are very few words learned as ideograms, such words as the following are learned in this way: were, has, have, does, goes, come. They are studied by S.O.S and are recorded in the notebook as they are found essential in construction of Dictation exercises.
5. Dictation. All dictation exercises are filed under this section. The sequence of presentation is essentially the same as that of the previous section: presentation of letters, words, and practice in reading stories containing words in which previously presented phonograms are recognized and rules and generalization are applied. Exercises for development of the Syllable Concept and Dictionary Technique are included as incidental projects in lessons of a few minutes each while the introduction of new phonograms is proceeding.

Diphthongs are introduced to the pupil as they occur in the book chosen as a basis for the work at this point. The pupil is to read these books being studied in the room of the remedial teacher only. Each diphthong is typed at the top of a strip of tagboard followed by practice words which the pupil gradually learns to read.

A series of readers is now selected for study:

Ideally, the matter presented to be read by the pupil from now on should contain only words which the pupil has never seen before but which fall under headings already mastered. . . . The pupil studies the first sentence, very soon a paragraph or page, and is told in advance any word for which he is not responsible. He asks for help on any word that he does not know. The help given demands quick thought by the teacher (Gillingham & Stillman, 1946, p. 113).

No guessing of a word from the context of the sentence is allowed.

Toward the end of the period of building up reading skills by the acquisition of phonograms, drill is begun on sight-words the teacher has previously told to the student.

Gradually, books selected by the teacher may be given to the pupil for reading at home. The pupil is encouraged then to read all that he can of the material in use in the classroom and to select his own books for reading enjoyment.

Evaluation of progress is an ongoing procedure with the alert teacher constantly aware of a child's level of development and degree of facility on a number of separate but related series of skills. Gillingham has developed a phonics proficiency scale which provides a more systematic, though unstandardized measure. It provides an assessment of mastery of words phonetic for reading and spelling, words phonetic for spelling only, and multiple spellings, and is presented along with the development of teaching procedures.

In addition to the formal procedures developed by Gillingham (as outlined above), she makes other pertinent comments regarding difficulties children may have with spelling and handwriting and offers specific suggestions. She notes that the majority of children who have difficulty with reading are poor spellers even after they master the skill of reading. The basis of the remedial spelling program is a strong foundation in phonics. After that is acquired, work is begun in establishing good oral spelling through ear training. Exercises are used so that consonant and vowel sounds, rhyming words, and different word endings may be heard. Nonphonetic words are taught through nonsense tricks and jingles, drill, and general spelling rules. For example, amusing rhymes may help the child to learn the spelling of difficult words.

Advice to Mice

Don't nibble spice
Sugared rice
Is twice as nice
For little mice.

(Gillingham & Stillman, 1936, p. 64.)

Much dictionary work is to be done. As skill in dictionary work increases, the child is encouraged to look up words. He is also encouraged to trace, copy, and write to dictation. The goal of the spelling remediation process is to enable the child to express himself independently in writing. From word sequences the child should progress to short sentences. It is important that his ideas are expressed by written symbols. The teacher should write the symbols first; the child should rewrite them later. Gradually the child should progress to writing compositions.

To remedy handwriting problems, Gillingham (1936) feels that the teacher must first determine which hand is to be used. Then the position of the paper and the hand is practiced repeatedly. Exercises such as freehand loops follow. Proper slant is developed through these exercises. Kinesthetic training is stressed. Lines, circles, and squares are drawn while the students eyes are closed. Letters are analyzed as to their proportions, straight lines, and curves.

Using the blackboard as a model, the child works daily on various letters. Drill is strongly advised until the child has mentally matched each letter with its form. Either cursive or manuscript writing may be taught in this manner, but according to Gillingham cursive writing is much easier for the child with confused dominance because there is less of a chance for reversals.

In review of the Alphabetic System, two points should be stated. Initially, Gillingham felt that children who were capable of learning by visual methods should do so. However, in "correspondence" (1958), she noted the difficulties children have with spelling and concluded that the kinesthetic and auditory stimuli provided in her program would prevent such difficulties. Therefore, she advised that all children be exposed to the Alphabetic System. Since his research has indicated that auditory discrimination of most sounds is not achieved until the end of the third grade, Wepman (1960) takes issue with this approach. Strang, McCullough, and Traxler (1967) feel that if a child can learn from the whole word method, it would be unfortunate to deny him the opportunity.

The Gillingham program has been critically evaluated by Dechant (1964), who feels the lack of meaningful activities renders the system unacceptable as a total reading program, and by Gates (1947, pp. 495–496), who offers the following disadvantages associated with the program:

1. Rigidity of procedures.
2. Forfeit of interest because of the lack of real reading.
3. Delay of meaningful material.
4. Tendency to develop labored reading with a great deal of lip movement.

Gates also points out that the children with whom this program would be used as a remedial technique often are caught up in small detail. With children who evidence auditory misperception, the program would serve to accentuate their deficits and could be extremely discouraging (Frostig, 1966).

Romalda Bishop Spalding

Spalding's (1957) method is a phonic approach to the teaching of reading, which she calls the Unified Phonics Method. Her program differs from other phonics approaches in that it does not start with reading. Instead of presenting reading first, Spalding advocates teaching the writing of the sounds of the spoken language by using the letters which represent the sounds. She states:

This direct approach from the *sounds* of the words the child knows and uses in speaking into the *written characters* which represent the sound is a direct, simple, logical explanation to him of the whole writing and reading process (Spalding, 1957, p. 27).

Spalding emphasizes writing of sounds to teach correct spelling and to enable the child to translate speech into written symbols. She says that she knows of no other book concerned with handwriting which consistently focuses upon the association between sound and letter form. Her emphasis upon writing as the logical beginning for the reading process stems from her belief that "motor patterns are stored in other areas of the brain, but in the same way that the symbols of written language are recorded" (p. 227). If a child cannot depend solely upon his visual recall, then, Spalding contends, learned kinesthetic controls and auditory recall should be reinforcing agents.

Spalding's Unified Phonics Method is not a remedial approach: rather, it is intended for use in the regular classroom beginning at the first-grade level. The approach, however, is adapted easily to the remedial situation, classroom or tutorial, and has been used by numerous special service persons. Spalding clearly states that her technique, while not considered by her remedial, is based upon Orton's theories of developmental language disorders: "Dr. Orton evolved his method—which is essentially the basis on which I have developed my method of teaching all children—to overcome these handicaps in children having severe disabilities" (p. 228). Following Orton's lead, Spalding believes that the habit of working from the engrams of only the dominant hemisphere can be established through the use of kinesthetic control and she therefore stresses handwriting. The purpose of the emphasis upon writing is the coordination of motor patterns and the reinforcement of visual recall by kinesthetic and aural recall so that laterality, which is important in achieving proficiency in language development, can be established. The fusion of the senses through the formation of the habitual usage of only one side of the brain aids in the attainment of unilateral hemisphere dominance.

Spalding suggests that her method of teaching should be used with first graders, who generally have not yet developed complete laterality. Orton (1937) reports that the most critical stages of language development occur between two to three and six to eight years of age. Gesell (1940) has come to the conclusion also that the greatest changes in laterality occur from three to seven years of age and that these changes are most frequently related to handedness. The importance of the period in language development and in achieving laterality, especially the use of a preferred hand, is taken into consideration by Spalding. She notes that the child tends to use first one and then the other side of the brain.

In spite of Spalding's emphasis upon writing, in practice her method remains essentially phonic in nature and she describes it as "a fully developed, highly successful method for teaching the basic techniques of the language, accurate speaking, spelling, writing and reading—as one integrated subject" (1957, p. 8). Spalding's rationale for phonics being the best approach to teaching reading is based on her contention that once a person has a good grasp of phonics each printed word automatically will sound out itself. The person will read with understanding and not merely by memorization, which often is the result of the sight word method. In this way children will be able to read and attack new words by reasoning and not merely by guessing. Moreover, children with phonic skills become independent in their reading much earlier than those without them, and there is less need for rigidly controlled vocabulary and constant repetition of the same words in text materials.

The Unified Phonics Method is much more than just a phonics method of sounds which entails tedious drills. The child is taught first to write the symbolic characters of the sounds which he hears, next he learns the spelling of the words, and only after this has taken place does the child learn to read. Once the child writes the word and sees it, Spalding believes reading will follow naturally, for learning the relation between the sounds of speech and their written symbols is the true process of reading. By recognizing the symbolic character and automatically associating the sound with the letters, the reader will be able to produce all words correctly. Therefore, the Unified Phonics Method combines speech, writing and spelling along with reading.

The material of the method consists of 70 phonograms. They are the single letters or letter combinations which represent 45 basic sounds used in the spoken language. The name of the letter is never mentioned but rather is known only through its phonetic sound. The phonograms are shown on cards. The teacher shows the card and produces the sound. The children view the card, produce the sound, and write the letter on paper. As soon as the children know the sounds and symbols, words from the Ayres list are dictated to them. No visual clues, such as pictures, are given along with these words. Spalding feels that if pictures are shown the children would tend to read the picture and not really learn the word. The word is simply given auditorially as a whole, not by syllables, and is not seen by the children until they write it down. While writing the word the child says one sound, writes it, says the next one, and so on, until he finishes the word. In this way he does not say the whole word at the beginning; thus he writes as fast as he speaks.

Spelling rules are taught as they come up in the words. Some of the letters may have more than one sound, such as *s*. In order to differentiate between the sounds of a single letter the child is taught to place a number over the letter to indicate which sound must be said. Some of the sounds also may be underlined to indicate certain things such as, *e* in *me* is underlined to point out that in Rule 4 *a, e, o,* and *u* say their names at the end of a syllable. After the word is dictated by the teacher, he then gives a sentence containing that word to help in identifying it. Although all of the words given are either in the children's spoken or "understood" vocabulary, further comprehension of the meaning is insured by having the child put the word in a sentence.

Words which are not phonetic are the only ones that are learned by memory. The reading of a sentence begins when the children have learned enough of these words to comprehend its meaning. However, none of these activities—writing, spelling, and reading—can take place until the children have correct handwriting and are free from any speech impediments. Spalding states, "Unless children write correctly they do not see the correct symbols for the sounds. The best time to stop wrong habits is before they begin" (p. 68). Therefore, correct handwriting is taught from the very beginning.

Spalding uses the face of the clock as a reference guide for the child so that he may produce the correct letter form (see Figure 1). In order to avoid confusions as in the letters p, b, and d, the clock is thought to be an easy reference point for the child. Spalding also gives clues such as "b begins with a line and d begins with a circle" (1957, p. 75). The child writes these while sounding them and "the kinesthetic feel of these two letters can keep children from reversing them" (p. 75). Orton (1937) says that the child, "by using the motion, consistently differentiates the confused pairs long before he can be sure of them by visual inspection alone" (p. 159).

TEACHING PROCEDURES

Spalding outlines her teaching procedures in nine fundamental points:

1. Teach the phonograms.
   a. Pupils are shown phonograms and say the associated sound in unison.
   b. Just after the phonogram is pronounced, the students write the letter symbol.
2. Avoid naming the letters; use only the phonetic sounds. Spalding feels this procedure facilitates the unification of speech, writing, and reading by eliminating the confusion accruing from using letter names.
3. Always refer to multiple letter phonograms, such as *ea, eigh, ou,* etc., by the sounds associated with them; never spell them letter by letter. The children should learn to think of these phonograms as distinct sounds, not as agglomerations of letters.
4. From the beginning of instruction teach and demand correct writing and pronounciation.
5. After the phonograms have been learned, dictate to the children words from the Ayres List for them to write.
   a. The students should say aloud each phonogram (sound) of short words or each syllable of longer words.
   b. Immediately after pronouncing the sounds or syllables, the children write the associated letter forms; their writing of the word marks the first time they have seen the word in its written form.
6. The basic rules of spelling are taught as the occasion and need arise; such rules are ultimately committed to memory.
7. Irregular forms of words, that is, words which cannot be analyzed phonetically and to which no spelling rules apply, must be taught as sight or "learned" words.
8. Spelling must be emphasized as the basic key to the understanding of both written and spoken language.
9. Reading from books is delayed until the children can read common words easily enough so that they may grasp the meaning of the material.

HANDWRITING PROCEDURES

In addition to presenting procedures for teaching the phonic reading and spelling elements of the program, Spalding provides detailed instructions for the teaching of handwriting. She makes various suggestions regarding writing position for both right-handed and left-handed children, mode of holding a pencil, and position for chalkboard writing. A resume of the specific techniques of teaching writing of letters follows:

1. All letters are to be placed on the line.

2. Letters are of only two sizes—tall or short. On paper with three lines for letters, the short ones fill the space between the base and middle lines, the tall ones reach two-thirds of the distance from the base line to the upper line.

3. Only six different pencil strokes are necessary for making the lower-case letters. Figure 1 illustrates the various strokes and the relative sizes of letters.

4. Manuscript letters are made by using the clock face as a reference. The children are told that a certain letter, for example, "c," is a short letter, begins on the clock face at 2 and goes up and around to the number 4. Figure 2 illustrates the procedure for making the letters "c" and "s." Instructions are given by Spalding for teaching all of the lower-case letters.

5. Capital letters in manuscript are taught after the lower-case letters have been learned and the techniques are not significantly different from those for teaching lower-case letters.

6. Numerals are taught using the basic procedures discussed above.

7. Cursive writing is an adaptation of manuscript writing with the manuscript being joined together through the five connecting strokes. Figure 3 demonstrates the connecting strokes, the manuscript lower-case alphabet, and the derived cursive lower-case alphabet.

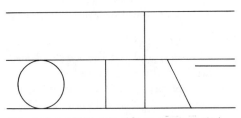

FIGURE 1.   (From Spalding, 1957. p. 74.)

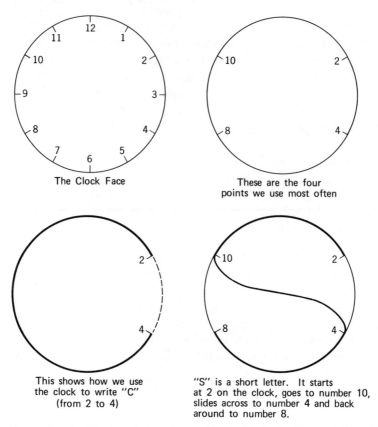

The Clock Face

These are the four
points we use most often

This shows how we use
the clock to write "C"
(from 2 to 4)

"S" is a short letter. It starts
at 2 on the clock, goes to number 10,
slides across to number 4 and back
around to number 8.

FIGURE 2.   Spalding's technique for teaching writing. (Spalding, 1957, p. 74.)

THE CHILD'S NOTEBOOK

Each child above the second-grade level is required by Spalding to
keep a written notebook, the first seven pages of which are taught in
all grades including the first. First- and second-grade children, however,
are not required to write these pages. The notebook is a reference book
for the phonograms and spelling and pronunciation rules.

1. **Page one.** On the first page of the notebook are the single consonants,
the single vowels (all long), and the five types of silent final *es*. Seven
spelling rules are written on the page: c before e, i or y says $\overset{2}{c}$, and if g
is before e, i, or y, it may say $\overset{2}{g}$. q is always written with the letter u
when we say the sound "kw." (The u is not considered a vowel here.)
The other spelling rules are concerned with the different silent final *es*.

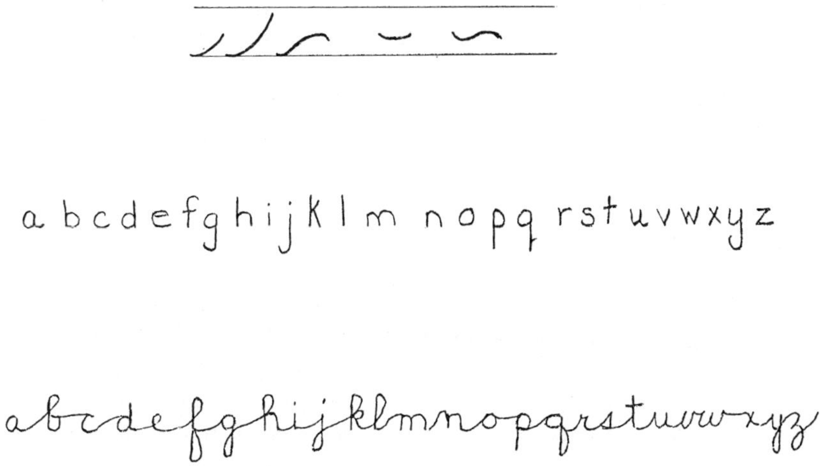

a b c d e f g h i j k l m n o p q r s t u v w x y z

abcdefghijklmnopqrstuvwxyz

FIGURE 3.   Cursive writing. (Spalding, 1957, p. 88–89.)

2. Page two. The second page is devoted to the five spellings of the "er" sound.

3. Page three. On the third page the child writes the rule governing the spelling of words having "ei" after "c" and its exceptions.

4. Page four. This page is devoted to the usual spelling of the sound "sh" when it appears at the beginning of any syllable other than the first, for example, sh, ti, si, ci.

5. Page five. The fifth page of the notebook demonstrates the doubling of final consonants when various endings are added to base words.

6. Page six. Page six indicates that words which end in one of the five different silent *es* drop the e when an ending beginning with a vowel is added.

7. Page seven. On page seven of his notebook, the child writes all of the phonograms not previously recorded in the notebook, namely, those not written on pages one and two.

With the completion of page seven, the child has in his notebook all of the 70 phonograms and a ready reference for all of the spelling rules, 26 in number. As noted previously, children above the second-grade level write these seven pages each year; first- and second-grade teachers provide the pages for their students by putting them on the chalkboard or on charts.

In conclusion, Spalding's Unified Phonics Method is well described by its title. It is a teaching method rather than a set of procedures, it is thoroughly phonic in approach, and it is unified in that an attempt is made to teach the child to coordinate or unify his kinesthetic and aural recall with his often faltering visual recall. For the child with auditory deficiencies, the demands placed upon his auditory modality by the method are often unrealistic and without extensive auditory perceptual training he will have great difficulty learning to read.

Conclusion

The methods characterized by the authors as auditory were discussed in the chapter; these are the methods devised by Gillingham and Stillman (1965) and Spalding (1957). In addition, the theories of Orton, related to hemispheric dominance and specific reading disability, were reviewed briefly because of his pivotal position in the development of the methods.

Two points should be restated:

1. The methods were termed auditory because of their assumption of auditory competency and their strong reliance upon the auditory modality as the principal input mode.

2. As a result of the emphasis upon auditory efficiency inherent in the methods, the child with auditory difficulties would be expected to perform relatively poorly when taught by these methods. For that child with good auditory and kinesthetic input modes but poor visual abilities, the methods appear to be methods of choice—Gillingham and Stillman's in the intensive remedial situation, Spalding's in the less intensive, more episodic clinical situation.

References

Dechant, E. V. *Improving the teaching of reading.* Englewood Cliffs, N.J.: Prentice-Hall, 1964.

Eisenson, J. Correlates of aphasia in adults. In L. E. Travis, *Handbook of speech pathology,* New York: Appleton-Century-Crofts, 1957.

Eisenson, J., Auer, J., & Irwin, J. V. *The psychology of communication.* New York: Appleton-Century-Crofts, 1963.

Frostig, M. The needs of teachers for specialized information on reading. In W. M. Cruickshank. *The teacher of brain injured children.* Syracuse, N.Y.: Syracuse University Press, 1966.

Gates, A. I. *The improvement of reading.* (3rd ed.) New York: Macmillan, 1947.

Gesell, A. *The first five years of life.* New York: Harper & Row, 1940.

Gillingham, A. Correspondence. *Elementary English,* 1958, **35,** 119–122.

Gillingham, A., & Stillman, B. *Remedial work for reading, spelling, and penmanship.* New York: Hackett & Wilhelms, 1936.

―――. *Remedial work for reading, spelling and penmanship.* (6th ed.) New York: Hackett & Wilhelms, 1946.

―――. *Remedial training for children with specific disability in reading, spelling, and penmanship.* (7th ed.) Cambridge, Mass.: Educators Publishing Service, 1965.

McGinnis, M. *Aphasic children: Identification and education by the association method.* Washington, D.C.: Volta Bureau, 1963.

Orton, S. *Reading, writing and speech problems in children.* New York: Norton, 1937.

―――. The sight reading method of teaching reading, as a source of reading disability. *Journal of Educational Psychology,* 1929, **20,** 135–143.

―――. A neurological explanation of the reading disability. *Education Record,* 1939, **20,** Supplement 12, 58–68.

Osgood, C. E., & Miron, M. S. *Approaches to the study of aphasia.* Urbana: University of Illinois Press, 1963.

Penfield, W., & Roberts, L. *Speech and brain mechanisms.* Princeton, N.J.: Princeton University Press, 1959.

Russell, R. W., & Espir, M. L. E. *Traumatic aphasia.* Oxford University Press, 1961.

Spalding, R. B., & Spalding, W. T. *The writing road to reading.* New York: Morrow, 1957.

Strang, R., McCullough, C., & Traxler, A. *The improvement of reading.* New York: McGraw-Hill, 1967.

Wepman, J. M. Auditory discrimination, speech and reading, *Elementary School Journal,* 1960, **60,** 245–247.

CHAPTER VIII

A STRUCTURED SYSTEM

Barry, Lehtinen, Cruickshank, and others have noted that some children with specific learning disorders have need for structure in their educational environment. In general, these authors are concerned about the need for structure and organization in the pupils' physical surroundings. Such thinking has led to the separation of hyperactive children from their classmates by provision of isolation cubicles, to the elimination of all nonessential and possibly distracting stimuli in the immediate setting, and to the initiation of rigid, minute-by-minute daily schedules. Structure may also be provided by the meticulous sequencing of material to be learned. No subject is more dependent upon structure and sequence than the English language. The meaningfulness of any sentence is related directly to the order or sequence of words within it. The system devised by Fitzgerald and modified by Pugh is a highly structured, predominantly visual method for teaching the sequence of English to children with severe auditory problems. Although originally developed for use with deaf and hard of hearing children, the method is recommended for those children with adequate hearing who might profit from such an approach. The procedures can facilitate the mastery of the sequence of the language in children with either auditory or visual modality problems. Therefore the criterion for selection of this system is: Does the child exhibit inadequate syntax in oral or written language? The Fitzgerald-Pugh system can be used in conjunction with any of the other methods discussed, although it is probably more closely related to the language development systems than to the others.

Fitzgerald, who lost her hearing before her speech was fully established, was thus personally aware of the difficulties involved in language development when input problems exist. She retained what speech she had acquired and in 1906 graduated from Gallaudet College. For seventeen years, Fitzgerald taught in the manual department of the Wisconsin School for the Deaf and continued to work with the deaf at state schools in Louisiana, Arkansas, Virginia, Georgia, and Texas. She conducted summer classes for teachers and was active in the field until her death in 1940.

A concern with the educational needs of deaf children was expressed in Fitzgerald's early work (1912, 1918). She concluded that their need for language was great and that its development had to be emphasized in their training. Since she felt that insufficient practice was the basis for most language problems, the use of meaningful drill was suggested as an essential means for teaching language arts. Therefore, practice and more practice was necessary to perfect language. Expectedly, drill became an important aspect of the Fitzgerald method of teaching "straight language." Because drills are emphasized in her method, one should not think that Fitzgerald advocated an unnatural or mechanical approach to language acquisition, for she strongly cautioned teachers against the development of a merely memorized language. Drill is a part of the method, but mechanical learning is to be avoided.

The culmination of Fitzgerald's work is the book *Straight Language for the Deaf*, which was published originally in 1926 and which subsequently has undergone several revisions and a dozen printings. The steady, continuous demand for her book demonstrates the staying power of Fitzgerald's contribution; the book, now forty-two years old, still is widely used. *Straight Language* is actually an instructional manual dealing with three general areas: (1) nongrammatical aspects of language such as vocabulary building, calendar work, commonly used commands and expressions; (2) grammatical aspects of language such as the use of various parts of speech (pronouns, verbs, etc.); and (3) a presentation of the Fitzgerald Key. Our discussion includes Fitzgerald's ideas regarding nongrammatical aspects of language and a description of the Fitzgerald Key. We feel that the grammatical aspects of language are better covered in a discussion of the Key rather than in a separate section.

A list of guiding principles for teachers can be extracted from Fitzgerald's work and should be reviewed before proceeding with discussion of her system. It is noteworthy that many of the points she stresses are applicable to education in general. The list provides the reader with an understanding of her basic attitude toward instruction and is indicative of the spirit with which the Key is to be used. The guiding principles follow.

1. The teacher should be familiar with the work which comes just before and immediately after the particular grade level she expects to teach.

2. The teacher must not be so eager for the child to speak that the essential background for speech is ignored. Such ignorance leads to and encourages parrot-talk rather than language based on understanding.

3. The child's mental picture must be clear or the language he uses may become a jumble of memorized words which are meaningless to him.

4. When a child attempts to express himself orally, his teacher must be sure that he has acquired the language to fit his mental concept.

5. The child must be given the chance to absorb knowledge. When he exhibits interest, present him with materials and knowledge to satisfy his present need.

6. The child must realize the connection between language use and language understanding. Children are never expected to use words they do not understand.

7. When possible, provide the child with the opportunity to discover and correct his own mistakes.

8. Have the child attempt what he can be expected to do. Progress at his speed and level.

9. Do not abbreviate. The child cannot be expected to spell words correctly unless he sees them.

10. Insist upon neatness, paragraphing, correct punctuation, respect for margins, and sequence both of time and thought.

11. Be definite in your approach.

12. Learning should be meaningful; all possible mechanical repetition is to be strictly avoided.

Teaching Nongrammatical Aspects of Language

Probably the most interesting and pertinent aspects of nongrammatical language training discussed by Fitzgerald relate to suggestions for teaching children about the calendar, weather, commands, and expressions. Calendar work begins early in the program as a nonlanguage activity and is continued throughout the child's schooling. As he gains facility in language, his concepts regarding the calendar and weather become progressively more complex. At the same time, Fitzgerald warns against practicing calendar work so frequently that it becomes monotonous. Teaching the calendar aids in developing concepts of (1) morning and afternoon, (2) time sequence (dials are set for recess, dismissal, etc.), (3) adverbs, for example, "all day," "again," "several times," and "for a little while," so that they are recognized as "How Often" or "How Long" rather than "When", and (4) acquaintance with the names of the days and months.

A sample calendar should be drawn on a board (chalkboard, tagboard, or bulletin board) which is large enough to include appropriate pictures to designate the month. Fitzgerald is explicit in describing the calendar and where it should be placed in the classroom:

It should be remembered that the day grows old from left to right; therefore, the calendar should be on a south board, and for any changes in the weather during the day, the calendar square $(3'' \times 3'')$ should be divided vertically rather than horizontally (Fitzgerald, 1966, p. 7).

By placing the calendar on a south board, the east-west progression of the sun during the day is implicitly stated and at a later time in the program the direction names, east-west-north-south, are taught. Dividing the day with a vertical line to set off morning from afternoon emphasizes the left-right progression of the calendar, and no other marking off or crossing out of the days is permitted.

Another chart headed *Yesterday Was* and *Today Is* is used to emphasize the sequence of time. The teacher is cautioned not to point to a row of figures on the calendar and call it a week. If the teacher does point, the pupil may always think of a week as invariably starting with Sunday. *Tomorrow* is later added; then follows *Last* Sunday afternoon, *Next* Saturday morning, etc.

Oral reports on the weather begin as soon as possible, but care should be taken in using the terms "warm" and "cold" until concrete facts are available to substantiate these comparative adjectives. The thermometer is a good source for concrete data; therefore, it should be introduced as soon as feasible. When the child is ready, an exercise called *My Day* is used in a manner similar to the calendar work and correlates recall, connected language, written and oral expression.

Regarding the teaching of commands and expressions, Fitzgerald stresses several basic points. When commands are first taught, the child should not have to pretend he is carrying out the teacher's direction. If commanded "Comb your hair," he should be provided with a comb. Only after the child learns the meaning of some actual commands is he requested to "make believe." The phrase "I played" is used to express pretense. Fitzgerald notes that when a command calls for two or more things to be done in sequence, one must watch for any tendency to carry out the first part and then return to the starting place before taking the next step.

To teach expressions such as "thank you," "you are welcome," the phrases are printed on charts placed in the room so that they can be referred to when the occasion arises. The cards bearing the expressions are moved from time to time so that the child will not associate them with position rather than the printed form. "Goodbye" and "Good Morning" are placed initially near the door. Activities pertaining to commands and expressions as well as calendar work are continued through intermediate and upper grades.

The Fitzgerald Key

This section provides readers with a limited knowledge of the Key, some understanding of its use, and an idea for whom the system might be appropriate. It is important to note again that no attempt should be made to implement any method presented in this book without first consulting the original sources. And in the case of the Key, a visit to a local educational facility for the deaf, where the key can be seen in use, would be beneficial.

A highly structured visual system of language instruction for deaf children is presented in *Straight Language*. Fitzgerald maintains that deaf children need a visual guide to follow in structuring sentences because they frequently are unable to hear their errors in construction. The deaf child uses the visual cues to compensate for his inadequate hearing sense. Fitzgerald's system encourages compensation through headings which describe the content and provide the sequence necessary for the development of verbal language. These ordered headings comprise a sentence pattern, and the pattern of headings is the Fitzgerald Key. This method probably is suitable for hearing children who also experience difficulty in monitoring and who necessarily would profit from the visual reinforcement inherent in the Key.

The Key is written in yellow washable paint across the top of the most prominent blackboard in the classroom. At first only two headings are used (Who: What:); later, additional headings are introduced

(Whose: How Many: What Kind Of: Color: Whom: What:). The Key becomes increasingly more complex as the child develops proficiency and as his needs dictate. But the Key is used for all grades and for all subjects. The key words are arranged in the order which corresponds to their use in the English language. Fitzgerald's rationale for this approach follows:

Understanding precedes use. We draw a line between the understanding of language and the use of language, but we insist that visualization and understanding of language go hand in hand as the child proceeds to acquire language. We have proven to our satisfaction that classification of words and thoughts (under key-words and the few symbols we use) and the understanding that follows hasten, to say the least, the child's grasp of and spontaneous use of English (1966, p. 4).

The Key is supplemented by several symbols used to identify some parts of speech. The symbols are:

$=$	verb	$\leftrightarrow$	conjunctive
$=$	infinitive	$\top$	pronoun
$\rightleftharpoons$	present participle	$\sqcap$	adjective

With regards to the objections occasionally raised against the use of symbols, Fitzgerald defends her use of them in the following passage:

We have found that the children sense the difference between these parts of speech more easily when their symbols are used than when verb, adjective, etc., are introduced in conjunction with the key-words, which key-words present definite *thoughts*. The teacher always uses the names of the parts of speech when referring to the symbols (1966, p. 21).

The average width for each group of headings painted on the blackboard is 16 inches. Usually they are made wider for younger children and are reduced gradually toward the average. The depth of each group of headings is always 6 inches, which permits four lines 1½ inches apart and which allows space to accommodate the four key-words in the fifth space. (A cursory look at the headings in Table 1 indicates that the fifth space is occupied by How far:, How often:, How long:, and How much:. The 6-inch depth is required so that they will all fit within the allotted space.) Symbols which represent parts of speech are placed below the space set aside for the key words. The Why: of the fifth space is dropped 1½ inches below the lowest of the other key words, or 7½ inches from the top of the key. Eventually the key is transferred from the blackboard to paper when the child is ready.

USE OF THE KEY

Fitzgerald offers a number of considerations regarding the use of the Key:

1. The Key helps in phrasing.
2. Suggested command: Say it with the Key.
3. See that children point to the correct key-word.
4. See that they point to the side to show modifiers. In "Weldon has blue eyes," the pointer is placed to the left of What for *blue* and then directly under What for *eyes*.
5. Do not write connected language in the Key when it is being worked out. Follow the Key as a pattern.
6. Do not help the child with what he wants to say and then have him place the statement in the Key. Let him work it out for himself.
7. Have the child face the class as he points to the Key.
8. Add to the Key as fast as the children can visualize the thoughts back of the key-words—but no faster (1966, p. 62).

In *Straight Language*, Fitzgerald immediately classifies new vocabulary under certain headings. Two of the earliest headings apply to nouns: Who: for humans; and What: for nouns applying to animals and to inanimate objects. For young children, Fitzgerald tells teachers to hold up familiar objects or pictures, say their names aloud in order to capitalize on any auditory skills that may be present, and place them under the headings Who: or What: An example exercise is provided below:

Who:	What:

Place these words (or objects or pictures) under the proper heading.

top	ball	mother
boy	car	dog
baby	spoon	cat

After the children have grasped this concept, new categories are added to the Key, such as How Many:, What Color:, Where:, and Whose:.

This collection of headings is referred to as the Primary Key. An example is provided below:

Whose:	Who: What:	How many:	What kind of:	Color:	Whom: What:

=

I	see	a	big	red	ball
Tommy	made	a		green	car

The child can master the use of the Primary Key without knowing how to speak. As the child progresses in silent reading, he will begin gradually to sense the meanings back of the key words.

Soon after words under these headings are introduced, rules for their order in noun phrases are presented. The first rules are:

How Many:	What:	
How Many:	What Color:	What:

Thus the sequence, or order of the language is acquired. An example of this rule might be:

How Many:	What:	
five	dogs	

How Many:	What Color:	What:
five	brown	dogs

Later, as the children master the Whose: category heading, they learn that the possessive nouns and the possessive pronouns replace the How Many: category, rather than precede it. The rule is:

Whose:	What:	

not

Whose:	How Many:	What:

Example:

Whose:	What:
Tom's	coat

not

Whose:	How Many:	What:
Tom's	one	coat

As the vocabulary grows, the children learn "qualifying adjectives," which include such words as large, pretty, new, beautiful, old, and interesting. These words are referred to by the teacher as adjectives. Since there is no appropriate key word, they are classified under the adjective symbol ⊓. A new rule for noun-phrase order is now required:

How Many: :   What Color: What:
                  ⊓

Using the symbol = for verbs, the teacher can build sentences like the following under these headings:

Who: What: =	How Many:		What Color: ⊓		Whom: What:	Where:
I	see	three	big	blue	balls.	
Bob	ran					to school.
John	bought	a	little		car	

Additional examples at the primary level are included in the completed primary worksheet presented as Table 1. The Key becomes increasingly complex as the pupil progresses; traditional terms such as subject, indirect object, and direct object are added to the Key. Advanced headings and a demonstration of their use are offered in Table 2.

Fitzgerald used the Key until it was no longer needed by the child. The method was not used in isolation but rather was incorporated into the teaching of other academic subjects. The following outline gives the sequence used in teaching vocabulary to children.

A. Words are classified
   1. Who: is introduced—using real people, then pictures and finally just words.
   2. What: is introduced in the same manner as Who:
   3. How Many:
      a. Teach the symbols and number words of cardinal numbers.
      b. The words a, the, some, many are taught.
   4. What Color:
      a. Colors are learned.
      b. In describing, How Many: always precedes What Color: for example, Three red balls.
   5. Verbs, adjectives, pronouns, connectives, and infinitives are classified.

Table 1

Whose: Who: What: ==	Whose: Whom: What: ( ) Whom:	What: Whom:	Where:	From: For: With: How: Why:	How far: How often: How long: How much:	When:
The Americans took		the fort		from the British.		
Early took		the ball	from the baby.			
Jack picked up		the pencils		for Miss Blocker.		
I bought		some oranges		for Miss Tinnin.		
I bought		some material for a blouse.				
Melvin went			to the store	for some bread.		
Doyle went			to the doctor's			
Mr. Saylor went			to Bastrop	with Miss Kramer		yesterday.
We saw		Mr. Saylor	in Mr. Brace's car.	in Mr. Brace's car.		
The boys walked					ten miles Saturday afternoon.	
We go			to rhythm		twice a week.	
I love		Mother			very much.	
Hayden likes		apple pie			better than ice cream.	
Miss Creath went			to the beauty parlor	to get a shampoo and a set.		Saturday
Myra was crying				because she was lonesome.		this morning

Table 2

Subject: Verb:	Indirect Object:	Direct Object:	Where:	From: / For: / With: / How:	Why:	How far: / How often: / How long: / How much: / When:
Betty wrote			on the blackboard			just now
		what / she / did				
		in the sewing room / yesterday.				this morning
Miss Compton asked	me	why / I / did not go / to Dallas / Easter.				
Frank stayed			in the hospital			yesterday / until / the doctor / came.
Elbert was	too sleepy / to study.					last night
Elbert was	so sleepy / that / he / could not study.					last night
Dan ran				so fast / that / I / could not keep up		

    a. Drill verbs—see, saw, have, has, etc.
    b. Nondrill verbs.
    c. After mastery of a few nouns, verbs should be added to form
       phrases and sentences.
  6. Who: and Whose:. Possessives of nouns are taught before pos-
     sessives of pronouns.
  7. Where:, When:, How Long:, How Often:, Why:, etc.
     These are introduced as the children are ready for them.
B. Further classification of words or phrases.
  1. Unclassified lists are written horizontally.
  2. Classified lists are written vertically.
C. Obtain original lists from children. Omit How:.
D. Classify words and phrases according to key-words and symbols
   (written).
  1. Always maintain the order of the Key.
  2. Teach the articles a, an, the.
E. Plurals of What: and Who:
  1. Those with the simple "s" ending (balls, apples).
  2. Those that don't change (deer, sheep).
  3. Unusual plural forms (men, women).
  4. Plurals which require changes in letters (babies, knives).
F. Analyze words in context (and phrases), for example, John opened
   the *box* (What:). John walked *into the box* (Where:).
G. Classify all new vocabulary on the blackboard using the Key.
H. Require that second- and third-grade students keep a vocabulary
   book as outlined by the teacher.

A Linguistic Analysis of Fitzgerald's Noun Phrase

A method of testing the adequacy of Fitzgerald's plan for teaching
language would be to evaluate the structures taught in the Key in terms
of the concepts of modern linguistics. Fitzgerald's work appeared too
early to have been influenced greatly by modern linguistic theories.
She derived much of her method for presenting grammatical facts from
her own observation of normal language and of the difficulties encountered in the language of deaf people. It should be noted that such
direct observation of normal language is the method generally advocated
by linguists themselves, so it is not surprising that Fitzgerald's work
parallels the work of some linguists rather closely.

Although many aspects of Fitzgerald's work can be evaluated in terms
of structural linguistic concepts, only one is analyzed in this section—the

Table 3   A Comparison of the Order of Noun Modifiers According to Fitzgerald and Hill

Hill's Classes of Noun Modifiers

Fitzgerald's Sequence of Categories	VI	Vb	Va	IV	III	II	I
Whose:	"all" "both" "half"	Possessive nouns	articles / Possessive pronouns				
How Many:				Numerals and numerical phrases			
Qualifying Adjectives					"True" adjectives: "beautiful"	Size: Shape	Noun adjectives: "wood," "wooden"
What Color:						Colors	

236

elements of the noun phrase. It should be noted, however, that transformational-generative grammar, as explained by Chomsky (1957), offers promise of being able to alter the Fitzgerald system so that it would be more flexible and so that it would make English seem more logical to individuals who have trouble understanding the intricacies of this complex language. Since transformational-generative grammars still need refining by the linguists, our analysis is oriented toward structural-grammar, which has been more thoroughly studied.

A description of the order of modifiers in noun phrases, which bears striking similarity to Fitzgerald's presentation, is that of the structural linguist Hill (1958). The following is his sample noun phrase illustrating the order of noun modifiers in English:

VI V IV III II   I   N
All the ten fine old stone houses

As one may observe, Hill's Class I consists of the modifiers that occur nearest to the noun being modified, Class II includes modifiers twice removed from the noun, and so on. Table 3 demonstrates the relationship between the sequences given by Fitzgerald and Hill. The linearity of the relationship indicates close, although not perfect agreement.

A further illustration of this relationship is provided by Table 4. Hill's sample phrase was amended to read "All the ten fine grey stone houses" and his order of modification was plotted against the sequential order of Fitzgerald's categories. The resultant matrix once again reveals the high degree of similarity.

The authors feel the analysis indicates that Fitzgerald's system of rules for the order of modifiers in noun phrases bears up well under

Table 4   An Example of the Fitzgerald-Key–Structural-Linguistics Relationship

		Hill's Classes of Noun Modifiers						
		VI	V	IV	III	II	I	N
Fitzgerald's Categories	How Many:	All	the	ten				
	⊓					fine		stone
	What Color:					grey		
	What:							houses

evaluation on a structural linguistic basis. The linguistic system does allow for some sentences that Fitzgerald's system could not produce, but it also allows some nongrammatical sentences that Fitzgerald would not permit.

The Contributions of Pugh

Pugh (1947) offers a modification of the system perfected by Fitzgerald. The contents of her book are illustrated through the Fitzgerald Key. While the chapters in *Straight Language* are presented in more or less logical order, the content of *Steps in Language Development* is organized in a definite developmental sequence. The principles set down in *Straight Language* are adhered to rigorously. In addition to the Key, Pugh uses the identifying symbols, with some modification, and the sequence of presentation of the parts of speech suggested by Fitzgerald. For example, an initial distinction is made between people and inanimate objects or animals; then nouns, pronouns, adjectives, and eventually direct objects are presented.

The material given in *Steps in Language Development* is arranged into a series of steps to be taken in teaching language to deaf children. The content is outlined clearly and precisely. Viewed collectively, the sequence resembles a set of instructional units. The book is a workbook, thus teachers probably will find it quite helpful in implementing a structured approach to teaching language. Actually the books by Pugh and Fitzgerald complement one another so well that teachers who choose to use the Key are encouraged to use both.

References

Chomsky, N. *Syntactic structures.* The Hague: Mouton, 1957.

Fitzgerald, E. Manual spelling and English. *American Annals of the Deaf,* 1912, **57,** 197–203.

————. Language building in the primary grades. *American Annals of the Deaf,* 1918, **63,** 342–353.

————. *Straight language for the deaf.* Washington, D.C.: The Volta Bureau, 1966.

Hill. A. A. *Introduction to linguistic structures. From sound to sentence in English.* New York: Harcourt, Brace, 1958.

Pugh, B. *Steps in language development.* Washington, D.C.: The Volta Bureau, 1947.

CHAPTER IX

THE TEST-RELATED SYSTEMS

The training systems reviewed in this chapter are directly related to the diagnostic assessment instruments associated with them. For example, various activities in the Frostig-Horne Program are recommended when the results of the Frostig Test indicate specific deficits. By the same token, poor performance on subtests of the ITPA reveals those areas of psycholinguistic ability to be emphasized in a curriculum such as Hartman's Preschool Diagnostic Language Program. The selection of either system is dependent upon the profiles obtained for children on the appropriate test battery. Children who score low on the Eye-Motor Coordination subtest of the Frostig Test should be provided with the activities suggested by Frostig to improve that skill. Other children with poor scores on Auditory Decoding from the ITPA should be trained in that area. As the reader may note, no attempt is made to categorize children by type of learning disability but only to utilize their test scores.

These systems could appropriately have been presented in other chapters. The Frostig Program is a perceptual-motor system; the ITPA Program is a language development system. Because, however, these are the only curricula directly dependent upon associated tests, they are discussed separately. Kephart suggests using results of the Purdue Perceptual-Motor Survey in planning remediation. His scale, however, is not as standardized, scaled, or formal as the Frostig Test and the ITPA.

Frostig Program in Visual Perception

Marianne Frostig, founder of the Marianne Frostig Center of Educational Therapy, Los Angeles, California, has developed a facility which provides professional training and treatment of children with learning disabilities. Frostig's work in visual perception has gained national recognition. The recognition is based in part upon the fact that she, with others, has designed a widely used test of visual perception and has prepared a training program to accompany this measure. One should not assume, however, that Frostig's interest in visual perception results in a remedial approach which emphasizes that process to the exclusion of others. On the contrary, Frostig's current (Frostig, 1966, 1967a, 1967b, 1968; Frostig & Maslow, 1968) writings evidence increased concern for the treatment of auditory and motor problems. Recognizing that perceptual adequacy may be fundamental to academic success, Frostig's main interest centers around the development of perceptual skills rather than in providing instruction specifically in reading, spelling, and writing.

Although Frostig (1967a) maintains that knowledge of subject matter is important, she does not think this knowledge alone provides enough information to formulate optimal educational programs for learning disabled children. A detailed analysis of the learner cannot be neglected; styles of learning, preferred sensory channels, and areas of perceptual and cognitive deficits or strengths must be determined if the child is to be taught effectively. Once sufficient information about the learner has been acquired, curricula may be adapted, selected, or developed which are appropriate to him.

Because knowledge of the child's learning patterns is considered important, Frostig (1967a, 1967b), using an adapted Guilford model, suggests a comprehensive testing program which includes administration of the following battery: the Developmental Test of Visual Perception (DTVP), the Wepman Test of Auditory Discrimination, the Illinois Test of Psycholinguistic Abilities, and the Weschler Intelligence Test for Children. In addition, the child's motor adequacy is assessed by use of the *Oseretsky Tests of Motor Proficiency,* or a similar measure. Frostig

(1967a) recognizes that these tests, including her own, have been criticized with some justification, but suggests that:

. . . it is better to make mistakes than to do nothing when ground has to be broken.

It is important to be aware of the flaws of the new tests with which we measure abilities, but it is equally important to be aware of the need for measuring specific learning abilities even though the tests have not yet been perfected. By being aware of the deficiencies of the tests, we may add additional measures to make up for these deficiencies (p. 18).

A rigid adherence to test results is not recommended by Frostig; she suggests that observation of the child's classroom behavior is necessary to expand, confirm, or refute test findings. Formal testing, nonetheless, is considered by her to be one of the important sources of information concerning the child's level of functioning and of his areas of strength or weakness on certain measures. Concomitant with this belief, however, is her caution that "test results should always be taken with a tablespoon of salt" (Frostig, 1967a, p. 19).

THE DEVELOPMENTAL TEST OF VISUAL PERCEPTION

According to Frostig and Horne (1964), perception is one of the prime psychological functions without which "all but the simplest body functions, such as breathing and elimination, would stop and survival would be impossible" (p. 7). In short, perception is the ability to recognize stimuli and includes not only reception from outside the body but also the capacity to interpret and identify sensory impressions by correlating them with other experiences. Perception takes place not in the receiving organ (the eye, ear, etc.) but in the brain itself. Although no specific causative factor for inadequate perceptual development has been identified, Frostig and Horne have pointed out that a disability in visual perception may be the result of either delayed maturation, actual cerebral injury, or genetic and environmental factors.

Contrary to some writers, Frostig as well as Getman and Barsch maintain that most learning is acquired through the visual channel; and if development in visual perception, which occurs between the ages of $3\frac{1}{2}$ to $7\frac{1}{2}$ years, is hindered, some cognitive deficits will result. Examples of possible handicaps include difficulty in recognizing objects and their relationship to each other in space as well as the development of distortions which make the world appear unstable and unpredictable. The acquisition of these and other perceptual problems increases the probability that the child will experience some degree of emotional disturbance and eventual academic failure.

The test's development was a natural outgrowth of Frostig's expressed concern with the need for acquiring more detailed information about children with learning problems. The Developmental Test of Visual Perception (Frostig et al., 1964) was formulated to facilitate the early detection of visual perception impairments and addresses attention to both the degree and kind of deviation. The present discussion of the test includes (1) a description of the instrument itself and (2) an overview of standardization information.

Description of the Instrument. The measure, published originally in 1961, has seen two revisions. Test items were constructed to interest children in the three to nine year age range. Item analyses were used to sequence the items along an easy to difficult continuum. Administration time is less than an hour for either individuals or small groups of children.

Five subtests were developed in an attempt to measure a variety of visual perception skills. Criteria for inclusion of these particular perceptual abilities are:

1. They are critical for the acquisition of school learning.
2. They affect the total organism to a much greater degree than some other functions, such as color vision or pure tone discrimination.
3. They develop relatively early in life.
4. They are frequently disturbed in children diagnosed as neurologically handicapped.
5. They are suitable for group testing.
6. And, we have observed that training in these areas is very frequently successful (Frostig et al., 1961, p. 384).

The five relatively independent areas of visual perception which comprise the subtests of the current form of the Frostig test are (1) eye-motor coordination, (2) figure ground, (3) form constancy, (4) position in space, and (5) spatial relations.

1. Eye-Motor or Visual-Motor Coordination. The ability to integrate vision with movements of the body, particularly with the fine visual-motor skills necessary for success with pencil and paper activities, is involved in this subtest. Continuous straight, curved, or angled lines are drawn between boundaries of various widths or from point to point without guidelines. One example of these tasks requires the child to draw

a continuous pencil line between two pictures of houses without violating specified boundaries (Figure 1. I). In Frostig's opinion, adequate visual-motor coordination is an important prerequisite for reading and is essential for writing.

2. Figure Ground. This subtest is offered as a measure of the ability to select from a mass of stimuli a particular center of attention (the figure) and to disregard the rest of the stimuli (the ground). One task, included in the test, requires that the child outline in colored pencil the stars in a figure composed of superimposed stars and circles (Figure 1, II). Confusion of the lines of the two forms may be indicative of a figure-ground difficulty. Frostig suggests that the ability to distinguish figure from ground is essential for the analysis and synthesis of written words, phrases, and paragraphs.

3. Form Constancy. The ability measured is that of recognizing that a figure may vary in size, texture, or position without altering its basic form. For example, a circle may have a ½- or a 1-inch diameter, but it remains a circle. In this instance, the child is presented a page on which a collection of forms is printed. One task requires that the child locate and outline as many circles as he can find. The circles, however, vary in size and texture and must be distinguished from other geometric forms. According to Frostig, adequate shape and size constancy is necessary for the recognition of familiar words seen in an unfamiliar context, color, size, or style of print.

4. Position in Space. Involved in this subtest is the ability to distinguish a particular form from other figures as it is presented in an identical, rotated, or reversed position. One task presents a series of printed half moons to the child, who is asked to specify the one that faces a direction different from the others (Figure 1, III). Frostig maintains that mastery of position in space is needed to differentiate letters which have the same form but different positions—such as b and d.

5. Spatial Relations. The ability of perceive the position of two or more objects in relation to oneself and to each other is measured by this subtest. In one item, the child is provided an example in which lines have been drawn among nine points in such a way as to form a pattern. The task requires that the child duplicate the pattern (Figure 1, IV). Spatial adequacy is assumed by Frostig to be necessary for the recognition of letters in a word and words in a sentence.

The DTVP yields two kinds of scaled scores—the Perceptual Quotient (PQ) and the Perceptual Age (PA). In addition, raw scores on the subtests may be converted to scaled scores. The PQ is indicative of the child's level of visual ability when compared with that of his agemates. A PQ of 90 is the suggested cutoff score below which a kindergarten

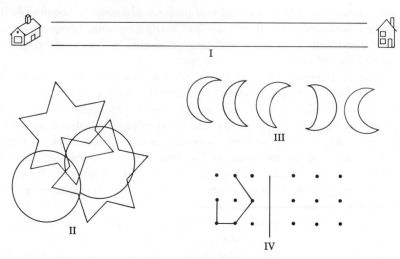

FIGURE 1.   Selected items from the *Developmental Test of Visual Perception*. (Published with the permission of Consulting Psychologist Press.)

child should receive special training. The distinction can be made, therefore, between children who may require training in visual perception and those who do not need special training. The PA, on the other hand, estimates the developmental level of the child. Since age equivalents are not related to chronological age, the PA in itself neither predicts the child's ability to profit from training nor indicates his need for training (Frostig et al., 1964). Thus the test is constructed to provide the educator with useful information which includes (1) an estimation of the over-all visual perception adequacy of the child and (2) a delimitation of the distinct perceptual areas in need of training.

Standardization Information. The present discussion centers on the standardization sample, administration procedures, validity, and reliability.

1. Standardization Sample. Frostig et al. (1964) have pointed out quite fairly that the standardization sample, 2116 unselected school children, for the latest edition of the test (the third) was not representative. Even though the test's authors mentioned the desirability of a broader-based standardization sample, its absence remains one deficiency in the measure. For example, the subjects were exclusively children from white middle-class homes. The published normative data, therefore, will best

permit comparisons of a given child's performance with this particular sample. His rank among children in the general population cannot be estimated with confidence. Certainly it could not be so estimated if the test were used in population centers having large concentrations of culturally disadvantaged children.

2. Subtest Independence. The Frostig Test is assumed to measure five distinct aspects of visual perception, and the remedial programs, which will be discussed shortly, were prepared to correspond with the five subtest areas. Consequently, specific perceptual deficits, as indicated from the test profile, suggest the use of specific materials designed to develop or train those particular perceptual deficits. Hence profile or scatter analysis is essential to the meaningful interpretation of DTVP results.

Scatter analysis is predicated upon the independence of the subtests, an independence somewhat supported by correlation studies of Frostig et al. (1964), Silverstein (1965), and Olson (1966b), which generally report intercorrelations of less than .50 among the five subtests. The factor analysis of the DTVP by Corah and Powell (1963) and Olson (1969) provided contradictory evidence which prompted their conclusion that although scatter analysis of the subtests is of questionable value, the PQ, a pooled figure to which each subtest contributes, may be a useful criterion of perceptual development. Additional research is necessary to demonstrate with certainty the independence of the DTVP subtests.

3. Administration Procedures. While the suggested examination procedures for the DTVP appear to be generally acceptable, some revisions have been advised. If children devote too much time to the individual test items, the teacher is at a loss as to what to do. To remedy this situation, Anderson (1965) has proposed the provision of time limits or specific instructions for use with laggards. Anderson considers the directions for administering and scoring satisfactory, but he states that the test material's esthetic quality ranges from "mediocre to poor." Austin (1965) was concerned that the time required to administer the test might be too lengthy for young children and that some of the vocabulary used in the directions was perhaps inappropriate. Most reports on the test, however, express no disquietude regarding the administration procedures.

4. Validity. Correlation coefficients of .44, .50, and .50 between the Frostig Test and teacher ratings of classroom adjustment, motor coordination, and intellectual functioning are offered by Frostig et al. (1963) in support of the test's validity. Subsequent investigations have established the relationship between the DTVP and numerous measures of

intelligence and academic achievement. Authors who have used the test with different samples of children include: Sprague (1963) and Rosen (1966), first grade; Olson (1966a, 1966b), second grade; Olson (1966c), third grade; Frostig et al. (1964), kindergarten through second grade; Bryan (1964), kindergarten through third grade; Allen, Dickman, and Haupt (1966), mentally retarded; Frostig (1962, 1963), brain injured; Abercrombie (1964), physically handicapped; Schellenberg (1963), poor readers. Should the test be used with mentally retarded children, review should be made of the cautions outlined by Allen, Jones, and Haupt (1965).

Summation of the findings, which relate to reading ability or readiness, indicate two things about the DTVP:

a. The DTVP adequately predicts reading readiness at the first-grade level, but not the level of achievement attained in the first grade. Bryan (1964), to the contrary, found the DTVP to be a better predictor of reading success than either reading readiness or IQ at this grade level.

b. It is related to a "small degree" with second- and third-grade reading ability. The predictive value of the DTVP at these levels is not as high as that of IQ, however.

Generally, the reported correlation coefficients between the DTVP and various intelligence measures range in the .30s and .40s. Additional work is required before the validity of the test can be firmly established.

5. Reliability. Three test-retest reliability studies, based upon two or three week intervals, are reported (Frostig et al., 1964). The resultant reliability coefficients for the total scores were .98, .80, and .69. Split-half reliability also was obtained for various age levels. Coefficients ranged from .78 at the 8–9 year level to .89 at the 5–6 level. The reliability coefficients for the total test generally lie above the accepted minimum of .80.

Frostig et al. (1964) reported studies that pertain to the reliability of the subtests and are based upon the test performance of kindergarten and first-grade children. These reliability coefficients which were derived by the test-retest method generally failed to achieve .70. Coefficients associated with Eye-Motor Coordination and Figure Ground were below .40 and .46, respectively. Constancy of Shape at the kindergarten, not the first-grade level was the only subtest which had a reliability coefficient exceeding .70. An additional investigation which used the split-half procedure for estimating reliability of the subtests was presented. In this case, relatively low coefficients were found for Position in Space at varying age levels (r = .35 to .70); coefficients associated with Eye-Motor Coordination were either .59 or .60; but those associated with the other subtests ranged from .65 to .96.

Frostig-Horne Program in Visual Perception

Description of the Training Program. While the Frostig Test contributed to the diagnosis of the child's perceptual assets and disabilities, the Frostig-Horne (1964) materials provide a well structured developmental program aimed at remediation of specific areas of perceptual weakness. The materials are recommended by Frostig for use with children in kindergarten and first grade as preparation for reading and other more complex visual activities as well as for use with children who have problems in perception. Modifications of the program are included in the manual for most types of exceptional children, and the procedure is set forth in explicit, carefully worded directions.

The program may be used remedially as well as developmentally. Remediation should begin immediately after evaluation of the visual perception areas, for early identification is necessary to prevent academic failure and concomitant emotional disturbance.

Not only does the program provide training in each of the five areas of measured visual perception, but it also suggests techniques for developing gross and fine muscle coordination, training eye movements, and enhancing body image and concept, skills which are basic to adequate perceptual functioning. In the *Teacher's Guide* (Frostig & Horne 1964), these latter activities are arranged in order of difficulty under the five areas and are to be used to prepare the child for the fine motor paper and pencil worksheets or as supplemental techniques.

Eye-Motor. Children who have eye-motor problems experience difficulty when they reach for items, dress themselves, or attempt movements which depend heavily upon visual adequacy. The supplemental procedures, which involve eye movement training, are followed up by 90 Frostig worksheets. The exercises include coloring, tracing, and the drawing of straight, curved, or broken lines between boundaries which become increasingly more narrow and are ultimately eliminated by the end of this section.

Figure-Ground. Problems in this area may cause the child to be disorganized and inattentive because of inability to screen out superfluous environmental stimuli. Numerous worksheets are provided which require the child to trace lines and to identify figures printed on increasingly complex backgrounds. Recognition of intersecting and hidden figures as well as figure completion and assembly activities are used in the training program.

PERCEPTUAL CONSTANCY. Inability of the child to perceive constancy of shapes and sizes can make his environment seem unstable and inconsistent. A familiar symbol may not be recognized when presented in a different color, size, form, or context. Worksheets provide exercise in the matching, discrimination, and categorizing of various forms and animals.

POSITION IN SPACE. Reversal problems such as the confusion of b and d, 42 and 24, "on" and "no" frequently result from inability to interpret position. Training in body image, body schema, and body concepts precedes the use of worksheets. In Frostig's program, awareness of the body's position in relation to objects is promoted by encouraging the child to crawl correctly under, over, and around various pieces of classroom furniture. Additional exercises are suggested which help develop the sense of directions in space, such as right, left, before, behind, over, under. After the child can perform these activities successfully, worksheets are introduced.

SPATIAL RELATIONS. Disabilities in this area can make it impossible to sequence sufficient perceptual information for word writing, arithmetic, and map reading. Worksheets are provided which afford practice in visually oriented sequential problems such as figure completion, recall of sequence, assembly of parts, and figure copying. Exercises concerned with spatial relations are complex and to an extent involve the perceptual abilities of the other areas.

The positive tone and creative presentation of the worksheets elicit teacher enthusiasm, and the "games" which foster high motivation and help maintain success furnish step by step progression in terms of difficulty and flexibility. These techniques make it possible for the child to progress at his own rate. In accordance with the present authors' experience, the work periods are sufficiently short to maintain the attention and tolerance of young children.

Use of the program is possible with a variety of groups of children who possess social-cultural, emotional, sensory, or neurological handicaps and it is useful also with groups who are heterogeneous in terms of mental ability. When limitations of the program are considered, acknowledgement is made that although perceptual training helps prepare a child for higher cognitive development, such training does not insure successful performance in higher cognitive processes. Seldom is a program comprehensive enough to meet the many needs of the developing child; instead, it must be used in combination with other programs and activities for maximum growth and development. However, Frostig's program is one of the few organized approaches to the assessment and remediation of these difficulties and many educators faced with the assessment and remediation of perceptual disorders use it.

Evaluation of the Training Program. Whereas the DTVP has prompted a steady accumulation of research, comparatively few studies have sought to evaluate the efficacy of the Frostig-Horne training program. When attempts have been made, the researchers tend to make variations in the program rather than implementing the techniques exactly as prescribed by Frostig; a few, including Klein (1967), have reported that extensive innovations were required before the children could cope satisfactorily with the worksheet exercises.

Teachers in Missouri who used the materials with kindergarten children observed improvements in many areas of visual perception and reported that the progress seemed to be effective in the promotion of reading and number readiness (Grade Teacher, 1965). The observations of these teachers, however, are refuted by Jacobs (1968), who found the program exerted little remedial influence upon kindergarten and prekindergarten youngsters. Jacobs concluded that the materials were most effective when used with first-grade culturally disadvantaged children.

A controlled study investigating the influence of visual perception training on first-grade reading achievement was reported by Rosen. The experimental Ss were trained using the Frostig-Horne materials for 29 days, 30 minutes per day, while the control Ss received the regular reading instruction. Rosen concludes:

> Each analysis revealed improvement in these perceptual capabilities trained; however, improvements in these abilities did not reflect themselves in comparable superior performance in criterion reading measures in experimental groups. Indeed, in two of the analysis control groups excelled experimental Ss in an important reading capability involving comprehension of ideas found in a short paragraph. It appears that additional time devoted to reading instruction was more important for reading achievement in this particular capability than time devoted to the types of perceptual training in this investigation (1966, p. 985).

Although the materials have been used with some types of exceptional children, the implications at this time are most inconclusive. In a study involving brain-injured children who were cerebral palsied Tyson (1963) found that the program in general was successful. This led to the implication that the approach was particularly desirable for young children with suspected visual-motor disturbance. Allen, Dickman, and

Haupt (1966) used the Frostig-Horne program for one semester with ten educable mental retardates. Six other retardates served as the control group. The authors concluded that the work resulted in discernible improvement on three of five subtests. Nonsignificant differences between groups were found on the other two subtests, Eye-Motor Coordination and Spatial Relations. However, an error was found in the published analysis of variance table which, when corrected, reduced the differences on the three subtests to insignificance. Therefore, contrary to the conclusions of the authors, the use of these materials with this sample of retardates apparently did not yield marked improvements in perceptual performance.

In summary, assessments of the Frostig-Horne training program differ, rendering additional research necessary in order to conclusively establish its efficacy. At present, the reactions of educators and researchers who have used the program vary widely regarding the effect of such training on the development of basic academic skills. Continued experimentation is recommended.

The Preschool Diagnostic Language Program

The Preschool Diagnostic Language Program, developed for culturally disadvantaged children and published as a curriculum guide in an experimental edition, is based upon the clinical model of the Illinois Test of Psycholinguistic Abilities and utilizes information from that test in structuring a compensatory program (Hartman, 1966). The approach outlined in the program is intended to (1) be introduced in compensatory preschool programs, (2) proceed from a specific diagnosis of educational malfunctioning in perception, cognition and language, (3) provide specific sequential programing in areas of weakness, and (4) be entirely usable and manageable by the average preschool teacher (Hartman, 1966, pp. 1-2).

Although the program was devised for culturally disadvantaged children who are better described as language deprived rather than language disordered, perusal of the curriculum guide indicates that the program would be equally beneficial for young children with language learning disorders. The program is still being evaluated by the Preschool and Primary Education Project of the Pennsylvania Department of Public Instruction and therefore must still be considered experimental. Teachers are encouraged, however, to explore the usefulness of the program not only in classes for culturally disadvantaged children, but in classes wherever the methods suggested would be applicable.

The 1961 ITPA is the primary diagnostic test battery used in the program and, as such, serves two functions. First, the results of the test provide the individual diagnoses upon which the program is structured. Second, the ITPA is used to measure the individual child's progress in the program; it is therefore one of the methods used in evaluating the effectiveness of the PDLP. Hartman (1966) is fair and justified in stating the disadvantages of total dependence upon the ITPA as a diagnostic and therapeutic-validation instrument. His comments are not new but they are statements which deserve iteration: the test does not provide information relative to the tactile-kinesthetic modalities; the theory upon which it is based represents assumptions and hypotheses; and the subtests may not measure the theoretical constructs which are purportedly assessed. Although the Revised Edition of the ITPA (Kirk, McCarthy, & Kirk, 1968) has been welcomed as a much needed extension and refinement of the 1961 Experimental Edition, the new instrument is open to the same criticisms posed by Hartman.

The Osgood model of language function upon which the 1961 and 1968 editions of the ITPA are based is presented in Chapter II. Thorough repetition of the discussion does not appear necessary, but a description of the clinical model of the ITPA will aid in understanding the test. The 1968 edition includes all of the former test and will be used in the future in lieu of the 1961 edition, thus we discuss only the newer test, although it was not used by Hartman. Following Hartman's principles, however, there is no reason to feel that the PDLP could not be implemented using the 1968 ITPA as the diagnostic instrument.

The Clinical Model of the ITPA

The model for the 1968 ITPA, shown in Figure 2, is based on the theoretical model of language devised by Osgood and encompasses three dimensions: psycholinguistic processes, levels of organization, and channels of communication (Kirk, McCarthy, & Kirk, 1968).

Psycholinguistic Processes. The first dimension of the test model encompasses the acquisition and use of the habits required for normal language usage. The three main sets of habits are reception, expression, and organization or association. Kirk, McCarthy, and Kirk (1968) define reception (decoding) as the ability necessary in order to obtain meaning from either visual or auditory symbols. Expression (encoding) refers to the ability required to express meaning either vocally or through gestures. Association is the ability to organize and manipulate linguistic symbols in a meaningful fashion. Examples of activities which demonstrate association ability include word associations, analogies, and simi-

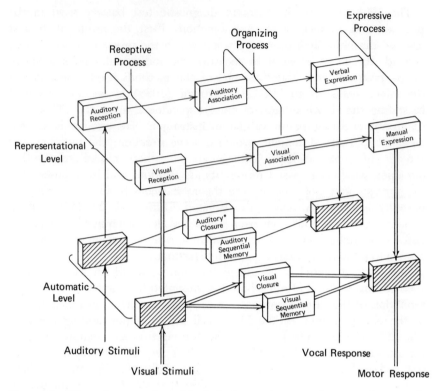

FIGURE 2.   Three-dimensional model of the ITPA. (From Kirk, McCarthy, & Kirk, 1968, p. 8.)

larities. Association appears to be comparable to the function of language which Myklebust (1954) terms "inner language."

Levels of Organization. The ITPA model includes a dimension that describes the functional complexity of the organism, namely, the two levels of language organization. The first level, the Automatic, mediates activities that require first the retention of linguistic symbol sequences and second the execution of automatic habit-chains. The second function is closure, and both grammatical and visual closure are tested. The former function, memory, is assessed by the test in both the auditory and visual aspects.

A child in the echo babble stage of speech development functions at the Automatic level because he is able to imitate but has no established meanings for his vocalizations. As the child develops greater language facility, he still relies upon this level for the complex receptive and expressive sequencing of sounds within words, words within sentences, whether oral or written.

The second and more complex level of organization is the Representational, which mediates activities requiring the meaning or significance of auditory or visual symbols. When the child learns the meaning of a linguistic signal and when he uses it in a symbolic or meaningful way, he is operating at the Representational level. Thus this level is directly comparable to the corresponding level of the Osgood model.

Channels of Language Input and Output. The third dimension of the ITPA describes the sensory motor path through which language is transmitted. The dimension is divided into the modes of input—auditory and visual—the modes of output—vocal and motor—and the combinations of auditory-vocal and visual-motor. No provisions have been made for other combinations of input and output modes, such as auditory-motor, visual-vocal, tactile-motor.

The Relationship of the Levels, Processes, and Modes. It may be noted from the model (Figure 2) that a relationship between levels and processes is implied. Processes are those learned activities imposed upon the nervous system at any level of organization. Osgood has hypothesized that a higher order of learning is required as the organizational complexity of the levels increases. For example, in permanently modifying the complex neural organization of the Representational level through learning, a qualitatively different type of decoding or reception results than is found at the Automatic level. The former is meaningful; the latter is not.

PRINCIPAL FEATURES OF THE PROGRAM

The primary characteristic of the Preschool Diagnostic Language Program is the utilization of the ITPA to structure individual programs of training. The second characteristic of the PDLP is the stages through which the program moves: a developmental stage and a remedial stage.

The Developmental Stage of the PDLP. The initial, developmental stage of the program may last from six weeks to three or four months and has as its goals the following:

1. Interpreting individual ITPA profiles in terms of possible intra-class remedial groupings.

2. Informally assessing the *accuracy* of ITPA scores and the *severity* and level of identified disability areas.

3. Preparing materials and room for remedial groupings.

4. "Trying out" various remedial groupings.

5. Getting children familiar with the type of "work" routines demanded during the remedial phase of the experimental language program (Hartman, 1966, 11–12).

During the first few months of the developmental stage of the program, teachers will be concerned most about diagnosing the language needs of the children, developing, on the basis of diagnosed needs, the initial remedial groupings, and generally preparing for the remedial stage of the program.

DIAGNOSING LANGUAGE NEEDS. Since children placed in a program such as this have been given the ITPA previous to enrollment, the results of the testing provide the basis for the initial remedial groupings. The teacher, however, is charged with the responsibility of assessing the accuracy of the test results and he, therefore, must use a systematic, albeit informal method of testing the children. In this way, the test results may be verified and supplemented. Informal procedures of assessing the child's language function are given in Chapters III and IV and are not repeated here, although review of the informal techniques of assessment may be helpful. The article by Wiseman (1965) and Bateman's (1968) monograph are also of interest.

In addition to verifying the ITPA results through informal testing, the teacher must rate the severity of each child's disabilities. The severity ratings along with the knowledge of areas of disability are used in developing the initial remedial groups. Severity ratings range from severe disability to moderate disability to disability noted; ratings are designated by different X symbols in the following manner:

1. X^1 represents a severe disability, namely, a delay of one year or more, on an ITPA subtest.

2. X^2 designates moderate disability, that is, a language age delay of less than one year but below CA.

3. X^3 is used to denote the presence of a disability when informal testing techniques are used and when the delay cannot be quantitatively delimited.

Many activities are listed by Hartman (1966) as samples of techniques through which the teacher may arrive at severity ratings. For example, he states that a child has a severe disability in auditory decoding if he cannot answer correctly such questions as:

Do you rain?
Do you smoke?
Do you run?
Do you bark?
Do airplanes fly?
Do cars cry?
Do babies eat?
Do bicycles drink?

The reader who is familiar with the ITPA will notice that the preceding questions comprise the first eight items of the Auditory Decoding subtest. In the same fashion, the sample questions for the other areas to be tested are taken directly from the ITPA.

DEVELOPING INITIAL REMEDIAL GROUPINGS. The teacher uses the information obtained from the results of the ITPA and from informal procedures to structure the initial remedial groups. The main purpose of such grouping is to enable the teacher to plan activities for discrete disabilities. The number of remedial groupings will vary, but a few guiding principles can be stated. More than three or four groups cannot be handled at one time; some grouping of common disabilities, therefore, must be developed. The teacher will have to be present during all activities pertaining to remediation of auditory and vocal areas, but he will not necessarily have to participate actively in all tasks related to the visual and motor areas.

For a hypothetic group of children, Hartman illustrates how the teacher might initially set up remedial groups and how the different "stations" in the classroom could be established. He hypothesized first three groups of children:

1. Group I—Children with visual decoding and/or visual-motor problems *and* some common auditory problems.
2. Group II—Children with auditory decoding and/or auditory-vocal problems *and* some common visual problems.
3. Group III—Children with other disabilities, not fitting into Group I or II.

For these three groups the teacher would set up three stations in the classroom, as follows:

1. Station I—Visual-motor association (the most severe single visual disability in the class).
2. Station II—Visual decoding and visual-motor sequencing.
3. Station III—All auditory disability (teacher supervised).

Group I would move through the sequence of the three stations daily. Group II would remain together at Station III, the auditory station, and Group III would be what Hartman calls a "feeder" group, that is, the children would not rotate as a unit but would be assigned to stations related to their disabilities.

The example given above is merely an illustration of how the initial remedial groups might be effected, but no example should be ideal when, in reality, groupings are seldom ideal. No system of grouping is going to be adequate for every child in a class; some children will exhibit profiles of abilities and disabilities that preclude their inclusion. Such children should be in the group which best fits their needs and should receive as much individual tutoring as feasible.

The Remedial Stage. Preparation for the remedial stage of the Preschool Diagnostic Language Program comprises the steps used in planning traditional programs: scheduling, preparing the room, gathering materials, and orienting the children. Three sample schedules for three different classes, given by Hartman (1966), are presented here. Schedule Sample I reflects the presence of auditory-vocal association deficits in all or most of the children and enough visual-motor sequencing problems in Group I that appropriate activities are repeated. One may observe that the program is scheduled for one hour per day, although it could be used for a longer period of time.

Schedule Sample I   (One Day)

Time	Group I	Group II	Group III
9:00– 9:20	Auditory Decoding Auditory-Vocal Automatic Vocal Encoding	Visual-Motor Assn. Motor Encoding	Visual Decoding Visual-Motor Sequencing
9:20– 9:40	Visual Decoding Visual-Motor Sequencing	Auditory Decoding Auditory-Vocal Sequencing Auditory-Vocal Automatic	Visual-Motor Assn. Motor Encoding
9:40– 9:50	Visual-Motor Sequencing	Motor Encoding	Auditory-Vocal Automatic
9:50–10:05	Whole Class—Auditory-Vocal Association		

Schedule Sample II   (One Week)

Disability Areas	Monday	Tuesday	Wednesday	Thursday	Friday
Auditory Decoding	Groups I, II, III	Groups I, II (together)			Groups I, III
Auditory-Vocal Association	Group I	Group I			Group I
Auditory-Vocal Automatic	Groups I, II, III	Groups II, III (together)	SAME AS MONDAY	SAME AS TUESDAY	Groups I, III (together)
Auditory-Vocal Sequencing	Groups II, III	Groups II, III (together)			No groups
Vocal Encoding	Groups I, II	Groups I, II (together)			Group II
Visual Decoding	Groups I, II, III	Groups I, III (together)			Groups I, III
Visual-Motor Association	Groups II, III	Groups II, III			Groups I, III
Visual-Motor Sequencing	Group II	Groups I, II			Group III
Motor Encoding	Group III	Group III			No groups

Schedule Sample II is divided into the nine disability areas defined by the 1961 ITPA and shows groups working together and apart on various days. Apparently Groups I and II have more severe auditory deficits than Group III, and this staggered schedule allows the teacher to work with those groups as much as possible.

The teacher who prepared Schedule III set up remedial groupings for each day and handled two auditory stations per day. No remedial groups having one defined type of membership were established. Also, it is apparent that the vocal and motor encoding problems in the class are not significant enough to warrant separate stations.

Scheduling and preparing the classroom go hand in hand, both being dependent upon the types of language disabilities presented by the children. Usually three or four separate stations are needed in the classroom. In addition to the permanent stations set up, the teacher may wish to establish temporary and/or permanent substations. A sample class-

Schedule Sample III (One Week)

| Names | Language Stations | | | | |
| | I | II | III | IV | V |
	Aud. Dec. Aud.-Voc. Assn. Aud.-Voc. Seq.	Aud.-Voc. Assn. Aud.-Voc. Auto. Aud.-Voc. Seq.	Vis. Dec. Vis.-Mot. Seq.	Vis.-Mot. Assn. Vis.-Mot. Seq.	Vis. Dec. Vis.-Mot. Seq.
Adams, Barry	M-Tu	W-Th-F	M-Tu	M-F	W-F
Baker, Mary	M-F-	—	M-F	—	M-F
Brody, Bill	W-F	M	M-Tu	Tu-F	M-F
Cohen, Larry	M-F	M-F	M	Tu-W	Th-F
Ellis, Harry	W-Th-F	M-Tu	W-Th-F	M-Tu	—
Gary, Linda	—	M-Tu	W-Th-F	M-F(2)*	—
etc.					

*(2) goes to station *twice* a day.

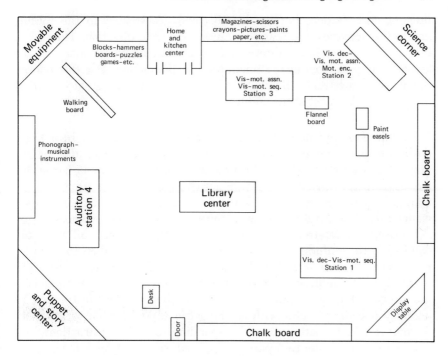

FIGURE 3. Sample classroom layout.

room layout, taken from Hartman (1966) and shown in Figure 3, illustrates the method used by one teacher in arranging the classroom. It can be seen that:

1. Three independent or nonsupervised visual stations were established.
2. Stations were located to take advantage of chalkboards and places where materials are stored.
3. A library table was centrally located so that children who finished their tasks early could go to look at pictures at this table.
4. The auditory station could easily use the puppet, story, and music equipment and materials in the room (Hartman, 1966, 37–38).

The time and effort expended in scheduling and arranging the class are wasted if the children do not know where they are to go and what they are supposed to do when they reach the different stations. Some type of system must be established for changing stations and the stations must be set up so that the children can begin work as soon as they are seated. Initially, the teacher will need to give directions to the children at each station, but as they become accustomed to the routine and to the activities, they can work with very little direction. The exception is, of course, the auditory and vocal stations where many of the activities require continual student-teacher interaction. For this reason, the teacher constructs the daily schedule so that the greater part of his time may be spent at the auditory station.

Specific Training Activities. Activity planning in the Preschool Diagnostic Language Program does not differ substantially from the suggestions given by Kirk (1966) and Wiseman (1965). Wiseman, in particular, has developed a series of language activities which lends itself to summarization and which is divided into five major sections: decoding, association, encoding, automatic or closure processes, and memory.

Decoding is referred to by Wiseman (1965) as the ability of the child to gather information from his environment and then to comprehend what he has seen and heard. For remedial purposes, decoding is divided into auditory and visual components, and training activities are suggested ranging from the simple to the complex. Instruction in auditory decoding begins with teaching the child to listen to a variety of sounds, discriminating sounds, responding to verbal instructions, and comprehending sentences, paragraphs, and stories. Visual clues, such as objects or pictures, are used in the initial stages of remediation but are later removed. Visual decoding training also begins with very simple activities and proceeds to more difficult tasks, such as identifying objects and pictures; identifying color, forms, letters, and numbers; learning similarities and differences; categorizing by visual features; and explaining action in pictures.

Association is the process used while manipulating concepts to form new ideas, including activities that demonstrate parallel or analogous ideas such as the awareness that carpenters and bricklayers both build houses. Transferring concepts from one experience to another is an associative process. Using addition combinations while buying candy at the store exemplifies such transfer. Seeing relationships between two objects at both the concrete and abstract level is also such a process. For example, an airplane and a car are alike in that both have wheels and windows (concrete level), but they are also both means of transportation (abstract level) (Wiseman, 1965, 21–22).

Suggestions made by Wiseman related to the improvement of associative abilities are concerned with either auditory association or visual association. Auditory association refers to the transference of ideas which have been received through the auditory channel and generally requires a vocal response. The child is asked to categorize or classify various objects or events, for example, "Name all the foods you can think of." He is then required to reverse the classification process when he is asked to what group three different objects belong, for example, "Chair, bed, and couch all belong to what group?" The child may be taught to identify similarities and differences and to describe such characteristics; concrete associations are emphasized at the beginning, more abstract associations are emphasized later in the program.

Visual association is defined by Wiseman as the ability to draw relationships between ideas presented visually; the suggestions made for training in this area are similar to those described under visual decoding remediation. Sorting activities and the teaching of visual similarities and differences are stressed initially. Later, the child is taught to arrange picture cards according to the context of a story.

The third area of remediation is encoding or the ability to generate and express ideas. Wiseman noted that mere verbal fluency may be confused with the more productive and complex encoding process; chatter should not be accepted as a substitute for meaningful language usage. The authors have noted that often children who seem to be quite fluent experience great difficulty when required to give relevant, meaningful responses in a structured situation, for example, when being administered the Vocal Encoding subtest of the ITPA. Training in vocal encoding begins with vocabulary-building tasks—asking the child to label or name a variety of objects and pictures. The suggestions given by Wiseman from this point forward are rather sketchy and deal with many aspects of vocal expression, answering questions in complex sentences, having the child teach a skill or concept to his classmates, and structuring problem-solving sessions. The activities related to the improvement of motor encoding (the expression of ideas through gestures) begin with imitative movements and progress through following directions, identifying body parts, right-left discrimination training, and all types of pantomiming.

Training in automatic or closure processes comprises the fourth area of remediation. Wiseman stated:

[M]uch of what the very young child learns is at a non-meaningful level. That is, he is not consciously aware of many associations he makes between the auditory and visual stimuli which constantly bombard him. However, the fact that he is a part of an environment that contains large numbers of redundancies and the fact that his central nervous system is structured so that his behavior takes these repetitions into account describe this important learning process. This *automatic* process is the accidental, nonpurposeful acquisition of the subtleties of the environment. For example, correct grammatical construction is the result of an unconscious assimilation and imitation of language patterns gradually habituated into an automatic form of behavior (1965, pp. 22–23).

When disabilities occur in the automatic processes, a child may exhibit a variety of problems, ranging from difficulties with temporal and distance orientation to an inability to blend sound elements into a meaningful whole to produce a word.

Activities suggested for training in the automatic process are discussed under auditory closure and visual closure; all are devoted to forming meaningful wholes from nonmeaningful parts. In training auditory closure, the teacher begins with auditory sound blending—discrete sound elements are produced, such as d-o-g, and the child selects a picture of a dog. Visual clues may be eliminated and the child is forced to rely more and more on his auditory ability, although additional clues may be given such as embedding the sound sequence to be blended in a meaningful sentence ("The boy pets the d-o-g"). Later in the program the child is taught paired-word associates, big-little, good-bad, etc., in the hope that when the stimulus word is given its associate will be evoked automatically, thereby supposedly strengthening the closure process.

The suggestions given by Wiseman for the training of visual closure are related to facilitating visual recognition of familiar pictures even when the complete visual stimulus is not present but only significant parts of it. The first tasks set for the child are the identification of silhouettes and slightly distorted shadows of familiar objects. Incomplete line drawings and pictures with parts erased are presented to the child for immediate recognition. Other activities include having the child complete and identify dot-to-dot line drawings.

The last area of remediation discussed by Wiseman (1965) is memory, which he notes has general and sequential elements found in both the auditory and visual channels or modes. General memory is the ability to retain global forms of information, for example, reading a paragraph and recalling its content. Sequential memory, on the other hand, refers to the ability to recall stimulus events in a specified order, such as the letters in a word. Wiseman says:

There are two general types of responses to be considered when working to improve the memory process: recognition and recall. Recognition responses refer to a less complex memory process that entails choosing the correct answer from several possible choices. . . . The child with a deficient memory may need an initial choice of items to organize the memory process and prepare a "set." Recall answers emanate from the individual with no cues other than those provided by the content of a question such as, "Who discovered

America?" This is a higher level, more complex form of mental functioning and demands far more cognitive sophistication. Both recognition and recall are important, but recall is the ultimate educational goal (1965, p. 23).

The nature of responses elicited while he worked to improve memory led Wiseman to state that activities should stress immediate, intermediate, and long-term memory functions. He suggests that auditory memory may be improved by exercises in imitation, following sequential directions, and all sorts of auditory repetitive activities. Short-term recall is stressed in the program he outlines, but one assumes that he introduces at a later time activities requiring long-term memory. Improvement of visual memory is facilitated through tasks that require the child to recall what he has seen, be it a page of pictures, geometric forms, letters, words, or numerals, and to give evidence of recall by drawing, naming, or arranging stimulus items.

RESEARCH ON ITPA PROGRAMS

There is at present a significant body of research dealing with the use of the ITPA as a diagnostic instrument, and the general tenor of this research indicates that the test may be used to delineate various groups of children and to provide a more effective method of differential diagnosis (Bateman, 1963; Ferrier, 1963; Kass, 1962; McCarthy, 1965; Myers, 1965; Olson, 1961). The research related to remediation based upon results of the ITPA is more limited but again seems to indicate that structured training can effect beneficial changes in children's performance on the ITPA (Hart, 1963; Hermann, 1962; Smith, 1962; Painter, 1964).

With the exception of one study (Painter, 1964), very little research has been published regarding the efficiency of ITPA remedial programs in effecting significant gains on other measures of language development or upon tests of academic achievement. We have little evidence at this time, therefore, to assume that the initiation of an ITPA remediation program will have significant effects upon the academic deficiencies of learning disabled children in a school setting. Sutton (1963) indicated that visual memory tests correlate with reading tests when the visual memory test is similar to the reading task; perhaps the same phenomenon obtains in remediation, that is, the closer the training is to remedial reading, the greater the progress of the student will be. Language therapists, however, continue to report informally that children in programs devoted to ITPA and Frostig regimes of remediation make substantial gains in academic skill areas. Such contentions should be submitted to careful and thorough investigation in an effort to determine whether children with specific learning disabilities make greater progress under a process-oriented training program, such as the ITPA or Frostig, or with a task-oriented program, such as the Gillingham or McGinnis.

In the next few years there undoubtedly will appear a rash of studies using the 1968 revision of the ITPA. Hopefully, this new body of research will move beyond the territory covered from 1961 to the present. There seems little profit in attempting to categorize groups of children with learning disabilities; the authors feel that the 1961 ITPA has demonstrated its efficiency in revealing specific language deficits. The new edition of the test purportedly will do the same job in a more discrete, detailed, and reliable fashion, but in general it will accomplish the same, not a new, task.

References

Abercrombie, M. L. J. Visual, perceptual, and visuo-motor impairment in physically handicapped children: VI. Marianne Frostig Development Test of Visual Perception. *Perceptual and Motor Skills*, 1964, **18**, 561–625 (Monograph Supplement 3-V18).

Allen, R. M., Dickman, I., & Haupt, T. A pilot study of the immediate effectiveness of the Frostig-Horne training program with educable retardates. *Exceptional Children*, 1966, **31**, 41.

———, Jones, R. W., & Haupt, T. D. A note of caution for the research use of the Frostig test with mentally retarded children. *Perceptual and Motor Skills*, 1965, **21**, 237–238.

Anderson, J. M. Test and reviews. In O. K. Buros (Ed.), *Mental measurement year book*. (6th ed.) Highland Park, N.J.: Gryphon, 1965.

Austin, M. C. Test and reviews. In O. K. Buros (Ed.) *Mental measurement year book*. (6th ed.) Highland Park, N.J.: Gryphon, 1965.

Bateman, B. D. Reading and psycholinguistic processes of partially seeing children. *CEC Research Monographs*, Series A, No. 5, 1963.

——— Interpretation of the 1961 Illinois Test of Psycholinguistic Abilities. Seattle, Wash.: Special Child Publications, 1968.

Bryan, Q. R. Relative importance of intelligence and visual perception in predicting reading achievement. *California Journal of Educational Research*, 1964, **15**, 44–48.

Corah, N. L., & Powell, B. J. A factor analytic study of the Frostig Developmental Test of Visual Perception. *Perceptual and Motor Skills*, 1963, **16**, 59–63.

Ferrier, E. E. An investigation of the ITPA performance of children with functional defects of articulation. *Exceptional Children*, 1966, **32**, 625–631.

Frostig, M. Brain damage. I. Diagnostic problems. *American Journal of Orthopsychiatry*, 1962 ,**32**, 279–280.

———. Visual perception in the brain-injury child. *American Journal of Orthopsychiatry*, 1963, **33**, 665–671.

————. The needs of teachers for specialized information on reading. In W. Cruick-shank, *The teacher of brain-injured children.* Syracuse, N.Y.: Syracuse University Press, 1966. pp. 87–109.

————. Testing as a basis for educational therapy. *Journal of Special Education,* 1967, **2**, 15–34. (a)

————. Education of children with learning disabilities. In E. C. Frierson and W. B. Barbe. *Educating children with learning disabilities.* New York: Appleton-Century-Crofts, 1967. 387–398. (b)

————. Education for children with learning disabilities. In H. Myklebust, *Progress in learning disabilities.* Vol I. New York: Grune & Stratton, 1968. pp. 234–266.

————, & Horne, D. *The Frostig program for the development of visual perception: Teacher's guide.* Chicago: Follett. 1964.

————. *The developmental program in visual perception: Intermediate pictures and patterns.* Chicago: Follett, 1966. (a)

————. *The developmental program in visual perception: Advanced pictures and patterns.* Chicago: Follett, 1966. (b)

————, Lefever, D. W., & Whittlesey, J. R. B. A developmental test of visual perception for evaluating normal and neurologically handicapped children. *Perception and Motor Skills,* 1961, **12**, 383–394.

————. Disturbances in visual perception, *Journal of Educational Research,* 1963, 3, 160–162.

————, & Maslow, P. Language training: A form of ability training. *Journal of Learning Disabilities,* 1968, **1**, 105–114.

————, Maslow, P., Lefever, D. W., & Whittlesey, J. R. B. *The Marianne Frostig Developmental Test of Visual Perception, 1963 standardization.* Palo Alto, Cal.: Consulting Psychologist, 1964.

————, Miller, A. M., & Horne, D. *The developmental program of visual perception: Beginning pictures and patterns.* Chicago: Follett, 1966.

Grade Teacher unsigned article. When the mind can't see what the eye sees. *Grade Teacher,* 1965, **83**, 82–85.

Hart, N. W. M. The differential diagnosis of the psycholinguistic abilities of the cerebral palsied child and effective remedial procedures. *Special Schools Bulletin,* No. 2, Brisbane, Australia, 1963.

Hartman, A. S. *Preschool diagnostic language program.* Harrisburg, Pa.: Department of Public Instruction, 1966.

Hermann, A. An experimental approach to the educability of psycholinguistic functions in children. Unpublished masters thesis, University of Illinois, 1963.

Jacobs, J. J. An evaluation of the Frostig visual-perceptual training program. *Journal of the Association for Supervision and Curriculum Development,* 1968, **25**, 332–340.

Kass, C. E. Psycholinguistic disabilities of children with reading problems. *Exceptional Children,* 1966, **32**, 533–541.

Kirk, S. A. *The diagnosis and remediation of psycholinguistic disabilities.* Urbana: University of Illinois Press, 1966.

————, McCarthy, J. J., & Kirk, W. D. *Illinois Test of Psycholinguistic Abilities, Revised Edition, Examiner's Manual.* Urbana: University of Illinois Press, 1968.

Klein, G. Practical applications for perceptual training. *Exceptional Children,* 1967, **34,** 50–55.

McCarthy, J. M. Patterns of psycholinguistic development of mongoloid and non-mongoloid severely retarded children. Unpublished doctoral dissertation, University of Illinois, 1965.

Myers, P. I. A study of language disabilities in cerebral palsied children. *Journal of Speech and Hearing Research,* 1965, **8,** 129–137.

Olson, A. Relation of achievement test scores and specific reading abilities to The Frostig Test of Visual Perception. *The Optometric Weekly,* 1966, 33. (a)

———. The Frostig Development Test of Visual Perception as a predictor of specific reading abilities with second grade children. *Elementary English,* 1966, **43,** 869–872. (b)

———. School achievement, reading ability, and specific visual perceptual skills in third grade. *Reading Teacher,* 1966, **19,** 490–492. (c)

———. Factor Analytic Studies of the Frostig Developmental Test of Visual Perception. *Journal of Special Education,* 1969, **2,** 429–433.

Olson, J. L. Deaf and sensory aphasic children. *Exceptional Children,* 1961, **27,** 422–424.

Painter, G. The effect of a rhythmic and sensory motor activity program on perceptual motor spatial abilities of kindergarten children. *Exceptional Children,* 1966, **33,** 113–119.

Rosen, C. L. An experimental study of visual perceptual training and reading achievement in first grade. *Perceptual and Motor Skills,* 1966, **22,** 979–986.

Schellenberg, E. D. A study of the relationship between visual-motor perception and reading disabilities of third grade pupils. *Dissertation Abstracts,* 1963, **23,** 3785–3786.

Silverstein, A. B. Variance components in the developmental tests of visual perception. *Percptual and Motor Skills,* 1965, **20,** 973–976.

Smith, J. O. Effects of a group language development program upon the psycholinguistic abilities of educable mental retardates. *Special Education Research Monographs,* No. 1, George Peabody College for Teachers, 1962.

Sprague, R. H. Learning difficulties for first grade children diagnosed by the Frostig visual perceptual tests. *Dissertation Abstracts,* 1964, **25,** 4006–4007.

Sutton, P. R. The relationship of visualization ability to reading. Unpublished masters thesis, University of Illinois, 1963.

Tyson, M. C. Pilot study of remedial visuo-motor training. *Special Education,* 1963, **52,** 22–25.

Wiseman, D. E. A classroom procedure for identifying and remediating language problems. *Mental Retardation,* 1965, **3,** 20–24.

CHAPTER X

A NEUROLOGICAL
ORGANIZATION SYSTEM

In the remedial perceptual-motor systems discussed in Chapter IV, training of perceptual abilities and of motor abilities is emphasized equally. The implication is that these functions are closely related and that improvement in one area stimulates improvement in the other area. Specific tasks, therefore, are designed to make use of both abilities simultaneously, resulting in increased integration between perception and motor response. In some systems, however, the emphasis of training is upon the development of motoric integration and coordination, the inference being that perception is to a considerable extent the by-product of motoric adequacy. Only one such system is discussed in this chapter—that arising from the work of Delacato and Doman.

Delacato and Doman work with children diagnosed as brain injured at the Institutes for the Achievement of Human Potential, in Chestnut Hill, Pennsylvania, which they co-direct. The training program at the Institutes is based upon a theoretical principle referred to as Neurological

Organization and is an outgrowth of their dissatisfaction with the results achieved by the methods of speech and physical therapy generally applied to brain damaged children (Doman, Spitz, Zucman, & Delacato, 1960). Ultimately, their theory for remediation can be traced back to Orton's theory of neurological organization introduced in 1928; however, Orton presented little information relative to treatment and prevention of learning disabilities. The influence of Temple Fay, a noted Philadelphia neurologist, enabled Delacato to form his rationale for the treatment and prevention of reading and language retardation (Delacato, 1959, pp. 10–12). Delacato's principle of neurological organization, diagnostic procedures, and treatment techniques is discussed in the chapter. An evaluation of the method is also included.

Principle of Neurological Organization

The concept of Neurological Organization, the cornerstone of the Delacato approach, is based on the theory that neurological development follows the biogenetic postulate that "ontogeny recapitulates phylogeny" (Delacato, 1959, 1963); that is, that individual human development repeats the pattern of man's evolutionary development. Delacato (1959) concludes:

Neurological organization is that physiologically optimum condition which exists uniquely and most completely in man and is the result of a total and uninterrupted ontogenetic neural development. The development recapitulates the phylogenetic neural development of man (p. 19).

Subsequently, Delacato's basic premise is that if man does *not* follow the sequential continuum of neurological development, he will exhibit problems of mobility and/or communication.

Delacato (1959, 1963) traces the phylogenetic development of the brain from the lowest level of living vertebrates (such as sharks and rays whose functions and movements are controlled by the spinal cord and medulla), through amphibians which have developed a larger pons and more dominant midbrain, to the primates (monkeys and apes) who have developed a larger and more dominant cortex.

Relative to man, Delacato (1963, p. 47–67) suggests that the development of the human brain follows a fairly consistent pattern. Beginning before birth and ending around the eighth year of life, neurological functions gradually develop vertically from spinal cord to cortex as myelinization takes place. During gestation and up to the time of birth the spinal cord and medulla oblongata are the upper reaches of neuro-logical organization. Within this organization is found muscle tone, reflex movement, and other reflexes necessary for life. At this level of organiza-tion the infant has movement, but no mobility. His movements are trunkal in nature and are not directed toward any object; his reflex activities such as sucking and crying are of a survival nature. Movements at this level resemble those of a fish.

The next developmental stage begins when the infant is about four months old. At this time, he is on an amphibianlike level, which is the responsibility of the pons. The infant's mobility is homolateral crawling; his vision is bi-ocular; and his hearing is bi-aural. Movements resemble those of a reptile.

The next stage of neurological development is called the midbrain level. When at this level the child is about ten months old. His mobility

Table 1 Comparison of Phylogenetic Neurological Development with Human Neurological Development[a]

	Highest Neurological Level	Mobility	Vision	Audition
Newborn infant	Medulla	Trunkal mvmt.	Reflex	Reflex
Fish	Medulla	Trunkal mvmt.	Reflex	Reflex
Four-month-old infant	Pons	Homolateral crawling	Bi-ocular	Bi-aural
Amphibian	Pons	Homolateral crawling	Bi-ocular	Bi-aural
Ten-month-old infant	Midbrain	Cross-pattern creeping	Binocular yoking	Binaural
Reptile	Midbrain	Cross-pattern creeping	Binocular yoking	Binaural
One-year-old infant	Early cortex	Crude walking	Early fusion	Early stereo-phonic
Primate	Early cortex	Crude walking	Early fusion	Early stereo-phonic
Eight-year-old (who speaks, reads, and writes)	Cortical hemi-spheric dominance	Cross-pattern walking	Stereopsis with predominant eye	Stereophonic hearing with pre-dominant ear

[a] Delacato, 1963, pp. 66–67.

is marked by cross-pattern creeping; his vision is binocular and eye yoking has begun. Hearing is binaural.

Neurologically, the one-year-old child has entered the level of the early cortex. His movements resemble those of a primate. He is able to walk crudely. There is an early fusion of the eyes taking place and the hearing is stereophonic.

The normal eight-year-old has developed cortical hemispheric dominance. He has a cross-pattern walk, a predominant eye, hand, foot, and stereophonic hearing with a predominant ear. He can read and write well. The comparison of phylogenetic neurological development and human neurological development as presented by Delacato is given in Table 1.

Man's neurological growth continues considerably beyond that of primates and man alone develops the use of symbolic language. Of particular significance for Delacato is the fact that man is the only creature which has developed hemispheric dominance in neurological function. Delacato has prepared tables showing the duration and se-

Table 2   The Doman-Delacato Developmental Language Scale

Stage	Level	Basic Characteristic	Age Range	Brain Stage
I Crying	1. Crying—a reflex creation of sound which, in itself, conveys no meaning other than to indicate the existence of life	Reflex—non-volitional	Birth	Medulla and spinal cord
II Alarm crying	2. Crying of a nature which seeks to protect life	Vital—to protect the mechanism from threat	3 to 20 weeks	Pons
III Gnostic sound	3. The ability to create meaningful sounds which indicate mood without words	Gnostic—meaningful goal directed	16 to 60 weeks	Midbrain

Table 2   (Continued)

Stage	Level	Basic Characteristic	Age Range	Brain Stage
IV Symbolic sound language	4. The ability to initiate and say two meaningful and understandable words	Depth of meaning	36 to 80 weeks	Human cortex
	5. The ability to use two words in combination plus a 10 to 25 word vocabulary	Depth of meaning exclusive to man	50 to 120 weeks	Human cortex
	6. The ability to form meaningful sentences which are grammatically incorrect or incomplete plus a vocabulary of more than 200 words		75 to 200 weeks	
	7. The ability to create meaningful sentences which are complete and grammatically correct plus an innumerable vocabulary		150 to 350 weeks	

quence of the various stages of growth through which a normal child moves in the course of mobility and language development (Tables 2 and 3). With the completion of these developmental processes, usually by the age of eight years, a child is said to have achieved a state of Neurological Organization. If injury to the brain occurs at any level or if environmental factors restrict the child's development in his natural progression, the child will show evidence of neurological dysfunction

Table 3   The Doman-Delacato Developmental Mobility Scale

Stage	Level	Age Range	Brain Level
I Movement without mobility	1. (Rolling over) 2. (Moving in a circle or backward)	4 to 20 weeks	Medulla and spinal cord
II Crawling	3. (Crawling without pattern) 4. (Crawling homologously) 5. (Crawling homolaterally) 6. (Crawling cross pattern)	6 to 40 weeks	Pons
III Creeping	7. (Creeping without pattern) 8. (Creeping homologously) 9. (Creeping homolaterally) 10. (Creeping cross pattern)	16 to 60 weeks	Midbrain
IV Walking	11. (Cruising—walking holding onto objects) 12. (Walking—without help and without pattern) 13. (Walking cross pattern)	40 to 100 weeks	Cortex

or disorganization in either language or mobility. Children who have problems in language, particularly in reading, almost always demonstrate incomplete attainment of cortical hemispheric dominance. Children who do not establish this dominance usually also evidence incomplete development at one or more preceding stages of brain development.

According to the theory of Neurological Organization, never are all the cells of the brain damaged; those that remain intact can be trained to take over the functions of the ones that have been destroyed. Such a supposition leads naturally to optimism regarding the benefits of treatment.

Diagnostic Procedures

Children with suspected brain damage or neurological dysfunction first are seen at the Institutes for a three-day complete diagnostic evaluation. A detailed history of the child's development is taken, including prenatal and perinatal factors, childhood diseases and injuries, motor and speech development, sleep patterns and tonality (Delacato, 1963). The child then undergoes clinical examination proceeding from subcortical to cortical levels and then to laterality.

THE DEVELOPMENTAL HISTORY

The parental questionnaire often suggests the etiological factors which in turn can lead to greater diagnostic validity. Conditions during pregnancy are considered of great importance. In addition to traumatic incidences and the Rh factor, the presence of spotting, measles, great weight gain, or illness on the part of the mother are of utmost importance in making a diagnosis. Many aspects of the birth process are taken into consideration. The length and severity of labor, the type and amount of anesthesia used, and the type of presentation are important. Often the birth cry and the time it takes place are overlooked, but they are also important.

Information relative to early childhood development and diseases is collected. Delacato is concerned particularily about feeding, sleep, and elimination patterns during the first six months of life. A history of febrile infections is always noted. The opportunity for and the amount of mobility of the child during the early months are considered. Constant motion or not enough movement may be a factor in a child's faulty neurological organization. The modes of crawling, creeping, and walking as well as the ages of onset are noted. Frequently the age and mode of crawling cannot be accurately determined unless a baby book or pediatric records are available.

Case history information concerning the child's mode of moving is generally obtained from the mother. Detailed information is gathered relative to the child's behavior in climbing since climbing often is an indication of the amount of creeping a child has done. Information as to the age of walking as well as the age of talking ideally should come from records.

THE CLINICAL EXAMINATION

Delacato's diagnostic approach proceeds from evaluation of subcortical to the cortical levels—then to laterality since this procedure retraces the course of neurological organization and is representative of the sequence of treatment involved. Tests such as the Wechsler Intelligence Scale for Children are given, as are measures of language, reading, and math. As a result of this testing, the intelligence quotient is known, and the potential for performance can be estimated. In addition to standardized tests, evaluative procedures associated with Delacato-Doman follow.

Pons Level. It is imperative that the child be observed during sleep. If the child is well developed at the pons level he sleeps correctly. Delacato (1963) states that as the head is turned while the child sleeps, one of the following behaviors should occur:

1. As the head is turned the body configuration should reverse itself and the child should remain asleep.
2. As the head is turned the child should resist its turning and should return to the original position and the child should remain asleep.
3. The child should awaken (p. 83).

If the child allows his head to be turned, does not awaken, and his body configuration does not change, it is assumed that he is not well organized at the level of the pons. Children who are not organized at the pontine and medullar level are usually quite severely disabled.

Midbrain Level. The next stage of evaluation is the midbrain level. When a child is unable to cross-pattern creep correctly, his eyes are not yoked yet, and he is unable to produce the sound components that make up his native language, organization at the midbrain level has not been completely established.

Early Cortex Level. The early cortex level is evaluated next. If a child is well organized at this level, he is able to cross-pattern walk correctly and smoothly. He can oppose the thumb and forefinger of each hand easily with no significant difference between the hands.

The child's overall performance in the areas of general physical activity and play is evaluated next. He should be able to play with the toys and playground equipment found in the average nursery school and be cautious of the dangers in his physical environment.

At this level of evaluation the child should have a thorough vision test that involves tests for muscle imbalance, both lateral and vertical at far and near points, fusion, fusion ranges, accommodation, and convergence. The eyes are tested separately, but while the tested eye is perceiving the target, the eye not being tested is seeing the same background. The child well organized at the level of the cortex should be able to succeed on these tests unless there is some pathological deterrent.

Cortical Hemispheric Dominance. Delacato next evaluates the area of cortical hemispheric dominance, an evaluation accomplished by ascer-

Table 4   Doman–Delacato Neurological Developmental Profile

(Writing) Expressive or Motor   (Reading) Receptive or Sensory

Brain Stage	TERM FRAME	COLUMN A MOBILITY	COLUMN B LANGUAGE	COLUMN C MANUAL COMPETENCE	COLUMN D VISUAL COMPETENCE	COLUMN E AUDITORY COMPETENCE	COLUMN F TACTILE COMPETENCE
VII (CORTEX)	Superior 36 Mon. / Average 72 Mon. / Slow 96 Mon.	Using a leg in a skilled role which is consistent with the dominant hemisphere	Complete vocabulary and proper sentence structure	Using a hand to write which is consistent with the dominant hemisphere	Reading words using a dominant eye consistent with the dominant hemisphere	Understanding of complete vocabulary and proper sentences with proper ear	Tactile identification of objects using a hand consistent with hemispheric dominance
VI (CORTEX)	Superior 22 Mon. / Average 46 Mon. / Slow 67 Mon.	Walking and running in complete cross pattern	2000 words of language and short sentences	Bimanual function with one hand in a dominant role	Identification of visual symbols and letters within experi- (STEREOPSIS)	Understanding of 2000 words and simple sentences (STEREOPHONY-S)	Description of objects by tactile means (STEREOGNOSIS)
V (CORTEX)	Superior 13 Mon. / Average 28 Mon. / Slow 45 Mon.	Walking with arms freed from the primary balance role	10 to 25 words of language and two word couplets	Cortical opposition bilaterally and simultaneously	Differentiation of similar but unlike simple visual symbols	Understanding of 10 to 25 words and two word couplets	Tactile differentiation of similar but unlike objects
IV	Superior 8 Mon. / Average 16 Mon. / Slow 26 Mon.	Walking with arms used in a primary balance role most frequently at or above shoulder height	Two words of speech used spontaneously and meaningfully	Cortical opposition in either hand	Convergence of vision resulting in simple depth perception	Understanding of two words of speech	Tactile understanding of the third dimension in objects which appear to be flat
III (MIDBRAIN)	Superior 4 Mon. / Average 8 Mon. / Slow 13 Mon.	Creeping on hands and knees, culminating in cross pattern creeping	Creation of meaningful sounds	Prehensile grasp	Appreciation of detail within a configuration	Appreciation of meaningful sounds	Appreciation of gnostic sensation
II (PONS)	Superior 1 Mon. / Average 2.5 Mon. / Slow 4.5 Mon.	Crawling in the prone position culminating in cross pattern crawling	Vital crying in response to threats to life	Vital release	Outline perception	Vital response to threatening sounds	Perception of vital sensation
I (MEDULLA and CORD)	Birth	Movement of arms and legs without bodily movement.	Birth cry and crying	Grasp reflex	Light reflex	Startle reflex	Babinski reflex

taining the dominant hand, eye, and foot. To find the dominant eye is not as simple as one may think. However, the dominant eye must be determined because an eye-hand relationship is considered a prerequisite to language development.

The evaluation of cortical hemispheric organization consists of tasks such as throwing a ball, using scissors, tracing a circle, and picking up various objects to see which is the dominant hand. Parents are asked to observe the child while eating, writing, and brushing his teeth. To determine the dominant foot, the child kicks a ball, steps onto a chair, walks forward and backward, walks up steps, picks up small objects with his toes, and occasionally traces a circle with a pencil held between his toes. The assumption behind these tasks is that the child tends to use his preferred hand or foot.

Data acquired from the evaluation are recorded on The Doman-Delacato Developmental Profile (Doman, Delacato, & Doman, 1964), a copy of which is included as Table 4. The profile permits a child's performance in six areas of expressive and receptive behavior to be displayed conveniently. The areas include: mobility, language, manual competence, visual competence, auditory competence, and tactile competence. The profile is presented to demonstrate the dimensions and extent of the Institutes' evaluation process; *use of the profile in educational or clinical settings is not recommended where personnel is without specific training in the use of this particular profile.*

Treatment Techniques

Establishment of the level of dysfunction, using the developmental profile, is followed by therapy which is based on the assumption that a specific therapeutic experience will affect the development of a specific brain level. Treatment begins at the child's diagnostically determined level of neurological development, at which the child fails. The child must master each successive level before he moves on to the next level; the test for crawling, therefore, is the mastery of crawling.

The principles of treatment consist of:

a. Permitting the child normal developmental opportunities in areas in which the responsible brain level was undamaged;

b. Externally imposing the bodily patterns of activity which were the responsibility of damaged brain levels; and

c. Utilizing additional factors to enhance neurological organization (Doman et al., 1960, p. 257).

The method of treating the brain itself instead of the results of the brain injury was developed at the Institutes and is called "patterning." A group of patterning movements was devised to manipulate the limbs of brain-injured children to produce movements which are the responsibility of the damaged level. The levels considered are medulla, pons, midbrain, and cortex. Patterning (the manipulation of arms, legs, and head) is based on the theory that all cells in an area of the brain are not usually affected by injury and that activation of live cells is possible. Intensity, duration, and frequency of the exercises will enable the brain to receive the sensory messages. Delacato (1957) defines this method as "treating a central problem where it exists, in the central nervous system, not in the peripheral areas" (p. 8). According to Doman et al. (1960), the movements used in patterning are modifications of the developmental patterns of A. L. Gesell and T. Fay. The patterning process is illustrated in Figure 1.

PREREMEDIAL LEVEL

Medulla Level. At the preremedial level, the principles of treatment are applied to the specific levels of neurological development as follows (Delacato, 1963). For the child whose mobility is severely impaired and who is disorganized at spinal cord and medulla level, opportunity is provided to use the basic reflex movements available to him by placing him on the floor for most of the day. In addition, undulating, fishlike movements are imposed on the child's body for prescribed periods during the day.

Pons Level. The same procedures are used at the level of pons with homolateral patterning being administered; this consists of having several adults work the child's limbs for him rhythmically while he lies face down on a table. One person turns his head from side to side, while another flexes the arm and leg on the side to which the head has been turned, and a third person extends the limbs on the opposite side. Proper sleeping patterns are prescribed at this level also. The development of biocular vision is aided by having the child follow a self-directed visual stimulus with each eye being occluded for three or four one-minute periods a day for two or three weeks.

Midbrain Level. At the midbrain level, the aim of treatment is the mastery of bilateral activity. A summary of useful activities follows.

Cross-pattern creeping is taught; practice time for this activity varies from ten minutes to one hour per day. Training for visual yoking of the eyes is facilitated when the child follows a visual stimulus which he or others is moving. Music, tonal discrimination and memory, and sound games are used with children who have articulation problems and difficulty with phonetic elements.

START—in UP position at (1) and DOWN position at (3)

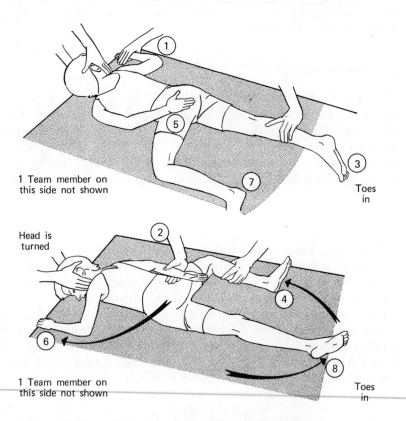

Head faces
UP arm

1 Team member on
this side not shown

Toes
in

Head is
turned

1 Team member on
this side not shown

Toes
in

Team members move, as follows: 1 + 3 to 2 + 4   5 + 7 to 6 + 8

FIGURE 1.   (a) Cross-pattern—three-man team. (b) Homolateral pattern—five-man team.

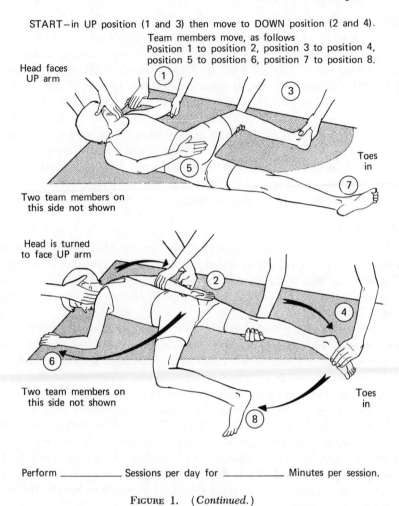

START—in UP position (1 and 3) then move to DOWN position (2 and 4).

Team members move, as follows
Position 1 to position 2, position 3 to position 4,
position 5 to position 6, position 7 to position 8.

Head faces
UP arm

Toes
in

Two team members on
this side not shown

Head is turned
to face UP arm

Two team members on
this side not shown

Toes
in

Perform _____ Sessions per day for _____ Minutes per session.

FIGURE 1.   (*Continued.*)

Early Cortical Level. At the cortical level, patterning consists of daily ten-minute or more practice periods in cross-pattern walking depending upon the diagnosis. Visually the child should be developing stereopsis through playground games which require that he learn about spatial relations. He also must develop comfortable near-point vision if he is to become ready to read, and simple table activities such as crayoning are suggested.

Cortical Hemispheric Dominance. The final stage of neurological development is attained when cortical hemispheric dominance is established.

At this level, patterns of sleep consistent with sidedness are emphasized Activities such as kicking, stepping off, and hurdling are used to help develop a dominant foot. Skills such as throwing, cutting, using tools, and picking up objects are used to develop handedness. Eye dominance is taught through the use of games involving telescopes for far-point vision and microscopes for near-point vision. Delacato also favors the use of a device called a Stereo-Reader manufactured by the Keystone View Company. It has the effect of occlusion while giving the illusion that both eyes are seeing the training material. This material consists of exercise cards of visual-motor activities, word families, visual discrimination, phrase reading, reading for interest, and speed reading. Two twenty-minute periods per day are usually prescribed.

REMEDIAL LEVEL

The foregoing procedures comprise the preremedial period. In theory when the neurological organization is complete, the problem is overcome. The only function of the remedial teacher is to bring the child as quickly as possible up to a level which will enable him to go into the regular class.

Delacato (1963) recommends specific rules for remedial teaching. In both speech and reading, a child should be introduced first to whole words which arise out of his experience. The next step is to help the child recognize words by their relationship to other words and to the meaning of the sentence, that is, from context clues. Following this step, he moves on to analyzing the smaller components that make up a word, and lastly to phonetic analysis. Thus reading instruction should proceed from concepts and whole words down to its finer elements. When a child reaches a plateau, the teacher should go back to the conceptual whole and begin the process again. As it is repeated, the cycle should become longer until the child is ready to handle the work of the regular classroom.

Appraisal of the Delacato Method

Both the theoretical base and the treatment techniques employed by Doman and Delacato have stimulated considerable interest and controversy in the professional and popular press. In defense of the efficacy of his habilitation system, Delacato (1966) refers to the studies of Carrick and Watson; Mariam; Masterman; McGrath; Kabot; Vivian; Glaeser, DeWaide, and Levi; Noonan; Alcuin; and Miracle. These investigations are offered by Delacato as a scientific appraisal of his method; the results are interpreted by their respective authors as demonstrations of the positive relationship between reading achievement and his suggested techniques.

Robbins and Glass (1967), however, are highly critical of the basic assumptions of the theory, notably the position on Neurological Organization, and of the eleven studies offered by Delacato in defense of his system. The research designs, choice of statistical procedures, sampling techniques, and other technical aspects used in the studies cited are systematically challenged. Their criticisms cast considerable doubt upon the otherwise encouraging results of the reported studies. Specific probable sources of invalidity for these and other pertinent experiments reviewed by Robbins and Glass are presented in Table 5. In addition to the relevance to the Delacato system, the reader will find the Robbins and Glass monograph interesting for its critical analysis of such topics as laterality, cerebral dominance, and handedness. Additional research is available which also fails to support the Institutes' position relative to the acquisition of reading (Robbins, 1966; Stephens, Cunningham, & Stigler, 1967).

Kershner's (1968) study which used matched groups of trainable retardates yielded a curious finding. After approximately five months of training using Delacato's techniques the experimental group was found to have significantly outperformed their controls in mobility (the ability to creep and crawl) and on the Peabody Picture Vocabulary Test, but was found to be no better than the control group in motor development as determined by performance on an adapted form of the Vineland-Oseretsky Motor Development Tests. Interpretation leads to the rather strange conclusion that the training techniques which were essentially motor or perceptual-motor and devoid of any language activities resulted in increased vocabulary comprehension while simultaneously producing no comparable improvement in motor development. The control group was involved in a considerable physical education program in an attempt to control for Hawthorne effect; Kershner suggests, perhaps with justification, that this accounts for the results relative to the motor development variable.

Freeman (1967) has offered a distillation of objections to the Institutes' methods which are expressed frequently by professional individuals and groups. These objections, published in the *Journal of the American Medical Association*, are listed below; the reader is referred to Freeman's article for a detailed discussion of each item.

1. A tendency on the Institutes' part to ignore the natural clinical course of some patients with brain injuries.

Table 5 Probable Sources of Invalidity for the Eleven Experiments Being Reviewed

Source of Invalidity	Delacato (1959) Piper	Delacato (1963)	Sister Edwin	Master-man	Mc-Grath	Noonan	Kabot	Glaeser	Aleulin	Miracle
History			X	X				X		
Maturation	X	X			X	X				
Testing	X	X			X					
Instrumentation							X			
Regression	X	X		X	X	X				
Selection			X	X	X		X	X	X	X
Experimental mortality	X							X		
Inappropriate or inadequate statistical analysis	X	X	X							

2. Assumption that their methods treat the brain itself, whereas other methods are "symptomatic."

3. Assumption that because the "full potential of the brain" is not known one can conclude that each child not "genetically defective" may have above average intellectual potential.

4. The policy which makes parents therapists.

5. The forceful prevention of self-motivated activities of the child.

6. Assertions which may increase parental anxiety and concern, such as:

a. The threat of the child's death.

b. The implication that a variety of almost universal child-rearing practices may damage a child's potential.

c. The implication that there is a need for absolutely rigid performance of "patterning" to obtain successful results.

7. Assumption that improvements are due to specific factors.

8. The test instrument (the Doman-Delacato Profile).

9. Statistical defects in the reported studies which were referred to previously in Table 5.

Because of the controversy engendered by the objections listed, the Institutes have become increasingly alienated from medical, psychological, educational, and parental national organizations. During the spring of 1968, an "official statement" which was critical of the Institutes was approved by the American Academy for Cerebral Palsy, American Academy of Physical Medicine and Rehabilitation, American Congress of Rehabilitation Medicine, Canadian Association for Children with Learning Disabilities, Canadian Association for Retarded Children, Canadian Rehabilitation Council for the Disabled, National Association for Retarded Children, American Academy of Pediatrics, American Academy of Neurology, and the American Association on Mental Deficiency (Drake, 1968). The Institutes' official reply to the "official statement" and to criticisms by Freeman, Robbins, and Glass is presented in a series of articles published in *Human Potential* (1968a, 1968b, 1968c, 1968d), a publication of the Institutes.

This book is limited to discussion of methods; a detailed review of the research which is pertinent to this method's evaluation can be found in the original studies and the cited critiques. A reading of these primary sources is necessary for personal evaluation of the system's efficacy. That professional opinions as well as research findings differ regarding the value of a particular remedial technique is a common occurrence in education. Studies that do not support the work of others who train at the perceptual-motor level also exist. Since these workers have not made the all-encompassing claims for cures maintained by the Institutes, they remain firmly associated with the professional community. Conclusive evidence of this method's value, however, will be established by the patient accumulation of future research findings. Fortunately, the nature of the interest in this subject is such that additional studies are assured.

References

Delacato, C. H. The non-surgical central approach to the central problem. Monograph published in 1957 in Philadelphia, Pennsylvania.

————. *The treatment and prevention of reading problems.* Springfield, Ill.: Thomas, 1959.

————. *The diagnosis and treatment of speech and reading problems.* Springfield, Ill.: Thomas, 1963.

————. *Neurological organization and reading.* Springfield, Ill.: Thomas, 1966.

Doman, G. J., Delacato, C. H., & Doman, R. *The Doman-Delacato Developmental Profile.* Philadelphia, Pa.: Institutes for the Achievement of Human Potential, 1964.

Doman, R. J., Spitz, E. B., Zucman, E., & Delacato, C. H. Children with severe brain injuries. *Journal of the American Medical Association,* 1960, **174,** 257–262.

Drake, D. C. Ten agencies rap institute for retarded. *The Philadelphia Inquirer,* May 7, 1968.

Human Potential. Institutes' official reply, 1968, 1, 301–306. (a)

————. Institutes' official statement. 1968, 1, 307–310. (b)

————. Letters to and about the Institutes, 1968, 1, 311–331. (c)

————. Editorial statement. 1969. 1, 332–333. (d)

Kershner, J. R. Doman-Delacato's theory of neurological organization applied with retarded children. *Exceptional Children,* 1968, **34,** 441–452.

Robbins, M. P. A study of the validity of Delacato's theory of neurological organization. *Exceptional Children,* 1966, **32,** 517–523.

———— & Glass, G. V. The Doman-Delacato rationale: A critical analysis. Research paper, Laboratory of Educational Research, University of Colorado, Boulder, August, 1967.

————. The Doman-Delacato rationale: A critical analysis. In J. Hellmuth (Ed.). *Educational therapy.* Seattle, Wash.: *Special Child* (in press).

Stephens, W. E., Cunningham, E. S., & Stigler, B. J. Reading readiness and eye hand preference patterns in first grade children. *Exceptional Children,* 1967, **33,** 481–488.

CHAPTER XI

THE METHODS AND THE MODEL

Traditionally, the last chapter of a textbook summarizes previously presented material with an effort being made to draw logical conclusions and to point the way toward future study. Summarizing the various teaching methods and techniques which have been presented here would not do justice to the individual systems, nor would it enable the authors to draw over-all conclusions regarding the methods. Rather we present a summary in terms of relating the teaching methods to the composite model of language function discussed in Chapter II. In this way we feel that similarities and contrasts among methods can be demonstrated effectively. In approaching this task it appeared easier and less confusing to take apart the model along the lines of the levels of language organization, processes, and sensory modalities in order to place within the model the different methods. Such an approach resulted in nine tables rather than one and each of the tables is discussed in turn.

Decoding

Beginning at the lower left-hand corner of the model (see Chapter II, Figure 1), one encounters first decoding at the projection level. Since most authors agree with Osgood in stating that the projection level is not amenable to learning, the first level in which the teacher is interested is integration. Table 1 presents the authors who emphasize training in decoding at the integration level, whether the sensory modality be visual, auditory, tactile, or kinesthetic. Most of the authors who emphasize decoding at this level are more concerned with vision than with other modalities. In fact, only two writers, Freidus and Barsch, stress tactile decoding. Decoding at the integration level refers to the reception of nonmeaningful, although organized or patterned stimuli. The ability to match colors, forms, sounds, objects, and so on, through the utilization

Table 1   Authors Who Emphasize Decoding at the Integration Level

The Decoding Process			
Visual	Auditory	Tactile	Kinesthetic
Barry	Barry		
Barsch		Barsch	Barsch
Cruickshank			
Freidus	Freidus	Freidus	Freidus
Frostig			
Getman			Getman
ITPA	ITPA		
Kephart			Kephart
Lehtinen			
Myklebust	Myklebust		

of the various sensory modalities is mediated at this level. All types of discrimination tasks and many of the activities described by the authors in Chapter IV—Perceptual Motor Systems—are typical of decoding at the integration level.

Differences among authors begin to become apparent as we move up the language model to decoding at the representational level and one finds that many of those who emphasized decoding at the lower level no longer stress decoding. Table 2 shows the relatively small number of authors (as compared with those in Table 1) who emphasize representational level decoding. The table also indicates that the visual and auditory modalities are about equally emphasized, although few authors are concerned with the tactile and kinesthetic modalities. Decoding at the representational level refers to the reception of meaningful stimuli; discrimination and matching are no longer the primary activities involved, although adequate decoding at the representational level is dependent upon adequate decoding at the integration level. Obviously, one cannot apprehend the meaning or significance of a symbol unless one is able to discriminate.

Inspection of Tables 1 and 2 reveals the similarities among Barry, Freidus, Myklebust, and the ITPA systems and the contrast between them and other authors such as Barsch, Frostig, and Getman. The greatest point of contrast is the division among authors along the line drawn between the levels of language and to a lesser extent along the lines

Table 2 Authors Who Emphasize Decoding at the Representational Level

The Decoding Process		
Visual	Auditory	Tactile
Barry	Barry	
		Barsch
Freidus	Freidus	Freidus
ITPA	ITPA	
Lehtinen		
	McGinnis	
Myklebust	Myklebust	

drawn among the input-output modes. Barry, Freidus, Myklebust, and the ITPA appears to stress both visual and auditory decoding at both levels of organization, whereas Barsch, Frostig, Getman, and Kephart are more concerned with visual decoding and motor encoding at the integration level. The reader should recall, however, that because of other similarities and differences among their methods all of these authors are not included in the same chapter. For example, Freidus and Myklebust are discussed in different sections because their basic orientations are dissimilar; Myklebust in the last analysis is concerned primarily with oral and written language, whereas Freidus leans toward an emphasis upon the development of the perceptual motor skills. The tables also reveal that Barsch and Freidus are the only two authors who consistently stress training tactile and/or kinesthetic decoding at either level of language.

Encoding

In some respects the obverse of decoding is encoding or expression and the next two tables are concerned with the latter process. In Table 3 one may find the authors who emphasize encoding at the integration level, that is, the ability to express certain vocal or nonvocal motor acts which, in themselves, are not meaningful. For example, the production of sounds, digits, or words without meaning is typical of vocal encoding at this level. Copying designs or performing skilled motor

Table 3   Authors Who Emphasize Encoding at the Integration Level

The Encoding Process	
Vocal	Motor
Barry	
	Barsch
	Delacato
	Freidus
	Frostig
	Getman
	Kephart
McGinnis	
Myklebust	

acts are the nonvocal, or so-called motor counterparts of vocal encoding at the integration level. Table 4 presents a review of the authors who stress training in the encoding process at the representational level, training which includes activities involving meaningful vocal, graphic, and/or motor responses. The expression of ideas through the media of oral language, writing, and gestures typifies encoding at the representational level.

By comparing Tables 1 and 2 with Tables 3 and 4, it becomes apparent that most authors who emphasize visual decoding, whether at the integration or representational level, also stress motor encoding, while those authors who are concerned primarily with auditory decoding tend to stress vocal encoding. For example, all of the writers discussed under the rubric of perceptual motor systems emphasize the visual-motor mode of input and output, but those authors who are included in the language development systems seem primarily concerned with the auditory-vocal channel of communication. It is interesting to note also that a few individual writers cut across modality-bound lines, the most notable being Freidus, Myklebust, and the ITPA systems.

Table 4   Authors Who Emphasize Encoding at the Representational Level

The Encoding Process		
Vocal	Graphic	Motor
Barry		Barry
Fitzgerald	Fitzgerald	
Freidus		Freidus
ITPA		ITPA
Myklebust	Myklebust	Myklebust
Pugh	Pugh	

Association

Whereas decoding tasks are primarily receptive and encoding tasks are essentially expressive, associational activities involve important elements of both reception and expression and cannot be divided arbitrarily. In actuality most tests of decoding or encoding involve sòme association ability, as do activities which are developed to improve either decoding or encoding. Such contamination results from having to provide the child with a stimulus and having to evaluate his response. In these tasks either the input or output modality is deemphasized so that one may assess the child's behavior in that process which is under scrutiny. Other activities, however, emphasize to the same degree both the decoding of a stimulus and the encoding of a response and the assumption is made that it is the association between the two which is of primary importance. On the other hand, decoding and encoding requirements may be held at a minimal level while the nature of the association becomes more and more complex and difficult, as in analogy tests. At the integration level of language these association tasks are nonmeaningful and include such tasks as copying designs, learning sound-letter and letter-sound combinations, or learning to associate pictures with objects. Following are examples of common association activities:

1. Auditory-motor. Writing individual letters, numbers, nonsense syllables from dictation.
2. Auditory-visual. Matching sounds with pictures or letters.
3. Visual-vocal. Saying aloud the sound of a particular letter presented graphically.
4. Visual-motor. Copying geometric forms, letters, and so on.
5. Auditory-vocal. Imitating sounds or words.

Authors who emphasize the perfection of cross-modality associations at the integration level of language are presented in Table 5. Inspection of the table reveals that the authors who are concerned with the teaching of academic skills stress association in all input-output combinations, a phenomenon which occurs because many of these authors suggest the use of a phonics approach to reading. In fact, the greatest difference among the authors listed in Table 5 is related to the types of material they employ in strengthening association ability; Gillingham, McGinnis,

Table 5   Authors Who Emphasize Association at the Integration Level

Association Process				
Auditory-Vocal	Auditory-Motor	Auditory-Visual	Visual-Vocal	Visual-Motor
Barry	Barry			
				Barsch
				Cruickshank
				Freidus
				Frostig
				Getman
Gillingham[a]	Gillingham	Gillingham	Gillingham	Gillingham
				Kephart
				Lehtinen
McGinnis	McGinnis	McGinnis	McGinnis	
Myklebust	Myklebust			
Spalding[a]	Spalding	Spalding	Spalding	Spalding

[a] Gillingham and Spalding emphasize sound-letter and letter-sound combinations using all input-output modalities.

and Spalding use letters and words, the majority of the other authors uses a variety of materials. The aim of the former is to improve academic skills, that of the latter to improve basic learning processes regardless of the kind of material employed.

The association process at the representational level differs from the process at the integration level in that the associations formed are meaningful in terms of dealing with concepts rather than with simple discriminations or percepts. The authors who emphasize the association process at the representational level are primarily interested in the formation of meaningful auditory and/or visual associations. The activities they

Table 6   Authors Who Emphasize Association at the Representational Level

	Association Process	
Auditory	Visual	Tactile-Kinesthetic
Barry	Barry	
Fernald[a]	Fernald	Fernald
Freidus	Freidus	
ITPA	ITPA	
McGinnis		
Myklebust	Myklebust	

[a] Fernald emphasizes simultaneous association across all input-output modalities.

suggest include categorization, classification, and sorting tasks as well as the identification and description of similarities and differences among objects, pictures, words, and ideas. In comparing Tables 5 and 6, the reader may observe that many authors who emphasize association at the integration level do not stress the ability at the representational level. In general, most of those who employ a phonics approach to reading remediation are not shown in Table 6 because their orientation presumes that their students are well able to generalize, abstract, and form meaningful associations. Rather, they feel that the children need specific assistance only in forming those associations between letters and sounds in which the presentation of one will come to evoke the recall of the other. The remaining authors shown in Table 6 acknowledge the cognitive (as opposed to integration level) disorders presented by many children with specific learning disabilities and they have developed techniques for assisting these children.

Closure

The closure or automatic functions evolve from the redundancies in the environment which lead to overlearned and unconscious associations like those that are necessary for correct grammatical construction, proper syntax, or sound blending. Though adequate closure probably is an element in the mastery of most perceptocognitive habits, only a few of the authors discussed provide particular suggestions for the development or perfection of the closure function, and they are presented in Table 7.

Table 7   Authors Who Emphasize Automatic or Closure Functions

Closure Functions	
Auditory	Visual
	Frostig
Gillingham	
ITPA	ITPA
Myklebust	

Wiseman, in his ITPA curriculum, details activities which facilitate the closure function in both the auditory and visual channels. While not specifically mentioning closure, many of the remedial procedures suggested by Myklebust are based upon Gestalt principles. These include his use of sentence completion exercises and activities which require the recognition of familiar words from their configurations. Because of her heavy emphasis upon the training of sound blending, Gillingham is included among the authors who implement closure activities even though she, like Myklebust, does not refer to the term by name in her writings. The figure completion activities suggested by Frostig for training in spatial relations are decidedly closure tasks. Undoubtedly, other authors could be listed in Table 7 because they may mention, incidentally, tasks which incorporate the closure function; only those presented in Table 7, however, appear to stress the need for training in closure.

Memory

Most persons who have developed instructional systems recognize the positive influence of memory upon learning and have attempted to develop the function. Since these authors tend to emphasize different dimensions of memory, considerable variety exists among the types of training tasks proposed. For example, one person may be interested primarily in the sequential aspects of visual memory at the integration level of language, whereas another may center his attention upon auditory memory at the representational level. Therefore, the general characteristics of any memory deficit in children with learning disorders must be determined before the selection of appropriate remedial procedures. Once this is done, as with other types of learning disorders, the teacher can familiarize himself with work of those writers who address themselves to the particular aspect of the problem presented by the child. Table 8 was prepared to demonstrate the relative positions regarding memory training of the authors included in this book. Although they

Table 8   Authors Who Emphasize Memory Functions

| | Memory Functions | | | |
| | Auditory | | Visual | |
	Sequential	Nonsequential	Sequential	Nonsequential
Representational level	Freidus ITPA Myklebust	ITPA Myklebust	Freidus ITPA Myklebust	Barsch ITPA
Integration level	Barry ITPA	ITPA	Barsch Frostig ITPA Kephart Myklebust	Barsch Getman ITPA

all express interest in memory functions, the focus of their interest differs markedly.

Because the activities suggested by Wiseman parallel the ITPA and Osgood models, they bear resemblance to the functions of memory postulated in the composite model and subsequently provide for training along most dimensions of memory. The remedial activities suggested by Wiseman are related to both auditory and visual channels at each level of language. Concern with problems of storage and retrieval (memory) leads Freidus and Myklebust to emphasize the association of present sensory information and past meaningful experience. Myklebust's interest in auditory memory centers around problems in reauditorization and word selection, both involving meaningful language. In training visual memory, he uses nonmeaningful as well as meaningful materials and suggests a variety of techniques including the use of large print, color coding, flashlight pointers, and numerous auditory and tactile reinforcements.

According to Barry, training in auditory memory is often necessary. Her activities are, however, characteristic of tasks at the integration level in that imitation (short-term recall) of rhythms and nonsense syllables, among other similar tasks, is predominant. Practice in visual memory at the integration level is recommended by Getman, who attempts to develop greater awareness of size and form, increased speed in visual recognition, increased span of form recognition, and more adequate retention of visual images. Barsch also suggests specific activities to train visual memory in both its sequential and nonsequential aspects, although only nonsequential recall is stressed at the representational level. Selected parts of the Frostig-Horne training program in visual perception, especially those related to spatial relations, depend heavily upon visual memory. These activities involve imitation and recall of sequences. Kephart does not specifically mention memory training; he is included in Table 8, however, because of the large amount of training he describes which requires the child to reproduce forms using pegboards, matchsticks, and chalkboards.

Feedback

Feedback, the function by which the child monitors his own responses to alter or correct them, is recognized by most authors as an important facet of learning. This self-correcting or self-adjusting phenomenon is operant in the auditory, visual, tactile, and kinesthetic modalities at both the meaningful and nonmeaningful levels of language. Some authors, like Freidus and Kephart, make feedback a fundamental principle within their concepts of learning disabilities, while others either refer briefly to the subject or make no mention at all of the function. Authors who utilize feedback theory directly or whose techniques strongly reflect feedback theory are presented in Table 9.

Freidus bases her approach directly upon a servomechanistic model and subsequently recommends self-correcting materials or at least materials which reduce the probability of error, such as form boards. Whenever appropriate, the child is asked to check his answers, productions, or other responses for errors, distortions, and so on. One may find in Freidus' writings numerous activities which are suitable for training the feedback function in various modalities at both levels of language.

Kephart also uses a servo model and considers feedback essential to the formation of an adequate perceptual-motor match. Consistent with his model, the activities he offers are designed to provide strong visual and tactile-kinesthetic feedback at the integration level.

The other authors shown in Table 9 may or may not mention feedback directly, and few of them include feedback within their models of the learning process. Many of the tasks they recommend, however, have built into them the function of feedback; for example, they may require the child to match pictures with written words or simultaneously talk and write, techniques recommended by McGinnis and Fitzgerald and Pugh, respectively.

Table 9   Authors Who Emphasize Feedback Function

	Feedback Functions		
	Auditory	Visual	Tactile-Kinesthetic
Representational level	Freidus McGinnis Myklebust	Fitzgerald Freidus Pugh	Freidus
Integration level	Freidus McGinnis Myklebust	Barsch Freidus Getman Kephart Lehtinen Myklebust	Barsch Freidus Getman Kephart

Summary

In this chapter we have undertaken the task of relating the various methods and techniques previously discussed to the composite model of language function. At best this is a difficult assignment, fraught with making judgments regarding the authors' suggested techniques, judgments with which the writers may not agree. If one is to use a theoretical frame of reference within which to view learning disabilities from evaluation through remediation, it follows that the model of choice must be related to assessment and remedial procedures. Obviously there is no real necessity for using any of the specific methods or systems discussed in this book. The trained and competent teacher could implement the results of formal and informal evaluation without having to select from the different methods presented. It seems just as obvious, however, that using an already developed system of remediation is more economic and convenient in the long run. All that is required is that the teacher choose techniques which are appropriate for a child with a particular set of specific learning disabilities. In order to do this, we feel that the teacher or therapist must have general knowledge regarding the area of specific learning disabilities, evaluation techniques, and remedial procedures, all of which must be integrated within a frame of reference and ideally could be presented in schematic or diagrammatic fashion.

As stated in earlier chapters, learning disabilities do not exist in neat, tight compartments; they overlap and interrelate in such a way that often each child appears to exhibit his own unique syndrome. Such children may be grouped in spite of their uniqueness, although the groupings must be flexible and dynamic. A child with visual perception problems and oral language delay may be grouped with different children, depending upon which aspect of his difficulty is under scrutiny. When the teacher is working with the children in a specific group, for example, those needing visual perceptual training, there is no reason why the teacher should spend his time devising techniques of remediation when he could so easily select procedures already developed by authors such Kephart, Frostig, Barsch, or Getman.

In this book we have presented a concept of learning disorders, evaluation procedures, and a review of many methods and techniques developed by leaders in the field. Throughout we have attempted to relate the information to a theoretical frame of reference termed the composite model. The success of this approach now depends upon the response of the individual teachers and therapists who endeavor to implement the philosophy of assessment and remediation presented.

GLOSSARY

Acalculia. See *Dyscalculia.*

Agnosia. Loss of or impairment of the ability to recognize objects or events presented through the various modalities when the sense organ is not significantly defective.

    Auditory. Inability to recognize sounds or combinations of sounds without regard to their meaning.

    Tactile (Astereognosis). Disorder of body orientations; characterized by inability to recognize stimuli through the sense of touch.

    Visual. Inability to recognize objects by sight.

    Autotopagnosia. Disorder of body orientation; characterized by inability to identify body parts.

Agraphia. See *Dysgraphia.*

Alexia. See *Dyslexia.*

Aniseikonia. A condition in which images formed on the retinas of the two eyes are unequal in size or shape.

Anomia. Inability to appropriately name objects, persons, activities; classically refers to difficulty in recalling nouns.

Anoxia. Deficient amount of oxygen in the tissues of a part of the body or in the bloodstream supplying such part.

Aphasia. See *Dysphasia.*

Apraxia. See *Dyspraxia.*

Articulation. The production of speech sounds by modifying the breath stream through movements of the lips, tongue, and velum.

Astereognosis. See *Agnosia.*

Astigmatism. A defect in the curvature of the lens causing distorted images.

Auditory agnosia. See *Agnosia.*

Auditory memory span. The number of items that can be recalled from oral stimulation; includes immediate and delayed recall of digits, words, sentences, and paragraphs or free and controlled recall (latter entails questions pertaining to content).

Autotopagnosis. See *Agnosia.*

Bilateral. Involving both sides.

Body concept. See *Body image.*

Body image. The concept and awareness of one's own body as it relates to orientation, movement, and other behavior.

Body schema. See *Body image.*

Central nervous system. The neural tissue which comprises the brain and spinal cord.

Cerebral cortex. The gray matter composing the external layer of the brain, which is responsible for the integration of stimuli received and responses made.

Cerebral dominance. The state in which one hemisphere of the brain is more involved in the mediation of various functions than the other hemisphere; a theory expostulated largely by Orton, Delacato, and Travis that one hemisphere is a dominant controller; right-hemisphere dominant and ambidexterous people show mixed dominance.

Cerebrum. The extensive portion of the brain which comprises the cerebral hemispheres. That part of the brain other than the brain stem and cerebellum.

Channels of communication. The sensory-motor pathways through which language is transmitted, e.g., auditory-vocal, visual-motor, among other possible combinations.

Choreoathetosis. A nervous disorder affecting motor control centers, characterized by regular, involuntary, jerky movements.

Circumlocution. Literally to speak around the point; inability to present ideas in a concise and clear manner.

Closure. A behavior that signifies pattern completion; the mechanism responsible for the automatic completion of familiar events.

Cognition. Intellectual activities as distinguished from feeling or willing.

Color coding. A teaching technique which uses colors to facilitate learning; e.g., designating each of the sounds in English with a different color or using particular colors for the various parts of speech.

Conceptualization. The ability to infer from what is observable.

Congenital. Present at birth; usually a defect of either familial or exogenous origin which exists at the time of birth.

Contralateral. On the opposite side.

Convulsive disorder. A clinical syndrome, the central feature of which is recurrent seizures or convulsions; recurrent disturbances of consciousness, with or without muscular components, and accompanied by changes in the electrical potentials of the brain.

Cortex. See *Cerebral cortex.*

Crawling. A means of locomotion in which the trunk is in contact with the surface.

Creeping. A means of locomotion on hands and knees with the trunk free of the surface.

Cross-pattern. A highly integrated movement in which arms and legs operate in a alternating fashion; e.g., in walking, as the right leg extends, the right arm swings back while comparable body parts on the left side are in reverse positions.

Cutaneous. Pertaining to the skin.

Cybernetic system. See *Feedback.*

Decoding. The receptive habits in the language process, e.g., sensory acuity, awareness, discrimination, vocabulary comprehension.

Directionality. Awareness of the up-and-down axis (verticality) and awareness of the relative position of one side of the body versus the other (laterality).

Discrimination. The act of distinguishing differences among stimuli.

Dissociation. Inability to synthesize separate elements into integrated meaningful wholes.

Distractibility. Forced responsiveness to extraneous stimuli.

Dyscalculia. Loss of inability to calculate, to manipulate number symbols, or to do simple arithmetic.

Dysfunction. Abnormal or imperfect behavior of an organ.

Dysgraphia. Impairment in spontaneous writing, the ability to copy being intact.

Dyslexia. Impairment in the ability to read; generally believed to be the result of cerebral lesions.

Dysphasia. Disorders of linguistic symbolization; the partial or complete loss of ability to speak (expressive dysphasia) or to comprehend the spoken word (receptive dysphasia); generally believed to be the result of injury, disease, or maldevelopment of the brain.

Dyspraxia. Partial loss of the ability to perform purposeful movements in a coordinated manner in the absence of paralysis, cerebral palsy, or sensory loss.

Echolalia. Senseless repetition of words or sounds.

EEG. See *Electroencephalogy.*

Electroencephalogy. Technique of recording brain waves for the purpose of detecting pathological conditions.

Emotional lability. Unstable feelings, emotions, and moods characterized by rapid shifts from one extreme to the other.

Encoding. The expressive habits in the language process, i.e., response formation including word selection, syntax, grammar, and the actual motor production of the response.

Engram. A memory trace or pattern supposedly left in the brain cells following a mental stimulus.

Epilepsy. See *Convulsive disorder.*

Etiology. The cause of an abnormal condition.

Evocative mechanism. Habits formed when external or response events occurring with high frequency or temporal contiguity; closure function is apparent and once initiated these activities tend to complete themselves in a fairly predictive fashion, e.g., the completion of the sentence "the boy ran up the . . ." is probably included in the following set: hill, alley, road, path, etc.

Expressive dysphasia. See *Dysphasia.*

External feedback. See *Feedback.*

Feedback. The process of monitoring and modifying one's own responses; a cybernetic system; includes both an internal form where part of the response pattern is fed back into the system prior to effecting the response and an external form where the overt response is monitored.

Figure-ground. Tendency of one part of a perceptual configuration to stand out clearly while the remainder forms a background.

Formulation. The organization of relevant elements of a specific project into a clear and concise pattern.

Graphic. Pertaining to writing.

Gustatory. Pertaining to taste.

Handedness. Refers to hand preference of an individual.

Hemorrhage. Bleeding.

Homolateral. Pertaining to one side.

Homologous. Pertaining to body structures which have the same origin in different species, e.g., the arm of a man and the wing of birds.

Hyperactivity. Disorganized, disruptive, and unpredictable behavior; overreaction to stimuli.

Hyperkinetic. See *Hyperactivity.*

Hypoactivity. Insufficient motor activity characterized by lethargy.

Hypokinetic. See *Hypoactivity.*

Ideation. Reflective thought; the organization of concepts into meaningful relationships.

Imagery. Representation of images.

Impulsivity. The initiation of sudden action without sufficient forethought or prudence.

Initial teaching alphabet. An alphabet of 44 characters, each of which represents a single English phoneme.

Inner language. Develops prior to receptive and expressive language; initially concerned with the formation of simple concepts as evidenced in the child's play activities; later more complex relationships evolve and the child plays with toys in a meaningful fashion.

Integration. (1) The second level of organization postulated by Osgood, which organizes and sequences both incoming and outgoing neural events. (2) In the composite model (chapter II), imitative behaviors are included along with Osgood's predictive and evocative activities. (3) To Wepman, the mediating processes of the CNS including the memory bank.

Internal feedback. See *Feedback.*

i.t.a. See *Initial teaching alphabet.*

Kinesthesia. The sense by which muscular movements are perceived.

Language. An arbitrary system of vocal symbols by which ideas are conveyed.

Language processes. The habits associated with decoding, association, and encoding of symbolic, including perceptual, information.

Laterality. Sidedness. See also *Directionality.*

Lesion. Any hurt, wound, or local degeneration.

Linguistics. The science of languages; the study of human speech including the units, structure, and modification of language or languages.

Linguistic approaches to reading. The relationship between the words as printed and the sounds for which the letters are conventional signs is emphasized; goal is to develop automatic association between letters and sounds.

Localization. The discovery of the locality of a disease; the hypothesis which assigns specific actions or functions to particular areas of the brain; establishing separate and individual centers in the brain for controlling speech, vision, audition, etc.

Locomotion. Movement from one place to another.

Medulla oblongata. The portion of the brain directly above the spinal cord.

Memory. The function of reviving past experience related to objects, places, people, events, and so on. Short-term or immediate memory refers to memory of what has been presented within the preceding few seconds.

Midbrain. Also *mesencephalon;* the portion of the brain directly above the pons.

Modality. An avenue of acquiring sensation; visual, auditory, tactile, kinesthetic, olfactory, and gustatory are the most common sense modalities.

Model. A diagrammatic representation of a concept.

Morphology. That aspect of linguistics which deals with meaningful units in the language code.

Motility. The range and speed of motion.

Motor. Pertaining to the origin or execution of muscular activity.

Movigenics. The motor-based curriculum developed by Barsch for children with specific learning disorders.

Multisensory. Generally applied to training procedures which simultaneously utilize more than one sense modality.

Myelinization. The production of the soft material surrounding the axon of a nerve fiber.

Neuron. A unit of the nervous system consisting of the cell body, nucleus, and cell membrane.

Nystagmus. A continuous rolling movement of the eyeball.

Ocular. Pertaining to the eye.

Olfactory. Pertaining to the sensation of smell.

Ontogeny. The developmental history of an individual organism.

Organicity. Dysfunction due to structural changes in the central nervous system.

Paradigm. See *Model.*

Paroxysmal. Pertaining to a spasm or convulsion.

Partitive. In grammar, a word or form such as few, some, any.

Pathology. A diseased, disordered, or abnormal condition of the organism or of any of its parts.

Patterning. The regimen of development exercises proposed by Delacato for the treatment of motor and learning disorders.

Perception. Recognition of a quality without distinguishing meaning, which is the result of a complex set of reactions including sensory stimulation, organization within the nervous system, and memory; an immediate or intuitive judgment involving subtle discriminations.

Perinatal. The period of life from the twenty-first week of gestation to the second month after birth.

Perseveration. The tendency for a specific act of behavior to continue after it is no longer appropriate; related to difficulty in shifting from one task to another.

Phonation. The production of vocalization, distinguished from articulation.

Phoneme. A group of closely related speech sounds all of which are generally regarded as the same sound, e.g., /t/ in top and in stop is one phoneme, although it is produced differently in the two words.

Phonics. The system of relating speech sounds to specific letters or letter combinations.

Phonogram. A letter symbol that represents a speech sound.

Phylogeny. The origin and development of a species, distinguished from ontogeny.

Pons. The portion of the brain directly above the medulla oblongata.

Predictive mechanisms. Mechanisms formed at the integration level of language which, according to Osgood, account for the learning of automatic and serial behavior.

Prenatal. Pertaining to the period preceding birth.

Process-oriented methods. Those methods emphasizing the processes of language, such as decoding, encoding, and memory; distinguished from task-oriented methods.

Projection level. According to Osgood, the lowest level of language organization; represents the simple, reflexive, sensory response to a stimulus.

Proprioception. The reception of stimuli arising within the body; sensation is received by nerve endings in muscles, tendons, and joints which are sensitive to alterations in muscular tension.

Propositional speech. The production of meaningful units of speech, usually sentences, which are used to communicate a specific idea.

Protocol. The original records of the results of testing.

Psychomotor. Pertaining to the motor effects of psychological processes. Psychomotor tests are tests of motor skill which depends upon sensory or perceptual motor coordination.

Reauditorization. A term used by Myklebust to denote the retrieval of auditory images.

Representational level. According to Osgood, the highest level of language organization; imparts meaning to what is received by the senses.

Representational mediation process. The process whereby the incoming stimulus is invested with meaning; a process which eventuates in encoding.

Response. The overt reaction to a stimulus.

Revisualization. A term used by Myklebust to denote the retrieval of visual images.

Schema. See *Model.*

Self-concept. A person's idea of himself; the person's feeling about the way he views himself is included; comparable to Myklebust's concept of self-perception.

Sensory acuity. The ability to respond to sensation at normal levels of intensity.

Sensory-motor (sensorimotor). Pertaining to the combined functioning of sense modalities and motor mechanisms; distinguished from psychomotor.

Sensory signal. A pattern of stimuli to which the organism responds.

Servomechanism or *servosystem.* A control system which includes input, feedback, and output; the response of the servomechanism to the signals received regulates the input so that the output may also be regulated.

Spatial orientation. Awareness of space around the person in terms of distance, form, direction, and position.

Speech. Audible communication through a system of arbitrary vocal symbols.

Stereopsis. The perception of objects in three dimensions.

Stimulability. The ability to respond appropriately after stimulation; imitation.

Stimulus. An external event which causes physiological change in the sense organ.

Strauss syndrome. The cluster of symptoms characterizing the "brain-injured" child; includes hyperactivity, distractibility, and impulsivity.

Strephosymbolia. Literally, "twisted symbols"; used as a synonym for dyslexia.

Structural reading. A reading method devised by Catherine Stern, based upon the child's own spoken vocabulary.

Substantive. In grammar, a word which denotes existence, such as the verb "to be"; a noun or group of words used as a noun.

Symbol. Something that represents or stands for something else; restricted to association of symbol and concept or idea; distinguished from sign.

Symptom. A manifestation of disordered functioning; applied to both physiological and psychological aspects.

Symptomatology. Pertaining to the symptoms presented by the individual.

Syndrome. The cluster or pattern of symptoms which characterizes a specific disorder.

Synergy. The combining of elementary motor processes into a complex coordinant movement.

Syntax. The way in which words are ordered, relative to one another, to form phrases, clauses, or sentences.

Tachistoscope. A mechanical device which provides brief, timed exposure of visual material.

Tactile. Pertaining to the sense of touch; also tactual.

Task-oriented methods. Teaching methods which emphasize the content of material to be learned, such as reading and arithmetic; distinguished from process-oriented methods.

Thought. A covert activity involving symbols.

Trauma. Any wound or injury, especially an organic injury.

Unilateral. On one side; usually applied to the body.

VAKT. A multisensory teaching method involving visual, auditory, kinesthetic, and tactile sense modalities; the Fernald "hand-kinesthetic" method.

Vertical. Pertaining to the axis from head to foot of the human body.

Vestibular. Pertaining to the sensory mechanism for the perception of the organism's relation to gravity.

Visual-motor. The ability to relate visual stimuli to motor responses in an appropriate way.

Word blindness. An inability to recognize or recall letters and words.

Word deafness. An inability to recall or recognize auditory equivalents of spoken words.

AUTHOR INDEX

SUBJECT INDEX